SUPPLEMENT 58

Control of Pig Reproduction VI

Proceedings of the Sixth International Conference
on Pig Reproduction

University of Missouri-Columbia
June 2001

Edited by:
R. D. Geisert, H. Niemann and C. Doberska

COVER ILLUSTRATION

Laser scanning confocal micrograph of filamentous actin in a pig embryo at the
hatched blastocyst stage; image is digitally embellished with global blastomeres.
Courtesy of J. R. Dobrinsky, Germplasm and Gamete Physiology Laboratory,
Agricultural Research Services, US Department of Agriculture, Beltsville, MD
20705, USA

Published by the Society for Reproduction and Fertility
2001

First published 2001
ISSN 0449 3087
ISBN 0 906545 38 2

SOCIETY FOR REPRODUCTION AND FERTILITY

The Society for Reproduction and Fertility publishes *Reproduction* and supplements. Supplements, which are distinct from the regular issues, are not associated with any particular volume and are known by their serial number and date.

Published by **the Society for Reproduction and Fertility**

Managing Editor	Christine Doberska
Editorial Assistants	Rachel Ashen
	Elisabeth Stevens

www.srf-reproduction.org./journal

Agents for distribution:
Portland Customer Services, Commerce Way, Colchester, CO2 8HP, Essex, UK;
Tel: 44(0) 1206 796351; FAX: 44(0) 1206 799331; e-mail: sales@portland-services.com

Printed by Cambridge University Press

Contents

Preface   v

Acknowledgements   vi

DEVELOPMENT OF THE FOLLICLE AND CORPUS LUTEUM
Chairman R. R. Kraeling

Nutritional regulators of the hypothalamic–pituitary axis in pigs
C. R. Barb, R. R. Kraeling and G. B. Rampacek   1–15

Apoptosis during folliculogenesis in pigs
H. D. Guthrie and W. M. Garrett   17–29

Ovarian follicular growth in sows
M. C. Lucy, J. Liu, C. K. Boyd and C. J. Bracken   31–45

Formation and early development of the corpus luteum in pigs
B. D. Murphy, N. Gévry, T. Ruiz-Cortés, F. Coté, B. R. Downey and
J. Sirois   47–63

OOCYTE DEVELOPMENT IN VITRO AND IN VIVO
Chairman B. N. Day

Mammalian gonadal differentiation: the pig model
E. Pailhoux, B. Mandon-Pepin and C. Cotinot   65–80

In vitro development of pig preantral follicles
E. E. Telfer   81–90

Maturation of pig oocytes in vivo and in vitro
R. Moor and Y. Dai   91–104

Basic mechanisms of fertilization and parthenogenesis in pigs
R. S. Prather   105–112

FERTILIZATION IN VIVO AND IN VITRO
Chairman R. D. Geisert

Phagocytosis of boar spermatozoa in vitro and in vivo
H. Woelders and A. Matthijs   113–127

Involvement of oviduct in sperm capacitation and oocyte development
in pigs
H. Rodriguez-Martinez, P. Tienthai, K. Suzuki, H. Funahashi, H. Ekwall
and A. Johannisson   129–145

Gamete adhesion molecules
D. J. Miller and H. R. Burkin   147–158

In vitro fertilization and embryo development in pigs
L. R. Abeydeera   159–173

EMBRYONIC AND PLACENTAL DEVELOPMENT

Chairman R. M. Roberts

Gene expression during pre- and peri-implantation embryonic development
in pigs
P. Maddox-Hyttel, A. Dinnyés, J. Laurincik, D. Rath, H. Niemann,
C. Rosenkranz and I. Wilmut   175–189

Functional analysis of autocrine and paracrine signalling at the
uterine–conceptus interface in pigs
L. A. Jaeger, G. A. Johnson, H. Ka, J. G. Garlow, R. C. Burghardt,
T. E. Spencer and F. W. Bazer   191–207

Histological and immunohistochemical events during placentation in pigs
V. Dantzer and H. Winther   209–222

GESTATION AND PARTURITION

Chairman G. R. Foxcroft

Comparative aspects of placental efficiency
M. E. Wilson and S. P. Ford   223–232

Causes and consequences of fetal growth retardation in pigs
C. J. Ashworth, A. M. Finch, K. R. Page, M. O. Nwagwu and H. J. McArdle   233–246

Prenatal development as a predisposing factor for perinatal losses in pigs
T. van der Lende, E. F. Knol and J. I. Leenhouwers   247–261

Endocrine regulation of periparturient behaviour in pigs
C. L. Gilbert   263–276

NEW TECHNOLOGIES

Chairman H. Niemann

Applying functional genomic research to the study of pig reproduction
D. Pomp, A. R. Caetano, G. R. Bertani, C. D. Gladney and R. K. Johnson   277–292

Cloning pigs: advances and applications
I. A. Polejaeva   293–300

Deep intrauterine insemination and embryo transfer in pigs
E. A. Martinez, J. M. Vazquez, J. Roca, X. Lucas, M. A. Gil and J. L. Vazquez   301–311

Transgenic alteration of sow milk to improve piglet growth and health
M. B. Wheeler, G. T. Bleck and S. M. Donovan   313–324

Cryopreservation of pig embryos: adaptation of vitrification technology
for embryo transfer
J. R. Dobrinsky   325–333

Author index   335

Subject index   337

Preface

The Sixth International Conference on Pig Reproduction was held at the University of Missouri-Columbia, USA on 3–6 June 2001. The Conference continued the established tradition of holding meetings at four-year intervals to provide a forum to discuss the latest developments in pig reproductive biology and the application of this information to improvements in swine fertility.

This was the third time that the University of Missouri has hosted the Conference and the success of the meeting was again a testament to the hard work of the Local Organizing Committee led by Dr Randy Prather. Delegates were again provided with an excellent environment for both scientific and social interactions, and not even the torrential rain of Missouri dampened the spirits of the meeting.

The International Organizing Committee continued to take the primary responsibility for the development of the scientific program, led by Rod Geisert. Wide consultations across the research community resulted in a comprehensive programme representing the very latest developments in swine reproductive biology and reproductive technology. The main scientific programme included six sessions and 25 invited speakers from eight different countries. The Conference was attended by 215 delegates from 21 countries who presented results of their recent research in 89 posters during the meeting. The overall programme also included a well-attended Pre-Conference Workshop that discussed the biological basis for improvements in breeding herd performance.

The IOC has again co-operated with the Society for Reproduction, and specifically Christine Doberska, in the publication of the main invited lectures of the Sixth International Conference on Pig Reproduction as Supplement 58 of *Reproduction*. We are again confident that the timely publication of these papers will provide an important source of information to the research and teaching community. Although space limitations and publication costs do not allow the publication of the abstracts of posters in *Supplement 58*, the full text of these abstracts can be downloaded from the Conference web-site at http://www.asrc.agri.missouri.edu/icpr/ and we thank the LOC for making this possible.

G. R. Foxcroft
Chair, International Organizing Committee

Acknowledgements

The Organizing Committee is most grateful for the contributions made by the invited speakers through the quality of their presentations and development of manuscripts contained within the Supplement for the VIth International Conference on Pig Reproduction. The Committee is also appreciative of the efforts made by the many delegates who presented posters of their current research and contributed to the lively discussion during the presentations and poster sessions. We would like to thank Drs R. R. Kraeling, B. N. Day, R. D. Geisert, R. M. Roberts, G. R. Foxcroft and H. Niemann for serving as Chairmen of the sessions and Dr Chris Polge for summarizing the presentations at the end of the conference.

The success of the Conference was in great part due to the continuous efforts of the Local Organizing Committee at the University of Missouri. We are indebted to the efforts of R. S. Prather, B. N. Day and the many other faculty, graduate students, and staff who volunteered their time to serve as hosts for the scientific and social events that made the conference a truly international event for those interested in improving pig reproduction in the new century.

This Conference could not have occurred without the financial support of ALPHARMA, ARS (USDA), Continental Plastics Corp., Dekalb Choice Genetics, CSREES (USDA), InterAg, Intervet Inc., IMV International Corp., Minitube of America, National Pig Development (USA), Pig Improvement Company, Pharmacia & UpJohn Co. and Thorn Bioscience, to whom the Conference Organising Committee extends our sincere thanks.

Finally, we would like to acknowledge the major contributions that Drs G. R. Foxcroft and B. N. Day have made to the continuing success of the International Conference on Pig Reproduction. Their insight and leadership as retiring founding members of the International Organizing Committee will be surely missed.

C.J. Ashworth, B.N. Day,
G.R. Foxcroft, R.D. Geisert,
R.R. Kraeling, T. van de Lende,
H. Niemann, R.S. Prather
International Organizing Committee

Reproduction Supplement 58, 1–15

Nutritional regulators of the hypothalamic–pituitary axis in pigs

C. R. Barb[1], R. R. Kraeling[1] and G. B. Rampacek[2]

[1]Animal Physiology Research Unit, USDA/ARS, Richard B. Russell Agriculture Research Center, PO Box 5677, Athens, GA 30604, USA; and [2]Animal and Dairy Science Department, University of Georgia, Athens, GA 30602, USA

Nutritional signals are detected by the central nervous system (CNS) and translated by the neuroendocrine system into signals that alter secretion of LH and growth hormone (GH). Furthermore, these signals directly affect the activity of the pituitary gland independently of CNS input. Insulin-like growth factor I (IGF-I), insulin, leptin and specific metabolites, such as glucose and free fatty acids (FFA), are potential signals of the metabolic status to the brain–pituitary axis. Intravenous injection of a lipid emulsion or glucose suppressed the GH and LH response to GH releasing hormone (GHRH) and GnRH, respectively. Insulin and IGF-I regulation of LH and GH secretion occur at the pituitary gland. Feed deprivation for 24 h suppressed leptin secretion without affecting LH or GH secretion, whereas central administration of leptin resulted in a decrease in feed intake and an increase in GH secretion. Oestrogen-induced leptin gene expression in adipose tissue increased with age and adiposity in pigs. Leptin stimulated GnRH release from hypothalamic tissue *in vitro*. These results identify putative signals that link metabolic status and neuroendocrine control of growth and reproduction by altering endocrine function during periods of fasting, feed restriction and lactation.

Neuroendocrine control of LH and GH secretion

It is generally accepted that there are two modes of LH secretion in pigs (Kraeling and Barb, 1990): pulsatile secretion and surge secretion. These patterns of LH secretion reflect the pattern of GnRH released from neurosecretory neurones within the hypothalamus into the hypothalamic–hypophysial portal system (Goodman, 1988). An LH pulse and an LH surge generator are located within the CNS of pigs (Kraeling and Barb, 1990). The importance of pulsatile GnRH and LH secretion was demonstrated by Lutz *et al.* (1984) and Pressing *et al.* (1992) who induced precocious oestrus and ovulation in intact prepubertal gilts by giving i.v. injections of GnRH at 1 h intervals. In addition, administration of GnRH at 1 h intervals to anoestrous postpartum sows induced oestrus and ovulation (Cox and Britt, 1988). Wetsel *et al.* (1992) reported intrinsic pulsatile secretory activity of immortalized GnRH neurones *in vitro*. Thus, GnRH neurones secrete their product in an autonomous episodic frequency, but interoceptive and exteroceptive factors detected by the CNS are translated by the

Email: rbarb@saa.ars.usda.gov

neuroendocrine system into signals that alter the pattern of GnRH and subsequent LH secretion. For example, interoceptive signals, such as gonadal and adrenal steroids, metabolites, and other neuronal signals, act to modulate pulse frequency and amplitude of GnRH pulses.

Many of the interoceptive signals that regulate GnRH and LH secretion also modulate GH secretion. Of particular importance is the role of nutrition and metabolic status in maintaining reproductive function, but also in modulating the GH-releasing hormone (GHRH)–somatostatin–GH axis and subsequent growth. It is well established that the onset of puberty is linked to the attainment of a critical body weight or metabolic mass, indicating an association between mechanisms regulating energy balance and the reproductive and growth axis.

Metabolism and the endocrine system

The importance of nutrition and metabolic state in maintaining reproductive function is well established. The onset of puberty may be linked to attainment of a critical body weight or a minimum percentage of body fat (Frisch, 1984). Alternatively, metabolic mass and food intake, or its correlated metabolic rate, may be the triggering mechanism (Frisch, 1984). Cameron et al. (1985) reported that transition from a fed to a fasting state occurred more rapidly in the juvenile than in the mature monkey. Cameron et al. (1985) suggested that the dynamic fluctuations in plasma hormones and substrates that occur during postprandial and postabsorptive periods provide signals to the brain that link metabolic status to activation of the reproductive system. Nutritional perturbations delay the onset of puberty, interfere with normal oestrous cycles and alter LH secretion in pigs (for a review, see Prunier and Quesnel, 2000a).

The GH response to nutritional status is variable in pigs. Buonomo et al. (1988) reported that serum GH concentrations increased after 48 h of fasting in barrows. In contrast, Booth (1990) reported that feed restriction for 8–14 days failed to affect serum GH concentrations in prepubertal gilts. Acute feed deprivation failed to influence GH secretion during a 28 h fast, although serum GH secretion increased after feeding was resumed. Similarly, Armstrong and Britt (1987) reported that GH secretion increased during the postprandial period in feed restricted gilts. However, antagonism of glucose utilization increased basal and mean serum GH concentrations, but not GH pulse frequency and amplitude (Barb et al., 2001). Thus, GH response to energy availability is equivocal.

Collectively, these data demonstrate that nutritional status affects endocrine function. Contemporary models of energy regulation emphasize physiological signals that control energy intake, partitioning and expenditure, and their sites of action. It is hypothesized that mechanisms regulating energy balance are sensitive to metabolic signals generated by changes in oxidation of metabolic fuels and could account for positive correlations between body fat, fertility and endocrine function (Wade et al., 1996). Identification of specific metabolic signals that influence the reproductive and growth axis remains elusive, primarily because of the large number of substances from the periphery that may act centrally to modify neuronal activity. Similar to the study by Cameron et al. (1985) on primates, Barb et al. (1997) reported that transition from a fed to fasting state occurred more rapidly in prepubertal than in mature gilts. Different temporal relationships between circulating blood concentrations of glucose, free fatty acids (FFA), ketones, insulin and IGF-I in mature and prepubertal pigs were probably related to a greater glucose production rate, higher metabolic rate, smaller energy reserves and greater growth requirements in prepubertal gilts. In a subsequent study, acute fasting suppressed leptin secretion in prepubertal gilts (Barb et al., 2001). Thus, glucose, FFA, IGF-I, insulin and leptin may provide peripheral signals to the brain that link metabolic status to activation of the reproductive system and modulation of the growth axis. The intent of this review is to present evidence for nutritional control of the hypothalamic–pituitary axis and putative sites of action of specific metabolites and metabolic hormones in modulating LH and GH secretion. The effects of nutrition and feed restriction on reproductive function in pigs will not be discussed. For further information on nutrition and reproductive function in pigs see Cosgrove and Foxcroft (1996) and Prunier and Quesnel (2000a,b).

Nutritional mediators of LH and GH secretion

Roles of glucose and insulin

Numerous reports have led to the proposal that blood glucose concentration is an accurate reflection and index of the collective effects of energy on reproduction and growth. Moreover, changes in gluconeogenesis may be the mechanism by which altered energy metabolism affects the neuroendocrine axis in pigs. In support of this idea, Barb *et al.* (1997) suggested that the ability of pigs to maintain euglycaemia during acute fasting was primarily due to rapid mobilization of alternative energy stores, such as FFA. This mobilization of energy stores may account for the failure of acute feed deprivation to affect LH secretion. Booth (1990) demonstrated that administration of glucose to feed-restricted gilts induced a rapid increase in episodic LH secretion similar to that observed in response to resumed feeding. In contrast, the LH response to GnRH was lower in satiated prepubertal gilts that received an i.v. injection of glucose compared with that of saline-treated gilts (Barb *et al.*, 1991). These conflicting results may, in part, be related to nutritional state, which has a profound effect on circulating concentrations of metabolites and metabolic hormones. These factors could alter the hypothalamic–pituitary response to glucose challenge.

Blocking of glycolysis with 2-deoxy-D-glucose resulted in a marked reduction in LH pulse frequency and an increase in serum GH concentrations in prepubertal gilts (Barb *et al.*, 2001). Furthermore, an i.v. bolus of glucose suppressed the GH response to GHRH in gilts (Barb *et al.*, 1991) and exposure of pig pituitary cells in culture to 300 or 600 mg glucose dl⁻¹ suppressed the LH and GH responses to GnRH and GHRH, respectively (Barb *et al.*, 1995; Tables 1 and 2). The above studies support the hypothesis that glucose is a primary regulator of LH and GH secretion, and that the pituitary gland is a potential site of action.

The physiological relevance of the decrease in serum insulin concentrations during fasting is not clear (Barb *et al.*, 1997). In primiparous lactating sows (Rojkittikhun *et al.*, 1993a) and prepubertal gilts (Barb *et al.*, 2001), a 24 h fast did not affect LH secretion, although serum insulin concentrations were suppressed compared with those of animals that were fed. Increased dietary energy and insulin treatment in gilts at the follicular phase resulted in an increase in serum LH and FSH concentrations, but this effect did not occur in the absence of increased dietary energy (Cox *et al.*, 1987). Rojkittikhun *et al.* (1993b) reported that insulin treatment increased plasma LH concentrations but did not affect LH pulse frequency during the weaning to oestrus interval in primiparous sows. One model used to study the effect of insulin on the hypothalamic–pituitary axis is the diabetes-induced animal. In diabetic ovariectomized gilts, withdrawal of insulin therapy for 4 days prevented the oestradiol-induced preovulatory-like LH surge, but did not affect pulsatile LH secretion (Angell *et al.*, 1996). This finding indicates that diabetes mellitus alters the sensitivity of the hypothalamic–pituitary axis to oestradiol and the responsiveness of the pituitary gland to GnRH. Pituitary cell culture experiments confirmed that the sensitivity of the pituitary gland to GnRH decreased after removal of insulin therapy for 7 days in diabetic pigs (Angell *et al.*, 1996; Table 1).

Table 1. Effects of glucose, free fatty acids or diabetes on LH and GH secretion in the pig

Animal	Hormone	Metabolite[a]	Route	Type response	Result	Reference
Prepubertal gilt	LH	Glucose (1g kg^{-1})	i.v.	GnRH challenge	Decreased	Barb et al., 1991
		Liposyn (3 ml kg^{-1})	i.v.	GnRH challenge	Decreased	Barb et al., 1991
		Liposyn (3 ml kg^{-1}) per h for 9 h	i.v.	Pulse amplitude	Increased	Barb et al., 1991
OVX prepubertal gilt, R	LH	Glucose	i.v.	Pulsatile	Increased	Booth, 1990
OVX diabetic gilt, no insulin	LH	Glucose		Oestradiol-induced surge	Decreased	Angell et al., 1996
	LH	Glucose		Pulsatile secretion	No effect	Angell et al., 1996
Diabetic gilt, no insulin	LH	Glucose		Pulsatile secretion	Increased	Cox et al., 1994
OVX prepubertal gilt	GH	Glucose (1 g kg^{-1})	i.v.	GHRH challenge	Decreased	Barb et al., 1991
	GH	Liposyn (3 ml kg^{-1})	i.v.	GHRH challenge	Decreased	Barb et al., 1991
	GH	Liposyn (3 ml kg^{-1}) per h for 9 h	i.v.	Pulsatile	Increased	Barb et al., 1991
OVX diabetic gilt	GH	Blood glucose (465 mg dl^{-1})		Pulsatile secretion	Increased	Barb et al., 1992

OVX: ovariectomized; R: feed-restricted.

[a] 10% Liposym II; Abbott Laboratories, North Chicago, IL.

Table 2. Effects of glucose, oleic or linoleic acids on basal, GnRH and GHRH-induced LH and GH secretion from anterior pituitary cells in culture from prepubertal gilts[a]

	Hormone	Metabolite	Dose	Result
Basal secretion				
	LH	Glucose	300, 600 mg dl^{-1}	No effect
	GH	Glucose	100, 300, 600 mg dl^{-1}	No effect
	LH	Oleic acid	10^{-7}, 10^{-6}, 10^{-5}, 10^{-4} mol l^{-1}	Increased
	LH	Linoleic acid	10^{-6}, 10^{-5}, 10^{-4} mol l^{-1}	Increased
	GH	Oleic acid	10^{-11}, 10^{-9} mol l^{-1}	Decreased
			10^{-7}, 10^{-5} mol l^{-1}	Increased
	GH	Linoleic acid	10^{-9} mol l^{-1}	Increased
Response to GnRH				
	LH	Glucose	600 mg dl^{-1}	Decreased
	LH	Oleic acid	10^{-6}, 10^{-5}, 10^{-4} mol l^{-1}	Decreased
	LH	Linoleic acid	10^{-5} mol l^{-1}	Decreased
Response to GHRH				
	GH	Glucose	100, 300, 600 mg dl^{-1}	Decreased
	GH	Oleic acid	10^{-11}, 10^{-9}, 10^{-7}, 10^{-5} mol l^{-1}	Decreased
	GH	Linoleic acid	10^{-11}, 10^{-9}, 10^{-7}, 10^{-5} mol l^{-1}	Decreased

[a]From Barb *et al.* (1995).

Mean serum GH concentrations and GH pulse frequency were greater in gilts with poorly controlled diabetes than in control pigs. Serum insulin concentrations were lower (0.3 ± 0.02 versus 0.9 ± 0.05 ng ml^{-1}; $P < 0.0001$) and plasma glucose concentrations were higher (465 ± 17 versus 82 ± 17 mg dl^{-1}; $P < 0.05$) in diabetic pigs than in control pigs (Barb *et al.*, 1992). The increase in GH secretion may be due, in part, to higher ($P < 0.0002$) glucose concentrations in the cerebrospinal fluid of diabetic pigs (162 ± 14 mg dl^{-1}) compared with control pigs (51 ± 3 mg dl^{-1}), which alters GHRH and somatostatin secretion from the hypothalamus, which in turn alters pituitary somatotrope activity (Barb *et al.*, 1992).

Two studies were conducted to investigate the idea that insulin acts at either the CNS or pituitary gland to alter LH and GH secretion. Central administration of insulin at doses of 1–100 µg failed to change LH and GH secretion in ovariectomized prepubertal gilts (Barb *et al.*, 1996; Fig. 1). However, insulin suppressed basal GH secretion and the GH response to GHRH for anterior pituitary cells in culture from 180-day-old gilts (C. R. Barb, J. B. Barrett and R. R. Kraeling, unpublished; Fig. 2). Thus, the influence of insulin on the LH and GH axis appears to be a manifestation of plasma glucose concentration. However, subtle effects of insulin on the sensitivity of the pituitary gland to hypothalamic secretagogues cannot be discounted (Tables 3 and 4).

Role of FFA

In pigs, feed deprivation results in a rapid onset of FFA mobilization from peripheral fat deposits, but maintenance of euglycaemia indicates an increase in hydrolysis of triglycerides and FFA oxidation resulting in glucose sparing (Barb *et al.*, 1997). Armstrong and Britt (1987) reported that chronic feed restriction in gilts resulted in cessation of oestrous cycles and lower concentrations of plasma insulin, increased concentrations of FFA and reduced LH pulse

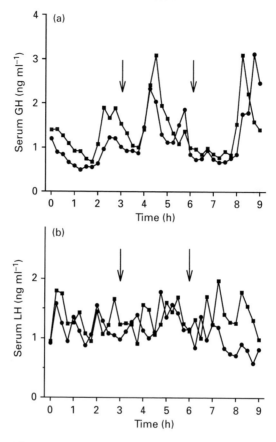

Fig. 1. Concentrations of serum (a) GH and (b) LH in ovariectomized prepubertal gilts receiving intracerebroventricular injection of saline (■; $n = 4$) or 1 µg insulin (●; $n = 4$) at 3 h and 6 h (arrows). Pooled standard errors for LH = 0.2 ng ml^{-1} and GH = 0.5 ng ml^{-1}.

frequency compared with those of control gilts. Booth (1990) reported similar results in prepubertal gilts that were feed-restricted for 8 days, whereas in prepubertal gilts subjected to short-term fasting, serum concentrations of FFA increased, but there was no change in LH or GH secretion compared with control gilts (Barb *et al.*, 2001). In primiparous lactating sows, concentrations of serum FFA increased on day 12 and day 20 of lactation and this was associated with increased fat mobilization and protein catabolism (Armstrong *et al.*, 1986). Sows that remained anoestrous after weaning had increased plasma glucose concentrations and lower serum concentrations of FFA on day 12 and day 20 than those of oestrous sows. The authors speculated that aberrations in energy metabolism during lactation might have predisposed sows to anoestrus after weaning.

Therefore, do alterations in serum concentrations of FFA influence hypothalamic–pituitary function? In prepubertal gilts, i.v. infusion of a lipid emulsion enhanced the LH response to

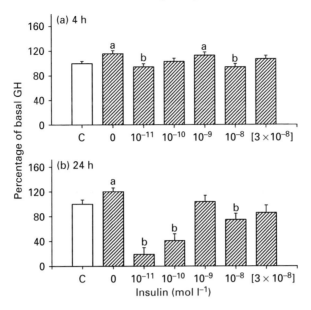

Fig. 2. Effect of insulin $(0–3 \times 10^{-8}$ mol $l^{-1})$ on growth hormone-releasing hormone (GHRH)-induced $(10^{-6}$ mol $l^{-1})$ GH secretion in pig pituitary cells during (a) 4 h or (b) 24 h culture periods. Values are mean ± standard errors ($n = 8–12$ wells per treatment). C: control = basal secretion in the absence of treatment. [a]Significantly different from the control ($P < 0.05$). [b]Significantly different from GHRH alone ($P < 0.05$).

GnRH, but suppressed the GH response to GHRH, whereas infusion of the lipid emulsion at 1 h intervals increased serum LH pulse amplitude and GH pulse frequency (Barb *et al.*, 1991; Table 1). The hourly fluctuations in serum concentrations of FFA may have synchronized the endogenous rhythm of GHRH and somatostatin secretion from the hypothalamus and, subsequently, altered somatotrope activity. Cultured pig pituitary cells were used to determine whether the effects of FFA *in vivo* occur at the pituitary gland without benefit of CNS input. Oleic and linoleic acids increased basal LH release. In contrast, oleic acid suppressed GnRH-induced release of LH (Table 2). This response was equivocal for linoleic acid (Barb *et al.*, 1995). It is difficult to explain the differences between the *in vivo* and *in vitro* results. One possibility is that other hypothalamic factors *in vivo* may have altered pituitary gland responsiveness to GnRH (Barb *et al.*, 1991). Alternatively, the lipid emulsion infused in the *in vivo* study (Barb *et al.*, 1991) consisted of linoleic, oleic, palmitic, linolenic and stearic acids, whereas the effects of oleic or linoleic acid alone were evaluated in the *in vitro* study (Barb *et al.*, 1995). Oleic and linoleic acids act directly on the anterior pituitary cells to alter basal and GHRH-induced GH release (Barb *et al.*, 1995; Table 2). Moreover, this event seems to be mediated at the plasma membrane, because oleic and linoleic acids do not block the forskolin-induced release of GH (Barb *et al.*, 1995). Thus, the above findings may explain, in part, the altered neuroendocrine activity observed during periods of fasting, feed restriction and lactation.

Table 3. Effects of leptin, insulin-like growth factor I (IGF-I) or insulin treatment on *in vitro* basal, GnRH and GHRH-induced LH and GH secretion from anterior pituitary cells and GnRH secretion from hypothalamic tissue

Animal[a]	Hormone	Metabolic hormone	Culture	Dose	Result	References
Basal secretion						
Prepubertal gilt	LH	Leptin	Pituitary	10^{-14}, 10^{-13}, 10^{-11}, 10^{-10}, 10^{-9}, 10^{-8}, 10^{-6} mol l^{-1}	Increased	Barb *et al.*, 1999
	GH	Leptin		10^{-6}, 10^{-7} mol l^{-1}	Increased	Barb *et al.*, 1998
Gilt	LH	IGF-I	Pituitary			Whitley *et al.*, 1995
Follicular phase				10^{-11}, 10^{-10}, 10^{-9} mol l^{-1}	Increased	
Luteal phase				10^{-11} mol l^{-1}	Increased	
OVX				10^{-11}, 10^{-10} mol l^{-1}	Increased	
Prepubertal gilt	GH	IGF-I	Pituitary			
4 h				10^{-9}, 10^{-8}, 3×10^{-8} mol l^{-1}	Increased	C. R. Barb, J. B. Barrett and
24 h				10^{-11}, 10^{-10}, 10^{-9}, 10^{-8}, 3×10^{-8} mol l^{-1}	Decreased	R. R. Kraeling, unpublished
Prepubertal gilt	GH	Insulin	Pituitary			
4 h				10^{-11} mol l^{-1}	Decreased	C. R. Barb, J. B. Barrett and
24 h				10^{-11}, 10^{-10}, 10^{-9}, 10^{-8}, 3×10^{-8} mol l^{-1}	Decreased	R. R. Kraeling, unpublished
OVX	GnRH	Leptin	Hypothalamic–preoptic area	10^{-12}, 10^{-10}, 10^{-6} mol l^{-1}	Increased	Barb *et al.*, 1999
Response to GnRH						
Prepubertal gilt	LH	Leptin	Pituitary	10^{-7} mol l^{-1}	Decreased	Barb *et al.*, 1999
Gilt	LH	IGF-I	Pituitary			Whitley *et al.*, 1995
Follicular				10^{-11}, 10^{-10}, 10^{-9}, 10^{-8}, 3×10^{-8} mol l^{-1}	No effect	
Luteal				10^{-11}, 10^{-10}, 10^{-9}, 10^{-8}, 3×10^{-8} mol l^{-1}	No effect	
OVX				10^{-11}, 10^{-10}, 10^{-9}, 10^{-8}, 3×10^{-8} mol l^{-1}	No effect	
Response to GHRH						
Prepubertal gilt	GH	Leptin	Pituitary	10^{-11}, 10^{-9} mol l^{-1}	Decreased	Barb *et al.*, 1998
Prepubertal gilt	GH	IGF-I	Pituitary		No effect	
4 h				10^{-11}, 10^{-10}, 10^{-9}, 10^{-8}, 3×10^{-8} mol l^{-1}	No effect	C. R. Barb, J. B. Barrett and
24h				10^{-11}, 10^{-10}, 10^{-8}, 3×10^{-8} mol l^{-1}	Decreased	R. R. Kraeling, unpublished
Prepubertal gilt	GH	Insulin	Pituitary			
4 h				10^{-11}, 10^{-8} mol l^{-1}	Decreased	C. R. Barb, J. B. Barrett and
24h				10^{-11}, 10^{-10}, 10^{-8} mol l^{-1}	Decreased	R. R. Kraeling, unpublished

[a]OVX: ovariectomized.

Role of IGF-I

IGF-I appears particularly suitable for a role in linking somatic growth and development to activation of the reproductive axis. IGF-I exerts neurotrophic and mitogenic effects in the brain via interaction with specific receptors (Sara and Hall, 1990). Although type I IGF receptors are distributed widely throughout the brain, they are more concentrated in the median eminence (Werther *et al.*, 1990) indicating that, in this region, IGF-I is involved in functions other than cellular differentiation. Although IGF-I concentrations in the postnatal hypothalamus appear to be independent of peripheral concentrations (Rotwein *et al.*, 1988), circulating concentrations of IGF-I increased during pubertal development in pigs (Lee *et al.*, 1991). It is now clear that the peripubertal increase in serum IGF-I concentration is from hypothalamic, hepatic (Handelsman *et al.*, 1987) and adipose tissue (Wolverton *et al.*, 1992). Moreover, the pubertal increase in circulating IGF-I concentrations (Lee *et al.*, 1991) occurs concomitantly with an age-related decrease in pituitary response to GHRH (Dubreuil *et al.*, 1987) and an increase in LH secretion (Lutz *et al.*, 1984). These observations indicate that IGF-I may modulate hypothalamic release of GnRH and GHRH–somatostatin and pituitary responsiveness to hypothalamic hormones.

It is proposed that IGF-I acts, in a feedback loop, directly on the pituitary gland and brain to regulate LH and GH secretion. Although most evidence indicates that the effect of IGF-I on the release of pituitary hormones occurs in the CNS, subtle effects on the anterior pituitary cannot be discounted. Hiney *et al.* (1991) reported that IGF-I elicited GnRH release from the median eminence *in vitro*. The release of GnRH is greater after IGF-I than after IGF-II or insulin administration, indicating that IGF-I is the primary signal (Hiney *et al.*, 1991). In addition, release of GnRH from the median eminence, which is devoid of GnRH cell bodies, indicates that activation of gene expression by IGF-I is not involved. In rats, intracerebroventricular administration of IGF-I suppressed pulsatile GH secretion and stimulated brain somatostatin release (Abe *et al.*, 1983). IGF-I inhibited both acute release of GH and GH mRNA content in rat pituitary cells *in vitro* (Yamashita and Melmed, 1986). Moreover, intracerebroventricular administration of IGF-I suppressed GH secretion in pig fetuses (Spencer *et al.*, 1991; Table 4). In a recent experiment, intracerebroventricular administration of 10 µg IGF-I failed to alter LH and GH secretion in ovariectomized prepubertal gilts. Mean serum LH and GH concentrations before treatment were 0.8 ± 0.2 and 1.7 ± 0.6 ng ml^{-1} and after treatment were 1.0 ± 0.2 and 1.7 ± 0.6 ng ml^{-1}, respectively (Barb *et al.*, 1996). Doses up to 75 µg IGF-I failed to alter LH and GH secretion (Barb *et al.*, 1996). IGF-I suppressed basal GH secretion (Table 3) and the GH response to GHRH from pig pituitary cells in culture (C. R. Barb, J. B. Barrett and R. R. Kraeling, unpublished; Fig. 3). Furthermore, Whitley *et al.* (1995) reported that IGF-I-induced LH secretion was greater in pituitary cells from gilts at the follicular phase compared with cells from gilts at the luteal phase and ovariectomized gilts (Table 3). Thus, under certain physiological conditions, such as steroid milieu or nutritional status, endogenous IGF-I may contribute to the regulation of LH and GH secretion from the anterior pituitary in pigs.

Role of leptin

Leptin, secreted by adipose tissue in response to changes in energy availability, serves as a circulating signal of nutritional status and has a profound influence on regulation of the neuroendocrine axis and appetite in rodents (Casanueva and Dieguez, 1999; Ahima and Flier,

Table 4. Effects of leptin, insulin-like growth factor I (IGF-I) or insulin treatment on LH and GH secretion *in vivo*

Animal	Hormone	Hormone and dose	Route	Results	References
Prepubertal gilt	LH	Leptin: 10, 50 or 100 g	ICV	No effect	Barb *et al.*, 1999
	GH	Leptin: 10, 50 or 100 g	ICV	Increased	Barb *et al.*, 1998
OVX prepubertal	LH	IGF-I: 0.1, 1, 10, 25 or 75 g	ICV	No effect	Barb *et al.*, 1996
	GH	IGF-I: 0.1, 1, 10, 25 or 75 g	ICV	No effect	Barb *et al.*, 1996
Fetal pig	GH	IGF-I: 1.5 g	ICV	Decreased	Spencer *et al.*, 1991
OVX prepubertal	LH	Insulin: 1, 10 or 100 g	ICV	No effect	Barb *et al.*, 1996
	GH	Insulin: 1, 10 or 100 g	ICV	No effect	Barb *et al.*, 1996
Barrow	GH	Insulin: 0.3 iu kg^{-1} body weight	i.v.	Increased	Bonneau 1993
OVX gilt	LH	Insulin: 6 ng	ICV	Increased	Cox *et al.*, 1990
OVX gilt	GH	Insulin: 3, 6 or 12 ng	ICV	No effect	Barb *et al.*, 1990
Postpartum sow	LH	Insulin: 0.5 iu kg^{-1} body weight	i.v.	No effect	Rojkittikhun *et al.*, 1993b
Gilt follicular phase	LH	Insulin: 0.1 iu kg^{-1} body weight 4 × day +9, 960 kcal Me day^{-1}	i.v.	Increased	Cox *et al.*, 1987
	LH	Insulin: 0.1 iu kg^{-1} body weight 4 × day +5, 771 kcal Me day^{-1}	i.v.	No effect	Cox *et al.*, 1987

OVX: ovariectomized; Me: metabolizable energy; ICV: intracerebroventricular.

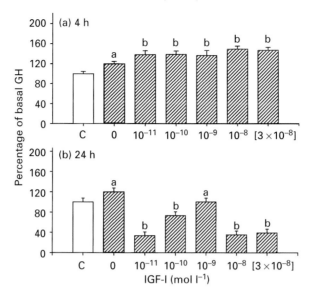

Fig. 3. Effect of insulin-like growth factor I (IGF-I) ($0–3 \times 10^{-8}$ mol l^{-1}) on growth hormone-releasing hormone (GHRH)-induced (10^{-6} mol l^{-1}) GH secretion in pig pituitary cells during (a) 4 h or (b) 24 h culture periods. Values are mean ± standard errors ($n = 8–12$ wells per treatment). C: control = basal secretion in the absence of treatment. [a]Significantly different from the control ($P < 0.05$). [b]Significantly different from GHRH alone ($P < 0.05$).

2000). We reported that serum leptin concentrations increased with age (Qian *et al.*, 1999) and decreased in response to feed deprivation (Barb *et al.*, 2001). In the ovariectomized prepubertal gilt, oestrogen-induced leptin mRNA expression in adipose tissue occurred at the time of expected puberty in intact gilts (Qian *et al.*, 1999) and was associated with greater LH secretion (Barb *et al.*, 2000). Furthermore, expression of the long form leptin receptor (OB-Rl) mRNA in the hypothalamus had increased by 3.5 months of age and remained high at 6 months of age in the prepubertal gilt demonstrating an age-dependent increase in OB-Rl expression (Lin *et al.*, 2001). Thus, leptin may be an important link between metabolic status and the neuroendocrine system.

Gonadotrophin secretion. The multifaceted effects of leptin appear to be mediated by the hypothalamus. In pigs, the presence of biologically active leptin receptors in the hypothalamus and pituitary gland indicate that leptin acts through the hypothalamic–pituitary axis (Lin *et al.*, 2000). In support of this proposal, leptin increased LH secretion from pig pituitary cells *in vitro* and GnRH release from hypothalamic tissue *in vitro* (Barb *et al.*, 1999; Table 3). Co-localization of leptin receptor mRNA with neuropeptide Y (NPY) gene expression provides strong evidence that hypothalamic NPY is a potential target for leptin (Cunningham *et al.*, 1999). In pigs, central administration of NPY suppressed LH secretion (Barb, 1999). However, fertility was restored only partially in the *ob/ob* mouse with a homozygous null mutation for NPY (Erickson *et al.*, 1996). In addition, leptin failed to affect *in vitro* NPY release from pig hypothalamic–preoptic area tissue fragments (C. R. Barb, unpublished). Therefore, the action of leptin at the CNS may be mediated via other hypothalamic factors in addition to NPY.

Growth hormone axis. Growth hormone, unlike other pituitary hormones, exerts biological effects on most tissues in the body and plays an important role in the regulation of metabolism and energy balance (Etherton and Bauman, 1998). Altered GH secretion is associated with changes in body composition, metabolism and fasting (Muller *et al.*, 1999). A common factor associated with all of the above situations is a change in adiposity or change in energy metabolism.

We assessed the role of leptin in modulating GH secretion by intracerebroventricular administration of leptin to pigs that had been fed. GH secretion increased markedly in pigs that were fed normally, and maximum concentrations of GH occurred at 15–30 min after intracerebroventricular injection (Barb *et al.*, 1998), which is similar to the GH response to exogenously administered GHRF (Barb *et al.*, 1991; Table 4). More-over, central admin-istration of leptin reduced feed intake in a dose-dependent manner and this effect was still apparent at 48 h after leptin treatment (Barb *et al.*, 1998). In addition to a hypothalamic site of action, we demonstrated that leptin stimulated basal GH secretion and inhibited GHRH-induced GH secretion from pituitary cells in culture (Barb *et al.*, 1998; Table 3). Taken together, these results support the hypothesis that adipose tissue secretes a protein signal that acts on the CNS to regulate GH secretion and feed intake.

Leptin, a metabolic signal, regulates LH and GH secretion. In pigs, pulsatile leptin secretion decreased significantly after 24 h of a 28 h fast with no subsequent change in LH and GH secretion or in subcutaneous back fat thickness. However, plasma glucose and serum insulin and IGF-I concentrations were lower in fasted animals compared with control animals (Barb *et al.*, 2001). Prepubertal gilts were treated with 2-deoxy-D-glucose, a competitive inhibitor of glycolysis, to determine whether the effects of metabolic fuel restriction on LH and GH secretion were due to reduced serum leptin concentrations. Treatment with 2-deoxy-D-glucose increased mean serum GH concentrations, but failed to affect the frequency and amplitude of GH pulses. However, 2-deoxy-D-glucose suppressed LH pulse frequency, but failed to alter mean serum LH concentrations and LH pulse amplitude. Serum leptin concentrations were unchanged by 2-deoxy-D-glucose treatment (Barb *et al.*, 2001). These results indicate that acute effects of energy deprivation on LH and GH secretion are independent of changes in serum leptin concentrations and that there are two distinct sites at which leptin and glucose modulate the neuroendocrine axis.

Conclusion

Evidence has been presented that supports the concept that metabolites and metabolic hormones affect both hypothalamic hormone secretion and, hence, anterior pituitary function and anterior pituitary hormone secretion, directly. In general, glucose, FFA, insulin and IGF-I act primarily at the anterior pituitary gland to modulate pituitary responsiveness to GHRH and GnRH, whereas there are two distinct sites of action for leptin in regulating LH and GH secretion. Although leptin is an important metabolic signal, other metabolic cues, such as glucose, FFA, insulin and IGF-I, may play a role in modulating the neuroendocrine axis during pubertal development, lactation and during periods of acute and chronic undernutrition (Fig. 4).

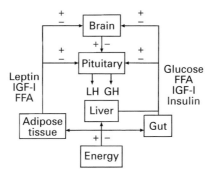

Fig. 4. Putative sites of action for metabolic fuels and metabolic hormones in neuroendocrine control of LH and GH secretion in pigs. Changes in circulating concentrations of glucose, free fatty acids (FFA), insulin, insulin-like growth factor I (IGF-I) and leptin in response to energy availability can be both inhibitory and stimulatory to LH and GH secretion.

References

Abe H, Molitch ME, Van Wyk JJ and Underwood LE (1983) Human growth hormone and somatomedin C suppress the spontaneous release of growth hormone in unanesthetized rats *Endocrinology* **113** 1319–1324

Ahima RS and Flier JS (2000) Leptin *Annual Review of Physiology* **62** 413–437

Angell CA, Tubbs RC, Moore AB, Barb CR and Cox NM (1996) Depressed luteinizing hormone response to estradiol *in vivo* and gonadotropin-releasing hormone *in vitro* in experimentally diabetic swine *Domestic Animal Endocrinology* **13** 453–463

Armstrong JD and Britt JH (1987) Nutritionally-induced anestrus in gilts: metabolic and endocrine changes associated with cessation and resumption of estrous cycles *Journal of Animal Science* **65** 508–523

Armstrong JD, Britt JH and Kraeling RR (1986) Effect of restriction of energy during lactation on body condition, energy metabolism, endocrine changes and reproductive performance in primaparous sows *Journal of Animal Science* **63** 1915–1925

Barb CR (1999) The brain–pituitary–adipocyte axis: role of leptin in modulating neuroendocrine function *Journal of Animal Science* **77** 1249–1257

Barb CR, Cox NM, Matamoros IA, Kraeling RR and Rampacek GB (1990) Growth hormone (GH) secretion after intracerebroventricular (ICV) administrations of insulin (INS) in the gilt *Journal of Animal Science* **68** (Supplement 1) 310 (Abstract)

Barb CR, Kraeling RR, Barrett JB, Rampacek GB, Campbell RM and Mowles TF (1991) Serum glucose and free fatty acids modulate growth hormone and luteinizing hormone secretion in the pig *Proceedings of the Society for Experimental Biology and Medicine* **198** 636–642

Barb CR, Cox NM, Carlton CA, Chang WJ and Randle RF (1992) Growth hormone secretion, serum, and cerebral spinal fluid insulin and insulin-like growth factor-1 concentrations in pigs with streptozotocin-induced diabetes mellitus *Proceedings of the Society for Experimental Biology and Medicine* **201** 223–228

Barb CR, Kraeling RR and Rampacek GB (1995) Glucose and free fatty acid modulation of growth hormone and luteinizing hormone secretion by cultured porcine pituitary cells *Journal of Animal Science* **73** 1416–1423

Barb CR, Kraeling RR and Rampacek GB (1996) Luteinizing hormone and growth hormone (GH) secretion after intracerebroventricular (ICV) administration of IGF-I or insulin (INS) in the prepuberal gilt *Journal of Animal Science* **74** (Supplement 1) 240 (Abstract)

Barb CR, Kraeling RR, Rampacek GB and Dove CR (1997) Metabolic changes during the transition from the fed to the acute feed-deprived state in prepuberal and mature gilts *Journal of Animal Science* **75** 781–789

Barb CR, Yan X, Azian MJ, Kraeling RR, Rampacek GB and Ramsay TG (1998) Recombinant porcine leptin reduced feed intake and stimulates growth hormone secretion in swine *Domestic Animal Endocrinology* **15** 77–86

Barb CR, Barrett JB, Kraeling RR and Rampacek GB (1999) Role of leptin in modulating neuroendocrine function: a metabolic link between the brain–pituitary and adipose tissue *Reproduction in Domestic Animals* **34** 111–125

Barb CR, Kraeling RR, Rampacek GB and Estienne MJ (2000) Current concepts of the onset of puberty in the gilt *Reproduction in Domestic Animals* (Supplement 6) 82–89

Barb CR, Barrett JB, Kraeling RR and Rampacek GB (2001) Serum leptin concentrations, luteinizing hormone and growth hormone secretion during feed and metabolic fuel restriction in the prepuberal gilt *Domestic Animal Endocrinology* **20** 47–63

Bonneau M (1993) Growth hormone response to GRF and insulin-induced hypoglycemia in Yorkshire and Meishan pigs *American Journal of Physiology: Endocrinology and Metabolism* **264** E54–E59

Booth PJ (1990) Metabolic influences on hypothalamic–pituitary ovarian function in the pig *Journal of Reproduction and Fertility Supplement* **40** 89–100

Buonomo FC, Grohs DL, Baile CA and Campion DR (1988) Determination of circulating levels of insulin-like growth factor II (IGF-II) in swine *Domestic Animal Endocrinology* **5** 323–329

Cameron JL, Koerker DJ and Steiner RA (1985) Metabolic changes during maturation of male monkeys: possible sign for onset of puberty *American Journal of Physiology* **249** E385–E391

Casanueva FF and Dieguez C (1999) Neuroendocrine regulation and actions of leptin *Frontiers in Neuroendocrinology* **20** 317–363

Cosgrove JR and Foxcroft GR (1996) Nutrition and reproduction in the pig: ovarian aetiology *Animal Reproduction Science* **42** 131–141

Cox NM and Britt JH (1988) Pulsatile administration of gonadotropin releasing hormone to lactating sows: endocrine changes associated with induction of fertile estrus *Biology of Reproduction* **27** 1126–1137

Cox NM, Stuart MJ, Althen TG, Bennett WA and Miller HW (1987) Enhancement of ovulation rate in gilts by increasing dietary energy and administering insulin during follicular growth *Journal of Animal Science* **64** 507–516

Cox NM, Barb CR, Kesner PJ, Kraeling RR, Matamoros IA and Rampacek GB (1990) Effects of intracerebroventricular administration of insulin on luteinizing hormone in gilts *Journal of Reproduction and Fertility Supplement* **40** 63 (Abstract)

Cox NM, Meurer KA, Carlton CA, Tubbs RC and Mannis DP (1994) Effect of diabetes mellitus during the luteal phase of the oestrous cycle on preovulatory follicular function, ovulation and gondatrophins in gilts *Journal of Reproduction and Fertility* **101** 77–86

Cunningham MJ, Clifton DK and Steiner RA (1999) Leptin's action on the reproductive axis: perspectives and mechanisms *Biology of Reproduction* **60** 216–222

Dubreuil P, Pelletier G, Petitclerc D, Lapierre H, Couture Y, Brazeau P, Gaudreau P and Morisset J (1987) Influence of age and sex on basal secretion of growth hormone (GH) and on GH-induced release by porcine GH-releasing factor pGRF(1-29NH2) in growing pigs *Domestic Animal Endocrinology* **4** 299–307

Erickson JC, Hollopeter G and Palmiter RD (1996) Attenuation of the obesity syndrome of ob/ob mice by the loss of neuropeptide Y *Science* **274** 1704–1707

Etherton TD and Bauman DE (1998) Biology of somatotropin in growth and lactation of domestic animals *Physiological Reviews* **78** 745–761

Frisch RE (1984) Body fat, puberty and fertility *Biological Reviews* **59** 161–188

Handelsman DJ, Spaliviero JA, Scott CD and Baxter RC (1987) Hormonal regulation of the peripubertal surge of insulin-like growth factor-I in the rat *Endocrinology* **120** 491–496

Goodman RL (1988) Neuroendocrine control of the ovine estrus cycle. In *The Physiology of Reproduction*, Vol 1, pp 1929–1970 Eds E Knobil, JD Neill, LL Ewing, GS Greenwald, CL Markert and DW Pfaff. Raven Press, New York

Hiney JK, Ojeda SR and Dees WL (1991) Insulin-like growth factor-I: a possible metabolic signal involved in the regulation of female puberty *Neuroendocrinology* **54** 420–423

Kraeling RR and Barb CR (1990) Hypothalamic control of gonadotrophin and prolactin secretion in pigs *Journal of Reproduction and Fertility Supplement* **40** 3–7

Lee CY, Bazer FW, Etherton TD and Simmen FA (1991) Ontogeny of insulin-like growth factors (IGF-I and IGF-II) and IGF-binding proteins in porcine serum during fetal and postnatal development *Endocrinology* **128** 2336–2344

Lin J, Barb CR, Matteri RL, Kraeling RR, Chen X, Meinersmann RJ and Rampacek GB (2000) Long form leptin receptor mRNA expression in the brain, pituitary and other tissues in the pig *Domestic Animal Endocrinology* **19** 53–61

Lin J, Barb CR, Kraeling RR and Rampacek GB (2001) Developmental changes in the long form leptin receptor and related neuropeptide gene expression in the pig brain *Biology of Reproduction* **64** 1614–1618

Lutz JB, Rampacek GB, Kraeling RR and Pinkert CA (1984) Serum luteinizing hormone and estrogen profiles before puberty in the gilt *Journal of Animal Science* **58** 686–691

Muller EE, Locatelli V and Cocchi D (1999) Neuroendocrine control of growth hormone secretion *Physiological Reviews* **79** 511–607

Pressing A, Dial GD, Esbenshade KL and Stroud CM (1992) Hourly administration of GnRH to prepubertal gilts: endocrine and ovulatory responses from 70 to 190 days of age *Journal of Animal Science* **70** 232–242

Prunier A and Quesnel H (2000a) Nutritional influences on the hormonal control of reproduction in female pigs *Livestock Production Science* **63** 1–16

Prunier A and Quesnel H (2000b) Influence of the nutritional status on ovarian development in female pigs *Animal Reproduction Science* **60–61** 185–197

Qian H, Barb CR, Compton MM, Hausman GJ, Azain MJ, Kraeling RR and Baile CA (1999) Leptin mRNA expression and serum leptin concentrations as influenced by age, weight and estradiol in pigs *Domestic Animal Endocrinology* **16** 135–143

Rojkittikhun T, Uvnäs-Moberg K and Einarsson S (1993a) Plasma oxytocin, prolactin, insulin and LH after 24 h of fasting and after refeeding in lactating sows *Acta Physiologica Scandinavica* **148** 413–419

Rojkittikhun T, Einarsson S, Zilinskas H, Edqvist LE, Uvnäs-Moberg K and Lundeheim N (1993b) Effects of insulin administration at weaning on hormonal patterns and reproductive performance in primiparous sows *Zentralblatt fur Veterinarmedizin Reihe A* **40** 161–168

Rotwein P, Burgess JD, Milbrandt JD and Krause JE (1988) Differential expression of insulin-like growth factor genes in rat central nervous system *Proceedings National Academy of Sciences USA* **85** 265–269

Sara VR and Hall K (1990) Insulin-like growth factors and their binding proteins *Physiological Reviews* **70** 591–614

Spencer GSG, Macdonald AA, Buttle HL, Moore LG and Carlyle SS (1991) Intracerebral administration of insulin-like growth factor I decreases circulating growth hormone levels in the fetal pig *Acta Endocrinologica (Copenhagen)* **124** 563–568

Wade GN, Schneider JE and Li HY (1996) Control of fertility by metabolic cues *American Journal of Physiology* **270** E1–E19

Werther GA, Abate M, Hogg A *et al.* (1990) Localization of insulin-like growth factor-I mRNA in rat brain by *in situ* hybridization – relationship to IGF-I receptors *Molecular Endocrinology* **4** 773–778

Wetsel WC, Valenca MM, Merchenthaler I, Liposits Z, Lopez FJ, Weiner RI, Mellon PL and Negro-Vilar A (1992) Intrinsic pulsatile secretory activity of immortalized luteinizing hormone-releasing hormone-secreting neurons *Proceedings National Academy of Sciences USA* **89** 4149–4153

Whitley NC, Barb CR, Utley RV, Popwell JM, Kraeling RR and Rampacek GB (1995) Influence of stage of the estrous cycle on insulin-like growth factor-I modulation of luteinizing hormone secretion in the gilt *Biology of Reproduction* **53** 1359–1364

Wolverton CK, Azain MJ, Duffy JY, White ME and Ramsay TG (1992) Influence of somatotropin on lipid metabolism and IGF gene expression in porcine adipose tissue *American Journal of Physiology* **263** E637–E645

Yamashita S and Melmed S (1986) Insulin-like growth factor I action on rat anterior pituitary cells: suppression of growth hormone secretion and messenger ribonucleic acid levels *Endocrinology* **118** 176–182

Reproduction Supplement **58**, 17–29

Apoptosis during folliculogenesis in pigs

H. D. Guthrie and W. M. Garrett

Germplasm and Gamete Physiology Laboratory, Agricultural Research Service,
US Department of Agriculture, Beltsville, MD 20705, USA

The number of female germ cells in pig fetuses decreases by 70% between day 50 after mating and day 300 after birth. Approximately 55% of antral follicles undergo degeneration (atresia) except during the 3 days before oestrus, when only 15% of the follicles survive to ovulate. Apoptosis, a form of programmed cell death, is recognized as the mechanism of germ cell death and follicle atresia at all stages of folliculogenesis. The internucleosomal cleavage of genomic DNA caused by caspase-induced deoxyribonuclease activity was measured in pig granulosa cells by DNA fluorescence flow cytometry, densitometry of fluorescently labelled internucleosomal DNA fragments and immunohistochemical analysis of the 3′ end labelling of de-oxyribonuclease-nicked DNA on frozen tissue sections. Follicular atresia during the 3 days before oestrus is associated with a 60–70% decrease in the secretion of FSH. In granulosa cells, apoptosis is associated with decreased cell proliferation and reduced production of oestradiol and inhibin. In cultured pig granulosa cells, FSH and IGF-I are anti-apoptotic and a caspase inhibitor blocked apoptosis, thereby providing evidence of caspase activity. Oocytes in most follicles have resumed meiotic maturation; therefore, one role for apoptosis and follicle atresia may be to act as a barrier to ovulation of oocytes that have not remained in meiotic arrest.

Mechanism of apoptosis

Apoptosis or programmed cell death is a physiological process that is essential for the successful development and survival of multicellular organisms (Vaux, 1993). The distinguishing characteristic of apoptosis is the ordered disassembly of cells from within a remodelling process required to remove cells that have completed their functions and are no longer needed, or that fail to develop properly, or that are damaged genetically. Apoptosis is triggered by environmental or physiological stimuli, or by withdrawal of trophic factors. As the predominant form of physiological cell death in eukaryotic cells, apoptosis requires energy utilization and is often regulated at the level of transcription or translation. These features of apoptosis distinguish it from necrosis, a pathological form of cell death, which is a result of injury and is characterized by swelling of the cell, activation of an immune response and lysis (Arends *et al.*, 1990).

Physiological induction of apoptosis follows two general pathways: negative induction by survival factor withdrawal (Fig. 1a) and positive induction by specific ligand binding to a plasma membrane receptor (Fig. 1b). Six major components in these pathways have been

Email: dave@anri.barc.usda.gov

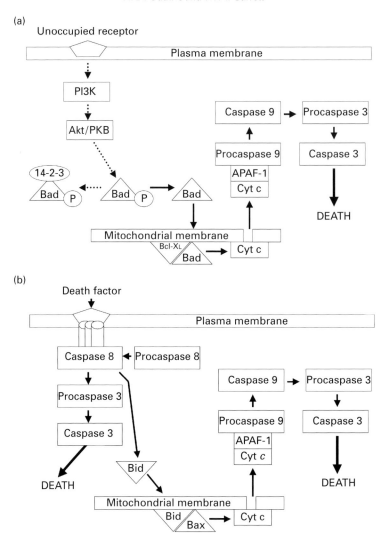

Fig. 1. Model for apoptosis pathway in pigs. (a) Negative induction by with-drawal of trophic or cell survival factors and (b) positive induction by specific ligand binding to plasma membrane receptors. In the negative induction pathway, receptor occupancy maintains a phosphorylation signal trans-duction pathway to sequester phosphorylated pro-apoptotic B-cell lymphoma/leukaemia-2 (Bcl-2) family proteins, such as Bcl-X$_L$/Bcl-2-associated death promoter (Bad) in the cytosol. If the receptor for a survival factor, such as FSH or insulin-like growth factor (IGF-I), is vacated then the phosphorylation signal transduction pathway is disabled; Bad is dephosphorylated and translocated to the mitochondrion. As a consequence of binding with an anti-apoptotic protein, such as Bcl-2 and Bcl-2-related gene-x long form (Bcl-X$_L$), the outer mitochondrial membrane is destabilized and cytochrome *c* (Cyt *c*) escapes to initiate caspase activation. In the positive induction pathway, ligands, such as tumour necrosis factor, Fas and angiotensin II, occupy their membrane receptors to cause aggregation (trimerization) of plasma membrane receptors and orient receptor cytosolic-death domains into a configuration that recruits adaptor proteins to promote the binding and activation of procaspases. Pro-apoptotic Bcl-2 proteins localized in the

described to execute pro-apoptotic or anti-apoptotic processes in mammalian species. These components are: (i) plasma membrane receptors for cell survival factors and cell death factors; (ii) the B-cell lymphoma/leukaemia 2 (Bcl-2) family of proteins; (iii) cytochrome *c*; (iv) apoptotic protease-activating factor 1 (APAF-1); (v) cysteinyl aspartate-specific proteases (caspases, interleukin-1β-converting enzyme family); and (vi) inhibitory apoptosis proteins (IAP) (for reviews, see Ashkenazi and Dixit, 1998; Thornberry and Lazebnik, 1998; Desagher and Martinou, 2000; Guthrie and Garrett, 2000a).

Results from other studies indicate that the mitochondrion is a major target for the Bcl-2 proteins (Desagher and Martinou, 2000). Currently, 24 Bcl-2 proteins have been identified in mammals. Each member of the family contains at least one of four regions of Bcl-2 homology that permit Bcl-2 proteins to form homo- and heterodimers to regulate each other. The Bcl-2 proteins possess either anti-apoptotic or pro-apoptotic function. For the most part, the anti-apoptotic members bind to the outer mitochondrial membranes and the pro-apoptotic members are distributed in both the cytosol and mitochondria. The primary mechanism by which Bcl-2 proteins regulate apoptosis is by controlling the release of cytochrome *c* from the mitochondrion into the cytosol, where it coordinates the activation of caspases. The release of cytochrome *c* from the mitochondrion initiates the 'caspase cascade' and serves as the critical point of control for apoptosis. In the cytosol, cytochrome *c* forms a complex with APAF-1, dATP and procaspase 9 resulting in proteolytic activation of 'initiator' caspases, such as caspase 9. Caspase 9 subsequently activates downstream 'effector' caspases, such as caspase 3, which functions to degrade cellular components or activate other substrates (Fig. 2) by proteolytic attack (Enari *et al.*, 1998).

Caspases are responsible for the inactivation or activation of protein activities that lead to the death or disassembly of affected cells, and are present as inactive pro-enzymes, most of which are activated by proteolytic cleavage themselves (Cohen, 1997; Miller, 1997). The execution phase of caspase activity is represented by caspase 3 which, serving as a substrate for initiator caspases, amplifies the earlier cell death signals, resulting in cleavage of vital cellular proteins for completion of the cell death pathway (Fig. 2).

The specific substrate targets of the execution phase of apoptosis that affect the final dis-assembly of the cell are varied. The actions and substrates include disruption of micro-filaments (GAS2), cytoskeletal components (actin and fodrin), chromosome structure (lamin), the cell cycle (retinoblastoma protein), DNA repair (poly[ADP]-ribose polymerase), low density lipoprotein receptor expression (sterol regulatory element-binding proteins 1 and 2) and signal transduction (catalytic subunit of DNA protein kinase). The chromatin in the nucleus is supported by a scaffold of protein designated as the nuclear matrix. The final stages of apoptosis are characterized by the activation in the nucleus of a deoxyribonuclease, which cleaves DNA between nucleosomes into internucleosomal fragments.

The IAP family are cytoplasmic proteins that bind to, and inhibit the activity of, specific caspases that function in the cell death pathway (Roy *et al.*, 1997).

---

cytosol, such as Bcl-2-related death gene (Bid), are activated by caspase action mediated through the Fas/ tumour necrosis factor apoptosis signal and are translocated to the mitochondrion for heterodimerization with other proapoptotic proteins such as Bcl-2 associated-x-gene (Bax) to destabilize the outer mitochondrial membrane resulting in the release of cytochrome *c*. The positive induction pathway can initiate a 'caspase cascade' that results in a death process that can be independent of or dependent on changes in mitochondrial stability. Akt: serine-threonine kinase; APAF-1: apoptotic protease-activating factor 1; PI3K: phosphatidylinositide-3-OH kinase; PKB: protein kinase B.

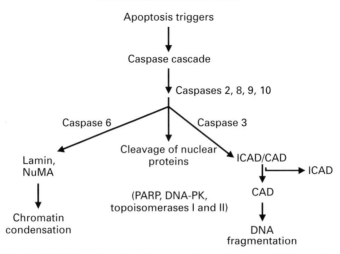

Fig. 2. Model for the role of caspases in nuclear apoptotic events showing the specific substrate targets of the execution phase of apoptosis leading to cleavage of genomic DNA into internucleosomal fragments. CAD: caspase-activated DNase; DNA-PK: DNA-dependent protein kinase; ICAD: inhibitor of CAD; NuMA: nuclear-mitotic apparatus protein; PARP: poly(ADP-ribose) polymerase.

Folliculogenesis and apoptosis

In pigs, the number of germ cells per female reaches a maximum of 1.2×10^6 in the fetus at day 50 after mating and then decreases sharply to 5.0×10^5 at parturition (Fig. 3). Germ cell development is dynamic in the fetus with proliferation, meiotic arrest, primordial follicle formation, primordial follicle activation and germ cell death occurring simultaneously in the same ovaries. In the ovaries of pig fetuses, about 5% of oocytes are undergoing apoptosis as indicated by the presence of pyknotic nuclei (Black and Erickson, 1968). Although germ cell death has not been studied extensively in pigs, in laboratory species it has been established that during early stages of oogenesis and folliculogenesis, apoptosis plays the primary role in oocyte degeneration (Pesce *et al.*, 1993; Pesce and De Felici, 1994). Bcl-2 knockout mice have reduced numbers of primordial follicles (Ratts *et al.*, 1995), and targeted overexpression of Bcl-2 in mouse ovarian somatic cells leads to reduced follicular atresia and increased litter size (Hsu *et al.*, 1996). After parturition, the number of germ cells per female decreased at a slower rate to 2.0×10^5 at day 300 of age (Fig. 3). In pigs, preantral follicle growth begins within 10 days of birth (Erickson, 1967). Antral follicles are first observed histologically at about day 65 of age and emerge from the ovarian surface at about day 80 of age (Erickson, 1967; H. D. Guthrie, unpublished). We found that Bcl-2 was not expressed in germ cells and that expression was greatest in stromal cells located in the ovarian cortex surrounding primordial follicles and in the granulosa cells of primordial and preantral follicles (Garrett and Guthrie, 1999). This finding indicates that Bcl-2 mediates its survival effect indirectly through stromal cell survival factors.

Granulosa cell apoptosis is the underlying molecular mechanism of follicular atresia (Hughes and Gorospe, 1991; Tilly *et al.*, 1991; Guthrie *et al.*, 1995). The incidence of follicular atresia, determined by pyknotic nuclei in granulosa cells, is lowest among primordial follicles ($\leqslant 6\%$) and preantral follicles ($\leqslant 17\%$), and greatest among antral

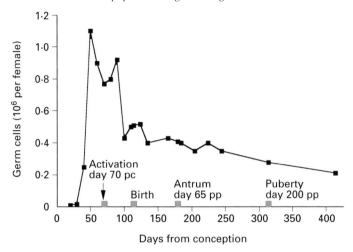

Fig. 3. Changes in the number of germ cells during folliculogenesis in female pigs showing key stages in development. Primordial follicle activation was first detected at day 70 post coitum (pc) and follicle antrum formation was first detected at day 65 post partum (pp) (modified from Erickson, 1967; Black and Erickson, 1968).

follicles, averaging 55% in pre- and postpubertal gilts (Erickson, 1967; Dalin, 1987). The formation of antral follicles and the increased incidence of atresia during prepubertal development is coincident with a 60% decrease in mean plasma concentrations of FSH and LH between day 60 and day 120 of age (Guthrie and Garrett, 2000a).

Ovarian regulation of atresia and apoptosis

Biochemical characteristics of atresia and apoptosis have been investigated to discover causative factors and markers in an attempt to identify follicles in early stages of atresia. Results from studies of ovarian gene expression *in vivo* and *in vitro* have indicated that ovarian products, such as steroid hormones, transforming growth factor family members, insulin-like growth factor I (IGF-I), IGF-binding proteins and inhibins could play a role in the atretic process and apoptosis.

Steroid hormones

Follicles that contain $\geq 10\%$ of apoptotic granulosa cells were found to have very low follicular fluid concentrations of oestradiol (1–5 ng ml^{-1}; Guthrie *et al.*, 1995). Among non-atretic follicles, oestradiol concentrations were inversely related to the percentage of apoptotic (%A_0) granulosa cells ($r = -0.45$; $P = 0.01$; Fig. 4) at the beginning of a follicular phase, on day 1 after withdrawal of altrenogest and on day 6 of the oestrous cycle (Guthrie *et al.*, 1995). It was concluded that low follicular fluid concentrations of oestradiol are a very early predictor of atresia. Loss of aromatase activity and enzyme protein (Guthrie and Garrett, 2000a) in granulosa cells is an important characteristic of atresia in follicles and may be mediated, in part, at transcription (Tilly *et al.*, 1992a).

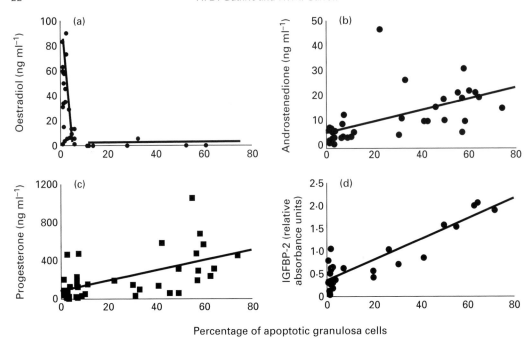

Percentage of apoptotic granulosa cells

Fig. 4. Linear regression of follicular fluid concentrations of (a) oestradiol, (b) androstenedione, (c) progesterone and (d) IGF binding protein 2 (IGFBP-2) on granulosa cell apoptosis in individual medium-sized nonatretic (< 10% apoptotic granulosa cells) and atretic (≥ 10% apoptotic granulosa cells) follicles in pigs (modified from Guthrie *et al.*, 1995).

Progesterone and androstenedione content of atretic follicles is similar to, or greater than, that of nonatretic follicles on days 6–7 of the oestrous cycle (Guthrie *et al.*, 1995). Androstenedione and progesterone is were produced continuously *in vivo* in the follicular fluid as follicles became increasingly atretic as indicated by a greater proportion of apoptotic granulosa cells (Fig. 4). These results are in agreement with findings indicating that atretic pig follicles in culture release similar or greater amounts of androgen or progesterone to healthy follicles (Guthrie *et al.*, 1995). The ability of atretic follicles to continue production of androgens and progesterone is probably due to the ability of theca cells to retain specific binding and steroid responsiveness to LH even in advanced stages of atresia, whereas specific binding of FSH in granulosa cells disappears relatively early during atresia (Tsafriri and Braw, 1984). The loss of specific binding of FSH in granulosa cells of atretic follicles may account, in part, for the loss of aromatase activity. Similarly, granulosa cells from atretic pig follicles were no longer able to release cAMP in response to exogenous gonadotrophins (Guthrie and Garrett, 2000a). In small pig follicles, expression of LH receptor and FSH receptor transcripts was localized to the theca interna and granulosa cells, respectively (Guthrie and Garrett, 2000a). In atretic follicles, LH receptor was expressed weakly in theca cells, whereas there was no expression of FSH receptor in granulosa cells (Guthrie and Garrett, 2000a).

Steroids modulate apoptosis in cultured granulosa cells of rats (Hsueh *et al.*, 1994). Progesterone acting through a novel membrane receptor was shown to inhibit apoptosis in cultured granulosa cells of rats (Peluso and Pappalardo, 1994). In addition, the anti-apoptotic effect of epidermal growth factor (EGF) might also act by stimulating progesterone production. Progesterone production by pig granulosa cells *in vitro* was inversely related to apoptosis in the presence of FSH or IGF-I (Guthrie *et al.*, 1998). This is in contrast to the positive correlation between follicular fluid concentrations of progesterone and the percentage of apoptotic granulosa cells during early stages of atresia *in vivo* (Guthrie *et al.*, 1995).

In an attempt to clarify the role of progesterone in relation to apoptosis, the relationship between apoptosis and progesterone production in pig granulosa cells was examined using inhibitors of progesterone production and apoptosis. Although trilostane inhibited FSH-induced progesterone production, it did not affect the anti-apoptotic effect of FSH. When apoptosis was inhibited using the general caspase inhibitor benzyloxycarbonyl-valinyl-alaninyl-aspartyl fluoromethylketone (Guthrie *et al.*, 2000), no effect on progesterone production was found. These results indicate that apoptosis and progesterone production are regulated independently by FSH in pig granulosa cells. In addition, although EGF also increased progesterone production in cultured pig granulosa cells, it did not have an anti-apoptotic effect (H. D. Guthrie, unpublished).

Atresia is regulated by oestrogens and androgens in laboratory species (Tsafriri and Braw, 1984). Oestradiol benzoate was shown to block apoptosis in granulosa cells after the withdrawal of diethylstilbestrol (DES) in hypophysectomized, DES-treated, immature female rats (Billig *et al.*, 1993). Furthermore, simultaneous treatment with testosterone prevented the anti-atretogenic effect of oestradiol benzoate, indicating that an interaction between locally produced oestrogen and androgen could regulate processes that trigger apoptosis and atresia. Further studies are required to determine the role of ovarian steroids on apoptosis and the atretic process in pigs.

Role of inhibin and activin

Apart from the initial primary role of inhibin as an endocrine regulator of pituitary function and of activin as a stimulator of pituitary cell FSH secretion (de Jong, 1988), evidence from granulosa cell culture indicates that inhibin and activin, dimers of inhibin–activin α and β subunits, act as intra-ovarian paracrine factors, regulating multiple facets of follicular development (Hillier, 1991; Findlay, 1994). Other studies have shown that increased expression of inhibin–activin subunits is associated with follicle growth during the early luteal phase of the oestrous cycle in pigs (Guthrie *et al.*, 1997; Garrett *et al.*, 2000). Multiple molecular forms of inhibin or the α subunit are detectable in follicular fluid of atretic and nonatretic follicles during the follicular and the early luteal phase of the oestrous cycle (Guthrie *et al.*, 1997). The high molecular mass forms of inhibin dimer (227, 121, 69 kDa) were more abundant in nonatretic follicles than in atretic follicles, indicating a higher rate of inhibin synthesis. Expression of α and β subunit mRNAs, and cytochrome P450 aromatase protein increased by 102, 93 and 238%, respectively, as nonatretic follicles grew from the 1–2 mm into the 3–5 mm size class (Garrett *et al.*, 2000). In addition, expression of α and β subunit mRNAs was positively correlated with the expression of a marker for cell proliferation, proliferation-associated nuclear antigen Ki-67 protein (α: $r = 0.571$, $P = 0.0001$; and β: $r = 0.594$, $P = 0.0001$). In contrast, as follicle atresia increased, as indicated by granulosa cell apoptosis, from the nonatretic to the late atretic stage, the expression of α and β subunit mRNAs, cytochrome P450 aromatase protein and cell proliferation-associated nuclear antigen Ki-67 protein decreased by 70, 83, 66 and 69%, respectively (Garrett *et al.*, 2000). These results indicate that granulosa cell proliferation and follicle growth are linked to the expression of inhibin–activin subunits. However, atresia was associated with a general decline in granulosa cell biosynthetic activity. In contrast, other findings indicate an atretogenic role for activin *in vivo* (Woodruff *et al.*, 1990) and *in vitro* (Ford and Howard, 1997). However, these results might also be explained by stimulation of androgen production by theca interna or by a blockade of terminal granulosa cell differentiation.

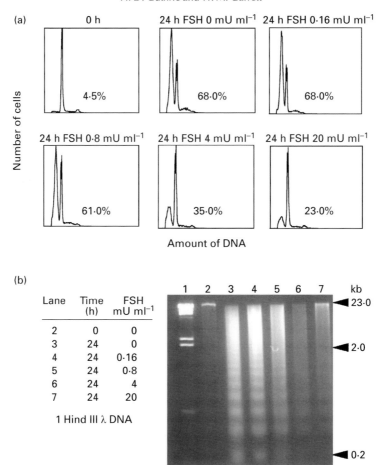

Fig. 5. Attenuating effect of FSH on apoptosis during 24 h culture of pig granulosa cells. (a) DNA histograms showing percentages of granulosa cells and (b) DNA internucleosomal cleavage showing low molecular weight DNA (< 23 kbp) fragments fractionated by agarose gel electrophoresis of DNA extracted from cells before culture (lane 2) and after culture (lanes 3–7). The absence of internucleosomal DNA fragments in lane 2 shows that the incidence of endogenous endonuclease activity was low before culture. DNA extracted from cells cultured for 24 h (lanes 3–7) shows an increase in DNA internucleosomal cleavage relative to noncultured cells and the attenuating effect of FSH (modified from Guthrie *et al.*, 1998).

FSH and growth factors in vitro

Various growth factor pathways have been implicated in the growth, cell proliferation and differentiated cell functions of follicles (Hammond *et al.*, 1993). Culture of granulosa cells or follicles from untreated or equine chorionic gonadotrophin (eCG)-treated rats have been useful models for the study of granulosa cell apoptosis because the granulosa cells in these experimental models undergo spontaneous or culture-induced apoptosis (Tilly *et al.*, 1992b; Chun *et al.*, 1994). Gonadotrophins, EGF, transforming growth factor α, basic fibroblast growth factor and IGF-I have been described as follicle survival or anti-apoptotic factors capable of suppressing granulosa cell DNA fragmentation in rats (Hsueh *et al.*, 1994).

Pig granulosa cells, like those of rats, undergo spontaneous or culture-induced apoptosis, and were used to test the hypothesis that FSH and IGF-I are anti-apoptotic, cell survival factors (Guthrie *et al.*, 1998). Representative DNA histograms of granulosa cells isolated from one pig (Fig. 5a) show that the percentage of apoptotic granulosa cells increased from 4.5% in freshly isolated cells to 68.0% after 24 h in culture. Apoptosis in granulosa cells decreased by half ($P < 0.01$) in the presence of FSH (4 NIH-S1 mU ml^{-1}) and reached a plateau between 4 and 20 FSH mU ml^{-1}. During the 24 h culture period, genomic DNA was cleaved into inter-nucleosomal fragments forming 'DNA ladders' characteristic of deoxyribonuclease activity (Fig. 5b, lane 3). Internucleosomal cleavage was attenuated by 50% in the presence of FSH (Fig. 5b, lanes 6 and 7). IGF-I was also found to have an anti-apoptotic effect on granulosa cells (Guthrie *et al.*, 1998). Apoptosis decreased by 50% in cells subjected to 50–250 ng IGF-I ml^{-1} compared with cells cultured for 24 h in the absence of IGF-I.

There are biologically significant differences in the regulation of apoptosis in isolated pig and rat granulosa cells. In rats, IGF-I and FSH did not attenuate apoptosis in cultured granulosa cells (Tilly *et al.*, 1992a; Hsueh *et al.*, 1994). In contrast, Guthrie *et al.* (1998) found that both FSH and IGF-I attenuated apoptosis in pig granulosa cells, but that EGF was not effective (H. D. Guthrie, unpublished). In rats, apoptosis in granulosa cells was attenuated only when FSH and IGF-I were added to the culture of intact preovulatory follicles (Tilly *et al.*, 1992a; Chun *et al.*, 1994). A review of several studies in rats and pigs indicates that apoptosis decreased in culture conditions that promoted granulosa cell proliferation (Guthrie and Garrett, 2000a).

The role of FSH in vivo

Administration of charcoal-stripped pig follicular fluid induced changes in circulating concentrations of FSH in pigs indicating that FSH may play a critical role in maintaining a nonatretic population of follicles (Guthrie *et al.*, 1987, 1988). A decrease in circulating concentrations of FSH of 60% after treatment with charcoal-stripped pig follicular fluid (compared with charcoal-stripped pig serum) was associated with a reduction ($P < 0.05$) in total ovarian mass (by 39%) and of fluid volume (by 59%), and with a reduction ($P < 0.05$) in the number of 3–5 mm follicles from 29.6 to 2.9 per gilt (93% decrease). Follicles remaining after treatment with charcoal-stripped pig follicular fluid were opaque, which is indicative of atresia (Guthrie *et al.*, 1987). In another experiment, administration of FSH free of LH activity resulted in an increase ($P < 0.05$) in the number of 3–6 mm follicles compared with the saline control group (59.0 versus 30.8 per gilt, 48% increase) and restored the number of 3–6 mm follicles to that observed in the saline control group after charcoal-stripped pig follicular fluid treatment (0.2 versus 36.2 per gilt). There is a similar relationship between FSH secretion and the number of small and medium-sized follicles during the follicular phase and the periovulatory period of the next oestrous cycle. Selection and growth of the ovulatory cohort of follicles was accompanied by a 60–70% decrease in circulating concentrations of FSH and by atresia of non-ovulatory follicles and suspension of their replacement until after ovulation (Guthrie *et al.*, 1995; Guthrie and Garrett, 2000a). Regrowth of 3–5 mm follicles after ovulation is temporally related to increased circulating concentrations of FSH (Guthrie and Garrett, 2000a). During the cell differentiation required for the maturation of ovulatory follicles, FSH appears to become less important as these events progress in the presence of low concentrations of plasma FSH and granulosa cell FSH receptor. The critical factor for the survival of ovulatory follicles may be the greater LH-responsiveness of ovulatory follicles, compared with non-ovulatory follicles, in terms of increased granulosa and theca cell LH receptor expression (Guthrie and Garrett, 2000a), LH binding and increased granulosa LH-sensitive adenylate cyclase activity (Channing et al., 1982; Foxcroft and Hunter, 1985; Guthrie et al., 1995; Guthrie and Garrett, 2000a). On the basis of the effects of FSH treatment in vitro and regulation of FSH secretion in vivo, we conclude that FSH plays a role in growth and survival of small and medium-sized follicles by stimulation of granulosa cell proliferation and attenuation of granulosa cell apoptosis.

Follicular IGF and IGFBP

Although follicle atresia may be a result of decreased circulating concentrations of FSH and a reduction in the number of FSH receptors in the follicle population (Guthrie and Garrett, 2000a), an increase in the number of inhibitory IGF-I binding proteins (IGFBP) in granulosa cells may also play a role in biological neutralization of IGF-I (Hammond et al., 1993). Analysis of follicular fluid from follicles recovered during preovulatory maturation and during the early luteal phase showed that the amount of follicular fluid IGFBP-2 present was three-fold greater in atretic than in nonatretic follicles (Guthrie et al., 1995). The quantity of IGFBP-2 was positively correlated with the percentage of apoptotic granulosa cells per follicle, during preovulatory maturation ($r = 0.73$; $P \leqslant 0.001$) and during the early luteal phase ($r = 0.90$; $P \leqslant 0.001$; Fig. 4). Therefore, in several mammalian species, production or accumulation of IGFBP-2 may play a role in follicular atresia and granulosa cell apoptosis (Guthrie et al., 1995). In studies of gene expression in relation to atresia and apoptosis, it is clear that follicular cell proliferation and atresia are regulated by a complex interaction between the granulosa, theca interna and factors originating from the systemic circulation.

Apoptotic pathway

There is some evidence that caspase activity is associated with culture-induced apoptosis in pig granulosa cells (Guthrie et al., 2000). The percentage of apoptotic granulosa cells increased ($P < 0.05$) from 2.3% in freshly harvested granulosa cells to 33% after 24 h in culture. The caspase inhibitor benzyloxycarbonyl-valinyl-alaninyl-aspartyl fluoro methylke-tone reduced apoptosis to 3%, which is similar to that in non-cultured cells. Reduction of granulosa cell apoptosis had no significant effect on steroidogenic activity during the culture period. Both APAF-1 and cytochrome c are expressed in cultured mouse granulosa cells and caspase 3 was activated during culture-induced apoptosis (Robles et al., 1999). Further support for the role of caspases in ovarian apoptosis is that the expression of caspase 3 is associated with apoptosis in atretic follicles of rats (Flaws et al., 1995). A new anti-apoptotic pathway, the IAP protein family, has been found in the ovaries of mice and rats. These proteins may play an important regulatory role in granulosa cell apoptosis and follicle atresia because in rats two IAPs, X-link inhibitor of apoptosis (XIAP) and human inhibitor of apoptosis protein 2 (HIAP-2), are localized in the cytoplasm and nuclei of granulosa and theca cells of healthy follicles and had decreased to low and non-detectable values in granulosa and theca cells, respectively, in atretic follicles (Li et al., 1998). Another IAP, neuronal apoptosis inhibitory protein mRNA was strongly expressed in granulosa cells that were not undergoing apoptosis (Matsumoto et al., 1999). A physiological role of IAPs is strongly supported by the observation that expression of neuronal apoptosis inhibitory protein was increased 2.4-fold after the administration of equine chorionic gonadotrophin (eCG) and hCG, a treatment known to inhibit granulosa cell apoptosis both in vitro and in vivo. Evidence for the operation of the positive induction pathway is also present in ovarian tissue with expression of Fas and the Fas ligand in atretic follicles of the rat (Hakuno et al., 1996; Kim et al., 1998).

Other signal transduction pathways may play a role in granulosa cell apoptosis and follicular atresia. An intense localization of angiotensin II receptor was found in atretic follicles of rats (Daud *et al.*, 1988). Expression of the angiotensin II receptor in granulosa cells may be inhibited by FSH in healthy follicles (Pucell *et al.*, 1988). If FSH support or FSH receptor function is lost, the angiotensin II receptor may be expressed and play a role in regulation of the atretic follicle. However, it remains to be established whether angiotensin II receptors are expressed as a result of atresia or whether expression of the receptors is involved in the mechanism of granulosa cell apoptosis. Although only limited studies have been conducted in pigs, clearly the physiologically regulated expression of the six major components of the apoptotic pathway are operating in the ovarian follicle and support the hypothesis that granulosa cell apoptosis is regulated through both negative and positive induction pathways.

Conclusion

The rationale for the production of so many germ cells during early fetal life and their subsequent loss in pigs and other species is unknown. One explanation of the importance of apoptosis and follicular atresia is that oocytes may have a limited finite lifespan when they reach full size. Up to 70% of oocytes in 3–5 mm diameter follicles have initiated germinal vesicle breakdown (GVBD) in prepubertal (Day and Funahashi, 1996; Grupen *et al.*, 1997; H. D. Guthrie, unpublished) and post-pubertal gilts (Brüssow *et al.*, 1996; Guthrie and Garrett, 2000b). The incidence of GVBD did not differ significantly between atretic and nonatretic follicles before the start of ovulatory follicle maturation; however, follicles containing oocytes undergoing GVBD are eliminated before the preovulatory LH surge (Guthrie and Garrett, 2000b). Therefore, apoptosis and follicle atresia may be physiologically important as a barrier to ovulation of oocytes that have not remained in meiotic arrest during the period of rapid maturation of the ovulatory cohort.

References

Arends ML, Morris RG and Wyllie AH (1990) Apoptosis. The role of the endonuclease *American Journal of Pathology* **136** 593–608

Ashkenazi A and Dixit VM (1998) Death receptors: signaling and modulation *Science* **281** 1305–1308

Billig H, Furuta I and Hsueh AJW (1993) Estrogens inhibit and androgens enhance ovarian granulosa cell apoptosis *Endocrinology* **133** 2204–2212

Black JL and Erickson BH (1968) Oogenesis and ovarian development in the prenatal pig *Anatomical Record* **161** 45–56

Brüssow K-P, Torner H, Rátky J, Kanitz W and Köchling W (1996) Aspects of follicular development and intrafollicular oocyte maturation in gilts *Reproduction in Domestic Animals* **31** 555–563

Channing CP, Anderson LD, Hoover DJ, Kolena J, Osteen KG, Pomerantz SH and Tanabe K (1982) The role of nonsteroidal regulators in control of oocyte and follicular maturation *Recent Progress in Hormone Research* **38** 331–408

Chun S-Y, Billig H, Tilly JL, Fututa I, Tsafriri A and Hsueh AJW

(1994) Gonadotropin suppression of apoptosis in cultured preovulatory follicles: mediatory role of endogenous insulin-like growth factor I *Endocrinology* **135** 1845–1853

Cohen GM (1997) Caspases: the executioners of apoptosis *Biochemical Journal* **326** 1–16

Dalin A-M (1987) Ovarian follicular activity during the luteal phase in gilts *Journal of Veterinary Medicine Series A* **34** 592–601

Daud AI, Bumpus FM and Husain A (1988) Evidence for selective expression of angiotensin II receptors on atretic follicles in the rat ovary: an autoradiographic study *Endocrinology* **122** 2727–2733

Day BN and Funahashi H (1996) *In vitro* maturation and fertilization of pig oocytes. In *Biotechnology's Role in the Genetic Improvement of Farm Animals* pp 125–144 Eds RH Miller, VG Pursel and HD Norman. Beltsville Symposia in Agricultural Research XX, American Society of Animal Science, Savoy, IL

de Jong FH (1988) Inhibin: fact or artifact *Molecular and Cellular Endocrinology* **13** 1–10

Desagher S and Martinou JC (2000) Mitochondria as the

central control point of apoptosis *Trends in Cell Biology* **10** 369–377

Enari M, Sakahira H, Yokoyama H, Okawa K, Iwamatsu A and Nagata S (1998) A caspase-activated DNase that degrades DNA during apoptosis, and its inhibitor ICAD *Nature* **391** 43–50

Erickson BH (1967) Radioresponse of the pre-puberal porcine ovary *International Journal of Radiation Biology* **13** 57–67

Findlay JK (1994) Peripheral and local regulators of folliculogenesis *Reproduction, Fertility and Development* **6** 127–139

Flaws JA, Tilly JL, Hirshfield AN, Tilly KI, DeSanti A, Trbovich AM and Kugu K (1995) Interleukin-1 beta-converting enzyme-related proteases (IRPs) and mammalian cell death: dissociation of IRP-induced oligonucleosomal endonuclease activity from morphological apoptosis in granulosa cells of the ovarian follicle *Endocrinology* **136** 5042–5053

Ford JJ and Howard HJ (1997) Activin inhibition of estradiol and progesterone production in porcine granulosa cells *Journal of Animal Science* **75** 761–766

Foxcroft GR and Hunter MC (1985) Basic physiology of follicular maturation in the pig *Journal of Reproduction and Fertility Supplement* **33** 1–19

Garrett WM and Guthrie HD (1999) Expression of Bcl-2 and 3-hydroxysteroid dehydrogenase protein during oocyte and follicle development in foetal and post-natal pig ovaries *Reproduction, Fertility and Development* **11** 463–470

Garrett WM, Mack SO, Rohan RM and Guthrie HD (2000) *In situ* analysis of the changes in expression of porcine ovarian inhibin subunit messenger ribonucleic acids during the early luteal phase *Journal of Reproduction and Fertility* **118** 235–242

Grupen CG, Nagashima H and Nottle MB (1997) Asynchronous meiotic progression in porcine oocytes matured *in vitro*: a cause of polyspermic fertilization? *Reproduction, Fertility and Development* **9** 187–191

Guthrie HD and Garrett WM (2000a) Factors regulating apoptosis during folliculogenesis in pigs *Proceedings of the American Society of Animal Science* http://www.asas.org/jas/symposia/proceedings/0933.pdf

Guthrie HD and Garrett WM (2000b) Changes in porcine oocyte germinal vesicle development as follicles approach preovulatory maturity *Theriogenology* **54** 389–399

Guthrie HD, Bolt DJ, Kiracofe GH and Miller KF (1987) Ovarian response to injections of charcoal-extracted porcine follicular fluid and porcine FSH in gilts fed a progesterone agonist, altrenogest *Journal of Animal Science* **64** 816–826

Guthrie HD, Bolt DJ, Kiracofe GH and Miller KF (1988) Effect of charcoal-extracted porcine follicular fluid and 17β-estradiol on follicular growth and plasma gonadotropins in gilts fed a progesterone agonist (altrenogest) *Biology of Reproduction* **38** 750–755

Guthrie HD, Grimes RW, Cooper BS and Hammond JM (1995) Follicular atresia in pigs: measurement and physiology *Journal of Animal Science* **73** 2834–2844

Guthrie HD, Ireland JLH, Good TEM and Ireland JJ (1997) Expression of different molecular weight forms of

inhibin in atretic and nonatretic follicles during the early luteal phase and altrenogest-synchronized follicular phase in pigs *Biology of Reproduction* **56** 870–877

Guthrie HD, Garrett WM and Cooper BS (1998) Follicle-stimulating hormone and insulin-like growth factor-I attenuate apoptosis in cultured porcine granulosa cells *Biology of Reproduction* **58** 390–396

Guthrie HD, Garrett WM and Cooper BS (2000) Inhibition of apoptosis in cultured porcine granulosa cells by inhibitors of caspase and serine protease activity *Theriogenology* **54** 731–740

Hammond JM, Samaras SE, Grimes R, Leighton J, Barber J, Canning SF and Guthrie HD (1993) The role of insulin-like growth factors and epidermal growth factor-related peptides in intraovarian regulation in the pig ovary *Journal of Reproduction and Fertility* **48** 117–125

Hakuno N, Koji T, Yano T, Kobayashi N, Tsutsumi O, Taketani Y and Nakane PJ (1996) Fas/APO-1/CD95 system as a mediator of granulosa cell apoptosis in ovarian follicle atresia *Endocrinology* **137** 1938–1948

Hillier SG (1991) Regulatory functions for inhibin and activin in human ovaries *Journal of Endocrinology* **131** 171–175

Hsu SY, Lai RJ-M, Finegold M and Hsueh AJW (1996) Targeted overexpression of Bcl-2 in ovaries of transgenic mice leads to decreased follicle apoptosis, enhanced folliculogenesis and increased germ cell tumorigenesis *Endocrinology* **137** 4837–4843

Hsueh AJ, Billig H and Tsafiri A (1994) Ovarian follicle atresia: a hormonally controlled apoptotic process *Endocrine Reviews* **15** 707–724

Hughes FM, Jr and Gorospe WC (1991) Biochemical identification of apoptosis (programmed cell death) in granulosa cells: evidence for a potential mechanism underlying follicular atresia *Endocrinology* **129** 2415–2422

Kim JM, Boone DL, Auyeung A and Tsang BK (1998) Granulosa cell apoptosis induced at the penultimate stage of follicular development is associated with increased levels of Fas and Fas ligand in the rat ovary *Biology of Reproduction* **58** 1170–1176

Li J, Kim J-M, Liston R, Li M, Miyazaki T, Mackenzie AE, Korneluk RG and Tsang BK (1998) Expression of inhibitor of apoptosis proteins (IAPs) in rat granulosa cells during ovarian follicular development and atresia *Endocrinology* **139** 1321–1328

Matsumoto K, Nakayama T, Sakai H, Tanemura K, Osuga H, Sato E and Ikeda J-E (1999) Neuronal apoptosis inhibitory protein (NAIP) may enhance the survival of granulosa cells thus indirectly affecting oocyte survival *Molecular Reproduction and Development* **54** 103–111

Miller DK (1997) The role of the caspase family of cysteine proteases in apoptosis *Seminars in Immunology* **9** 35–49

Peluso JJ and Pappalardo A (1994) Progesterone and cell–cell adhesion interact to regulate rat granulosa cell apoptosis *Biochemical Cell Biology* **72** 547–551

Pesce M and De Felici M (1994) Apoptosis in mouse primordial germ cells: a study by transmission and scanning electron microscope *Anatomy and Embryology* (Berlin) **189** 435–440

Pesce M, Farrace MG, Piacentini M, Dolci S and De Felici M (1993) Stem cell factor and leukemia inhibitory factor promote germ cell survival by suppressing programmed cell death (apoptosis) *Development* **118** 1089–1094

Pucell AG, Bumpus FM and Husain A (1988) Regulation of angiotensin II receptors in cultured rat ovarian granulosa cells by follicle-stimulating hormone and angiotensin II *Journal of Biological Chemistry* **263** 11 954–11 961

Ratts VS, Flaws JA, Kolp R, Sorenson CM and Tilly JL (1995) Ablation of bcl-2 gene expression decreases the numbers of oocytes and primordial follicles established in the post-natal female mouse gonad *Endocrinology* **136** 3665–3668

Robles R, Tao XJ, Trbovich AM, Maravel DV, Nahum R, Perez GI, Tilly KI and Tilly JL (1999) Localization, regulation and possible consequences of apoptotic protease-activating factor-1 (Apaf-1) expression in granulosa cells of the mouse ovary *Endocrinology* **140** 2641–2644

Roy N, Deveraux QL, Takahashi R, Salvesen GS and Reed JC (1997) The c-IAP-1 and c-IAP-2 proteins are direct inhibitors of specific caspases *EMBO Journal* **16** 6914–6925

Thornberry NA and Lazebnik Y (1998) Caspases: enemies within *Science* **281** 1312–1316

Tilly JL, Kowalski KI, Johnson AL and Hsueh AJW (1991) Involvement of apoptosis in ovarian follicular atresia and postovulatory regression *Endocrinology* **129** 2799–2801

Tilly JL, Kowalski KI, Schomberg DW and Hsueh AJW (1992a) Apoptosis in atretic ovarian follicles is associated with selective decreases in messenger ribonucleic acid transcripts for gonadotropin receptors and cytochrome P450 aromatase *Endocrinology* **131** 1670–1676

Tilly JL, Billig H, Kowalski KI and Hsueh AJW (1992b) Epidermal growth factor and basic fibroblast growth factor suppress the spontaneous onset of apoptosis in cultured rat ovarian granulosa cells and follicles by a tyrosine kinase-dependent mechanism *Molecular Endocrinology* **6** 1942–1950

Tsafriri A and Braw RH (1984) Experimental approaches to atresia in mammals. In *Oxford Reviews of Reproductive Biology* pp 226–265 Ed. JR Clarke. Clarendon Press, Oxford

Vaux DL (1993) Toward an understanding of the molecular mechanisms of physiological cell death *Proceedings National Academy of Sciences USA* **90** 786–789

Woodruff TK, Lyon RJ, Hansen SE, Rice GC and Mayo KE (1990) Inhibin and activin locally regulate rat ovarian folliculogenesis *Endocrinology* **127** 3196–3205

Reproduction Supplement **58**, 31–45

Ovarian follicular growth in sows*

M. C. Lucy, J. Liu, C. K. Boyd and C. J. Bracken

164 Animal Sciences Research Center, University of Missouri-Columbia, MO 65211, USA

The resumption of ovarian follicular development during lactation and after weaning in sows is a complex process that ultimately determines rebreeding efficiency of sows. Ovarian follicular development before weaning is heterogeneous because multiple patterns of development are observed when individual sows are compared. Sows can have relatively inactive ovaries before weaning with follicles of < 2 mm in diameter. Other sows have non-ovulatory follicular waves in which follicles grow to approximately 5 mm and subsequently regress before weaning. Sows may also have preovulatory follicular development and ovulation, or may develop cystic ovaries before weaning. Weaning is a random event relative to follicular development on the ovary. Therefore, variation in the weaning to oestrus interval in sows is caused by weaning at random stages of follicular development. Most sows experience a rapid period of follicular growth after weaning and return to oestrus within 3–7 days. Delayed intervals to oestrus after weaning are associated with inactive ovaries before weaning (follicles < 2 mm in diameter) or weaning during the regression phase of a follicular wave. An integrated model for follicular growth and oestrus in weaned sows should include endocrine mechanisms (that is, individual differences in insulin, insulin-like growth factor I (IGF-I), LH and FSH), behavioural mechanisms (relationship between follicular growth and the initiation of oestrus) and morphological mechanisms (that is, timing of weaning relative to ovarian follicular development).

Introduction

Sows must return to oestrus after weaning so that they can be inseminated and establish a new pregnancy. The return to oestrus normally occurs within 3–7 days after weaning and ovulation occurs near the end of oestrus (Soede and Kemp, 1997). Even under optimal conditions, the variation in the interval to oestrus after weaning and the variation in the time of ovulation relative to oestrus are far too great (Flowers and Esbenshade, 1993; Kemp and Soede, 1997). Oestrous detection and insemination must be performed on each of the days that sows are expected to return to oestrus. Furthermore, sows must be inseminated twice to ensure an optimum conception rate and litter size because ovulation is not precisely timed relative to the onset of oestrus. The poor timing of reproductive events places significant demands on labour for oestrous detection and insemination, and wastes semen because sows are inseminated two or more times. Little is known about the factors that cause the variation in the

---

*Contribution from the Missouri Agricultural Experiment Station. Journal Series Number 13,156
Email: LucyM@missouri.edu

weaning to oestrus interval or the weaning to ovulation interval in sows. If we could manage follicular populations in sows then it may be possible to reduce the variation in the interval from weaning to oestrus or ovulation. This reduction would benefit the producer by shortening the period of oestrous detection and insemination and possibly eliminate the need for double inseminations if a precise synchronization of ovulation can be achieved.

Ovarian morphology before and after weaning in sows

Follicular growth before weaning in sows

Follicular growth before weaning in sows has been studied intensely and several authors have reviewed the literature (Edwards, 1982; Britt *et al.*, 1985; Varley and Foxcroft, 1990). There is a steady increase in the diameter of ovarian follicles, but few follicles are > 5 mm in diameter before week 3 of lactation. After week 3 of lactation, the number of 5 mm follicles increases, but follicles > 5 mm do not generally develop in lactating sows.

The classical data on follicular growth in sows were collected from sows killed at specific stages of lactation. Therefore, only one observation of the ovaries could be made on each sow. Gross changes in follicle size could be measured (that is, progressively larger follicles during later lactation), but patterns of follicular growth within a sow could not be elucidated. Ovarian ultrasonography revolutionized the study of ovarian function in cattle, sheep and horses because follicular growth could be studied each day in individual animals (Pierson *et al.*, 1988). Ultrasonography can also be performed each day in sows. The ovary of gilts or first parity sows can be examined by attaching a flexible handle to the ultrasound probe. Second or greater parity sows can be palpated manually through the rectum (similar to cattle). Owing to the large number of follicles, the examinations are videotaped and played later for frame-by-frame viewing, digitizing and data collection. The timing of hormonal events relative to follicular growth at oestrus (Soede and Kemp, 1997) and critical windows of insemination relative to ovulation have been described (Soede *et al.*, 1995).

Lucy *et al.* (1999) performed an ultrasonographic and endocrine study of 31 sows before and after weaning. Sows were examined by ultrasonography each day from day –7 before weaning until ovulation after weaning (weaning = day 0). Four patterns of ovarian follicular growth were observed. The first two patterns of development were ovulation before weaning and the formation of cystic follicles before weaning. The third pattern of follicular development (ovarian inactivity) was characterized by extremely small follicles (< 2 mm diameter). The follicles in sows with inactive ovaries may grow and regress, but their development cannot be tracked using ultrasonography because they are too small. The fourth pattern of follicular development is perhaps the most unique and interesting. On the basis of ultrasonographic examinations performed each day in individual sows, synchronized waves of ovarian follicular growth were observed before weaning. The wave consisted of a cohort of 20–30 follicles that grew from a diameter of 2 mm (limit of detection by ultrasonography) to 4–6 mm (co-dominant follicles). The co-dominant follicles then regressed and were replaced by a new wave of follicles. The ultrasonographic data were in agreement with classical observations that show that follicles rarely exceed a diameter of 5 mm before weaning. However, there did not appear to be a steady progression of larger and larger follicles. Instead, follicles grew in waves with each wave of follicular growth creating broad peaks of follicular activity. Anoestrous cattle also have non-ovulatory follicular waves during lactation (Ginther *et al.*, 1996). However, in anoestrous cattle, a dominant follicle is selected from the cohort and then after selection the dominant follicle fails to ovulate. In both pigs and cattle, the follicular cohort (pigs) or the dominant follicle (cattle) will ovulate once the suppressive effects of lactation are either removed (that is, weaning in sows) or reduced (later lactation in cattle).

Follicular growth after weaning in oestrous sows

Sows typically have follicles of 2–5 mm in diameter when they are weaned. Weaning causes a rapid development of preovulatory follicles (Palmer *et al.*, 1965; Cox and Britt, 1982; Dyck, 1983). The follicles are maximally steroidogenic at 6–7 mm when sows come into oestrus (Liu *et al.*, 2000). Follicles grow slightly larger (7–8 mm) before ovulation (Soede *et al.*, 1998). Using ICI 33828, Day and Longenecker (1968) showed that pig follicles could grow from an immature stage to preovulatory size in 5 days. Numerous studies have demonstrated a rapid return to oestrus and ovulation in lactating sows treated with equine chorionic gonadotrophin (eCG), combinations of eCG and hCG, or GnRH (Esbenshade *et al.*, 1990). Although sows can be hormonally stimulated into oestrus, the interval from treatment to the onset of oestrus is variable. Likewise, there can be a large variation in the weaning to oestrus interval in the absence of any hormonal treatment. Some of the variability is caused by an imprecise relationship between oestrus and ovulation in pigs (Soede and Kemp, 1997). Therefore, the actual interval to ovulation after weaning may be more or less precise than the interval to oestrus. ten Napel *et al.* (1995) successfully shortened the duration of the weaning to oestrus interval by using genetic selection in primiparous sows. However, the decrease in the weaning to oestrus interval was due to a decrease in the number of sows with extremely long weaning to oestrus intervals. In other words, the mean interval from weaning to oestrus decreased because outliers with extremely long weaning to oestrus intervals were eliminated. The distribution of sows in oestrus within 1 week was essentially unchanged by genetic selection.

The variation in the weaning to oestrus interval is probably caused by the variation in pre-weaning follicular development in sows. The first two pre-weaning patterns of ovarian follicular development (pre-weaning ovulation and pre-weaning cystic ovary) occur in a small percentage of sows. Nevertheless, these pre-weaning patterns are important because sows that have ovulated before weaning or that have developed cystic ovaries before weaning will theoretically not show signs of oestrus after weaning. The third pattern of pre-weaning development (ovarian inactivity) probably causes a long interval from weaning to oestrus in sows. We have observed this type of development in 'normal' sows, but it may be more common in undernourished or low-body condition sows (Prunier and Quesnel, 2000), or in sows exposed to heat stress. A preliminary experiment was carried out using ten sows exposed to either thermoneutral conditions (21°C, 60% relative humidity; *n* = 5) or heat stress (32°C, 60% relative humidity; *n* = 5) during lactation. All sows were weaned at approximately 21 days and moved to thermoneutral conditions. Populations of follicles at weaning were distinctly different for thermoneutral and heat-stressed sows. At weaning, thermoneutral sows had nearly 40 follicles that were 4–5 mm in diameter (Fig. 1). On successive days after weaning, this group of follicles developed into progressively larger size classes (6–7 mm and then 8 mm). Heat-stressed sows did not have any 4–5 mm follicles at weaning. All of the follicles in the heat-stressed sows were < 2–3 mm in diameter. As a consequence, subsequent follicular growth was delayed in the heat-stressed sows. In fact, the heat-stressed sows required 4 days after weaning to develop the same number of 4–5 mm follicles that were found in the thermoneutral sows on the day of weaning. This delay in follicular development resulted in delayed oestrus in the heat-stressed sows compared with thermoneutral sows.

If follicles of a sow are developing in synchronized waves before weaning (fourth pattern), the interval to oestrus after weaning will depend on the stage of follicular development of the cohort at weaning. Sows weaned during the development of a follicular cohort will return to oestrus first because weaning is timed with the development of a group of follicles. Sows weaned when the cohort is regressing may return to oestrus later because a new wave of follicles must develop and replace the regressing cohort.

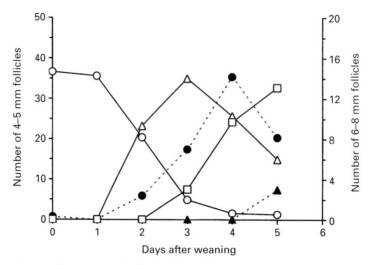

Fig. 1. The number of follicles within different diameter ranges for sows exposed to either thermoneutral conditions (○, 4–5 mm follicles; △, 6–7 mm follicles; □, 8 mm follicles; 21°C) or heat stress (●, 4–5 mm follicles; ▲, 6–7 mm follicles; 32°C) during lactation. Sows were moved to thermoneutral conditions after weaning and the number of follicles was counted using ultrasonography. Note the reduced number of 4–5 mm follicles in heat-stressed sows at weaning (day 0). Complete development of the 4–5 mm follicle pool required 4 days in heat-stressed sows. Subsequent follicular development (growth of follicles to 6–7 mm in diameter) was also delayed in heat-stressed sows.

Ultrasound images and endocrine data that demonstrate the effect of pre-weaning follicular development on interval to ovulation after weaning are shown for two sows (Fig. 2). Sow no. 134-2 ovulated 5 days after weaning, whereas sow no. 120-1 ovulated 7 days after weaning. The ultrasound images show that sow no. 134-2 had smaller ovarian follicles 2 days before weaning (day –2) compared with sow no. 120-1. However, the cohort of follicles underwent rapid development for the next 2 days so that at the time of weaning (day 0), plasma oestradiol concentrations had already increased in sow no. 134-2. Although sow no. 120-1 had follicles of a similar size before weaning, the follicles were marginally oestrogenic and may not have responded to the increase in LH after weaning because they were atretic. Both sows had decreased FSH concentrations after weaning, an increase in oestradiol and an LH surge. However, the increase in oestradiol and the LH surge occurred earlier in sow no. 134-2 than in sow no. 120-1. Ovulation in sow no.134-2 was completed by day 5.

The effect of pre-weaning follicular development and follicular development shortly after weaning on the interval to oestrus and ovulation can be clearly seen when populations of follicles are studied in weaned sows. Lucy et al. (1999) examined the average diameter of the follicular cohort in sows with different weaning to ovulation intervals (Fig. 3). The average follicular diameter for sows with different weaning to ovulation intervals was the same at the time of weaning. However, after weaning, follicular development occurred earlier in sows that ovulated on day 5 after weaning than in sows that ovulated on day 7 or day 9 after weaning. The analysis demonstrated that the growth curves for the preovulatory follicles were parallel. In other words, the rate of growth of the preovulatory follicular cohort was the same regardless of the weaning to ovulation interval. This pattern of development is different from

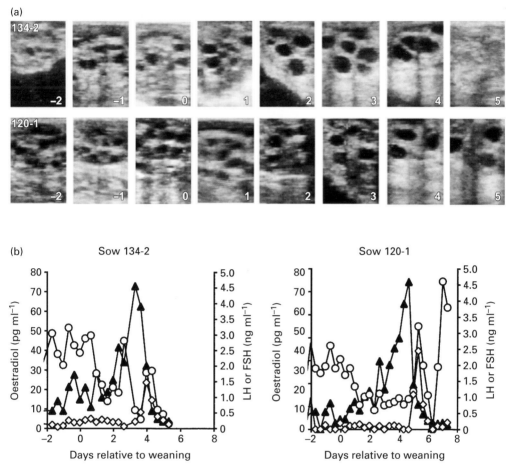

Fig. 2. (a) Daily ultrasonographic images of sows numbered134-2 and 120-1 from day –2 to day 5 after weaning. (b) Plasma concentrations of oestradiol (▲), FSH (○) and LH (◇) from these sows (2 days before weaning (day –2) until ovulation). Sow number 134-2 ovulated on day 5 after weaning. Note the presence of follicles visible by ultrasonography on day 4 and the absence of visible follicles on day 5 (ovulation). Sow number 120-1 ovulated on day 7 after weaning. Preovulatory follicles were visible on day 5, but these follicles did not ovulate for another 2 days. Sow number 134-2 had smaller ovarian follicles 2 days before weaning compared with sow number 120-1. However, the cohort of follicles in sow number 134-2 underwent rapid development for the subsequent 2 days so that at the time of weaning, plasma oestradiol concentrations were already increased (day 0). An increase in plasma oestradiol was not observed in sow number 120-1. The follicles in sow number 120-1 may have been atretic co-dominant follicles that were unable to respond to the increase in LH after weaning. Both sows had decreased plasma FSH concentrations and an increase in oestradiol and an LH surge after weaning.

an alternative possibility in which the rate of preovulatory follicular growth is simply slower in sows that ovulate later after weaning (that is, growth curves have different slopes for sows with different intervals to ovulation). There appears to be a mixed population of follicles on the ovary at weaning. Some of the follicles will participate in the preovulatory follicular wave, whereas other follicles will regress. We assume that healthy follicles (non-atretic) participate in the follicular wave. The average diameter of the healthy follicle pool may be impossible to determine unless the ovary is monitored carefully for several days before ovulation. When

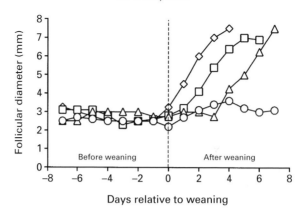

Fig. 3. Least square means for follicular diameter after weaning in sows. Sows were grouped on the basis of the number of days to ovulation after weaning (5 days: ◇ (SEM = 0.5), 7 days: □ (SEM = 0.3), 9 days: △ (SEM = 0.5) and anoestrus: ○ (SEM = 0.3)). Sows ovulating at 5 days after weaning initiated a follicular wave soon after weaning. There was a delay in the initiation of follicular growth in sows ovulating later. Anoestrous sows failed to develop preovulatory follicles.

plasma oestradiol concentrations were studied, it was found that follicles of sows with the shortest intervals to ovulation had greater oestrogenic activity before weaning and an earlier increase in preovulatory oestradiol concentrations (Lucy *et al.*, 1999). Thus, the entire process of preovulatory follicular development begins before a sow is weaned.

The population of preovulatory follicles that will ultimately participate in ovulation is clearly established by day 3 after weaning. Sows in a commercial herd were studied to determine factors affecting follicular populations and the interval to ovulation after weaning (Bracken *et al.*, 1999). Ovaries were examined by ultrasonography each day beginning on day 3 after weaning and twice each day from day 4.5 until ovulation. Sows with short intervals to ovulation (≤ 6.5 days) had follicular populations on day 3 after weaning that were more advanced (comprised larger follicles) when compared with sows with long (≥ 9 days) intervals to ovulation (Fig. 4). Follicular populations in sows with intermediate (7–8 days) intervals to ovulation were intermediate in size when compared with sows with short or long intervals to ovulation. Production factors (that is, parity and body condition score) known to influence the interval to oestrus and ovulation had a predictable effect on follicular growth within 3 days after weaning in sows (that is, sows with low body condition score and first parity had populations of follicles shifted toward smaller sizes on day 3). Thus, follicular populations by day 3 after weaning are predictive of the time of ovulation in sows.

Follicular growth in anoestrous sows

Ovarian follicular development in anoestrous sows can be monitored each day using ultrasonography. On the basis of ultrasonographic data, anoestrous sows can be classified as either type I anoestrus or type II anoestrus. In type I anoestrus, sows have 1–2 mm follicles at weaning. However, a follicular cohort does not develop after the sow is weaned. Instead, ovarian follicular populations remain at approximately the same size throughout the first week after weaning. Sows fail to come into oestrus because they do not have preovulatory follicles.

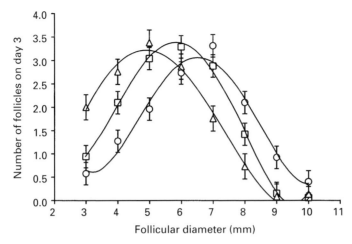

Fig. 4. The average number of 3–10 mm follicles on day 3 after weaning for each follicular diameter in sows with short (○, ≤ 6.5 days; *n* = 48), medium (□, 7–8 days; *n* = 48) or long (△ ≥ 9 day; *n* = 39) intervals to ovulation. Symbols and error bars represent least square means and standard errors. The lines represent the fourth-order polynomial regression curves that were fitted to the original data.

Type II anoestrus is an alternative pattern of follicular growth in anoestrous sows. Sows with type II anoestrus initiate follicular growth after weaning. The follicles grow to approximately 5 mm and then fail to progress to a preovulatory size (7–8 mm). The cohort that develops after weaning eventually regresses and a second wave of follicular growth begins. Langendijk *et al.* (2000) studied follicular growth using ultrasonography and reported type II anoestrus in a population of weaned sows. Oestrous sows had follicular growth from 2.3 mm (day 0) to 5.4 mm in diameter (day 4) after weaning. Type II anoestrous sows had follicular growth from 2.4 mm (day 0) to 4 mm in diameter (day 4) after weaning but failed to develop preovulatory follicles.

Follicular growth in sows with cystic ovaries

Cystic ovaries develop rapidly in sows (Fig. 5). Generally, follicles predetermined to become cysts grow to a diameter of 8–9 mm (slightly larger than expected preovulatory size follicles in sows), stop growing (plateau phase) and then fail to ovulate on the day of expected ovulation (approximately 2 days after reaching mature size). The plasma oestradiol concentrations decrease and plasma FSH concentrations increase before the follicles undergo rapid growth culminating in the cystic condition (20–30 mm ovarian follicles). The period of cystic follicle development was associated with progesterone secretion from the ovary perhaps arising from the cysts themselves or from corpora lutea formed after the ovulation in some follicles within the follicular cohort. Lucy *et al.* (1999) reported that cysts regressed approximately 1 week after formation and a new cohort of follicles was formed.

Endocrine mechanisms controlling follicular growth

Gonadotrophins before weaning

The inhibition of LH secretion by lactation prevents preovulatory follicular development in sows before weaning (Britt *et al.*, 1985; Varley and Foxcroft, 1990). Weaning soon after

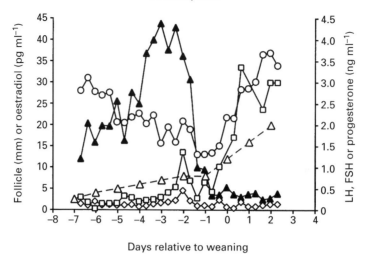

Fig. 5. Follicular diameter (△), and plasma concentrations of oestradiol (▲), progesterone (□), LH (◇) and FSH (○) in a sow developing cystic ovaries before weaning. The sow had follicular development before weaning and an increase in oestradiol. There was an LH surge on day −2 that was associated with the ovulation of some follicles and a subsequent increase in progesterone. Other follicles formed cysts on the ovary.

farrowing (zero-weaning) leads to increased LH secretion and enhanced (although cystic) follicular growth (DeRensis et al., 1993). In suckled sows, LH secretion initially increases after farrowing, but then decreases (DeRensis et al., 1993; Sesti and Britt, 1994). During this time, the releasable pool of LH remains constant (Sesti and Britt, 1994). However, in time, LH secretion increases (Edwards and Day, 1984), perhaps because of reduced suckling stimulus as the litter matures (Edwards, 1982; Britt et al., 1985; Quesnel and Prunier, 1995). The increase in LH secretion is believed to stimulate follicular growth and may explain why sows have progressively larger follicles during late lactation. Follicles that develop during lactation are capable of preovulatory follicular growth and ovulation when stimulated with GnRH or eCG (Britt et al., 1985).

The secretion of LH can be modified by nutritional and environmental inputs (Einarsson and Rojkittikhun, 1993; van den Brand et al., 2000), which can lead to decreased follicular growth (associated with reduced LH secretion) in sows that are under-fed (Koketsu et al., 1998; Quesnel et al., 1998) or exposed to high environmental temperatures (Armstrong et al., 1984). In contrast to LH, the secretion of FSH is not inhibited during lactation (Britt et al., 1985). Therefore, as with other farm animals, FSH shows some autonomy and appears to be regulated more tightly by ovarian factors (possibly oestradiol, inhibin or both).

Changes in plasma FSH and oestradiol concentrations coincide with the development of follicles before as well as after weaning. Plasma concentrations of FSH and oestradiol are shown for two sows before weaning (Fig. 6). In each sow, follicular development is coincident with an increase in plasma oestradiol concentrations and a decrease in plasma FSH concentrations. Greatest concentrations of oestradiol in the vena cava were associated with co-dominant follicles during the pre-weaning follicular wave. Regression of the follicular wave led to a decrease in plasma oestradiol and an increase in plasma FSH concentrations. The peaks of follicular activity were preceded by an increase in FSH that presumably stimulates a new wave of follicular development. In this sense, follicular waves before weaning in sows

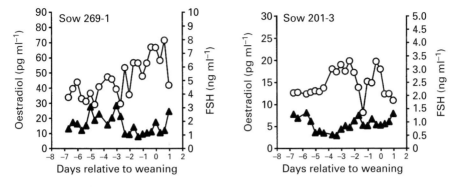

Fig. 6. Plasma oestradiol (▲) and FSH (○) concentrations on the days before weaning (day −7 to day 0) in two sows (numbers 269-1 and 201-3). In sow number 269-1, the maximum diameter of the cohort of follicles was from day −6 to day −2 and then the follicles regressed on day −1 and day 0. The oestradiol and FSH concentrations indicate that the follicles on day −2 had become atretic co-dominant follicles because oestradiol decreased and FSH increased. The maximum diameter of the cohort of co-dominant follicles in sow number 201-3 was from day −7 to day −5 and these follicles regressed and a new wave began on day −3 to day 0. Again, the decrease in oestradiol and the increase in FSH on day −5 indicate that the cohort of co-dominant follicles had become atretic (loss of dominance).

are similar to those observed in cattle because an increase in FSH precedes the follicular wave (Ginther *et al.*, 1996).

Gonadotrophins after weaning

Basal LH concentrations and the number of LH peaks increase after weaning (Cox and Britt, 1982; Edwards, 1982; Shaw and Foxcroft, 1985). The increase in LH pulsatility is believed to drive follicular growth toward ovulation. Concentrations of FSH initially increase after weaning, but then decrease as preovulatory follicles develop (Edwards, 1982; Shaw and Foxcroft, 1985).

We have also observed a decrease in FSH coincident with an increase in follicular growth and an increase in oestradiol in weaned sows (Fig. 2). Although LH is important for follicular growth, there is variability in the patterns of LH secretion in sows before and after weaning, and a high correlation between intensity of LH secretion and interval to oestrus has not been found. In studies of weaned sows, neither Shaw and Foxcroft (1985) nor DeRensis and Foxcroft (1999) obtained a correlation between characteristics of LH secretion after weaning and interval to oestrus or follicular growth. Similarly, FSH before or after weaning was not correlated with the interval to oestrus after weaning. However, these findings do not exclude the possibility that there are differences in gonadotrophin secretion between oestrous and anoestrous sows. In a study of FSH and inhibin, Trout *et al.* (1992) found increased FSH and inhibin in sows that underwent oestrus after weaning. Both oestrous and anoestrous sows had decreasing concentrations of FSH and increasing concentrations of inhibin after weaning. However, in anoestrous sows these changes were not associated with maturation of follicles and expression of oestrus.

Metabolic hormones controlling follicular growth

Most reproductive studies of the weaned sow have focused on LH and FSH because gonadotrophins play a role in preovulatory follicular development (Flowers *et al.*, 1991).

Metabolic hormones like insulin, IGFs and leptin are also involved by either directly influencing hypothalamic–pituitary function (Barb *et al.*, this supplement) or by affecting gonadotrophin action at the ovary. IGF-I and -II are the ligands for the IGF system (Jones and Clemmons, 1995) and both are structurally related to insulin. Their actions are similar to each other because they are similar in structure and amino acid sequence. However, IGF-II has lower potency than IGF-I for tyrosine kinase signalling through the type I IGF receptor. Neither IGF-I nor IGF-II has insulin-like metabolic effects unless present at extremely high concentrations. Likewise, insulin does not have IGF-like effects unless present at extremely high concentrations. Nevertheless, both insulin and the IGFs share some functional similarity in terms of their effects on ovarian cells. Granulosa and theca cells express insulin receptors as well as type I and type II IGF receptors (Liu *et al.*, 2000; Prunier and Quesnel, 2000). Thus, insulin, IGF-I and IGF-II can act directly on ovarian cells. The pig follicle also expresses IGF-I (granulosa cell layer) and IGF-II (theca cell layer). The intraovarian expression of the IGFs adds an additional component to the ovarian IGF system (see below). When acting alone, IGF-I, IGF-II and insulin cause growth, differentiation and survival of ovarian cells (Poretsky *et al.*, 1999; Schams *et al.*, 1999; Lucy, 2000). However, the most important actions of ovarian IGFs as well as insulin, are observed when the IGFs and insulin act synergistically with the gonadotrophins (LaVoie *et al.*, 1999; Sekar *et al.*, 2000; Zhang *et al.*, 2000). The synergistic relationship between the IGFs and insulin with gonadotrophins is observed for a variety of cellular functions, including mitogenesis and steroidogenesis. The synergism is caused by the ability of IGFs and insulin to increase the number of gonadotrophin receptors and increase the activity of gonadotrophin receptor second messenger systems. At the same time, gonadotrophins increase type I IGF receptor expression and may increase IGF-I synthesis in granulosa cells. Both insulin and IGF-I may play a role in follicular development during periods of under-feeding or weight loss because undernutrition causes a decrease in plasma concentrations of IGF-I and insulin (IGF-II is influenced less by undernutrition). According to the hypothesis, plasma insulin and IGF-I act in an endocrine manner to affect ovarian cells. The decrease in plasma IGF-I and insulin concentrations during undernutrition decreases the responsiveness of the ovary to gonadotrophins and ultimately leads to a decrease in follicular growth (Cox, 1997; Prunier and Quesnel, 2000). Mao *et al.* (1999) decreased plasma insulin and IGF-I concentrations with feed restriction and then failed to find a correlation between LH and follicular growth in sows treated with GnRH. Likewise, Cosgrove *et al.* (1992) found that re-alimentation of feed-restricted gilts could increase follicular growth in the absence of a change in LH secretion. The change in follicular development was associated with greater plasma IGF-I and insulin concentrations in the re-alimented group. Thus, feeding increases the responsiveness of the ovary to LH through its effects on insulin and IGF-I.

Gene expression within follicles as a mechanism to control follicular growth

Gonadotrophin receptors

The ability of gonadotrophins to act on ovarian follicles depends on the expression of gonadotrophin receptors in ovarian cells. In the preovulatory follicles, the LH receptor is expressed in both granulosa and theca cell layers (Yuan *et al.*, 1996; Liu *et al.*, 2000). The amount of LH receptor mRNA increases as follicles develop from 2 mm to 6 mm in diameter (Fig. 7). In 8 mm follicles (after the LH surge), LH receptor mRNA is not expressed. The increasing intensity of LH receptor signals reflects the increased dependence of the preovulatory follicle on LH and is also associated with an increase in aromatase mRNA in the granulosa cell layer (Fig. 7). In contrast, FSH receptor mRNA is markedly reduced in 4 mm

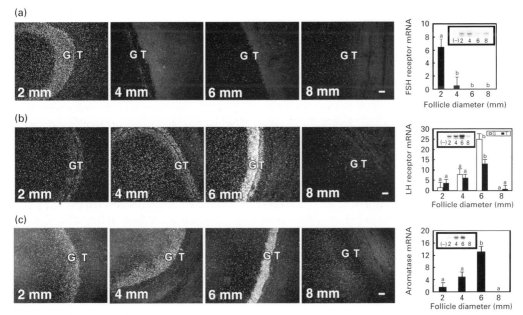

Fig. 7. *In situ* hybridization of (a) FSH receptor, (b) LH receptor and (c) aromatase in follicles 2, 4, 6 and 8 mm in diameter collected from sows after weaning (Liu *et al.*, 2000). The images were obtained using darkfield microscopy. G: granulosa cells; T: theca cells. Least square means (± SEM) for quantification of mRNA signal from *in situ* hybridization are shown in the far-right panel. [ab]Within mRNA and cell layers, bars with different superscripts were significantly different at *P* < 0.05 (Duncan's multiple range test). The inset shows the autoradiograph of the ribonuclease protection assay (20, 10 and 10 µg RNA for FSH receptor, LH receptor and aromatase, respectively). (–): negative control. The amount of LH receptor mRNA increased as follicles developed from 2 mm to 6 mm in diameter (b). The LH receptor mRNA was not expressed in 8 mm follicles (after the LH surge). The increasing intensity of LH receptor signal reflects the increased dependence of the preovulatory follicle on LH and was associated with an increase in aromatase mRNA in the granulosa cell layer (c). In contrast, the FSH receptor mRNA was markedly decreased in 4 mm follicles and absent in follicles larger than 4 mm (a). Therefore, the preovulatory follicles switched from FSH- to LH-dependence. Scale bars represent 120 µm.

follicles and absent in follicles of > 4 mm in diameter (Fig. 7). Therefore, the preovulatory follicle releases itself from its dependence on FSH. Smaller follicles on the ovary continue to express FSH receptor, but FSH concentrations are reduced as larger follicles (growing independently of FSH) suppress FSH secretion to basal values.

The molecular analyses are in agreement with classical studies of FSH dependence of preovulatory follicles. Guthrie *et al.* (1988) treated gilts with highly purified pig FSH and found that the FSH-treated gilts had greater numbers of 3–6 mm follicles, but the number of 7–8 mm follicles and plasma concentrations of oestradiol were not increased when compared with controls. Esbenshade *et al.* (1990) reviewed studies showing that purified pig LH could induce oestrus in sows and gilts, but only when higher doses were administered. Lower doses of LH could induce oestrus when a combination of LH and FSH were used. These data indicate that pig follicles are dependent on FSH and LH for follicular growth. The follicles switch from FSH- to LH-dependence at the 2–4 mm stage.

Liu *et al.* (2000) measured gene expression in follicles from sows after weaning. To our knowledge, gene expression in ovarian follicles has not been measured before weaning. We propose that gene expression in follicles is developmentally regulated and is similar in sows before and after weaning. If this is the case, then follicular growth in lactating sows is initially FSH dependent. At the peak of follicular development during lactation (5 mm follicles), the follicles switch from an FSH-dependent state to an LH-dependent state. The LH-dependent follicles are oestrogenic and can suppress FSH secretion (dominance phase) (Fig. 6). However, inadequate LH pulsatility during lactation leads to atresia of the LH-dependent large (5 mm) follicles (loss-of-dominance phase). Atresia in the large follicle pool leads to an increase in FSH that triggers a new follicular wave. If sows are weaned at the peak of the follicular wave then the LH-dependent follicles continue to grow (that is, develop from 5 mm follicles to the preovulatory stage) because LH pulsatility increases immediately after weaning. We predict that the weaning to ovulation interval in these sows is short, because most the follicular development is completed before weaning. Sows weaned at the beginning of a follicular wave (shortly after the large follicle pool becomes atretic) would be expected to have a long interval from weaning to ovulation.

Expression of ovarian growth factor and its role in follicular development

IGF-I and IGF-II, their receptors (type I and type II IGF receptors) and IGF-binding proteins (IGFBP-1 to -6) regulate growth, differentiation and apoptosis of ovarian cells (Poretsky *et al.*, 1999; Schams *et al.*, 1999; Lucy, 2000). IGFs can originate from endocrine sources or they may be produced locally within the follicle. Under normal physiological conditions, a threshold of IGF-I protein in follicular fluid may be met by local (paracrine/autocrine) and endocrine sources of IGF-I. In general, IGFs and IGFBPs are localized to specific cell layers (granulosa and (or) theca) within developing follicles. The location of specific components of the IGF system corresponds to the location of LH receptors and FSH receptors within the developing follicles. The co-localization of IGF and gonadotrophin receptor genes indicates a coordination of gonadotrophin and IGF action within the ovary that may control growth, differentiation and steroidogenesis of theca and granulosa cells.

Liu *et al.* (2000) measured the mRNA expression of gonadotrophin receptors, steroidogenic enzymes and IGF system genes during the maturation and differentiation of preovulatory follicles in the sow. Four developmental patterns of gene expression were observed for the ovarian mRNA. The first developmental pattern of gene expression was correlated with the oestrogenic capacity of the follicle and included genes for oestrogen biosynthesis, IGF-II and LH receptor. The second developmental pattern of gene expression was inversely correlated with follicular growth and included genes with decreased expression in large follicles (FSH receptor, IGFBP-2 and GH receptor). The third developmental pattern was constitutive (that is, no obvious developmental pattern; IGF-I and type I IGF receptor) and the fourth developmental pattern was increased expression after oestrus and the LH surge (IGFBP-4 and type II IGF receptor).

The IGF-I and type I IGF receptor mRNA were expressed constitutively (that is, no change in expression for 2–8 mm follicles). The pattern of IGF-I and type I IGF receptor gene expression is in agreement with studies in several species (Poretsky *et al.*, 1999; Lucy, 2000) and supports the observation that IGF-I expression in follicles is not correlated with follicular growth. The lack of a correlation between IGF-I and follicular growth does not mean that IGF-I is not physiologically important within the preovulatory follicle. Indeed, numerous gonadotrophin-dependent and gonadotrophin-independent actions of IGF-I have been described for both granulosa and theca cells. The lack of developmental regulation for type I IGF receptor gene expression indicates that IGF-I is required throughout the preovulatory period and highlights the importance of IGF-I and the type I IGF receptor for all phases of follicular growth.

Expression of IGF-II was high in the theca of 6 mm follicles when the greatest concentrations of oestradiol were observed in follicular fluid. The increase in IGF-II as well as the increase in steroidogenic enzymes was associated with an increase in LH receptor mRNA in both granulosa and theca interna cells of 6 mm follicles (Fig. 7). The steroidogenic enzyme and LH receptor mRNA underwent a precipitous decrease in follicles at the 8 mm stage after sows were observed in oestrus and apparently had an LH surge. However, IGF-II mRNA remained high in 8 mm follicles. The maintenance of IGF-II gene expression indicates that IGF-II may have additional functions in either ovulation or luteinization.

The availability of IGF in biological systems is modulated by IGFBPs. Six different IGFBPs, as well as four different IGFBP-related proteins, have been characterized (Jones and Clemmons, 1995). Each IGFBP has a unique pattern of tissue distribution and regulation. The IGFBPs modulate the interaction of IGF-I and IGF-II with their receptors and may regulate cell growth and differentiation by titrating the trophic effects of IGF (Poretsky *et al.*, 1999; Lucy, 2000). Liu *et al.* (2000) examined the regulation of IGFBP-2 and -4 in the sow ovary. Expression of IGFBP-2 was inversely correlated with the diameter of the follicles (that is, IGFBP-2 mRNA decreased in large preovulatory follicles). Thus, the potential for IGF-I or IGF-II action in large follicles is enhanced by the coordinated decrease in IGFBP-2 gene expression because IGF-I action in preovulatory follicles may be greater when IGFBP concentrations are decreased (Spicer and Chamberlain, 1999). The IGFBP-4 mRNA was similar in 2, 4 and 6 mm follicles and increased in both granulosa and theca interna cells of 8 mm follicles. LH stimulated IGFBP-4 mRNA expression *in vitro* (Armstrong *et al.*, 1998) and the increase in IGFBP-4 that was observed may have been caused by the LH surge in sows with 8 mm follicles. Given the large increase in IGFBP-4 mRNA immediately preceding ovulation (8 mm follicle), we predict that IGFBP-4 may play a role in the luteinization of ovarian cells and (or) ovulation.

Conclusions

There are numerous factors that control follicular growth, and ultimately the weaning to oestrus interval and the weaning to ovulation interval in sows. Pre-weaning follicular growth is heterogeneous because sows can experience near complete ovarian inactivity, wave-like patterns of follicular growth, cystic ovaries, or they may develop preovulatory follicles and ovulate. Gonadotrophins (LH and FSH) and metabolic hormones (insulin and IGF-I) act synergistically to promote follicular growth. Ovarian inactivity may be the result of a combination of low IGF-I and insulin concentrations, and low LH pulsatility during lactation. Conversely, the development of cystic ovaries or pre-weaning ovulation may be caused by a combination of high IGF-I and insulin concentrations, and high LH pulsatility. In many sows, follicles grow in cohorts that reach 5 mm in diameter. Follicles may cease growing at about 5 mm because they are LH dependent and LH pulsatility is low during lactation. Eventually, the 5 mm follicles regress because they cannot survive physiologically without LH. Regression of the follicular cohort results in an increase in FSH that triggers the development of a new group of follicles. LH pulsatility increases within 4 h after weaning and the increase in LH stimulates follicular development. Diameters of ovarian follicles after weaning increase beyond the 5 mm stage because LH pulsatility increases and the increase in LH rescues an LH-dependent cohort of follicles. Growth of ovarian follicles after weaning leads to an increase in oestradiol and a decrease in FSH. The decrease in FSH prevents the development of small follicles during the preovulatory period and ensures that only LH-dependent follicles (> 5 mm) will continue development. Sows with ovarian inactivity (all follicles < 2 mm) may not respond to the increase in LH after weaning because they express only low amounts of LH receptor in their follicles. An integrated model that includes gonadotrophins, metabolic hormones and growth factors, cyclical patterns of follicular growth before weaning, and developmental regulation of gonadotrophin receptors, growth factors, and growth factor receptors may be necessary to explain follicular growth, interval to oestrus and interval to ovulation after weaning in sows.

References

Armstrong DG, Baxter G, Gutierrez CG, Hogg CO, Glazyrin AL, Campbell BK, Bramley TA and Webb R (1998) Insulin-like growth factor binding protein-2 and -4 messenger ribonucleic acid expression in bovine ovarian follicles: effect of gonadotropins and development status *Endocrinology* **139** 2146–2154

Armstrong JD, Britt JH and Cox NM (1984) Seasonal differences in body condition, energy intake, post-weaning follicular growth, LH and rebreeding performance in primiparous sows *Journal of Animal Science* **59** (Supplement 1) 338 (Abstract)

Bracken CJ, Lamberson WR, Lucy MC and Safranski TJ (1999) Factors affecting the timing of ovulation in weaned sows *Journal of Animal Science* **77** (Supplement 1) 75 (Abstract)

Britt JH, Armstrong JD, Cox NM and Esbenshade KL (1985) Control of follicular development during and after lactation in sows *Journal of Reproduction and Fertility Supplement* **33** 37–54

Cosgrove JR, Tilton JE, Hunter MG and Foxcroft GR (1992) Gonadotropin-independent mechanisms participate in ovarian responses to realimentation in feed-restricted prepubertal gilts *Biology of Reproduction* **47** 736–745

Cox NM (1997) Control of follicular development and ovulation rate in pigs *Journal of Reproduction and Fertility Supplement* **52** 31–46

Cox NM and Britt JH (1982) Relationships between endogenous gonadotropin-releasing hormone, gonadotropins and follicular development after weaning in sows *Biology of Reproduction* **27** 70–78

Day BN and Longenecker DE (1968) Synchronization of estrus and superovulation in swine with ICI 33828 and pregnant mare serum. In *VIth International Congress on Reproduction and Artificial Insemination* Volume II pp 1419–1421 Ed. C Thibault. National Institute of Agricultural Research, Jouy-en-Josas

DeRensis F and Foxcroft GR (1999) Correlation between LH response to challenges with GnRH and naloxone during lactation, and LH secretion and follicular development after weaning in the sows *Animal Reproduction Science* **56** 143–152

DeRensis F, Hunter MG and Foxcroft GR (1993) Suckling-induced inhibition of luteinizing hormone secretion and follicular development in the early postpartum sow *Biology of Reproduction* **48** 964–969

Dyck GW (1983) Postweaning changes in the reproductive tract of the sow *Canadian Journal of Animal Science* **63** 571–577

Edwards S (1982) The endocrinology of the post-partum sow. In *Control of Pig Reproduction* pp 439–458 Eds. DJA Cole and GR Foxcroft. Butterworth Scientific, Boston

Edwards S and Day BN (1984) Characterization of the LH secretion pattern during lactation in the pig *Journal of Animal Science* **59** (Supplement 1) 343 (Abstract)

Einarsson S and Rojkittikhun T (1993) Effects of nutrition on pregnant and lactating sows *Journal of Reproduction and Fertility Supplement* **48** 229–239

Esbenshade KL, Ziecik AJ and Britt JH (1990) Regulation and action of gonadotropins in pigs *Journal of Reproduction and Fertility Supplement* **40** 19–32

Flowers WL and Esbenshade KL (1993) Optimizing management of natural and artificial matings in swine *Journal of Reproduction and Fertility Supplement* **48** 217–228

Flowers B, Cantley TC, Martin MJ and Day BN (1991) Episodic secretion of gonadotropins and ovarian steroids in jugular and utero–ovarian vein plasma during the follicular phase of the oestrous cycle in gilts *Journal of Reproduction and Fertility* **91** 101–112

Ginther OJ, Wiltbank MC, Fricke PM, Gibbons JR and Kot K (1996) Selection of the dominant follicle in cattle *Biology of Reproduction* **55** 1187–1194

Guthrie HD, Bolt DJ, Kiracofe GH and Miller KF (1988) Ovarian response to injections of charcoal-extracted porcine follicular fluid and porcine follicle-stimulating hormone in gilts fed a progesterone agonist (altrenogest) *Biology of Reproduction* **55** 750–755

Jones JI and Clemmons DR (1995) Insulin-like growth factors and their binding proteins: biological actions *Endocrine Reviews* **16** 3–33

Kemp B and Soede NM (1997) Consequences of variation in interval from insemination to ovulation on fertilization in pigs *Journal of Reproduction and Fertility Supplement* **52** 79–89

Koketsu Y, Dial GD, Pettigrew JE, Xue J, Yang H and Lucia T (1998) Influence of lactation length and feed intake on reproductive performance and blood concentrations of glucose, insulin and luteinizing hormone in primiparous sows *Animal Reproduction Science* **52** 153–163

Langendijk P, van den Brand H, Soede NM and Kemp B (2000) Effect of boar contact on follicular development and on estrus expression after weaning in primiparous sows *Theriogenology* **54** 1295–1303

LaVoie HA, Garmey JC and Veldhuis JD (1999) Mechanisms of insulin-like growth factor I augmentation of follicle-stimulating hormone-induced porcine steroidogenic acute regulatory protein gene promoter activity in granulosa cells *Endocrinology* **140** 146–153

Liu J, Koenigsfeld AT, Cantley TC, Boyd CK, Kobayashi Y and Lucy MC (2000) Growth and initiation of steroidogenesis in porcine follicles are associated with unique patterns of gene expression for individual components of the ovarian insulin-like growth factor system *Biology of Reproduction* **63** 942–952

Lucy MC (2000) Regulation of ovarian follicular growth by somatotropin and insulin-like growth factors in cattle *Journal of Dairy Science* **83** 1635–1647

Lucy MC, Liu J, Koenigsfeld AT, Cantley TC and Keisler DH (1999) Ultrasonically-measured ovarian follicular development in weaned sows *Biology of Reproduction* **60** (Supplement 1) 166 (Abstract)

Mao J, Zak LJ, Cosgrove JR, Shostak S and Foxcroft GR (1999) Reproductive, metabolic and endocrine responses to feed restriction and GnRH treatment in primiparous, lactating sows *Journal of Animal Science* **77** 725–735

Palmer WM, Teague HS and Venzke WG (1965) Microscopic observations on the reproductive tract of the sow during lactation and early postweaning *Journal of Animal Science* **24** 541–545

Pierson RA, Kastelic JP and Ginther OJ (1988) Basic principles and techniques for transrectal ultrasonography in cattle and horses *Theriogenology* **29** 3–20

Poretsky L, Cataldo NA, Rosenwaks Z and Giudice LC (1999) The insulin-related ovarian regulatory system in health and disease *Endocrine Reviews* **20** 535–582

Prunier A and Quesnel H (2000) Influence of the nutritional status on ovarian development in female pigs *Animal Reproduction Science* **60–61** 185–197

Quesnel H and Prunier A (1995) Endocrine bases of lactational anoestrus in the sow *Reproduction, Nutrition and Development* **35** 395–414

Quesnel H, Pasquier A, Mounier AM and Prunier A (1998) Influence of feed restriction during lactation on gonadotropic hormones and ovarian development in primiparous sows *Journal of Animal Science* **76** 856–863

Schams D, Berisha B, Kosmann M, Einspanier R and Amselgruber WM (1999) Possible role of growth hormone, IGFs and IGF-binding proteins in the regulation of ovarian function in large farm animals *Domestic Animal Endocrinology* **17** 279–285

Sekar N, Garmey JC and Veldhuis JD (2000) Mechanisms underlying the steroidogenic synergy of insulin and luteinizing hormone in porcine granulosa cells: joint amplification of pivotal sterol-regulatory genes encoding the low-density lipoprotein (LDL) receptor, steroidogenic acute regulatory (stAR) protein and cytochrome P450 side-chain cleavage (P450scc) enzyme *Molecular and Cellular Endocrinology* **159** 25–35

Sesti LAC and Britt JH (1994) Secretion of gonadotropins and estimated releasable pools of gonadotropin-releasing hormone and gonadotropins during establishment of

suckling-induced inhibition of gonadotropin secretion in the sow *Biology of Reproduction* **50** 1078–1086

Shaw HJ and Foxcroft GR (1985) Relationships between LH, FSH and prolactin secretion, and reproductive activity in the weaned sow *Journal of Reproduction and Fertility* **75** 17–28

Soede NM and Kemp B (1997) Expression of oestrus and timing of ovulation in pigs *Journal of Reproduction and Fertility Supplement* **52** 91–103

Soede NM, Wetzels CC, Zondag W, deKoning MA and Kemp B (1995) Effects of time of insemination relative to ovulation, and determined by ultrasonography, on fertilization rate and accessory sperm count in sows *Journal of Reproduction and Fertility* **104** 99–106

Soede NM, Hazeleger W and Kemp B (1998) Follicle size and the process of ovulation in sows as studied with ultrasound *Reproduction in Domestic Animals* **33** 239–244

Spicer LJ and Chamberlain CS (1999) Insulin-like growth factor binding protein-3: its biological effect on bovine granulosa cells *Domestic Animal Endocrinology* **16** 19–29

ten Napel J, deVries AG, Buiting GAJ, Luiting P, Merks JWM and Brascamp EW (1995) Genetics of the interval from weaning to estrus in first-litter sows: distribution of data, direct response of selection, and heritability *Journal of Animal Science* **73** 2193–2203

Trout WE, Killen JH, Christenson RK, Schanbacher BD and Ford JJ (1992) Effects of weaning on concentrations of inhibin in follicular fluid and plasma of sows *Journal of Reproduction and Fertility* **94** 107–114

van den Brand H, Dieleman SJ, Soede NM and Kemp B (2000) Dietary energy source at two feeding levels during lactation of primiparous sows: I. Effects on glucose, insulin and luteinizing hormone and on follicle development, weaning-to-estrus interval, and ovulation rate *Journal Animal Science* **78** 396–404

Varley MA and Foxcroft GR (1990) Endocrinology of the lactating and weaned sow *Journal of Reproduction and Fertility Supplement* **40** 47–61

Yuan, W, Lucy MC and Smith MF (1996) Messenger ribonucleic acid for insulin-like growth factors-I and -II, insulin-like growth factor binding protein-2, gonadotropin receptors, and steroidogenic enzymes in porcine follicles *Biology of Reproduction* **55** 1045–1054

Zhang G, Garmey JC and Veldhuis JD (2000) Interactive stimulation by luteinizing hormone and insulin of the steroidogenic acute regulatory (StAR) protein and 17α-hydroxylase/17,20-lyase (CYP17) genes in porcine theca cells *Endocrinology* **141** 2735–2742

Reproduction Supplement **58**, 47–63

Formation and early development of the corpus luteum in pigs

B. D. Murphy[1], N. Gévry[1], T. Ruiz-Cortés[1], F. Coté[2], B. R. Downey[2] and J. Sirois[1]

[1]*Centre de Recherche en Reproduction Animale, Faculté de Médecine Vétérinaire, Université de Montréal, 3200 Rue Sicotte, St-Hyacinthe, Québec J2S 7C6, Canada; and* [2]*Department of Animal Science, McGill University, Ste-Anne de Bellevue Québec, Canada*

Numerous corpora lutea form from the multiple follicles that ovulate during the oestrous cycle of pigs. Vascular elements invade the follicle from the theca compartment, first centripetally, and subsequently by lateral branching of centripetal veins and arteries. The vessels are the vehicle for dispersion of steroidogenic theca cells throughout the corpus luteum. Mitosis occurs in both the theca and granulosa layers before ovulation, and in luteal cells well into the luteal phase. Luteal cell proliferation undergoes gradual restriction as the corpus luteum matures, but the mechanisms of exit from the cell cycle are unknown. The extracellular ligands that direct luteinization and maintain the corpus luteum include LH, prolactin, insulin and insulin-like growth factors (IGFs). These ligands induce qualitative and quantitative changes in steroid output, with progesterone as the principal product. These changes upregulate the cholesterol synthetic pathways to increase substrate availability. The intracellular regulation of luteinization is complex. A model is presented in which LH stimulates arachidonic and lineoleic acid metabolism to produce ligands for the nuclear proteins of the peripheral peroxisome activator receptor family. These ligands have downstream effects on cell differentiation and exit from the cell cycle. Luteal function is maintained by interactions among ligands, cholesterol regulatory proteins and constitutively expressed and regulated transcription factors.

Introduction

The success of gestation in the pig is entwined inextricably with the establishment and maintenance of the corpus luteum. This complex transitory organ develops from follicles as a consequence of ovulation and secretes the progesterone necessary for creating a uterine environment hospitable for survival of embryos and fetuses. Pigs differ from ruminants because the corpus luteum is required for the entire 16 weeks of gestation. Its importance is underlined by the fact that its principal synthetic product, progesterone, can, by itself, maintain gestation in ovariectomized gilts. The focus of this review is the process of luteinization and its aim is to identify the principal unanswered questions about luteal differentiation in pigs. Where possible, answers to these questions are proposed.

Corner (1919) described both the theca and granulosa precursors of luteal cells and the

Email: murphyb@medvet.umontreal.ca

histomorphological changes that follow ovulation and result in redistribution of theca cells within the corpus luteum. Both the final destinations of theca cells and the process of luteal angiogenesis, their proposed vehicle of dispersion, are not understood completely. Luteinization is believed to represent terminal differentiation of the granulosa component of the follicle, but little is known about the mechanisms for exit of luteal cells from the cell cycle in any species, and its timing in pigs has not been addressed. Furthermore, the mechanisms effecting the logarithmic increase in steroid output that occurs within a few days after the commencement of luteinization are only beginning to be recognized.

Formation of the pig corpus luteum

Preovulatory follicle development in the pig has been investigated extensively (for review see Cox, 1997). A well-documented finding is heterogeneity of the developmental process (Grant *et al.*, 1989), resulting in asynchrony in ovulation and consequent corpus luteum formation (Pope *et al.*, 1990). Ovulation and luteinization have been studied less. The evolution of a pig follicle to a young corpus luteum is shown (Fig. 1). The period from the onset of the LH surge to first ovulation was estimated as a mean of 44 h (Soede *et al.*, 1994) and in equine chorionic gonadotrophin (eCG)–hCG-treated gilts, the mean interval ranges from 34 to 48 h (Hunter, 1972). During the period between the ovulatory stimulus and expulsion of the ovum, the follicle undergoes changes, including hyperaemia and theca cell hypertrophy. There is rearrangement of the compact layers of granulosa cells to looser associations, characterized by reduced intercellular contact (Fig. 2a,b). Vascular remodelling begins before ovulation and incipient invagination occurs at the sites of major vein and artery complexes (Fig. 1). In samples taken approximately 24 h after ovulation, vascular and associated thecal tissues have not yet breached the follicle wall, but the regions of invagination are still substantially deeper and wider than in preovulatory follicles (Corner, 1919). Soon thereafter, there is evidence of focal decomposition of the follicle wall (Corner, 1919) and invasion of vascular elements into the granulosa compartment. The vascular components spearhead the invasion at the apices of the invaginations and bear theca cells to the lumen of the follicle (Fig. 1). Lateral vascularization throughout the former granulosa compartment occurs, apparently concomitant with the centripetal growth of the arteries and veins.

Corner (1919) described the invasion of the follicle compartment by the vascular elements and theca. He reported the dispersion of thecal cells throughout the luteal parenchyma, where they become disseminated singly or in groups of two or three among the granulosa descendants. Furthermore, Corner (1919) noted that many thecal cells remain near the periphery of the follicle or associate with the vessels that have invaded. His identification was based on the morphological characteristics of these cells and their responses to fixatives. Although the contribution of theca cells to the corpus luteum is not disputed, their ultimate fate and distribution have not been confirmed. It is assumed, but has not been shown conclusively, that theca cells become the small luteal cells that can be separated from their larger counterparts, presumably granulosa cell descendants, on density gradients (Pitzel *et al.*, 1990). There are no definitive markers that can be recognized after the differentiation of the theca precursors into theca–luteal cells. Understanding the fate of theca–luteal cells will allow better understanding of the important processes in luteal formation, the persistence of cell division, angiogenesis and migration of theca cells.

Ligand induction and maintenance of luteinization

In pigs, luteinization and maintenance of the corpus luteum depends on members of at least three protein families: the gonadotrophins, the cytokine–prolactin family and the family of

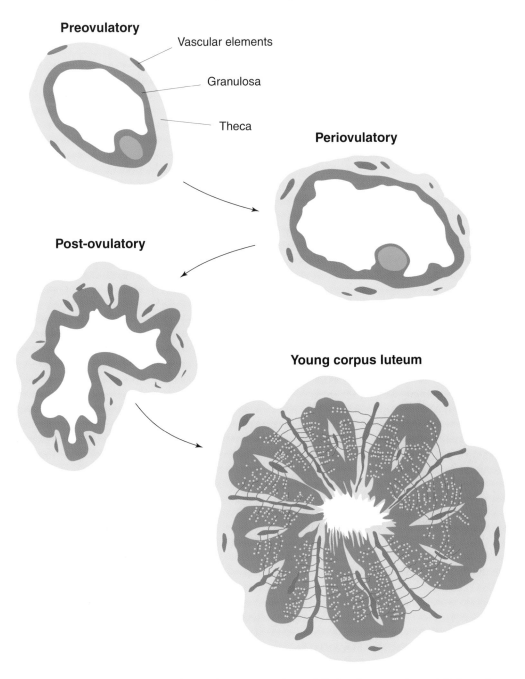

Fig. 1. Development of a pig corpus luteum from a preovulatory follicle. The preovulatory follicle undergoes hyperaemia and enlargement (periovulatory stage) before expulsion of the ovum (post-ovulatory stage) and formation of the young corpus luteum. The granulosa compartment is depicted in blue, the theca and its descendants in yellow, and the vascular elements in red. Incipient intrusion of the vascular elements occurs during the periovulatory period, but the theca–granulosa barrier is not breached until after ovulation. The vascular elements invade the corpus luteum in a centripetal direction, as well as laterally into the luteal parenchyma. Blood vessels are believed to carry theca cells into the luteal parenchyma and to disperse them throughout the corpus luteum.

B. D. Murphy et al.

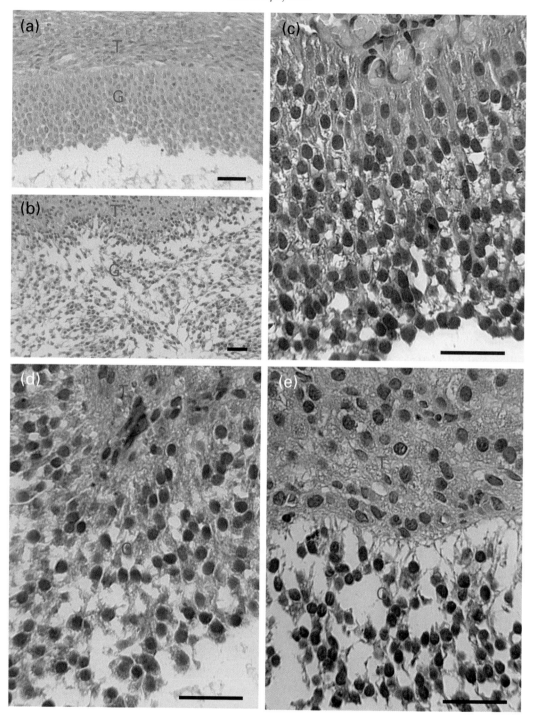

Fig. 2. Photomicrographs of the periovulatory period in follicles from gilts treated with hCG to induce ovulation. Expression of proliferating cell nuclear antigen (PCNA), a marker for cell division, was identified by immunohistochemistry. In all panels cell nuclei with the characteristic brown diaminobenzidine stain are positive for PCNA. (a) Cross-section through a large antral (7 mm in diameter) pig follicle subjected to immunolocalization procedures but not exposed to the anti-PCNA antibody. (b) Theca–granulosa interface at

insulin and insulin-like growth factors (IGFs). The proximal stimulus for ovulation is the preovulatory release of LH from the pituitary, as in other mammals. In most of the species studied, including pigs (Coté *et al.*, 2001), gonadotrophins provoke expression of an inducible form of the cyclo-oxygenase enzyme (COX-2) by the granulosa cells that catalyses the first rate-limiting step in conversion of arachidonic acid to prostaglandins (Sirois and Richards, 1992). The sequence of COX-2 expression after ovulation has not been investigated in pigs, but it is clearly present and inducible in the corpus luteum at days 9 and 17 of the oestrous cycle (Diaz *et al.*, 2000). A second catalytic route for arachidonic acid is via the lipoxygenase enzymes, resulting in hydroxyeicosatetranoic acids (HETEs). Pharmacological interruption of this pathway reduces the rate of ovulation in pigs (Downey *et al.*, 1998).

The LH surge is the stimulus for initiation of other events in luteinization, particularly the qualitative and quantitative changes in steroidogenesis. Studies of hypophysectomy in pigs have shown that the pituitary is necessary for luteal support throughout gestation, that LH is essential in the early corpus luteum and that prolactin plays an important role later in pregnancy (Li *et al.*, 1989). Both LH and prolactin have luteotrophic effects on pig granulosa cells *in vitro* (Chedrese *et al.*, 1988).

Luteinization of pig granulosa cells *in vitro* occurs only when serum is present in the medium (Picton *et al.*, 1999). Serum-borne elements, particularly insulin and IGFs, contribute to luteinization and support of the corpus luteum during the luteal phase. Plasma membranes of pig luteal cells have receptors for IGF-I, and IGF-I binding proteins are expressed differentially in the pig corpus luteum throughout the luteal phase (Wandji *et al.*, 2000a). Insulin and IGFs are essential for the steroidogenic changes that characterize luteal formation *in vitro* (Pescador *et al.*, 1999; Sekar *et al.*, 2000). Most of the downstream genes that are modulated by these ligands in the corpus luteum have not yet been identified.

Angiogenesis in the pig corpus luteum

The source of the vasculature that perfuses and maintains the pig corpus luteum is the veins and arteries that invade after ovulation. Histological evidence indicates that the major vessels grow rapidly in a centripetal direction, arriving at the antrum of the former follicle (Fig. 1). Lateral development from the invading vascular components also occurs rapidly (Corner, 1919). The morphology and regulation of angiogenesis in the corpus luteum are the subject of at least five recent reviews (for example see Fraser and Lunn, 2001). Although none of these reviews considers pigs, the principles are expected to apply to this species. The rate of neovascularization in the corpus luteum appears to be higher than for any known tissue, including human tumours. A current view of regulation suggests that LH precipitates the angiogenic cascade (Fraser and Lunn, 2001). However, the principal stimulus inducing neovascularization is hypoxia, and a case has been made for hypoxia as an angiogenic stimulus in corpora lutea (Reynolds *et al.*, 2000). Results in other species implicate acidic and basic fibroblast growth factors (a and bFGFs), particularly bFGFs, and vascular endothelial growth factor (VEGF) as the key mediators of luteal angiogenesis (Reynolds *et al.*, 2000). The source of the FGFs is presumed to be the luteinized granulosa cells (Reynolds *et al.*, 2000) and this is consistent with the pattern of occurrence of FGF mRNA in pig follicles and corpora lutea (Guthridge *et al.*, 1992). VEGF is thought to stimulate proliferation of endothelial cells

---

Fig. 2. continued
38 h after hCG treatment, showing the dispersion of the granulosa layers at approximately 3 h before expected ovulation. (c) Cross-section of an 8 mm follicle taken from an untreated gilt and (d) 24 h after hCG and (e) 38 h after hCG administration. T: theca compartment. G: granulosa compartment. Scale bars represent 25 μm.

(Fraser and Lunn, 2001) and migration of endothelial cells into the granulosa parenchyma (Reynolds *et al.*, 2000). Its source may be theca-derived pericytes (Reynolds *et al.*, 2000) or granulosa–luteal cells (Fraser and Lunn, 2001). VEGF is found in pig follicular fluid and is produced by pig follicles during gonadotrophin-stimulated development (Barboni *et al.*, 2000). Both the theca and granulosa compartments contribute, but the latter predominates in overall VEGF synthesis (Barboni *et al.*, 2000). LH greatly reduces expression of VEGF by pig granulosa cells, both *in vivo* and *in vitro* (Barboni *et al.*, 2000). These findings contrast with the current view that LH drives angiogenesis via induction of VEGF and its downstream targets in granulosa cells (Fraser and Lunn, 2001). Whether this anomaly reflects differences in experimental design or fundamental differences among pig, ruminant and primate angiogenesis deserves further investigation. Connective tissue growth factor (CTGF) and a tumour inhibitor, MAC-25, have recently emerged as potential modulators of angiogenesis in pig corpora lutea (Wandji *et al.*, 2000b). Although there are some intriguing new findings, the nature of angiogenic stimuli and processes in formation of pig corpora lutea remain unknown.

Luteinization and exit from the cell cycle

Luteinization is the final phase in differentiation of theca and granulosa cells, a process that begins with formation of the primordial follicle before birth. There is much evidence that pig follicular growth results from hyperplasia of granulosa cells (Morbeck *et al.*, 1992). After ovulation, the prevailing view, derived from other species, is that luteinization results in exit of granulosa cells from the cell cycle. Reprogramming from the proliferative to the differentiated state in rat granulosa cells is complete within 5–7 h after the LH surge (Richards, 2001a). Although functional changes in mammalian theca cells have been described, little is known about their proliferation during luteinization *in vivo*. In pigs, both theca (Englehardt *et al.*, 1991) and granulosa cells (Pescador *et al.*, 1999; Picton *et al.*, 1999) proliferate and undergo luteinization when cultured with serum. This luteinization, defined as the loss of cytochrome P450aromatase expression and synthesis of large amounts of progesterone as the principal steroid product, can be avoided by culture in serum-free, insulin-supplemented medium (Picton *et al.*, 1999). Granulosa cells incubated under the latter conditions continue to proliferate, albeit somewhat less robustly than in the presence of serum.

Much of the growth of the pig corpus luteum is the result of cellular hypertrophy (Corner, 1919; Ricke *et al.*, 1999) and little information is available on the contribution of cell proliferation. Corner (1919) confirmed that cell division was occurring by observation of the mitotic spindle in theca cells of the periovulatory follicle and in follicles undergoing luteinization. We recently examined cell proliferation by immunohistochemistry using a mitotic marker, proliferating cell nuclear antigen (PCNA), in gilts treated with hCG to induce ovulation (B. D. Murphy, F. Coté, J. Sirois and B. R. Downey, unpublished). Late preovulatory follicles (6–8 mm in diameter) displayed the mitotic signal in many cells of the theca. The granulosa cell compartment consists of compact layers of cells, all of which express PCNA strongly (Fig. 2c). At 24 h after hCG administration, the theca cells are hypertrophied and display numerous PCNA positive cells (Fig. 2d). The granulosa layer is expanded; there is loss of the compactness of the cell layers and evidence of mitosis throughout (Fig. 2d). Ovaries removed at 30 and 34 h after hCG administration display greater dissociation of the granulosa cell layers, while retaining the same pattern of mitosis in the theca and the granulosa compartments (data not shown). At 38 h after hCG administration, a few hours before expected ovulation, the rate of mitosis has increased in the theca layers (Fig. 2e). The granulosa cells are nearly dissociated (Fig. 2b); however, the PCNA signal is present, particularly in the most interior layers of cells (Fig. 2e).

Ricke *et al.* (1999) demonstrated extensive mitosis in the corpus luteum during the first 4 days after ovulation. About 25–40% of the mitotic cells are derived from the theca or granulosa, whereas the other mitotic cells represent proliferation of vascular elements (Ricke *et al.*, 1999). Co-localization of mitotic and steroidogenic enzyme signals indicates that luteal steroidogenesis and cell division occur in proliferating cells, particularly early in luteal development. Over the lifespan of the corpus luteum, the labelling index decreases (Ricke *et al.*, 1999) and the mitotic signal is observed rarely in large luteal cells. Thus, it appears that terminal differentiation occurs in the pig corpus luteum. Nonetheless, it is equally apparent that the rat model of rapid and irreversible exit from the cell cycle soon after the ovulatory stimulus (Richards *et al.*, 1998) does not apply to pigs. A more appropriate model includes continued mitosis of the steroidogenic cells well into the luteal phase, with increasing restriction in the capacity to proliferate.

The mechanisms of terminal differentiation in the corpus luteum have begun to be studied, mostly in rodents (Richards *et al.*, 1998; Richards, 2001a,b). The initiation of mitotic division is under the control of members of the retinoblastoma protein family, retinoblastoma protein (pRb), p107 and p130 (Classen and Dyson, 2001). In the hyperphosphorylated state, these proteins permit cell division by liberating the transcription factors of the E2F family, which then upregulate the genes responsible for progression of the cell cycle. Hypophosphorylation of these proteins results in mitotic quiescence by the opposite mechanism, the sequestering of E2Fs (Morgan, 1995). In luteinization, a general pattern emerges in which pRb and p130 are dephosphorylated, thereby impairing the expression and activity of positive regulators of the cell cycle, cyclins D1, D2 and E (Green *et al.*, 2000; Hampl *et al.*, 2000). A second level of regulation is recognized, on the basis of a phenotype of luteal disruption in mice bearing the null mutation for p27[Kip1] (Kikokawa *et al.*, 1996), a member of one of the two families of inhibitors of the cyclin-dependent kinases (Zhu and Skoultchi, 2001). In these mice, differentiation of luteal cells appears to occur, as indicated by cytochrome P450side chain cleavage (P450scc) expression, and cyclin D2 activity is repressed; however, active DNA synthesis persists (Tong *et al.*, 1998). Further evidence for a role for these repressors of cyclin-dependent kinases (CDKs) comes from a study which showed that expression of p27[Kip1] and p21[Cip1] is increased in granulosa cells of hypophysectomized rats treated with ovulatory doses of hCG (Robker and Richards, 1998). The expression of p27 proteins remains high throughout the lifespan of the corpus luteum in pregnant mice (Hampl *et al.*, 2000). CDK4, expressed in mouse granulosa cells and in the mouse corpus luteum of gestation, complexes with p27 and cyclin D3 (Hampl *et al.*, 2000). A different disruption in the luteal phenotype emerged after null mutation of CDK4, which enhanced expression of p27[Kip1] (Tsutsui *et al.*, 1999). It took the form of entrapment of oocytes and aberrant luteal organisation. Cell cycle regulators can participate in both cell proliferation and differentiation, and CDKs regulate transcription of genes that result in differentiation in some tissues (Zhu and Skoultchi, 2001), which could explain the phenotype of the CDK4 knockout mice.

Although progress has been made, our knowledge remains rudimentary. There is no specific information on exit from the cell cycle for pigs, and there is no information on the cell cycle dynamics of theca cells in development of the corpus luteum.

Differentiation of theca and granulosa cells into their luteal counterparts

Granulosa and theca cells undergo functional differentiation during luteinization. In most of the species studied, the theca of the follicle responds to LH stimulation by synthesis of androgens. These diffuse across the basement membrane to the granulosa compartment where they are aromatized to oestrogens, under the influence of FSH. The latter portion of the scheme occurs in pigs, as 3β-hydroxysteroid dehydrogenase (3β-HSD), which converts pregnenolone to progesterone, is found in the theca of the growing follicle only (Driancourt *et al.*, 1998). However, pig follicles deviate from the general pattern because the theca cells express aromatase and produce oestrogens that complement the production of granulosa cells (Tsang *et al.*, 1985). In many species, oestrogen concentrations are low or absent in the corpus luteum. In contrast, P450aromatase expression persists in pig corpora lutea (Meduri *et al.*, 1996) and large and small cells of pig corpora lutea maintain the capability to secrete oestrogen (Lemon and Loir, 1977). However, luteinization in pigs engenders alteration of the pattern of steroid synthesis in favour of progesterone, particularly the granulosa cells (Lavoie *et al.*, 1997), as indicated by the early acquisition of the expression of P450scc, which converts cholesterol to pregnenolone, and of 3β-HSD (Meduri *et al.*, 1996). This change is accompanied by a large increase in total steroid output, which requires an extensive increase in the supply of cholesterol, the substrate for steroid synthesis. In pigs, luteinization is characterized by coordinated upregulation of cholesterol synthesis, importation and intracellular trafficking genes, including the low density lipoprotein receptor and sterol carrier protein 2 (Lavoie *et al.*, 1997), steroidogenic acute regulatory protein (StAR), P450scc (Lavoie *et al.*, 1997; Pescador *et al.*, 1997, 1999) and Niemann-Pick C1 protein (Song *et al.*, 1998). Expression of StAR is a key event in granulosa cell remodelling (Pescador *et al.*, 1997, 1999); thus, factors that control this transition are believed to be essential regulators of luteinization.

The pattern of expression of gonadotrophin receptors changes as a pig follicle becomes a corpus luteum. The FSH receptors present on granulosa cells of the follicle are lost during luteinization (Liu *et al.*, 1998). Binding analysis of LH receptors indicated an initial downregulation, relative to granulosa cells from periovulatory follicles, followed by recovery in the number of receptors as the luteal phase progresses (Gebarowska *et al.*, 1997). Autoradiographic studies indicate that hCG binding in newly formed corpora lutea is mainly peripheral and is more widespread in mid-cycle corpora lutea (Gebarowska *et al.*, 1997). Immunohistochemical localization of the LH receptor supports this interpretation of the early stage: downregulation after ovulation and restriction of the signal to the periphery and to the presumed theca-derived component of the corpus luteum (Meduri *et al.*, 1996). However, the analyses diverge at this point, as immunolocalization using a monoclonal antibody indicates that, although the LH receptor signal increases at mid-cycle, it is present at the spokes of vascular invasion only, interpreted as restriction to the theca descendants (Meduri *et al.*, 1996). In contrast, *in situ* analysis indicates that both large and small cells throughout the pig corpus luteum contain LH receptor mRNA (Yuan and Lucy, 1996). Furthermore, LH receptor mRNA and protein were highly abundant, as demonstrated by RT–PCR and immunolocalization in large and small cell populations isolated from pig corpus luteum (Kaminski *et al.*, 2000). Data from the corpus luteum and the large number of studies demonstrating luteinized granulosa cell responses to LH (Murphy and Silavin, 1989) provide evidence for the persistence of the LH receptor on both theca and granulosa descendants in pig corpora lutea.

Transcriptional regulation of luteinization

The subject of transduction of signals and signalling pathways involved in luteinization has been reviewed recently (Murphy, 2000). Hence, in the present review, greater emphasis is placed on gene transcription and its role in the intricacies of corpus luteum formation. Transcription is not the sole regulator of gene expression, but it is clearly the most significant. It is a complex process that includes chromatin modification, coactivator recruitment, and synthesis and activation of transcription factors. Frequently, two or more transcription factors interact to produce differential expression of a gene. As noted above, luteal formation involves changes in the expression of numerous known, and presumably many more unknown, gene products. It is not within the scope of this review to consider all permutations; thus, we will focus on factors known to act on genes related to steroidogenesis and to provision of steroid substrate. Where pertinent, factors involved in differentiation and exit from the cell cycle are also discussed.

The classic linear route for transduction of gonadotrophin signals is via cAMP activation of protein kinase A and subsequent phosphorylation of cAMP response binding protein (CREB; Richards, 2001b). CREB exists in three isoforms and is considered to be synthesized constitutively (Zeleznik and Somers, 1999). Phosphorylated CREB transactivates gonadotrophin-regulated steroidogenic genes including P450scc (Watanabe *et al.*, 1994) and P450aromatase (Michael *et al.*, 1997). StAR transcription, which is dependent on cAMP (Stocco, 2001), is modulated by CREB phosphorylation (D. M. Stocco, personal communication). Similarly, transcription of pig Niemann–Pick C protein 1 (NPC-1) is CREB-dependent (N. Gévry and B. D. Murphy, unpublished). Little is known about CREB expression in pigs, other than that its coding sequence is found in the pig genome (R. L. Mattari and J. A. Carroll; GenBank Accession U95009). Notwithstanding, in primates, CREB expression is abolished in granulosa cells during luteinization (Somers *et al.*, 1995). These observations are consistent with a model in which LH acts through cAMP to initiate luteinization of granulosa cells, which then become refractory to this messenger (Zeleznik and Somers, 1999). This view is not compatible with observations that LH and cAMP can stimulate progesterone from large and small pig luteal cells *in vitro* (Hunter, 1981) and that exogenous LH increases circulating progesterone concentrations from the pig corpus luteum (Watson and Maule Walker, 1978).

Among the transcription factors implicated clearly in luteinization is the CCAAT/enhancer binding protein β (C/EBP-β). C/EBP-β expression is induced rapidly in rat granulosa cells in response to an ovulatory dose of hCG (Sirois and Richards, 1993), and granulosa cells in the C/EBP-β knockout mice do not luteinize (Sterneck *et al.*, 1997). Furthermore, antisense inhibition of C/EBP-β expression interferes with ovulation and luteinization in rats, with no apparent reduction in COX-2 expression (Pall *et al.*, 1997). C/EBP-β is a transactivator of StAR transcription (Reinhart *et al.*, 1999). C/EBP-β is present in pigs and its expression changes during adipocyte differentiation *in vitro* (Yu and Hausman, 1998). Therefore, it is likely that C/EBP-β expression will prove to be a vital controlling factor in luteinization in pigs.

The six transcription factors (GATA 1–6) of the GATA family are proteins with two zinc fingers that bind to the consensus promoter elements (A/T)GATA(A/G) (Molkentin, 2000). The GATA-1, -2 and -3 subfamily regulates haematopoeisis and lymphopoiesis primarily, whereas the subfamily comprising GATA-4, -5 and -6 is expressed in endoderm-derived tissues, including the cardiovascular and digestive systems (Molkentin, 2000). Modulation of the abundance of GATA transcription factors is associated with luteinization in mice and expression of one isoform, GATA-4, is reduced in the follicle after ovulation, whereas GATA-6 is expressed highly in both developing and mature corpora lutea (Heikinheimo *et al.*, 1997). In contrast, GATA-4 is expressed constitutively in rat granulosa cells and interacts with acutely regulated C/EBP-β in induction of StAR transcription (Silverman *et al.*, 1999). GATA-4 induces transcription of both StAR and P450aromatase in mouse ovaries (Tremblay and Viger, 2001). Deletion and mutational analysis of the mouse StAR promoter demonstrated that the GATA-4 element interacts with other enhancers, including steroid factor 1 (SF-1) and AP-1, in translating the cAMP stimulus (Wooten-Kee and Clark, 2000). Both the pig StAR and NPC-1 (N. Gévry and B. D. Murphy, unpublished) promoters have GATA response elements within the first 200 bp upstream of the ATG transcription start site. Given the importance of StAR and NPC-1 for luteinization in pigs, it is likely that GATA-directed transcription contributes to the synthesis of progesterone in this species.

Other transcription factors essential to luteal steroidogenesis are the sterol regulatory element binding proteins (SREBPs). There are three known isoforms of this basic-helix-loop-helix-leucine zipper protein: SREBP-1a and -1c (also known as ADD-1) are the products of alternative splicing, whereas SREBP-2 arises from a second gene (Osborne, 2000). The SREBPs are present in cells as integral membrane proteins embedded in the endoplasmic reticular or nuclear membranes (Brown and Goldstein, 1999). In the event of intracellular sterol depletion, a second element, sterol cleavage-activating protein, cleaves the N-terminal SREBP fragment, which then relocates to the nucleus and interacts with decanucleotide segments of the gene promoters (Brown and Goldstein, 1999). Transcription of genes associated with increased intracellular cholesterol is induced, including the cascade for *de novo* cholesterol synthesis and those related to low density lipoprotein (LDL) receptor-mediated cholesterol importation. Given the increases in cholesterol required to accomplish luteal synthesis of progesterone, it is not surprising that SREBP isoforms are important regulators of *de novo* synthesis and importation of cholesterol into the corpus luteum (Lopez and McLean, 1999; Shea-Eaton *et al.*, 2001). In addition, over-expression of transcriptionally active SREBP-1a, -1c and -2 increases transcription of StAR (Christenson *et al.*, 2001; Shea-Eaton *et al.*, 2001) and SREBP-1a synergizes with cAMP induction of StAR transcription (Z. T. Ruiz-Cortes and B. D. Murphy, unpublished). Nevertheless, basal StAR transcription in human granulosa lutein cells appears to be unaffected by sterol depletion or repletion and, thus, the physiological significance of SREBP in regulation of StAR is unclear (Christenson *et al.*, 2001). SREBPs appear to have the greatest effects on transcription in concert with other factors and may also integrate endocrine signals. Recent evidence indicates that cAMP may act via CREB to amplify SREBP-mediated transcription of HMG-CoA-reductase (Dooley *et al.*, 1999). Downstream signals in the mitogen-activated kinase pathway stimulate SREBP-induced transcription of the LDL promoter directly (Kotzka *et al.*, 2000). Induction of StAR transcription involves interaction of SREBP with Yin Yang 1 (YY1) (Christenson *et al.*, 2001) and the orphan nuclear receptor of the steroid–thyroid superfamily, SF-1 (Shea-Eaton *et al.*, 2001). Thus, the SREBPs are important in luteinization. They may act on cholesterol homeostasis genes in the corpus luteum and also on transcription of StAR, a key step in luteinization of granulosa cells.

SF-1 is implicated in luteinization and steroidogenesis (Wehrenberg *et al.*, 1997). It is essential for expression of StAR, key steroidogenic enzymes (Hanley *et al.*, 2000) and nonsteroidogenic proteins specific to bovine luteinization (Ivell *et al.*, 1999). In equine follicles, SF-1 expression decreases between the ovulatory stimulus and expulsion of the oocyte (Boerboom *et al.*, 2000). In rat granulosa cells, a reduction in SF-1 expression occurs concomitantly with the decrease in P450aromatase expression (Fitzpatrick *et al.*, 1997). SF-1 expression recovers during early development of the ovine corpus luteum and is expressed constitutively during the mid-luteal phase (Juengel *et al.*, 1998). Pig SF-1 has been identified and sequenced, and is present in the pig corpus luteum of pregnancy (Pilon *et al.*, 1998). Its pattern of expression during luteal formation has not been investigated.

The peroxisome proliferator-activated receptors (PPARs), another group of receptors of the steroid–thyroid superfamily, are potential effectors of luteinization. Three distinct isoforms, PPARα, γ and δ (also known as PPARβ) are recognized. Each is encoded by a separate gene and has different patterns of tissue and developmental distribution (Chinetti *et al.*, 2000). PPARs require a ligand to be activated and after activation, they form heterodimers with the retinoic acid X receptor (RXR) and interact with specific PPAR response elements in the promoter regions of target genes (Chinetti *et al.*, 2000). Natural ligands include eicosanoides derived from arachidonic acid catalysed by COX-2 (for example 15-deoxy-D-12-14-prostaglandin J2 (PGJ2) and prostacyclin) and 15-hydroxyeicosatetranoic acid (15-HETE), derived from catalysis of lipo-oxygenase (Chinetti *et al.*, 2000). Linoleic acid metabolites, including 9- and 12-hydroxydecadanoic acid (9- and 12-HODE), which are also catalysed by lipo-oxygenases, also serve as natural ligands (Chinetti *et al.*, 2000). The thiazolidinedione family of synthetic compounds, the members of which are effective in treatment of non-insulin dependent diabetes, are high affinity ligands for PPARγ. Two splice variants of PPARγ are recognized, and PPARγ2 is expressed highly in adipose tissue and involved in terminal differentiation of adipocytes (Hansen *et al.*, 1999). In adipose tissue, a PPARγ-induced cell cycle inhibition occurs in tandem with an increase in intracellular concentrations of p27[Kip1] (Motomura *et al.*, 2000; Wakino *et al.*, 2000), which, as noted above, is related to the mechanism of cell cycle exit during luteinization in mice and rats (Robker and Richards, 1998). PPARδ has been implicated in adipocyte proliferation (Hansen *et al.*, 2000). All three PPARs are expressed in pigs (Grindflek *et al.*, 1998; Houseknecht *et al.*, 1998; Ding *et al.*, 2000). PPARα transactivates pig HMG-CoA reductase (Ortiz *et al.*, 1999). PPARγ mRNA is present in pig granulosa cells during luteinization *in vitro* (Z. T. Ruiz-Cortés and B. D. Murphy, unpublished). Furthermore, a role for PPARγ in luteinization is apparent, on the basis of studies that demonstrate stage-specific expression in bovine luteal cells (Lohrke *et al.*, 1998; Viergutz *et al.*, 2000). A preliminary report indicates that PPARγ is expressed in theca and granulosa cells of pig preovulatory follicles and appears to be related to luteal differentiation (Schoppee *et al.*, 2000). Mechanistic information comes from studies of bovine luteal cells (Lohrke *et al.*, 1998) and pig granulosa cells (Gasic *et al.*, 1998; Schoppee *et al.*, 2000) in which trogladizone (a thiazolidinedione) and PGJ2 cause dose-dependent increases in steroid synthesis. Trogladizone also interferes with 3β-HSD expression in pig granulosa cells (Gasic *et al.*, 1998); it is not known whether this is mediated by PPARγ. Trogladizone reduces P450aromatase expression and activity in human granulosa cells (Mu *et al.*, 2000) and PGJ2 interferes with the cell cycle in bovine luteal cells (Viergutz *et al.*, 2000), thereby further implicating this receptor in luteinization.

Expression of PPARs is induced by other transcription factors involved in luteinization. C/EBPα upregulates PPARγ (Wu *et al.*, 1999), as do endogenous lipid ligands produced as a result of SREBP expression (Patel *et al.*, 2001). In similar experiments, over-expression of SREBP induced transcription of PPARγ (Fajas *et al.*, 1999). PPARs may also influence corpus luteum formation and function by interactions with CREB (Mizukami and Taniguchi, 1997). Over-expression of SREBPs enhances transactivation of target genes by PPARγ (Fajas *et al.*, 1999). Mice bearing the null mutation for PPARα have disrupted expression of SREBP-regulated cholesterol and fatty acid metabolism genes (Patel *et al.*, 2001). Thus, the PPAR family of nuclear receptors is involved in the process of luteinization and understanding its impact awaits further experimentation.

Conclusion: models and mechanisms of formation of the pig corpus luteum

Several pieces in the 'puzzle of luteinization' are now in place, but not enough for the full picture to emerge. An attempt can be made, albeit rife with speculation, to model the changes and mechanisms of early luteal development from the theca and granulosa components of preovulatory pig follicles. The events that are known to occur in pig theca cells during luteinization *in vivo* after the LH surge, steroid synthesis, proliferation, hypertrophy and migration, are shown (Fig. 3a). LH and cAMP upregulate StAR and other steroidogenic enzymes in the theca (Zhang *et al.*, 2000), presumably working through the linear pathway via phosphorylation of CREB. StAR and steroidogenic enzymes require the orphan nuclear receptor SF-1 for their expression. Serum and growth factors are potent stimulators of theca cell mitosis (May *et al.*, 1992), acting via tyrosine kinases, protein kinase C and mitogen-activated kinase pathways. Theca cell hypertrophy is observed during luteal formation

(a)　Theca cells, 0–72 h after the ovulatory stimulus

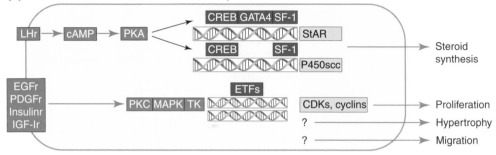

(b)　Granulosa cells, 0–72 h after the ovulatory stimulus

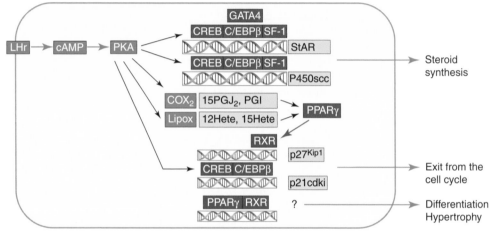

(c)　Cells of the corpus luteum through the luteal phase

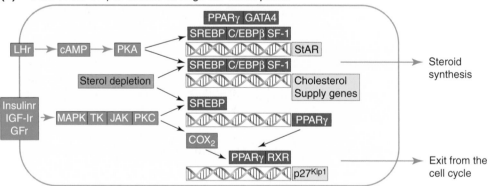

Fig. 3. Summary of the changes and regulation of luteinization in pigs. Elements in red are ligand pathways, blue are transcription factors and yellow are examples of regulated genes. (a) Theca cell between the preovulatory surge and approximately 24 h after ovulation. (b) Granulosa cell over the same period as in (a). (c) Generalized luteal cell during the early luteal phase. LHr: LH receptor; PKA: protein kinase A; CREB: cAMP response binding protein; GATA4: transcription factor GATA4; SF-1: steroid factor 1; StAR: steroidogenic acute regulatory protein; P450scc: cytochrome P450 side chain cleavage protein; EGFr: epidermal growth factor receptor; PDGFr: platelet-derived growth factor receptor; Insulinr: insulin receptor; IGF-Ir: insulin-like growth factor I receptor; PKC: protein kinase C; MAPK: mitogen-activated protein kinase; TK: tyrosine kinase; ETF: ETF transcription factor family; CDK: cyclin-dependent kinase; C/EBPβ: CCAAT/enhancer binding protein β; COX$_2$: cyclo-oxygenase enzyme; Lipox: lipo-oxygenase; PPARγ: peroxisome proliferator-activated receptor γ;

(Corner, 1919) and the migration of theca cells into the granulosa compartment is described in detail above. The factors controlling these profound and important changes are not currently known.

More is known about early events in granulosa cell differentiation, but a coherent synthesis eludes us. An attempt to reconcile available findings is shown (Fig. 3b). LH receptors appear at the antral follicle stage and respond to the ovulatory surge by expression of a number of genes, including COX-2. Given the role of lipoxygenase in ovulation (Downey *et al.*, 1998), its products may also be present during early luteinization. Both enzymes produce ligands for PPARγ, which induces differentiation and exit from the cell cycle in adipocytes. Therefore, PPARγ may serve multiple roles in granulosa cell luteinization: induction of differentiation, stimulation of steroidogenesis and initiation of exit from the cell cycle. Not represented in the scheme (Fig. 3b) are the roles of insulin and growth factors, which synergize with LH to convert granulosa cells to the luteal phenotype. In early luteinization in other species, CREB isoforms are present, and cAMP and CREB upregulate StAR expression and enzymes in the steroidogenic cascade. LH induces expression of C/EBP-β in preovulatory follicles, and this factor, together with GATA-4 and SF-1, enhances the transcription of StAR. The morphological evidence indicates that hypertrophy of granulosa cells is present as early as 24 h after ovulation or by 72 h after the ovulatory stimulus. The cellular events of hypertrophy and their mechanisms of control are not well understood.

The corpus luteum continues to evolve over its lifespan and, likewise, its regulation undergoes an evolution. Given the differential origin and variation in cell size of pig luteal cells, differing regulatory mechanisms must also exist. For simplicity, these have been generalized (Fig. 3c). The pituitary factors, LH and prolactin, are necessary for continued luteal steroidogenesis. If, as in other species, CREB is not expressed during luteinization, LH and cAMP must be acting through other mechanisms, perhaps independent of protein kinase A (Richards, 2001b). A role for SREBP is proposed via its classic effects on the genes that supply cholesterol, regulated by intracellular sterol concentrations. It may have a second role in transcriptional regulation of PPARγ expression, and SREBP may be involved in expression of ligands that activate PPARγ. As noted above, COX-2 expression is evident during the mid- and late luteal phases of the pig oestrous cycle (Diaz *et al.*, 2000) and may be a further source of ligands for PPARγ. This receptor then has pleiotropic effects on the luteal cell, ensuring the completion of differentiation and exit from the cell cycle, and stimulating steroidogenesis directly. Growth factors and insulin participate in sterol homeostasis and in steroid synthesis via their effects on StAR and receptor-mediated importation of extracellular cholesterol.

The original work described in this review was funded by CIHR grants MT-11018 to B. D. Murphy and MT-13190 to J. Sirois, and by a NSERC Strategic Grant 202133-97 to B. D. Murphy and B. R. Downey. Z. T. Ruiz-Cortés is on leave from Universidad de Antioqua, Colombia. The authors are grateful to M. Dobias for technical assistance and S. Ledoux for artwork.

Fig. 3. continued
15PGJ2: 15-deoxy-D-12-14-prostaglandin J2; PGI: prostaglandin I; 12Hete: 12-hydroxyeicosatetranoic acid; 15Hete: 15-hydroxyeicosatetranoic acid; RXR: retinoic acid X receptor; SREBP: sterol regulatory element binding protein; GFr: growth factor receptor; JAK: janus kinase.

References

Barboni B, Turriani M, Galeati G, Spinaci M, Bacci ML, Forni M and Mattioli M (2000) Vascular endothelial growth factor production in growing pig antral follicles *Biology of Reproduction* **63** 858–864

Boerboom D, Pilon N, Behdjani R, Silversides DW and Sirois J (2000) Expression and regulation of transcripts encoding two members of the NR5A nuclear receptor subfamily of orphan nuclear receptors, steroidogenic factor-1 and NR5A2, in equine ovarian cells during the ovulatory process *Endocrinology* **141** 4647–4656

Brown MS and Goldstein JL (1999) A proteolytic pathway that controls the cholesterol content of membranes, cells, and blood *Proceedings National Academy of Sciences USA* **96** 11 041–11 048

Chedrese PJ, Rajkumar K, Ly H and Murphy BD (1988) Dose response of luteinized porcine granulosa cells *in vitro* to prolactin: dependency on pre-exposure to human chorionic gonadotrophin *Canadian Journal of Physiology and Pharmacology* **66** 1337–1340

Chinetti G, Fruchart JC and Staels B (2000) Peroxisome proliferator-activated receptors (PPARs): nuclear receptors at the crossroads between lipid metabolism and inflammation *Inflammation Research* **49** 497–505

Christenson LK, Osborne TF, McAllister JM and Strauss JF, III (2001) Conditional response of human steroidogenic acute regulatory protein gene promoter of sterol regulatory element binding protein 1a *Endocrinology* **142** 28–36

Classen M and Dyson N (2001) p107 and p130: versatile proteins with interesting pockets *Experimental Cell Research* **264** 135–147

Corner GW (1919) On the origin of the corpus luteum of the sow from both granulosa and theca interna *American Journal of Anatomy* **27** 117–183

Coté F, Sirois J, Doré M and Downey BR (2001) Induction of prostaglandin G/H synthase-2 in preovulatory follicles of equine chorionic gonadotropin/human chorionic gonadotropin treated prepubertal gilts *Biology of Reproduction* **63** (Supplement 1) 161 (Abstract)

Cox NM (1997) Control of follicular development and ovulation rate in pigs *Journal of Reproduction and Fertility Supplement* **52** 31–46

Diaz FJ, Crenshaw TD and Wiltbank MC (2000) Prostaglandin F2a induces distinct physiological responses in porcine corpora lutea after acquisition of luteolytic capacity *Biology of Reproduction* **63** 1504–1512

Ding ST, Schinckel AP, Weber TE and Mersmann HJ (2000) Expression of porcine transcription factors and genes related to fatty acid metabolism in different tissues and genetic populations *Journal of Animal Science* **78** 2127–2134

Dooley KA, Bennett MK and Osborne TF (1999) A critical role for cAMP response element-binding protein (CREB) as a co-activator in sterol-regulated transcription of 3-hydroxy-3-methylglutaryl coenzyme A synthase promoter *Journal of Biological Chemistry* **274** 5285–5291

Downey BR, Mootoo JE and Doyle SE (1998) A role for lipoxygenase metabolites of arachidonic acid in porcine ovulation *Animal Reproduction Science* **49** 269–279

Driancourt MA, Quesnel H, Meduri G, Prunier A and Hermier D (1998) Luteinization and proteolysis in ovarian follicles of Meishan and Large White gilts during the preovulatory period *Journal of Reproduction and Fertility* **114** 287–297

du Mesnil du Buisson F and Dauzier L (1957) Influence d'ovariectomie chez la truie pendant la gestation *Compte Rendu Société de Biologie* **151** 311–313

Ellicott AR and Dzuik PJ (1973) Minimum daily dose of progesterone and plasma concentration for maintenance of pregnancy in ovariectomized gilts *Biology of Reproduction* **9** 300–304

Englehardt H, Gore-Langton RE and Armstrong DT (1991) Luteinization of porcine theca cells *in vitro*. *Molecular and Cellular Endocrinology* **75** 237–245

Fajas L, Schoonjans K, Gelman L et al. (1999) Regulation of peroxisome proliferator-activated receptor gamma expression by adipocyte differentiation and determination factor 1/sterol regulatory element binding protein 1: implications for adipocyte differentiation and metabolism *Molecular and Cellular Biology* **19** 5495–5503

Fitzpatrick SL, Carlone DL, Robker RL and Richards JS (1997) Expression of aromatase in the ovary: down-regulation of mRNA by the ovulatory luteinizing hormone surge *Steroids* **62** 197–206

Fraser HM and Lunn SF (2001) Regulation and manipulation of angiogenesis in the primate corpus luteum *Reproduction* **121** 355–362

Gasic S, Bodenburg Y, Nagamani M, Green A and Urban RJ (1998) Troglitazone inhibits progesterone production in porcine granulosa cells *Endocrinology* **139** 4962–4966

Gebarowska D, Ziecik AJ and Gregoraszczuk EL (1997) Luteinizing hormone receptors on granulosa cells from preovulatory follicles and luteal cells throughout the oestrous cycle of pigs *Animal Reproduction Science* **49** 191–205

Grant SA, Hunter MG and Foxcroft GR (1989) Morphological and biochemical characteristics during ovarian follicular development in the pig *Journal of Reproduction and Fertility* **86** 171–183

Green C, Chatterjee R, McGarrigle HHG, Ahmed F and Thomas NSB (2000) p107 is active in the nucleolus of non-dividing human granulosa lutein cells *Journal of Molecular Endocrinology* **25** 275–286

Grindflek E, Sundvold H, Klungland H and Lien S (1998) Characterisation of porcine peroxisome proliferator-activated receptors gamma 1 and gamma 2: detection of breed and age differences in gene expression *Biochemical and Biophysical Research Communications* **249** 713–718

Guthridge M, Schmitt J, Bertolini J, Cowling J, Runting A, Katsahambas S, Drummond AE and Hearn MT (1992) Studies on basic fibroblast growth factor (FGF-beta) gene expression in the rat and pig ovary using *in situ* hybridization and quantitative reverse transcriptase–polymerase chain reaction techniques7 *EXS (Basel)* **61** 219–229

Hampl A, Pachernik J and Dvorak P (2000) Levels and

interactions of p27, cyclin D3 and CDK4 during the formation and maintenance of the corpus luteum in mice *Biology of Reproduction* **62** 1393–1401

Hanley NA, Ikeda Y, Luo X and Parker KL (2000) Steroidogenic factor 1 (SF-1) is essential for ovarian development and function *Cellular and Molecular Endocrinology* **163** 27–32

Hansen JB, Petersen RK, Larsen BM, Bartkova J, Alsner J and Kristiansen K (1999) Activation of peroxisome proliferator-activated receptor gamma bypasses the function of the retinoblastoma protein in adipocyte differentiation *Journal of Biological Chemistry* **274** 2386–2393

Hansen JB, Zhang H, Rasmussen TH, Petersen RK, Flindt EN and Kristiansen K (2000) Peroxisome proliferator activator receptor delta (PPARdelta)-mediated regulation of preadipocyte proliferation and gene expression is dependent on cAMP signaling *Journal of Biological Chemistry* **276** 3175–3182

Heikinheimo M, Ermolaeva M, Bielinska M, Rahman NA, Narita N, Huhtaniemi IT, Tapanainen JS and Wilson DB (1997) Expression and hormonal regulation of transcription factors GATA-4 and GATA-6 in the mouse ovary *Endocrinology* **138** 3505–3514

Houseknecht KL, Bidwell CA, Portocarrero CP and Spurlock ME (1998) Expression and cDNA cloning of porcine peroxisome proliferator-activated receptor gamma (PPARgamma) *Gene* **225** 89–96

Hunter MG (1981) Responsiveness *in vitro* of porcine luteal tissue recovered at two stages of the luteal phase *Journal of Reproduction and Fertility* **63** 471–476

Hunter RHF (1972) Ovulation in the pig: timing in response to injection of human chorionic gonadotrophin *Research in Veterinary Science* **13** 356–361

Ivell R, Bathgate R and Walther N (1999) Luteal peptides and their genes as important markers of ovarian differentiation *Journal of Reproduction and Fertility Supplement* **54** 207–216

Juengel JL, Larrick TL, Meberg BM and Niswender GD (1998) Luteal expression of steroidogenic factor-1 mRNA during the estrous cycle and in response to luteotropic and luteolytic stimuli in ewes *Endocrine* **9** 227–232

Kaminski T, Gawronska B, Derecka K, Okrasa S and Przala J (2000) Gene expression and peptide localization for LH/hCG receptor in porcine small and large luteal cells: possible regulation by opioid peptides *Journal of Physiology and Pharmacology* **51** 359–368

Kikokawa H, Kineman RD, Manova-Todorova KO *et al.* (1996) Enhanced growth of mice lacking cyclin-dependent kinase inhibitor function of p27(Kip1) *Cell* **31** 721–732

Kotzka J, Muller-Wieland D, Roth G, Kremer L, Munck M, Schurmann S, Knebel B and Krone W (2000) Sterol regulatory element binding proteins (SREBP)-1a and SREBP-2 are linked to the MAP-kinase cascade *Journal of Lipid Research* **41** 99–108

Lavoie HA, Benoit AM, Garmey JC, Dailey RL, Wright DJ and Veldhuis JD (1997) Coordinate developmental expression of genes regulating sterol economy and cholesterol side chain cleavage in the porcine ovary *Biology of Reproduction* **57** 402–407

Lemon M and Loir L (1977) Steroid release *in vitro* by two luteal cell types in the corpus luteum of the pregnant sow *Journal of Endocrinology* **72** 351–359

Li Y, Molina JR, Klindt J, Bolt DJ and Anderson LL (1989) Prolactin maintains relaxin and progesterone secretion by aging corpora lutea after hypophysial stalk transection or hypophysectomy in the pig *Endocrinology* **124** 1294–1304

Liu J, Aronow BJ, Witte DP, Pope WF and La Barbera AR (1998) Cyclic and maturation-dependent regulation of follicle-stimulating hormone receptor and luteinizing hormone receptor messenger ribonucleic acid expression in the porcine ovary *Biology of Reproduction* **58** 648–658

Lohrke B, Viergutz T, Shahi SK, Pohland R, Wollenhaupt K, Goldammer T, Walzel H and Kanitz W (1998) Detection and functional characterisation of the transcription factor peroxisome proliferator-activated receptor gamma in lutein cells *Journal of Endocrinology* **159** 429–439

Lopez D and McLean MP (1999) Sterol regulatory element-binding protein-1a binds to cis elements in the promoter of the rat high density lipoprotein receptor SR-BI gene *Endocrinology* **140** 5669–5681

May JV, Bridge AJ, Gotcher ED and Gangrade BK (1992) The regulation of porcine theca cell proliferation *in vitro*: synergistic actions of epidermal growth factor and platelet-derived growth factor *Endocrinology* **131** 689–697

Meduri G, Vu Hai MT, Jolivet A, Takemori S, Kominami S, Driancourt MA and Milgrom E (1996) Comparison of cellular distribution of LH receptors and steroidogenic enzymes in the porcine ovary *Journal of Endocrinology* **148** 435–446

Michael MD, Michael LF and Simpson ER (1997) A CRE-like sequence that binds CREB and contributes to cAMP-dependent regulation of the proximal promoter of the human aromatase P450 (CYP19) gene *Molecular and Cellular Endocrinology* **134** 147–156

Mizukami J and Taniguchi T (1997) The antidiabetic agent thiazolidinedione stimulates the interaction between PPAR gamma and CBP *Biochemical and Biophysical Research Communications* **240** 61–64

Molkentin JD (2000) The zinc-finger containing transcription factors GATA-4, -5 and -6 *Journal of Biological Chemistry* **50** 38 949–38 952

Morbeck DE, Esbenshade KL, Flowers WL and Britt JH (1992) Kinetics of follicle growth in the prepubertal gilt *Biology of Reproduction* **47** 485–491

Morgan DO (1995) Principles of CDK regulation *Nature* **374** 131–134

Motomura W, Okumura T, Takahashi N, Obara T and Kohgo Y (2000) Activation of peroxisome proliferator-activated receptor gamma by troglitazone inhibits cell growth through the increase of p27KiP1 in human pancreatic carcinoma cells *Cancer Research* **60** 5558–5564

Mu YM, Yanase T, Nishi Y, Waseda N, Oda T, Tanaka A, Takayanagi R and Nawata H (2000) Insulin sensitizer, troglitazone, directly inhibits aromatase activity in human ovarian granulosa cells *Biochemical and Biophysical Research Communications* **271** 710–713

Murphy BD (2000) Models of luteinization *Biology of Reproduction* **63** 2–11

Murphy BD and Silavin SL (1989) Luteotropic agents and steroid substrate utilization *Oxford Reviews of Reproductive Biology* **11** 180–223

Ortiz JA, Mallolas J, Nicot C, Bofarull J, Rodriguez JC, Hegardt FG, Haro D and Marrero PF (1999) Isolation of pig mitochondrial 3-hydroxy-3-methylglutaryl-CoA synthase gene promoter: characterization of a peroxisome proliferator-responsive element *Biochemical Journal* **337** 329–335

Osborne TF (2000) Sterol regulatory element binding proteins (SREBPS): key regulators of nutritional homeostasis and insulin action *Journal of Biological Chemistry* **275** 32 379–32 382

Pall M, Hellberg P, Brannstrom M, Mikuni M, Peterson CM, Sundfeldt K, Norden B, Hedin L and Enerback S (1997) The transcription factor C/EBP-β and its role in ovarian function; evidence for direct involvement in the ovulatory process *EMBO Journal* **16** 5273–5279

Patel DD, Knight BL, Wiggins D, Humphreys SM and Gibbons GF (2001) Disturbances in the normal regulation of SREBP-sensitive genes in PPARalpha-deficient mice *Journal of Lipid Research* **42** 328–337

Pescador N, Stocco DM and Murphy BD (1997) Follicle-stimulating hormone and intracellular second messengers regulate steroidogenic acute regulatory protein (StAR) mRNA in luteinized granulosa cells *Biology of Reproduction* **57** 660–668

Pescador N, Stocco DM and Murphy BD (1999) Growth factor modulation of steroidogenic acute regulatory protein and luteinization in the pig ovary *Biology of Reproduction* **60** 1453–1461

Picton HM, Campbell BK and Hunter MG (1999) Maintenance of oestradiol production and expression of cytochrome P450 aromatase enzyme mRNA in long-term serum-free cultures of pig granulosa cells *Journal of Reproduction and Fertility* **115** 67–77

Pilon N, Behdjani R, Daneau I, Lussier JG and Silversides DW (1998) Porcine steroidogenic factor-1 gene (pSF-1) expression and analysis of embryonic pig gonads during sexual differentiation *Endocrinology* **139** 3803–3812

Pitzel L, Hubertus J and Wuttke W (1990) Effects of oxytocin on *in vitro* steroid release of midstage small and large porcine luteal cells *Endocrinology* **126** 2343–2349

Pope WF, Xie S, Broermann DM and Nephew KP (1990) Causes and consequences of early embryonic diversity in pigs *Journal of Reproduction and Fertility Supplement* **40** 251–260

Reinhart AJ, Williams SC, Clark BJ and Stocco DM (1999) SF-1 steroidogenic factor-1 and C/EPB-β CCAAT/Enhancer binding protein-β cooperate to regulate the murine StAR (steroidogenic acute regulatory protein) promoter *Molecular Endocrinology* **13** 729–741

Reynolds LP, Grazul-Bilska AT and Redmer DA (2000) Angiogenesis in the corpus luteum *Endocrine* **12** 1–9

Richards JS (2001a) Graafian follicle function and luteinization in nonprimates *Journal of the Society for Gynecologic Investigation* **8** (Supplement 1) S21–S23

Richards JS (2001b) New signaling pathways for hormones and cyclic adenosine 3'5'-monophosphate action in endocrine cells *Journal of Molecular Endocrinology* **15** 209–218

Richards JS, Russell DL, Robker RL, Dajee M and Alliston TN (1998) Molecular mechanisms of ovulation and luteinization *Molecular and Cellular Endocrinology* **145** 47–54

Ricke WA, Redmer DA and Reynolds LP (1999) Growth and cellular proliferation of pig corpora lutea throughout the estrous cycle *Journal of Reproduction and Fertility* **117** 369–377

Robker RL and Richards JS (1998) Hormone-induced proliferation and differentiation of granulosa cells: a coordinated balance between cell cycle regulators D2 and p27Kip1 *Molecular Endocrinology* **12** 924–940

Schoppee PD, Guthrie HD and Veldhuis JD (2000) Expression of peroxisome proliferator activated receptor γ (PPARγ) is associated with specific stages of follicular cell differentiation in porcine ovaries *Biology of Reproduction* **62** (Supplement 1) 195–196

Sekar N, Garmey JC and Veldhuis JD (2000) Mechanisms underlying the steroidogenic synergy of insulin and luteinizing hormone in porcine granulosa cells: joint amplification of pivotal sterol-regulatory genes encoding the low-density lipoprotein (LDL) receptor, steroidogenic acute regulatory (stAR) protein and cytochrome P450 side-chain cleavage (P450scc) enzyme *Molecular and Cellular Endocrinology* **159** 25–35

Shea-Eaton WK, Trinidad MJ, Lopez D, Nackley A and McLean MP (2001) Sterol regulatory element binding protein-1a regulation of the steroidogenic acute regulatory protein gene *Endocrinology* **142** 1525–1533

Silverman E, Eimerl S and Orly J (1999) CCAAT enhancer-binding protein β and GATA-4 binding regions within the promoter of the steroidogenic acute regulatory protein (StAR) gene are required for transcription in ovarian cells *Journal of Biological Chemistry* **274** 17 987–17 996

Sirois J and Richards JS (1992) Purification and characterization of a novel, distinct isoform of prostaglandin endoperoxide synthase induced by human chorionic gonadotropin in granulosa cells of rat preovulatory follicles *Journal of Biological Chemistry* **267** 6382–6388

Sirois J and Richards JS (1993) Transcriptional regulation of the rat prostaglandin endoperoxidase synthase 2 gene in granulosa cells *Journal of Biological Chemistry* **268** 21 931–21 938

Soede NM, Helmond A and Kemp B (1994) Periovulatory profiles of oestradiol, LH and progesterone in relation to oestrus and embryonic mortality in multiparous sows using transrectal ultrasonography to detect ovulation *Journal of Reproduction and Fertility* **101** 633–641

Somers JP, Benyo DF, Little-Ihrig LL and Zeleznik AJ (1995) Luteinization in primates is accompanied by a loss of a 43-kilodalton adenosine 3'5'-monophosphate response element binding protein isoform *Endocrinology* **136** 4262–4268

Song J-H, Dobias M, Pescador N and Murphy BD (1998) Luteinization and gonadotrophins upregulate the Niemann-Pick gene in the porcine ovary *Biology of Reproduction* **58** (Supplement 1) 188 (Abstract)

Sterneck E, Tessarollo L and Johnson PF (1997) An essential role for C/EBPβ in female reproduction *Genes and Development* **11** 2153–2162

Stocco DM (2001) StAR protein and the regulation of steroid hormone biosynthesis *Annual Reviews of Physiology* **63** 193–213

Tong W, Kiyokawa H, Soos TJ, Park MS, Soares VC, Manova K, Pollard JW and Koff A (1998) The absence of P27Kip1, an inhibitor of G1 cyclin-dependent kinases, uncouples differentiation and growth arrest during the granulosa-luteal transition *Cell Growth and Differentiation* **9** 787–794

Tremblay JJ and Viger RS (2001) GATA factors differentially activate multiple gonadal promoters through conserved GATA regulatory elements *Endocrinology* **142** 977–986

Tsang BK, Ainsworth L, Downey BR and Marcus GJ (1985) Differential production of steroids by dispersed granulosa and theca interna cells from developing preovulatory follicle in pigs *Journal of Reproduction and Fertility* **74** 459–471

Tsutsui T, Hesabi B, Moons DS, Pandolfi PP, Hansel KS, Koff A and Kiyokawa H (1999) Targeted disruption of CDK4 delays cell cycle entry with enhanced p27^Kip1 activity *Molecular and Cellular Biology* **19** 7011–7019

Viergutz T, Loehrke B, Poehland R, Becker F and Kanitz W (2000) Relationship between different stages of the corpus luteum and the expression of the peroxisome proliferator-activated receptor gamma protein in bovine large lutein cells *Journal of Reproduction and Fertility* **118** 153–161

Wakino S, Kintscher U, Kim S, Yin F, Hsueh WA and Law RE (2000) Peroxisome proliferator-activated receptor gamma ligands inhibit retinoblastoma phosphorylation and G1 → S transition in vascular smooth muscle cells *Journal of Biological Chemistry* **275** 22 435–22 441

Wandji SA, Gadsby JE, Simmen FA, Barber JA and Hammond JM (2000a) Porcine ovarian cells express messenger ribonucleic acids for the acid-labile subunit and insulin-like growth factor binding protein-3 during follicular and luteal phases of the estrous cycle *Endocrinology* **141** 2638–2647

Wandji SA, Gadsby JE, Barber JA and Hammond JM (2000b) Messenger ribonucleic acids for MAC25 and connective tissue growth factor (CTGF) are inversely regulated during folliculogenesis and early luteogenesis *Endocrinology* **141** 2648–2657

Watanabe N, Inoue H and Fujii-Kuriyama Y (1994) Regulatory mechanisms of the cAMP-dependent and cell specific expression of human steroidogenic P450scc (CYPA11) gene *European Journal of Biochemistry* **222** 825–834

Watson J and Maule Walker FM (1978) Progesterone secretion by the corpus luteum of the early pregnant pig during superfusion *in vitro* with PGF-2alpha, LH and oestradiol *Journal of Reproduction and Fertility* **52** 209–212

Wehrenberg U, Wulff C, Husen B, Ken-ichirou M and Rune GM (1997) The expression of SF-1/Ad4BP is related to the process of luteinization in the marmoset (*Callithrix jacchus*) ovary *Histochemistry and Cell Biology* **107** 345–350

Wooten-Kee CR and Clark BJ (2000) Steroidogenic factor-1 influences protein-deoxyribonucleic acid interactions within the cyclic adenosine 3′5′-monophosphate-responsive regions of the murine steroidogenic acute regulatory protein gene *Endocrinology* **141** 1345–1355

Wu Z, Rosen ED, Brun R, Hauser S, Adelmant G, Troy AE, McKeon C, Darlington GJ and Spiegelman BM (1999) Cross-regulation of C/EBP alpha and PPAR gamma controls the transcriptional pathway of adipogenesis and insulin sensitivity *Molecular Cell* **3** 151–158

Yu ZK and Hausman GJ (1998) Expression of CCAAT/enhancer binding proteins during porcine preadipocyte differentiation *Experimental Cell Research* **15** 343–349

Yuan W and Lucy MC (1996) Messenger ribonucleic acid expression for growth hormone receptor, luteinizing hormone receptor, and steroidogenic enzymes during the estrous cycle and pregnancy in porcine and bovine corpora lutea *Domestic Animal Endocrinology* **13** 431–444

Zeleznik AJ and Somers JP (1999) Regulation of the primate corpus luteum: cellular and molecular prospectives *Trends in Endocrinology and Metabolism* **10** 189–193

Zhang G, Garmey JC and Veldhuis JD (2000) Interactive stimulation by luteinizing hormone and insulin of the steroidogenic acute regulatory (StAR) protein and 17alpha- hydroxylase/17,20-lyase (CYP17) genes in porcine theca cells *Endocrinology* **141** 2735–2742

Zhu L and Skoultchi AI (2001) Coordinating cell proliferation and differentiation *Current Opinion in Genetics and Development* **10** 91–97

Reproduction Supplement **58**, 65–80

Mammalian gonadal differentiation: the pig model

E. Pailhoux, B. Mandon-Pepin and C. Cotinot

Unité de Biologie du Développement et Biotechnologies, Bâtiment J.Poly. INRA, 78350 Jouy en Josas, France

In mammals, testicular differentiation is initiated by SRY (the sex-determining region of the Y chromosome) gene expression in Sertoli cell precursors, followed by upregulation of the SOX9 gene (SRY-related HMG box gene 9). Subsequently, differentiated testis produces two hormones that induce sexual differentiation of the internal and external genital tract. Knowledge of the molecular mechanisms involved in gonadal differentiation has increased greatly over the past decade. Several genes are involved in genital ridge formation in both sexes, and others act specifically in testicular or ovarian developmental pathways. As for other mammals, relatively few data are available on the first steps of ovarian differentiation in pigs. In this review, the expression profiles of most genes known to be involved in gonadal differentiation in pigs will be presented and compared with those observed in mice. The main feature of gonadal differentiation in the pig is fetal steroidogenesis, especially cytochrome P450 aromatase gene organization and expression. Another specific feature of gonadal differentiation in pigs is the appearance of numerous cases of XX sex-reversed animals. This intersex condition occurs as early as day 50 after coitus, during embryogenesis, and appears to be triggered genetically. It leads to a wide range of phenotypes, strikingly similar to those observed in humans. Identification of the genes involved in this pathology will improve our knowledge of mammalian gonadal differentiation and may allow the eradication of this genetic disease in pigs.

Introduction

In pigs, as in other mammals, sexual differentiation is achieved following two imbricated steps (Fig. 1). The first step leads to gonadal formation from a bipotential primordium localized at the anterior part of the mesonephros: the urogenital ridge. This developmental event, called sex determination, depends on XX or XY chromosomal status determined at the time of fertilization. The presence of a single gene on the Y chromosome, SRY, is sufficient to induce testicular differentiation (Sinclair *et al.*, 1990). In females, the absence of SRY testis-determining factor and the presence of two X chromosomes allows formation of the ovaries. The second step of sexual differentiation, known as secondary differentiation, leads to the development of internal and external genitalia. The internal ducts of males and females arise from the Wolffian and Müllerian anlagen, respectively. Female differentiation has been

---

Email: pailhoux@biotec.jouy.inra.fr

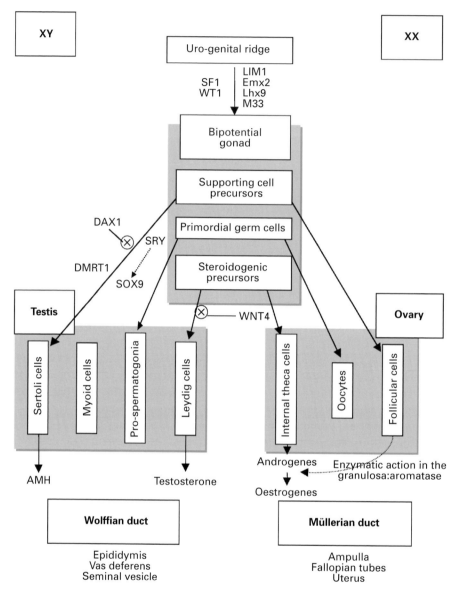

Fig. 1. Simplified representation of mammalian sexual differentiation. The left part of the figure shows male development and the right part shows the female pathway. The different steps in this developmental process are boxed, from upper to lower, chromosomal sex, gonadal sex and internal phenotypic sex. The central part of the scheme represents the sex-specific fate of the different gonadal cell types in the bipotential gonad. Their differentiated counterparts are indicated in the final gonad (testis or ovary). Myoid cells of the testis have no precursors in the bipotential gonads because they migrate from the mesonephros. Principal genes implicated in gonadal differentiation are indicated. Crossed circles depict inhibitory regulations. LIM1 = Lhx1: LIM homeobox gene 1; Lhx9: LIM homeobox gene 9; Emx2: empty spiracles, *Drosophila* homologue 2; M33 = CBX2: chromobox homologue 2, *Drosophila* polycomb class; SF1: steroidogenic factor 1; WT1: Wilms' tumour gene 1; DAX1: DSS-AHC critical region on the X chromosome, gene 1; SRY: sex-determining region of Y chromosome; SOX9: SRY-related HMG box gene 9; DMRT1: doublesex- and Mab-3-related transcription factor 1; WNT4: wingless-type MMTV integration site family, member 4; AMH: anti-Müllerian hormone.

considered as the default pathway, which is 'overridden' in males by two testicular hormones: the anti-Müllerian hormone (AMH) and testosterone (Jost *et al.*, 1973). The production of AMH by Sertoli cells acts to suppress the Müllerian ducts, thereby preventing the formation of Fallopian tubes and uteri in males, whereas testosterone, secreted by Leydig cells, induces the formation of epididymis, vas deferens and seminal vesicles. The same process of a default pathway is involved in the formation of external genitalia (urethra, prostate gland, penis and scrotum), which differentiate from the urogenital sinus only in the presence of a male hormone: dihydrotestosterone.

This review will focus essentially on the first step of mammalian sexual differentiation, which is determined genetically. Firstly, the genes involved in this primary pathway will be described and their expression patterns in male and female pigs will be compared with those described in other species. In a second section, results concerning XX sex reversal, an abnormal gonadal differentiation observed frequently in pigs, will be presented.

Molecular basis of gonadal differentiation

The testis-determining factor: SRY

All the genes involved in gonadal differentiation have been discovered during the past decade. In 1990, the first, SRY, was isolated after 25 years of research. Indeed, Ferguson-Smith (1966) predicted that after uneven crossover between sex chromosomes during male meiosis, the testis-determining factor (TDF) could translocate from Y to X and cause sex reversal in humans. After numerous genetic studies on sex-reversed patients, a candidate gene was found in a 35 kb Y DNA fragment present in an XX male patient: SRY (Sinclair *et al.*, 1990). Thereafter, two pieces of experimental evidence were collected proving that SRY is TDF: (i) the open reading frame of SRY presents a mutation in XY female patients with gonadal dysgenesis (Cameron and Sinclair, 1997); and (ii) a 14.6 kb fragment containing the murine homologue (*Sry*) reverses the sex of XX mice when added by transgenesis (Koopman *et al.*, 1991). This intronless gene has been found in most mammalian species and represents the master gene in testicular differentiation. In pigs it has been located in the distal portion of the short arm of the Y chromosome (p12–p13), which is a conserved chromosomal position compared with that of humans (Yang *et al.*, 1993). SRY encodes a nuclear factor encompassing a conserved DNA binding domain of 79 amino acids (HMG box). Surprisingly, outside this domain, the SRY protein is poorly conserved among mammals, a fact that is particularly true for humans and mice (Whitfield *et al.*, 1993). Despite 10 years of research, the biological target of SRY and its molecular mechanism of action remain unknown.

The other genes

Sex determination appears to be a complex process involving two types of genes: some of the genes are implicated in the formation of the genital ridges in both sexes, whereas others are involved specifically in testis or ovary differentiation. To date, six genes encoding transcription factors have been classified in the first group: Wilms' tumour gene 1 (WT1), steroidogenic factor 1 (SF1), three homeobox genes (LIM1, Emx2 and Lhx9) and M33, a mouse homologue of the *Drosophila* polycomb genes. Five genes belong to the second group: the testis determining factor SRY, the SRY-related HMG box gene 9 (SOX9), the X-linked gene DAX1, DMRT1 and a gene of the Wnt/Wingless family WNT4.

Genes involved in early gonadogenesis. WT1 was first discovered in humans by genetic analysis of patients affected by renal failure (Wilms' tumour) associated with an XY sex reversal phenotype (Gessler *et al.*, 1990; Pelletier *et al.*, 1991). The implication of WT1 in urogenital ridge formation was demonstrated clearly by knockout experiments in mice (Kreidberg *et al.*, 1993). Indeed, homozygous mutant embryos revealed failure in gonad and kidney development. The 10 exon WT1 gene contains two alternative spliced regions, one in exon 5 and a second in exon 9, giving rise to the addition or suppression of three amino acids: lysine-threonine-serine: KTS (Haber *et al.*, 1991). Therefore, WT1 encodes four distinct transcription factors, each containing four zinc finger domains. In addition to their DNA binding activity, WT1 proteins might also bind RNA and act as post-transcriptional regulators (Caricasole *et al.*, 1996; Bardeesy and Pelletier, 1998). WT1 transcripts are expressed very early in the mesonephros, then in the genital ridges and their expression persists in the gonad of both sexes throughout life (Pritchard-Jones *et al.*, 1990; Payen *et al.*, 1996). In addition to the involvement of WT1 in genital ridge formation, WT1 isoform without KTS can regulate the gene encoding AMH (Nachtigal *et al.*, 1998). The biological significance of isoform ratios (with or without KTS) has been brought to light by studying patients with Frasier syndrome (Barbaux *et al.*, 1997). In this syndrome, XY sex reversal is a consequence of intronic mutation preventing the production of the KTS-containing isoforms, thereby altering the isoform ratios in heterozygous affected patients. In conclusion, according to the expression pattern and the complexity of this gene, it is clear that WT1 is a key factor in gonadal formation and testis differentiation in mammals.

The nuclear hormone receptor SF1 homologous to the *Drosophila* fushi-tarazu factor 1 (Ftz-F1), also termed Ad4BP (adrenal 4 binding protein), was first isolated as a common regulator of cytochrome P450 steroid hydroxylases in the gonads and adrenal cortex (Lala *et al.*, 1992; Morohashi *et al.*, 1992). In the testis, expression of SF1 has been identified in Leydig cells as well as in Sertoli cells, where it contributes to maintaining high AMH expression (Shen *et al.*, 1994; Arango *et al.*, 1999). Another critical role in gonadal and adrenal development has been demonstrated by knockout experiments: mice lacking SF1 are devoid of gonads and adrenal glands (Luo *et al.*, 1994). Recently, a similar phenotype has been described in an XY woman patient harbouring a heterozygous 2 bp substitution in the DNA binding domain of SF1 (Achermann *et al.*, 1999). Hence, it is clear that SF1 is implicated at numerous steps in sexual differentiation as it regulates a large array of genes involved in gonadal formation and hormonal synthesis.

In addition to WT1 and SF1, four other genes involved in urogenital ridge formation have been identified by knockout experiments in mice. Three of these genes belong to the homeobox gene family. Lhx9 invalidation results in failure in gonad formation without any additional major developmental defects (Birk *et al.*, 2000). Invalidation of the other two genes leads to a more marked change in the phenotype, with an absence of head structures for LIM1, and of kidneys and gonads for LIM1 and Emx2 (Shawlot and Behringer, 1995; Miyamoto *et al.*, 1997). The last gene in this group, M33, is one of the *Drosophila* polycomb genes. M33 null mice underwent a significant delay in gonadogenesis, leading to male-to-female sex reversal in XY fetuses (Katoh-Fukui *et al.*, 1998). The involvement of these genes in urogenital ridge formation has been demonstrated clearly in gene disruption experiments, but this strategy makes it impossible to reveal other putative functions later in sexual differentiation (such as WT1 and SF1). Conditional knockout will be needed to gain further information.

Sex differentiating genes. The Y specific gene SRY initiates a cascade of gene regulations resulting in maleness. One of the most important genes downstream from SRY is SOX9, which encodes a key transcription factor for testicular differentiation. SOX9 was first isolated by studying patients with a bone developmental defect, campomelic dysplasia, associated with 75% of XY individuals with a male-to-female sex reversal (Foster *et al.*, 1994; Wagner *et al.*,

1994). The structure of SOX9 is that of a typical transcription factor with a DNA binding domain (HMG box) and a transcriptional trans-activating domain (Südbeck *et al.*, 1996). From an evolutionary viewpoint, the structure and expression pattern of SOX9 appear to be highly conserved among mammals as well as in other vertebrates, such as birds and reptiles (Kent *et al.*, 1996; Morais da Silva *et al.*, 1996; Western *et al.*, 1999). A high expression of SOX9 is always correlated with testicular differentiation, independent of the presence of SRY. Abnormal upregulation of SOX9 in XX individuals is associated with female-to-male sex reversal in humans and mice (Huang *et al.*, 1999; Bishop *et al.*, 2000). It is now clear that SOX9 lies at a crucial step in testis formation and that progress in the understanding of this differentiation pathway could result from studies on its transcriptional regulation. However, defects in the expression of SOX9 leading to sex reversal indicate that there may be long range regulatory elements distributed as far as 1 Mb upstream from the coding region of the gene (Wunderle *et al.*, 1998; Pfeifer *et al.*, 1999). This fact has also been pointed out in XX mice with the description of the Odsex (ocular degeneration with sex reversal) mutation consisting of a 150 kb deletion localized at about 1 Mb upstream from *Sox9*. The authors conclude that the deletion encloses a female specific repressor binding site in this 5' region (Bishop *et al.*, 2000), strengthening the suspicion that male specific genes such as SOX9 may be repressed in XX individuals (McElreavey *et al.*, 1993).

One putative repressor of male genes was discovered in 1994 by studying XY sex-reversed female patients harbouring a partial duplication (band p21) of their X chromosome (Bardoni *et al.*, 1994). In this dosage-sensitive sex reversal region (DSS), the DAX1 gene (DSS-AHC critical region on the X chromosome) appears to be the best candidate for triggering the absence of testicular differentiation by acting antagonistically to SRY (Swain *et al.*, 1998). This possibility was confirmed by the characterization of the *Dax-1* expression pattern in mice, which was expressed more highly in ovaries than in testes (Swain *et al.*, 1996). According to all these results, DAX1 was assumed to be a potential ovarian differentiating factor until the observation of *Dax-1*-null mice. Surprisingly, the disruption of *Dax-1* in female mice does not prevent ovarian differentiation or fertility (Yu *et al.*, 1998). In contrast, male spermatogenesis is affected in XY *Dax-1 –/Y* mice.

A true ovarian determining gene was discovered by knockout experiments of *Wnt-4*, a signalling protein of the Wnt/Wingless family (Vainio *et al.*, 1999). Homozygous disruption of *Wnt-4* triggers the development of Leydig cells and steroidogenesis in female gonads. In contrast, sexual differentiation in *Wnt-4 –/–* males appears to be normal at birth. The female dimorphic expression pattern of *Wnt-4* in mice also provides evidence for an ovary-differentiating role of this gene (Vainio *et al.*, 1999).

In conclusion, many factors involved in gonadal differentiation have been isolated and characterized over the past decade, but there may be other factors that are still unknown. For example, the genetic aetiology of many cases of sex reversal in humans and mammalian species remains to be elucidated and does not appear to be the result of mutations within known genes (Vaiman and Pailhoux, 2000). Monosomic deletions of chromosome 9p associated with male-to-female XY sex reversal in humans have indicated the possible role of DMRT1 in testis differentiation (Calvari *et al.*, 2000; Ottolenghi *et al.*, 2000). This gene, which is homologous to doublesex in *Drosophila* and mab-3 in *Caenorhabditis* (Raymond *et al.*, 1998), plays a crucial role in testis formation in reptiles and birds (Raymond *et al.*, 1999; Kettlewell *et al.*, 2000).

Relationships among sex differentiating genes (Fig. 2)

Many studies have focussed on transcriptional regulation of the AMH gene. Indeed, AMH is the first hormone secreted by the differentiated testis. Two binding sites, one for SF1 and the

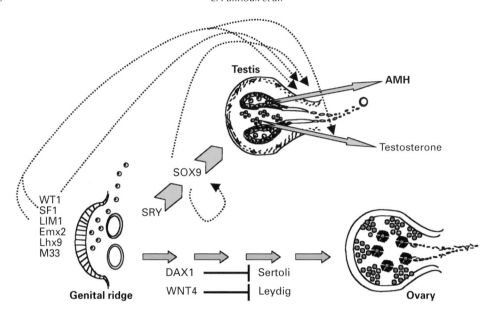

Fig. 2. Gene epistasis in gonadal formation. The upper part represents the male pathway initiated by SRY, with SOX9 as a key testicular factor. Dotted arrows indicate its role in AMH upregulation. AMH expression is also controlled positively by SF1 and WT1. The lower part shows the female pathway, including two male pathway inhibitors, DAX1 and WNT4. The six genes on the left are involved in genital ridge formation. LIM1 = Lhx1: LIM homeobox gene 1; Lhx9: LIM homeobox gene 9; Emx2: empty spiracles, *Drosophila* homologue 2; M33 = CBX2: chromobox homologue 2, *Drosophila* polycomb class; SF1: steroidogenic factor 1; WT1: Wilms' tumour gene 1; DAX1: DSS-AHC critical region on the X chromosome, gene 1; SRY: sex-determining region of Y chromosome; SOX9: SRY-related HMG box gene 9; WNT4: wingless-type MMTV integration site family, member 4; AMH: anti-Müllerian hormone.

other for SOX9, are highly conserved in the promoter region of the AMH gene among different mammalian species (Shen *et al.*, 1994). By targeted mutagenesis of these binding sites *in vivo*, it has been shown that, in mice, SOX9 triggers AMH expression and SF1 enhances it (Arango *et al.*, 1999). DAX1 and WT1 (-KTS) might also act as negative and positive modulators on AMH transcription through protein interaction with SF1 (Nachtigal *et al.*, 1998).

In conclusion, SOX9 is a key gene in mammalian sexual differentiation. Some questions remain to be answered. How is this gene upregulated in males and downregulated in females? What is the link between SRY and SOX9? Also, other than AMH, what male genes are regulated specifically by SOX9?

Gonadal differentiation: a cellular viewpoint

During the past 4 years, interesting results have been obtained using a co-culture system of gonads with mesonephri from a transgenic strain ubiquitously expressing β-galactosidase. Firstly, it has been shown that migration of mesonephric cells takes place into XY but not XX gonads from day 11.5 to day 16.5 after coitus in mice (Martineau *et al.*, 1997). The signal that triggers migration operates over long distances and behaves as a chemoattractant. By culturing XX gonads with XY gonads at their surfaces, as a sandwich, mesonephric cell migration into the XX tissue took place. After this migration, the XX gonads organized cord structures and acquired male-specific patterns of gene expression (Tilmann and Capel, 1999). The migrating mesonephric cells give rise to three types of cell population in XY gonads: myoid, endothelial and some closely associated with endothelial cells. Finally, by using XX gonads transgenic for SRY, it has been shown that this migration event depends on the SRY gene and represents the earliest physiological sign of SRY action (Capel *et al.*, 1999).

The pig: a particular model of mammals?

To date, most of the gene expression patterns described have been observed in mice. In pigs, four studies present the time course of sex-determining genes during gonadal development (Daneau *et al.*, 1996; Parma *et al.*, 1997, 1999; Pilon *et al.*, 1998). The main results of these studies are summarized (Fig. 3) and compared with expression profiles in mice. No significant differences are noticeable for three genes: SOX9, DAX1 and AMH. There are three notable differences between these two species, two in males and one in females. In female mice, SF1 expression is stopped between germ cell meiosis (day 13.5 after coitus) and the beginning of folliculogenesis (day 18.5 after coitus) (Ikeda *et al.*, 1994). In pigs, SF1 is expressed continuously in gonads of both sexes from the time of formation of genital ridges (day 23 after coitus). Different levels of expression between sexes (high in males versus low in females) have been found using northern blot analysis at later stages (days 45–52 after coitus) (Pilon *et al.*, 1998). In mice, transcription of the SRY gene has been detected during a very short period of 2 days (days 10.5–12.5 after coitus) (Jeske *et al.*, 1995). Conversely, in pigs, SRY is expressed over a longer period of about 3 weeks. Expression persists > 2 weeks after the first sign of Sertoli cell differentiation (day 28 after coitus in pigs) (Parma *et al.*, 1999). The role of this persistence of SRY in domestic species is unknown but it could suggest the involvement of this gene in other developmental testicular processes, such as inhibition of male germ cell meiosis. The main difference is in the expression of aromatase. In pigs, P450 aromatase transcripts are detected very early in testicular differentiation, at the same time as AMH expression (Parma *et al.*, 1999). In mice, there is no expression of aromatase until birth in both sexes and in sheep and goats an expression peak is observed between gonadal differentiation and germ cell meiosis, but only in the female fetuses (Payen *et al.*, 1996; E. Pailhoux, personal observation). Of the species studied, the pig appears to be unique as far as P450 aromatase is concerned. There are three distinct functional genes encoding three isoforms (type I: ovary; type II: placenta; and type III: embryo), with presumed differences in substrate specificities, expression, activity and mode of regulation (Graddy *et al.*, 2000). The testicular isoform appears to be the same as that expressed in the adult ovary (Conley *et al.*, 1996). The testicular isoform also appears to be active, as oestrone sulphate was first detected in male pig fetuses at day 31 after coitus (Raeside *et al.*, 1993). This fetal production of oestrogens by the testis remains poorly understood. One putative cellular target could be the gonocytes, as proposed by Parma *et al.* (1999). In addition to aromatase, it seems that the entire fetal steroidogenic pathway is different in pigs compared with other mammalian species. We recently tested the expression of 3β-hydroxysteroid dehydrogenase (3β-HSD) in gonads of male, female and intersex fetuses at days 50 and 70 after coitus and found similar high expression in all the samples tested. Also surprising was the expression profile of WNT4 (Fig. 5), which appears to be slightly higher in females, although a significant expression was also detected in males, in contrast to the case in mice. In conclusion, it appears that the specific steroidogenesis observed in pigs must be investigated further to gain a better understanding of the role these hormones play in the formation and maintenance of functional gonads and reproductive organs.

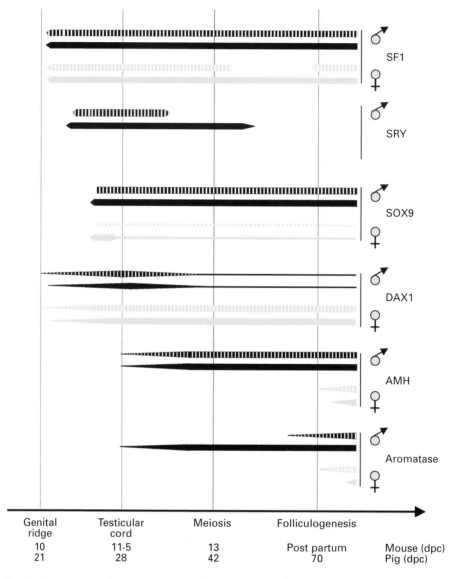

Fig. 3. Time course of gene expression during mouse and pig gonadal differentiation. The width of the lines is proportional to the relative expression. For each gene indicated on the right, the expression in gonads of male mice (striped black), male pigs (black), female mice (striped grey) and female pigs (grey) is shown during four main developmental processes, as indicated under the arrow symbolizing the time course of development. dpc: indicates the days after coitus at which these developmental processes occur. SF1: steroidogenic factor 1; SRY: sex-determining region of Y chromosome; SOX9: SRY-related HMG box gene 9; DAX1: DSS-AHC critical region on the X chromosome, gene 1; AMH: anti-Müllerian hormone.

Genes involved in ovary development

In the presence of two X chromosomes, the indifferent embryonic gonad develops into an ovary. Ovarian differentiation, germ cell meiosis and folliculogenesis begin during fetal life in pigs. Other key events, such as follicular growth and atresia, which occur throughout

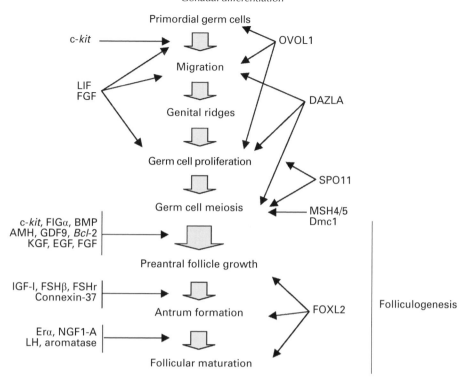

Fig. 4. Schematic representation of ovarian differentiation and function. Four main steps of germ cell life are represented (migration, proliferation, meiosis and maturation). A non-exhaustive list of factors involved in different steps is indicated on both sides of the diagram. OVOL1: OVO, *Drosophila* homologue-like 1; LIF: leukaemia inhibitory factor; FGF: fibroblast growth factor; DAZLA: deleted in azoospermia-like, autosomal; SPO11: *Saccharomyces cerevisiae* homologue of SPO11; MSH4/5: MutS *Escherichia coli* homologue 4/5; Dmc1: disrupted meiotic cDNA 1, yeast homologue; FOXL2: forkhead transcription factor L2; FIGα: factor in the germ line, alpha; BMP: bone morphogenetic protein; AMH: anti-Müllerian hormone; GDF9: growth/differentiation factor 9; *Bcl*-2: B-cell Cll/lymphoma 2; KGF: keratinocyte growth factor; EGF: epidermal growth factor; IGF-I: insulin-like growth factor I; FSHβ: follicle-stimulating hormone, beta polypeptide; FSHr: FSH receptor; Erα: oestrogen receptor alpha; NGF1-A: nerve growth factor 1-A; and LH: luteinizing hormone.

prepubertal and reproductive life, are also initiated during fetal life. Four major phases can be distinguished: migration, proliferation and meiosis of the germ cells, and folliculogenesis. These steps are under the control of several transcription factors, growth and paracrine factors, and hormones (Fig. 4).

In pigs, urogenital ridge formation begins at day 21 after coitus (Pelliniemi, 1985). The migration and proliferation of germ cells depend on co-ordinated expression and interaction of different genes. Two factors: c-kit and c-kit ligand (stem cell factor; SCF) play a central role in the migration and colonization of germ cells to the developing genital ridge. SCF controls the early germ-line population and is an essential requirement for primordial germ cell survival (Godin *et al.*, 1991). Leukaemia inhibitory factor (LIF) is crucial for primary germ cell development (Donovan, 1994). It can stimulate primary germ cell proliferation in culture and may regulate primordial germ cell survival and proliferation *in vivo*. Apoptosis is responsible for primordial germ cell attrition in the developing fetal ovary. LIF might support primordial germ cell survival by preventing primordial germ cell apoptosis (De Felici and Pesce, 1994). Another gene of interest during this step is the DAZLA gene. Indeed, the disruption of the DAZLA gene leads to a loss of germ cells and complete absence of male and female gamete production (Ruggiu *et al.*, 1997). DAZLA transcripts are localized in germ cells before meiosis and at the time meiosis begins. In the ovary, transcripts are not restricted to germ cells, but are found in somatic cells of primordial follicles (granulosa) as well.

Several genes have been shown to be involved in germ cell meiosis from day 42 after coitus in pigs. As oocytes transit from pachytene to diplotene before arresting, DNA repair proteins and other factors are required for proper chromosome alignment and recombination. Oogonia lacking MSH5 (homologue of bacterial MutS) or DMC1 (homologue of RecA) do not complete meiosis and are invariably lost from the ovary before diplotene. Null mice for Msh5 (Edelmann *et al.*, 1999) are viable but sterile. Meiosis in these mice is affected due to disruption of chromosome pairing in prophase I. The ovaries of Msh5 –/– females are normal in size at birth but degenerate progressively to become rudimentary, concomitant with the decrease in the number of oocytes from before day 3 post partum until adulthood. Null mutation of Dmc1 genes showed that homozygous mutant males and females are sterile, with arrest of gametogenesis in the first meiotic prophase (Habu *et al.*, 1996). In Dmc1 –/– female mice, normal differentiation of oogenesis was aborted in embryos and germ cells disappeared in the adult ovary.

Primordial follicles are formed perinatally in mammalian ovaries and the first appears at about day 70 after coitus in pigs. Folliculogenesis requires careful orchestration of developmental programmes in germ and somatic cells, as well as the interactions between them. In the initial stage of folliculogenesis, paracrine factors promote growth of the oocyte and adjacent somatic cells. FIGα (factor in the germ line alpha), a germline cell-specific factor (Soyal *et al.*, 2000), is crucial for the initial formation of primordial follicles. Mouse lines lacking FIGα have primordial follicles that are not formed at birth and a massive depletion of oocytes, resulting in shrunken ovaries and female sterility. In addition, many growth factors, fibroblast growth factor 8 (FGF8) and several members of the transforming growth factor β (TGFβ) family have been implicated in regulating early folliculogenesis. One factor, anti-Müllerian hormone (AMH), is expressed in granulosa cells surrounding oocytes and has been implicated in the recruitment of primordial follicles into the growth phase of folliculogenesis (Durlinger *et al.*, 1999). Other members of the TGFβ family, GDF9A (growth/differentiation factor 9) and BMP15 (bone morphogenetic protein 15), are first expressed in oocytes in primary follicles (McGrath *et al.*, 1995; Dube *et al.*, 1998). Female mice deficient in GDF9A are infertile because of an early block in folliculogenesis at the type 3b primary follicle stage. BMP15 is an oocyte-derived growth factor essential for female fertility. Natural mutation in this gene (Inverdale sheep carrying FecXI mutation) causes both increased ovulation rate and infertility phenotypes in a dosage-sensitive manner (Galloway *et al.*, 2000). Finally, the absence of gonadotrophins leads to atretic follicles that disappear from the ovary.

The female pig gonad remains undifferentiated histologically until day 28 after coitus and final histological differentiation of the ovary is achieved by day 44 after coitus when the cortical cords have been organized and the medullary cords have degenerated (Pelliniemi and Lauteala, 1981). We analysed temporal expression of some of these genes involved in mammalian ovary development by RT–PCR. As examples, the results of three of these genes presenting typical expression profiles are summarized (Fig. 5). The ovarian-determining gene WNT4 was expressed as early as day 37 after coitus and throughout fetal life in both sexes, with a relatively higher expression in females. DMC1, which is essential for meiotic recombination, was first expressed during meiosis, between day 45 and day 52 after coitus, began to decrease at day 70 after coitus (last studied stage during fetal life) and was expressed

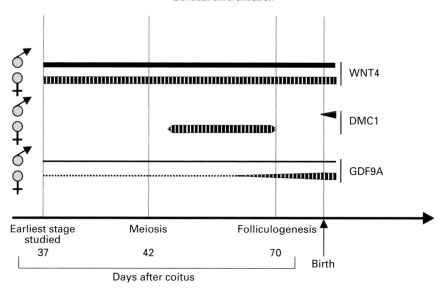

Fig. 5. Example of expression profiles of ovarian genes in pigs. These genes are involved in three different developmental steps: WNT4: ovarian differentiation; DMC1: germ cell meiosis; GDF-9A: folliculogenesis. The width of the lines is proportional to the expression. For each gene, the expression is shown for males (full line) and females (striped line). WNT4: wingless-type MMTV integration site family, member 4; DMC1: disrupted meiotic cDNA 1; GDF9A: growth/differentiation factor 9A.

in gonads of 5-week-old males. GDF9A, described as an oocyte-derived paracrine factor important for growth of follicles beyond the primary stage, increased at the beginning of folliculogenesis (day 65 after coitus).

These studies demonstrate that several genes, whether restricted in their expression to the ovary or expressed preferentially in the ovary, constitute critical determinants in ovarian development. Further investigations are also in progress, such as suppressive subtractive hybridization during the different stages of pig fetal ovarian development to isolate genes that are expressed differentially at key stages of ovarian development (before meiosis, during meiosis and during folliculogenesis).

Anomalous sexual development: sex reversal

In parallel with the classic scheme of sex differentiation in mammals, exceptions exist where XX individuals develop testes in the absence of the Y chromosome and, conversely, XY individuals without testes have been described. Such individuals have been observed in numerous mammalian species including humans, pigs, goats, horses, dogs, mice, marsupials and moles, and are called sex-reserved or intersexes (Pailhoux *et al.*, 1994a,b; Sanchez *et al.*, 1996; Whitworth *et al.*, 1996; Meyers-Wallen *et al.*, 1999; Bishop *et al.*, 2000; Buoen *et al.*, 2000; Sarafoglou and Ostrer, 2000). Some of these individuals result from mutations in the SRY gene (XY female) or from translocation of SRY to the X chromosome or autosomes (XX male). However, most sex-reversed individuals result from alterations of X-linked or autosomal genes remaining for the most part unknown. The genes known to be involved in sex determination, such as SRY, WT-1, DAX-1 and SOX9, have been isolated by genetic analysis of sex-reversed patients.

In pigs, the frequency of intersexuality ranges from 0.1 to 0.5% of females and may reach up to 20% in isolated herds. The animals described are mainly adults that were detected either by the breeder because of abnormal external genitalia or at slaughter through discovery of one or two abdominal testes. At slaughter, the incidence of intersexuality is > 0.2% of the total European pig population. In practical terms, instances of intersexuality represent a source of direct loss in the breeding herd resulting from sterility, genital infections reducing growth and viability and downgrading of carcasses for so-called boar taint. In addition, such animals may provoke losses due to their aggressive behaviour.

Intersex pigs are masculinized genetic females with a 38, XX chromosome constitution. We studied about 50 adult animals from an experimental breeding herd at INRA (Institut National de la Recherche Agronomique), where about 1% of females are intersexes, to elucidate the genetic aetiology of the pig sex reversal condition. PCR was used to test the DNA from blood and gonadal biopsies of intersex animals for the presence of cryptic Y chromosome-specific sequences, particularly the SRY gene. Intersex pigs result from three situations: the presence of XX and XY cells within the same animal (4%); the presence of a small fragment of the Y chromosome (containing the SRY gene) in XX individuals (2%); and the presence of an autosomal or X-linked mutation affecting genes in the sex-determining pathway or mimicking their effects (94%) (Pailhoux et al., 1997).

A genetic approach was attempted using genome scanning of resource families to isolate genes involved in intersexuality in pigs. Analyses indicate that sex reversal in this species is controlled multigenically and five regions of the genome appear to be involved (E. Pailhoux, personal observation). Some of these regions correspond to regions described previously in humans, which also confer abnormal sex determination.

Phenotypically, all the animals studied ranged from true hermaphrodites (48%) to males with (50%) and without (2%) ambiguities. True hermaphrodites with both testicular and ovarian tissue in the same animal or in the same gonad have been observed and a few rare cases of pregnancy in these hermaphrodite sows have been obtained (Pailhoux et al., 1997). Of the 50 animals observed, only one was a male without ambiguities. This phenotype, which was characterized by an external and internal male type genitalia, has not been described previously in pigs. The only visible defect was a unilateral cryptorchidism. From histological observations of gonadal biopsies, intersex gonads can be divided into different phenotypes. The most primitive type consists of unorganized tissue with neither ovarian nor testicular structures. The second type contains cords in interstitial stroma and thus resembles the sexually indifferent phase of embryonic gonadal differentiation. The third type occurs as a testis or an ovotestis and resembles the normal testis but with cords that are thinner and devoid of germ cells. The fourth type is similar but more rudimentary. The fifth occurs as an ovary or an ovotestis and consists of variable ovarian tissue (Pailhoux et al., 1997). This broad variability of gonadal phenotypes is one of the main features of this pathology. The precise classification of the different cases of intersexuality in pigs reveals strong similarity with observations in human sex-reversed patients.

Pig fetuses were studied during gonadal development to determine the onset of the pathology (Fig. 6). The fetuses were obtained by crossing parents that had produced intersexes previously in their progeny. These molecular and histological investigations revealed that as early as day 50 after coitus, intersex gonads could differ from normal ovaries and present expression profiles of the male type for SOX9, AMH and P450 aromatase genes. Variability in gonadal phenotypes was observed at all the developmental stages tested, even within the same animal. The degeneration of germ cells observed in the testicular portion of all the intersex gonads was observed just after birth. The development of both non-functional ovaries and testis in intersex individuals with complete female chromosomes indicates that defective

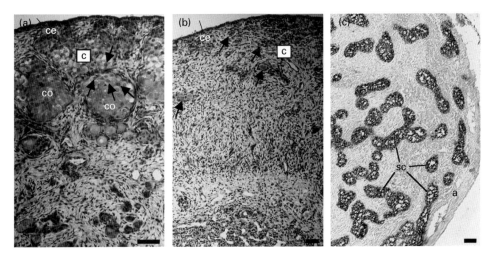

Fig. 6. Light micrograph of three gonadal sections from XX pigs. (a) Normal ovary at day 70 after coitus. (b) Ovary of an intersex pig at day 70 after coitus. Note the hypoplasia of the ovarian cortex associated with the reduction of germ cell number. (c) Immunohistological detection of anti-Müllerian hormone (AMH) in seminiferous tubules of a fetal XX sex-reversed gonad at day 50 after coitus. ce: coelomic epithelium; c: ovarian cortex; co: ovigerous cord; sc: seminiferous cord. The arrows show the germ cells. Scale bars represent 50 μm.

genes are involved in normal females, both in inhibition of male gonadal differentiation and maintenance of ovarian differentiation. Indeed, the ovarian pathway had been initiated in these gonads, but was altered and gave rise to severe ovarian dysfunction leading in some cases to complete transdifferentiation. Molecular identification of the genes involved in this pathology of XX sex reversal will greatly increase our understanding of sex determination and gonadal differentiation in mammals.

Conclusion

Our knowledge of the molecular mechanisms involved in mammalian gonadal differentiation has been improved greatly by the isolation and study of numerous genes. To date, the male pathway has been better characterized as a result of the discovery of two main genes: the testis-determining factor SRY and the Sertoli cell-specific factor SOX9. There is little information on the ovarian-determining pathway and very few factors have been identified. WNT4 is one factor that has been identified and appears to be an inhibitory testis factor. Likewise, two mutations (odsex in mice and polled intersex syndrome in goats) are indicative of the existence of this type of factor. Indeed, they reveal that XX sex reversal could be the result of suppression of such inhibitory effects. Similarly, investigations of pig intersexuality could give some insight into this type of gene. A better understanding of this pathology in pigs will also offer breeders the possibility of eradicating intersexuality and enhancing female fertility. Indeed, genes involved in ovarian sex reversal are likely to be critical factors in ovarian differentiation and function. Other interesting approaches for isolating ovarian-specific genes are being produced by the new transcriptome technologies. The systematic differential screening of transcripts involved in the crucial steps of ovarian differentiation (meiosis, folliculogenesis) along with delimitation of chromosomal segments implicated in reproductive quantitative trait loci will certainly improve the control of female fertility.

The authors would like to acknowledge the help of their collaborators in studies of pig intersexuality: A. Barbosa, J. Bussière, P. Dando, M. Fellous, M. Georges, J-M. Gogué, J. Gruand, P. Guillouet, C. Legault, C. Nezer, P. Parma, L. Pelliniemi, N. Servel and B. Vigier.

References

Achermann JC, Ito M, Ito M, Hindmarsh PC and Jameson JL (1999) A mutation in the gene encoding steroidogenic factor-1 causes XY sex reversal and adrenal failure in humans *Nature Genetics* **22** 125–126

Arango NA, Lovell-Badge R and Behringer RR (1999) Targeted mutagenesis of the endogenous mouse Mis gene promoter: *in vivo* definition of genetic pathways of vertebrate sexual development *Cell* **99** 409–419

Barbaux S, Niaudet P, Gubler MC et al. (1997) Donor splice-site mutations in WT1 are responsible for Frasier syndrome *Nature Genetics* **17** 467–470

Bardeesy N and Pelletier J (1998) Overlapping RNA and DNA binding domains of the wt1 tumor suppressor gene product *Nucleic Acids Research* **26** 1784–1792

Bardoni B, Zanaria E, Guioli S et al. (1994) A dosage sensitive locus at chromosome Xp21 is involved in male to female sex reversal *Nature Genetics* **7** 497–501

Birk OS, Casiano DE, Wassif CA et al. (2000) The LIM homeobox gene Lhx9 is essential for mouse gonad formation *Nature* **403** 909–913

Bishop CE, Whitworth DJ, Qin Y, Agoulnik AI, Agoulnik IU, Harrison WR, Behringer RR and Overbeek PA (2000) A transgenic insertion upstream of sox9 is associated with dominant XX sex reversal in the mouse *Nature Genetics* **26** 490–494

Buoen LC, Zhang TQ, Weber AF and Ruth GR (2000) SRY-negative, XX intersex horses: the need for pedigree studies to examine the mode of inheritance of the condition *Equine Veterinary Journal* **32** 78–81

Calvari V, Bertini V, De Grandi A et al. (2000) A new submicroscopic deletion that refines the 9p region for sex reversal *Genomics* **65** 203–212

Cameron FJ and Sinclair AH (1997) Mutations in SRY and SOX9: testis-determining genes *Human Mutation* **9** 388–395

Capel B, Albrecht KH, Washburn LL and Eicher EM (1999) Migration of mesonephric cells into the mammalian gonad depends on Sry *Mechanisms of Development* **84** 127–131

Caricasole A, Duarte A, Larsson SH, Hastie ND, Little M, Holmes G, Todorov I and Ward A (1996) RNA binding by the Wilms tumor suppressor zinc finger proteins *Proceedings National Academy of Sciences USA* **93** 7562–7566

Conley AJ, Corbin CJ, Hinshelwood MM, Liu Z, Simpson ER, Ford JJ and Harada N (1996) Functional aromatase expression in porcine adrenal gland and testis *Biology of Reproduction* **54** 497–505

Daneau I, Ethier JF, Lussier JG and Silversides DW (1996) Porcine SRY gene locus and genital ridge expression *Biology of Reproduction* **55** 47–53

De Felici M and Pesce M (1994) Growth factors in mouse primordial germ cell migration and proliferation *Progress in Growth Factor Research* **5** 135–143

Donovan PJ (1994) Growth factor regulation of mouse primordial germ cell development *Current Topics in Developmental Biology* **29** 189–225

Dube JL, Wang P, Elvin J, Lyons KM, Celeste AJ and Matzuk MM (1998) The bone morphogenetic protein 15 gene is X-linked and expressed in oocytes *Molecular Endocrinology* **12** 1809–1817

Durlinger AL, Kramer P, Karels B, de Jong FH, Uilenbroek JT, Grootegoed JA and Themmen AP (1999) Control of primordial follicle recruitment by anti-Mullerian hormone in the mouse ovary *Endocrinology* **140** 5789–5796

Edelmann W, Cohen PE, Kneitz B, Winand N, Lia M, Heyer J, Kolodner R, Pollard JW and Kucherlapati R (1999) Mammalian MutS homologue 5 is required for chromosome pairing in meiosis *Nature Genetics* **21** 123–127

Ferguson-Smith MA (1966) X-Y chromosomal interchange in the aetiology of true hermaphroditism and of XX Klinefelter's syndrome *Lancet* **2** 475–476

Foster JW, Dominguez-Steglich MA, Guioli S et al. (1994) Campomelic dysplasia and autosomal sex reversal caused by mutations in an SRY-related gene *Nature* **372** 525–530

Galloway SM, McNatty KP, Cambridge LM et al. (2000) Mutations in an oocyte-derived growth factor gene (BMP15) cause increased ovulation rate and infertility in a dosage-sensitive manner *Nature Genetics* **25** 279–283

Gessler M, Poustka A, Cavenee W, Neve RL, Orkin SH and Bruns GA (1990) Homozygous deletion in Wilms tumours of a zinc-finger gene identified by chromosome jumping *Nature* **343** 774–778

Godin I, Deed R, Cooke J, Zsebo K, Dexter M and Wylie CC (1991) Effects of the steel gene product on mouse primordial germ cells in culture *Nature* **352** 807–809

Graddy LG, Kowalski AA, Simmen FA, Davis SL, Baumgartner WW and Simmen RC (2000) Multiple isoforms of porcine aromatase are encoded by three distinct genes *Journal of Steroid Biochemistry and Molecular Biology* **73** 49–57

Haber DA, Sohn RL, Buckler AJ, Pelletier J, Call KM and Housman DE (1991) Alternative splicing and genomic structure of the Wilms tumor gene WT1 *Proceedings National Academy of Sciences USA* **88** 9618–9622

Habu T, Taki T, West A, Nishimune Y and Morita T (1996) The mouse and human homologs of DMC1, the yeast meiosis-specific homologous recombination gene, have a common unique form of exon-skipped transcript in meiosis *Nucleic Acids Research* **24** 470–477

Huang B, Wang S, Ning Y, Lamb AN and Bartley J (1999) Autosomal XX sex reversal caused by duplication of SOX9 *American Journal of Medical Genetics* **87** 349–353

Ikeda Y, Shen WH, Ingraham HA and Parker KL (1994)

Developmental expression of mouse steroidogenic factor-1, an essential regulator of the steroid hydroxylases *Molecular Endocrinology* **8** 654–662

Jeske YW, Bowles J, Greenfield A and Koopman P (1995) Expression of a linear Sry transcript in the mouse genital ridge *Nature Genetics* **10** 480–482

Jost A, Vigier B, Prépin J and Perchellet JP (1973) Studies on sex differentiation in mammals *Recent Progress in Hormone Research* **29** 1–41

Katoh-Fukui Y, Tsuchiya R, Shiroishi T, Nakahara Y, Hashimoto N, Noguchi K and Higashinakagawa T (1998) Male-to-female sex reversal in M33 mutant mice *Nature* **393** 688–692

Kent J, Wheatley SC, Andrews JE, Sinclair AH and Koopman P (1996) A male-specific role for SOX9 in vertebrate sex determination *Development* **122** 2813–2822

Kettlewell JR, Raymond CS and Zarkower D (2000) Temperature-dependent expression of turtle Dmrt1 prior to sexual differentiation *Genesis* **26** 174–178

Koopman P, Gubbay J, Vivian N, Goodfellow P and Lovell-Badge R (1991) Male development of chromosomally female mice transgenic for Sry *Nature* **351** 117–121

Kreidberg JA, Sariola H, Loring JM, Maeda M, Pelletier J, Housman D and Jaenisch R (1993) WT-1 is required for early kidney development *Cell* **74** 679–691

Lala DS, Rice DA and Parker KL (1992) Steroidogenic factor I, a key regulator of steroidogenic enzyme expression, is the mouse homolog of fushi tarazu-factor I *Molecular Endocrinology* **6** 1249–1258

Luo X, Ikeda Y and Parker KL (1994) A cell-specific nuclear receptor is essential for adrenal and gonadal development and sexual differentiation *Cell* **77** 481–490

McElreavey K, Vilain E, Abbas N, Herskowitz I and Fellous M (1993) A regulatory cascade hypothesis for mammalian sex determination: SRY represses a negative regulator of male development *Proceedings National Academy of Sciences USA* **90** 3368–3372

McGrath SA, Esquela AF and Lee SJ (1995) Oocyte-specific expression of growth/differentiation factor-9 *Molecular Endocrinology* **9** 131–136

Martineau J, Nordqvist K, Tilmann C, Lovell-Badge R and Capel B (1997) Male-specific cell migration into the developing gonad *Current Biology* **7** 958–968

Meyers-Wallen VN, Schlafer D, Barr I, Lovell-Badge R and Keyzner A (1999) Sry-negative XX sex reversal in purebred dogs *Molecular Reproduction and Development* **53** 266–273

Miyamoto N, Yoshida M, Kuratani S, Matsuo I and Aizawa S (1997) Defects of urogenital development in mice lacking Emx2 *Development* **124** 1653–1664

Morais da Silva S, Hacker A, Harley V, Goodfellow P, Swain A and Lovell-Badge R (1996) Sox9 expression during gonadal development implies a conserved role for the gene in testis differentiation in mammals and birds *Nature Genetics* **14** 62–68

Morohashi K, Honda S, Inomata Y, Handa H and Omura T (1992) A common trans-acting factor, Ad4-binding protein, to the promoters of steroidogenic P-450s *Journal of Biological Chemistry* **267** 17 913–17 919

Nachtigal MW, Hirokawa Y, Enyeart-VanHouten DL, Flanagan JN, Hammer GD and Ingraham HA (1998) Wilms' tumor 1 and Dax-1 modulate the orphan nuclear receptor SF-1 in sex-specific gene expression *Cell* **93** 445–454

Ottolenghi C, Veitia R, Quintana-Murci L, Torchard D, Scapoli L, Souleyreau-Therville N, Beckmann J, Fellous M and McElreavey K (2000) The region on 9p associated with 46,XY sex reversal contains several transcripts expressed in the urogenital system and a novel doublesex-related domain *Genomics* **64** 170–178

Pailhoux E, Cribiu EP, Chaffaux S, Darre R, Fellous M and Cotinot C (1994a) Molecular analysis of 60,XX pseudohermaphrodite polled goats for the presence of SRY and ZFY genes *Journal of Reproduction and Fertility* **100** 491–496

Pailhoux E, Popescu PC, Parma P, Boscher J, Legault C, Molteni L, Fellous M and Cotinot C (1994b) Genetic analysis of 38XX males with genital ambiguities and true hermaphrodites in pigs *Animal Genetics* **25** 299–305

Pailhoux E, Pelliniemi L, Barbosa A, Parma P, Kuopio T and Cotinot C (1997) Relevance of intersexuality to breeding and reproductive biotechnology programs; XX sex reversal in pigs *Theriogenology* **47** 93–102

Parma P, Pailhoux E, Puissant C and Cotinot C (1997) Porcine Dax-1 gene: isolation and expression during gonadal development *Molecular and Cellular Endocrinology* **135** 49–58

Parma P, Pailhoux E and Cotinot C (1999) Reverse transcription-polymerase chain reaction analysis of genes involved in gonadal differentiation in pigs *Biology of Reproduction* **61** 741–748

Payen E, Pailhoux E, Abou Merhi R, Gianquinto L, Kirszenbaum M, Locatelli A and Cotinot C (1996) Characterization of ovine SRY transcript and developmental expression of genes involved in sexual differentiation *International Journal of Developmental Biology* **40** 567–575

Pelletier J, Bruening W, Li FP, Haber DA, Glaser T and Housman DE (1991) WT1 mutations contribute to abnormal genital system development and hereditary Wilms' tumour *Nature* **353** 431–434

Pelliniemi LJ (1985) Sexual differentiation of the pig gonad *Archives d'Anatomie Microscopique et de Morphologie Expérimentale* **74** 76–80

Pelliniemi LJ and Lauteala L (1981) Development of sexual dimorphism in the embryonic gonad *Human Genetics* **58** 64–67

Pfeifer D, Kist R, Dewar K, Devon K, Lander ES, Birren B, Korniszewski L, Back E and Scherer G (1999) Campomelic dysplasia translocation breakpoints are scattered over 1 Mb proximal to SOX9: evidence for an extended control region *American Journal of Human Genetics* **65** 111–124

Pilon N, Behdjani R, Daneau I, Lussier JG and Silversides DW (1998) Porcine steroidogenic factor-1 gene (pSF-1) expression and analysis of embryonic pig gonads during sexual differentiation *Endocrinology* **139** 3803–3812

Pritchard-Jones K, Fleming S, Davidson D *et al.* (1990) The candidate Wilms' tumour gene is involved in genitourinary development *Nature* **346** 194–197

Raeside JI, Wilkinson CR and Farkas G (1993) Ontogenesis of estrogen secretion by porcine fetal testes *Acta Endocrinologica* **128** 549–554

Raymond CS, Shamu CE, Shen MM, Seifert KJ, Hirsch B, Hodgkin J and Zarkower D (1998) Evidence for evolutionary conservation of sex-determining genes *Nature* **391** 691–695

Raymond CS, Kettlewell JR, Hirsch B, Bardwell VJ and Zarkower D (1999) Expression of Dmrt1 in the genital ridge of mouse and chicken embryos suggests a role in vertebrate sexual development *Developmental Biology* **215** 208–220

Ruggiu M, Speed R, Taggart M, McKay SJ, Kilanowski F, Saunders P, Dorin J and Cooke HJ (1997) The mouse Dazla gene encodes a cytoplasmic protein essential for gametogenesis *Nature* **389** 73–77

Sanchez A, Bullejos M, Burgos M, Hera C, Stamatopoulos C, Diaz De la Guardia R and Jimenez R (1996) Females of four mole species of genus Talpa (insectivora, mammalia) are true hermaphrodites with ovotestes *Molecular Reproduction and Development* **44** 289–294

Sarafoglou K and Ostrer H (2000) Clinical review 111: familial sex reversal: a review *Journal of Clinical Endocrinology and Metabolism* **85** 483–493

Shawlot W and Behringer RR (1995) Requirement for Lim1 in head-organizer function *Nature* **374** 425–430

Shen WH, Moore CC, Ikeda Y, Parker KL and Ingraham HA (1994) Nuclear receptor steroidogenic factor 1 regulates the mullerian inhibiting substance gene: a link to the sex determination cascade *Cell* **77** 651–661

Sinclair AH, Berta P, Palmer MS *et al.* (1990) A gene from the human sex-determining region encodes a protein with homology to a conserved DNA-binding motif *Nature* **346** 240–244

Soyal SM, Amleh A and Dean J (2000) FIGalpha, a germ cell-specific transcription factor required for ovarian follicle formation *Development* **127** 4645–4654

Südbeck P, Schmitz ML, Baeuerle PA and Scherer G (1996) Sex reversal by loss of the C-terminal transactivation domain of human SOX9 *Nature Genetics* **13** 230–232

Swain A, Zanaria E, Hacker A, Lovell-Badge R and Camerino G (1996) Mouse Dax1 expression is consistent with a role in sex determination as well as in adrenal and hypothalamus function *Nature Genetics* **12** 404–409

Swain A, Narvaez V, Burgoyne P, Camerino G and Lovell-Badge R (1998) Dax1 antagonizes Sry action in mammalian sex determination *Nature* **391** 761–767

Tilmann C and Capel B (1999) Mesonephric cell migration induces testis cord formation and Sertoli cell differentiation in the mammalian gonad *Development* **126** 2883–2890

Vaiman D and Pailhoux E (2000) Mammalian sex reversal and intersexuality. Deciphering the sex-determination cascade *Trends in Genetics* **16** 488–494

Vainio S, Heikkila M, Kispert A, Chin N and McMahon AP (1999) Female development in mammals is regulated by Wnt-4 signalling *Nature* **397** 405–409

Wagner T, Wirth J, Meyer J *et al.* (1994) Autosomal sex reversal and campomelic dysplasia are caused by mutations in and around the SRY-related gene SOX9 *Cell* **79** 1111–1120

Western PS, Harry JL, Graves JA and Sinclair AH (1999) Temperature-dependent sex determination: upregulation of SOX9 expression after commitment to male development *Developmental Dynamics* **214** 171–177

Whitfield LS, Lovell-Badge R and Goodfellow PN (1993) Rapid sequence evolution of the mammalian sex-determining gene SRY *Nature* **364** 713–715

Whitworth DJ, Shaw G and Renfree MB (1996) Gonadal sex reversal of the developing marsupial ovary *in vivo* and *in vitro*. *Development* **122** 4057–4063

Wunderle VM, Critcher R, Hastie N, Goodfellow PN and Schedl A (1998) Deletion of long-range regulatory elements upstream of SOX9 causes campomelic dysplasia *Proceedings National Academy of Sciences USA* **95** 10 649–10 654

Yang H, Fries R and Stranzinger G (1993) The sex-determining region Y (SRY) gene is mapped to p12-p13 of the Y chromosome in pig (*Sus scrofa domestica*) by *in situ* hybridization *Animal Genetics* **24** 297–300

Yu RN, Ito M, Saunders TL, Camper SA and Jameson JL (1998) Role of Ahch in gonadal development and gametogenesis *Nature Genetics* **20** 353–357

Reproduction Supplement **58**, 81–90

In vitro development of pig preantral follicles

E. E. Telfer

Institute of Cell and Molecular Biology, University of Edinburgh, King's Buildings, Mayfield Road, Edinburgh EH9 3JR, UK

A limiting factor to realizing the full potential of many of the new reproductive techniques is the lack of abundant numbers of fertilizable oocytes. This problem could be addressed by using the large source of oocytes available from preantral and primordial follicles by developing systems for *in vitro* growth. *In vitro* systems that use early growing follicles as a source of oocytes have been developed for laboratory species and these have been successful in producing live young. If successful, *in vitro* growth in association with *in vitro* maturation (IVM) and cryopreservation would optimize *in vitro* production systems. *In vitro* growth systems that support the growth of pig preantral follicles have been developed and have been successful in producing meiotically competent oocytes but, to date, no live young have been produced. However, these systems remain to be characterized and their main application is as experimental models to study the processes of early oocyte and follicle development. This review provides an overview of culture systems that have been developed for domestic species and discusses how these are furthering our basic knowledge of early follicular development, as well as considering the benefits and potential problems associated with *in vitro* growth systems.

Introduction

The ability to grow mature oocytes from immature oocytes *in vitro* is the ambition of many people involved in animal production. The idea of harvesting immature oocytes for growth *in vitro* is not a new one and over the past decade techniques have been developed for isolating and culturing preantral follicles from a range of rodent species (Roy and Greenwald 1985, 1989; Eppig and Schroeder, 1989; Torrance *et al.*, 1989; Nayudu and Osborn, 1992; Spears *et al.*, 1994; Cortvrindt *et al.*, 1996). The limited success of the rodent system for production of viable offspring (Eppig and Schroeder, 1989) has resulted in many attempts to develop similar methods for applications in humans (Abir *et al.*, 1997; Wright *et al.*, 1999) and domestic species (for reviews see Telfer, 1998; Telfer *et al.*, 1999; Van den Hurk *et al.*, 2000). Progress has been slow in developing culture systems to support oocyte development from non-rodent species. Indeed, follicle culture promises much but so far there has been no real progress in applying these techniques to animals with follicles that undergo a long period of growth. Culture conditions for these species will be complex and dynamic, as they must promote oocyte growth, acquisition of developmental competence and appropriate genomic

Email: Evelyn.Telfer@ed.ac.uk

maturation (genomic imprinting). The slow progress in developing culture systems has been due mainly to a lack of knowledge of the basic mechanisms that control follicle and oocyte development in these species. Therefore, the main application of *in vitro* growth systems at this time is as experimental models to gain valuable insight into factors regulating follicle and oocyte development.

Selection of follicles for *in vitro* growth

The ovarian follicle, which comprises an oocyte and its companion somatic cells, is the functional unit of the mammalian ovary. By or shortly after the birth of female mammals there is a large store of primordial follicles that constitutes the only reserve of germ cells in the postnatal ovary. The number of primordial follicles varies with age, species and breed but, in general, larger species have more follicles than do smaller species (Jones and Krohn, 1961; Gosden and Telfer, 1987a,b). By the time the female reaches puberty about 75% of the original store of primordial follicles will have degenerated (Erickson, 1966; Gosden and Telfer, 1987b). This loss represents an enormous wastage of genetic material, but even after puberty only a small number of follicles will ever be used and the rest will degenerate at the antral stage of development (Faddy *et al.*, 1987; Gosden and Telfer, 1987b). Therefore, there are large numbers of immature (primordial and preantral) follicles at all ages that are a potential source of follicles for *in vitro* growth.

It is not known whether all immature follicles are capable of development *in vitro* or whether there is an optimal population that can be selected. However, primordial and early preantral (primary) follicles are a more homogeneous group than later preantral and antral follicles, as at these developmental stages there is a low rate of degeneration. The degree of apoptotic cell death in the granulosa cells of pig follicles ranging from 100 µm to 3.3 mm in diameter has been examined (F. Ghafari and E. E. Telfer, unpublished) and it was found that in follicles ≤ 500 µm in diameter there is little apoptotic cell death but, thereafter, > 50% of follicles show signs of apoptosis. Similar results were found using bovine follicles, in which about 90% of antral follicles were already undergoing apoptotic cell death at the time of isolation, whereas < 10% of isolated preantral and early antral follicles showed any signs of apoptosis (Telfer *et al.*, 1998). Thus, to obtain maximum numbers of follicles that have not been compromised it is best to isolate primordial or early preantral follicles.

Methods of isolating immature follicles

Primordial follicles

Primordial follicles are the most abundant population of oocytes in the ovary at any age (Gosden and Telfer, 1987b), but they are also the follicles about which least is known and they are difficult to isolate. Primordial follicles can be isolated from the ovaries of rodents and piglets using proteolytic enzyme digestion (Greenwald and Moor, 1989), but the enzymatic techniques lead to degradation of the basement membrane and result in detachment of granulosa cells from the oocyte. There are as yet no reliable methods for isolating intact primordial follicles and so most of the culture work involving primordial follicles has relied on the isolation of clumps or slices of ovarian cortex, as these sections are composed almost entirely of primordial follicles (Braw-Tal and Yossefi, 1997; Fortune *et al.*, 1998). The isolation and culture of primordial follicles remains the ideal but it is likely to be some time before this can be achieved and a more realistic starting point is preantral follicles.

Preantral follicles

Several methods have been developed for isolation of preantral follicles from rodent ovaries, which involve either tissue disaggregation by enzymes or microdissection. Enzymatic digestion using collagenase and DNase has been used successfully to isolate follicles from mice (Eppig and Schroeder, 1989; Torrance *et al.*, 1989; Eppig and Telfer, 1993), hamsters (Roy and Greenwald, 1985) and rats (Daniel *et al.*, 1989). Such methods have allowed large numbers of early developing preantral follicles to be collected from rodents for culture to the stage at which the oocytes can resume meiotic maturation and be fertilized (Eppig, 1994; Eppig and O'Brien, 1998). However, the enzyme treatment compromises the integrity of the basement membrane and detaches adherent theca cells so these units are actually granulosa cell–oocyte complexes and not intact follicles. A microdissection technique has to be used to isolate intact follicles from rodent ovaries (Spears *et al.*, 1994); this is relatively straightforward as the stromal tissue is soft.

The large-scale isolation of preantral follicles from domestic species has been more difficult to achieve (for reviews see Telfer, 1996; Telfer *et al.*, 1999; Van den Hurk *et al.*, 2000). The ovaries of domestic species are fibrous in nature and, therefore, techniques that work in rodents cannot be readily applied. Proteolytic enzymes have been used to isolate follicles from pig (Telfer, 1996) and horse (Telfer and Watson, 2000) ovaries but the most effective and reliable method for isolating preantral follicles from domestic species is by microdissection from ovarian cortical slices (McCaffery *et al.*, 2000) (Fig. 1). The most effective method for isolating preantral follicles from pig ovaries is by microdissection from cortical slices, as this method allows the isolation of morphologically 'normal' follicles with intact basement membranes and maintains theca–granulosa–oocyte interactions (Van den Hurk *et al.*, 1998). The disadvantage of this method of isolation is that it is slow, labour intensive and provides a relatively low yield.

In vitro growth systems

Several culture systems have been devised that support development *in vitro* of immature follicles from rodents. The most successful system in terms of production of developmentally competent oocytes is that developed by Eppig and Schroeder (1989). In this system, granulosa cell–oocyte complexes from immature mice can be grown on a collagen matrix under serum-free conditions for up to 12 days. During this growth period many of the oocytes acquire developmental competence. Indeed, it has been calculated that using this technique of *in vitro* growth and subsequent IVM it is possible to obtain four times as many blastocysts per animal as can be produced by IVM of *in vivo*-derived oocytes (Eppig and O'Brien, 1998). Although these results are impressive, they should be treated with caution, as a high rate of blastocyst formation does not predict the rate of successful development to live young.

The development of an *in vitro* system that supports oocyte and follicle growth in domestic species is much more ambitious because oocyte development occurs over a much longer time compared with that in laboratory animals, and follicles are large (Fig. 2). The ideal *in vitro* system for oocyte growth would be a system in which isolated oocytes could achieve growth and developmental competence in defined media without the follicle unit. However, oocyte growth is dependent upon gap junction-mediated communication between the oocyte and its companion granulosa cells, and the rate of growth is related directly to the number of granulosa cells coupled to the oocyte (Herlands and Schultz, 1984). Therefore, the intimate physiological connections between oocytes and somatic cells within the follicle are essential for normal development of the oocyte. Alternatively, the next best option would be to culture

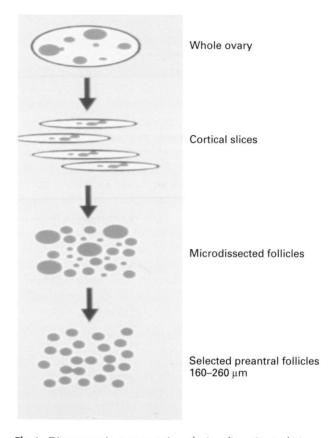

Whole ovary

Cortical slices

Microdissected follicles

Selected preantral follicles
160–260 μm

Fig. 1. Diagrammatic representation of microdissection technique
for isolating pig preantral follicles. Ovaries are sliced into
cortical sections (avoiding large antral follicles as much as
possible). Preantral follicles are dissected from the surrounding
stroma using needles and then selected by size (160–260 μm in
diameter).

granulosa cell–oocyte complexes similar to those described above (Eppig and Schroeder,
1989), in which the whole follicle unit is not required for the oocyte to acquire developmental
competence. To date, culture of granulosa cell–oocyte complexes has not been successful for
domestic species and the whole follicle unit appears to be required for at least part of the
culture period. Methods for culturing intact ovarian follicles have been developed in rodent
systems (Nayudu and Osborn, 1992; Spears *et al.*, 1994) and the advantage of these methods
is that they can provide valuable information about the interaction of all components of the
follicle unit.

Culture systems that support some elements of oocyte and follicle growth in follicles from
cattle (Gutierrez *et al.*, 2000; McCaffrey *et al.*, 2000), pigs (Hirao *et al.*, 1994; Telfer *et al.*, 2000;
Wu *et al.*, 2000) and sheep (Cecconi *et al.*, 1999; Newton *et al.*, 1999) have been developed
(Telfer, 1998; Van den Hurk *et al.*, 2000). Most of these systems are at the stage of defining
conditions for the early stages of follicle growth and all use an intact follicle unit. Systems to
support the development of pig oocytes are more advanced than those for other large animal
species (Hirao *et al.*, 1994; Telfer *et al.*, 2000; Wu *et al.*, 2000) (Fig. 3). Oocytes from pig

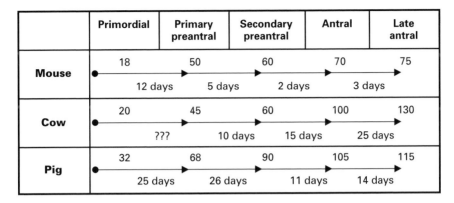

	Primordial	Primary preantral	Secondary preantral	Antral	Late antral
Mouse	18	50	60	70	75
	12 days	5 days	2 days	3 days	
Cow	20	45	60	100	130
	???	10 days	15 days	25 days	
Pig	32	68	90	105	115
	25 days	26 days	11 days	14 days	

Fig. 2. Oocyte diameters in micrometres (µm) (top line) for each stage of follicle development and time taken to reach each stage (bottom line) for mice, cows and pigs.

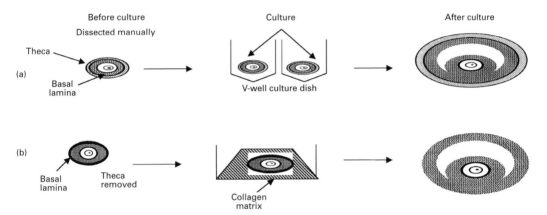

Fig. 3. Diagrammatic representation of follicle culture systems for pig preantral follicles. (a) Intact follicles (210–260 µm in diameter) are microdissected and placed in individual culture wells. During culture, antral formation occurs and in the presence of serum approximately 19% of the oocytes recovered are capable of reaching metaphase II (Telfer *et al.*, 2000). (b) Theca cells are removed and follicles are cultured in a supported three-dimensional collagen matrix (Hirao *et al.*, 1994). Antral formation occurs during culture and approximately 40% of the oocytes that reach 110 µm in diameter after 16 days in culture reach metaphase II.

preantral follicles have been grown within a collagen gel matrix and some acquired meiotic competence once they reached a diameter of approximately 100 µm (Hirao *et al.*, 1994). A culture period of 16 days was required to achieve this level of growth and even then only 3.5% of the complexes cultured developed an oocyte with a diameter > 110 µm and only 1.3% of oocytes from the initially cultured follicular structures were capable of reaching metaphase II after IVM (Hirao *et al.*, 1994). This low rate of success to resume and progress in meiotic maturation will be the result of many factors, but the principal factors are likely to be: (i) the selection and stage of follicles that start the culture; and (ii) the culture conditions.

Telfer *et al.* (2000) cultured pig preantral follicles for up to 20 days and demonstrated that when follicles were cultured in serum conditions, meiotically competent oocytes could be harvested. The ability to reach the metaphase II stage after *in vitro* growth was dependent on the starting size of the follicle and the presence of serum in the medium. All oocytes that acquired meiotic competence were derived from follicles that started the culture at a diameter of 210–260 μm and were cultured in the presence of serum. Oocytes derived from follicles that were 160–210 μm in diameter at the start of culture were unable to reach metaphase II, whether they were cultured with or without fetal calf serum (FCS). This finding shows that the development of meiotic competence during *in vitro* growth is dependent on the starting population of follicles and the culture conditions, with the presence of serum factors being beneficial. Clearly, it would be more beneficial to have a serum-free culture system so that conditions can be defined. One of the difficulties with a serum-free culture system has been the high degree of apoptosis that occurs under these conditions; however, addition of ascorbic acid on a daily basis to serum-free medium prevents apoptosis in cultured bovine (Thomas *et al.*, 2001) and pig (M. Bark and E. E. Telfer, unpublished) follicles.

Wu *et al.* (2000) reported that isolated pig preantral follicles (range 200–310 μm in diameter) have been cultured for 4 days and that after this period a proportion of oocytes were capable of maturation and fertilization, and blastocysts were produced. This study reported that optimum conditions for oocyte development during this short culture period were when three follicles were cultured per well in North Carolina State University 23 medium (NCSU 23) containing 7.5% pig serum and 1.5 ng FSH ml^{-1}. Under these conditions, 68% of cumulus–oocyte complexes (COCs) were recovered for IVM and oocyte maturation rates were 51%, with 13% of oocytes developing to blastocysts after fertilization. The growth rate reported by Wu *et al.* (2000) is exceptionally fast, as the equivalent development *in vivo* would take several weeks. Such an extreme acceleration of oocyte development *in vitro* has not been observed in any other species and it is not known whether normal development occurred (Wu *et al.*, 2000).

From all the culture systems that have been developed for pigs and other domestic species it is emerging that the maintenance of cellular interactions between the oocyte and granulosa cells, and the granulosa cells and theca cells, is important for oocyte development *in vitro*. The culture systems reported by Hirao *et al.* (1994) and Telfer *et al.* (2000) show evidence of antral formation after a few days in culture (Fig. 4a) and that the connections between the differentiated cumulus cells and oocyte remain intact during culture (Hirao *et al.*, 1994; Fig. 4b). Meiotic and cytoplasmic maturation of oocytes grown *in vitro* will be unsuccessful if the somatic cells fail to maintain their interaction with the oocyte and undergo normal differentiation during *in vitro* growth of follicles. A greater understanding of oocyte–granulosa cell interactions and theca–granulosa cell interactions is required to improve culture systems for follicle and oocyte development.

Development of markers to evaluate oocyte and follicle quality

A major concern about accelerating the rate of oocyte development *in vitro* is whether this leads to the development of abnormal oocytes. Oocyte development is co-ordinated with somatic cell development and so requires developmentally regulated signals; a culture system may interfere with normal signalling pathways. Non-invasive markers are required to determine the developmental potential of *in vitro*-grown oocytes to improve culture systems for follicles and oocytes from pigs and other domestic species. Ideally, cellular markers of somatic cell differentiation and oocyte development would be used that could be related to normal *in vivo* development. There are various candidate markers such as intra-ovarian growth factors (insulin-like growth factors (IGFs), activins and inhibins) and oocyte-specific factors such as growth differentiation factor 9 (GDF-9). These factors are all essential for early follicular development and their pattern of expression is likely to give some clue as to the developmental status of the follicle or oocyte. However, the presence or absence of any of

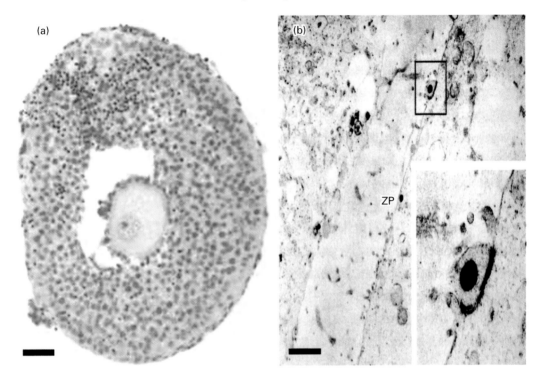

Fig. 4. (a) Histological section of pig preantral follicle after 6 days of culture. Note antral formation and detachment of the theca layer. (b) Electron micrograph of a pig oocyte cultured for 16 days *in vitro*. Reproduced from Hirao *et al.* (1994). Note the presence of a contact (inset) between the oocyte and cumulus cell process that traverses the zona pellucida (ZP). Scale bars represent (a) 50 μm and (b) 20 μm.

these factors at any single time point is unlikely to provide information on the health of an oocyte or follicle.

The development of oocytes *in vitro* to a stage at which they can support normal embryonic development is dependent on the oocyte reaching the appropriate stage of development to respond to the endocrine and paracrine signals responsible for the induction of maturation. In pigs, cattle and sheep this will be over a period of at least 28 days. Therefore, some non-invasive indicator of follicle health is required. When follicles are being monitored individually *in vitro*, medium can be monitored at regular intervals and, therefore, any secreted factors that might indicate follicle or oocyte health could be measured easily.

In our recent studies, we have been examining the secretion of matrix metalloproteinases (MMP-2 and -9) and tissue inhibitors of metalloproteinases (TIMP-1 and -2) as markers of follicle health. During follicular growth, maintenance of the follicle wall is facilitated by MMPs. MMPs are zinc- and calcium-dependent enzymes that are capable of degrading the protein components of the extracellular matrix. MMPs are regulated by TIMPs and are also responsible for the reconstruction of the follicle wall at the time of ovulation, and during corpus luteum formation and development (Zhao and Luck, 1996). The main follicular sources of MMPs and TIMPs are thought to be the granulosa and theca cells (Smith *et al.*, 1994; Zhao and Luck, 1996), but TIMP activity has also been found in oocytes (Bagavandoss, 1998). Balanced production of MMPs and TIMPs is essential for normal follicular development; therefore, their secretion pattern during culture might provide evidence of follicle or oocyte health. Our studies indicate that there is a relationship between the secretion patterns of MMP-2, MMP-9, TIMP-1 and TIMP-2, and the morphological criteria of health status of the follicle or oocyte (McCaffery *et al.*, 2000).

The secretion of MMP-9, TIMP-1 and TIMP-2 has been correlated with morphologically healthy follicles (McCaffery *et al.*, 2000). These factors may be useful in assessing follicle viability during prolonged cultures; however, the ultimate test of whether oocyte development *in vitro* has progressed normally is whether live young are produced after fertilization.

Future prospects and problems

The development of follicle culture systems has allowed many studies to be carried out on the basic mechanisms of oocyte and follicle development. Rodent culture systems have provided information on factors secreted by oocytes, which led to the discovery of GDF-9, an oocyte-specific factor that regulates early follicle development (Vanderhyden *et al.*, 1992). The development of systems for domestic species is leading to the elucidation of some basic mechanisms of early oocyte and follicle development (McCaffrey *et al.*, 2000; Thomas *et al.*, 2001). Clearly, there is potential to develop these culture systems from the experimental model phase to the production phase but there are serious concerns that immature oocytes harvested for *in vitro* growth may be developmentally compromised and may result in the production of unhealthy offspring.

It is now clear that the long-term health of an individual can be influenced by fetal–maternal interactions (Nathanielsz, 1999) and that any factors that stress the preimplantation embryo could adversely affect fetal–maternal interactions, resulting in problems for the offspring. Some assisted reproductive technologies that involve the culture of oocytes or embryos can lead to problems in the fetus or offspring. High birth weights and abnormal fetal development have been observed in calves and lambs produced by IVM and IVF, or by *in vitro* culture of embryos (Behboodi *et al.*, 1995). The abnormalities observed were associated initially with the technique of nuclear transfer (Willadsen *et al.*, 1991) but it is now clear that these features can arise from *in vitro* culture of embryos (Walker *et al.*, 1992, 1996). These features have been characterized as large offspring syndrome (Walker *et al.*, 1996; Thompson, 1997; Young *et al.*, 1998; Sinclair *et al.*, 1999), which is also associated with an increased rate of abortion, increased duration of gestation, physical abnormalities and increased mortality and morbidity (Walker *et al.*, 1996; Thompson, 1997).

The identification of a link between embryo manipulation and various abnormalities raises the question of the safety of these techniques and it is not known whether using immature oocytes for *in vitro* production would exacerbate this. Mice produced from preantral follicles grown *in vitro* appear to be normal at birth but no follow-up studies of any mice produced in this way have been conducted. There is one report that a single mouse (indeed, to date the only animal produced in such a way) produced from a primordial follicle grown *in vitro* (Eppig and O'Brien, 1996) suffered from obesity, liver problems and neurological damage in adulthood (Eppig and O'Brien, 1998). Whether these problems are in any way connected to the *in vitro* production methods or are entirely random cannot yet be answered, but it does raise questions as to the safety of these techniques and suggests that we should proceed with caution from the experimental application to production using these techniques. The application of new molecular techniques to screen early oocytes and embryos for normal expression patterns will be critical to the development and application of *in vitro* growth techniques. The use of appropriate micro-arrays will be instrumental to ensure the generation of embryos with normal expression patterns and should increase the likelihood of obtaining normal offspring.

Conclusion

The culture of immature follicles holds much promise. In conjunction with cryopreservation techniques, culture of immature follicles has the potential to optimize *in vitro* production systems. However, our understanding of the conditions that allow normal development of oocytes is still at an early stage. The main benefits of these culture systems are in obtaining information to improve our understanding of the mechanisms that control oocyte growth, accumulation of regulatory factors and acquisition of competence to undergo fertilization and embryogenesis.

The author would like to acknowledge grant support from BBSRC, MAFF, MRC, The Wellcome Trust, Pig Improvement Company and MLC.

References

Abir R, Franks S, Mobberley MA, Moore PA, Margara RA and Winston RML (1997) Mechanical isolation and *in vitro* growth of preantral and small antral human follicles *Fertility and Sterility* **68** 682–688

Bagavandoss P (1998) Differential distribution of gelatinases and tissue inhibitor of metalloproteinase-1 in the rat ovary *Journal of Endocrinology* **158** 221–228

Behboodi E, Anderson GB, Bondurant RH, Cargill SL, Kreuscher BR, Medrano JF and Murray JD (1995) Birth of large calves that developed from *in vitro* derived embryos *Theriogenology* **44** 227–232

Braw-Tal R and Yossefi S (1997) Studies *in vivo* and *in vitro* on the initiation of follicle growth in the bovine ovary *Journal of Reproduction and Fertility* **109** 165–171

Cecconi S, Barboni B, Coccia M and Mattioli M (1999) *In vitro* development of sheep preantral follicles *Biology of Reproduction* **60** 594–601

Cortvrindt R, Smitz J and van Steirtegham AC (1996) *In vitro* maturation, fertilization and embryo development of immature oocytes from early preantral follicles from prepubertal mice in a simplified culture system *Human Reproduction* **12** 2656–2666

Daniel SA, Armstrong DT and Gore-Langton RE (1989) Growth and development of rat oocytes *in vitro. Gamete Research* **24** 109–121

Eppig JJ (1994) Further reflections on culture systems for the growth of oocytes *in vitro. Human Reproduction* **9** 969–976

Eppig JJ and O'Brien MJ (1996) Development *in vitro* of mouse oocytes from primordial follicles *Biology of Reproduction* **54** 197–207

Eppig JJ and O'Brien MJ (1998) Comparison of preimplantation developmental competence after mouse oocyte growth development *in vitro* and *in vivo. Theriogenology* **49** 415–422

Eppig JJ and Schroeder AC (1989) Capacity of mouse oocytes from preantral follicles to undergo embryogenesis and development to live young after growth, maturation, and fertilization *in vitro. Biology of Reproduction* **41** 268–276

Eppig JJ and Telfer EE (1993) Isolation and culture of oocytes *Methods in Enzymology* **225** 77–84

Erickson BH (1966) Development and senescence of the postnatal bovine ovary *Journal of Animal Science* **25** 800–805

Faddy MJ, Telfer EE and Gosden RG (1987) The kinetics of preantral follicle development in ovaries of CBA/Ca mice during the first 14 weeks of life *Cell and Tissue Kinetics* **20** 551–560

Fortune JE, Kito S and Wandji SA (1998) Activation of bovine and baboon primordial follicles *in vitro. Theriogenology* **49** 441–449

Gosden RG and Telfer E (1987a) Scaling of follicular sizes in mammalian ovaries *Journal of Zoology* **211** 157–168

Gosden RG and Telfer E (1987b) Numbers of follicles and oocytes in mammalian ovaries and their allometric relationships *Journal of Zoology* **211** 169–175

Greenwald GS and Moor RM (1989) Isolation and preliminary characterization of pig primordial follicles *Journal of Reproduction and Fertility* **87** 561–571

Gutierrez C, Ralph JH, Telfer EE, Wilmut I and Webb R (2000) Growth and antrum formation of bovine preantral follicles in long-term culture *Biology of Reproduction* **62** 1322–1328

Herlands RL and Schultz RM (1984) Regulation of mouse oocyte growth: probable nutritional role for intercellular communication between follicle cells and oocytes in oocyte growth *Journal of Experimental Zoology* **229** 317–325

Hirao Y, Nagai T, Kubo M, Miyano T and Kato S (1994) *In vitro* growth and maturation of pig oocytes *Journal of Reproduction and Fertility* **100** 333–339

Jones EC and Krohn PL (1961) The relationship between age and numbers of oocytes and fertility in virgin and multiparous mice *Journal of Endocrinology* **21** 469–495

McCaffery FH, Leask R, Riley SC and Telfer EE (2000) Culture of bovine preantral follicles in a serum free system: markers for assessment of growth and development *Biology of Reproduction* **63** 267–273

Nathanielsz PW (1999) *Life in the Womb: the Origin of Health and Disease* Promethean Press, Ithaca

Nayudu PL and Osborn SM (1992) Factors influencing the rate of preantral and antral growth of mouse ovarian follicles *in vitro. Journal of Reproduction and Fertility* **95** 349–362

Newton H, Picton H and Gosden RG (1999) *In vitro* growth of oocyte–granulosa cell complexes isolated from cryopreserved ovine tissue *Journal of Reproduction and Fertility* **115** 141–150

Roy SK and Greenwald GS (1985) An enzymatic method for dissociation of intact follicles from the hamster ovary: histological and quantitative aspects *Biology of Reproduction* **32** 203–215

Roy SK and Greenwald GS (1989) Hormonal requirements for the growth and differentiation of hamster preantral follicles in long-term culture *Journal of Reproduction and Fertility* **87** 103–114

Sinclair KD, McEvoy TG, Maxfield EK, Maltin CA, Young LE, Wilmut I, Broadbent PJ and Robinson JJ (1999) Aberrant fetal growth and development after *in vitro* culture of sheep zygotes *Journal of Reproduction and Fertility* **116** 177–186

Smith GW, Goetz TL, Anthony RV and Smith MF (1994) Molecular cloning of an ovine ovarian tissue inhibitor of metalloproteinases: ontogeny of mRNA expression and *in situ* localisation within preovulatory follicles and luteal tissue *Endocrinology* **134** 344–352

Spears N, Boland NI, Murray AA and Gosden RG (1994) Mouse oocytes derived from *in vitro* grown primary ovarian follicles are fertile *Human Reproduction* **9** 527–532

Telfer EE (1996) The development of methods for isolation and culture of preantral follicles from bovine and porcine ovaries *Theriogenology* **45** 101–110

Telfer EE (1998) *In vitro* models for oocyte development *Theriogenology* **49** 451–460

Telfer EE and Watson ED (2000) Isolation of preantral follicles from mare ovaries *Journal of Reproduction and Fertility Supplement* **56** 447–453

Telfer EE, Binnie JP and Jordan LB (1998) Effect of follicle size on the onset of apoptotic cell death in cultured bovine ovarian follicles *Theriogenology* **49** 357 (Abstract)

Telfer EE, Webb R, Moor RM and Gosden RG (1999) New approaches to increasing oocyte yield from ruminants *Animal Science* **68** 285–298

Telfer EE, Binnie JP, McCaffery F and Campbell BK (2000) *In vitro* development of oocytes from porcine and bovine primary follicles *Molecular and Cellular Endocrinology* **163** 117–123

Thomas FH, Leask R, Sršen V, Riley SC, Spears N and Telfer EE (2001) Effect of ascorbic acid on health and morphology of bovine preantral follicles during long-term culture *Reproduction* **122** 487–495

Thompson JG (1997) Comparison between *in vivo* derived and *in vitro* produced pre-elongation embryos from domestic ruminants *Reproduction, Fertility and Development* **9** 341–354

Torrance C, Telfer E and Gosden RG (1989) Quantitative study of the development of isolated mouse pre-antral follicles in collagen gel culture *Journal of Reproduction and Fertility* **87** 367–374

Van den Hurk R, Spek ER, Hage WJ, Fair T, Ralph JH and Schotanus K (1998) Ultrastructure and viability of isolated bovine preantral follicles *Human Reproduction Update* **4** 833–841

Van den Hurk R, Abir R, Telfer EE and Bevers MM (2000) Primate and bovine immature oocytes and follicles as sources of fertilisable oocytes *Human Reproduction Update* **6** 457–474

Vanderhyden BC, Telfer EE and Eppig JJ (1992) Mouse oocytes promote the proliferation of granulosa cells from preantral and antral follicles *in vitro*. *Biology of Reproduction* **46** 1196–1204

Walker SK, Heard TM and Seamark RF (1992) *In vitro* culture of sheep embryos without co-culture: successes and perspectives *Theriogenology* **37** 111–126

Walker SK, Hartwich KM and Seamark RF (1996) The production of unusually large offspring following embryo manipulation: concepts and challenges *Theriogenology* **45** 111–120

Willadsen SM, Janzen RE, McAllister RJ, Shea BF, Hamilton G and McDermand D (1991) The viability of late morulae and blastocysts produced by nuclear transplantation in cattle *Theriogenology* **36** 161–170

Wright CS, Hovatta O, Margtara R, Trew G, Winston RM, Franks S and Hardy K (1999) Effects of follicle-stimulating hormone and serum substitution on the *in-vitro* growth of human ovarian follicles *Human Reproduction* **14** 1555–1562

Wu J, Emery BR and Carrell DT (2000) *In vitro* growth, maturation, fertilization, and embryonic development of oocytes from porcine preantral follicles *Biology of Reproduction* **64** 375–381

Young LE, Sinclair KD and Wilmut I (1998) Large offspring syndrome in cattle and sheep *Reviews of Reproduction* **3** 155–163

Zhao Y and Luck MR, (1996) Bovine granulosa cells express ECM proteins and their regulators during luteinisation in culture *Reproduction, Fertility and Development* **8** 259–226

Reproduction Supplement **58**, 91–104

Maturation of pig oocytes *in vivo* and *in vitro*

R. Moor and Y. Dai*

The Babraham Institute, Babraham, Cambridge CB2 4AT, UK

In this review the concept that the origins of embryonic failure occur during oocyte development is explored. The four factors that determine oocyte viability, namely a normal growth phase, adequate follicle cell support during maturation, the completion of intracellular reprogramming before fertilization and the functioning of oocyte surveillance mechanisms, form the four sections of this review. The viability of pig oocytes at the end of the growth phase is compromised by presumptive spontaneous meiotic progression and by morphological heterogeneity. Determining the percentage and identity of viable dictyate oocytes, and identifying the reasons for the loss of viability, are key areas of future investigation. Although the requirement for follicle cell support during maturation is already established, little is yet known about the underlying signals and their transmission to the oocyte. The analysis of the action and nature of somatic signals will provide the foundation for further advances in the maturation of oocytes *in vitro*. Signalling cascades in oocytes control both the translation of masked mRNA and the modification and spatial localization of resultant proteins. The interdependent nature of this control system explains why inappropriate signals during maturation lead to subsequent embryonic mortality. Chromosomal errors during meiosis and early mitosis accumulate because of the leaky nature of the checkpoint system during the maternally regulated part of development: effective cell cycle surveillance is established only after the activation of the embryonic genome. In summary, we emphasize that the quality of the dictyate oocyte and the provision of appropriate signals *in vitro* are the principal determinants of maturational success.

Introduction

The female germ cell population is specialized because its numbers are fixed in prenatal life and decline progressively thereafter by either atresia or ovulation. Although the pig conforms to this pattern of germ cell behaviour, its cellular population of approximately 2×10^5 primordial follicles is larger than that in many other mammals (Gosden and Telfer, 1987). Despite this apparent advantage, only a small fraction of pig oocytes will develop into live offspring in the lifespan of the sow. Most of the oocyte population (> 99%) will be lost at

*Correspondence
Email: daiy@bbsrc.ac.uk

various stages of oogenesis by the process of programmed cell death. As the loss of oocytes by atresia forms the subject of other contributions to this symposium it will not be discussed further in this review. Instead, we shall focus on the competence of the remaining oocytes, coupled with a consideration of the effectiveness of potential surveillance mechanisms that function in the maintenance of oocyte quality. The underpinning proposition is that the normal progression of early embryogenesis depends absolutely on a complex but ordered series of events during oogenesis. This protracted period of oocyte development includes an early mitotic phase of germ cell multiplication, the transition from mitosis to meiosis, meiotic arrest, genetic recombination, primordial cell inactivity, oocyte growth and a final culminating phase of intense cellular reorganization during maturation. The introduction of a haploid sperm nucleus at fertilization restores the diploid status of the egg and drives meiosis to its conclusion. The high incidence of early embryonic mortality in pigs indicates that this elaborate series of cellular events may often undergo aberrant changes that are not invariably detected by oocyte surveillance mechanisms (for reviews see Perry, 1954; Wilmut et al., 1986).

In addition to their normal development in vivo, oocytes from antral follicles have, over the past 20 years, been used for the in vitro production of embryos (for reviews see Hasler et al., 1995; Galli and Lazzari, 1996). Despite numerous studies in a variety of different animals, the percentage of offspring produced in vitro remains < 20%. Although a significant part of the embryonic mortality associated with in vitro systems may be a result of the inherent quality of the oocytes, the remainder appears to be associated with imperfect in vitro technology. The causes of these imperfections can be ascribed broadly to three general deficiencies: there is an inadequate understanding of the intracellular processes underlying oocyte development, many studies contain a number of variables and many use inadequate methods of experimental assessment. For example, using measures of success such as fertilization, cleavage or cavitation are at best imperfect and often obscure subtle cellular abnormalities that contribute to later embryonic mortality. The concepts of limiting the number of experimental variables and using rigorous endpoints such as live births is of particular relevance to pigs, in which disappointingly few in vitro-produced embryos develop to term (Mattioli et al., 1989; Funahashi and Day, 1997; Kikuchi and Kashiwazaki, 1999).

The aim of this review is to emphasize deficiencies in our understanding of both the oocyte and the processes involved in its acquisition of developmental competence during maturation. In particular, the review will pose the following questions: to what extent are G2-stage pig oocytes in antral follicles developmentally compromised? What intrafollicular signals confer developmental capacity on oocytes and through what general mechanisms do the intracellular signals act? Finally, what surveillance mechanisms exist to detect defects in oocytes during their passage from germ cells to mature metaphase II oocytes? References to current in vitro protocols will be made only where such considerations illuminate significant issues about oocyte quality, intrafollicular signalling or cellular surveillance.

Heterogeneity and developmental competence in oocyte populations

Heterogeneity and follicular dynamics

It is axiomatic that heterogeneity is an essential feature of folliculogenesis in the ovaries of all mammals. Whether there are differences in the pool of primordial follicles is uncertain and raises the question of how and which follicles are recruited from this large reserve population into the growing classes. We postulate, but have not proven, that follicles differ even within the primordial pool. Regardless of the accuracy or otherwise of this hypothesis, there is no dispute about the importance of follicular heterogeneity once growth has been initiated. Pig

follicles develop over a number of months from a structure composed of a single layer of flattened somatic cells to a complex multi-compartmental antral follicle in a highly ordered series of stages (Morbeck *et al.*, 1994). Changes in the oocyte parallel these somatic cell developments. Genes are activated in a stage-specific manner; some of the resultant mRNA is translated immediately and the proteins are used to support the remarkable 200-fold increase in the volume of the developing oocyte. Other newly synthesized proteins are exported to form the zona pellucida or to act as signals between the growing oocyte and its associated follicle cells. However, not all the mRNA is translated and as the oocyte grows it accumulates large quantities of de-adenylated transcripts that are complexed with protein and stored in the cytoplasm (Gosden *et al.*, 1995). It is this masked mRNA that will ultimately drive both the process of maturation and all the developmental events that occur before activation of the embryonic genome. Therefore, there can be no doubt that heterogeneity exists not only during all stages of folliculogenesis but is also an essential component of the ovarian regulatory system. However, should the oocyte be regarded as entering a homogeneous population once its growth phase is complete? Furthermore, if there are morphological differences between fully grown oocytes, can these be correlated with the subsequent developmental capacity of the egg?

Heterogeneity within the fully grown dictyate oocyte population

Knowledge about the inherent quality of oocytes removed from follicles by clinicians and research workers for the *in vitro* production of embryos is an important unresolved problem. Clearly, until this intractable question is resolved no definitive statements can be made about the absolute quality of either human or animal *in vitro* embryo production techniques. Questions about oocyte quality, especially in humans and cattle, have exercised workers for many years and have been the subject of a substantial number of papers all describing different methods that purport to identify healthy oocytes. However, with the exception of identifying grossly abnormal oocytes, no technique has yet been devised to distinguish oocytes with developmental competence from those that are inherently incapable of supporting development to term (Hyttel *et al.*, 1997). Indirect evidence that a significant proportion of fully grown oocytes might be developmentally incompetent comes primarily from humans, in which approximately 20% of aspirated oocytes have been classified as morphologically degenerate (for review see Moor *et al.*, 1998). Even when these oocytes are excluded, the number of babies produced from the remaining morphologically normal oocytes by *in vitro* maturation is still remarkably low. Moreover, genetic analyses on early cleavage stage embryos reveal a high incidence of chromosomal abnormality, indicating that many oocytes may be inherently genetically defective in humans. It is important to determine whether high percentages of genetically defective oocytes occur in other species also, or whether chromosomal abnormalities are predominantly a problem associated with the extended lifespan of humans.

In pigs, questions about oocyte homogeneity have focussed primarily on observed differences in the configuration of chromatin in the nucleus of fully grown oocytes and are based on a seminal paper by Motlik and Fulka (1976). These studies were carried out on the ovaries of 24 superovulated gilts that were examined at 4 h intervals after administration of hCG and from oocytes cultured *in vitro*. A total of 156 oocytes was examined before or within 4 h of hCG injection and 145 (94%) exhibited a GVI type chromatin pattern: the remaining 11 oocytes displayed advanced stages of germinal vesicle breakdown (GVIV or early diakinesis). In contrast, the results of more recent studies using the same classification system indicate that an exceptionally low percentage (approximately 30%) of oocytes collected from medium-sized follicles of prepuberal gilts or from sows in the luteal or early follicular phase remain in an

inactive GVI state (see Funahashi and Day, 1997; Prather and Day, 1998; Guthrie and Garrett, 2000). Excluding possible differences in classification between the two groups of investigators, what could now account for this spectacular increase in the apparent spontaneous resumption of meiosis in pig oocytes from follicles 3–6 mm in diameter? The age of the pigs at death, the size and nature of the follicles selected for aspiration, their hormonal milieu and the composition of modern pig diets are among the possible explanations for the observed differences (Ding and Foxcroft, 1994; Hunter, 2000). Clearly, more research is needed on the causes of this presumptive precocious meiotic resumption. These studies could be preceded very profitably by an updating of the original follicle classifications using accurately staged oocytes taken directly from normal and synchronized pigs and three-dimensional nuclear reconstructions using modern confocal techniques.

It has been suggested that differences between GVI- and GVII-stage oocytes affect their subsequent maturation and development (Grupen and Nagashima, 1997; Prather and Day, 1998). To circumvent this, three approaches have been used to induce meiotic homogeneity before induction of the maturation process. The first approach has been to administer gonadotrophin (eCG) to gilts 72 h before oocyte collection. In the second approach, oocytes have been preincubated for 12 h without gonadotrophins. The third approach has been to expose oocytes to dibutyryl cyclic adenosine 3',5'-monophosphate (dbcAMP) or hypoxanthine to induce synchronization (Miyano *et al.*, 1995; Funahashi and Day, 1997; Prather and Day, 1998). These meiotic synchronization protocols are of interest because they indicate that the GVI to GVII transition is readily reversible. However, both approaches also expose the oocytes to potentially damaging problems. The administration of gonadotrophins to ungulate oocytes can induce the premature unmasking of some mRNAs followed by precocious protein synthesis and a subsequent reduction in embryonic development (Moor *et al.*, 1985). Equally, even the method of LH delivery *in vivo* appears to influence the subsequent developmental competence of oocytes *in vivo* (Oussaid *et al.*, 1997). These experiments (Fig. 1) show that the administration of LH as a single bolus rather than in a pulsatile manner to sheep had no measurable effect on the completion of meiosis or on fertilization. However, the advantages of a pulsatile form of LH administration were not apparent until early development, when significantly more blastocysts ($P < 0.01$) were formed.

Taken together the above two studies indicate that exogenous hormone therapy can compromise egg quality and embryonic development. However, if used correctly gonadotrophins not only assist in the imposition of nuclear homogeneity (Funahashi and Day, 1997) but may also act to prime the oocyte before maturation. This postulated requirement for pre-maturation priming is considered by some investigators to occur in the period immediately preceding the release of LH and to be important for cytoplasmic maturation; pre-maturation priming plays no role in the regulation of the meiotic cell cycle (for review see Moor *et al.*, 1998). There is some evidence of a small beneficial effect of pre-maturation priming in primates, cattle and also in pig oocytes, in which FSH priming increases development to the morula stage and beyond (Bolamba and Sirard, 2000).

In conclusion, it appears that the questions of oocyte viability may be complicated in pigs by problems associated with the spontaneous resumption of meiosis in oocytes from intermediate-sized follicles. This abnormality adds a further specialized challenge to the key problem of determining what percentage of fully grown oocytes is inherently capable of ultimately supporting development to term. Until this question is resolved, it will be impossible to be certain of the extent to which improvements can be made to our current methods of maturing oocytes *in vitro*. The resolution of this key question is likely to be expedited by the power of modern fluorescence-activated *in situ* hybridization (FISH) techniques for chromosome analysis (Munne *et al.*, 1995; Harper and Delhanty, 1996).

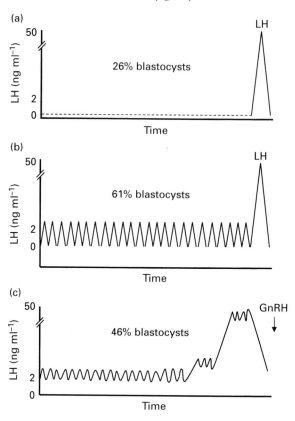

Fig. 1. An illustration that the mode of LH release in the 24 h preceding the LH surge in sheep (pre-maturation period) influences the subsequent developmental capacity of matured oocytes. (a) Inhibition of GnRH and, thus, LH pulsatility, was induced in the 24 h before maturation with the antagonist antarelix: oocyte maturation and ovulation were thereafter induced by a single injection of LH. (b) Inhibition of natural LH pulsatility during the late follicular phase using antarelix. However, hourly injections of LH induced artificial pulsatility in the 24 h before a single ovulatory injection of LH. (c) Untreated controls. Rates of blastocyst development were significantly higher in the groups of animals whose oocytes had been exposed to pulsatile LH administration in the 24 h before induction of maturation (graphs constructed from data presented by Oussaid *et al.*, 1997).

Follicular signals and intercellular communication

The first requirement for the production of a viable egg is the growth and development of a competent dictyate oocyte and the second is for appropriate somatic cell support. A number of questions are raised by this assertion: is this support cell-type specific; what is the nature of the required support; when is it required; and by what pathways is the support delivered to the oocyte?

Follicular contribution to oocyte competence

The question of whether and when follicle cell support is required during maturation is not new (for review see Moor and Warnes, 1978). Using *in vivo* approaches, Moor and Warnes (1978) showed that oocytes denied follicular support for the first third of the maturation period failed to develop into fetuses, although meiotic cycle progression was not inhibited. By linking these results with those derived from biochemical analyses of gene expression and cell fusion, it is now widely accepted that mammalian follicles generate inhibitory signals until after the LH surge (Dekel, 1996). Thereafter, positive follicular signals that are generated in the first third of maturation (inductive phase) initiate a phase of intracellular reprogramming that is completed in the second phase of maturation (cytoplasmic reprogramming phase). In addition to the provision of specialized signals for the completion of maturation, follicle cells also provide essential nutrient and metabolic support to the oocyte throughout the entire period of oocyte development. In the oocytes of domestic animals, this follicular cell support is required not only for growth but also for normal intracellular function, such as the maintenance of ionic balances in the cell and the maintenance of mRNA masking and stability (for reviews see Moor, 1983; Motlik and Fulka, 1986; Mattioli, 1994). Therefore, successful maturation of pig oocytes *in vivo* or *in vitro* depends on the presence of follicle cells able to generate and transmit the correct sequence of signals and support to induce and maintain the intracellular maturation programme.

Signals and signalling pathways during maturation

The oocyte membrane is remarkably poorly equipped to transport many of the metabolic products required by the oocyte (see Moor, 1983). Instead, substrates such as nucleotides, amino acids and phospholipids enter the oocyte cytoplasm through an extensive network of gap junctions. In pigs, cell coupling between the oocyte and the associated coronal cells is maintained throughout most of the maturation period. Its premature disruption *in vitro* does not affect meiotic progression but disrupts cytoplasmic maturation, fertilization and development totally (Mattioli *et al.*, 1988; Mori *et al.*, 2000). Although this loss of developmental potential is due in part to the intracellular depletion of essential molecules, junctional disruption also blocks the transmission of specific signals including those associated with calcium regulation and FSH stimulation (Fagbohun and Downs, 1991; Kaufman and Homa, 1993). The extent to which other intracellular regulators depend on junctional transport is unclear because of our lack of knowledge about the mode of action, or indeed even the nature, of many of the key signalling molecules. Studies on the somatic signals, their transmission and their intracellular action are likely to provide some of the more rewarding areas for future research on pig oocytes. These areas of study should include not only the somatic compartment but should also focus on receptors and electric potentials within the nuclear and cell membranes (Mattioli, 1994); this latter focus is important as membrane events affect polarity and cellular compartmentalization in amphibian, and probably also in mammalian, oocytes (see Berridge, 1988). A small number of examples will suffice to indicate both the complexity and the limits of our current knowledge on signalling during oocyte maturation. Oestrogen receptors have been located in oocytes (Wu *et al.*, 1992) and oestrogen is also dominant in early preovulatory follicles. Inserting 17α-hydroxylase inhibitors into ovine follicles in the early preovulatory phase subverts the normal steroid biosynthetic pathway. This change has no effect on meiotic progression but compromises early embryogenesis greatly by altering the synthesis of a small number of proteins in the oocyte (Osborn and Moor, 1983). Although oestrogens are important during the early phase of maturation, progesterone is required in the second phase of maturation to maintain junctional

communication between the oocyte and the adjacent corona cells (Mattioli *et al.*, 1988). Future analyses on steroid signalling will need to take into account the likelihood that the relationship between the oocyte and its steroid milieu is highly dynamic and may not even be of a direct nature. Likewise, growth factors and cytokines appear to have certain beneficial effects on oocytes matured *in vitro* but it is likely that the action of these might be on the follicle cells rather than directly on the oocyte. In addition to the above well-established signalling molecules, other more localized intrafollicular signalling systems may also be important. For example, after the LH surge, maturing oocytes secrete two major gelatinases and the associated follicle cells secrete the corresponding metalloproteinase tissue inhibitors (Brenner *et al.*, 1989; Smith *et al.*, 1999). The results of Funahashi *et al.* (1997) indicate that this interaction between oocyte matrix metalloproteinases (MMPs) and follicle cell inhibitors (tissue inhibitors of matrix metalloproteinases; TIMPs) may act as an activator during maturation (Fig. 2). Their results show firstly that TIMP acts during maturation only and is without effect if added after fertilization. Moreover, TIMP has no effect on cell cycle progression or fertilization but instead acts solely to induce a significant improvement in early development.

In conclusion, we believe that the unique contribution made by the follicle cells, often through intercellular communication, to oocyte development is clearly established. The intimacy of this oocyte–follicle interdependency is demonstrated graphically by the finding that the calcium stores of pig oocytes are rapidly depleted when they are removed from the follicle (Petr *et al.*, 2001). Although it is apparent that a diverse range of somatic signals, ranging from inorganic ions to proteins, is involved in oocyte regulation, much remains to be discovered about the nature and action of both the inhibitory and stimulatory signalling systems. Moreover, it is apparent that many signals exert subtle effects that are not apparent until blastulation or beyond: this fact highlights the importance of using appropriate endpoints in signalling studies. Until both the full range of nutrients and instructive signals are identified, it will continue to be necessary to provide oocytes with appropriate signals by resorting to the inclusion of follicle cells in maturation systems (Staigmiller and Moor, 1984; Mattioli *et al.*, 1989). However, the ultimate success of this cellular supplementation approach depends on the precision with which the culture system enables the follicle cells to mimic their counterparts *in vivo*. We consider that too little attention is given to this requirement in the design of *in vitro* maturation systems.

Oocyte responses to intrafollicular signals

The purpose of signals directed at oocytes in preovulatory follicles is to drive the two parallel programmes of meiotic progression and cytoplasmic reprogramming. These two programmes can, to a significant extent, occur independently of each other. However, it is only when both are synchronized that developmental competence is attained by the mature oocyte. Although the protein products required for each programme differ, the intracellular signalling pathways and their targets in the oocyte are comparable. In somatic cells, the ultimate role of most signals is either to regulate transcription or to alter the activity of the gene products by protein modification. In contrast, in fully grown oocytes the signalling pathways converge not on DNA regulation but on the mobilization and translation of masked mRNA, as virtually no transcription occurs in oocytes during maturation. Intracellular signals in oocytes are involved with the selection of appropriate stored transcripts for translation at precise times and in controlling the level and duration of translation. In addition to regulating translation, signals also act to control the activity of the resultant proteins by post-translational modification and to localize proteins to specific cellular compartments. Abnormalities in any of these regulatory steps may induce discontinuities in the maturation process with resultant failures during development. The

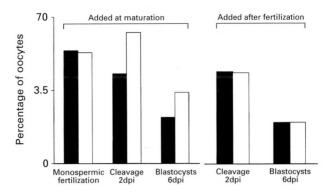

Fig. 2. Effect on early development of adding tissue inhibitor of metalloproteinase protein 1 (TIMP-1) to the medium used for maturation or culture of pig oocytes and embryos. ■: control; □: added TIMP-1; 2dpi: day 2 after implantation; 6dpi: day 6 after implantation. Addition of TIMP-1 during oocyte maturation enhanced embryo cleavage and blastulation. In contrast, addition of TIMP-1 during embryo culture had no effect on development (constructed from data published by Funahashi *et al.*, 1997).

cytoplasmic reprogramming events controlled by stored mRNA extend to almost every component of the oocyte. The process of cytoplasmic reprogramming includes changes to the plasma membrane, changes to the position of intracellular organelles, synthesis of new products required for fertilization and early development, and the control of meiotic cycle events.

The progression of the meiotic cycle is unique because the nature of this form of cell division is entirely different from that in all other cells in the body. The complexity of the various specialized regulatory events that operate in maturing pig oocytes can be illustrated by reference to the events that occur during progress through the first meiotic M-phase. During this phase the G2-block is removed, chromatin condenses, the nuclear membrane disassembles, a spindle is formed, homologous chromosomes separate (while sister chromatids remain tightly adherent) and meiosis progresses from metaphase I to metaphase II with no intervening S-phase. The complexity and precision with which translational mechanisms control the availability of molecules involved in driving events that occur in the first M-phase are shown (Fig. 3).

The results presented (Fig. 3) highlight the fact that relevant mRNAs for meiosis are recruited at different times, for different durations and at different levels. Although the resultant new protein synthesis is essential for meiotic progression in pig oocytes, it is important to stress that not all controls are imposed on the translation process itself. Meiotic regulation includes both a temporal and spatial component. The time dimension is characterized by the synthesis and destruction of specific cell-cycle regulators at specific stages in meiosis. However, the modification and spatial localization of these molecules is equally important for the regulation of meiosis as the time of their synthesis (see Pines, 1999).

Molecules controlling the first meiotic M-phase

There is strong evidence that two tyrosine kinases, p34^{cdc2} (MPF) and mitogen-activated protein kinase (MAPK), act in concert to induce G2- to M-phase progression in pig oocytes (Inoue *et al.*, 1998; Motlik *et al.*, 1998; Lee *et al.*, 2000a). In the case of MPF kinase, the catalytic subunit (p34^{cdc2}) is stored in the oocyte as an inactive protein. The regulatory subunit

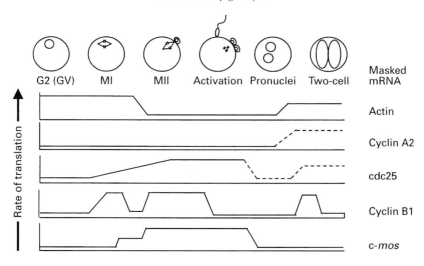

G2 (GV)   MI   MII   Activation   Pronuclei   Two-cell   Masked mRNA

Actin

Cyclin A2

cdc25

Cyclin B1

c-*mos*

Rate of translation

Fig. 3. The complex series of translational patterns generated by the mobilization of some of the masked mRNAs required to drive the cell cycle from the G2- (germinal vesicle) to the MII-stage of meiosis. The diagram illustrates the rate of translation of five species of mRNA plotted against the different stages of oocyte and egg development in pigs. Although the mRNAs shown represent a small fraction of the total pool of stored message only, nevertheless the unique nature of the translational pattern for each separate mRNA species is clearly shown.

(cyclin B1) requires *de novo* synthesis and complexing with the catalytic subunit during the late G2-phase. The MPF complex must then be activated by the removal of phosphates from Thr14 and Tyr15 of the $p34^{cdc2}$ molecule before translocation to the nucleus, where it exerts many of its major effects. In contrast, the two MAPK kinases (ERK1 and ERK2) are stored as proteins in the cytoplasm of pig oocytes and become activated by phosphorylation and selective relocation (see Inoue *et al.*, 1998). The MAPK cascade is important in many cell types, including pig oocytes, for the translocation of extrafollicular signals to their intracellular targets (Inoue *et al.*, 1998). It is by examining the detail of how each translocational event, phosphorylation step and protein localization process is controlled that a full appreciation of the maturation process can be most easily gained. For example, the master cell cycle kinase regulator (MPF kinase) requires both the synthesis of B-type cyclin and dephosphorylation before it acquires enzyme activity in pig oocytes: the phosphatase required for MPF dephosphorylation is coded for by the cdc25 gene. The requirement for both cyclin B and cdc25 mRNA translation for entry into metaphase I in pig oocytes has been demonstrated by both direct mRNA injection (Fig. 4) and by antisense-mediated arrest of translation in dictyate oocytes (Dai *et al.*, 2000). Thus, injection of mRNA coding only for either the B type cyclin (pig cyclin B1 or B2) or for the cdc25c protein on its own has only a limited effect on the induction of premature nuclear membrane breakdown (GVBD). In contrast, the injection of both cyclin B1 and cdc25 mRNA together induces premature GVBD in most oocytes (Y. Dai and R.M. Moor, unpublished).

Although both these results and those involving injection of antisense DNA (Dai *et al.*, 2000) confirm that cdc25 translation is required for GVBD, they provide no indication of how this translational event is regulated. Comparative studies on the pig cdc25 gene reveal that cdc25 mRNA in the oocyte differs from that in somatic cells. Moreover, these differences are retricted to the 3′ untranslated region (3′ UTR): oocyte-specific cdc25 mRNA contains a 400

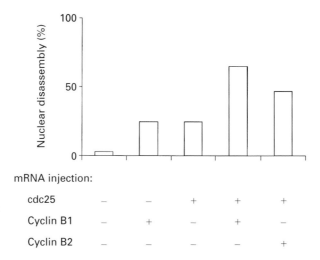

Fig. 4. Evidence that the synthesis of both a B-type cyclin and cdc25 protein is required for nuclear membrane breakdown (GVBD) in pig oocytes is provided by the microinjection of a dictyate (GV) oocyte with mRNA followed by confocal examination 15 h later ($n = 30$–54 oocytes per group). Injection of either cyclin B1 or cdc25 mRNA alone induces premature nuclear membrane disassembly in 25% of oocytes. In contrast, injecting cdc25 and cyclin B1 together increases the percentage of premature nuclear membrane breakdown to $> 65\%$ (Y. Dai and R. M. Moor, unpublished).

nucleotide 3' UTR extension not found in any somatic cell (Newman and Dai, 1997). This unique segment of untranslated sequence contains the motifs that repress translation of the cdc25 mRNA throughout early growth and until the precise time in diakinesis when synthesis of cdc25 protein is required. At this point, RNA binding proteins, possibly modified by phosphorylation, bind to the cytoplasmic polyadenylation elements (CPEs) and the hexanucleotide polyadenylation signal within the extended 3' UTR of the stored cdc25 transcripts. The resultant RNA–protein interactions induce polyadenylation and the loading of the cdc25 mRNA onto polysomes for translation (Y. Dai, C. Lee and R. M. Moor, unpublished). By analogy with other systems it is probable, but has not been proven, that so-called zipcode proteins also bind to motifs in the extended 3' UTR to ensure the accurate localization of the proteins. The newly synthesized cdc25 protein requires phosphorylation before translocation to the nucleus, where it exerts its primary action on the MPF molecule (Hoffman *et al.*, 1993; Dai *et al.*, 2000). In the absence of cdc25 synthesis in pig oocytes, nuclear membrane disassembly (GVBD) in late diakenesis is prevented (Dai *et al.*, 2000).

The example of cdc25 regulation shows that a range of phosphorylation cascades and translocation events is required to control the synthesis of this single phosphate. Inappropriate signals provided during *in vitro* maturation are likely to impair or distort one or more of the regulatory cascades that determine the correct temporal and spatial organisation of these events within the oocyte. Equally elaborate but entirely different sets of molecules are required both for the assembly of the spindle (Lee *et al.*, 2000b) and for the accurate segregation of homologues at anaphase I (Y. Dai and R. M. Moor, unpublished). Aberrations in any of these processes, or in any of those that drive cytoplasmic maturation, generally also result in segregation errors, chromosomal imbalances or other developmental failures.

Checkpoint surveillance in pig oocytes

Checkpoint mechanisms in somatic cells operate to eliminate errors during mitosis (Hartwell and Weinert, 1989). These mechanisms ensure that the progression of the cell cycle is error-free; if errors are detected by the surveillance mechanisms then mitosis is arrested to enable the error to be corrected or the cell to enter the apoptotic pathway. Mitotic cells are blocked from entering M-phase if replication is incomplete or if the cells contain damaged DNA. Likewise, segregation of sister chromatids is prevented in M-phase if abnormalities are detected in the spindle. Finally, replication is prevented in S-phase if segregation is incomplete (for review see Clarke and Gimenez-Abian, 2000). The question of what surveillance mechanism operates in oocytes to detect defects in meiosis I is particularly relevant for two reasons. Firstly, sister chromatids do not separate during the first meiotic M-phase, thereby raising important questions about the events monitored by meiotic checkpoints. Secondly, the high incidence of chromosomal non-disjunction associated with meiotic MI in humans (Angell, 1997) raises questions about the effectiveness of the entire surveillance system in oocytes.

Bradshaw *et al.* (1995) introduced an extensive set of lesions into dictyate oocytes immediately before maturation to determine whether checkpoints would prevent entry into M-phase. However, neither damaged DNA nor the introduction of unreplicated DNA into fully grown oocytes prevented chromatin condensation and nuclear membrane breakdown (Fulka *et al.*, 2000). Although it is clear from studies on *Drosophila* (Roeder and Bailis, 2000) that checkpoints monitor the process of genetic recombination, there is no evidence that additional checkpoints monitor the integrity of DNA in fully grown dictyate oocytes of mammals. The search for meiotic M-phase checkpoints has been particularly intensive both because of the absence of checkpoints in dictyate oocytes and because of the unique chromosome segregation system that operates in the first meiotic metaphase. Cell fusion analyses, drug-induced spindle lesions, mutational targeting of DNA repair genes, DNA damage and genetically induced chromosomal imbalances have all been used in a variety of species, including the pig, to identify M-phase checkpoints. Using precisely staged mouse oocytes, Fulka *et al.* (1995) showed that the fusion of early metaphase I oocytes (before the capture of microtubules by kinetochores) to oocytes at later metaphase I stages invariably delayed the onset of chromosome segregation in the more advanced partner. The results of that study indicate that oocytes may emit 'wait' signals before kinetochore–microtubule attachment. These inhibitor signals disappear after kinetochore attachment and the chromosome segregation machinery is activated. This conclusion is supported by results from mice homologous for the targeted disruption of DNA mismatch repair genes (Woods and Hodge, 1999). However, other studies raise the possibility that the target for the sensing mechanism in the spindle checkpoint is dependent on microtubule tension rather than on kinetochore attachment itself (see Le-Maire-Adkins and Rouke, 1997; Yu and Muszynski, 1999). The presence of the spindle checkpoint is in contrast to the absence of a surveillance system for DNA damage during M-phase (Fulka *et al.*, 2000).

In conclusion, these surveillance results indicate that despite the presence of checkpoints during recombination and in M-phase, a surprisingly high proportion of mature human oocytes contain chromosomal errors (Hassold *et al.*, 1996). As meiotic checkpoints appear leaky, it is a reasonable expectation that this would be compensated for by the presence of powerful checkpoints during early cleavage. Not only is this not the case but recent studies indicate that errors actually accumulate during early cleavage (Handyside and Delhanty, 1997; Munne and Cohen, 1998; Harrison and Kuo, 2000). Indeed, it appears possible that effective surveillance in embryos is not established until after activation of the embryonic genome at the mid-cleavage transition.

Future perspectives

The development of pig embryos depends on three inter-linked processes, each dependent on the error-free completion of the preceding process. The first phase involving primordial cell selection and completion of growth offers the long-term potential for the induction of growth *in vitro*. Although *in vitro* growth would increase the number of fully grown oocytes available for maturation, this does not appear to be a high priority as exceptionally large numbers of pig ovaries are invariably available from commercially killed gilts. However, the development of methods for distinguishing between viable and developmentally compromised dictyate oocytes is a high priority. This methodology will be of central importance both in the selection of a homogeneous and viable population of oocytes for *in vitro* maturation and in the understanding of the link between oocyte quality and embryonic mortality *in vivo*. The problems of spontaneous resumption of meiosis in intermediate-sized antral follicles appear to be more acute in pig oocytes than in other species and this increases the concern about the quality of dictyate oocytes in pigs. Sensitive FISH methods of chromosome analysis, coupled with follicle dissection, now offer important opportunities for making significant progress in studies on the quality and heterogeneity of pig oocytes. However, it is possible that the elimination of genetically compromised oocytes will, on its own, be insufficient to ensure the optimal developmental potential of pig oocytes matured *in vitro*. A pre-maturation period of differentiation may be required before fully grown oocytes have the ability to respond to the full range of maturation signals.

The follicle cell compartment is our second recommended focus for future research on maturation. It is apparent that information on the nature, generation, transmission and action of intrafollicular signals is presently inadequate. Furthermore, it is entirely possible that the current expedient of adding follicular tissue to maturation systems *in vitro* might not provide the full range of signals to the oocyte. This is likely to be especially relevant if the maturation systems are not designed specifically to ensure normal follicle cell function. Modern methods of molecular analysis should now be used in studies on intrafollicular signalling systems. We anticipate that a systematic analysis of intrafollicular signals, coupled with methods of selecting and priming dictyate oocytes, will be central to the development of successful methods of *in vitro* maturation. However, success will be conditional on the use of rigorous experimental protocols and reliable biological endpoints for assessing factors that confer developmental competence on maturing oocytes.

The authors would like to thank L. Notton and K. Waterton for the artwork and for the preparation of the manuscript. Financial support from the BBSRC is gratefully acknowledged.

References

Angell R (1997) First-meiotic-division nondisjunction in human oocytes *American Journal of Human Genetics* **61** 23–32

Berridge MJ (1988) Inositol lipids and calcium signalling *Proceedings of the Royal Society of London (Biology)* **234** 359–378

Bolamba D and Sirard MA (2000) Ovulation and follicular growth in gonadotropin-treated gilts followed by *in vitro* fertilization and development of their oocytes *Theriogenology* **53** 1421–1437

Bradshaw J, Jung T, Julka J, Jr and Moor RM (1995) UV irradiation of chromosomal DNA and its effect upon MPF and meiosis in mammalian oocytes *Molecular Reproduction and Development* **41** 503–512

Brenner CA, Adler RR and Rappolee DA (1989) Genes for extracellular matrix-degrading metalloproteinases and their inhibitor, TIMP, are expressed during early mammalian development *Genes and Development* **3** 848–859

Clarke DJ and Gimenez-Abian JF (2000) Checkpoints controlling mitosis *Bioessays* **22** 351–363

Dai Y, Lee C, Hutchings A, Sun Y and Moor RM (2000) Selective requirements for Cdc25C protein synthesis during meiotic progression in porcine oocytes *Biology of Reproduction* **62** 519–532

Dekel N (1996) Protein phosphorylation/dephosphorylation in the meiotic cell cycle of mammalian oocytes *Reviews of Reproduction* **1** 82–88

Ding J and Foxcroft GR (1994) Conditioned media produced by follicular shells of different maturity affect maturation of pig oocytes *Biology of Reproduction* **50** 1377–1384

Fagbohun CF and Downs SM (1991) Metabolic and ligand-stimulated meiotic maturation in the mouse oocyte–cumulus cell complex *Biology of Reproduction* **45** 851–859

Fulka J, Jr, Moor RM and Fulka J (1995) Mouse oocyte maturation: meiotic checkpoints *Journal of Experimental Cell Research* **219** 414–419

Fulka J, Jr, Tesarik J, Loi P and Moor RM (2000) Manipulating the human embryo: cell cycle checkpoint controls *Cloning* **2** 1–7

Funahashi H and Day BN (1997) Advances in *in vitro* production of pig embryos *Journal of Reproduction and Fertility Supplement* **52** 271–283

Funahashi H, McIntush EW, Smith MF and Day BN (1997) Effect of tissue inhibitor of metalloproteinase (TIMP-1) on early development of swine oocytes matured and fertilized *in vitro*. *Theriogenology* **47** 277 Abstract

Galli C and Lazzari G (1996) Practical aspects of IVM/IVF in cattle *Animal Reproduction Science* **42** 371–379

Gosden RG (1995) Oocyte development throughout life. In *Cambridge Reviews in Human Reproduction, Gametes – The Oocyte* pp 73–80 Eds JG Grudzinskas and JL Yovich. Cambridge University Press, Cambridge

Gosden RG and Telfer E (1987) Number of follicles and oocytes in mammalian ovaries and their allometric relationships *Journal of Zoology* **211** 169–175

Grupen CG and Nagashima H (1997) Asynchronous meiotic progression in porcine oocytes matured *in vitro*: a cause of polyspermic fertilization? *Reproduction, Fertility and Development* **9** 187–191

Guthrie HD and Garrett WM (2000) Changes in porcine oocyte germinal vesicle development as follicles approach preovulatory maturity *Theriogenology* **54** 389–399

Handyside AH and Delhanty JD (1997) Preimplantation genetic diagnosis: strategies and surprises *Trends in Genetics* **13** 270–275

Harper JC and Delhanty JD (1996) Detection of chromosomal abnormalities in human preimplantation embryos using FISH *Journal of Assisted Reproduction and Genetics* **13** 137–139

Harrison RH and Kuo HC (2000) Lack of cell cycle checkpoints in human cleavage stage embryos revealed by a clonal pattern of chromosomal mosaicism analysed by sequential multicolour FISH *Zygote* **8** 217–224

Hartwell LH and Weinert TA (1989) Checkpoints: controls that ensure the order of cell cycle events *Science* **246** 629–634

Hasler JF, Henderson WB, Hurtgen PJ et al. (1995) Production, freezing and transfer of bovine IVF embryos and subsequent calving results *Theriogenology* **43** 141–152

Hassold T and Abruzzo M (1996) Human aneuploidy: incidence, origin, and etiology *Environmental and Molecular Mutagenesis* **28** 167–175

Hoffmann I, Clarke PR, Marcote MJ, Karsenti E and Draetta G (1993) Phosphorylation and activation of human cdc25C by cdc2-cyclin B and its involvement in the self-amplification of MPF at mitosis *EMBO Journal* **12** 53–63

Hunter MG (2000) Oocyte maturation and ovum quality in pigs *Reviews of Reproduction* **5** 122–130

Hyttel P, Fair T, Callesen H and Greve T (1997) Oocyte growth, capacitation and final maturation in cattle *Theriogenology* **47** 23–32

Inoue M, Naito K, Nakayama T and Sato E (1998) Mitogen-activated protein kinase translocates into the germinal vesicle and induces germinal vesicle breakdown in porcine oocytes *Biology of Reproduction* **58** 130–136

Kaufman ML and Homa ST (1993) Defining a role for calcium in the resumption and progression of meiosis in the pig oocytes *Journal of Experimental Zoology* **265** 69–76

Kikuchi K and Kashiwazaki N (1999) Developmental competence after transfer to recipients, of porcine oocytes matured, fertilized and cultured *in vitro*. *Biology of Reproduction* **60** 336–340

Lee J, Miyano T and Moor RM (2000a) Localisation of phosphorylated MAP kinase during the transition from meiosis I to meiosis II in pig oocytes *Zygote* **8** 119–125

Lee J, Miyano T and Moor RM (2000b) Spindle formation and dynamics of γ-tubulin and nuclear mitotic apparatus protein distribution during meiosis in pig and mouse oocytes *Biology of Reproduction* **62** 1184–1192

LeMaire-Adkins R and Radke K (1997) Lack of checkpoint control at the metaphase/anaphase transition: a mechanism of meiotic nondisjunction in mammalian females *Journal of Cell Biology* **139** 1611–1619

Mattioli M (1994) Transduction mechanisms for gonadotrophin-induced oocyte maturation in mammals *Zygote* **2** 347–349

Mattioli M, Galeati G, Bacci ML and Seren E (1988) Follicular factors influence oocyte fertilizability by modulating the intercellular co-operation between cumulus cells and oocytes *Gamete Research* **21** 223–232

Mattioli M, Galeati G, Bacci ML and Seren E (1989) Developmental competence of pig oocytes matured and fertilized *in vitro*. *Theriogenology* **31** 1201–1207

Miyano T, Ebihara M, Goto Y, Hirao Y, Nagai T and Kato S (1995) Inhibitory action of hypoxanthine on meiotic resumption of denuded pig follicular oocytes *in vitro*. *Journal of Experimental Zoology* **273** 70–75

Moor RM (1983) Contact, signalling and cooperation between follicle cells and dictyate oocytes in mammals. In *Current Problems in Germ Cell Differentiation* pp 307–326 Eds A McLaren and CC Wylie. Cambridge University Press, Cambridge

Moor RM and Warnes GM (1978) Regulation of oocyte maturation in mammals. In *Control of Ovulation* pp 159–176 Eds DB Crighton, GR Foxcroft, NB Haynes and GE Lamming. Butterworths, London

Moor RM, Osborn JC and Crosby IM (1985) Gonadotrophin-induced abnormalities in sheep oocytes after superovulation *Journal of Reproduction and Fertility* **74** 167–172

Moor RM, Dai Y, Lee C and Fulka J, Jr (1998) Oocyte maturation and embryonic failure *Human Reproduction* **4** 23–236

Morbeck DE, Esbenshade KL, Flowers WL and Britt JH (1994) Kinetics of follicle growth in the prepubertal gilt *Biology of Reproduction* **47** 485–491

Mori T, Amano T and Shimizu H (2000) Roles of gap junctional communication of cumulus cells in cytoplasmic maturation of porcine oocytes cultured *in vitro*. *Biology of Reproduction* **62** 913–919

Motlik J and Fulka J (1976) Breakdown of the germinal vesicle in pig oocytes *in vivo* and *in vitro*. *Journal of Experimental Zoology* **198** 155–162

Motlik J and Fulka J (1986) Factors affecting meiotic competence in pig oocytes *Theriogenology* **25** 87–96

Motlik J, Pavlok A, Kubelka M, Kalous J and Kala P (1998) Interplay between CDC2 kinase and map kinase pathway during maturation of mammalian oocytes *Theriogenology* **49** 461–469

Munne S and Cohen J (1998) Chromosome abnormalities in human embryos *Human Reproduction Update* **4** 842–855

Munne S, Alikani M, Tomkin G, Grifo J and Cohen J (1995) Embryo morphology, developmental rates and maternal age are correlated with chromosomal abnormalities *Fertility and Sterility* **64** 382–391

Newman B and Dai Y (1997) Transcription of *c-mos* protooncogene in the pig involves both tissue-specific promoters and alternative polyadenylation sites *Molecular Reproduction and Development* **44** 275–288

Osborn JC and Moor RM (1983) The role of steroid signals in the maturation of mammalian oocytes *Journal of Steroid Biochemistry* **19** 133–137

Oussaid B, Mariana JC and Poulin N (1997) Effect of LH pulses during the follicular phase on developmental competence of sheep oocytes 13th Scientific Meeting, European Embryo Transfer Association *Edition Fondation Marcel Merieux, Lyon* 190

Perry JS (1954) Fecundity and embryonic mortality in pigs *Journal of Embryology and Experimental Morphology* **2** 308–322

Petr J, Rozinek J, Hruban V, Jilek F, Sedmikova M, Vanourkova Z and Nemecek Z (2001) Ultrastructural localization of calcium deposits during *in vitro* culture of pig oocytes *Molecular Reproduction and Development* **58** 196–204

Pines J (1999) Four dimensional control of the cell cycle *Nature Cell Biology* **1** 73–79

Prather RS and Day BN (1998) Practical considerations for the *in vitro* production of pig embryos *Theriogenology* **49** 23–32

Roeder GS and Bailis JM (2000) The pachytene checkpoint *Trends in Genetics* **16** 395–403

Smith MF, McIntush EW, Ricke WA, Kojima FN and Smith GW (1999) Regulation of ovarian extracellular matrix remodelling by metalloproteinases and their tissue inhibitors: effects on follicular development ovulation and luteal function *Journal of Reproduction and Fertility Supplement* **54** 367–381

Staigmiller RB and Moor RM (1984) Effect of follicle cells on the maturation and developmental competence of ovine oocytes matured outside the follicle *Gamete Research* **9** 221–229

Wilmut I, Sales DI and Ashworth CJ (1986) Maternal and embryonic factors associated with prenatal loss in mammals *Journal of Reproduction and Fertility* **76** 851–864

Woods LM and Hodges CA (1999) Chromosomal influence on meiotic spindle assembly: abnormal meiosis I in female Mlh1 mutant mice *Journal of Cell Biology* **145** 1395–1406

Wu T, Wang L and Wan Y (1992) Expression of estrogen-receptor gene in mouse oocyte and during embryogenesis *Molecular Reproduction and Development* **33** 407–412

Yu HG and Muszynski MG (1999) The maize homologue of the cell cycle checkpoint protein MAD2 reveals kinetochore substructure and contrasting mitotic and meiotic localization patterns *Journal of Cell Biology* **145** 425–435

Reproduction Supplement **58**, 105–112

Basic mechanisms of fertilization and parthenogenesis in pigs

R. S. Prather

*Food for the 21st Century, 162 ASRC, Department of Animal Sciences,
University of Missouri-Columbia, Columbia, MO 65211, USA*

Fertilization of the egg, or oocyte, initiates the entire developmental process, but while the mechanism by which the spermatozoa triggers the oocyte to resume meiosis has been studied extensively, conclusions about this process are still elusive. Some workers have suggested that a molecule on the surface of the spermatozoon may interact with a receptor on the plasma membrane of the oocyte, thereby triggering the oocyte to resume meiosis. Other workers have focused on a factor or factors located in the cytoplasm of the spermatozoa that is deposited into the cytoplasm of the oocyte. A hallmark response to fertilization in mammals is an increase in the cytoplasmic concentration of free Ca^{2+} in the oocyte. Many additional studies have focused on treatments that will induce the oocyte to resume meiosis without being fertilized. The process of resumption of meiosis without a spermatozoon is generally referred to as activation or parthenogenesis. Activation of the oocyte is very important for a number of oocyte- or embryo-related technologies including intracytoplasmic sperm injection (ICSI) and cloning by nuclear transfer. This review will focus on what is known about fertilization and methods to mimic this process, with an emphasis on pigs.

Introduction

Pig oocytes are arrested at metaphase II of meiosis when ovulated. Fertilization induces the resumption of meiosis, or activates the oocyte, resulting in an oocyte with a single pronucleus and two polar bodies (Fig. 1). Although the downstream events of fertilization have been well characterized, there is still debate as to what triggers activation. The two competing theories are: (i) that sperm binding to the plasma membrane triggers oocyte activation; and (ii) that a factor is deposited into the cytoplasm of the oocyte at sperm–oocyte fusion and that this factor triggers oocyte activation. Proponents of either of these theories admit that complete oocyte activation may be triggered by a combination of these events. A complete understanding of the process of fertilization is needed because failure of adequate fertilization would be disastrous for the reproductive process. In addition, many oocyte- or embryo-related technologies rely on adequate activation of the oocyte. These technologies include *in vitro* fertilization (IVF), intracytoplasmic sperm injection (ICSI) and nuclear transfer. Many reviews have been written on the mechanisms of oocyte activation in other species such as mice and sea urchins (Swann and Lai, 1997; Macháty and Prather, 1998; Macháty *et al.*, 1999a: Parrington, 2001); thus, the focus of the present review will be on pig oocytes.

Email: PratherR@Missouri.Edu.

R. S. Prather

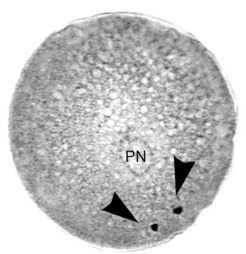

Fig. 1. Parthenogenetically activated pig oocyte. This oocyte has a single pronucleus (PN) and two polar bodies (arrowheads). Photo courtesy of L. Lai.

Activation by fertilization

As stated above, one of the hallmarks of fertilization is the release of intracellular Ca^{2+}. A series of Ca^{2+} bursts or oscillations generally follows this first Ca^{2+} transient and continues until the time the pronuclei form. The amplitude and frequency of the Ca^{2+} bursts are generally consistent within an oocyte, but do vary between oocytes. Although the Ca^{2+} transients are the main feature of fertilization, there are many other cellular and subcellular events that participate in this process. Some of the following features are species-specific; however, for context they will all be presented with a later focus on pigs.

The events of activation have been broken down into two classes: early and late events. Early events include: a sodium influx (Dale *et al.*, 1978), hyperpolarization of the membrane (Miyazaki and Igusa, 1982) and Ca^{2+} entry through voltage-gated Ca^{2+} channels (Chambers, 1989), followed by an explosive release of Ca^{2+} starting at the point of sperm–oocyte fusion. These Ca^{2+} releases may be mediated by inositol triphosphate or ryanodine receptors on the endoplasmic reticulum. The first burst of Ca^{2+} also causes exocytosis of the cortical granules. It is thought that the contents of the cortical granules modify the zona pellucida such that additional spermatozoa cannot bind to or penetrate the zona pellucida. In mammals, there are a series of intracellular free Ca^{2+} oscillations after fertilization. The oscillations are coupled with a Ca^{2+} influx and, in pigs, this influx may be mediated by a *trp* gene homologue (Macháty *et al.*, this supplement). Late events include an increase in intracellular pH, polyadenylation and translation of pre-existing mRNAs, resulting in an increase in protein synthesis as well as a change in the quality of the proteins in the oocyte, a decrease in the activity of maturation-promoting factor (MPF), cytostatic factor, mitogen-activated protein kinase (MAPK), myosin light chain kinase (MLCK) and glutathione concentration. If these early and late events occur, then the oocyte will develop pronuclei and begin the developmental programme.

Parthenogenetic activation

As stated earlier, many manipulations performed on oocytes bypass the normal fertilization process. The two most prominent procedures include ICSI and nuclear transfer. Thus, it is imperative that we understand the normal responses to fertilization so that we can attempt to mimic them and activate the oocytes parthenogenetically for ICSI and nuclear transfer. The Ca^{2+}-dependent and -independent methods of parthenogenetic activation, combination treatments, as well as specific applications to ICSI and nuclear transfer, will be discussed.

Calcium-dependent activation

Early studies in mouse oocytes showed that stimulating protein kinase C with phorbol esters induced a series of Ca^{2+} oscillations, and that this was followed by pronuclear formation and, in some cases, limited development. There are numerous ways to induce an intracellular Ca^{2+} transient in pig oocytes, including injection of Ca^{2+} (Macháty *et al.*, 1996), electrically porating the plasma membrane in the presence of extracellular Ca^{2+} (Prather *et al.*, 1989; Sun *et al.*, 1992), treatment with ionophores (Wang *et al.*, 1998a,b, 1999), thimerosal (Macháty *et al.*, 1997a) or ethanol (Didion *et al.*, 1990), stimulation of guanine nucleotide binding proteins (Macháty *et al.*, 1997b) and injection of inositol triphosphate, cyclic-ADPribose (Macháty *et al.*, 1997c) or a crude sperm extract (Macháty *et al.*, 2000). Each of these treatments attacks a different pathway or point on a pathway that results in a Ca^{2+} transient.

These observations illustrate why the data on what activates an oocyte at fertilization are so difficult to interpret: many different pathways have the capacity to activate the egg (even nitric oxide has been implicated; Kuo *et al.*, 2000). This is further illustrated by studies in which the mRNA encoding the muscarinic M1 receptor was injected into the cytoplasm of unfertilized oocytes (Macháty *et al.*, 1997b; Kim *et al.*, 1998). After time for translation and insertion into the plasma membrane, the oocytes were treated with acetylcholine. Acetylcholine activated the guanine protein-coupled receptor, which probably activated phospholipase C. Phospholipase C then probably acted on phosphatidyl inositol bisphosphate to yield inositol triphosphate and diacylglycerol. The inositol triphosphate bound to inositol triphosphate receptors located on the endoplasmic reticulum and released Ca^{2+} into the cytoplasm. This Ca^{2+} release caused release of the cortical granules into the extracellular space, a decrease in histone H1 kinase activity, a shift in protein profiles consistent with fertilization and pronuclear formation (Macháty *et al.*, 1997b; Kim *et al.*, 1998). Furthermore, oocytes activated in this manner could develop to the blastocyst stage and these blastocysts had nucleoli and mitochondria that had morphologies consistent with normal blastocyst stage embryos (Kim *et al.*, 1998).

Although a simple electrical pulse in the presence of Ca^{2+} will generally induce an oocyte to begin the developmental process, the pattern of events associated with normal fertilization is not always followed. Normally, histone H1 kinase activity decreases after fertilization and stays low until the first cleavage; however, with electrical activation H1 kinase activity initially decreases, but increases later in the first cell cycle (Leal and Liu, 1998). Although a single electrical pulse provides a single Ca^{2+} transient that is sufficient to induce development to the blastocyst stage, it is thought that the quality (amplitude and frequency) of the Ca^{2+} transient or transients is very important and may determine the degree of development after stimulation (Ozil, 1990).

As stated earlier, there is an increase in intracellular pH at fertilization in many lower species such as the sea urchin. However, this has not been demonstrated at fertilization in mammals. Recently, Ruddock *et al.* (2000a) observed an increase in intracellular pH when pig oocytes were treated with 7% (v/v) ethanol or A23187 and there appears to be more than one mechanism regulating the change in pH. Similar observations were made in murine and bovine oocytes (Ruddock *et al.*, 2000b). However, the increase in intracellular pH in pigs is independent of intracellular Ca^{2+} concentration (Ruddock *et al.*, 2001).

Calcium-independent activation

Although intracellular Ca^{2+} is released at fertilization, this is not a requisite for activation of the oocyte. Indeed, the early studies on treatment with phorbol esters were not consistent with phosphorylation status; cells in metaphase have proteins that are already phosphorylated and need to be dephosphorylated to push the cell into the next interphase (histones, nuclear lamins). Thus, studies that have evaluated treatments that would decrease the phosphorylation status or inhibit phosphorylation would appear to be more relevant. Inhibition of MAPK, MPF and MLCK (Green *et al.*, 1999) has resulted in pronuclear formation of pig oocytes. In contrast, stimulation of protein kinase C (Sun *et al.*, 1997) resulted in cortical granule release, but not pronuclear formation, whereas stimulation of tyrosine kinase activity resulted in both cortical granule release and pronuclear formation (Kim *et al.*, 1999).

In addition to the treatments that inhibit kinase activity, other treatments can result in oocyte activation. One of the more popular techniques is to inhibit protein synthesis. As cyclin B is being made continually and this manufacture is necessary for maintaining high concentrations of MPF, inhibiting the production of cyclin B will cause MPF activity to decrease. This lower MPF activity results in the resumption of meiosis by the oocyte and formation of a pronucleus. This response may be species-specific as Nussbaum and Prather (1995) found that cycloheximide treatment alone did not result in activation, but when used in combination with an electrical pulse, it enhanced the rates of pig oocyte development; in other species, activation can be induced with the cycloheximide treatment only (Macháty and Prather, 1998).

In relation to altering MPF activity, the cyclin-dependent kinase inhibitor butyrolactone I can result in cleavage rates of 40%. However, when combined with an electrical pulse, butyrolactone I can result in 59% of the treated oocytes progressing to the blastocyst stage (Dinnyes *et al.*, 1999).

Combination treatments

As stated above, attacking more than one point on the pathway can result in improved rates of pronuclear formation, as well as improved rates of development. A combination of an electrical pulse and cycloheximide is superior to either treatment alone in promoting pronuclear formation (Nussbaum and Prather, 1995). Similarly, Grocholova *et al.* (1997) used a combination of A23187 and cycloheximide to improve development of parthenogenetic oocytes. For the thimerosal treatment to result in pronuclear formation the action on the sulphydryl groups must be reversed or the spindle will be damaged irreversibly. To facilitate that reversal, thimerosal followed by dithiothreitol treatment results in Ca^{2+} release and 42% of oocytes developing to the compact morula or blastocyst stage (Macháty *et al.*, 1997b). Thimerosal causes Ca^{2+} oscillations and no development if not reversed with dithiothreitol (Macháty *et al.*, 1999b).

Another treatment that is often used when development of parthenogenotes is desired is cytochalasin B. It is not known whether cytochalasin B affects any of the Ca^{2+} pathways, but it does depolymerize microfilaments and, thus, prevents polar body emission. Retaining the second polar body should result in a doubling of the number of chromosomes in the developing embryo. Cha *et al.* (1997) increased the percentage of 2n chromosome spreads by treating the activated oocytes with cytochalasin B. Jolliff and Prather (1997) used electrical activation followed by cytochalasin B and obtained fairly normal *in vivo* development to day 12. Kure-bayashi *et al.* (2000) found that development could proceed to day 29 *in vivo*. The lack of further development is probably a result of genomic imprinting (Reik and Walter, 2001).

Although some of these treatments result in cortical granule release they do not prevent subsequent fertilization (Wang *et al.*, 1997, 1998a,b). Thus, there is much to learn about the zona pellucida and methods of inducing hardening.

In conclusion, the most widely used method of activation for nuclear transfer is electrical activation (Prather *et al.*, 1989). Variations to a single pulse of electricity have been added to improve the rates of development (Liu and Moor, 1997).

Activation for ICSI or nuclear transfer

A variety of different activation parameters has been used for ICSI and nuclear transfer. In some cases the injection procedure for ICSI activates the oocyte. Martin (2000) produced an ICSI-derived piglet without any activation stimuli to the *in vivo*-matured oocytes other than injection of a fresh spermatozoon. In contrast, Kolbe and Holtz (2000) used Ca^{2+} ionophore to activate *in vivo*-matured ICSI oocytes. Lai *et al.* (in press) obtained a piglet when electrical activation was applied after injection of the spermatozoon; the oocytes did not develop as well without the electrical application.

Oocytes must be enucleated for nuclear transfer. One of the common chemicals used in the enucleation is bisbenzimide. Unfortunately, exposure to this compound has deleterious effects on the development of pig oocytes to the blastocyst stage (Tao *et al.*, 2000). Thus, compounds used for enucleation might limit development of nuclear transfer and parthenogenetic embryos.

In many cases there is a benefit to fusing the donor cell to the recipient oocyte or microinjecting the nucleus into the oocyte, before the oocyte is actually activated. Miyoshi *et al.* (2000a) found that a delay of 3 h between fusion and activation improved the rate of blastocyst formation. Tao *et al.* (1999a) used microinjection to transfer the nuclei and attempted to delay the activation up to 4 h after the microinjection while using a Ca^{2+}-free medium. The Ca^{2+}-free condition was detrimental to development. The rates of development to the blastocyst stage after nuclear transfer have been as low as 3% (Miyoshi *et al.*, 2000b). When presumptive G0 fibroblast cells were transferred to oocytes and electrically activated, only 7% formed blastocysts (Tao *et al.*, 1999b). Betthauser *et al.* (2000) reported 4–8% blastocysts resulting from nuclear transfers that were activated by ionophore followed by 6-dimethylaminopurine. Recently, Kühholzer *et al.* (2001) reported almost 20% blastocysts from electrically activated oocytes. In addition, oocytes from sows resulted in higher rates of development to the blastocyst stage compared with oocytes from gilts. Polejaeva *et al.* (2000) used natural fertilization to achieve normal activation. Nuclear transfer was generally performed as described above with electrical activation. However, the nuclei were transferred to enucleated fertilized oocytes after electrical activation. Thus, the nuclei were transferred to sperm-activated oocytes, which resulted in a number of live born piglets. Onishi *et al.* (2000) produced live pigs by electrical activation and microinjection of oocytes, but did not report on development to the blastocyst stage. Park *et al.* (in press) produced 9–16% blastocysts with two electrical pulses to fuse and activate the oocytes, resulting in five nuclear transfer-derived piglets.

Conclusion

In conclusion, there are a number of methods that can be used to activate pig oocytes artificially. These methods often attack different pathways that lead to parthenogenesis (Fig. 2). These include Ca^{2+}-dependent and -independent processes. As there are so many pathways in oocytes that can be stimulated to trigger the resumption of meiosis, it might be concluded that

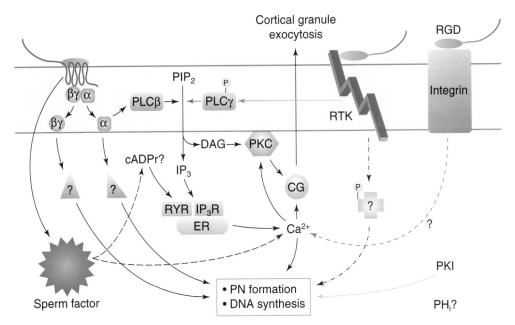

Fig. 2. Summary of pathways that may be activated at fertilization or parthenogenesis. Description of the pathways is included throughout the text. PIP_2: phosphatidyl inositol bisphosphate; DAG: diacylglycerol; cADPr: cyclic ADP ribose; IP_3: inositol trisphosphate; RYR: ryanodine receptor; IP_3R: inositol trisphosphate receptor; PN: pronuclear; PKC: protein kinase C; ER: endoplasmic reticulum; CG: cortical granule; RTK: receptor tyrosine kinase; PLC: phospholipase C; α, β, γ: α, β, γ subunits of a G-protein coupled receptor; p: phosphorylation; PKI: protein kinase inhibitor; RGD: arginine-glycine-aspartic acid peptide.

the oocyte is poised to progress to interphase. Upsetting this apparently delicate balance required for maintenance of the oocyte in metaphase can be accomplished via a variety of methods. Generally, if more than one pathway that results in activation is attacked, greater rates of development to the blastocyst stage can be obtained. Further advancements in the understanding of the basic mechanisms of fertilization will aid in designing strategies to artificially activate pig oocytes for ICSI and nuclear transfer.

References

Betthauser J, Forsberg E, Augenstein M et al. (2000) Production of cloned pigs from *in vitro* systems *Nature Biotechnology* **18** 1055–1059

Cha KS, Kim NH, Lee SM, Baik CS, Lee HT and Chung KS (1997) Effect of cytochalasin B and cycloheximide on the activation rate, chromosome constituent and *in vitro* development of porcine oocytes following parthenogenetic stimulation *Reproduction, Fertility and Development* **9** 441–446

Chambers EL (1989) Fertilization in voltage-clamped sea urchin eggs. In *Mechanisms of Egg Activation* pp 1–18 Eds R Nuccitelli, GN Cherr and WH Clark. Plenum Press, New York

Dale B, DeFelice LJ and Taglieti V (1978) Membrane noise and conductance increase during single spermatozoon–egg interactions *Nature* **275** 217–219

Didion BA, Martin MJ and Markert CL (1990)

Parthenogenetic activation of mouse and pig oocytes matured *in vitro*. *Theriogenology* **33** 1165–1175

Dinnyes A, Hirao Y and Nagai T (1999) Parthenogenetic activation of porcine oocytes by electric pulse and/or butyrolactone I treatment *Cloning* **1** 209–216

Green KM, Kim JH, Wang WH, Day BN and Prather RS (1999) Effect of myosin light chain kinase, protein kinase A, and protein kinase C inhibition of porcine oocyte activation *Biology of Reproduction* **61** 111–119

Grocholova R, Petr J, Rozinek J and Jilek F (1997) The protein phosphatase inhibitor okadaic acid inhibits exit from metaphase II in parthenogenetically activated pig oocytes *Journal of Experimental Zoology* **277** 49–56

Jolliff WJ and Prather RS (1997) Parthenogenic development of *in vitro*-matured, *in vivo*-cultured porcine oocytes beyond blastocyst *Biology of Reproduction* **56** 544–548

Kim JH, Machatý Z, Cabot RA, Han YM, Do HJ and Prather RS (1998) Development of pig oocytes activated by stimulation of an exogenous G protein–coupled receptor *Biology of Reproduction* **59** 655–660

Kim JH, Do HJ, Wang WH, Machatý Z, Han YM, Day BN and Prather RS (1999) A protein tyrosine phosphatase inhibitor, sodium orthovanadate, causes parthenogenetic activation of pig oocytes via an increase in protein tyrosine kinase activity *Biology of Reproduction* **61** 900–905

Kolbe T and Holtz W (2000) Birth of a piglet derived from an oocyte fertilized by intracytoplasmic sperm injection (ICSI) *Animal Reproduction Science* **64** 97–102

Kühholzer B, Hawley RJ, Lai L, Kolber-Simonds D and Prather RS (2001) Clonal lines of transgenic fibroblast cells derived from the same fetus result in different development when used for nuclear transfer in pigs *Biology of Reproduction* **64** 1695–1698

Kuo RC, Baxter GT, Thompson SH, Strickers SA, Patton C, Bonaventura J and Epel D (2000) NO is necessary and sufficient for egg activation at fertilization *Nature* **406** 633–636

Kure-bayashi S, Miyake M, Okada K and Kato S (2000) Successful implantation of *in vitro*-matured, electroactivated oocytes in the pig *Theriogenology* **53** 1105–1119

Lai L, Sun Q, Wu G, Murphy CN, Kühholzer B, Park KW, Bonk AJ, Day BN and Prather RS Development of porcine embryos and offspring after ICSI with liposome transfected or non-transfected sperm into *in vitro* matured oocytes *Zygote* (in press)

Leal CL and Liu L (1998) Differential effects of kinase inhibitor and electrical stimulus on activation and histone H1 kinase activity in pig oocytes *Animal Reproduction Science* **52** 51–61

Liu L and Moor RM (1997) Factors affecting electrical activation of porcine oocytes matured *in vitro*. *Animal Reproduction Science* **48** 67–80

Machatý Z and Prather RS (1998) Strategies for activating nuclear transfer oocytes *Reproduction, Fertility and Development* **10** 599–613

Machatý Z, Funahashi H, Mayes MA, Day BN and Prather RS (1996) Effects of injecting calcium chloride into *in vitro*-matured porcine oocytes *Biology of Reproduction* **54** 316–322

Machatý Z, Wang WH, Day BN and Prather RS (1997a) Complete activation of porcine oocytes induced by the sulfhydryl reagent, thimerosal *Biology of Reproduction* **57** 1123–1127

Machatý Z, Mayes MA, Kovacs LG, Balatti PA, Kim JH and Prather RS (1997b) Activation of porcine oocytes via an exogenously introduced rat muscarinic M1 receptor *Biology of Reproduction* **57** 85–91

Machatý Z, Funahashi H, Day BN and Prather RS (1997c) Developmental changes in the intracellular calcium release mechanisms in porcine oocytes *Biology of Reproduction* **56** 921–930

Machatý Z, Rickords LF and Prather RS (1999a) Parthenogenetic activation of porcine oocytes after nuclear transfer *Cloning* **1** 101–109

Machatý Z, Wang WH, Day BN and Prather RS (1999b)

Calcium release and subsequent development induced by modification of sulfhydryl groups in porcine oocytes *Biology of Reproduction* **60** 1384–1391

Machatý Z, Bonk AJ, Kühholzer B and Prather RS (2000) Porcine oocyte activation induced by a cytosolic sperm factor *Molecular Reproduction and Development* **57** 290–295

Martin MJ (2000) Development of *in vivo*-matured porcine oocytes following intracytoplasmic sperm injection *Biology of Reproduction* **63** 109–112

Miyazaki S and Igusa Y (1982) Ca-mediated activation of a K current at fertilization of golden hamster eggs *Proceedings National Academy of Sciences USA* **79** 931–935

Miyoshi K, Saeki K and Sato E (2000a) Improvement in development of porcine embryos reconstituted with cells from blastocyst-derived cell lines and enucleated oocytes by optimization of reconstruction methods *Cloning* **2** 175–184

Miyoshi K, Taguchi Y, Sendai Y, Hoshi H and Sato E (2000b) Establishment of a porcine cell line from *in vitro*-produced blastocysts and transfer of the cells into enucleated oocytes *Biology of Reproduction* **62** 1640–1646

Nussbaum DJ and Prather RS (1995) Differential effects of protein synthesis inhibitors on porcine oocyte activation *Molecular Reproduction and Development* **41** 70–75

Onishi A, Iwamoto M, Akita T, Mikawa S, Takeda K, Awata T, Hanada H and Perry AC (2000) Pig cloning by microinjection of fetal fibroblast nuclei *Science* **289** 1188–1190

Ozil JP (1990) The parthenogenetic development of rabbit oocytes after repetitive pulsatile electrical stimulation *Development* **109** 117–127

Park K-W, Cheong H-T, Lai L *et al.* (2001) Production of nuclear transfer-derived swine that express the enhanced green fluorescent protein *Animal Biotechnology* (in press)

Parrington J (2001) Does a soluble sperm factor trigger calcium release in the egg at fertilization? *Journal of Andrology* **22** 1–11

Polejaeva IA, Chen SH, Vaught TD *et al.* (2000) Cloned pigs produced by nuclear transfer from adult somatic cells *Nature* **407** 29–30

Prather RS, Simms MM and First NL (1989) Nuclear transplantation in early pig embryos *Biology of Reproduction* **41** 414–418

Reik W and Walter J (2001) Genomic imprinting: parental influence on the genome *Nature Genetics* **2** 21–32

Ruddock NT, Machatý Z, Milanick M and Prather RS (2000a) Mechanism of intracellular pH increase during parthenogenetic activation of *in vitro* matured porcine oocytes *Biology of Reproduction* **63** 488–492

Ruddock NT, Machatý Z and Prather RS (2000b) Intracellular pH increases accompany parthenogenetic activation of porcine, bovine and murine oocytes *Reproduction, Fertility and Development* **12** 201–207

Ruddock NT, Machatý Z, Cabot R and Prather RS (2001) Porcine oocyte activation: the differing roles of calcium and pH *Molecular Reproduction and Development* **59** 227–234

Sun FZ, Hoyland J, Huang X, Mason W and Moor RM

(1992) A comparison of intracellular changes in porcine eggs after fertilization and electroactivation *Development* **115** 947–956

Sun QY, Wang WH, Hosoe M, Taniguchi T, Chen DY, Shioya Y (1997) Activation of protein kinase C induces cortical granule exocytosis in a calcium-independent manner, but not resumption of cell cycle in porcine oocytes *Development, Growth and Differentiation* **39** 523–529

Swann K and Lai FA (1997) A novel signaling mechanism for generating Ca^{2+} oscillations at fertilization in mammals *Bioessays* **19** 371–378

Tao T, Macháty Z, Boquest AC, Day BN and Prather RS (1999a) Development of pig embryos reconstructed by microinjection of cultured fetal fibroblast cells into *in vitro* matured oocytes *Animal Reproduction Science* **56** 133–141

Tao T, Boquest AC, Macháty Z, Petersen AL, Day BN and Prather RS (1999b) Development of pig embryos by nuclear transfer of cultured fibroblast cells *Cloning* **1** 55–62

Tao T, Macháty Z, Abeydeera LR, Day BN and Prather RS (2000) Optimisation of porcine oocyte activation following nuclear transfer *Zygote* **8** 69–77

Wang WH, Sun QY, Hosoe M, Shioya Y and Day BN (1997) Quantified analysis of cortical granule distribution and exocytosis of porcine oocytes during meiotic maturation and activation *Biology of Reproduction* **56** 1376–1382

Wang WH, Abeydeera LR, Prather RS and Day BN (1998a) Functional analysis of activation of porcine oocytes by spermatozoa, calcium ionophore and electric pulse *Molecular Reproduction and Development* **51** 346–353

Wang WH, Macháty Z, Abeydeera LR, Prather RS and Day BN (1998b) Parthenogenetic activation of pig oocytes with calcium ionophore and the block to sperm penetration after activation *Biology of Reproduction* **58** 1357–1366

Wang WH, Macháty Z, Ruddock N, Abeydeera LR, Boquest AC, Prather RS and Day BN (1999) Activation of porcine oocytes with calcium ionophore: effects of extracellular calcium *Molecular Reproduction and Development* **53** 99–107

Reproduction Supplement 58, 113–127

Phagocytosis of boar spermatozoa *in vitro* and *in vivo*

H. Woelders and A. Matthijs

Institute for Animal Science and Health (ID-Lelystad), PO Box 65, 8200 AB Lelystad, The Netherlands

For successful conception, fertilization-competent spermatozoa must be present at the site of fertilization in adequate numbers until ovulation has taken place. In pigs, a large volume of semen is delivered into the uterus. Most, if not all, of the inseminated liquid is voided from the vulva within a few hours after insemination and approximately 45% of the spermatozoa are lost. Large numbers of spermatozoa are also lost due to phagocytosis by polymorphonuclear leukocytes (PMNs). In pigs, the recruitment of PMNs to the uterine lumen appears to be triggered by insemination of a volume of liquid, rather than by specific components of that liquid or by spermatozoa or seminal plasma. However, persistence of large numbers of PMNs in the uterine lumen at > 12 h after insemination appears to depend on the presence of spermatozoa in the inseminate. *In vitro* studies have indicated that damaged, killed or capacitated spermatozoa are not phagocytosed preferentially, but that capacitation treatment strongly reduced phagocytosis of spermatozoa. Recent studies have also shown that PMN recruitment and phagocytosis of spermatozoa *in vivo* can be reduced by addition of caffeine plus $CaCl_2$ to the inseminate, which appeared to have positive consequences for the longer term availability of spermatozoa at the site of fertilization.

Introduction

The purpose of insemination is to establish and maintain an adequate population of spermatozoa at the site of fertilization until ovulation has taken place. The number of spermatozoa used for artificial insemination (AI) of pigs is typically $2.5–3.0 \times 10^9$. There is interest in the pig AI industry to reduce the sperm dosage, but it is feared that this might be at the expense of fertilization, especially when sows ovulate a long time after insemination. The duration of the period between insemination and ovulation can be quite long, as the time of ovulation relative to the onset of oestrous behaviour cannot be predicted exactly and varies greatly among sows (Soede *et al.*, 1995). Studies have shown that at the sperm dosage used at present, the results of fertilization are good when ovulation takes place within 24 h after insemination. When ovulation takes place > 24 h after insemination, the farrowing rate decreases appreciably (Soede *et al.*, 1995). This effect was not prevented by using a sperm dosage as high as 6×10^9 spermatozoa per insemination (Steverink *et al.*, 1997). It is important to understand the dynamics in the sperm populations in the genital tract after

Email: h.woelders@id.wag-ur.nl

insemination to optimize the number of inseminations per oestrus and the sperm dosage per insemination.

The dynamics of sperm populations in the uterus and oviducts of pigs have been investigated extensively. One of the striking features is the rapid decrease in the number of spermatozoa in the genital tract after insemination (du Mesnil du Buisson and Dauzier, 1955a; First *et al.*, 1968; Pursel *et al.*, 1978). The large volume of the ejaculate and the large number of spermatozoa inundate the length of the uterine horns with semen to enable a build-up of adequate sperm populations in the uterotubal junctions and oviducts. However, the uterine horns must be cleared for the receipt of the embryos, which may arrive as early as 48 h after ovulation. A number of recent studies have contributed to our understanding of the involvement of polymorphonuclear leukocytes (PMNs) in the clearance of spermatozoa from the uterus of sows. These studies have dealt with subjects including mechanisms of recruitment of PMNs to the uterine lumen, mechanisms of attachment of spermatozoa to PMNs and the possibility of modulating the phagocytosis of boar spermatozoa *in vitro* and *in vivo*, which is discussed in this review.

Sperm transport

Cervix and uterus

In natural mating and artificial insemination of pigs the semen is deposited in the cervix, corpus uteri and uterine horns (Burger, 1952; du Mesnil du Buisson and Dauzier, 1955b). Pressure exerted during insemination as well as contractions of the uterine horns facilitate the flow of the semen into and through the length of the horns (Burger, 1952; Baker and Degen, 1972). Some of the semen may be lost by backflow during insemination. Loss of semen during artificial insemination can be minimized by using an inseminate volume of 100 ml rather than 200 ml (Baker *et al.*, 1968). However, these authors suggested that an inseminate volume of 20 ml may be too small for optimal transport of spermatozoa to the tip of the uterine horn. The large volume of the ejaculate of boars ensures that spermatozoa are washed into the horns; indeed, the entire length of the uterine horns is inundated with semen (Burger, 1952).

No significant amount of bulk fluid can be recovered when the uterine horns are inspected a few hours after insemination (du Mesnil du Buisson and Dauzier, 1955a; Hunter, 1981). Originally, it was believed that much or all of the liquid introduced into the uterus is resorbed by the genital tract (du Mesnil du Buisson and Dauzier, 1955a; First *et al.*, 1968; Engelhardt *et al.*, 1997). However, Blandau and Gaddum-Rosse (1974) stated that most of the semen is discharged through the vulva within 2 h after mating. Viring and Einarsson (1981) collected the backflow using colostomy bags attached around the vulva and found that the backflow of semen during the first few hours after insemination can be quite large. More recent studies have shown that the cumulative volume of backflow is equal to the inseminate volume on average (Kamerman, 1994; Steverink *et al.*, 1998; Matthijs *et al.*, 2000a). This finding indicates that none or very little of the inseminated liquid is resorbed by the uterus. It could be argued that the resorption of liquid by epithelia depends on the availability of the appropriate salts. The extender Beltsville thawing solution (BTS; Johnson *et al.*, 1988), which we have used in our studies, contains glucose as its primary osmotic support. However, comparable volumes of backflow were recovered after insemination with either BTS, Tyrode's *in vitro* fertilization (IVF) medium, phosphate buffered saline (PBS) or human infant oral rehydration solution (A. Matthijs, unpublished); the same appears to be true for seminal plasma after natural mating (Viring and Einarsson, 1981).

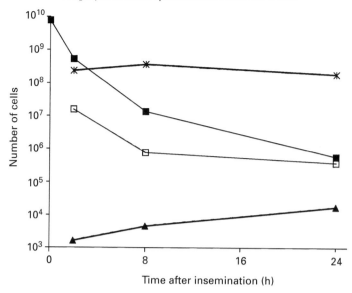

Fig. 1. Number of spermatozoa in uterus (■), uterotubal junction (□) and oviducts (▲), and number of polymorphonuclear leukocytes in the uterus (*), from 0 h to 24 h after insemination of gilts. Note logarithmic scale on *y* axis. Data from Pursel *et al.* (1978).

Although almost the entire volume of inseminate is lost by backflow, it is obvious that not all of the spermatozoa are lost with it. Apparently, many spermatozoa are able to move from the bulk liquid into the mucus lining the epithelium and are retained. Viring and Einarsson (1981) estimated that approximately one-third of the inseminated spermatozoa is lost by backflow of semen after natural mating. After artificial insemination with an inseminate volume of 80 ml, up to 45% of the inseminated spermatozoa are lost within 4 h after insemination (Kamerman, 1994; Steverink *et al.*, 1998; Matthijs *et al.*, 2000a).

The number of spermatozoa in the uterus decreases markedly within a few hours after insemination (du Mesnil du Buisson and Dauzier, 1955a; First *et al.*, 1968; Pursel *et al.*, 1978) (Fig. 1). Initially, the backflow of semen plays a major role in this reduction. Phagocytosis of spermatozoa by PMNs is another important mechanism. Although First *et al.* (1968) did not observe phagocytosis of spermatozoa before 8 h after insemination, there is increasing evidence that phagocytosis of spermatozoa starts soon after insemination and that it is the major mechanism of clearance of spermatozoa from the genital tract (Lovell and Getty, 1968; Pursel *et al.*, 1978; Rozeboom *et al.*, 1998, 1999; Matthijs *et al.*, 2000a).

The oviducts

Spermatozoa appear in the oviducts as early as 5–15 min after insemination (Burger, 1952; Baker and Degen, 1972). Dead spermatozoa are also transported to the oviducts, but less efficiently than are live spermatozoa (First *et al.*, 1968; Baker and Degen, 1972; Viring, 1980). Radioactive molecules of different sizes, including macromolecules, that were added to the inseminate were traced in the oviducts of sows killed at 1 h after insemination (Einarsson *et al.*, 1980; Viring *et al.*, 1980). By interrupting sperm transport to the isthmus at different times after mating, Hunter (1981) demonstrated that early transport of spermatozoa to the isthmus within the first 30 min after mating is rapid enough to allow fertilization of oocytes. The number of spermatozoa available in the isthmus continued to increase after that time, as after the first 30 min, the number of accessory spermatozoa on the oocytes increased when sperm transport was allowed to continue for longer. Moreover, a prolonged build-up of the isthmus population of spermatozoa for at least 60 min was required to provide a sperm population that could be maintained at a sufficient level for > 24 h in gilts that were inseminated 1 day too early. The sperm population in the oviducts is maintained and increased by ongoing sperm migration from the uterine horns and uterotubal junction during the first 24 h after insemination (Rigby, 1966; Pursel et al., 1978). Baker and Degen (1972) stated that the uterus continues to supply spermatozoa to the oviducts, while at the same time spermatozoa are lost from the oviducts through the infundibulum to the peritoneal cavity. In other studies, the net size of the oviductal sperm population decreases from 2 h after insemination onwards, parallel with a rapid decrease in the number of spermatozoa in the uterus and uterotubal junction (Viring, 1980; Viring and Einarsson, 1981), or stays approximately constant over the first 24 h after insemination (First et al., 1968).

Blandau and Gaddum-Rosse (1974) reported that boluses of liquid are moved up the isthmus towards the isthmic–ampullar junction by continuous antiperistaltic contractions in the oviducts. Comparable waves in the ampulla carry the liquid up to the infundibulum. In addition, an upward directed ciliary beat contributes to the upward transport in the oviducts (Gaddum-Rosse and Blandau, 1973). These mechanisms probably contribute to the upward movement of spermatozoa in the isthmus towards the site of fertilization and, ultimately, towards the peritoneal cavity (Baker and Degen, 1972; Blandau and Gaddum-Rosse, 1974). Indeed, spermatozoa are found in all segments of the oviducts (du Mesnil du Buisson and Dauzier, 1955a; Viring, 1980; Viring and Einarsson, 1980, 1981). Hunter (1984) showed that shortly after insemination the number of spermatozoa present in the proximal part of the isthmus was high enough to support fertilization. However, when continuation of the supply of spermatozoa from the lower isthmus was obstructed by ligation, the population of spermatozoa in the proximal isthmus appeared to be depleted within several hours, as it could no longer support fertilization of oocytes a few hours after ligation. This finding indicates that either the higher isthmus sperm population is relatively small or that the spermatozoa are moved away by the upward transport relatively fast, such that this population is depleted quite rapidly when supply from the lower isthmus is obstructed. Indeed, most studies have indicated that more spermatozoa are found in the isthmus than in the ampulla and that more spermatozoa are found in the distal part of the isthmus, which is closest to the uterotubal junction, than in the proximal part of the isthmus (du Mesnil du Buisson and Dauzier, 1955a; Viring, 1980; Viring and Einarsson, 1980, 1981). Thus, it appears that spermatozoa are retarded in the distal isthmus such that a relatively large population of spermatozoa builds up and is maintained for a considerable time, while feeding a smaller sperm population in the higher isthmus, as spermatozoa are gradually moved upwards and are ultimately lost in the peritoneal cavity. The mechanisms of retardation are assumed to comprise physical obstruction (retained in crypts and crevices), binding to epithelium or suppression of motility by other mechanisms (Katz et al., 1989; Hunter, 1990; Suarez et al., 1991).

Recruitment of PMNs

Insemination of pigs triggers a massive influx of PMNs into the lumen of the uterus (Lovell and Getty, 1968; Pursel et al., 1978; Rozeboom et al., 1998, 1999; Matthijs et al., 2000a). Negligible numbers of PMNs are found in the lumen of the genital tract in sows in the luteal phase (Matthijs et al., 2000a). Considerable numbers of PMNs can be found in the lumen of uninseminated oestrous sows, but not as many as in inseminated sows (Matthijs et al., 2000a).

Extensive infiltration of PMNs into the basal region of the uterine epithelium of pigs occurs at pro-oestrus (Bischof *et al.*, 1994; Engelhardt *et al.*, 1997), which is probably generated under the direct or indirect control of sex hormones. Some studies have revealed a hormone-controlled synthesis of cytokines, such as the granulocyte–macrophage colony-stimulating factor (GM-CSF) and interleukin 6 (IL-6) in mice (Robertson and Seamark, 1992), and IL-8 in humans (Arici *et al.*, 1998). These cytokines are thought to be involved in the migration of PMNs into the endometrial stroma.

The number of PMNs recruited to the uterine lumen after insemination of sows is quite large. Matthijs *et al.* (2000a) studied the total number of PMNs recruited and the number of phagocytosed and non-phagocytosed spermatozoa. Colostomy bags were attached around the vulva to collect the backflow of semen and all parts of the genital tract were flushed after the sows were killed at 4 h after artificial insemination with 2.4×10^9 spermatozoa. In the inseminated sows, the total number of PMNs was at least nine times higher ($P < 0.01$) than in uninseminated oestrous sows. The total number of PMNs recovered was approximately $3–5 \times 10^9$, which is more than the number of inseminated spermatozoa. At 4 h after insemination, approximately 30 times more PMNs than non-phagocytosed spermatozoa were found in the uterus of sows. The numbers of PMNs found in the uterus were in accordance with those reported by Pursel *et al.* (1978). The number of PMNs reported by Matthijs *et al.* (2000a) was somewhat higher, but these workers used adult multiparous sows compared with nulliparous sows in the study of Pursel *et al.* (1978).

The recruitment of PMNs to the uterine lumen probably starts immediately after insemination. Lovell and Getty (1968) found no PMNs in the luminal contents of pigs at 10 min after mating, but found large numbers (only four times lower than the number of spermatozoa) at only 30 min after mating. Pursel *et al.* (1978) reported large numbers of PMNs in the uterine lumen at 2 h after insemination. Moreover, the backflow of semen collected in the first hour after insemination contained large numbers of PMNs (Matthijs *et al.*, 2000a).

In sows evaluated at 4 h after insemination, it was clear that the recruitment of PMNs was triggered by the intromission of liquid into the uterus, rather than by the presence of spermatozoa or seminal plasma (Matthijs *et al.*, 2000a). The number of PMNs recruited in sows inseminated with semen extender (BTS) only was not significantly different (in fact tended to be higher) from that in sows inseminated with extended boar semen or seminal plasma in BTS. The number of PMNs recovered from sows inseminated with Tyrode's medium, PBS or 'oral rehydration solution' was similar to the number of PMNs recovered from sows inseminated with BTS. These data demonstrate that it is not an active substance in BTS that is causing the PMN recruitment, but rather the intromission of a volume of liquid. These results are consistent with those of Rozeboom *et al.* (1998, 1999), who found no difference in the numbers of PMNs in uterine lavages collected at 6 h after insemination of gilts with either extended semen, seminal plasma or extender only. The results of Matthijs *et al.* (2000a) (at 4 h after insemination) indicated that seminal plasma may even have a dampening effect, as the inseminates that contained seminal plasma tended to have a lower PMN response than did the inseminates with little or no seminal plasma, although this difference was not significant. Rozeboom *et al.* (1998, 1999) did not find a suppressing effect of seminal plasma at 6 h after insemination, but did detect a significant effect of pure (undiluted) seminal plasma on the persistence of the PMNs in the uterus at 12–24 h after insemination. In contrast to the earlier PMN recruitment, the continuation of PMN recruitment appeared to be triggered specifically by spermatozoa, as Rozeboom *et al.* (1998, 1999) reported that large numbers of PMNs persisted from 12 h to 36 h after insemination only if the inseminate contained spermatozoa. By this time, most of the spermatozoa have already been cleared from the genital tract. Thus, this second wave of PMN recruitment does not have a role in the initial rapid loss of most of the spermatozoa, but may be needed for the final stage of clearing of the uterus in preparation for the arrival of the conceptuses.

Phagocytosis of spermatozoa

PMNs are the main phagocytes involved in the clearance of spermatozoa from the genital tract of pigs. Spermatozoa are found attached to and ingested by PMNs in the uterine lumen, whereas the number of free spermatozoa decreases markedly to just a few per cent of the inseminated number of spermatozoa within only a few hours (Lovell and Getty, 1968; First et al., 1968; Pursel et al., 1978; Viring, 1980; Kamerman, 1994) and reaches as low as 1% at 24 h after insemination (First et al., 1968; Pursel et al., 1978). The clearance of spermatozoa from the uterus after insemination has also been observed in other mammalian species. Uterine clearance is a normal physiological process that serves to prepare the uterus for the reception of the embryos, which may arrive as early as 48 h after ovulation in pigs (Oxenreider and Day, 1965).

Several authors have hypothesized that phagocytosis of spermatozoa may also be a mechanism for the selection of superior spermatozoa (for example see Symons, 1967; Cohen and Tyler, 1980; D'Cruz and Haas, 1995). One reason for this suggestion was the apparent redundancy of spermatozoa in most species. However, in terms of biomass or bioenergy the male ejaculate is not very extravagant (Kemp et al., 1990) and competition between males may have been a selection force to favour increased numbers of spermatozoa, at least in promiscuous species (Birkhead and Møller, 1998). Nevertheless, the large number of spermatozoa per ejaculate prompted the hypothesis that only a very small percentage of the spermatozoa are genetically intact (Cohen, 1973). Selection of human spermatozoa on the basis of their chromosomal defects has been reported (Ibrahim and Pedersen, 1988; Van Dyk et al., 2000). However, this selection is probably caused by selection of spermatozoa on the basis of cellular morphological or functional abnormalities that coincide with genetic defects. Such a coincidence can occur when local, temporal or patient-related conditions in the testes are unfavourable. Moreover, the results of IVF and intracytoplasmic sperm injection (ICSI) indicate that it is unlikely that most spermatozoa are genetically defective.

Another hypothesis is that senescent, dead or prematurely capacitated spermatozoa are ingested preferentially by phagocytes (for example see Symons, 1967; Cohen and Tyler, 1980; D'Cruz and Haas, 1995). However, in a recent study of phagocytosis of boar spermatozoa by PMNs in vitro, it was shown that damaged or dead spermatozoa are not targeted preferentially and that motile, intact spermatozoa were actually phagocytosed faster than were killed spermatozoa (Matthijs et al., 2000b). Moreover, in regular pig AI almost all the spermatozoa of a fresh inseminate are intact, whereas phagocytosis in sows in vivo starts almost immediately after insemination (Lovell and Getty, 1968; Pursel et al., 1978; Rozeboom et al., 1998, 1999; Matthijs et al., 2000a).

It is important to note that clearance of spermatozoa from the genital tract by PMNs is not a specific immune response. The female genital tract is fully capable of generating an immune response to foreign material (Hogarth, 1982). Moreover, spermatozoa are highly antigenic when introduced into the peripheral blood circulation (Hancock, 1981; Hogarth, 1982). However, insemination does not elicit a cell-mediated antibody immune response in healthy females (Hancock, 1981; Hogarth, 1982). It is very important that a classical immune response is prevented, as this would lead to the development of sterilizing anti-sperm immunity, which does occur sometimes as a pathological condition (Hogarth, 1982; Hancock, 1984; Haas and Beer, 1986). PMNs enhance their non-immunological receptors while migrating towards the lumen of the uterus (Targowski and Niemialtowski, 1986). In healthy females, spermatozoa in the female genital tract are not destroyed by the membrane attack complex of the complement system, although complement factors (Bedford and Witkin, 1983; Hasty *et al.*, 1994) and antibodies (Symons and Herbert, 1971; Hussein *et al.*, 1983; Haas and Beer, 1986) are present in the genital tract. Complement and antibody concentrations are low in fertile women and sows (Hussein *et al.*, 1983; Haas and Beer, 1986), although Cohen (1984) reported an increase in antibody concentrations during the massive influx of neutrophils in rabbits after insemination. It has been proposed that the blocking of sperm antigens by the so-called 'natural antibodies' (Hancock, 1981) might help to prevent a classical immune response. Furthermore, it has been reported that seminal plasma can have a suppressive effect on proliferation of lymphocytes (Bouvet *et al.*, 1987; Veselský *et al.*, 1991), antibody response (Dostál *et al.*, 1997), phagocytic activity (Lazarevic *et al.*, 1995) and complement activation (Chowdhury *et al.*, 1996). Moreover, in humans, glycosaminoglycans, such as heparin, which are present in the female genital tract, are also able to inhibit complement activation (Ekre *et al.*, 1992). In pigs, glycosaminoglycans can abolish the toxic effect of intact complement of sow serum on boar spermatozoa *in vitro* (A. Matthijs, unpublished). These mechanisms may help to prevent an immunological reaction of the female and protect the spermatozoa from being destroyed by the membrane attack complex.

In vitro studies: mechanisms of attachment

Opsonin-dependent phagocytosis

The phagocytosis of boar spermatozoa has been studied using an *in vitro* phagocytosis assay (Matthijs *et al.*, 2000b). The phagocytosis of spermatozoa was studied by challenging PMNs isolated from the peripheral blood of sows with boar spermatozoa in a controlled environment. These studies were used to gain insights into the role of opsonins in attachment and phagocytosis of spermatozoa, as well as the phagocytosis of spermatozoa of different health or capacitation status. These studies demonstrated that the presence of serum from sows was essential for phagocytosis of killed spermatozoa and also appeared to stimulate phagocytosis of fresh, intact spermatozoa. In Tyrode's medium containing sow serum with inactivated complement, approximately 70% of the spermatozoa were phagocytosed during 60 min of incubation with PMNs. However, in the absence of serum, the phagocytosis of killed (frozen–thawed) spermatozoa was almost completely absent. Inclusion of serum from other species (cattle and guinea-pigs) produced results comparable to medium without serum (virtual absence of phagocytosis of frozen–thawed spermatozoa). The effect of sow serum was retained, at least in part, after thorough washing of spermatozoa that had been pre-incubated with sow serum. These results demonstrate that species-specific components of sow serum, which are probably antibodies or complement factors, can bind to boar spermatozoa and mediate phagocytosis of spermatozoa by PMNs.

Active complement factors play only a modest role. Phagocytosis of spermatozoa was hardly affected by whether the serum used had been treated to inactivate complement. However, the presence of intact complement rapidly induced cell death and acrosomal vesiculation.

Another class of opsonins could be the so-called 'natural antibodies'. As discussed above, insemination of females does not usually elicit a specific immune response (Hancock, 1981; Hogarth, 1982; Haas and Beer, 1986), such that no specific anti-sperm antibodies are produced. However, antibodies reactive with sperm proteins have been described in blood serum of normal healthy fertile males and females in a number of mammalian species (for example see Symons, 1967; Tung *et al.*, 1976; Hancock, 1979). These antibodies are called

H. Woelders and A. Matthijs

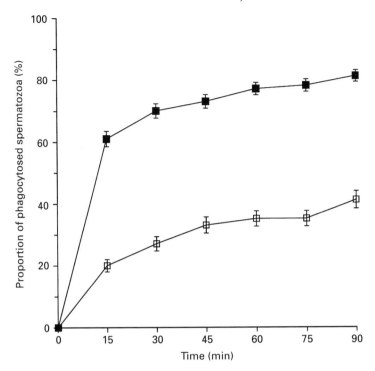

Fig. 2. Effect of *in vitro* capacitation treatment on the phagocytosis of boar spermatozoa by polymorphonuclear leukocytes *in vitro*. Fresh boar semen was obtained from the artificial insemination station at Bunnik, NL. Untreated semen (■) was compared with treated semen (□) (Matthijs *et al.*, 2000b).

'natural antibodies' to indicate that they are present in the blood of all animals, even when the animals have had no contact with the antigen, for example in juveniles.

Opsonin-independent phagocytosis of fresh spermatozoa

In contrast to killed spermatozoa, intact (untreated) spermatozoa were phagocytosed in the absence of serum (Matthijs *et al.*, 2000b). This finding indicates that ligands for PMN attachment are already present on the surface of spermatozoa. A possible mechanism of phagocyte attachment in the absence of added opsonins could be lectin–carbohydrate interactions, as has been described for the serum-independent phagocytosis of bacteria by neutrophils or macrophages (Ofec and Sharon, 1988). The complement receptor Cr3 (CD11b/CD18 β-integrin) on the surface of PMNs can act as a receptor for lectins (Gbarah *et al.*, 1991), as well as for specific carbohydrates (Thornton *et al.*, 1996). Other carbohydrate-recognizing lectin-like molecules have also been described (Weir *et al.*, 1981). There is a high incidence of glycosylated proteins and glycolipids, as well as carbohydrate-binding proteins, on the surface of mammalian spermatozoa (for example see Klint *et al.*, 1987; Macek and Shur, 1988; Dostàlovà *et al.*, 1994; Gadella *et al.*, 1994).

Influence of capacitation treatment

In the *in vitro* model, it was found that treatment of semen to induce capacitation *in vitro* resulted in a substantial reduction of sperm phagocytosis (Fig. 2; Matthijs *et al.*, 2000b). Thus, this treatment appears to induce a decreased number of binding sites for PMN attachment on the sperm surface. *In vitro* capacitation treatment of boar spermatozoa induces a great number of changes on the surface of the sperm membrane (Töpfer-Petersen *et al.*, 1990; Dostàlovà *et al.*, 1994; Gadella *et al.*, 1994; Ashworth *et al.*, 1995).

The conditions necessary for *in vitro* capacitation of boar spermatozoa have been well described (Yanagimachi, 1994; Harrison *et al.*, 1996). *In vivo* the uterine environment provides these conditions. Spermatozoa can be capacitated fully in the uterus without ascending to the oviducts (Imai *et al.*, 1979; Rath, 1992; Yanagimachi, 1994). Therefore, Matthijs *et al.* (2000b) suggested that the reduction of phagocytosis, as observed after *in vitro* capacitation treatment, could also be produced *in vivo* in the uterus. Thus, spermatozoa could acquire protection against phagocytosis while in the uterus, which would increase their chances of reaching the isthmus and taking part in fertilization.

Modulation of phagocytosis and recruitment

As discussed above, the clearance of spermatozoa from the uterus by phagocytosis of spermatozoa is a normal and necessary process. Nevertheless, it is an attractive proposition to inhibit or postpone the phagocytosis to some extent, so that perhaps successful artificial insemination could be achieved with a reduced dose of spermatozoa. For this reason we have been interested in substances that could affect phagocytosis of boar spermatozoa by PMNs.

In vitro *studies*

Several studies have shown that divalent cations such as Ca^{2+} and Mg^{2+} play an important role in the mechanism of adherence and ingestion of particles by PMNs (Cox and Karnovsky, 1973; Carrasco *et al.*, 1997). This is also true for boar spermatozoa; using an *in vitro* model we found complete inhibition of the ingestion of boar spermatozoa by PMNs in the presence of calcium chelator EDTA (data not shown; H. Woelders and A. Matthijs, unpublished).

EDTA inhibits phagocytosis through its effect on the phagocytotic activity of PMNs, whereas other classes of compound reduce the rate of phagocytosis by a direct effect on the spermatozoa. For example, glycosaminoglycans, notably heparin, reduced phagocytosis of boar spermatozoa by PMNs *in vitro* markedly (data not shown). However, the effect of glycosaminoglycans was lost when the cells were washed in a glycosaminoglycan-free medium. Caffeine is also able to reduce sperm phagocytosis by PMNs. In the *in vitro* phagocytosis model, 1 mmol caffeine l^{-1} reduced the rate of phagocytosis of boar spermatozoa (Fig. 3). The effect was observed immediately, but was stronger after the spermatozoa had been pre-incubated at 38°C in BTS in the presence of caffeine for 30 min. The pre-incubation was more effective when $CaCl_2$ was added (Fig. 3). The reduction of phagocytosis is due to an effect on the spermatozoa, rather than on the PMNs, as the reduction was obtained after the spermatozoa had been pre-incubated with caffeine. Treatment of the semen to induce capacitation also causes a strong reduction of phagocytosis *in vitro* (Matthijs *et al.*, 2000b). Caffeine may accelerate some of the changes related to sperm capacitation (Harrison *et al.*, 1993, 1996; Fraser, 1995). However, caffeine alone cannot induce capacitation. Moreover, capacitation cannot proceed in the presence of EDTA without added calcium (Fraser, 1992, 1995; Harkema *et al.*, 1998) and is also inhibited by the presence of seminal plasma (Nagai *et al.*, 1984; Fraser, 1992). The effect of caffeine on phagocytosis of spermatozoa was observed when boar spermatozoa were incubated in normal BTS in the presence of seminal plasma, although the effect of caffeine was more pronounced when $CaCl_2$ was added (Fig. 3). This finding indicates that capacitation is not a necessary

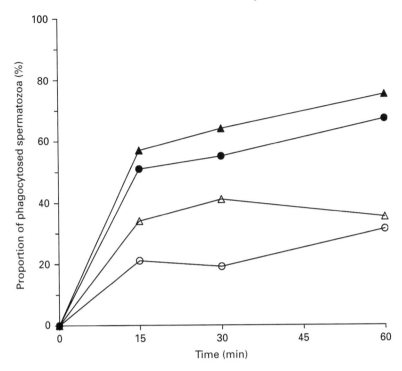

Fig. 3. Effect of pretreatment of boar spermatozoa with caffeine plus CaCl$_2$ on phagocytosis by polymorphonuclear leukocytes (PMNs) *in vitro*. Fresh boar semen was obtained from the artificial insemination station at Bunnik, NL. The spermatozoa were incubated for 30 min at 38°C in regular Beltsville thawing solution (BTS; ▲), or in BTS plus 6 mmol CaCl$_2$ l^{-1} (●), BTS plus 6 mmol CaCl$_2$ plus 1 mmol caffeine l^{-1} (○) or BTS with 1 mmol caffeine l^{-1} (△). The spermatozoa were challenged with PMNs in Tyrode's medium as described by Matthijs *et al.* (2000b).

precondition for the effect of caffeine on phagocytosis. However, it seems likely that there is overlap in the cell biological and biochemical mechanisms that lead to reduction of phagocytosis and capacitation, respectively. Caffeine is a phosphodiesterase inhibitor. Addition of dibutyryl cAMP, a membrane permeable analogue of cAMP, also resulted in a reduction of phagocytosis of boar spermatozoa by PMNs *in vitro* (A. Matthijs, unpublished). Therefore, it is likely that the effect of caffeine is mediated by an increase in the intracellular concentration of cyclic adenosine 3′,5′-monophosphate (cAMP).

In vivo studies: effect on number of spermatozoa and PMN recruitment

The possibility of reducing the phagocytosis of spermatozoa *in vivo* was tested in several insemination experiments. EDTA, which is effective *in vitro*, is a normal component of the boar semen extender BTS. Nevertheless, phagocytosis of spermatozoa appears to start shortly after insemination. This finding indicates that after much of the liquid of the inseminate has been voided, the free calcium concentration in the remaining uterine fluid is increased to concentrations that permit phagocytosis. In an attempt to over-ride this effect, we attempted to inhibit phagocytosis *in vivo* by using a high concentration of EDTA (25 mmol l^{-1}) in adapted BTS extender. At 4 h after insemination the number of non-phagocytosed spermatozoa found in the genital tract was not different from that in sows inseminated with extended semen in normal BTS. As brightly fluorescent spermatozoa (stained with Hoechst 33342) were used, the nuclei of phagocytosed spermatozoa could be recognized inside PMNs unless they were digested completely. In the *in vitro* model, spermatozoa were digested inside the PMNs within 1 h after phagocytosis. In the sows that received an inseminate containing 25 mmol EDTA l^{-1}, the number of non-phagocytosed spermatozoa found in the genital tract at 4 h after insemination was not different from that in the control group. However, the number of spermatozoa that could be recognized inside PMNs was much higher. These results indicate that the onset of phagocytosis was delayed initially by the extra EDTA, but that, once started, the rate of phagocytosis in the EDTA group was higher than that in the control group.

In the same experiment, a group of sows was included that were inseminated with inseminates containing caffeine plus $CaCl_2$ (Woelders *et al.*, 2000). In the caffeine plus $CaCl_2$ group, the number of non-phagocytosed spermatozoa present in the uterus at 4 h after insemination was 12 times higher ($P < 0.001$) than in the control group. It is possible that the phagocytosis of spermatozoa was reduced by the direct effect of caffeine plus $CaCl_2$ on spermatozoa, as observed in the *in vitro* phagocytosis model. In addition, the presence of $CaCl_2$ plus caffeine could potentially accelerate sperm capacitation in the uterus and thus influence sperm phagocytosis (compare with Fig. 2). However, a striking effect, which is likely to have contributed to the reduced loss of spermatozoa, was that the addition of caffeine plus $CaCl_2$ strongly reduced the recruitment of PMNs. The total number of PMNs found in animals at 4 h after insemination was three times lower ($P < 0.05$) in the caffeine plus $CaCl_2$ group than in the control group.

The PMNs are thought to be recruited from a large population in the basal region of the uterine epithelium (Bischof *et al.*, 1994; Engelhardt *et al.*, 1997). It is not known whether the reduction of recruitment is due to a direct effect of caffeine on the PMNs or to an effect of caffeine on the endometrium. It has been reported that phosphodiesterase inhibitors are able to restrict mobility and chemotactic activity of PMNs *in vitro* by increasing the intracellular, or perhaps also the extracellular, cAMP concentration (Hill *et al.*, 1975; Rivkin *et al.*, 1975; Carrasco *et al.*, 1997). *In vivo*, such a mechanism might result in restriction of the movement of PMNs from the endometrium into the uterine lumen. However, it does not necessarily inhibit the ability of PMNs to phagocytose once recruited. In fact, caffeine stimulates phagocytotic activity of PMNs, possibly by its ability to stimulate an increase in the intracellular concentration of free calcium in the PMNs (Carrasco *et al.*, 1997).

Although addition of caffeine plus $CaCl_2$ to the inseminate resulted in a much larger number of non-phagocytosed spermatozoa at 4 h after insemination, the number of spermatozoa recovered from the oviducts was not significantly different. However, it has been reported that the uterine sperm population can continue to play a role in replenishment of oviduct sperm populations for up to 24 h after insemination. Thus, the effect of caffeine plus $CaCl_2$ could be beneficial for increasing the likelihood of fertilization, especially when ovulation takes place a long time after insemination.

In vivo *studies: effects on fertilization*

In a subsequent insemination experiment, sows were inseminated with a reduced sperm dosage of only 0.5×10^9 spermatozoa either 26 h before ovulation or at 4 h after ovulation, as determined by transrectal ultrasonography (Woelders *et al.*, 2000). The sows received either inseminates containing caffeine plus $CaCl_2$, which was added just before insemination, or control inseminates ($n = 15$ or 16 per group). The sows were killed on day 5 after ovulation. The observed percentage of sows with > 80% fertilized oocytes (morphologically intact embryos as a percentage of total recovered oocytes plus embryos) in the caffeine plus $CaCl_2$ group was considerably higher than that in the control group, but the difference was not significant. The observed mean number of cells per embryo also appeared to be higher in the caffeine plus $CaCl_2$ group, but again, the difference was not significant. However, caffeine plus $CaCl_2$ resulted in a significantly greater number of accessory spermatozoa in the zonae pellucidae of oocytes of sows inseminated 26 h before ovulation. It was concluded from both insemination experiments that addition of caffeine plus $CaCl_2$ reduces the rate at which spermatozoa are eliminated from the genital tract. The greater number of accessory spermatozoa per embryo at 26 h after AI indicates that the number of spermatozoa in the oviducts remains sufficiently high for longer, which could have consequences for field fertility in pig AI and could potentially enable usage of a reduced sperm dosage.

Conclusion

PMNs play an important role in the clearance of spermatozoa from the uterine lumen. The phagocytosis of spermatozoa is not aimed specifically at removing dead, damaged or ageing spermatozoa. Fresh, intact spermatozoa are phagocytosed very rapidly *in vitro* as well as *in vivo*. However, incubation under capacitating conditions renders (a subpopulation of) the spermatozoa less vulnerable to phagocytosis.

Establishment of populations of spermatozoa in the uterotubal junctions and oviducts starts almost immediately after insemination. However, replenishment of these populations by ongoing migration of spermatozoa from the uterus can take place up to 24 h after insemination. This may be relevant for the likelihood of fertilization, especially when ovulation takes place a long time after insemination. It is possible to modulate PMN recruitment and phagocytosis of boar spermatozoa by addition of substances to the semen, for example, caffeine plus $CaCl_2$. An insemination study comparing inseminations with and without caffeine plus $CaCl_2$ indicated that the use of caffeine plus $CaCl_2$ could improve the fertility results or could enable the use of a reduced dosage of spermatozoa.

References

Arici A, Seli E, Senturk LM, Gutierrez LS, Oral E and Taylor HS (1998) Interleukin-8 in the human endometrium *Journal of Clinical Endocrinology and Metabolism* **83** 1783–1787

Ashworth PJC, Harrison RAP, Miller NGA, Plummer JM and Watson PF (1995) Flow cytometric detection of bicarbonate-induced changes in lectin binding in boar and ram sperm populations *Molecular Reproduction and Development* **40** 164–176

Baker RD and Degen (1972) Transport of live and dead boar spermatozoa within the reproductive tract of gilts *Journal of Reproduction and Fertility* **28** 369–377

Baker RD, Dziuk PJ and Norton HW (1968) Effect of volume of semen, number of sperm and drugs on transport of sperm in artificially inseminated sows *Journal of Animal Science* **27** 88–93

Bedford JM and Witkin SS (1983) Influence of complement depletion on sperm function in the female rabbit *Journal of Reproduction and Fertility* **69** 523–528

Birkhead TR and Møller AP (1998) *Sperm Competition and Sexual Selection* Academic Press, London

Bischof RJ, Brandon MR and Lee CS (1994) Studies on the distribution of immune cells in the uteri of prepubertal and cycling gilts *Journal of Reproduction and Fertility* **26** 111–129

Blandau RJ and Gaddum-Rosse P (1974) Mechanism of sperm transport in pig oviducts *Fertility and Sterility* **25** 61–67

Bouvet J-P, Couderc J and Pillot J (1987) *In vivo* and *in vitro* immunosuppressions in mice by a 100-110-Kd fraction from boar seminal plasma *American Journal of Reproductive Immunology* **14** 135–140

Burger JF (1952) Sex physiology of pigs *Onderstepoort Journal of Veterinary Research Supplement* **2** 116–131

Carrasco M, Del Rio M, Hernanz A and de la Fuente M (1997) Inhibition of human neutrophil functions by sulfated and nonsulfated cholecystokinin octapeptides *Peptides* **18** 415–422

Chowdhury NA, Kamada M, Takiwawa M and Mori H (1996) Complement-inhibiting activity of human seminal plasma and semen quality *Archives of Andrology* **36** 109–118

Cohen J (1973) Cross-overs, sperm redundancy and their close association *Heredity* **31** 408–413

Cohen J (1984) Immunological aspects of sperm selection and transport. In *Immunological Aspects of Reproduction in Mammals* pp 77–89 Ed. DB Crighton. Butterworths, Kent

Cohen J and Tyler KR (1980) Sperm populations in the female genital tract of the rabbit *Journal of Reproduction and Fertility* **60** 213–218

Cox JP and Karnovsky ML (1973) The depression of phagocytosis by exogenous cyclic nucleotides, prostaglandins, and theophylline *Journal of Cell Biology* **59** 480–490

D'Cruz OJ and Haas GG, Jr (1995) β₂-Integrin (CD11b/CD18) is the primary adhesive glycoprotein complex involved in neutrophil-mediated immune injury to human sperm *Biology of Reproduction* **53** 1118–1130

Dostál J, Veselský L, Marounek M, Zelezná B and Jonáková V (1997) Inhibition of bacterial and boar seminal immunosuppressive component in mice *Journal of Reproduction and Fertility* **111** 135–141

Dostàlovà Z, Calvete JC, Sans L and Töpfer-Petersen E (1994) Quantitation of boar spermadhesins in accessory sex gland fluids and on the surface of epididymal, ejaculated and capacitated spermatozoa *Biochimica et Biophysica Acta* **1200** 48–54

du Mesnil du Buisson F and Dauzier L (1955a) Distribution et résorption du sperme dans le tractus génital de la truie: survie des spermatozoïdes *Annales D'Endocrinologie* **16** 413–422

du Mesnil du Buisson F and Dauzier L (1955b) La remontée des spermatozoïdes du verrat dans le tractus génital de la truie en oestrus *Comte Rendus de la Société de Biologie* **148** 76–79

Einarsson S, Jones B, Larsson K and Viring S (1980) Distribution of small- and medium-sized molecules within the genital tract of artificially inseminated gilts *Journal of Reproduction and Fertility* **59** 453–457

Ekre HP, Naparstek Y, Lider O, Hydén P, Hägermark Ö, Nilsson T, Vlodavsky I and Cohen I (1992) Anti-inflammatory effects of heparin and its derivatives: inhibition of complement and of lymphocyte migration *Advances in Experimental Medicine and Biology* **313** 329–340

Engelhardt H, Croy BA and King GJ (1997) Role of uterine immune cells in early pregnancy in pigs *Journal of Reproduction and Fertility Supplement* **52** 115–131

First NL, Short RE, Peters JB and Stratman FW (1968) Transport and loss of boar spermatozoa in the reproductive tract of the sow *Journal of Animal Science* **27** 1037–1040

Fraser LR (1992) Requirements for successful mammalian sperm capacitation and fertilization *Archives of Pathology and Laboratory Medicine* **116** 345–350

Fraser LR (1995) Ionic control of sperm function *Reproduction, Fertility and Development* **7** 905–925

Gaddum-Rosse P and Blandau RJ (1973) *In vitro* studies on ciliary activity within the oviducts of the rabbit and pig *American Journal of Anatomy* **136** 91–104

Gadella BM, Gadella TWJ, Colenbrander B, van Golde LMG and Lopes-Cardozo M (1994) Visualization and quantification of glycolipid polarity dynamics in the plasma membrane of the mammalian spermatozoon *Journal of Cell Science* **107** 2151–2163

Gbarah A, Gahmberg G, Ofec I, Jacobi U and Sharon N (1991) Identification of the leukocyte adhesion molecules CD11 and CD18 as receptors for type 1-fimbriated (mannose-specific) *Escherichia coli. Infection and Immunity* **59** 4524–4530

Haas GG, Jr and Beer AE (1986) Immunologic influences on reproductive biology: sperm gametogenesis and maturation in the male and female genital tracts *Fertility and Sterility* **46** 753–765

Hancock RJT (1979) Complement fixing activities of normal mammalian sera for homologous and heterologous sperm *Journal of Reproductive Immunology* **1** 89–96

Hancock RJT (1981) Immunological aspects of reproduction in mammals *Oxford Reviews of Reproductive Biology* **3** 182–208

Hancock RJT (1984) Immune responses to sperm: recent developments. In *Immunological Aspects of Reproduction in Mammals* pp 55–76 Ed. DB Crighton. Buttersworth, London

Harkema W, Harrison RAP, Miller NGA, Topper EK and Woelders H (1998) Enhanced binding of zona pellucida proteins to the acrosomal region in response to fertilizing conditions: a flow cytometric study *Biology of Reproduction* **58** 421–430

Harrison RAP, Mairet B and Miller NGA (1993) Flow cytometric studies of bicarbonate-mediated Ca²⁺ influx in boar sperm populations *Molecular Reproduction and Development* **35** 197–208

Harrison RAP, Ashworth PJC and Miller NGA (1996) Bicarbonate/CO₂, an effector of capacitation, induces a rapid and reversible change in the lipid architecture of boar sperm plasma membranes *Molecular Reproduction and Development* **45** 378–391

Hasty LA, Lambris JD, Lessey BA, Pruksananonda K and Lyttle CR (1994) Hormonal regulation of complement components and receptors throughout the menstrual cycle *American Journal of Obstetrics and Gynecology* **170** 168–175

Hill HR, Estensen RD, Quie PG, Hogan NA and Goldberg ND (1975) Modulation of human neutrophil chemotactic responses by cyclic 3′,5′-guanosine monophosphate and cyclic 3′,5′-adenosine monophosphate *Metabolism* **24** 447–456

Hogarth PJ (1982) *Immunological Aspects of Mammalian Reproduction* pp 26–82. Blackie, Glasgow and London

Hunter RHF (1981) Sperm transport and reservoirs in the pig oviduct in relation to the time of ovulation *Journal of Reproduction and Fertility* **63** 109–117

Hunter RHF (1984) Pre-ovulatory arrest and peri-ovulatory redistribution of competent spermatozoa in the isthmus of the pig oviduct *Journal of Reproduction and Fertility* **72** 201–211

Hunter RHF (1990) Fertilization of pig eggs *in vivo* and *in vitro. Journal of Reproduction and Fertility Supplement* **40** 211–226

Hussein AM, Newby TJ, Stokes CR and Bourne FJ (1983) Quantitation and origin of immunoglobulins A, G and M in the secretions and fluids of the reproductive tract of the sow *Journal of Reproductive Immunology* **5** 17–26

Ibrahim ME and Pedersen H (1988) Acridine orange fluorescence as male fertility test *Archives of Andrology* **20** 125–129

Imai H, Niwa K and Iritani A (1979) Time requirement for capacitation of boar spermatozoa assessed by their ability to penetrate the zona-free hamster egg *Journal of Reproduction and Fertility* **56** 489–492

Johnson LA, Aalbers JG and Grooten HJG (1988) Artificial insemination of swine: fecundity of boar semen stored in beltsville TS (BTS), modified modena (MM), or MR-A and inseminated on one, three and four days after collection *Zuchthygiene* **23** 49–55

Kamerman E (1994) *Recovery of Spermatozoa From the Genital Tract of Sows After Insemination* (Dutch) Student thesis, Wageningen University *ID-Lelystad Report IVO-VOS* **297** ID-Lelystad Library, Lelystad

Katz DF, Drobnis EZ and Overstreet JW (1989) Factors regulating mammalian sperm migration through the female reproductive tract and oocyte vestments *Gamete Research* **22** 443–469

Kemp B, Vervoort FP, Bikker P, Janmaat J, Verstegen MWA and Grooten HJG (1990) Semen collection frequency and the energy metabolism of AI boars *Animal Reproduction Science* **22** 87–98

Klint M, Fridberger A, Menge A, Sällström J and Plöen L (1987) Boar sperm surface glycoproteins: isolation, localization, and temporal expression during spermatogenesis *Gamete Research* **17** 173–190

Lazarevic M, Skibinski G, Kelly R and James K (1995) Immunomodulatory effects of extracellular secretory vesicles isolated from bovine semen *Veterinary Immunology and Immunopathology* **44** 237–250

Lovell JW and Getty R (1968) Fate of semen in the uterus of the sow: histologic study of endometrium during the 27 hours after natural service *American Journal of Veterinary Research* **29** 609–625

Macek MB and Shur BD (1988) Protein–carbohydrate complementarity in mammalian gamete recognition *Gamete Research* **20** 93–109

Matthijs A, Hakze R, Postma A and Woelders H (2000a) Leukocyte recruitment and phagocytosis of boar spermatozoa. In *Boar Semen Preservation IV* pp 35–41 Eds LA Johnson and HD Guthrie. Allen Press Inc., Lawrence

Matthijs A, Harkema W, Engel B and Woelders H (2000b) *In vitro* phagocytosis of boar spermatozoa by neutrophils from peripheral blood of sows *Journal of Reproduction and Fertility* **120** 265–273

Nagai T, Niwa K and Iritani A (1984) Effect of sperm concentration during preincubation in a defined medium on fertilization *in vitro* of pig follicular oocytes *Journal of Reproduction and Fertility* **70** 271–275

Ofec I and Sharon N (1988) Lectinophagocytosis: a molecular mechanism of recognition between cell surface sugars and lectins in the phagocytosis of bacteria *Infection and Immunity* **56** 539–547

Oxenreider SL and Day BN (1965) Transport and cleavage of ova in swine *Journal of Animal Science* **24** 413–417

Pursel VG, Schulman LL and Johnson LA (1978) Distribution and morphology of fresh and frozen–thawed sperm in the reproductive tract of gilts after insemination *Biology of Reproduction* **19** 69–76

Rath D (1992) Experiments to improve *in vitro* fertilization techniques for *in vivo*-matured porcine oocytes *Theriogenology* **37** 885–896

Rigby JP (1966) The persistence of spermatozoa at the uterotubal junction of the sow *Journal of Reproduction and Fertility* **11** 153–155

Rivkin I, Rosenblatt J and Becker EL (1975) The role of cyclic AMP in the chemotactic responsiveness and spontaneous motility of rabbit peritoneal neutrophils. The inhibition of neutrophil movement and the elevation of cyclic AMP levels by catecholamines, prostaglandins, theophylline and cholera toxin *Journal of Immunology* **115** 1126–1134

Robertson SA and Seamark RF (1992) Granulocyte–macrophage colony stimulating factor (GM-CSF): one of a family of epithelial cell-derived cytokines in the preimplantation uterus *Reproduction, Fertility and Development* **4** 435–448

Rozeboom KJ, Troedsson MH and Crabo BG (1998) Characterization of uterine leukocyte infiltration in gilts after artificial insemination *Journal of Reproduction and Fertility* **114** 195–199

Rozeboom KJ, Troedsson MH, Molitor TW and Crabo BG (1999) The effect of spermatozoa and seminal plasma on leukocyte migration into the uterus of gilts *Journal of Animal Science* **77** 2201–2206

Soede NM, Wetzels CCH, Zondag W, De Koning MAI and Kemp B (1995) Effects of time of insemination relative to ovulation, as determined by ultrasonography, on fertilization rate and accessory sperm count in sows *Journal of Reproduction and Fertility* **104** 99–106

Steverink DWB, Soede NM, Bouwman EG and Kemp B (1997) Influence of insemination–ovulation interval and sperm cell dose on fertilization in sows *Journal of Reproduction and Fertility* **111** 165–171

Steverink DWB, Soede NM, Bouwman EG and Kemp B (1998) Semen backflow after insemination and its effect on fertilisation results in sows *Animal Reproduction Science* **54** 109–119

Suarez S, Redfern K, Raynor P, Martin F and Phillips DM (1991) Attachment of boar sperm to mucosal explants of oviducts *in vitro*: possible role in formation of a sperm reservoir *Biology of Reproduction* **44** 998–1004

Symons DBA (1967) Reaction of spermatozoa with uterine and serum globulin determined by immunofluorescence *Journal of Reproduction and Fertility* **14** 163–165

Symons DBA and Herbert J (1971) Incidence of immunoglobulins in fluids of the rabbit genital tracts and the distribution of IgG-globulin in the tissues of the female tract *Journal of Reproduction and Fertility* **24** 55–62

Targowski SP and Niemialtowski MN (1986) Appearance of Fc receptors on polymorphonuclear leukocytes after migration and their role in phagocytosis *Infection and Immunity* **52** 798–802

Thornton BP, Vetvicka V, Pitman M, Goldman RC and Ross GD (1996) Analysis of the sugar specificity and molecular location of the beta-glucan-binding lectin site of complement receptor type 3 (CD11b/CD18) *Journal of Immunology* **156** 1235–1246

Töpfer-Petersen E, Friess AE, Stoffel M and Schill WB (1990) Boar sperm membranes antigens. II. Reorganization of an integral membrane antigen during capacitation and acrosome reaction *Biochemistry* **93** 491–495

Tung KSK, Cooke WD, Jr, McCarty TA and Robitaille P (1976) Human sperm antigens and antisperm antibodies. II. Age-related incidence of antisperm antibodies *Clinical and Experimental Immunology* **25** 73–79

Van Dyk Q, Lanzendorf S, Kolm P, Hodgen GD and Mahony MC (2000) Incidence of aneuploid spermatozoa from subfertile men: selected with motility versus hemizona-bound *Human Reproduction* **15** 1529–1536

Veselský L, Cechová D, Hosková M, Stédra J, Holáň V and Stanék R (1991) *In vivo* and *in vitro* immunosuppresion by boar seminal vesicle fluid fraction *International Journal of Fertility* **36** 183–188

Viring S (1980) Distribution of live and dead spermatozoa in the genital tract of gilts at different times after insemination *Acta Veterinaria Scandinavica* **21** 587–597

Viring S and Einarsson S (1980) Influence of boar seminal plasma on the distribution of spermatozoa in the genital tract of gilts *Acta Veterinaria Scandinavica* **21** 598–606

Viring S and Einarsson S (1981) Sperm distribution within the genital tract of naturally inseminated gilts *Nordisk Veterinaermedicin* **33** 145–149

Viring S, Einarsson S, Jones B and Larsson K (1980) Transuterine transport of small- and medium-sized molecules deposited in the uterus in gilts *Journal of Reproduction and Fertility* **59** 459–462

Weir DM, Glass E and Steward J (1981) Recognition, adherence and phagocytosis *Annual Immunology (Institute Pasteur)* **132D** 131–149

Woelders H, Matthijs JJ, Bouwman, EG and Soede NM (2000) Caffeine plus Ca^{2+} reduces uterine leukocyte recruitment and sperm phagocytosis and improves fertility in pig AI *14th International Congress on Animal Reproduction Stockholm 2–6 July 2000 Proceedings* **2** 94 (Abstract 15:20)

Yanagimachi R (1994) Mammalian fertilization. In *The Physiology of Reproduction* pp 189–317 Eds E Knobil and JD Neill. Raven Press Ltd, New York

Reproduction Supplement 58, 129–145

Involvement of oviduct in sperm capacitation and oocyte development in pigs

H. Rodriguez-Martinez[1], P. Tienthai[1,2], K. Suzuki[3], H. Funahashi[4], H. Ekwall[2] and A. Johannisson[2]

Departments of [1]Obstetrics and Gynaecology and [2]Anatomy and Histology, Faculty of Veterinary Medicine, Swedish University of Agricultural Sciences (SLU), PO Box 7039, SE-750 07 Uppsala, Sweden; [3]Experimental Farm, Faculty of Agriculture, Hokkaido University, Sapporo 060-0811, Japan; and [4]Laboratory of Animal Reproduction, Faculty of Agriculture, Okayama University, Okayama 700-8530, Japan

An overview is presented on the structure and function of the pig oviduct in relation to sperm capacitation and oocyte development in vivo. In pigs, a functional sperm reservoir is established in the uterotubal junction–isthmus when sperm deposition occurs before ovulation. Capacitation is assumed to occur in this location, and spermatozoa progress towards the ampullary–isthmic junction at about the time of ovulation as a consequence of capacitation and hyperactivation. Preliminary data from our laboratory on viable spermatozoa retrieved from the sperm reservoir and the ampullary–isthmic junction of mated sows at pre- and periovulation oestrus showed that the largest subpopulation (60–90%) was of uncapacitated spermatozoa (using merocyanine-540), whereas 6–37% of the gated cells were capacitated spermatozoa. Incubation in a capacitation-inducing medium (bicarbonate-containing modified Brackett–Oliphant medium; mBO) for < 30 min effected capacitation readily, more markedly in ampullary–isthmic junction samples than in samples from the uterotubal junction, thereby indicating that uncapacitated spermatozoa responded to the addition of the effector bicarbonate at concentrations similar to those recorded in the periovulatory ampullary–isthmic junction in vivo. Addition of preovulatory isthmic oviductal fluid and hyaluronan under a similar incubation regimen maintained tubal sperm viability without obvious induction of capacitation. This finding indicates that, before ovulation, the intraluminal fluid of the sperm reservoir might delay sperm capacitation, perhaps because of its hyaluronan content. Evidence is presented that the sperm population in the oviduct undergoes capacitation under particular conditions in the upper tubal compartments. The diverse response of spermatozoa to capacitation stimuli helps to ensure full rates of fertilization in vivo. Data are also provided on the importance of final zona pellucida maturation in the pig oviduct to warrant proper zona pellucida reaction after sperm penetration, which would address in part the abnormal occurrence of polyspermy in in vitro fertilization of pigs.

Email: Heriberto.Rodriguez@og.slu.se

Introduction

Despite its fairly simple appearance, the pig oviduct is where essential reproductive processes occur, including the preparation of gametes for fertilization, fertilization and the initial phases of embryonic development. With the rapid development of *in vitro* assisted reproductive techniques, these processes can be performed in the laboratory with a reasonable degree of success. Spermatozoa can be capacitated, and oocytes from offal can be matured and fertilized. Further culture of the resulting zygotes allows production of early embryos that can be transferred, establish pregnancies and produce live offspring. These *in vitro* techniques, albeit suboptimal, have provided a large amount of valuable information on sperm capacitation, sperm–oocyte binding, oocyte maturation, fertilization and the early cleavage stages of newly developing embryos. However, failure of fertilization due to incomplete oocyte maturation and use of unphysiologically high numbers of capacitated spermatozoa can lead to lethal polyspermy and impaired developmental capability, and are major constraints during *in vitro* fertilization (IVF) in pigs. Owing to the conditions under which gamete preparation for fertilization, fertilization itself and early embryo development differ *in vitro* and *in vivo* (see Rodriguez-Martinez *et al.*, 1998), there is a need to examine the way in which the oviductal structure and function carry out these tasks. This is the intention of this review, which focuses on the formation of the tubal sperm reservoir, the occurrence of capacitation in tubal spermatozoa and some characteristics of prefertilization oocytes, particularly the zona pellucida.

General features of pig oviducts

The oviduct of a mature pig is approximately 25 cm in length and has a simple tubular histology, with an endosalpinx, a double-layered myosalpinx and a serosal mesosalpinx. The oviduct is divided into three main segments: the narrow isthmus (connected to the uterine horn via the uterotubal junction), the wider ampulla and the even broader, thin-walled infundibulum. The isthmus and ampulla are connected by an inconspicuous ampullary–isthmic junction, whereas the infundibulum is connected to the adovarian fimbriae and ovarian bursa by the abdominal opening (ostium). The endosalpinx is the inner non-glandular mucosa, the plicated lamina propria (Fig. 1a–f) of which is covered with a lining epithelium with ciliated (most cells) and non-ciliated (secretory) cells (Fig. 2b–f). Along this organ, towards the ostium, the longitudinal mucosal plicae acquire secondary and tertiary plicae, making the lumen more complex (Fig. 1c–f). The number of ciliated cells increases while the thickness of the internal, circular smooth muscle becomes thinner. The anatomical segments are considered to be particular tubal compartments that relate to specific functions such as the sperm reservoir (the uterotubal junction–adjacent isthmus), the site of fertilization (the ampullary–isthmic junction) and the area where ovum pick-up is performed (the fimbriae).

The tubal fluid

The intraluminal oviductal fluid provides the environment in which gametes are transported and matured, and where fertilization and early embryonic development occur. The tubal fluid is formed by specific oviductal secretions and by the passage of fluids and ions (Nichol *et al.*, 1992; Leese *et al.*, 2001). Tubal fluid differs from blood plasma in ionic composition (it is rich in K^+ and HCO_3^-), pH, osmolarity and macromolecular content, which vary with the hormonal environment (Nichol *et al.*, 1998). In the pig ampulla, concentrations of 33–35 mmol HCO_3^- l^{-1} can be recorded during periovulation (E. Ekstedt and H. Rodriguez-Martinez, unpublished).

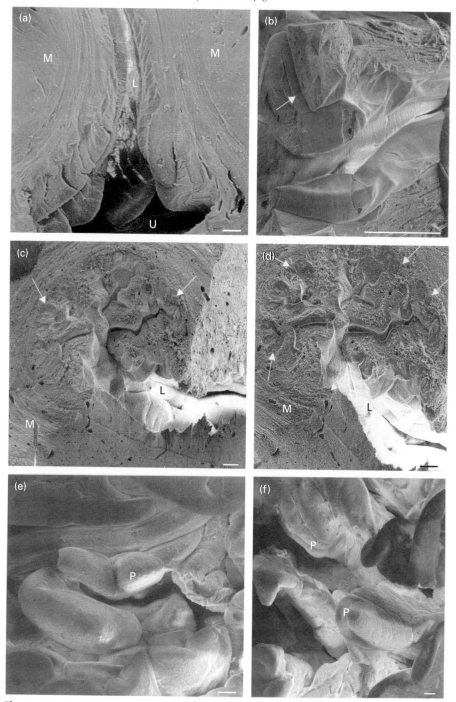

Fig. 1. Scanning electron micrographs of the main segments of the pig oviduct, with special reference to the tubal lumen. (a) A longitudinal section of the uterotubal junction. U: uterus; L: lumen; M: smooth muscle. (b) Open lumen of the uterotubal junction (arrow indicates deep folds), which together with the (c) adjacent isthmus (arrows indicate the deep furrows of the reservoir) builds up the periovulatory sperm reservoir. (d) Upper isthmus has secondary mucosal folds (arrows indicate deep furrows). (e) Lumen of the ampullary–isthmic junction and (f) ampulla with mucosal tertiary plicae (P). Scale bars represent (a) 5 mm, (b) 1 mm and (c–f) 100 μm.

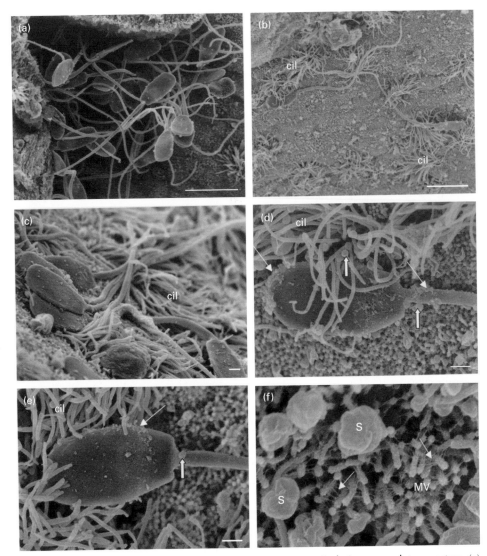

Fig. 2. Scanning electron micrographs of the pig sperm reservoir during preovulatory oestrus. (a) Clusters of spermatozoa in a deep furrow. (b) Spermatozoa apposed to the lining epithelium, with their heads towards the ciliated cells (cil). (c–e) Higher magnifications of spermatozoa in the reservoir depicting the relationship between ciliated cells and the sperm heads. Note the associated secretory droplets (thick arrows) and particulated material (thin arrows). (f) High magnification of the apical surface of secretory cells showing secretory droplets (S) and filament-like intraluminal material (arrows) between the microvilli (MV). Scale bars represent (a,b) 10 μm and (c–f) 1 μm.

By sampling of isthmic and ampullar segments *in vivo* using 1.2 mm indwelling chronic polyethylene catheters, ensheathed in 2.2 mm outer diameter Silastic tubing, placed surgically in the isthmus and ampulla with a partially modified technique after Kavanaugh *et al.* (1992), we recorded that fluid volume is highest during oestrus, and that the ampulla produces twice the volume that the isthmus does (Fig. 3), thereby reflecting its greater surface area (P. Tienthai and H. Rodriguez-Martinez, unpublished). The protein content of the oviductal fluid is about 10–15% of that in serum and originates from selective transudation (mostly at the ampulla)

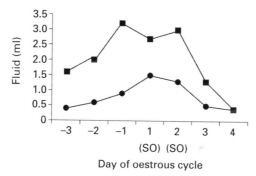

Fig. 3. Relative mean daily volumes of pig isthmic (●) and ampullar (■) fluid collected via indwelling catheters between pro-oestrus and metoestrus (*n* = 4 animals). SO: standing oestrus.

and, to a lesser extent, from the lining epithelium. Under oestrogen stimulation, especially during the periovulatory period, the lining epithelium produces specific glycoproteins (Hunter, 1994a; Buhi *et al.*, 1997) such as the oestrous-associated oviduct-specific glycoprotein (OSGP) (Leese *et al.*, 2001). During preovulation, mucopolysaccharides are also formed, particularly at the isthmic segment, where they obliterate the characteristically narrow lumen in which spermatozoa eventually reside (Johansson *et al.*, 2000; Rodriguez-Martinez, 2000). Glycosaminoglycans (GAGs) are also present in the tubal fluid, with a tendency to reach maximum concentrations during oestrus (Tienthai *et al.*, 2000). Heparan sulphate and the non-sulphated hyaluronan have been localized in the epithelium of the pig preovulatory reservoir, often near sperm clusters. Recent immunohistochemical investigations in our laboratory have indicated that the hyaluronan receptor CD44 and the enzymes hyaluronan synthase 3 and hyaluronidase 2 are localized in the lining epithelium of particular regions of the pig oviduct (P. Tienthai, A-S. Berqvist and H. Rodriguez-Martinez, unpublished). Hyaluronan has been related to the modulation of sperm capacitation (Suzuki *et al.*, 2000), the intratubal masking of spermatozoa, as a facilitator of sperm progression towards the site of fertilization and also as an attractant for spermatozoa during fertilization, although much evidence is yet circumstantial (see Rodriguez-Martinez, 2000). Mucopolysaccharides, GAGs and glycoproteins may have a function that is unique to the *in vivo* condition, increasing viscosity in the luminal fluid, thereby stabilizing the milieu surrounding the gametes and embryos in terms of fluid loss, osmotic changes, relationship to the epithelium and immunological protection.

The functional sperm reservoir

After deposition in the cervix, spermatozoa are transported rapidly through the uterus and colonize the first segment of the oviduct; $1–2 \times 10^8$ spermatozoa enter the uterotubal junction and the adjacent first isthmic segment within 15–20 min (see Hunter, 1990). Here, they form a substantial functional sperm reservoir in which most spermatozoa maintain normal ultrastructure and viability (Rodriguez-Martinez *et al.*, 1990; Mburu *et al.*, 1997). A certain number of these spermatozoa, usually several thousand, are released sequentially from the reservoir towards the site of fertilization at the ampullary–isthmic junction (Hunter, 1990; Mburu *et al.*, 1997). Of these, only a few spermatozoa reach the site of fertilization

(Hunter, 1995; Mburu *et al.*, 1997) and it is this marked decrease in sperm numbers along the tube that largely prevents polyspermy during fertilization. Most spermatozoa are localized in the narrow deep furrows in the reservoir (Figs 1c and 2a) and, thus, it seems that they make contact with the lining epithelium by their rostral region, as observed in oviducts fixed and processed conventionally for scanning electron microscopy (SEM) (Fig. 2b–e). However, when oviducts are cryofixed and observed under a cryo-SEM, spermatozoa are observed immersed in an amorphous intraluminal material (tubal fluid), rather than in direct contact with the epithelium (Rodriguez-Martinez *et al.*, 1998). Remnants of such secretory material can sometimes be seen among microvilli in samples fixed and processed conventionally (Fig. 2f).

The main function of the sperm reservoir is to ensure that at the time of fertilization adequate, although not excessive, numbers of fertile spermatozoa are present in the mid-oviduct. To achieve this goal the sperm reservoir entraps large numbers of spermatozoa in a restricted segment, the uterotubal junction–lower isthmus, which during the preovulatory period has a narrow lumen, an oedematous lamina propria, and is filled with a viscous tubal fluid. In addition, the reservoir maintains sperm viability and fertilizing capacity, escaping rejection by the female immune system and, presumably, modulates capacitation before ovulation. Finally, the reservoir prevents polyspermy by retaining spermatozoa and control-ling the release of spermatozoa towards the site of fertilization, either continuously or at a given, as yet unknown, signal.

The preovulatory sperm reservoir is built through the concerted action of several factors (see Hunter, 1990; Rodriguez-Martinez *et al.*, 1998), including purely mechanical (for example, the first segment encountered, deep folds, narrow lumen, viscous intraluminal fluid) and active interactions with this microenvironment. These interactions may inhibit sperm metabolism and, hence, motility, and stabilize the plasmalemma by specific signalling. Such interactions may occur with the surrounding fluid and include a decreased temperature or decreased pH and bicarbonate concentrations (Rodriguez-Martinez *et al.*, 1998; E. Ekstedt and H. Rodriguez-Martinez, unpublished). The selective binding of spermatozoa to the epithelium (Suarez, 1998) may account for a reduction in sperm motility, as determined *in vitro* (Suarez *et al.*, 1991) and, in species other than the pig, *in situ* (Smith, 1998).

Involvement of the oviduct in sperm capacitation

Several excellent reviews have been published on sperm capacitation, which is the predominant preparatory event for fertilization (Yanagimachi, 1994; Harrison, 1996; De Lamirande *et al.*, 1997). Sperm capacitation can be defined as a gradual, multi-step process that modifies the architecture of the intrinsically stable sperm plasma membrane (lipid order to disorder and protein relocation), including the removal of epididymal and seminal plasma proteins adsorbed to the sperm plasmalemma during ejaculation, thereby modifying its function in a varying number of cells within a given sperm population. Generally, capacita-tion includes the removal of membrane cholesterol and the reaction to specific signals by GAGs and glycoproteins, pH and Ca^{2+}-mediated mechanisms that occur during the sequential passage of spermatozoa in the female genital tract. Bicarbonate is a key effector molecule that elicits the earliest change that accompanies capacitation in pigs, this being the lipid disorder that initiates destabilization of the plasma membrane (Harrison, 1996, 1997; Harrison *et al.*, 1996; Gadella and Harrison, 2000). These membrane modifications precede specific changes in Ca^{2+} movement, motility patterns, such as hyperactivation, and exocytosis of the acrosome contents during the acrosome reaction, the latter of which is normally elicited upon contact with the zona pellucida (Berger *et al.*, 1989).

Sperm capacitation in the pig oviduct, assessed with fertilization as the endpoint, is thought to require 5–6 h after mating, but it could take < 2 h if semen deposition is performed at about the time of ovulation (Hunter, 1990). Data for IVF of pigs indicate that the time required for capacitation of boar spermatozoa *in vitro* may be < 4 h (Lynham and Harrison, 1998) and may be even shorter if cryopreserved spermatozoa are used. Surgical insemination of boar spermatozoa into the caudal isthmus and rostral ampulla during periovulation indicated that the caudal isthmus stimulated capacitation (observed as rates of fertilization) more readily than did the ampulla (Hunter *et al.*, 1998).

As boar spermatozoa inseminated at the onset of oestrus may be arrested and maintained viable in the sperm reservoir for ⩾ 36 h, the role of modulator of sperm capacitation has been ascribed to the reservoir. Capacitation can be modulated by either the intraluminal fluid or by contact between the apical membrane and the isthmic epithelial cells, or both (Suarez *et al.*, 1991; Smith, 1998). Oviductal fluid can reduce polyspermy in pig IVF, possibly owing to the inhibition of the acrosome reaction in the fertilization medium (Kim *et al.*, 1997). The oviductal fluid regulates the rate of capacitation *in vivo*, this being slower before ovulation than after ovulation (see Rodriguez-Martinez *et al.*, 1998). In addition, epithelial attachment delays rates of sperm capacitation in the reservoir (for review see Rodriguez-Martinez, 2000). Attachment prevents passive Ca^{2+} inflow to the spermatozoon, maintaining a low intracellular Ca^{2+} concentration (Dobrinski *et al.*, 1997). A reduction in the metabolism of spermatozoa and a delay in the occurrence of the membrane destabilization that results in capacitation (Harrison *et al.*, 1993) may extend the viability and fertilizing capacity of the stored spermatozoa. As most evidence has been collected *in vitro* (Harrison, 1996; Fazeli *et al.*, 1999), it remains to be determined more precisely how and when capacitation occurs *in vivo*.

With this intention, the status of sperm viability and capacitation was studied recently in spermatozoa retrieved by post-mortem flushing from the oviducts of nine sows removed at pre-, peri- or post-ovulation during standing oestrus. The sows (parity 2–5) were observed twice a day for spontaneous oestrus in the presence of fertile boars and were mated with one of two boars at 12 h after the observed onset of oestrus. The ovaries were explored periodically for preovulatory follicles by transrectal ultrasonography, as described by Mburu *et al.* (1995). The animals were killed at well-defined stages during oestrus, namely preovulation (at least 8 h before expected ovulation), periovulation (when follicles started to become less visible or were no longer visible with ultrasonography) or after ovulation (approximately 8 h after spontaneous ovulation). The oviducts were retrieved and kept at approximately 39°C during transportation to a nearby laboratory. The sperm reservoir segments (the uterotubal junction–adjacent lower isthmus) and the ampullary–isthmic junction were flushed with either modified Brackett–Oliphant medium (Brackett and Oliphant, 1975) without $NaHCO_3$, BSA or caffeine (300 mOsmol l^{-1}; control medium or mBO), or with mBO with bicarbonate–Ca^{2+}–BSA infused with 5% CO_2, pH 7.4, 300 mOsmol l^{-1} (treatment medium or mBO+) at 39°C to retrieve the spermatozoa in the 2 cm segments. The flushings were assessed quickly for the presence of spermatozoa (see Fig. 4c for a representative SEM view) and examined thereafter at various intervals within 60 min of incubation at 39°C for determination of capacitation status. The analyses included flow cytometry (on a FacsStar Plus flow cytometer equipped with standard optics; Becton Dickinson Immunochemistry Systems, San José, CA) of samples loaded with the membrane impermeable, fluorescent lipophilic dye merocyanine-540 (2.7 μmol l^{-1}; Molecular Probes Inc., Eugene, OR) and the membrane impermeable nucleic stain Yo-Pro-1 (25 nmol l^{-1}; Molecular Probes Inc.) (Harrison *et al.*, 1996), as well as incubation with chlortetracycline (Wang *et al.*, 1995). The rationale behind the use of merocyanine-540 was an attempt to recognize the degree of membrane lipid disorder, which is considered to be an early event in

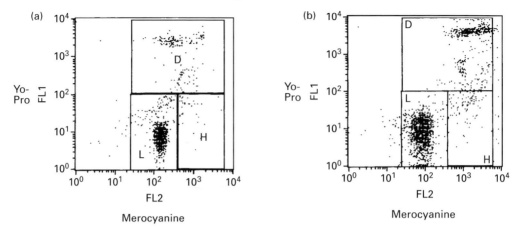

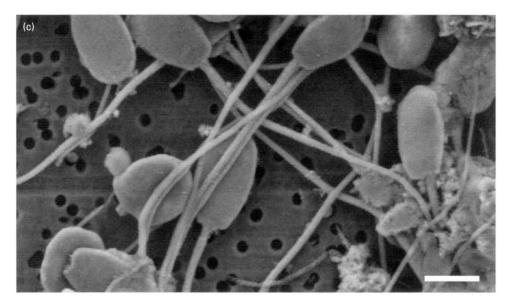

Fig. 4. Flow cytometric dot-plots of boar sperm populations retrieved from the pig sperm reservoir during preovulatory oestrus (a,b) and incubated in mBO+ containing 2.7 µmol merocyanine-540 l^{-1}, 25 nmol Yo-Pro-1 l^{-1}, 0.5 mg polyvinylalcohol (PVA) ml^{-1} and 0.5 mg polyvinylpyrrolidone (PVP) ml^{-1} for (a) 0 and (b) 30 min. Cells within quadrant 'L' are slightly fluorescent with merocyanine-540 (alive, uncapacitated spermatozoa), cells in quadrant 'H' are highly fluorescent with merocyanine-540 (capacitated spermatozoa) and cells in quadrant 'D' are fluorescent with Yo-Pro-1 (dead cells). (c) Scanning electron micrograph of representative spermatozoa retrieved by flushing. Scale bar represents 5 µm.

capacitation (Harrison, 1997; Gadella and Harrison, 2000). Thus, it was hoped that two different subpopulations of live cells, either slightly (low degree of disorder) or highly (high degree of disorder) fluorescent, would be detected on the basis of a mean 10^4 events measured per sample (range from 3×10^3 to 9×10^4 events; Fig. 4 a,b). In addition, it was hoped that different patterns of chlortetracycline fluorescence (a Ca^{2+} membrane-related event, at 100–200 spermatozoa per sample: uncapacitated (F pattern), capacitated (B pattern) and acrosome-reacted cells) could be distinguished with a light microscope equipped with

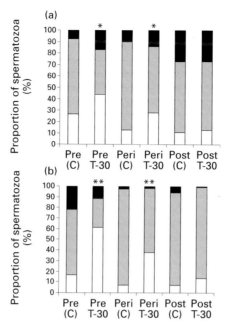

Fig. 5. Subpopulations of boar spermatozoa flushed from the (a) sperm reservoir and (b) ampullary–isthmic junction of sows at preovulatory (−8 h; Pre), periovulatory (± 4 h; Peri) and postovulatory (+8 h; Post) stages of standing oestrus. Spermatozoa were flushed with mBO medium (non-capacitating control; C), loaded with merocyanine-540 and Yo-Pro-1, and examined by flow cytometry. Spermatozoa were incubated thereafter with capacitating medium (mBO+; containing bicarbonate–Ca^{2+}–BSA) at 39°C for 30 min (T-30) and the flow cytometric analyses were repeated. The histograms depict the relative percentages of cells with high merocyanine-540 fluorescence (□: capacitated), low merocyanine-540 fluorescence (▨: viable, uncapacitated) and Yo-Pro-1 positive (■: dead) cells during control and treatment incubations. Significant differences were observed between control and treated spermatozoa retrieved from pre- and peri-ovulatory oviducts. *$P < 0.05$ and **$P < 0.01$.

epifluorescence optics. As a control procedure, semen collected from the same boars and extended in Beltsville thawing solution (BTS) at a concentration of 1×10^6 spermatozoa ml^{-1}, was separated by centrifugation through two layers of 40% (v/v) and 80% (v/v) Percoll–saline at 300 **g** for 15 min and the cleaned spermatozoa were subjected to incubation in mBO or mBO+ for up to 300 min. Capacitation status was examined at 5 and 30 min by flow cytometry (merocyanine-540) and at 15 and 300 min by chlortetracycline, as described above.

Flow cytometry studies of the viable (Yo-Pro-1 negative) spermatozoa retrieved from the sperm reservoir or the ampullary–isthmic junction (Fig. 5a,b) using control medium (control mBO) indicated that the largest subpopulation of spermatozoa (60–90%) was uncapacitated, which accounted for the low fluorescence of merocyanine-540. Only minor variations (not significant) in this subpopulation were observed between the different stages of standing oestrus (pre-, peri- or post-ovulation), as the subpopulation of capacitated spermatozoa ranged from 6% to 37% of the spermatozoa (Fig. 5a,b). Incubation for 30 min in the capacitation-inducing medium (treatment incubation in mBO+) increased the subpopulation of capacitated spermatozoa from the sperm reservoir markedly ($P < 0.05$), but particularly ($P < 0.01$) from the ampullary–isthmic junction at pre- and periovulation (Fig. 5a,b), indicating that spermatozoa might have been uncapacitated but were still viable and responsive to the addition of the effector or inducer bicarbonate (Suzuki *et al.*, 1994). Postovulatory spermatozoa were not affected significantly. In addition, the percentage of dead cells (Yo-Pro-1 positive cells) often increased with long-term incubation in mBO-capacitating medium compared with controls (Fig. 5a), a reaction that is probably effected by the bicarbonate in the medium, leading to extreme destabilization of the plasmalemma (Harrison *et al.*, 1993). The percentages of cell death were lower in the ampullary–isthmic junction (Fig. 5b) than in the sperm reservoir (Fig. 5a) at the peri- and postovulatory stages, but not at the preovulatory stage. Merocyanine-540 staining showed that there were changes in membrane fluidity in the spermatozoa before the chlortetracycline 'B pattern' was visible, after incubation in uncapacitating medium or capacitating medium, with the chlortetracycline 'B pattern' increasing significantly ($P < 0.05$) after only 60 min of incubation (data not shown). This finding indicates that capacitation follows a long sequence of events (Harrison, 1997) and that each technique shows a particular sequence. The analyses of the ejaculated spermatozoa from the same boars showed clearly that control mBO was not capacitating but that exposure to mBO+ induced significant ($P < 0.05$) capacitation changes (seven-fold) after only 15 min of incubation (data not shown). The chlortetracycline analyses were less clear in that changes were observed after 15 min but similar proportions were also observed after 300 min (data not shown).

Although the above results are from a restricted number of experiments and although tubal flushing does not allow selective retrieval of spermatozoa eventually bound or unbound to the tubal epithelium, the fact that only a small percentage ($< 30\%$) of spermatozoa showed early signs of capacitation (lipid disorder observed as an increase in merocyanine staining) indicates that capacitation *in vivo* might not occur in all spermatozoa at once, as is the case with IVF. Hence, these results support the suggestion by Harrison *et al.* (1993) that "…capacitation might represent a transient stage of (in)stability rather than a discrete physio- logical state: spermatozoa achieve fertilization only if they happen to be in this transient stage at the time of encountering the egg…". Therefore, these preliminary results would also be in line with previous findings (Rodriguez-Martinez *et al.*, 1998) supporting the suggestion by Smith (1998) that the preovulatory strategy of the isthmus is to delay capacitation rather than to promote it. However, several matters remain to be determined, such as whether the intraluminal secretion delays capacitation or whether this is done by the sperm–epithelium attachment, or alternatively, whether there is synergy between them. Fazeli *et al.* (1999) used tubal explants from prepubertal pigs to answer this question and concluded that only uncapacitated spermatozoa bind to the oviductal epithelium, whereas capacitated spermatozoa have a reduced binding capacity. In the light of our preliminary results this finding would imply that the flushing was able to retrieve many intact, bound spermatozoa (quite unlikely, in our experience) as well as unbound spermatozoa, which are usually found with disrupted membranes (Mburu *et al.*, 1997). As the percentage of capacitated spermatozoa was low at first reading with merocyanine-540 and even lower with chlortetracycline, the question arises of how many spermatozoa are actually bound or unbound *in vivo*. Perhaps it is not only the binding that is of importance, but also the medium in which the tubal spermatozoa are found.

In an attempt to answer this question, the effects of exogenous oestrous isthmic oviductal fluid, collected via chronic indwelling catheters, hyaluronan and homologous seminal plasma on the capacitation status of aliquots of flushings of tubal spermatozoa from the sperm reservoir were studied. Boar spermatozoa flushed from the sperm reservoir as described above were exposed to capacitating medium (mBO+) without (control) or with the addition of 20% (v/v) homologous isthmic oviductal fluid (collected from sows between late pro-oestrus and metoestrus using chronic indwelling catheters, as described above), 500 μg hyaluronan ml^{-1} (Hyonate; Bayer, Gothenburg) or 10% (v/v) homologous pooled seminal plasma from the same boars. After 5 and 30 min of incubation at 39°C, samples were loaded with merocyanine-540 or Yo-Pro-1 dye and analysed by flow cytometry. The relative changes in sperm subpopulations after incubation revealed that the percentages of capacitated spermatozoa (high merocyanine-540 fluorescence) in samples incubated with homologous isthmic oviductal fluid and hyaluronan were two- to four-fold lower ($P < 0.05$) than in controls (mBO+) at pre- and periovulatory periods after either 5 or 30 min of incubation, whereas no clear effect of seminal plasma was observed (data not shown). The number of dead cells was higher ($P < 0.05$) in all preparations than in controls, particularly when spermatozoa were exposed to seminal plasma ($P < 0.01$). The percentages of viable, uncapacitated cells remained unchanged during the 30 min of incubation in samples exposed to oviductal fluid and hyaluronan. However, after ovulation, no overall differences were noticed between controls and samples incubated with oviductal fluid, hyaluronan or seminal plasma. In comparison, oviductal fluid, hyaluronan and seminal plasma partially depressed the induction of capacitation in Percoll-cleaned freshly ejaculated spermatozoa, by incubation in bicarbonate–BSA-rich medium (mBO+, flow cytometry), although they did not reach control values and had a large percentage of destabilized (dead) cells. However, chlortetracycline did not provide the same temporal results as did flow cytometry measurements.

Exposure of frozen–thawed boar spermatozoa to 500 μg hyaluronan ml^{-1} *in vitro*, under conditions of pig IVF, decreases the incidence of polyspermy (Suzuki *et al.*, 2000), as well as inducing dose-related sperm capacitation (measured with chlortetracycline), without eliciting acrosome exocytosis (K. Suzuki, A. Asano, B. Eriksson, K. Niwa, H. Shimizu, T. Nagai and H. Rodriguez-Martinez, unpublished), thereby indicating that hyaluronan has a protective role relating to sperm viability for this category of preserved spermatozoa. In the above experiments, although there was a decrease in the percentage of capacitated cells compared with controls in samples exposed to oviductal fluid and hyaluronan, the percentages of viable, uncapacitated cells retrieved from the sperm reservoir were higher or remained unchanged during incubation. This finding indicates that the sperm reservoir fluid helps to maintain sperm viability, perhaps because of its hyaluronan content. However, more studies are required before conclusions can be drawn. Exposure to seminal plasma at similar concentrations has been demonstrated to maintain frozen–thawed boar spermatozoa in the chlortetra-cycline 'F pattern' and, furthermore, to counteract oocyte penetration by liquid-stored or frozen–thawed spermatozoa (K. Suzuki, A. Asano, B. Eriksson, K. Niwa, H. Shimizu, T. Nagai and H. Rodriguez-Martinez, unpublished). Such a preventive effect on capacitation was not observed in the tubal spermatozoa when chlortetracycline was used and it was also not clear with flow cytometry (merocyanine-540) analysis of ejaculated spermatozoa in the preliminary experiments reported in this review.

Progression of spermatozoa from the sperm reservoir

There is a sequential progression of boar spermatozoa from the reservoir towards the ampullary–isthmic junction in relation to ovulation (Mburu *et al.*, 1996, 1997). This pro-gression may be the consequence of several processes that are not necessarily mutually exclusive. Boar spermatozoa may achieve hyperactivation in the reservoir, detach from the epithelium and progress towards the ampullary–isthmic junction. To our knowledge, there is no evidence that this occurs in pigs *in vivo*. Furthermore, the lifespan of pig spermatozoa might be too short (Yanagimachi, 1994) to enable them to cover the distance to the ampullary–isthmic junction individually. However, a constant release and progression of spermatozoa that are not necessarily capacitated may occur as a consequence of a synergistic, concerted action of oedema resumption, changes in viscosity (perhaps in relation to hyaluronidase activity), an increased flow of tubal fluid and co-ordinated myosalpinx contractility towards the ampullary–isthmic junction (see Rodriguez-Martinez et al., 1998). Once they have left the sperm reservoir, spermatozoa may, probably on an individual basis and as an expression of the heterogeneity of the ejaculate, be readily capacitated, perhaps at very different rates, by the high concentrations of bicarbonate (> 30 mmol l^{-1}) present in the ampullary–isthmic junction (E. Ekstedt and H. Rodriguez-Martinez, unpublished). These concentrations are similar to those that facilitated capacitation in the spermatozoa flushed from the ampullary–isthmic junction (Fig. 5b) at pre- or periovulation (but not after ovulation, this being at > 8 h). Similar concentrations are used for ejaculated spermatozoa in pig IVF (Suzuki et al., 1994). Periovulatory fluid collected from the pig ampullary–isthmic junction increased the number of ejaculated spermatozoa depicting hyperactivation-like motility *in vitro* ('circling motility'; Nichol et al., 1997), thus supporting this hypothesis. Hormonal changes such as the action of preovulatory progesterone (Hunter, 1995) may underlie some of these mechanisms, rather than acting as a single signal triggering massive sperm progression.

No matter which mechanism is responsible, a regulation of the capacitation rate in the reservoir would ensure that appropriate numbers of fertilizing spermatozoa are present when ovulation occurs, thereby maximizing the likelihood of fertilization when sperm deposition is performed well ahead of ovulation, a common situation in pigs mated naturally. As capacitated spermatozoa have a relatively short lifespan (Yanagimachi, 1994), the likelihood of fertilization once they have left the reservoir and its stabilizing milieu depends largely on the number and location of viable spermatozoa along the oviduct mid-region, which is a fairly low number *in vivo*, according to Mburu et al. (1996). Considering the short period of ovulation (about 3 h) and the rapid transport of ova in pigs (< 1 h), there is a requirement for spermatozoa at different stages of capacitation to cover the area in which the ova may appear to provide the best chances for successful, timed fertilization. This requirement may also account for the large sperm population characteristic of pig ejaculates.

Role of the oviduct in oocyte pick-up, transport and oocyte development

Like the spermatozoon, the oocyte must reach full maturity before it is ready for fertilization and the inherent completion of meiosis and triggering of zygote cleavage. The preovulatory gonadotrophin surge signals release from meiotic arrest and completion of meiosis I, such that pig oocytes reach the metaphase II stage just before ovulation. At ovulation, oocytes are picked up by the cilia-covered fimbriae and guided through the infundibulum and ampulla (Oxenreider and Day, 1965; Alanko, 1974). The *in vivo* collection of oocytes in pigs is complex and is aided by the frictional large ovarian bursa and the contraction of selected muscles located in the mesosalpinx, such as the ligamentum infundibulo-cornuale. *In vivo*, the oocyte remains arrested at metaphase II until activated by fusion with the fertilizing spermatozoon (Alanko, 1974). In pigs, the rate of ampullar transport towards the ampullary–isthmic junction is fairly rapid (30–45 min) and the newly ovulated oocytes in their cumulus vestment aggregate within a 'cumulus plug' (Hancock, 1961), as shown (Fig. 6a–c). How oocyte pick-up and transport are regulated and elicited is still not clear as the ova are transported against a flow of tubal fluid. It is possible that the concerted action of an adhesive interaction between cumulus cells and the extracellular matrix they synthesize (Talbot et al.,

1999) (mainly hyaluronan) and ciliary beating, as well as myosalpingeal peristalsis (Rodriguez-Martinez *et al.*, 1982), are major agents. Eventually, final denudation of cumulus cells occurs, probably in relation to the presence of sperm hyaluronidase close to the plug, released by those spermatozoa that have broken acrosomes and are often observed in large numbers in the central lumen of the upper isthmus (Mburu *et al.*, 1997), exposing the zona pellucida to the tubal fluid (Fig. 6e). Molecules present in the oviductal lumen are involved in the development of the oocytes. Some of these are simple macromolecules, such as hyaluronan, which is present in the fluid during the entire period of tubal functionality, that is, until metoestrus (Tienthai *et al.*, 2000). Hyaluronan can support the development of pig oocytes fertilized *in vitro* up to the blastocyst stage (Kano *et al.*, 1998). Specific tubal proteins called 'porcine oviductal secretory proteins (POSPs)', produced *de novo* under oestrogen-dependence and occurring during late pro-oestrus, oestrus and metoestrus, become associated with the oocyte (Gandolfi, 1995; Buhi *et al.*, 1997, 2000). Ultrastructural studies have demonstrated that POSPs traverse the zona pellucida and associate with the oolemma and the plasma membrane of pig blastomeres (Buhi *et al.*, 1997, 2000). The role of such proteins is not fully understood but it is related to trophism, the enhancement of sperm–zona pellucida binding, extracellular matrix formation and prevention of premature hatching (Buhi *et al.*, 1997).

Impairment of fertilization in pigs

Capacitation represents a conflict between the maintenance of sperm viability and destabilization that, if expressed fully before the sperm–oocyte encounter, renders the spermatozoon infertile and ultimately causes cell death (Harrison, 1996). If insemination takes place > 24 h before ovulation, fertilization rates decrease, owing to low numbers of fertile spermatozoa present at the site of fertilization. Although sperm ageing has a clear effect on fertilization and conceptus development (Shaver and Martin-De Leon, 1977), oocyte ageing has been viewed as a major cause of fertilization failure in pigs (Kim *et al.*, 1996a). At sperm penetration, oocytes prevent the multiple entry of spermatozoa at the zona pellucida by the release of cortical granules, which cause a zona pellucida reaction. It is thought that postovulatory ageing of mammalian oocytes before sperm penetration may lead to polyspermy, owing to a non-functional cortical reaction mechanism, caused in turn by a delayed and incomplete exocytosis of the cortical granules (Hunter, 1994b). Although increasing progesterone concentrations after ovulation may be a causative factor, an increase in the number of spermatozoa ascending a more patent isthmus from the reservoir is the main cause of polyspermy (Hunter, 1994b), which is the major obstacle for optimal IVF in pigs. However, recent evidence indicates that the abnormally high incidence of polyspermic penetration of pig oocytes *in vitro* is probably not due to delayed or incomplete cortical granule exocytosis but to a delayed zona pellucida reaction, allowing simultaneous sperm penetration (Wang *et al.*, 1998). The surface morphology of the zona pellucida and the zona pellucida reactions at sperm penetration differs between *in vitro*-matured oocytes derived from offal and ovulated oocytes, as detected by SEM (Funahashi *et al.*, 2000). This observation can perhaps be explained in relation to the presence of additional macromolecules (Hedrick *et al.*, 1987) that make the outer surface of the zona pellucida smoother (Fig. 6d). The oestrogen-dependent oviductal glycoproteins secreted into the oviductal lumen are of particular interest (Brown and Cheng, 1986; Buhi *et al.*, 1997). These substances in the intraluminal oviductal fluid may be required for the final maturation of the zona pellucida in *in vitro*-matured pig oocytes, for example by providing an increased resistance to pronase digestion (Kim *et al.*, 1996b) or a reduction of polyspermy (Vatzias and Hagen, 1999) when *in*

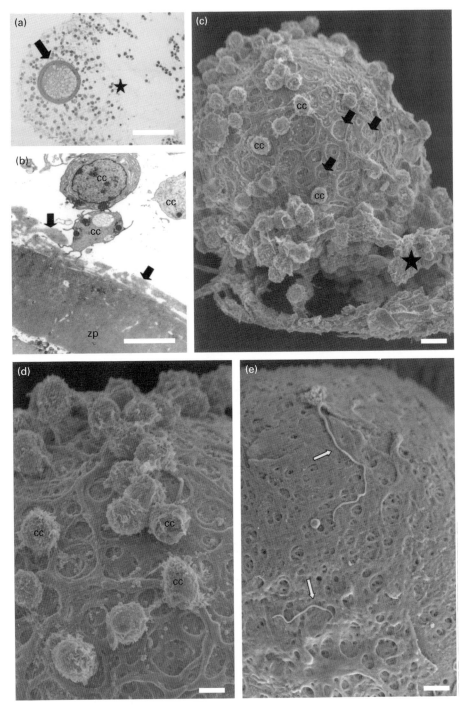

Fig. 6. Oocytes retrieved from pig ampullary–isthmic junction during periovulatory oestrus. (a) Low magnification photomicrograph of a partial view of an oocyte plug. Arrow: oocyte adjoined to the other oocytes (eight in total, not all included in the picture) by a cloud of extracellular inert material (star) among isolated cumulus cells. Spermatozoa do not seem to have reached the cloud yet. (b) Transmission electron micrograph of the oocyte in (a). Note the aspect of the zona pellucida (zp) with a spongy appearance (arrows)

vitro-matured oocytes are exposed to oviductal fluid. Funahashi *et al.* (2001) explored the ultrastructure of pig zonae pellucidae by transmission electron microscopy and confirmed that there are differences in the zona pellucida and the zona pellucida reaction at sperm penetration between *in vivo*- and *in vitro*-fertilized oocytes, with clear differences in network organization between the inner and outer zona pellucida. During final maturation, the zona pellucida of *in vivo*-ovulated oocytes may add oviductal glycoproteins, which allow the complete change in conformation of the inner zona pellucida that characterizes the zona pellucida reaction to occur.

Conclusion

The preliminary results presented in this review using merocyanine-540 dye and flow cytometry to monitor the early stages of sperm capacitation (lipid disorder in the sperm plasma membrane) showed that the largest subpopulation, 60–90%, of viable spermatozoa retrieved from the sperm reservoir and the ampullary–isthmic junction of mated sows at pre- and periovulation was uncapacitated. Incubation in a capacitation-inducing medium (mBO with bicarbonate–BSA) for < 30 min induced capacitation readily, more markedly in samples from the ampullary–isthmic junction than in those from the uterotubal junction. These results indicate that these uncapacitated spermatozoa were responsive to the addition of the effector bicarbonate at concentrations similar to those recorded in the periovulatory ampullary–isthmic junction *in vivo*. The addition of preovulatory isthmic oviductal fluid and hyaluronan under a similar incubation regimen appeared to retain the viability of tubal spermatozoa. This finding indicates that sperm reservoir fluid, perhaps because of its hyaluronan content, might be responsible for delaying sperm capacitation in the uterotubal junction–isthmus. In this study, evidence is provided for the need for a diverse response to capacitation by the sperm population in the oviduct *in vivo* that would ensure full rates of fertilization, indicating that caution is required when extrapolating results obtained solely from *in vitro* studies. On the basis of ultrastructural studies of the zona pellucida of *in vivo*- and *in vitro*-developed oocytes it is evident that the oviduct is also responsible for the final maturation of the zona pellucida by secreting specific glycoproteins that result in proper zona pellucida reaction after sperm penetration, and can explain in part the abnormal occurrence of polyspermy in pig IVF.

The skilled technical support of M. Ekwall and Å. Jansson is acknowledged. Funding has been provided by FORMAS, formerly the Swedish Council for Forestry and Agricultural Research (SJFR), the Swedish Farmers' Foundation for Agricultural Research (SLF), and the Swedish Foundation for International Cooperation in Research and Higher Education (STINT), through the SLU–Japan Programme on Reproductive Biotechnology, Sweden.

---

and cumulus cells (cc) still associated with the zona pellucida. (c) Scanning electron micrograph (SEM) of an oocyte as in (a) yet almost completely covered by cumulus cells (cc) and extracellular material (star). Note the rather wide fenestrations in the zona pellucida (arrows). (d) Higher magnification of (c) showing the outer surface of the zona pellucida with wide fenestrations left by the cumulus cell outgrowths. (e) SEM of another oocyte denuded of cumulus cells, depicting two sperm tails (arrows) that have penetrated the zona pellucida partially. Note the aspect of the outer zona pellucida and compare it with the amorphous cross-sectioned oocyte in (c). Scale bars represent (a) 100 μm, (b,d,e) 5 μm and (c) 10 μm.

References

Alanko M (1974) *Fertilization and Early Development of Ova in AI-Gilts, with Special Reference to the Role of Tubal Sperm Concentration: A Clinical and Experimental Study* PhD Thesis, University of Helsinki

Berger T, Turner DO, Meizel S and Heidrick JL (1989) The zona pellucida-induced acrosome reaction in boar sperm *Biology of Reproduction* **40** 525–530

Brackett BG and Oliphant G (1975) Capacitation of rabbit spermatozoa *in vitro. Biology of Reproduction* **12** 260–274

Brown CR and Cheng WKT (1986) Changes in composition of the porcine zona pellucida during development of the oocyte to the 2- to 4-cell embryo *Journal of Embryology and Experimental Morphology* **92** 183–191

Buhi WC, Alvarez IM and Kouba AJ (1997) Oviductal regulation of fertilization and early embryonic development *Journal of Reproduction and Fertility Supplement* **52** 285–300

Buhi WC, Alvarez IM and Kouba AJ (2000) Secreted proteins of the oviduct *Cells, Tissues, Organs* **166** 165–179

De Lamirande E, Leclerc P and Gagnon C (1997) Capacitation as a regulatory event that primes spermatozoa for the acrosome reaction and fertilization *Molecular Human Reproduction* **3** 175–194

Dobrinski I, Smith TT, Suarez SS and Ball BA (1997) Membrane contact with oviductal epithelium modulates the intracellular calcium concentration of equine spermatozoa *in vitro. Biology of Reproduction* **56** 861–869

Fazeli A, Duncan AE, Watson PF and Holt WV (1999) Sperm–oviduct interaction: induction of capacitation and preferential binding of uncapacitated spermatozoa to oviductal epithelial cells in porcine species *Biology of Reproduction* **60** 879–886

Funahashi H, Ekwall H and Rodriguez-Martinez H (2000) The zona reaction in porcine oocytes fertilized *in vivo* and *in vitro* as seen with scanning electron microscopy *Biology of Reproduction* **63** 1437–1442

Funahashi H, Ekwall H, Kikuchi K and Rodriguez-Martinez H (2001) Transmission electron microscopy studies of the zona reaction in pig oocytes fertilized *in vivo* and *in vitro. Reproduction* **122** 443–452

Gadella BM and Harrison RAP (2000) The capacitating agent bicarbonate induces protein kinase A-dependent changes in phospholipid transbilayer behaviour in the sperm plasma membrane *Development* **127** 2407–2420

Gandolfi F (1995) Functions of proteins secreted by oviduct epithelial cells *Microscopy Research Techniques* **32** 1–12

Hancock JL (1961) Fertilization in the pig *Journal of Reproduction and Fertility* **2** 307–331

Harrison RAP (1996) Capacitation mechanisms, and the role of capacitation as seen in eutherian mammals *Reproduction, Fertility and Development* **8** 581–594

Harrison RAP (1997) Sperm plasma membrane characteristics and boar semen fertility *Journal of Reproduction and Fertility Supplement* **52** 195–211

Harrison RAP, Mairet B and Miller NGA (1993) Flow cytometric studies of bicarbonate-mediated Ca^{2+} influx in boar sperm populations *Molecular Reproduction and Development* **35** 197–208

Harrison RAP, Ashworth PJC and Miller NGA (1996) Bicarbonate/CO_2, an effector of capacitation, induces a rapid and reversible change in the lipid architecture of boar sperm plasma membranes *Molecular Reproduction and Development* **45** 378–391

Hedrick JL, Wardrip NJ and Berger T (1987) Differences in the macromolecular composition of the zona pellucida isolated from pig oocytes, eggs, and zygotes *Journal of Experimental Zoology* **241** 257–262

Hunter RHF (1990) Fertilization of pig eggs *in vivo* and *in vitro. Journal of Reproduction and Fertility Supplement* **40** 211–226

Hunter RHF (1994a) Modulation of gamete and embryonic microenvironments by oviduct glycoproteins *Molecular Reproduction and Development* **39** 176–181

Hunter RHF (1994b) Causes for failure of fertilization in domestic species. In *Embryonic Mortality in Domestic Species* pp 1–22 Eds MT Zavy and RD Geisert. CRC Press, Boca Raton

Hunter RHF (1995) Ovarian endocrine control of sperm progression in the Fallopian tubes *Oxford Reviews of Reproductive Biology* **17** 85–124

Hunter RHF, Huang WT and Holtz W (1998) Regional influences of the Fallopian tubes on the rate of boar sperm capacitation in surgically inseminated gilts *Journal of Reproduction and Fertility* **114** 17–23

Johansson M, Tienthai P and Rodriguez-Martinez H (2000) Histochemistry and ultrastructure of the intraluminal mucus in the sperm reservoir of the pig oviduct *Journal of Reproduction and Development* **46** 183–192

Kano K, Miyano T and Kato A (1998) Effects of glycosaminoglycans on the development of *in vitro*-matured and fertilized porcine oocytes to the blastocyst stage *in vitro. Biology of Reproduction* **58** 1226–1232

Kavanaugh JF, Grippo AA and Killian GJ (1992) Cannulation of the bovine ampullary and isthmic oviduct *Journal of Investigative Surgery* **5** 11–17

Kim NH, Moon SJ, Prather RS and Day BN (1996a) Cytoskeletal alteration in aged porcine oocytes and parthenogenesis *Molecular Reproduction and Development* **43** 513–518

Kim NH, Funahashi H, Abeydeera LR, Moon SJ, Prather RS and Day BN (1996b) Effects of oviductal fluid on sperm penetration and cortical granule exocytosis during *in vitro* fertilization of porcine oocytes *Journal of Reproduction and Fertility* **107** 79–86

Kim NH, Day BN, Lim JG, Lee HT and Chung KS (1997) Effects of oviductal fluid and heparin on fertility and characteristics of porcine spermatozoa *Zygote* **5** 61–65

Leese HJ, Tay JI, Reischl J and Downing SJ (2001) Formation of Fallopian tubal fluid: role of a neglected epithelium *Reproduction* **121** 339–346

Lynham JA and Harrison RAP (1998) Use of stored eggs to assess boar sperm fertilizing functions *in vitro. Biology of Reproduction* **58** 539–550

Mburu JN, Einarsson S, Dalin AM and Rodriguez-Martinez H (1995) Ovulation as determined by transrectal ultrasonography in multiparous sows: relationships with oestrous symptoms and hormonal profiles *Journal of Veterinary Medicine A* **42** 285–292

Mburu JN, Einarsson S, Lundeheim N and Rodriguez-Martinez H (1996) Distribution, number and membrane integrity of spermatozoa in the pig oviduct in relation to spontaneous ovulation *Animal Reproduction Science* **45** 109–121

Mburu JN, Rodriguez-Martinez H and Einarsson S (1997) Changes in sperm ultrastructure and localisation in the porcine oviduct around ovulation *Animal Reproduction Science* **41** 137–148

Nichol R, Hunter RHF, Gardner DK, Leese HJ and Cooke GM (1992) Concentrations of energy substrates in oviductal fluid and blood plasma during the peri-ovulatory period *Journal of Reproduction and Fertility* **96** 699–707

Nichol R, Hunter RHF, De Lamirande E, Gagnon C and Cooke GM (1997) Motility of spermatozoa in hydro-salpingeal and follicular fluid of pigs *Journal of Reproduction and Fertility* **110** 79–86

Nichol R, Hunter RHF, Gardner DK, Partridge R, Leese HJ and Cooke GM (1998) Concentrations of energy substrates in oviductal fluid in unilaterally ovari-ectomized pigs *Research in Veterinary Science* **65** 263–264

Oxenreider SL and Day BN (1965) Transport and cleavage of ova in swine *Journal of Animal Science* **24** 413–417

Rodriguez-Martinez H (2000) The oviduct of the pig: do intraluminal glycosaminoglycans play a role in tubal function? In *Boar Semen Preservation IV* pp 153–163 Eds LA Johnson and HD Guthrie. Allen Press Inc., Lawrence

Rodriguez-Martinez H, Einarsson S and Larsson B (1982) Spontaneous motility of the oviduct in the anaesthetized pig *Journal of Reproduction and Fertility* **66** 615–624

Rodriguez-Martinez H, Nicander L, Viring S, Einarsson S and Larsson K (1990) Ultrastructure of the uterotubal junction in preovulatory pigs *Anatomia Histologia Embryologia* **19** 16–36

Rodriguez-Martinez H, Larsson B, Pertoft H and Kjellén L (1998) GAGs and spermatozoon competence *in vivo* and *in vitro*. In *Gametes: Development and Function* pp 239–274 Eds A Lauria, F Gandolfi, G Enne and L Gianaroli. Serono Symposium, Serono

Shaver EL and Martin-De Leon DC (1977) Effects of aging of sperm in the female and male reproductive tracts before

fertilization on the chromosome complement of the blastocyst *Aging Gametes* **16** 151–165

Smith TT (1998) The modulation of sperm function by the oviductal epithelium *Biology of Reproduction* **58** 1102–1104

Suarez SS (1998) The oviductal sperm reservoir in mammals *Biology of Reproduction* **58** 1105–1107

Suarez SS, Redferm K, Raynor P, Martin F and Philips DM (1991) Attachment of boar sperm to mucosal explants of oviduct *in vitro*: role in formation of a sperm reservoir *Biology of Reproduction* **44** 998–1004

Suzuki K, Ebihara M, Nagai T, Clarke NGE and Harrison RAP (1994) Importance of bicarbonate/CO_2 for fertilization of pig oocytes *in vitro* and synergism with caffeine *Reproduction, Fertility and Development* **6** 221–227

Suzuki K, Eriksson B, Shimizu H, Nagai T and Rodriguez-Martinez (2000) Effect of hyaluronan on monospermic penetration of porcine oocytes fertilized *in vitro*. *International Journal of Andrology* **23** 13–21

Talbot P, Geiske C and Knoll M (1999) Oocyte pickup by the mammalian oviduct *Molecular Biology of the Cell* **10** 5–8

Tienthai P, Kjellén L, Pertoft H, Suzuki K and Rodriguez-Martinez H (2000) Localisation and quantitation of hyaluronan and sulphated glycosaminoglycans in the tissues and intraluminal fluid of the pig oviduct *Reproduction, Fertility and Development* **12** 173–182

Vatzias G and Hagen DR (1999) Effects of porcine follicular fluid and oviduct-conditioned media on maturation and fertilization of porcine oocytes *in vitro*. *Biology of Reproduction* **60** 42–48

Wang WH, Abeydeera LR, Fraser LR and Niwa K (1995) Functional analysis using chlortetracycline fluorescence and *in vitro* fertilization of frozen–thawed ejaculated boar spermatozoa incubated in a protein-free chemically defined medium *Journal of Reproduction and Fertility* **104** 305–313

Wang WH, Abeydeera LR, Prather RS and Day BN (1998) Morphologic comparison of ovulated and *in vitro*-matured porcine oocytes, with particular reference to polyspermy after *in vitro* fertilization *Molecular Reproduction and Development* **49** 308–316

Yanagimachi R (1994) Mammalian fertilization. In *The Physiology of Reproduction* pp 189–317 Eds E Knobil and JD Neill. Raven Press, New York

Reproduction Supplement **58**, 147–158

Gamete adhesion molecules

D. J. Miller and H. R. Burkin

Department of Animal Sciences, University of Illinois at Urbana-Champaign, Urbana, IL 61801, USA

Despite the importance of fertilization for animal production, species preservation and controlling reproduction, the molecular basis underlying fertilization is not well understood. More progress has been made in mice than in other mammals, but targeted deletion of specific genes in the mouse has often yielded unexpected results. The pig is also a useful animal to study, as large numbers of pig gametes can be acquired easily. However, it appears that the pig zona pellucida proteins that bind to spermatozoa may not be homologues of ZP3, the mouse zona pellucida protein that spermatozoa bind to. Therefore, a zona pellucida receptor on spermatozoa that is important for mouse fertilization may be redundant, along with other receptors, in pig fertilization. In this review, the important steps of fertilization in pigs are discussed and the binding of pig gametes is compared with that of mouse gametes. In addition, the molecules that may be important for gamete adhesion are considered. New technical advances and creative ideas offer the opportunity to make important advances in this crucial area.

Introduction

Fertilization is one of the most intriguing biological events. Two haploid cells must attach in a specific manner; this attachment must signal a response from each gamete and the gametes must fuse together. More specifically, the spermatozoon must bind to the extracellular matrix (zona pellucida) of the oocyte, activate the release of a large specialized secretory vesicle (the acrosome) and penetrate this tough extracellular matrix. After penetrating the zona pellucida, the fertilizing spermatozoon must bind to and fuse with the oocyte, resulting in oocyte activation. During activation, the oocyte, previously suspended at metaphase II, completes meiosis and triggers mechanisms to prevent other spermatozoa from penetrating the zona pellucida and causing polyspermy. This complex series of cell interactions allows the formation of a new diploid cell (zygote) that can develop into the wide variety of tissues found in adult animals.

A better understanding of fertilization is vital for improving animal fertility. Once the stages of fertilization are clarified, specific tests to diagnose the causes of reduced fertility and therapies to treat specific causes can be developed. In addition, the fundamental information about fertilization can be used to develop more accurate laboratory tests that allow the identification and removal of subfertile animals from breeding herds. It may also be possible to develop new alternatives to control fertility. Finally, this information can be used to improve the success of *in vitro* fertilization.

Email: d-mille@uiuc.edu

The zona pellucida

Oocytes from a variety of vertebrates are surrounded by a glycoprotein coat. In mammals, this relatively thick protective coat is named the zona pellucida. In addition to protecting the developing embryo after fertilization, the zona pellucida binds only spermatozoa from a restricted number of species (Yanagimachi, 1994). Removal of the zona pellucida allows penetration of the oocyte by spermatozoa from a much broader range of species. These observations indicate that specific receptors mediate binding of spermatozoa to the zona pellucida.

Many lines of evidence indicate that the sperm-binding component on the zona pellucida is a carbohydrate. A study by Johnston *et al.* (1998) showed that the addition of synthetic carbohydrates to spermatozoa blocked the binding of spermatozoa to the zona pellucida. Fixed or denatured zona pellucida can bind spermatozoa, a characteristic not expected if protein is the binding component (Bleil and Wassarman, 1980).

The mouse zona pellucida

The mouse zona pellucida has been the most extensively studied. The zona pellucida is a product of the oocyte and is composed of three glycoproteins termed ZP1, ZP2 and ZP3, in order of migration on non-reducing SDS polyacrylamide gels. All zona pellucida glycoproteins run as broad bands on gels, due to their extensive and heterogeneous glycosylation. Each protein possesses both asparagine- and serine/threonine-linked oligosaccharides (Wassarman and Litscher, 2001). Related proteins are found in other mammals, and even in birds, amphibians and fish (Rankin and Dean, 2000).

Spermatozoa penetrate the zona pellucida by binding to glycoproteins on the zona pellucida and by releasing the acrosome, an unusual secretory vesicle that is present underneath the plasma membrane and stretched over the anterior region of the sperm nucleus (Yanagimachi, 1994). During the acrosome reaction, the outer acrosomal membrane fuses with the overlying plasma membrane, the contents of the acrosome are released and the inner acrosomal membrane becomes a delimiting sperm membrane. After the acrosome reaction, spermatozoa can penetrate the zona pellucida. Prematurely acrosome-reacted spermatozoa are unable to bind the zona pellucida, possibly because of the loss of the membrane that has the appropriate zona pellucida receptors (Yanagimachi, 1994).

In the fertilization of mice, evidence indicates that one zona pellucida glycoprotein, ZP3, binds acrosome-intact spermatozoa. If the zona pellucida is dissolved and soluble ZP3 is purified, ZP3 binds to acrosome-intact spermatozoa (Wassarman and Litscher, 2001). When spermatozoa are incubated with ZP3 in competitive binding assays, ZP3 blocks binding of spermatozoa to oocytes (Bleil and Wassarman, 1980). However, soluble ZP3 from fertilized eggs does not inhibit binding of spermatozoa to oocytes. The serine/threonine-linked oligosaccharides of ZP3 that bind spermatozoa are apparently modified at fertilization so that they are unable to bind spermatozoa (Florman and Wassarman, 1985).

The pig zona pellucida

The zona pellucida surrounding pig oocytes has been more difficult to study. The pig zona pellucida is composed of three glycoproteins that have been given various names (Table 1). The pig homologues of ZP1, ZP2 and ZP3 have been most recently termed ssZPB, ssZPA and ssZPC, respectively, in order of the size of the cDNAs encoding the proteins. The molecular weights of ssZPB and ssZPC overlap, a feature that makes their purification by preparative SDS–PAGE impossible (Nakano and Yonezawa, 2001). The only reported procedures for

Table 1. Nomenclature of vertebrate oocyte coat proteins (adapted from Rankin and Dean, 2000)

Species	Egg coat protein I	Egg coat protein II	Egg coat protein III
Mouse	ZP1	ZP2	ZP3
Pig	ssZPB/ZP3α	ssZPA/ZP1	ssZPC/ZP3β
Frog (*Xenopus laevis*)		gp69/ZP2/ZPA	gp43/ZP3/ZPC

purifying each glycoprotein require partial deglycosylation first. Removal of poly-lactosamine by endo-β-galactosidase allows separation of ssZPB and ssZPC (Yurewicz *et al.*, 1987; Yonezawa *et al.*, 1995). Although the partially deglycosylated ZPB retains some ability to bind spermatozoa, partial loss of sperm binding activity from ZPB or other zona glycoproteins could go undetected. Therefore, it is difficult to be certain that native ssZPC does not have sperm binding activity. Even ssZPB oligosaccharides that retain some binding activity require molar concentrations two to three orders of magnitude higher than for ssZPB to inhibit sperm–zona binding (Yurewicz *et al.*, 1991).

Considering this caveat, most evidence indicates that the mouse ZP1 homologue, ssZPB (the partially deglycosylated glycoprotein), binds spermatozoa; however, little binding activity has been ascribed to ssZPC, the mouse ZP3 homologue. Later experiments support a cooperative binding model, in which ssZPB requires the presence of some ssZPC to bind spermatozoa (Yurewicz *et al.*, 1998), and this finding is in agreement with the observations that some antibodies to ssZPC block sperm binding (Yurewicz *et al.*, 1998). The sperm binding activity of pig zona pellucida was first ascribed to serine-/threonine-linked oligosaccharides (Yurewicz *et al.*, 1991, 1992), but more recent data are not consistent with that finding. Asparagine-linked oligosaccharides were released from a mixture of ssZPB and ssZPC, and separated into neutral and acidic fractions. Only the neutral asparagine-linked sugars bound spermatozoa (Nakano and Yonezawa, 2001). Unfortunately, the precise oligosaccharide structure that binds spermatozoa was not resolved and there were over 30 different structures in this mixture. Further refinement of analytical approaches shows promise to resolve the oligosaccharide components in zona pellucida glycoproteins (Easton *et al.*, 2000). An advantage of studying the pig zona pellucida is the abundance of material that can be obtained for analysis. The major oligosaccharides in the pig zona pellucida have been described and it is apparent that the carbohydrate chains linked to mouse and pig zona glycoproteins are very different (Easton *et al.*, 2000; Nakano and Yonezawa, 2001).

Most studies attempting to identify the oligosaccharides that bind spermatozoa have used isolated and solubilized whole zonae pellucidae. This approach overlooks the finding that there is a heterogeneous distribution of glycosides within the zona pellucida (Aviles *et al.*, 2000). Some monosaccharides (for example, terminal α-galactose) cannot be detected by lectin staining in the outer portion of the zona pellucida and are not accessible until a spermatozoon has partially penetrated the zona pellucida (Aviles *et al.*, 2000). Therefore, one must be certain that oligosaccharide candidates proposed as receptors for acrosome-intact spermatozoa are located in the outer portion of the zona pellucida.

Receptors on spermatozoa for the zona pellucida

In contrast to the zona pellucida, which is a matrix made up of three glycoproteins, the surface of spermatozoa is a much more complex structure. The complexity of the sperm surface is probably one of the reasons why identifying the sperm proteins that bind to the zona pellucida has been very challenging. Another complication is that the binding of spermatozoa to the zona pellucida can be divided into two stages. Primary binding refers to the initial step in which acrosome-intact spermatozoa bind to the zona pellucida. After the acrosome reaction, a new membrane domain, the inner acrosomal membrane, is exposed and different receptors may allow spermatozoa to adhere to and penetrate the zona pellucida. Despite these difficulties, a number of candidates for zona pellucida receptors have been proposed, particularly for mouse spermatozoa.

Zona receptors on mouse spermatozoa

One possible zona pellucida receptor on mouse spermatozoa is sp56, a 56 kDa protein. This protein was first isolated on the basis of its affinity for ZP3 (Cheng *et al.*, 1994). Sequence analysis indicated that sp56 does not have a transmembrane domain (Bookbinder *et al.*, 1995). Recent studies revealed that sp56 is found within the acrosome so that although it cannot be involved in primary binding, it could potentially be exposed during the acrosome reaction and bind as a secondary receptor (Foster *et al.*, 1997). Early studies indicate that acrosome-reacted spermatozoa might bind only ZP2 (Bleil *et al.*, 1988), and this appears to be in conflict with the potential role of sp56 in binding ZP3 after the acrosome reaction. However, it is possible that sp56 binds ZP3 while spermatozoa are completing the acrosome reaction and, after the acrosome reaction is completed, sp56 is lost so that spermatozoa can bind only ZP2. There is evidence that sp56 is exposed gradually and then lost during the relatively slow exocytosis and dispersion of the acrosomal matrix during the acrosome reaction (Kim *et al.*, 2001).

A second possible candidate receptor with a molecular mass of 95 kDa was first identified by its ability to bind ZP3 after SDS-PAGE and transfer to a blot (Leyton and Saling, 1989a). A 95 kDa protein from human testis reported to be a human homologue of the mouse 95 kDa protein is very similar to c-mer (Burks *et al.*, 1995). The human sequence is controversial and the original mouse protein appears to be an unusual hexokinase (Bork, 1996; Kalab *et al.*, 1994; Tsai and Silver, 1996).

The zona receptor whose function has been studied in most detail is β1,4galactosyltransferase (GalTase) (Nixon *et al.*, 2000). This protein was named for the function with which it was first associated, that is, catalysing the addition of galactose to glycoproteins and glycolipids in the Golgi apparatus. More recent studies demonstrated that GalTase is also found on the plasma membrane of some cells, a location enabling it to act as a lectin and bind extracellular glycoconjugates that have N-acetylglucosamine residues presented in the proper context (Nixon *et al.*, 2000). The dual location of this zona pellucida receptor may be explained by the discovery of two forms of GalTase: a full-length form and a short form that results from translation from a downstream start site. The long form has an additional 13 amino acids on its cytoplasmic amino terminus that can apparently override the Golgi retention signal allowing some of the long form to move to the plasma membrane (Youakim *et al.*, 1994).

As a receptor on some cells, GalTase can bind specific extracellular glycoconjugates. GalTase on mouse spermatozoa binds ZP3, but not the other zona pellucida glycoproteins (Miller *et al.*, 1992). Reagents that inhibit GalTase block sperm binding to the zona pellucida (Nixon *et al.*, 2000). The ZP3 oligosaccharides that bind to GalTase, like those that bind to mouse spermatozoa, are linked to ZP3 through serine or threonine residues (Miller *et al.*, 1992). If these GalTase-binding oligosaccharides on ZP3 are removed or blocked, ZP3 does not bind to spermatozoa (Miller *et al.*, 1992).

However, when GalTase is eliminated by homologous recombination, spermatozoa from these mice remain fertile, indicating that there may be redundant receptors (Lu and Shur, 1997). The ability of spermatozoa from GalTase-null male mice to undergo the acrosome reaction and penetrate the zona pellucida *in vitro* is severely compromised (Lu and Shur, 1997).

Zona receptors on pig spermatozoa

Few studies on zona receptors of pig spermatozoa have been reported. Of the receptors described on the surface of mouse spermatozoa, GalTase is the only one that has been examined on pig spermatozoa. GalTase is present on the plasma membrane over the acrosome of pig spermatozoa (Larson and Miller, 1997). Although it binds to pig zona pellucida glycoproteins, GalTase binding is not required for fertilization in pigs. Reagents that inhibit GalTase and block mouse sperm–zona binding do not affect pig sperm–zona binding (Rebeiz and Miller, 1999). As GalTase binds the pig zona pellucida, it may be one of several receptors that function together in gamete binding. However, if other putative receptors are blocked, GalTase alone is not sufficient to allow spermatozoa to adhere to the zona pellucida (Rebeiz and Miller, 1999).

Several other proteins found on pig spermatozoa have been studied. A sperm protein named zonadhesin has affinity for the pig zona pellucida that is species-specific (Hardy and Garbers, 1994). This protein is particularly interesting because it is similar to other proteins that have been implicated in cell-to-cell and cell–matrix interactions (Hardy and Garbers, 1995). If zonadhesin is found within the acrosome, it may function in secondary binding of acrosome-reacted spermatozoa to the zona pellucida. The outcome of studies in which zonadhesin is blocked should be revealing.

There are several peripheral membrane sperm proteins that have been implicated in zona pellucida binding. These proteins may function as adhesive molecules but must couple to other transmembrane proteins to trigger signalling for the acrosome reaction. P47, a protein synthesized by testicular germ cells and the epididymis, has an affinity for the zona pellucida (Ensslin *et al.*, 1998). The consequences of blocking P47 have not been reported. A group of proteins named spermadhesins are produced in the testis, epididymis and accessory sex organs and some of these proteins bind to spermatozoa during epididymal passage or at ejaculation. These proteins have an affinity for a wide variety of ligands, including the zona pellucida (Jansen *et al.*, 2001). As they are peripheral membrane proteins, many are lost during capacitation (Calvete *et al.*, 1997). The necessity of spermadhesins produced by the accessory organs for fertilization is questionable, because removal of these glands does not affect fertility, and spermatozoa removed from the cauda epididymidis are fertile (Davies *et al.*, 1975; Hunter *et al.*, 1976).

One of the difficulties in assessing the function of zona pellucida receptor candidates is that some receptors may function as primary receptors on acrosome-intact spermatozoa, whereas others may act as secondary receptors on acrosome-reacted spermatozoa. The precise location of zona pellucida receptors on spermatozoa was addressed by labelling zona pellucida proteins directly with a bright fluorochrome and allowing labelled zona pellucida proteins to bind pig spermatozoa (Burkin and Miller, 2000). Dead spermatozoa were labelled with propidium iodide. Motile spermatozoa that excluded propidium iodide showed zona pellucida protein staining at the apical edge of spermatozoa (Fig. 1). No staining was observed when control proteins were labelled and incubated with spermatozoa. The staining with pig zona pellucida proteins was specific and saturable. The addition of excess unlabelled zona pellucida proteins displaced binding of labelled zona pellucida proteins.

No difference was observed in the labeling of capacitated compared with washed uncapacitated spermatozoa (Burkin and Miller, 2000). In contrast, when spermatozoa were

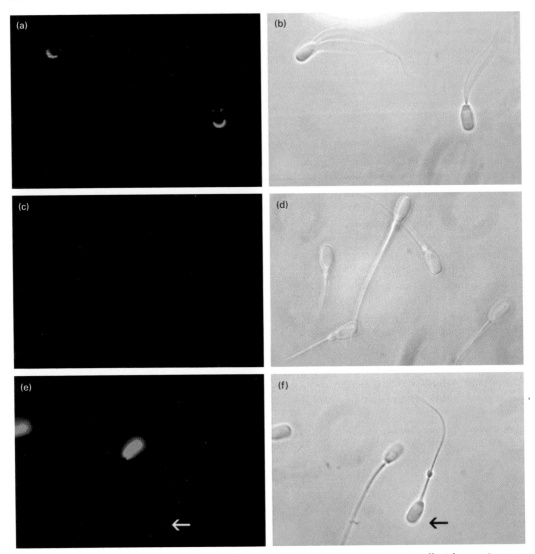

Fig. 1. Localization of solubilized zona pellucida proteins on live spermatozoa. Zona pellucida proteins were labelled with Alexa, a green fluorochrome. Labelled proteins and propidium iodide were added to live pig spermatozoa. Alexa-labelled zona pellucida proteins bound live, acrosome-intact spermatozoa over the anterior head region concentrated over the acrosomal ridge (a). The addition of a 100-fold excess of unlabelled zona pellucida proteins displaced the signal (c). The Alexa-labelled control glycoprotein, transferrin, did not bind to live spermatozoa indicated by the arrow (e,f). Dead spermatozoa stained with propidium iodide are visible because fluorescence images were captured using a filter set that allowed detection of both red and green fluorochromes simultaneously (a,c,e). Corresponding phase-contrast images are shown (b,d,f).

treated with the calcium ionophore A23187 to induce the acrosome reaction, zona pellucida protein binding was altered markedly. The entire apical half of the sperm head, including the region from the tip of the acrosome to the equatorial region, bound zona pellucida proteins (Fig. 2). This matched the region that bound zona pellucida proteins on fixed spermatozoa, probably because acrosomal zona pellucida binding proteins were exposed by fixation.

On the basis of these results, we predict that proteins on acrosome-intact spermatozoa involved in primary binding are located mainly on the plasma membrane overlying the apical ridge of the acrosome. The receptors on acrosome-reacted spermatozoa that are important for secondary binding are expected to be located over the entire acrosomal area of acrosome-reacted or fixed spermatozoa. Several of the receptor candidates studied appear to be located over the entire acrosomal area and, on the basis of zona protein binding, would be stronger candidates for secondary receptors than for primary receptors (Mori *et al.*, 1995; Ensslin *et al.*, 1998).

There are several candidates that may act as secondary receptors for acrosome-reacted spermatozoa, but there are fewer compelling candidates for zona pellucida receptors on acrosome intact spermatozoa. There are now more sophisticated biological tests of the function of putative zona pellucida receptors, such as gene knockouts in mice, a technique that will eventually be more common in other mammals. New approaches or a re-evaluation of the current approaches should enable additional candidates for primary zona receptors to be isolated.

The acrosome reaction and penetration of zona pellucida

Spermatozoa must undergo the exocytotic process, known as the acrosome reaction, to penetrate the zona pellucida. In mouse spermatozoa, acrosomal exocytosis is activated by ZP3 binding (Wassarman and Litscher, 2001). Although the oligosaccharides bind spermatozoa, the intact ZP3 glycoprotein is required to induce the acrosome reaction (Florman *et al.*, 1984). Interestingly, glycopeptides derived from pronase treatment of ZP3 can induce the acrosome reaction if a 'backbone' is provided by an antibody (Leyton and Saling, 1989b). This result led to the hypothesis that the function of the ZP3 protein backbone is to provide a scaffold for the sperm-binding oligosaccharides. Alternatively, the protein backbone could interact with a unique receptor that triggers the acrosome reaction.

ZP3 may trigger the acrosome reaction by activating the receptor that is important in initial binding. Alternatively, ZP3 may trigger the acrosome reaction by interacting with a second lower affinity receptor that is more important for signal transduction than initial binding. The only ZP3 receptor demonstrated to have a role in signal transduction is GalTase. Some GalTase antibodies are capable of clustering GalTase in a manner that appears to mimic ZP3 and trigger the acrosome reaction (Macek *et al.*, 1991). GalTase can bind two to three ZP3 molecules and some GalTase antibodies also appear to bind GalTase multivalently (Miller *et al.*, 1992). Monovalent Fab fragments do not induce the acrosome reaction but if the Fab fragments are made multivalent by addition of a second antibody, this complex induces the acrosome reaction. Aggregation of GalTase with antibodies activates heterotrimeric G proteins and triggers the acrosome reaction in a manner requiring pertussis toxin-sensitive G proteins (Gong *et al.*, 1995). This result is surprising as most G protein-coupled receptors have seven transmembrane domains and GalTase has only one. However, GalTase has clusters of basic amino acid residues that are necessary for G protein activation by traditional and non-traditional G protein-coupled receptors. At least one of these clusters of basic amino acid residues is required for G protein activation and GalTase signalling (Shi *et al.*, 2001).

An important role for GalTase in the acrosome reaction was confirmed by deleting GalTase by homologous recombination. Although spermatozoa from GalTase null mice bind to the zona pellucida, they acrosome react and penetrate the zona pellucida with only 7% of the frequency of control spermatozoa (Lu and Shur, 1997).

After the acrosome reaction, spermatozoa must remain stable on the zona pellucida in the secondary binding step. Some of the candidate receptors described above that have zona affinity and are found within the acrosome are good candidates for secondary receptors.

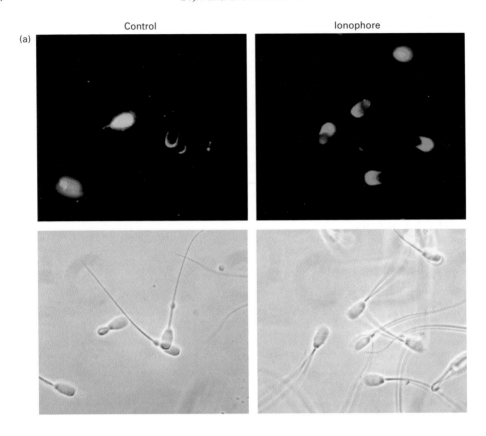

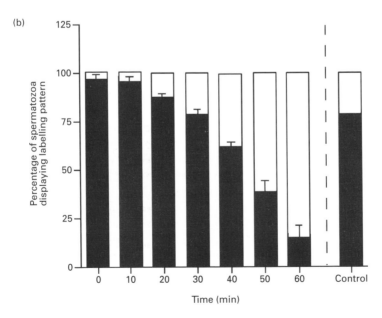

Fig. 2. For legend see opposite.

These candidates may function sequentially as the acrosome is exocytosed and the matrix is slowly dispersed. After the acrosome reaction, spermatozoa begin to penetrate the zona pellucida. This process requires a specialized hyperactivated motility to generate force to move through the zona pellucida (Yanagimachi, 1994). It also requires a localized dissolution of the zona pellucida, creating a penetration slit. There is considerable debate about whether zona penetration requires some hydrolysis of zona pellucida proteins or, apparently like penetration of the sea abalone egg coat (Kresge *et al.*, 2001), penetration does not require hydrolysis (Bedford, 1998).

In mice, there is evidence that ZP2 binds to acrosome-reacted spermatozoa to maintain spermatozoa on the zona pellucida (Bleil *et al.*, 1988). It is possible that ZP2 binds to components of the sperm acrosome, such as proacrosin and other proteases, to mediate secondary binding. Proacrosin is the zymogen form of acrosin, a serine protease that is abundant in the sperm acrosome (Jansen *et al.*, 2001). Proacrosin has affinity for sulphated fucose and sulphated zona pellucida proteins. The zona pellucida binding activity and enzyme activity of proacrosin are located in different regions of the molecule, and it is possible that both regions work in concert in adhesion and lysis of the zona pellucida during zona pellucida penetration. Gene knockout studies demonstrated that spermatozoa lacking proacrosin, although still fertile, are at a disadvantage compared with spermatozoa with normal amounts of proacrosin (Adham *et al.*, 1997). Another protein involved in secondary binding is PH-20, a sperm hyaluronidase that appears to have two functions. PH-20, present on the posterior head membrane of spermatozoa, can cleave hyaluronic acid in the matrix surrounding oocytes and, after the acrosome reaction, appears to be important for binding the zona pellucida (Myles and Primakoff, 1997). Blocking PH-20 prevents zona pellucida penetration (Myles and Primakoff, 1997; Yudin *et al.*, 1999).

Fusion of spermatozoa with the oocyte plasma membrane

Once inside the zona pellucida, spermatozoa bind to, and fuse with, the oocyte plasma membrane. A monoclonal antibody that inhibited sperm fusion to the plasma membrane of the oocyte provided the first step in identifying these adhesion molecules. This antibody reacted with a dimeric protein termed fertilin (Blobel *et al.*, 1992). Fertilin is a member of a growing family of molecules called ADAMs for their disintegrin and metalloprotease domains (adhesion, disintegrin and metalloprotease). The disintegrin domain is believed to interact with integrins on the oocyte membrane, specifically $\alpha6\beta1$ (Almeida *et al.*, 1995). Studies in

---

Fig. 2. Region of spermatozoa that binds zona pellucida proteins is increased in acrosome-reacting spermatozoa. Live, capacitated boar spermatozoa were incubated with the calcium ionophore A23187 to induce the acrosome reaction, followed by the addition of Alexa-labelled zona pellucida proteins and propidium iodide. The upper panels in (a) show fluorescence images of Alexa-labelled zona pellucida and propidium iodide, and the lower panels show corresponding phase-contrast images. Acrosome-reacted spermatozoa showed an increased area of zona pellucida protein binding, extending from the acrosomal ridge to the equatorial region of live spermatozoa, whereas controls without ionophore did not. For time course experiments (b), samples were removed at the specified times after the addition of ionophore. The percentage of live spermatozoa displaying zona pellucida binding in a thin band over the acrosomal ridge decreased with time (black bars), while the percentage displaying strong acrosomal fluorescence increased (white bars). Controls to which ionophore was not added were counted after 60 min. The graph shows the mean percentage of spermatozoa ± standard error. Regression analysis indicated a significant increase in the percentage of spermatozoa displaying strong fluorescence over the entire acrosomal region that was correlated with induction of the acrosome reaction.

mice with deletions in these genes produced by homologous recombination have yielded unexpected results. Spermatozoa from mice lacking fertilin-β have defects in transport through the oviduct and zona binding, but some spermatozoa can still fuse and activate oocytes (Cho *et al.*, 1998). Spermatozoa from knockouts of more recently described members of the ADAMs family were also defective in zona binding, but were not defective in oocyte membrane binding (Shamsadin *et al.*, 1999). As the ligand for these ADAMs family members was believed to be the integrin dimer α6β1, oocytes from animals lacking α6 were examined. These oocytes had no apparent defects in fertilization (Miller *et al.*, 2000). There may be redundant receptors that bind spermatozoa to the oocyte plasma membrane.

There are few studies of pig sperm binding to the oocyte plasma membrane. Pig oocytes express αv and β1 integrins on the surface membrane (Linfor and Berger, 2000). Several candidate ligands, described by their affinity for the oocyte membrane and their migration on SDS-PAGE, have been reported (Linfor and Berger, 2000; Sartini and Berger, 2000). Further studies to determine the biological importance of these adhesion molecules are necessary.

Egg activation and the block to polyspermy

After the spermatozoon binds and fuses with the oocyte plasma membrane, there is a release of calcium, a hallmark of fertilization (Yanagimachi, 1994). In mammals, there is a series of calcium oscillations that may be triggered by a sperm component that is released in the oocyte (Carroll, 2001). The cortical granules are released, the oocyte resumes and completes meiosis, and the sperm nucleus decondenses. As part of the block to polyspermy, the contents of the cortical granules act on the overlying zona pellucida. An enzyme that hydrolyses mouse ZP2 into two components is released, although it is not known how this proteolysis affects the function of ZP2 (Moller and Wassarman, 1989). A second enzyme, hexosaminidase B, is released from cortical granules during oocyte activation and acts on ZP3 (Miller *et al.*, 1993). This enzyme removes the terminal monosaccharide, *N*-acetylglucosamine, that binds GalTase. If hexosaminidase B is inhibited, polyspermic binding occurs (Miller *et al.*, 1993). There are few molecular studies of the block to polyspermic binding in pig oocytes, despite the high rate of polyspermy with *in vitro* fertilization in pigs.

Conclusion

Despite the importance of fertilization, a complete understanding of the receptors involved in gamete binding and fusion at the molecular level remains to be elucidated. The difficulty in obtaining sufficient material has made it problematic to determine the oligosaccharides from the zona pellucida that bind spermatozoa. Although it is apparent that soluble ZP3 is the only protein that binds acrosome-intact mouse spermatozoa, the zona pellucida protein that binds pig spermatozoa may not be the ZP3 homologue, but instead may be the homologue of mouse ZP1, known as ZPB. The complementary receptors for zona pellucida proteins on spermatozoa must be clarified. Studies of the identified receptor candidates must be completed and further studies are required to investigate new candidates. It is not clear how zona pellucida proteins are inactivated when the oocyte is fertilized and this causes difficulties for *in vitro* fertilization in pigs because of the high rates of polyspermy. New analytical techniques and novel approaches hold great promise for identifying molecules important for fertilization. The ability to modify animal genomes should enable the functions of old and new fertilization proteins to be tested and should help to resolve this enigma.

The authors apologize to those whose work was not cited due to space limitations. Work in the authors' laboratory was supported by the USDA National Research Initiative Competitive Grants Program, the National Science Foundation, and the National Institutes of Health.

References

Adham IM, Nayernia K and Engel W (1997) Spermatozoa lacking acrosin protein show delayed fertilization *Molecular Reproduction and Development* **46** 370–376

Almeida EAC, Huovila A-PJ, Sutherland AE et al. (1995) Mouse egg integrin α6β1 functions as a sperm receptor *Cell* **81** 1095–1104

Aviles M, Okinaga T, Shur BD and Ballesta J (2000) Differential expression of glycoside residues in the mammalian zona pellucida *Molecular Reproduction and Development* **57** 296–308

Bedford JM (1998) Mammalian fertilization misread? Sperm penetration of the eutherian zona pellucida is unlikely to be a lytic event *Biology of Reproduction* **59** 1275–1287

Bleil JD and Wassarman PM (1980) Mammalian sperm–egg interaction: identification of a glycoprotein in mouse egg zonae pellucidae possessing receptor activity for sperm *Cell* **20** 873–882

Bleil JD, Greve JM and Wassarman PM (1988) Identification of a secondary sperm receptor in the mouse egg zona pellucida: role in maintenance of binding of acrosome-reacted sperm to eggs *Developmental Biology* **128** 376–385

Blobel CP, Wolfsberg TG, Turck CW, Myles DG, Primakoff P and White JM (1992) A potential fusion peptide and an integrin ligand domain in a protein active in sperm–egg fusion *Nature* **356** 248–252

Bookbinder LH, Cheng A and Bleil JD (1995) Tissue- and species-specific expression of sp56, a mouse sperm fertilization protein *Science* **269** 86–89

Bork P (1996) Sperm–egg binding protein or proto-oncogene? *Science* **271** 1431–1432

Burkin HR and Miller DJ (2000) Zona pellucida protein binding ability of pig sperm during epididymal maturation and the acrosome reaction *Developmental Biology* **222** 99–109

Burks DJ, Carballada R, Moore HDM and Saling PM (1995) Interaction of a tyrosine kinase from human sperm with the zona pellucida at fertilization *Science* **269** 83–86

Calvete JJ, Ensslin M, Mburu J et al. (1997) Monoclonal antibodies against boar sperm zona pellucida-binding protein AWN-1. Characterization of a continuous antigenic determinant and immunolocalization of AWN epitopes in inseminated sows *Biology of Reproduction* **57** 735–742

Carroll J (2001) The initiation and regulation of Ca²⁺ signalling at fertilization in mammals *Seminars in Cell and Developmental Biology* **12** 37–43

Cheng A, Le T, Palacios M, Bookbinder LH, Wassarman PM, Suzuki F and Bleil JD (1994) Sperm–egg recognition in the mouse: characterization of sp56, a sperm protein having specific affinity for ZP3 *Journal of Cell Biology* **125** 867–878

Cho C, Bunch DO, Faure JE, Goulding EH, Eddy EM, Primakoff P and Myles DG (1998) Fertilization defects

in sperm from mice lacking fertilin β *Science* **281** 1857–1859

Davies DC, Hall G, Hibbitt G and Moore HD (1975) The removal of the seminal vesicles from the boar and the effects on the semen characteristics *Journal of Reproduction and Fertility* **43** 305–312

Easton RL, Patankar MS, Lattanzio FA, Leaven TH, Morris HR, Clark GF and Dell A (2000) Structural analysis of murine zona pellucida glycans. Evidence for the expression of core 2-type *O*-glycans and the Sdᵃ antigen *Journal of Biological Chemistry* **275** 7731–7742

Ensslin M, Vogel T, Calvete JJ, Thole HH, Schmidtke J, Matsuda T and Topfer-Petersen E (1998) Molecular cloning and characterization of P47, a novel boar sperm-associated zona pellucida-binding protein homologous to a family of mammalian secretory proteins *Biology of Reproduction* **58** 1057–1064

Florman HM and Wassarman PM (1985) *O*-linked oligosaccharides of mouse egg ZP3 account for its sperm receptor activity *Cell* **41** 313–324

Florman HM, Bechtol KB and Wassarman PM (1984) Enzymatic dissection of the functions of the mouse egg's receptor function for sperm *Developmental Biology* **106** 243–255

Foster J, Friday B, Maulit M, Blobel C, Winfrey V, Olson G, Kim K and Gerton G (1997) AM67, a secretory component of the guinea pig sperm acrosomal matrix, is related to mouse sperm protein sp56 and the complement component 4-binding proteins *Journal of Biological Chemistry* **272** 12 714–12 722

Gong XH, Dubois DH, Miller DJ and Shur BD (1995) Activation of a G protein complex by aggregation of β-1,4 galactosyltransferase on the surface of sperm *Science* **269** 1718–1721

Hardy DM and Garbers DL (1994) Species-specific binding of sperm proteins to the extracellular matrix (zona pellucida) of the egg *Journal of Biological Chemistry* **269** 19 000–19 004

Hardy DM and Garbers DL (1995) A sperm membrane protein that binds in a species-specific manner to the egg extracellular matrix is homologous to von Willebrand factor *Journal of Biological Chemistry* **270** 26 025–26 028

Hunter RH, Holtz W and Henfrey PJ (1976) Epididymal function in the boar in relation to the fertilizing ability of spermatozoa *Journal of Reproduction and Fertility* **46** 463–466

Jansen S, Ekhlasi-Hundrieser M and Topfer-Petersen E (2001) Sperm adhesion molecules: structure and function *Cells, Tissues, Organs* **168** 82–92

Johnston DS, Wright WW, Shaper JH, Hokke CH, Van den Eijnden DH and Joziasse DH (1998) Murine sperm–zona binding, a fucosyl residue is required for a high affinity sperm-binding ligand *Journal of Biological Chemistry* **273** 1888–1895

Kalab P, Visconti P, Leclerc P and Kopf GS (1994) p95, the major phosphotyrosine-containing protein in mouse spermatozoa, is a hexokinase with unique properties *Journal of Biological Chemistry* **269** 3810–3817

Kim KS, Foster JA and Gerton GL (2001) Differential release of guinea pig sperm acrosomal components during exocytosis *Biology of Reproduction* **64** 148–156

Kresge N, Vacquier VD and Stout CD (2001) Abalone lysin: the dissolving and evolving sperm protein *Bioessays* **23** 95–103

Larson JL and Miller DJ (1997) Sperm from a variety of mammalian species express β1,4-galactosyltransferase on their surface *Biology of Reproduction* **57** 442–453

Leyton L and Saling P (1989a) 95 kd sperm proteins bind ZP3 and serve as tyrosine kinase substrates in response to zona binding *Cell* **57** 1123–1130

Leyton L and Saling P (1989b) Evidence that aggregation of mouse sperm receptors by ZP3 triggers the acrosome reaction *Journal of Cell Biology* **108** 2163–2168

Linfor J and Berger T (2000) Potential role of αv and β1 integrins as oocyte adhesion molecules during fertilization in pigs *Journal of Reproduction and Fertility* **120** 65–72

Lu Q and Shur BD (1997) Sperm from β1,4-galactosyltransferase-null mice are refractory to ZP3-induced acrosome reaction and penetrate the zona pellucida poorly *Development* **124** 4121–4131

Macek MB, Lopez LC and Shur BD (1991) Aggregation of β-1,4-galactosyltransferase on mouse sperm induces the acrosome reaction *Developmental Biology* **147** 440–444

Miller BJ, Georges-Labouesse E, Primakoff P and Myles DG (2000) Normal fertilization occurs with eggs lacking the integrin α6β1 and is CD9-dependent *Journal of Cell Biology* **149** 1289–1296

Miller DJ, Gong XH, Decker G and Shur BD (1993) Egg cortical granule N-acetylglucosaminidase is required for the mouse zona block to polyspermy *Journal of Cell Biology* **123** 1431–1440

Miller DJ, Macek MB and Shur BD (1992) Complementarity between sperm surface β-1,4-galactosyltransferase and egg-coat ZP3 mediates sperm–egg binding *Nature* **357** 589–593

Moller CC and Wassarman PM (1989) Characterization of a proteinase that cleaves zona pellucida glycoprotein ZP2 following activation of mouse eggs *Developmental Biology* **132** 103–112

Mori E, Kashiwabara S, Baba T, Inagaki Y and Mori T (1995) Amino acid sequences of pig Sp38 and proacrosin required for binding to the zona pellucida *Developmental Biology* **168** 575–583

Myles DG and Primakoff P (1997) Why did the sperm cross the cumulus? To get to the oocyte. Functions of the sperm surface proteins PH-20 and fertilin in arriving at, and fusing with, the egg *Biology of Reproduction* **56** 320–327

Nakano M and Yonezawa N (2001) Localization of sperm ligand carbohydrate chains in pig zona pellucida glycoproteins *Cells, Tissues, Organs* **168** 65–75

Nixon B, Lu Q, Wassler M, Foote C, Ensslin M and Shur BD (2000) Galactosyltransferase function during mammalian fertilization *Cells, Tissues, Organs* **168** 46–57

Rankin T and Dean J (2000) The zona pellucida: using molecular genetics to study the mammalian egg coat *Reviews of Reproduction* **5** 114–121

Rebeiz M and Miller DJ (1999) Pig sperm surface β1,4galactosyltransferase binds to the zona pellucida but is not necessary or sufficient to mediate sperm–zona pellucida binding *Molecular Reproduction and Development* **54** 379–387

Sartini BL and Berger T (2000) Identification of homologous binding proteins in pig and bovine gametes *Molecular Reproduction and Development* **55** 446–451

Shamsadin R, Adham IM, Nayernia K, Heinlein UA, Oberwinkler H and Engel W (1999) Male mice deficient for germ-cell cyritestin are infertile *Biology of Reproduction* **61** 1445–1451

Shi X, Amindari S, Paruchuru K, Skalla D, Burkin H, Shur BD and Miller DJ (2001) Cell surface β-1,4-galactosyltransferase-I activates G protein-dependent exocytotic signaling *Development* **128** 645–654

Tsai J-Y and Silver L (1996) Sperm–egg binding protein or proto-oncogene *Science* **271** 1431–1432

Wassarman PM and Litscher ES (2001) Towards the molecular basis of sperm and egg interaction during mammalian fertilization *Cells, Tissues, Organs* **168** 36–45

Yanagimachi R (1994) Mammalian fertilization. In *Physiology of Reproduction, 2nd Edn* A189–A317 Eds E Knobil and JD Neill. Raven Press, New York

Yonezawa N, Aoki H, Hatanaka Y and Nakano M (1995) Involvement of N-linked carbohydrate chains of pig zona pellucida in sperm–egg binding *European Journal of Biochemistry* **233** 35–41

Youakim A, Dubois D and Shur B (1994) Localization of the long form of β-1,4-galactosyltransferase to the plasma membrane and Golgi complex of 3T3 and F9 cells by immunofluorescence confocal microscopy *Proceedings National Academy of Sciences USA* **91** 10913–10917

Yudin AI, Vandevoort CA, Li MW and Overstreet JW (1999) PH-20 but not acrosin is involved in sperm penetration of the macaque zona pellucida *Molecular Reproduction and Development* **53** 350–362

Yurewicz EC, Sacco AG and Subramanian MG (1987) Structural characterization of the M_r=55,000 antigen (ZP3) of pig oocyte zona pellucida *Journal of Biological Chemistry* **262** 564–571

Yurewicz EC, Pack BA and Sacco AG (1991) Isolation, composition and biological activity of sugar chains of pig oocyte zona pellucida 55 K glycoproteins *Molecular Reproduction and Development* **30** 126–134

Yurewicz EC, Pack BA and Sacco AG (1992) Pig oocyte zona pellucida Mr 55,000 glycoproteins: identification of O-glycosylated domains *Molecular Reproduction and Development* **33** 182–188

Yurewicz EC, Sacco AG, Gupta SK, Xu N and Gage DA (1998) Hetero-oligomerization-dependent binding of pig oocyte zona pellucida glycoproteins ZPB and ZPC to boar sperm membrane vesicles *Journal of Biological Chemistry* **273** 7488–7494

Reproduction Supplement **58**, 159–173

In vitro fertilization and embryo development in pigs

L. R. Abeydeera

PIC International, 2929 Seventh Street, Suite 130, Berkeley, CA 94710, USA

Considerable progress has been made in the *in vitro* production of pig embryos using improved methods for *in vitro* maturation (IVM) and fertilization (IVF). Despite the progress, polyspermic penetration remains a problem for *in vitro*-matured oocytes. Variation among boars, ejaculates and IVF protocols used in different laboratories appears to influence the incidence of polyspermy. Recent studies indicate that oviduct cells and their secretions play a role in reducing polyspermy. Very early attempts to culture *in vivo*-derived pig embryos met with little success and most were arrested at the four-cell stage. At present, many culture media are available that can overcome the four-cell block and support development to the blastocyst stage. In contrast, blastocyst development of *in vitro*-produced (IVP) embryos in these culture media varies significantly. Significant differences in morphology and numbers of cells have been observed in *in vitro*-produced blastocysts compared with *in vivo*-derived blastocysts. Surgical transfer of *in vitro*-produced embryos to recipient animals has resulted in acceptable pregnancy rates with moderate litter sizes. Although several systems are available for the generation of *in vitro*-produced embryos, the problems of polyspermy and poor embryo survival prevent large-scale production of embryos. Further research should be directed to improve oocyte and embryo quality, and to develop methods to minimize polyspermy through development of better IVM, IVF and embryo culture techniques.

Introduction

Owing to their physiological similarities to humans, pigs are increasingly important in biomedical research. Interest has grown in the use of transgenic pigs to produce specific proteins and as potential xenograft donors. Attempts to produce transgenic pigs by pronuclear microinjection require early embryos. Surgical collection of early embryos from donor animals is time-consuming, expensive and offers limited numbers of embryos. Therefore, it is important to produce large numbers of developmentally competent embryos by *in vitro* techniques for biomedical and basic research purposes.

Numerous reports describe maturation and fertilization of pig oocytes under *in vitro* conditions. Initially, nuclear maturation was achieved but problems with poor male pronuclear formation and high incidence of polyspermic penetration were observed routinely after *in vitro* fertilization (IVF) (Niwa, 1993; Funahashi and Day, 1997; Day *et al.*, 2000a). Oocyte maturation processes can be divided broadly into two aspects, namely nuclear and

Email: Labeydeera@PIC.com

Table 1. Sperm penetration obtained under various IVF conditions

IVF medium and supplements	Type of spermatozoa	Sperm concentration ($\times 10^6$ ml^{-1})	Type of oocyte	Penetration rate (%)	Reference
TCM + 10% FCS + 2 mmol caffeine l^{-1}	Fresh	2	In vivo (follicular) In vivo (ovulated)	80–100[a] 100[a]	Yoshida, 1987
BO + 0.1% BSA + 2 mmol caffeine l^{-1}	Frozen–thawed (epididymal)	24	IVM In vivo (ovulated)	42[a] 79[b]	Nagai et al., 1988
TCM + 10% FCS + 5 mmol caffeine l^{-1}	Frozen–thawed (ejaculated)	1 6 12 25 50	IVM	0 12 43 88 85	Wang et al., 1991
TCM + 10% FCS + 5 mmol caffeine l^{-1} TCM + 0.4% BSA + 5 mmol caffeine l^{-1}	Fresh Fresh	1 1	IVM IVM	94[a] 85[a]	Funahashi and Day, 1993
BO + 0.1% PVA + 5 mmol caffeine l^{-1}	Frozen–thawed (ejaculated)	4–5 7–8 10–12	IVM	28[a] 45[b] 44[b]	Wang et al., 1995
mTBM + 0.1% BSA mTBM + 0.1% BSA + 1 mmol caffeine l^{-1}	Frozen–thawed (ejaculated) Frozen–thawed (ejaculated)	1 1	IVM IVM	48[a] 96[b]	Abeydeera and Day, 1997a
TALP + 0.6% BSA	Fresh Frozen–thawed (ejaculated)	1 1	IVM IVM	71–100[a] 56–94[a]	Cordova et al., 1997

TCM: tissue culture medium; FCS: fetal calf serum; BO: Brackett and Oliphant medium; PVA: polyvinylalcohol; mTBM: modified Tris-buffered medium; TALP: Tyrode's albumin lactate pyruvate medium; IVM: in vitro-matured.
[a,b]Within a study, different superscripts indicate significant differences ($P \leq 0.05$).

cytoplasmic maturation. Although nuclear maturation appears to be normal, the degree of cytoplasmic maturation under those initial maturation conditions is unknown.

After many years of research, various modifications to the *in vitro* maturation (IVM) system have alleviated the problem of male pronuclear formation. However, polyspermy remains a major unresolved problem. It has not been established whether this abnormality is due to inadequate conditions during IVM, IVF or both. Despite the problem of polyspermy, successful production of pig embryos via *in vitro* techniques has improved markedly. Furthermore, transfer of embryos to recipient animals has resulted in acceptable pregnancy rates and litter sizes. This review will discuss recent progress in IVF and embryo culture techniques in pigs. It is envisaged that the development of new or optimization of existing *in vitro* techniques will result in further advances in embryo technology.

In vitro fertilization

Factors affecting sperm penetration

Fertilization medium and source of spermatozoa. Various types of fertilization medium, in conjunction with fresh or frozen–thawed spermatozoa at different concentrations, have been used to achieve *in vitro* penetration of pig oocytes (Table 1). Freshly ejaculated semen is still the main source of spermatozoa for routine IVF studies. Nevertheless, large variations among boars, as well as among different fractions within the same ejaculate, are observed in oocyte penetration and polyspermy (Xu *et al.*, 1996a,b). These authors found that the use of a specific sperm-rich fraction of the ejaculate can reduce the variability among different ejaculates collected from the same boar. Cryopreservation of semen from a single ejaculate would allow the optimization of IVF protocols and minimize the variability between trials. However, the same IVF protocol may not provide optimal conditions for frozen semen from other boars. It is necessary to optimize the IVF protocol for each individual batch of frozen semen to realise desirable IVF parameters because of variation in the ability of spermatozoa from different boars to withstand cryopreservation.

Bicarbonate concentration. Most IVF media contain $NaHCO_3$ concentrations that maintain a desirable pH under specific culture conditions. *In vivo*, spermatozoa undergo a process called capacitation before they are capable of penetrating an oocyte. Once ejaculated, spermatozoa are confronted with higher bicarbonate concentrations within the female tract, perhaps indicating a role for this ion (Harrison, 1996). In the presence of bicarbonate, a considerable number of sperm proteins become tyrosine-phosphorylated during *in vitro* capacitation (Flesch and Gadella, 2000). Bicarbonate concentration in IVF medium can influence the sperm penetration of pig oocytes (Table 2). Assessment of the functional status by chlortetracycline fluorescent staining indicated that HCO_3^- stimulated capacitation and acrosome reaction of spermatozoa in a concentration- and time-dependent manner (Abeydeera *et al.*, 1997). Suzuki *et al.* (1994a) showed that HCO_3^- was essential during IVF of pig oocytes under these conditions. However, successful sperm penetration in a Tris-buffered medium (Abeydeera and Day, 1997a,b) is evidence against the universal requirement for bicarbonate during pig IVF.

Calcium concentration. Extracellular Ca^{2+} is required for sperm capacitation and the ability to undergo an acrosome reaction (Flesch and Gadella, 2000). Current evidence indicates that calcium plays a critical role in modulating sperm function and is obligatory for successful fertilization in mammals (Fraser, 1995). Indeed, calcium is necessary during IVF of pig

Table 2. Sperm penetration of pig oocytes in the presence of bicarbonate

IVF condition	Bicarbonate (mmol l^{-1})	Penetration rate (%)	Reference
mBO + 0.1% PVA + 5 mmol caffeine l^{-1}	37	37[a]	Wang et al., 1995
	41	51[a]	
	45	76[b]	
	50	74[b]	
TCM + 10% FCS + 5 mmol caffeine l^{-1}	26	63[a]	Abeydeera et al., 1997
	36	88[b]	
	46	90[b]	
	56	88[b]	

mBO: modified Brackett and Oliphant medium; PVA: polyvinylalcohol; FCS: fetal calf serum; TCM: tissue culture medium.
[ab]Within a study, different superscripts indicate significant differences ($P < 0.05$).

Table 3. Effect of various types of macromolecule on fertilization parameters in pigs

Type of supplement	Penetration rate (%)	Polyspermy (%)
None	14[a]	5
PVA (5 mg ml^{-1})	19[ab]	15
PVP (5 mg ml^{-1})	27[b]	8
FCS (10%)	57[c]	79
BSA (5 mg ml^{-1})	77[d]	82

Data from Suzuki et al. (1994b).
PVA: polyvinylalcohol; PVP: polyvinylpyrrolidone; FCS: fetal calf serum.
[abcd]Different superscripts indicate significant differences among values ($P \leqslant 0.05$).

oocytes, as Abeydeera and Day (1997a) showed that penetration did not occur in its absence and that penetration rate increased with increasing concentrations of calcium.

Macromolecular supplements. Most pig IVF media are supplemented with fetal calf serum (FCS; Yoshida, 1987; Wang et al., 1991) or BSA (Nagai et al., 1988; Abeydeera and Day, 1997a) as a protein source but some studies have used polyvinylalcohol (PVA; Wang et al., 1995) or polyvinylpyrrolidone (PVP; Suzuki et al., 1994b) under defined conditions. Using modified Tyrode's medium containing 4.6 mmol CaCl$_2$ l^{-1} and 2 mmol caffeine l^{-1}, Suzuki et al. (1994b) showed that the type of macromolecule added during IVF has a significant influence on sperm penetration (Table 3). In addition, the amount of BSA or FCS added to IVF medium could also influence the fertilization rate.

Caffeine. Most pig IVF media are supplemented with caffeine, a phosphodiesterase inhibitor, which could increase cAMP within sperm cells, leading to capacitation (Flesch and Gadella, 2000). In a previous study, Wang et al. (1991) failed to obtain sperm penetration in the absence of caffeine and higher penetration rates were obtained at 2.5–10.0 mmol caffeine l^{-1} followed by a decrease at 20 mmol caffeine l^{-1} (Table 4). Nagai et al. (1994) obtained a similar pattern but failed to obtain penetration with 2 mmol caffeine l^{-1}. In contrast, recent

Table 4. Sperm penetration of pig oocytes in the presence of caffeine

IVF condition	Source of spermatozoa	Caffeine (mmol l^{-1})	Penetration rate (%)	Reference
TCM + FCS	Frozen–thawed (ejaculated)	0	0[a]	Wang *et al.*, 1991
		2.5	70[b]	
		5	89[c]	
		20	9[a]	
BO + BSA	Frozen–thawed (epididymal)	0	0[a]	Nagai *et al.*, 1994
		2	0[a]	
		5	45[b]	
		15	59[b]	
		20	32[c]	
mTBM + BSA	Frozen–thawed (ejaculated)	0	48[a]	Abeydeera and Day, 1997a
		1	96[b]	
		5	95[b]	
mBO + BSA	Frozen–thawed (ejaculated)	0	50[a]	Funahashi *et al.*, 2000
		1	98[b]	

TCM: tissue culture medium; FCS: fetal calf serum; mBO: modified Brackett and Oliphant medium; mTBM: modified Tris-buffered medium.
[abc]Within a study, different superscripts indicate significant differences ($P \leqslant 0.05$).

studies have shown penetration in about 50% of oocytes without caffeine (Abeydeera and Day, 1997a; Funahashi *et al.*, 2000). However, penetration rate was increased when caffeine was added during IVF. The disparity among these studies can be attributed to different IVF media or the type of spermatozoa used.

Preincubation of spermatozoa. Preincubation of spermatozoa at various concentrations (Nagai *et al.*, 1984) and the presence of pig follicular fluid during preincubation (Funahashi and Day, 1993) both influence fertilization parameters. Preincubation in the absence of pig follicular fluid stimulates sperm capacitation and results in higher penetration rate and polyspermy. In the presence of pig follicular fluid, capacitation and spontaneous acrosome reaction are stimulated in a concentration-dependent fashion. Such conditions effectively reduce the proportion of capacitated spermatozoa but maintain a high penetration rate with a low incidence of polyspermy. However, high concentrations (10%) of pig follicular fluid tend to reduce penetration by inducing a higher rate of spontaneous acrosome reaction (Funahashi and Day, 1993).

Sperm concentration and co-incubation interval. Penetration rate and polyspermy are also influenced by sperm concentration and duration of co-incubation with oocytes (Abeydeera and Day, 1997b). More spermatozoa are undergoing capacitation at higher sperm concentrations and may be responsible for the higher penetration rate. However, co-incubation of oocytes at a constant sperm concentration for a longer period allows sufficient sperm–oocyte interactions to result in a high incidence of sperm penetration. After reaching the highest penetration rate, a further increase in sperm concentration or co-incubation time tends to increase the incidence of polyspermic penetration.

Male pronuclear formation

Much research has been directed towards increasing the male pronuclear formation in pig oocytes after sperm penetration. Various modifications to IVM, such as supplementation of follicular fluid, co-culture with extroverted follicles, limited exposure to gonadotrophins or low NaCl concentration in culture medium have been used to improve the ability of oocytes to stimulate male pronuclear formation (see Day et al., 2000a). A significant improvement in male pronuclear formation was obtained after supplementation of maturation media with cysteine or glutathione (Yoshida et al., 1992). A later study showed that improvement in male pronuclear formation due to cysteine supplementation is correlated with higher concentrations of intracellular glutathione in matured oocytes (Yoshida et al., 1993). Synthesis of glutathione during oocyte maturation is a prerequisite for sperm nuclear chromatin decondensation and successful male pronuclear formation (Perreault et al., 1988). It appears that male pronuclear formation is compromised in oocytes with lower concentrations of intracellular glutathione.

Polyspermy

Despite the significant improvements in male pronuclear formation, polyspermy remains a major unresolved problem with IVF of pig oocytes. Under in vivo conditions, fertilization occurs within a few hours after ovulation and in most instances monospermic penetration ensues. Evidence from laboratory and farm animals indicates that the sperm:egg ratio at the time of initial penetration of the egg membranes is close to unity and this ratio increases only after the establishment of a zona block (Hunter, 1993). Under most IVF conditions, oocytes are always exposed to excessive numbers of spermatozoa, which may be a predisposing factor for multiple sperm penetrations. An ideal IVF system should result in a high penetration rate (> 80%) with a low incidence of polyspermy (< 10%). A tight correlation has been established between the absolute number of spermatozoa per oocyte at fertilization and the degree of polyspermy (Rath, 1992). Theoretically, the problem of polyspermy could be overcome by reducing the number of spermatozoa within the IVF droplets. However, in most cases, such adjustments are associated with a low oocyte penetration rate.

In mammals, sperm penetration triggers oocyte activation and subsequent cortical granule exocytosis leading to modification of the zona pellucida and block to polyspermy. Cortical granule density within the cytoplasm and exocytosis of these granules after sperm penetration in vitro appears to be similar between in vitro-matured and ovulated pig oocytes (Wang et al., 1998). However, the incidence of polyspermy is higher in in vitro-matured oocytes. The limited perivitelline space in in vitro-matured oocytes may interfere with the proper dispersal of cortical granule contents and delay the establishment of the zona block. It is possible that under IVF conditions, accessory spermatozoa gain entry before establishment of a functional zona block. Pig oocytes matured in Whitten's medium containing a low NaCl concentration resulted in oocytes with a wider perivitelline space that were less polyspermic (Funahashi et al., 1994a). Therefore, use of an IVM medium that results in matured oocytes with a wider perivitelline space may, at least in part, resolve the problem of polyspermy.

The in vivo counterparts of in vitro-matured oocytes are the mature oocytes from preovulatory follicles. Day et al. (2000b) examined the morphological, physical and fertilization parameters of in vitro-matured, ovulated and preovulatory oocytes (Table 5). For the properties evaluated, in vitro-matured oocytes are similar in quality to preovulatory oocytes. It is clear that after ovulation, major changes to the oocyte take place within the oviduct, which may be important in preventing polyspermy. Compared with controls, surgical transfer of in vitro-matured oocytes to an oestrous oviduct for 4 h resulted in similar

Table 5. Morphological, physical and fertilization parameters of ovulated, preovulatory and *in vitro*-matured pig oocytes

Parameter	Oocyte category		
	IVM	Preovulatory	Ovulated
Diameter (µm)	152[a]	157[a]	165[b]
Zona thickness (µm)	16[a]	16[a]	18[b]
Size of PVS (µm)	2.6[a]	2.6[a]	9.4[b]
Zona digestion time (min)	3–6[a]	3–6[a]	> 60[b]
Penetration rate (%)	85	82	93
Polyspermy (%)	64[a]	86[b]	28[c]

Data from Abeydeera *et al.* (1999).

PVS: perivitelline space.

[abc]Different superscripts within a row indicate significant differences ($P \leq 0.05$).

morphological and physical changes as observed in ovulated oocytes. Furthermore, oocytes exposed to the oviduct showed similar penetration rates (87 versus 83%) but a lower rate of polyspermy (26 versus 67%). Many *in vitro* studies have indicated the beneficial effects of oviduct cells and conditioned media in reducing polyspermy (Table 6). In these studies, oviductal cells were obtained from either prepubertal gilts or animals showing signs of oestrus. Vatzias and Hagen (1999) showed that supplementation of IVF medium with conditioned medium derived from periovulatory oviduct explant culture reduced the incidence of polyspermy compared with conditioned medium from mid-luteal phase oviduct explants and the control group. These results indicate strongly that oviductal secretions contain factors that interact with oocytes or spermatozoa to prevent or reduce entry of multiple spermatozoa.

The oviduct synthesizes and secretes multiple proteins in response to ovarian hormones, thereby creating a microenvironment capable of supporting the events of fertilization and embryo development. A variety of proteins synthesized and secreted by the pig oviduct have been identified (Buhi *et al.*, 2000). Most abundant is the oestrogen-dependent glycoprotein identified as pig oviduct-specific secretory glycoprotein (pOSP). Some other major synthesized proteins include protease inhibitors (tissue inhibitor of metalloproteinase 1 (TIMP-1), plasminogen activator inhibitor I), clusterin, growth factors and cytokines (Buhi *et al.*, 2000). The presence of pOSP in the zona pellucida and perivitelline space of oviductal oocytes and embryos indicates that it may have a physiological role during sperm–oocyte interaction (Buhi *et al.*, 1993). Exposure of oocytes to semi-purified pOSP (10 µg ml^{-1}) before and during fertilization significantly reduced the incidence of polyspermy (29 versus 61%) without compromising sperm penetration (63 versus 74%; Kouba *et al.*, 2000). There was no evidence of zona hardening but a reduction in sperm binding to zona pellucida was observed in the presence of pOSP. A different oviductal secretory product may be responsible for the zona hardening observed in ovulated oocytes. However, it is not clear whether the reduction of polyspermy by pOSP is due to its interaction with the oocyte or spermatozoa, as oocytes are exposed to the protein before and during fertilization. According to Suzuki *et al.* (2000), sperm preincubation or sperm–oocyte co-incubation in the presence of hyaluronic acid can reduce polyspermy. Hyaluronic acid has been localized in the tissues and intraluminal fluid of pig oviduct (Tienthai *et al.*, 2001), which indicates that it may be involved during *in vivo* fertilization. In addition to oviduct glycoproteins, hyaluronic acid may also play a role in modulation of sperm penetration and polyspermy.

L. R. Abeydeera

Table 6. Effect of pig oocyte or sperm exposure to oviduct cells or conditioned media before or during IVF on sperm penetration and polyspermy

Pre-fertilization conditions	Fertilization condition	Penetration rate (%)	Polyspermy (%)	Reference
Preincubation of IVM oocytes with POEC	IVF with (+) or without (−) POEC			Romar *et al.*, 2000
0 h	+	61	50[ab]	
0 h	−	77	57[b]	
2 h	+	59	41[a]	
4 h	+	66	24[a]	
3 h preincubation of IVM oocytes before IVF in				Bureau *et al.*, 2000
Medium only		90	45[a]	
Medium conditioned with POEC for 24 h		87	25[b]	
Medium with POEC added just before 3 h preincubation		93	37[a]	
None	Fertilization medium only (FM)	95	93[a]	Kano *et al.*, 1994
	FM + oviduct cell monolayer	85	64[b]	
	FM only	97	90[a]	
	FM + oviduct conditioned medium	90	73[b]	
Co-culture of spermatozoa with oviductal cells	Presence of oviduct cells during IVF			Nagai and Moor, 1990
0 h	−	89[a]	81[a]	
0 h	+	89[a]	85[a]	
1.0 h	+	94[a]	71[ab]	
2.5 h	+	84[a]	53[b]	
3.5 h	+	19[b]	14[c]	

IVM oocytes: *in vitro*-matured oocytes; POEC: pig oviduct epithelial cells.

[abc]Within a study, different superscripts indicate significant differences ($P \leqslant 0.05$).

Most pig IVF media are supplemented with caffeine, a phosphodiesterase inhibitor known to increase intracellular cAMP. A recent study, using frozen–thawed ejaculated semen, indicated that when IVF medium (modified Brackett and Oliphant medium; mBO) contained caffeine (1 mmol l^{-1}), almost all oocytes (98%) were penetrated, and 87% of penetrated oocytes were polyspermic (Funahashi *et al.*, 2000). However, when IVF medium was supplemented with fertilization-promoting peptide (FPP; 100 nmol l^{-1}) or adenosine (10 μmol l^{-1}) a high penetration rate (71–75%) was maintained with a significantly reduced frequency of polyspermy (20–25%). Furthermore, analysis of the functional state of spermatozoa exposed to these compounds revealed that FPP and adenosine stimulated capacitation but inhibited spontaneous acrosome reaction. In contrast, caffeine stimulated both capacitation and acrosome reaction. Accordingly, it may be possible to minimize the problem of polyspermic penetration by replacing the caffeine with FPP or adenosine.

The type of IVF medium may also affect the incidence of polyspermy (A. Kidson, personal communication). This worker examined fertilization parameters using either modified Tyrode's albumin lactate pyruvate (mTALP) or modified Tris-buffered medium (mTBM) as IVF medium. At a low sperm concentration (4×10^5 spermatozoa ml^{-1}), penetration (54 versus 32%) and polyspermy (40 versus 10%) were higher in mTALP than mTBM, respectively. A ten-fold higher sperm concentration increased penetration rates (82 versus 79%) similarly for mTALP and mTBM, respectively. Incidence of polyspermy was 76% for mTALP and 26% for mTBM. Therefore, medium and sperm concentration interact to produce different rates of polyspermy.

Developmental competence of pig embryos

Early attempts to culture *in vivo*-derived one-cell pig embryos in various culture media were consistently met with a developmental arrest at the four-cell stage (Davis, 1985). However, when collected at the four-cell stage and placed in culture, embryos continued development to the blastocyst stage. Numerous approaches have been used to circumvent the *in vitro* developmental block by using oviduct organ culture, co-culture with oviductal cells and oviductal fluid supplementation (see Day *et al.*, 2000a). In more recent studies, > 70% of *in vivo*-derived embryos developed to the blastocyst stage in modified Whitten's medium (mWM; Beckmann and Day, 1993), North Carolina State University 23 medium (NCSU 23; Petters and Wells, 1993), Iowa State University medium (ISU; Youngs *et al.*, 1993) and Beltsville embryo culture medium 3 (BECM-3; Dobrinsky *et al.*, 1996).

Type of culture medium and embryo development. Although various culture media have proven to be equally competent to support development of *in vivo*-derived embryos to the blastocyst stage, various degrees of success have been observed with *in vitro*-produced embryos, thus indicating the different sensitivity of these embryos to the type of culture medium. Abeydeera *et al.* (1999) compared the developmental ability of *in vitro*-matured and fertilized embryos in four different culture media. Highest (30%) and lowest (5%) proportions of blastocyst development were observed in NCSU and mWM, respectively, with the other two media (ISU and BECM) producing intermediate rates of blastocyst formation. One difference between NCSU and mWM is the presence of a higher sodium lactate concentration (25 mmol l^{-1}) in mWM. Supplementation of NCSU with 25 mmol sodium lactate l^{-1} significantly decreased blastocyst development (14 versus 32%). A similar lactate concentration has been found to be inhibitory to development of early stage pig embryos (Davis, 1985). However, reducing the lactate concentration in mWM did not improve blastocyst development. Blastocyst development in ISU (14%) was higher than in mWM (5%). Differences between these two media are the presence of low lactate concentrations (12.9 mmol l^{-1}) and absence of glucose in ISU medium. These results indicate that the presence of a higher concentration of lactate or glucose in mWM may be detrimental to the development of *in vitro*-matured and fertilized embryos. Indeed, culture of embryos in NCSU lacking glucose but supplemented with low concentrations of lactate (4.5 mmol l^{-1}) and pyruvate (0.33 mmol l^{-1}) for the first 72 h followed by NCSU with glucose for 72 h improved blastocyst development (L. R. Abeydeera, unpublished). It is concluded that NCSU appears to be the most suitable medium available for *in vitro* production of pig blastocysts, whereas other media are effective for culture of *in vivo*-derived embryos.

Table 7. Improvement in pig blastocyst development with modifications to the oocyte maturation medium

Maturation medium	Modification	Blastocysts (%)	Reference
NCSU 23 + 10% pFF	Control	9[a]	Funahashi et al., 1997a
	Preincubation in IVM medium for 12 h before addition of hormones	23[b]	
NCSU 37 + 10% pFF	Control	9[a]	Funahashi et al., 1997b
	cAMP for 20 h	22[b]	
NCSU 23 + 10% pFF	Control	18[a]	Abeydeera et al., 1998a
	Follicular shell pieces	36[b]	
TCM-199 + 25% pFF	Control	1[a]	Grupen et al., 1995
	500 µmol cysteamine l^{-1}	12[b]	
NSCU 23 + 10% pFF	Control	26[a]	Abeydeera et al., 1998b
	12.5 µmol BME l^{-1}	34[b]	
	25 µmol BME l^{-1}	41[b]	
NCSU 23 + 10% pFF	Control	21[a]	Abeydeera et al., 1998c
	1 ng EGF ml^{-1}	33[b]	
	10 ng EGF ml^{-1}	42[b]	
TCM-199 + 0.1% PVA	Control	22[a]	Abeydeera et al., 2000
	10 ng EGF ml^{-1}	37[b]	

NCSU: North Carolina State University; pFF: pig follicular fluid; IVM: in vitro maturation; TCM-199: tissue culture medium 199; BME: β-mercaptoethanol; EGF: epidermal growth factor; PVA: polyvinylalcohol.
[a,b]Within a study, different superscripts indicate significant differences ($P \leqslant 0.05$).

Embryo development with modifications to IVM medium. Production of blastocysts through IVM–IVF techniques has resulted in variable success. Many of the failures can be attributed to poor cytoplasmic maturation or a high incidence of polyspermy or both. However, improvements in embryo development to the blastocyst stage have been achieved by introducing various modifications to the IVM system (Table 7). Many of the effective modifications increased the intracellular glutathione concentration in oocytes and can be related to their developmental competence. After sperm penetration, some of the glutathione is used for sperm nuclear decondensation and oocytes with a higher glutathione content may retain more glutathione than do those with a low glutathione contents. Day et al. (2000a) suggested that intracellular glutathione could eliminate the oxidative damage caused by reactive oxygen species generated during culture in a conventional 5% CO_2 in air environment, which is detrimental to embryo development. Therefore, intracellular glutathione content of pig oocytes after IVM could be a potential biochemical marker to determine the effectiveness of an IVM system and subsequent developmental competence of oocytes.

Embryo development with modifications to IVF system. A significant improvement in blastocyst development has been observed when glutathione was supplemented during IVF in pigs (Boquest et al., 1999). The higher blastocyst yields did not appear to be related to an increase in glutathione concentrations in putative zygotes. Although the mechanism is not known, it is possible that extracellular glutathione may have effects on spermatozoa or oocytes or both. It was suggested that any detrimental effects on spermatozoa and oocytes by reactive oxygen species generated during IVF might have been counteracted by the presence of glutathione to ensure normal embryo development.

In a recent study, a higher rate of penetration (80 versus 57%) and blastocyst development (30 versus 8%) was observed when spermatozoa and oocytes were co-incubated in IVF medium for 10 min followed by transfer of oocytes with zona-bound spermatozoa to a fresh IVF medium for 5 h (Grupen and Nottle, 2000). It is surprising that this IVF strategy gave a higher penetration rate than controls. Intuitively, presence of spermatozoa for the entire co-incubation period would be expected to result in a similar or a higher penetration rate than the 10 min sperm–oocyte co-incubation method. Nevertheless, such an IVF strategy could reduce the detrimental effects caused by reactive oxygen species that may otherwise occur when spermatozoa and oocytes are left together for longer co-incubation periods. It would be worthwhile to re-examine and use such IVF techniques to produce pig embryos *in vitro*.

Embryo development with hyaluronic acid. An improvement in blastocyst development (70 versus 45%) was observed when *in vivo*-derived one- to two-cell stage pig embryos were cultured in the presence of hyaluronic acid (Miyano *et al.*, 1994). This stimulatory effect was not observed when culture medium contained a higher concentration (0.4 versus 1.5% w/v) of BSA, indicating that a factor or factors in BSA may become toxic to embryos at higher concentrations. Similarly, Kano *et al.* (1998) observed the beneficial effects of hyaluronic acid on blastocyst development of *in vitro*-matured and fertilized pig embryos. Hyaluronic acid has been localized in tissues and intraluminal fluid of pig oviduct (Tienthai *et al.*, 2001), which indicates a possible involvement during embryo development. Glycosaminoglycans promote the viability of pig oocytes (Sato *et al.*, 1990). The exact mechanism of hyaluronic acid-improved embryo development is not known. However, the involvement of hyaluronic acid in sustaining embryo viability should be considered in future work.

Embryo morphology and quality

Although the success achieved in improving the production of blastocysts by *in vitro* techniques is notable, distinct morphological differences have been observed between *in vitro*- and *in vivo*-produced embryos, including blastocysts (Wang *et al.*, 1999). Well-defined blastomeres in early stage embryos and a prominent inner cell mass in blastocysts are evident in embryos recovered *in vivo*. According to Papaioannou and Ebert (1988), the number of cells in *in vitro*-produced blastocysts is lower than in *in vivo*-produced blastocysts. It is possible that inadequate cytoplasmic maturation of *in vitro*-matured oocytes or suboptimal embryo culture conditions is responsible for the poor embryo quality. Transfer of *in vitro*-matured and fertilized zygotes to the oviducts of recipient animals and then recovery by retrogate flushing 5 days later resulted in blastocysts with cell numbers several-fold higher (106–136 versus 10–21) than blastocysts developed *in vitro* (Funahashi *et al.*, 1994b). In another study, the number of blastocyst cells after *in vitro* and *in vivo* development of *in vivo*-derived one- to two-cell embryos was examined (Machaty *et al.*, 1998). Compared with blastocysts developed in culture, a two-fold increase in cell number (25 versus 55) was observed for blastocysts developed *in vivo*. Collectively, the above findings indicate that suboptimal embryo culture conditions are likely to be the reason for low numbers of cells.

Recent evidence showed that partial inhibition of oxidative phosphorylation at the morula stage can significantly increase the proportion of blastocysts and their number of cells

Table 8. Results of transfer of *in vitro*-produced pig embryos

Source of spermatozoa	Embryonic stage	Piglets/recipients	Reference
Fresh	Two- to four-cell	9/1	Mattioli *et al.*, 1989
Fresh	Two- to four-cell	19/3	Funahashi *et al.*, 1997b
Frozen–thawed	Two- to four-cell	18/5	Abeydeera *et al.*, 1998a
Frozen–thawed	Two- to four-cell	7/1	Abeydeera *et al.*, 1998c
	Eight-cell to morula	11/2	
Frozen–thawed	⩾ One-cell	17/3	Kikuchi *et al.*, 1999
Frozen–thawed	Eight-cell to morula	82/12	Abeydeera *et al.*, 2000

(Machaty *et al.*, 2001). In the presence of inhibitors, it is assumed that the total ATP production by the embryo is low. A similar increase in blastocyst development and number of cells was also observed when morula stage embryos were cultured under low (5%) oxygen tension (Machaty *et al.*, 2001). In a previous study, no improvement in blastocyst development was observed when zygotes were cultured at a low oxygen tension for the entire culture period (Machaty *et al.*, 1998). The above findings indicate that ATP production in embryos after compaction may favour glycolysis over oxidative phosphorylation. In turn, it may be important to establish a sequential culture environment, 20% oxygen up to the morula stage and 5% oxygen for later stages, to reduce ATP production and generate better quality pig embryos *in vitro*.

Embryo transfer

Production of pig litters through embryo transfer techniques using *in vitro*-matured and fertilized embryos would eliminate the necessity of *in vivo*-derived embryos. Although initial embryo development can be achieved in culture, the ultimate test of their viability is to establish pregnancies and live births after transfer to recipient animals. Various degrees of success in pregnancies and live births have been achieved after transfer of *in vitro*-matured and fertilized embryos to the oviduct or uterus of recipient gilts (Table 8). A potential problem is asynchrony between the embryo and oviduct or uterus. Routine transfers with *in vitro*-produced embryos are performed to a recipient at least 24 h behind the embryonic age and accurate detection of oestrus is a critical factor. In addition, > 30 embryos are deposited in the oviduct or uterus at transfer. There is little information available about the ability of *in vitro*-produced embryos to hatch *in vivo*. Under *in vitro* conditions, < 10% of blastocysts hatch in NCSU 23 medium containing BSA (L. R. Abeydeera, unpublished). However, addition of 5–10% FCS at about days 4.5–5.0 of culture can increase hatching to 30–40%. Problems associated with *in vivo* hatching of *in vitro*-produced embryos could negatively affect the litter size. Therefore, development of embryo culture systems that stimulate hatching would probably improve pregnancy rate and litter size.

Fate of polyspermic oocytes

Polyspermic fertilization in mammals is considered pathological and usually results in early death of the zygote (Hunter, 1991). Recent studies indicate that polypronuclear oocytes produced from IVM–IVF cleave and develop to the blastocyst stage *in vitro* or *in vivo* at a rate similar to that of two-pronuclear oocytes (Han *et al.*, 1999a). However, they have fewer inner cell mass nuclei compared with blastocysts derived from oocytes with two pronuclei. It should be noted that polypronuclear oocytes used in the study of Han *et al.* (1999a) contained one female pronucleus and two male pronuclei. In contrast to blastocysts derived from two-pronuclear oocytes, some blastocysts developed from polypronuclear oocytes showed abnormal ploidy, including haploids, triploids and tetraploids. Interestingly, transfer of polypronuclear oocytes to recipients resulted in pregnancies (Han *et al.*, 1999b). At day 40 of pregnancy, 16 fetuses were recovered from three recipients that received polyspermic oocytes. Analysis of ploidy in eight fetuses revealed one triploid, one mosaic (diploid and tetraploid) and the remainder had diploid cells. When four pregnant recipients were allowed to continue beyond day 40, one recipient showed oestrus at day 60 and one on day 97. The remaining animals farrowed five live piglets with a normal ploidy. It seems that some of the polypronuclear pig oocytes possess an as yet unknown mechanism to prevent or correct their ploidy. The location of pronuclei within the cytoplasm of polypronuclear oocytes appears to have a significant effect on determining the ploidy of the resulting embryo before the first cell division (Han *et al.*, 1999b).

Conclusion

It is now possible to produce viable pig embryos through *in vitro* techniques. Supplementation with cysteine during oocyte maturation can alleviate the problem of poor male pronuclear formation. It may also be possible to reduce polyspermy, at least in part, by changing the NaCl concentration of culture medium. Consideration should also be given to exposure of oocytes to oviductal cells and their secretory products before or during sperm–oocyte interaction to reduce polyspermy. It may be necessary to replace caffeine with adenosine to stimulate sperm capacitation and realise normal penetration. A sequential embryo culture environment may improve the quality of blastocysts. It is envisaged that combinations of these improved systems will yield a higher proportion of viable blastocysts capable of establishing successful pregnancies and eventually reduce the number of embryos necessary per transfer. *In vitro* production of pig embryos, in conjunction with improvements in non-surgical embryo transfer techniques, has tremendous potential for basic research and commercial applications.

The author is very grateful to B. N. Day, D. L. Davis and J. E. Anderson for critical reading and editing of the manuscript.

References

Abeydeera LR and Day BN (1997a) *In vitro* penetration of pig oocytes in a modified Tris-buffered medium: effect of BSA, caffeine and calcium *Theriogenology* **48** 537–544

Abeydeera LR and Day BN (1997b) Fertilization and subsequent development *in vitro* of pig oocytes inseminated in a modified Tris-buffered medium with frozen–thawed ejaculated spermatozoa *Biology of Reproduction* **57** 729–734

Abeydeera LR, Funahashi H, Kim NH and Day BN (1997) Chlotetracycline fluorescence patterns and *in vitro* fertilization of frozen–thawed boar spermatozoa incubated under various bicarbonate concentrations *Zygote* **5** 117–125

Abeydeera LR, Wang WH, Cantley TC, Rieke A and Day BN (1998a) Coculture with follicular shell pieces can enhance the developmental competence of pig oocytes after *in vitro* fertilization: relevance to intracellular glutathione *Biology of Reproduction* **58** 213–218

Abeydeera LR, Wang WH, Cantley TC, Prather RS and Day BN (1998b) Presence of β-mercaptoethanol can increase the glutathione content of pig oocytes matured *in vitro* and the rate of blastocyst development after *in vitro* fertilization *Theriogenology* **50** 747–756

Abeydeera LR, Wang WH, Cantley TC, Rieke A, Prather RS and Day BN (1998c) Presence of epidermal growth factor during *in vitro* maturation of pig oocytes and embryo culture can modulate blastocyst development after *in vitro* fertilization *Molecular Reproduction and Development* **51** 395–401

Abeydeera LR, Prather RS and Day BN (1999) Developmental ability of *in vitro*-derived pig embryos in four different culture media *Biology of Reproduction* (Supplement) **60** 128 (Abstract)

Abeydeera LR, Wang WH, Cantley TC, Rieke A, Murphy CN, Prather RS and Day BN (2000) Development and viability of pig oocytes matured in a protein-free medium containing epidermal growth factor *Theriogenology* **54** 787–797

Beckmann LS and Day BN (1993) Effects of media NaCl concentration and osmolarity on the culture of early-stage porcine embryos and the viability of embryos cultured in a selected superior medium *Theriogenology* **39** 611–622

Boquest AC, Abeydeera LR, Wang WH and Day BN (1999) Effect of adding reduced glutathione during insemination on the development of porcine embryos *in vitro*. *Theriogenology* **51** 1311–1319

Buhi WC, O'Brien B, Alvarez IM, Erdos G and Dubois D (1993) Immunogold localization of porcine oviductal secretory proteins within the zona pellucida, perivitelline space, and plasma membrane of oviductal and uterine oocytes and early embryos *Biology of Reproduction* **48** 1274–1283

Buhi WC, Alvarez IM and Kouba AJ (2000) Secreted proteins of the oviduct *Cells, Tissues, Organs* **166** 165–179

Bureau M, Bailey JL and Sirard MA (2000) Influence of oviduct cells and conditioned media on porcine gametes *Zygote* **8** 139–144

Cordova A, Ducolomb Y, Jimenez I, Casas E, Bonilla E and Betancourt M (1997) *In vitro* fertilizing capacity of frozen–thawed boar semen *Theriogenology* **47** 1309–1317

Davis DL (1985) Culture and storage of pig embryos *Journal of Reproduction and Fertility Supplement* **33** 115–124

Day BN, Abeydeera LR and Prather RS (2000a) Recent progress in pig embryo production through *in vitro* maturation and fertilization techniques. In *Boar Semen Preservation IV* pp 81–92 Eds LA Johnson and HD Guthrie. Allen Press Inc., Kansas

Day BN, Abeydeera LR, Cantley TC, Rieke A and Murphy CN (2000b) Exposure of pig oocytes to estrus oviduct can influence the morphological, physical and *in vitro* fertilization parameters *Theriogenology* **53** 418 (Abstract)

Dobrinsky JR, Johnson LA and Rath D (1996) Development of a culture medium (BECM-3) for porcine embryos: effects of bovine serum albumin and fetal bovine serum on embryo development *Biology of Reproduction* **55** 1069–1074

Flesch FM and Gadella BM (2000) Dynamics of the mammalian sperm plasma membrane in the process of fertilization *Biochimica et Biophysica Acta* **1469** 197–235

Fraser LR (1995) Ionic control of sperm function *Reproduction, Fertility and Development* **7** 905–925

Funahashi H and Day BN (1993) Effects of follicular fluid at fertilization *in vitro* on sperm penetration in pig oocytes *Journal of Reproduction and Fertility* **99** 97–103

Funahashi H and Day BN (1997) Advances in *in vitro* production of pig embryos *Journal of Reproduction and Fertility Supplement* **52** 271–283

Funahashi H, Cantley TC, Stumpf TT, Terlouw SL and Day BN (1994a) Use of low-salt culture medium for *in vitro* maturation of porcine oocytes is associated with elevated oocyte glutathione levels and enhanced male pronuclear formation after *in vitro* fertilization *Biology of Reproduction* **51** 633–639

Funahashi H, Stumpf TT, Terlouw SL, Cantley TC, Rieke A and Day BN (1994b) Developmental ability of porcine oocytes matured and fertilized *in vitro*. *Theriogenology* **41** 1425–1433

Funahashi H, Cantley TC and Day BN (1997a) Preincubation of cumulus–oocyte complexes before exposure to gonadotropins improves the developmental competence of porcine embryos matured and fertilized *in vitro*. *Theriogenology* **47** 679–686

Funahashi H, Cantley TC and Day BN (1997b) Synchronization of meiosis in porcine oocytes by exposure to dibutyryl cyclic AMP improves developmental competence following *in vitro* fertilization *Biology of Reproduction* **57** 49–53

Funahashi H, Fujiwara T and Nagai T (2000) Modulation of the function of boar spermatozoa via adenosine and fertilization promoting peptide receptors reduces the incidence of polyspermic penetration into porcine oocytes *Biology of Reproduction* **63** 1157–1163

Grupen CG and Nottle MB (2000) A simple modification of the *in vitro* fertilization procedure improves the efficiency of *in vitro* pig embryo production *Theriogenology* **53** 422 (Abstract)

Grupen CG, Nagashima H and Nottle MB (1995) Cysteamine enhances *in vitro* development of porcine oocytes matured and fertilized *in vitro*. *Biology of Reproduction* **53** 173–178

Han YM, Abeydeera LR, Kim JH, Moon HB, Cabot RA, Day BN and Prather RS (1999a) Growth retardation of inner cell mass cells in polyspermic porcine embryos produced *in vitro*. *Biology of Reproduction* **60** 1110–1113

Han YM, Wang WH, Abeydeera LR, Petersen AL, Kim JH, Murphy C, Day BN and Prather RS (1999b) Pronuclear location before the first cell division determines ploidy of polyspermic pig embryos *Biology of Reproduction* **61** 1340–1346

Harrison RAP (1996) Capacitation mechanisms, and the role of capacitation as seen in eutherian mammals *Reproduction, Fertility and Development* **8** 581–594

Hunter RHF (1991) Oviduct function in pigs, with particular reference to the pathological condition of polyspermy *Molecular Reproduction and Development* **29** 385–391

Hunter RHF (1993) Sperm:egg ratios and putative molecular signals to modulate gamete interactions in polytocous mammals *Molecular Reproduction and Development* **35** 324–327

Kano K, Miyano T and Kato S (1994) Effect of oviduct epithelial cells on fertilization of pig oocytes *in vitro*. *Theriogenology* **42** 1061–1068

Kano K, Miyano T and Kato S (1998) Effects of glycosaminoglycans on the development of *in vitro*-matured and -fertilized porcine oocytes to the blastocyst stage *in vitro*. *Biology of Reproduction* **58** 1226–1232

Kikuchi K, Kaziwazaki N, Noguchi J, Shimada A, Takahashi R, Hirabayashi M, Shino M, Ueda M and Kaneko H (1999) Developmental competence, after transfer to recipients, of porcine oocytes matured, fertilized, and cultured *in vitro*. *Biology of Reproduction* **60** 336–340

Kouba AJ, Abeydeera LR, Alvarez IM, Day BN and Buhi WC (2000) Effects of the porcine oviduct-specific glycoprotein on fertilization, polyspermy and embryonic development *in vitro. Biology of Reproduction* **63** 242–250

Machaty Z, Day BN and Prather RS (1998) Development of early porcine embryos *in vitro* and *in vivo. Biology of Reproduction* **59** 451–455

Machaty Z, Thompson JG, Abeydeera LR, Day BN and Prather RS (2001) Inhibitors of mitochondrial ATP production at the time of compaction improve development of *in vitro* produced porcine embryos *Molecular Reproduction and Development* **58** 39–44

Mattioli M, Bacci ML, Galeati G and Seren E (1989) Developmental competence of pig oocytes matured and fertilized *in vitro. Theriogenology* **31** 1201–1207

Miyano T, Hiro-oka RE, Kano K, Miyake M, Kusunoki H and Kato S (1994) Effects of hyaluronic acid on the development of 1- and 2-cell porcine embryos to the blastocyst stage *in vitro. Theriogenology* **41** 1299–1305

Nagai T and Moor RM (1990) Effect of oviduct cells on the incidence of polyspermy in pig eggs fertilized *in vitro. Molecular Reproduction and Development* **26** 377–382

Nagai T, Niwa K and Iritani A (1984) Effect of sperm concentration during preincubation in a defined medium on fertilization *in vitro* of pig follicular oocytes *Journal of Reproduction and Fertility* **70** 271–275

Nagai T, Takahashi T, Masuda H, Shioya Y, Kuwayama M, Fukushima M, Iwasaki S and Hanada A (1988) *In-vitro* fertilization of pig oocytes by frozen boar spermatozoa *Journal of Reproduction and Fertility* **84** 585–591

Nagai T, Takenaka A, Mori T and Hirayama M (1994) Effects of caffeine and casein phosphopeptides on fertilization *in vitro* of pig oocytes matured in culture *Molecular Reproduction and Development* **37** 452–456

Niwa K (1993) Effectiveness of *in vitro* maturation and *in vitro* fertilization techniques in pigs *Journal of Reproduction and Fertility Supplement* **48** 49–59

Papaioannou VE and Ebert KM (1988) The preimplantation pig embryo: cell number and allocation to trophectoderm and inner cell mass of the blastocyst *in vivo* and *in vitro. Development* **102** 793–803

Perreault SD, Barbee RR and Slott VI (1988) Importance of glutathione in the acquisition and maintenance of sperm nuclear decondensing activity in maturing hamster oocytes. *Developmental Biology* **125** 181–186

Petters RM and Wells KD (1993) Culture of pig embryos *Journal of Reproduction and Fertility Supplement* **48** 61–73

Rath D (1992) Experiments to improve *in vitro* fertilization techniques for *in vivo*-matured porcine oocytes *Theriogenology* **37** 885–896

Romar R, Coy P, Matas C, Gadea J, Campos I, Selles E and Ruiz S (2000) *In vitro* fertilization of porcine oocytes pre-cultured in the presence of porcine oviductal epithelial cells *Theriogenology* **53** 431 (Abstract)

Sato E, Miyamoto H and Koide SS (1990) Glycosaminoglycans in porcine follicular fluid promoting viability of oocytes in culture *Molecular Reproduction and Development* **26** 391–397

Suzuki K, Ebihara M, Nagai T, Clarke NGE and Harrison RAP (1994a) Importance of bicarbonate/CO_2 for fertilization of pig oocytes *in vitro*, and synergism with

caffeine *Reproduction, Fertility and Development* **6** 221–227

Suzuki K, Mori T and Shimizu H (1994b) *In vitro* fertilization of porcine oocytes in chemically defined medium *Theriogenology* **42** 1357–1368

Suzuki K, Eriksson B, Shimizu H, Nagai T and Rodriguez-Martinez H (2000) Effect of hyaluronan on monospermic penetration of porcine oocytes fertilized *in vitro. Journal of Andrology* **23** 13–21

Tienthai P, Kjellen L, Pertoft H and Rodriguez-Martinez H (2001) Localisation and quantitation of hyaluronan and sulphated glycosaminoglycans in the tissues and intraluminal fluid of the pig oviduct *Reproduction, Fertility and Development* **12** 173–182

Vatzias G and Hagen DR (1999) Effects of porcine follicular fluid and oviduct-conditioned media on maturation and fertilization of porcine oocytes *in vitro. Biology of Reproduction* **60** 42–48

Wang WH, Niwa K and Okuda K (1991) *In-vitro* penetration of pig oocytes matured in culture by frozen–thawed ejaculated spermatozoa *Journal of Reproduction and Fertility* **93** 491–496

Wang WH, Abeydeera LR, Fraser LR and Niwa K (1995) Functional analysis using chlortetracycline fluorescence and *in vitro* fertilization of frozen–thawed ejaculated boar spermatozoa incubated in a protein-free chemically defined medium *Journal of Reproduction and Fertility* **104** 305–313

Wang WH, Abeydeera LR, Prather RS and Day BN (1998) Morphologic comparison of ovulated and *in vitro*-matured porcine oocytes, with particular reference to polyspermy after *in vitro* fertilization *Molecular Reproduction and Development* **49** 308–316

Wang WH, Abeydeera LR, Han YM, Prather RS and Day BN (1999) Morphologic evaluation and actin filament distribution in porcine embryos produced *in vitro* and *in vivo. Biology of Reproduction* **60** 1020–1028

Xu X, Ding J, Seth PC, Harbison DS and Foxcroft GR (1996a) *In vitro* fertilization of *in vitro* matured pig oocytes: effects of boar and ejaculate fraction *Theriogenology* **45** 745–755

Xu X, Seth PC, Harbison DS, Cheung AP and Foxcroft GR (1996b) Semen dilution for assessment of boar ejaculate quality in pig IVM and IVF systems *Theriogenology* **46** 1325–1337

Yoshida M (1987) *In vitro* fertilization of pig oocytes matured *in vivo. Japanese Journal of Veterinary Science* **49** 711–718

Yoshida M, Ishigaki K and Pursel VG (1992) Effect of maturation media on male pronucleus formation in pig oocytes matured *in vitro. Molecular Reproduction and Development* **31** 68–71

Yoshida M, Ishigaki K, Nagai T, Chikyu M and Pursel VG (1993) Glutathione concentration during maturation and after fertilization in pig oocytes: relevance to the ability of oocytes to form male pronucleus *Biology of Reproduction* **49** 89–94

Youngs CR, Ford SP, McGinnis LK and Anderson LH (1993) Investigations into the control of litter size in swine: I. Comparative studies on *in vitro* development of Meishan and Yorkshire preimplantation embryos *Journal of Animal Science* **71** 1561–1565

Reproduction Supplement **58**, 175–189

Gene expression during pre- and peri-implantation embryonic development in pigs

P. Maddox-Hyttel[1], A. Dinnyés[2], J. Laurincik[3,4], D. Rath[5],
H. Niemann[5], C. Rosenkranz[6] and I. Wilmut[2]

[1]*Department of Anatomy and Physiology, Royal Veterinary and Agricultural University,
1870 Frederiksberg C, Denmark;* [2]*Department of Gene Expression and Development,
Roslin Institute, Roslin, UK;* [3]*Constantin the Philosopher University and*
[4]*Research Institute of Animal Production, Nitra, Slovak Republic;* [5]*Department of Biotechnology,
Institute for Animal Science and Behaviour (FAL), Mariensee, 31535 Neustadt, Germany; and*
[6]*Veterinary University, Josef Baumann Gasse 1, A-1210 Vienna, Austria*

Embryo technological procedures such as *in vitro* production and cloning by
nuclear transfer are not as advanced in pigs as in cattle and cannot yet be
applied under field conditions. The present paper focuses on genome
activation in *in vivo*-derived, *in vitro*-produced and nuclear transfer pig
embryos with special emphasis on the development of embryonic nucleoli,
where the ribosomal RNA (rRNA) genes transcribed can be used as markers
for genome activity. In addition, contemporary data on gene expression in *in
vivo*-derived pig embryos are reviewed. In *in vivo*-derived pig embryos,
pronounced transcription is initiated at the four-cell stage (the third cell cycle
after fertilization), when nucleoli develop. In parallel with the development
of the nucleoli as a result of rRNA gene activation, a cascade of other genes is
also likely to be transcribed. However, apart from identification of transcripts
for the oestrogen receptor at the blastocyst stage, reports on mRNAs resulting
from initial transcription of the pig embryonic genome are lacking, in contrast
to the situation in cattle and, in particular, mice. More information is
available on gene expression during elongation of pig conceptuses, when the
genes for steroidogenic enzymes, extracellular matrix receptors, oestrogen
receptors, growth factors and their receptors, as well as retinol binding
protein and retinoic acid receptors, are expressed. Nucleolus development
appears to be disturbed in *in vitro*-produced pig embryos and in pig embryos
reconstructed by nuclear transfer of granulosa cells to enucleated metaphase
II oocytes produced by oocyte maturation *in vivo* or *in vitro*, which is
indicative of disturbances in activation of rRNA genes.

Introduction

Pig embryos present great challenges from an embryo technological viewpoint. *In vitro*
production (IVP) of pig embryos by *in vitro* maturation (IVM) of oocytes followed by *in vitro*

Email: poh@kvl.dk

fertilization (IVF) and *in vitro* culture (IVC) of the resultant embryos resulted in live offspring only recently (for reviews see Abeydeera *et al.*, 1998; Rath *et al.*, 1999; Day, 2000) and is still very inefficient. Successful cryopreservation of pig embryos has been accomplished using the open pulled straw method for vitrification (Vajta *et al.*, 1997; Berthelot *et al.*, 2000) and cytoskeletal stabilization (Dobrinsky *et al.*, 2000). Cloning of pigs by nuclear transfer of somatic cells has also presented a challenge that has been overcome only recently (Betthauser *et al.*, 2000; Onishi *et al.*, 2000; Polejaeva *et al.*, 2000). These difficulties indicate that pig embryos have a particular biology that is likely to differ in several respects from that of both ruminant domestic species and small rodents.

In cattle it is clear that IVP is associated with an increased incidence of calving problems and oversized calves (Kruip and den Dass, 1997). A potential background for this observation is that the pattern of expression of several genes of importance for initial embryonic development deviates in *in vitro*-produced bovine embryos (for review see Niemann and Wrenzycki, 2000). Likewise, it has been demonstrated that bovine embryos produced by nuclear transfer from somatic cells display deviating patterns of gene expression (Daniels *et al.*, 2000) that may be involved causally in the even more pronounced loss of both embryos and late fetuses that is associated with this procedure. Thus, basic knowledge of the patterns of gene expression during initial embryonic development under normal *in vivo* conditions has become an important tool in understanding how embryo technological procedures may cause deviations in gene expression that can be detrimental for further embryonic development.

In the present article, the data available on gene expression in pig embryos are reviewed and new data on the use of the development of the nucleolus as a marker for embryonic genome activation in pig embryos derived from IVP and nuclear transfer of somatic cells are presented.

Maternal to embryonic transition

The initial development of mammalian pre-implantation embryos is governed by gene transcripts and polypeptides produced by, and stored in, the oocyte, and the transition from maternal to embryonic control of development is a gradual event (for review see Thompson, 1996). Accordingly, using long-term incubation with [^{3}H]uridine, transcription has been observed during the first (Hay-Schmidt *et al.*, 2001) and second cell cycles in cattle (Plante *et al.*, 1994; Viuff *et al.*, 1996), well before the major transcriptional activation that occurs during the fourth cell cycle (Camous *et al.*, 1986). In pigs, the major transcriptional activation is observed during the third cell cycle (the four-cell stage; Tomanek *et al.*, 1989; Jarrel *et al.*, 1991; Hyttel *et al.*, 2000), but whether this activation is preceded by an earlier minor activation has not been investigated.

A more precise chronological description of the major transcriptional activation during the third cell cycle has been obtained by analyses of embryonic DNA and protein synthesis throughout this cell cycle (Schoenbeck *et al.*, 1992). The third cell cycle more or less lacks a G1 phase, as DNA synthesis (the S phase) commences within the first 2 h after cleavage to the four-cell stage; the S phase is completed at 16 h after cleavage and the prolonged G2 phase results in a total duration of the cell cycle of about 50 h. The synthesis of a number of proteins of maternal origin ceases at 10–14 h after cleavage to the four-cell stage and new proteins derived from embryonic transcripts appear at 16 h and, in particular, at 24 h after cleavage. Culture of four-cell; embryos with α-amanitin from early during the third cell cycle blocked the synthesis of the embryonic proteins from 16 h after cleavage, thus verifying their embryonic origin, but also resulted in persistence of maternal protein synthesis, indicating that embryonic transcription is required for downregulation of the maternally derived translation. Moreover, embryos cultured with α-amanitin from early during the third cell cycle did not cleave to the eight-cell stage, whereas embryos cultured with this substance from 24 h or 30 h after cleavage cleaved in 40 and 100% of cases, respectively. Hence, the embryonic protein synthesis occurring from 16 h to 30 h after cleavage is essential for further development. In accordance with these data on protein synthesis, incubation of embryos for 20 min in ^{3}[H]uridine followed by autoradiography has demonstrated that the major embryonic transcription is initiated between 10 h and 30 h after cleavage to the four-cell stage (Hyttel *et al.*, 2000).

Gene activation and expression in pig embryos

Pre-hatching development

There is little information on which genes are activated during pre-hatching development of pig embryos. As described above, significant α-amanitin-sensitive transcription for embryonic development occurs during the third cell cycle after fertilization (Schoenbeck *et al.*, 1992). The qualitative aspects of this transcription have not been investigated extensively. One candidate gene for transcription is cyclin B1, which forms part of the maturation-promoting factor (MPF; Jacobs, 1992) required for the G2 to M phase transition. The content of cyclin B1 transcripts has been examined in both *in vivo*-developed and *in vitro*-produced pig embryos throughout the third cell cycle after fertilization by RT–PCR (Anderson *et al.*, 1999). In both categories of embryos, there was a decrease in the amount of cyclin B1 transcripts during the cell cycle, and it was concluded that there is a continuous degradation of maternal cyclin B1 transcripts during the third cell cycle after fertilization without any detectable formation of embryonic transcripts. Thus, it appears that the cyclin B1 gene is not included in the cascade of gene activation that occurs during the third cell cycle after fertilization.

Oestrogen is important for transformation of pig morulae to the cavitated blastocyst stage (Niemann and Elsaesser, 1986) and administration of anti-oestrogen to the culture medium impaired the morulae to blastocyst transformation *in vitro* (Niemann and Elsaesser, 1987). Ying *et al.* (2000) investigated the presence of oestrogen receptor mRNA in pre-implantation pig embryos by RT–PCR. The transcript was identified in one-, two- and four-cell embryos, whereas it was not detected in five- to eight-cell embryos and morulae, but reappeared at the blastocyst stage. Ying *et al.* (2000) also localized the oestrogen receptor protein in one- and four-cell embryos by immunocytochemistry with a reduced staining intensity at the five- to eight-cell stage. However, the blastocysts did not display any immunoreactivity, indicating that there may be a lag phase before translation of the mRNA. It is thought that the transcripts found in the one- to four-cell embryos are of maternal origin, whereas in the blastocysts they are probably of embryonic origin.

Nucleolus development in pig embryos

It is common for the major transcriptional activation to occur in parallel with nucleolar formation, thereby indirectly signalling transcription of the ribosomal RNA (rRNA) genes (Camous *et al.*, 1986; Tomanek *et al.*, 1989). Transcription of the rRNA genes and subsequent processing of the transcripts result in formation of the nucleolus, which is the most prominent nuclear organelle and the site of formation of the ribosomal subunits. In pig embryos, nucleoli form towards the end of the third cell cycle after fertilization (Tomanek *et al.*, 1989; Hyttel *et al.*, 2000), whereas in cattle, nucleolar formation occurs towards the end of the fourth cell cycle (Camous *et al.*, 1986; Laurincik *et al.*, 2000). A minor activation of the rRNA genes, which is not associated with nucleolar development, has been demonstrated by fluorescence *in situ* hybridization (FISH) to occur during the third cell cycle in cattle (Viuff *et al.*, 1998).

The active ribosome-synthesizing nucleolus contains three main ultrastructural components: the fibrillar components, consisting of the fibrillar centres and the dense fibrillar component, and the granular component (for review see Wachtler and Stahl, 1993). These components of the fibrillo–granular nucleolus reflect the steps in the biosynthesis of ribosomes according to the following model: the fibrillar centres contain the enzymatic apparatus for transcription; the dense fibrillar component carries the primary unprocessed transcripts; and the granular component represents processed transcripts associated with proteins in the form of pre-ribosomal particles. As rRNA gene transcription is expressed in the ultrastructure of the nucleolus, the development of this organelle may serve as an indirect morphological marker of activation of the embryonic genome (Kopecny and Niemann, 1993).

Pig embryos display the first signs of development of fibrillar centres in the developing nucleoli towards the end of the third cell cycle (Tomanek *et al.*, 1989). Hyttel *et al.* (2000) analysed *in vivo*-developed pig zygotes and embryos by transmission electron microscopy to elucidate the chronology of this event in greater detail. After flushing from the oviducts, the zygotes and embryos were cultured into the subsequent cell cycle *in vitro* and were fixed at different intervals during the one-cell stage (first cell cycle; the zygotes were not cultured *in vitro*), the two-cell stage (second cell cycle), the four-cell stage (third cell cycle), the eight-cell stage (fourth cell cycle) and the 16-cell stage (fifth cell cycle).

The most prominent structural nuclear entities observed during the first two cell cycles were electron-dense spheres of packed fibrillar material, the nucleolus precursor bodies (NPBs; Fig. 1). NPBs were observed up to 10 h after cleavage to the four-cell stage, but at 20 and 30 h after cleavage, the nuclei displayed different stages of nucleolus formation, ranging from inactive NPBs to fibrillo–granular nucleoli presenting a dense fibrillar component, fibrillar centres and a granular component. Nucleolus formation was apparently initiated by the formation of the dense fibrillar component and the granular component, and later by the fibrillar centres on the surface of the NPBs. Fibrillo–granular nucleoli were formed at the start of the fifth cell cycle.

The nucleolus consists of the rRNA genes and their transcripts associated with proteins that play different roles in rRNA transcription and processing. We have analysed *in vivo*-developed pig zygotes and embryos fixed at different times during the first five cell cycles after fertilization to elucidate the protein composition of the nucleolus before and during activation of the rRNA genes. Antibodies against six important nucleolar proteins were applied on whole mounts that were analysed subsequently by confocal laser scanning microscopy (Hyttel *et al.*, 2000). The nucleolar proteins against which antibodies were applied were: topoisomerase I, RNA polymerase I, upstream binding factor (UBF), fibrillarin, nucleolin and nucleophosmin. Each of these proteins has a fairly well defined role in rRNA gene transcription and subsequent processing of the transcripts (Hyttel *et al.*, 2000). In brief, topoisomerase I uncoils the supercoiled DNA allowing transcription. RNA polymerase I, the binding of which to the rRNA genes is mediated by the transcription factor UBF, drives the actual transcription. Fibrillarin is probably involved in early processing of the transcripts, whereas nucleolin and nucleophosmin are involved in later processing. According to these functions, topoisomerase I, RNA polymerase I, UBF and fibrillarin have been localized to the fibrillar centres and the dense fibrillar component of the nucleolus in somatic cells, whereas nucleolin and nucleophosmin have been localized mainly to the granular component.

During the first cell cycle, labelling of nucleophosmin was localized to large shell-like bodies (Fig. 2). These bodies may be identical to the NPBs observed by transmission electron microscopy. The remaining proteins were not localized to nuclear entities. None of the

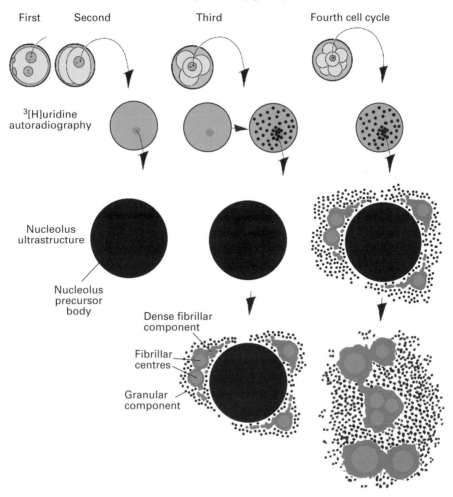

Fig. 1. Schematic illustration of the maternal–embryonic transition in a pre-implantation pig embryo as visualized using nucleolus development. Transcription, as evaluated by [H]uridine incorporation after 20 min incubation followed by autoradiography, is initiated during the third cell cycle, where silver grains become localized over both the nucleoplasm and the nucleolus. In parallel, the dense nucleolus precursor body is transformed gradually into a ribosome-synthesizing nucleolus with fibrillar centres, a dense fibrillar component and a granular component.

proteins were localized to nuclear entities during the second and early third cell cycles. The nucleophosmin observed during the first cell cycle is probably maternal proteins that target to the pronuclei and are degraded before or during the second cell cycle. RNA polymerase I was localized to discrete foci arranged in a shell-like pattern towards the end of the third cell cycle. This observation is in accordance with the observation by transmission electron microscopy of the first fibrillo–granular nucleoli established on the surface of the NPBs towards the end of this cell cycle. None of the remaining proteins were localized to nuclear entities. Early during the fourth cell cycle, labelling of topoisomerase I, RNA polymerase I, UBF and fibrillarin was localized to small foci arranged in a shell-like pattern, whereas labelling for nucleolin and

P. Maddox-Hyttel et al.

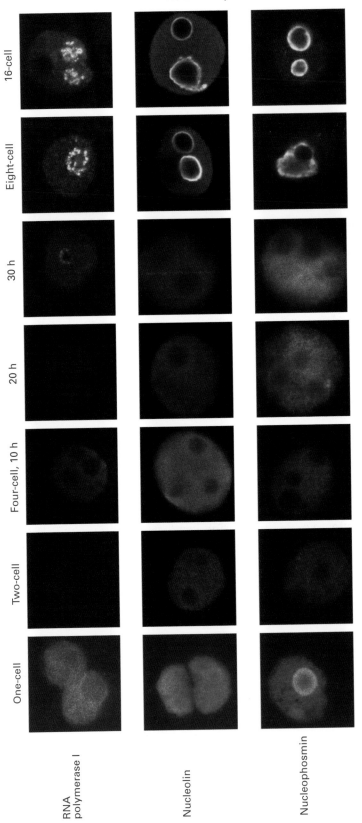

Fig. 2. Examples of the tentative localization of nucleolar proteins to the fibrillar nucleolar components (RNA polymerase I) and the granular nucleolar component (nucleolin and nucleophosmin). Each image represents an optical confocal section of a single nucleus of the developmental stage as indicated at the top, except for the one-cell stage of RNA polymerase I and nucleolin, where two pronuclei are shown. Note the nucleolar labelling of RNA polymerase I to the presumptive fibrillar components at 30 h after cleavage to the four-cell stage and the labelling of nucleolin and nucleophosmin to the presumptive granular component at the eight-cell stage.

nucleophosmin was localized to more or less shell-like bodies. Again, this labelling pattern is compatible with the presence of fibrillo–granular nucleoli on the surface of the NPBs with topoisomerase I, UBF, RNA polymerase I and fibrillarin being confined mainly to the fibrillar centres and the dense fibrillar component, and nucleolin and nucleophosmin to the dense fibrillar component and the granular component. Similar observations were made during the fifth cell cycle. The labelling patterns described above were very consistent within each developmental group. No embryos lacked labelling and unlabelled blastomeres were found in only a few embryos of the later stages.

In conclusion, the labelling patterns observed by immunocytochemistry are compatible with the formation of fibrillo–granular nucleoli towards the end of the third cell cycle.

Nucleolus development in in vitro-*produced pig embryos*

IVP of pig embryos resulted in live offspring only recently (for reviews see Abeydeera *et al.*, 1998; Rath *et al.*, 1999; Day, 2000) and the technique is still hampered by great inefficiencies. In general, the procedure results in development of about 35% of the collected immature oocytes to blastocysts; however, these blastocysts are characterized by variable and low numbers of cells. Moreover, pig IVF is associated with various rates of polyspermy (Wang *et al.*, 1998) and low rates of male pronucleus formation (Laurincik *et al.*, 1994; Prather and Day, 1998), and the process of IVC is associated with decreased cell numbers in the whole embryo as well as in the inner cell mass (Macháty *et al.*, 1998).

Proper activation of the embryonic genome is crucial for initial development and it is possible that this process is affected adversely in *in vitro*-produced pig embryos, as it is in cattle (for review see Niemann and Wrenzycki, 2000). Therefore, we aimed to evaluate the normality of genome activation in *in vitro*-produced pig embryos using nucleolus development as an indirect model.

The same panel of antibodies against key nucleolar proteins as was used for *in vivo*-derived embryos was used as a marker for nucleolus development and, hence, the activation of the rRNA genes (J. Laurincik, D. Rath, H. Niemann and P. Hyttel, unpublished). The embryos were produced according to the description of Rath *et al.* (1997, 1999). In brief, ovaries were obtained from a local abattoir and the contents of follicles 2–5 mm in diameter were aspirated and cumulus–oocyte complexes (COCs) with at least three cumulus cell layers were selected and placed into maturation medium (North Carolina State University (NCSU) 37 medium (Funahashi *et al.*, 1994, 1997) supplemented with dbcAMP, eCG, hCG and mercaptoethanol). After 24 h of incubation at 38.5°C and 5% CO_2 in humidified air, the COCs were placed into NCSU 37 medium without hormonal supplements and incubated for a further 24 h. For IVF, mature COCs were denuded mechanically and placed into Tyrode's albumin lactate pyruvate (TALP) fertilization medium (Bavister, 1981) supplemented with 3% bovine serum albumin and 1 μg sodium pyruvate ml^{-1}. Frozen epididymal semen was thawed, washed twice in TALP and the final concentration was set to 1500 spermatozoa per oocyte dissolved in 10 μl TALP. Spermatozoa were added to the oocytes and the resultant embryos were cultured for different times depending on the experimental design, to obtain different developmental stages.

The *in vitro*-produced embryos lacked labelling of nuclear entities for any of the proteins investigated during the first, second and third cell cycles after fertilization except for a few embryos showing labelling for fibrillarin and nucleolin towards the end of the third cycle. No labelling was observed during the fourth cycle, when strong labelling of the nucleolar compartment by all antibodies was expected from the results of studies of *in vivo*-developed embryos (Hyttel *et al.*, 2000). During the fifth cell cycle, about half of the embryos showed labelling of RNA polymerase I (Fig. 3) and a few had labelling for nucleolin, whereas no

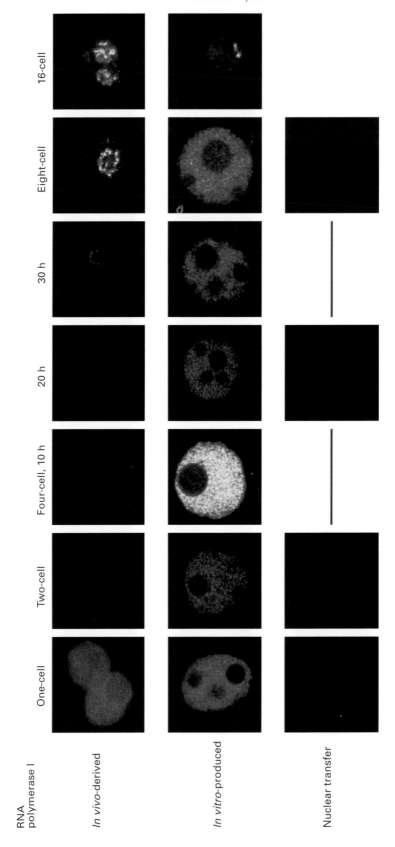

Fig. 3. Localization of RNA polymerase I in *in vivo*-derived, *in vitro*-produced and nuclear transfer pig embryos. Each image represents an optical confocal section of a single nucleus of the developmental stage indicated at the top. Note that the nucleolar localization of the protein in the *in vitro*-produced embryos is delayed until the 16-cell stage, whereas no localization is visible in the nuclear transfer embryos, which were analysed only up to the eight-cell stage. Nuclear transfer embryos were fixed at one time point only during the third cell cycle.

labelling was observed for the other proteins examined. These data show that nucleolus development is disturbed, indicating deviations in rRNA gene activation in *in vitro*-produced pig embryos.

Nucleolus development in pig nuclear transfer embryos

Except for the birth of a single piglet resulting from nuclear transfer from the blastomere of a four-cell embryo to an enucleated oocyte (Prather *et al.*, 1989), cloning by nuclear transfer was not accomplished until recently, when a litter of five piglets was born (Polejaeva *et al.*, 2000). Polejaeva *et al.* (2000) applied a double reconstruction technique in which the granulosa cell was first electrofused with a pre-activated *in vivo*-matured enucleated metaphase II oocyte and the reconstructed embryo was subsequently fused with a fertilized zygote enucleated at the pronuclear stage. Only 4% of the total number of fused reconstructed embryos in this trial and fewer from other trials survived to birth as live piglets. Nevertheless, other workers have obtained cloned piglets without serial nuclear transfer. Onishi *et al.* (2000) injected fetal fibroblast cells into the cytoplasm of *in vivo*-derived enucleated oocytes and obtained one live piglet. Betthauser *et al.* (2000) used *in vitro*-matured oocytes as an economical source of recipient oocytes, an improved activation method and a short *in vitro* culture of the cloned embryos to obtain four piglets from fetal body and genital ridge cells. In this case, activation was performed about 4 h after fusion. Two other studies have demonstrated that the use of *in vitro*-produced cytoplasts in combination with activation of cytoplasts before electrofusion and a blastocyst-derived cell line (Miyoshi *et al.*, 2000) or fetal fibroblasts (Koo *et al.*, 2000) can result in development of blastocysts *in vitro*. However, the efficiency of all these methods is low.

In cattle, fine structural investigations revealed only minor differences between somatic cell nuclear transfer embryos and *in vitro*-produced control embryos except that there was more cellular debris in the former (Heyman *et al.*, 1995). However, transcripts for certain genes of significance for embryonic development and implantation were lacking in a major proportion of nuclear transfer embryos (Daniels *et al.*, 2000). Very little is known about genome reactivation at nuclear transfer in pigs. Ouhibi *et al.* (1996) reported that nuclear transfer of pig ectodermal cells to enucleated metaphase II oocytes results in either complete or incomplete nucleolar remodelling. Thus, in some instances the active fibrillo–granular nucleolus of the ectodermal cell was transformed into a compact dense nucleolus precursor body, whereas in other cases it maintained the fibrillo–granular appearance. The reconstructed embryos were apparently transcriptionally quiescent in both cases. These data partially support the contention that after nuclear transfer the nucleolus is remodelled to an inactive entity in reconstructed embryos from cattle (Kanka *et al.*, 1991, 1999; King *et al.*, 1996; Lavoir *et al.*, 1997) and rabbits (Kanka *et al.*, 1996). The reformation of a functional nucleolus, indicating the reactivation of the rRNA genes, has been described less thoroughly. In rabbit embryos, fibrillo–granular nucleoli are established during the fourth cell cycle, corresponding to the normal rate of embryonic development in this species (Kanka *et al.*, 1996), whereas in bovine embryos fibrillo–granular nucleoli were reported during the third cell cycle, which is one cell cycle earlier than expected (Kanka *et al.*, 1999; Laurincik *et al.*, (in press)).

We have studied nucleolus development as an indirect model to elucidate the normality of genome reactivation in pig embryos reconstructed by nuclear transfer. Antibodies against RNA polymerase I and UBF as described earlier for the *in vivo*-derived embryos were used as markers for nucleolus development (Hyttel *et al.*, 2000). These two candidates were chosen as they, in particular UBF, were lacking during nucleolus reactivation in reconstructed embryos in a previous study of bovine somatic nuclear transfer embryos (Laurincik *et al.*, (in press)). Pig nuclear transfer embryos were produced by a relatively simple technique developed at the Roslin Institute (P. A. De Sousa, J. R. Dobrinsky, J. Zhu, A. Archibald, A. Ainslie, W. Bosma, J. Bowering, J. Bracken, P. Ferrier, J. Fletcher, B. Gasparrini, L. Harkness, P. Johnston, M. Ritchie, W. A. Ritchie, A. Travers, D. Albertini, A. Dinnyes, T. J. King and I. Wilmut, unpublished). In brief, *in vivo*-derived oocytes from superovulated gilts that ovulated 42–48 h after hCG administration or oocytes submitted to IVM for 42–44 h were denuded from cumulus cells, exposed to 7.5 µg cytochalasin B ml^{-1} and 5 µg Hoechst 33342 ml^{-1}, and enucleated at 39°C in Ca^{2+}-free Hepes-buffered NCSU 23 medium (Peters and Wells, 1993) containing 7.5 µg cytochalasin B ml^{-1}. Enucleation success was confirmed by ultraviolet irradiation. Enucleated oocyte cytoplasts were reconstructed with fetal fibroblast cells (serum-starved for 5 days) in Ca^{2+}-free Hepes-buffered NCSU 23 at 39°C, and fused by 3×80 µs electric pulses of 1.25 kV cm^{-1} in Ca^{2+}-free 0.3 mol mannitol l^{-1} and 100 µmol $MgCl_2$ l^{-1}. A delay of 2 h was applied between fusion and activation during which the reconstructed embryos were held in Ca^{2+}-free NCSU 23 supplemented with 7.5 µg cytochalasin B ml^{-1} at 39°C, in 5% CO_2 in air. Activation was achieved by 3×80 µs electric pulses of 1.0 kV cm^{-1} in 0.3 mol mannitol solution l^{-1} supplemented with 100 µmol $MgCl_2$ l^{-1} and 50 µmol $CaCl_2$ l^{-1}. Reconstructed embryos were cultured in NCSU 23 in groups of 20–40 per 500 µl medium under mineral oil in 5% CO_2 in air for 7 days, or transferred into synchronized recipients shortly after activation. *In vitro* culture of the fused embryos obtained from *in vivo*- or *in vitro*-derived oocytes using this method resulted in 58 and 41% cleavage, and 10 and 5% blastocyst development rates, respectively. Furthermore, the method was suitable for producing a healthy cloned piglet after co-transfer with parthenogenetically activated pig embryos (P. A. De Sousa, J. R. Dobrinsky, J. Zhu, A. Archibald, A. Ainslie, W. Bosma, J. Bowering, J. Bracken, P. Ferrier, J. Fletcher, B. Gasparrini, L. Harkness, P. Johnston, M. Ritchie, W. A. Ritchie, A. Travers, D. Albertini, A. Dinnyes, T. J. King and I. Wilmut, unpublished). Pig nuclear transfer embryos produced as described above were harvested for immunocytochemistry during the first, second, third and fourth cell cycle after fusion. None of the embryos produced from either *in vivo*- or *in vitro*-matured oocytes displayed labelling of either of the two proteins during these cell cycles. Again, these data show that nucleolus development is disturbed, indicating aberrations in the activation of the rRNA genes. Moreover, about one third of the reconstructed four- and eight-cell embryos derived from *in vivo*-matured cytoplasts presented one or more anucleated blastomeres, whereas this proportion was increased to about half in those originating from *in vitro*-matured cytoplasts.

Gene expression in pig conceptuses

During post-hatching and peri-implantation development

In pigs, the incidence of prenatal mortality ranges from 20% to 46% at term (Pope and First, 1985). Most of this loss occurs before day 20 of gestation (Geisert *et al.*, 1982) and, in particular, the period between day 11 and day 12, during which the peri-implantation conceptus undergoes rapid differentiation and expansion of the trophectoderm, appears to be critical (Geisert *et al.*, 1982; Stroband and Van der Lende, 1990). During elongation of the trophectoderm, pig conceptuses synthesize and secrete large amounts of oestrogen, which is probably the signal for recognition of pregnancy in pigs (Ford *et al.*, 1982; Geisert *et al.*, 1982, 1990). This important period of conceptus development is controlled by well-synchronized gene expression that has received greater attention than that in the pre-hatching embryo.

In a comprehensive study, Yelich *et al.* (1997a) investigated the content of mRNA encoding a number of developmentally important proteins in pig embryos in the period about the time of elongation by RT–PCR. The work included analyses of embryos from the spherical 2 mm stage of development up to the > 100 mm filamentous stage for mRNAs of the steroidogenic enzymes 17α-hydroxylase and aromatase, which are of importance for oestrogen synthesis, of brachyury, a transcription factor that can be used as a marker of mesoderm formation (Herrmann *et al.*, 1990), of the extracellular matrix receptor integrin β1, which is thought to be of importance for the morphological restructuring of the conceptus during rapid elongation, and a number of receptors for oestrogen, progesterone, oxytocin, $PGF_{2\alpha}$ and leukaemia inhibitory factor (LIF).

Conceptuses at all developmental stages from the 2 mm spherical stage onwards expressed 17α-hydroxylase and aromatase. Ko *et al.* (1994) demonstrated that transcripts for cytochrome P450 aromatase are present in high concentrations at days 10, 11 and 12 in pig conceptuses. The expression of the steroidogenic enzymes is in accordance with the need for oestrogen synthesis for maternal recognition of pregnancy.

Brachyury was not expressed in the small 2–4 mm spherical conceptuses, but was clearly evident from the 6 mm stage of development. Brachyury expression, which is a marker of mesoderm formation, appears to precede the morphological recognition of mesoderm, which is reported to occur at the 10 mm stage (Conley *et al.*, 1994).

Integrin β1 expression was evident from the 2 mm stage of development. Integrins serve as plasma membrane receptors for laminins (Rouslahti and Pierschbacher, 1987) and fibronectins (Chen *et al.*, 1985; Knudson *et al.*, 1986), both of which have roles in assembly of the extracellular matrix and, thus, for changes in cell shape and cell migration (Horwitz *et al.*, 1986; Tamkun *et al.*, 1986), which are important for elongation of pig conceptuses.

LIF receptor expression was evident in particular from the 6 mm stage of development onwards. In addition to its effect on cell differentiation, LIF may also stimulate cell proliferation in the inner cell mass and trophectoderm (Stewart, 1994; Lavranos *et al.*, 1995; Eckert *et al.*, 1997). Another possible role of LIF on elongating pig conceptuses is to enhance protease production (Harvey *et al.*, 1995); proteases serve in the modification of the extracellular matrix, which is required during the extensive morphological remodelling of conceptuses during elongation. mRNAs encoding the receptors for oestrogen, progesterone, $PGF_{2\alpha}$ and oxytocin were not detected in pig conceptuses at any stage of development.

Yelich *et al.* (1997b) investigated the possible role of retinoic acid for conceptus elongation by RT–PCR. This substance, which is a metabolite of retinol, is a powerful morphogen in early embryonic development. The conceptuses displayed mRNA for retinol binding protein (RBP) from the 2 mm stage of development and onwards. Accordingly, Trout *et al.* (1991) demonstrated that day 13–17 pig conceptuses present transcripts for RBP and *in situ* hybridization has shown that the transcripts are distributed uniformly in the inner cell mass and the trophectoderm. The transcripts for retinoic acid receptor α (RARα), RARβ and RARγ were evident from the 2 mm stage of development onwards.

Pig conceptuses also display transcripts for several growth factor receptors during peri-implantation development as demonstrated by Vaughan *et al.* (1992) using RT–PCR. Epidermal growth factor receptor (EGF receptor) was detected at all developmental stages from day 7 to day 22 of pregnancy. Transforming growth factor α (TGF-α) was expressed on days 8–12 only. In contrast, epidermal growth factor (EGF) was first expressed by the post-elongation conceptus at about day 15 of pregnancy. The expression pattern of TGF-α indicates a possible role for this factor during cellular remodelling of the blastocyst during elongation, whereas EGF is more likely to be involved in initial organ development.

Recently, it has also been reported that one of the important genes for organizing the longitudinal axis of the embryo, goosecoid, is expressed in the embryo of the pig conceptus (as opposed to the fetal membranes) during peri-implantation development (Meijer *et al.*, 2000). Goosecoid is a homeobox gene and is one of the first genes to be expressed in the vertebrate organizer regions and future dorsal regions of the embryo along the longitudinal axis (De Robertis *et al.*, 1994; Bouwmeester and Leyns, 1998). Meijer *et al.* (2000) found that goosecoid was expressed at all stages of pig embryonic development from day 9 to day 12 of pregnancy. On day 10, the transcripts were localized by *in situ* hybridization to one side of the epiblasts and expression was localized to a region anterior to the primitive streak on day 13.

Conclusion

Information about the patterns of gene expression during normal embryonic development *in vivo* is crucial to optimize the outcome of different embryo technological procedures. In pigs, there is a lack of knowledge about the qualitative aspects of gene expression during pre-hatching embryonic development, whereas more information is available on gene expression in relation to conceptus elongation and oestrogen secretion. Data presented here indicate that the pattern of embryonic nucleolus development may be disturbed in pre-implantation pig embryos produced either *in vitro* or by nuclear transfer, indicating that there are deviations in the activation of rRNA genes. In the near future, the application of cDNA array technology to analysis of embryonic gene expression will probably allow studies of the expression of thousands of genes and, thus, lead to a rapid expansion of the understanding of the sequential activation of the embryonic genome. However, it is of crucial importance to enter the field of proteomics to understand the significance of such data on functional genomics. After all, it is the proteins that determine the character of the cells and cell populations involved in initial embryonic development.

The projects were supported by the Bundesministerium für Wissenschaft und Verkehr der Republik Österreich GZ 45.023/1-III/B/8/98, The Danish Agricultural and Veterinary Research Council, Geron Biomed and through an Alexander von Humboldt fellowship.

References

Abeydeera LR, Johnson LA, Welch GR, Wang WH, Boquest AC, Cantley TC, Rieke A and Day BN (1998) Birth of piglets preselected for gender following *in vitro* fertilization of *in vitro* matured pig oocytes by X and Y chromosome bearing spermatozoa sorted by high speed flow cytometry *Theriogenology* **50** 981–988

Anderson JE, Matteri RL, Abeydeera LR, Day BN and Prather RS (1999) Cyclin B1 transcript quantitation over the maternal to zygotic transition in both *in vivo*- and *in vitro*-derived 4-cell porcine embryos *Biology of Reproduction* **61** 1460–1467

Bavister BD (1981) Substitution of a synthetic polymer for protein in a mammalian gamete culture system *Journal of Experimental Zoology* **217** 45–51

Berthelot F, Martinat-Botté F, Locatelli A, Perreau C and Terqui M (2000) Piglets born after vitrification of embryos using the open pulled straw method *Cryobiology* **41** 116–124

Betthauser J, Forsberg E, Augenstein M *et al.* (2000) Production of cloned pigs from *in vitro* systems *Nature Biotechnology* **18** 1055–1059

Bouwmeester T and Leyns L (1998) Vertebrate head induction by anterior primitive endoderm *BioEssays* **19** 855–863

Camous S, Kopecny V and Fléchon JE (1986)

Autoradiographic detection of the earliest stage of [3H]-uridine incorporation into the cow embryo *Biology of the Cell* **58** 195–200

Chen WT, Hasegawa E, Hasegawa T, Weinstock C and Yamada KM (1985) Development of cell–surface linkage complexes in cultured fibroblasts *Journal of Cell Biology* **100** 1103–1114

Conley AJ, Christenson LK, Ford SP and Christenson RK (1994) Immunocytochemical localization of cytochromes P450 17α-hydroxylase and aromatase in embryonic cell layers of the elongating porcine blastocyst *Endocrinology* **135** 2248–2254

Daniels R, Hall V and Trounson AO (2000) Analysis of gene transcription in bovine nuclear transfer embryos reconstructed with granulosa cells *Biology of Reproduction* **63** 1034–1040

Day BN (2000) Reproductive biotechnologies: current status in porcine reproduction *Animal Reproduction Science* **60–61** 161–172

De Robertis EM, Fainsod A, Gont LK and Steinbeisser H (1994) The evolution of vertebrate gastrulation *Development Supplement* 117–124

Dobrinsky JR, Pursel VG, Long CR and Johnson LA (2000) Birth of piglets after transfer of embryos cryopreserved by cytoskeletal stabilization and vitrification *Biology of Reproduction* **62** 564–570

Eckert J, Tao T and Niemann H (1997) Ratio of inner cell mass and trophoblastic cells in blastocysts derived from porcine 4- and 8-cell embryos and isolated blastomeres cultured *in vitro* in the presence or absence of protein and human leukemia inhibitory factor *Biology of Reproduction* **57** 552–560

Ford SP, Christenson RK and Ford JJ (1982) Uterine blood flow and uterine arterial, venous and luminal concentrations of oestrogens on days 11, 13 and 15 after oestrus in pregnant and non-pregnant sows *Journal of Reproduction and Fertility* **64** 185–190

Funahashi H, Cantley TC, Stumpf TT, Terlouw SL and Day BN (1994) Use of low salt culture medium for *in vitro* maturation of porcine oocytes is associated with elevated oocyte glutathione levels and enhanced male pronuclear formation after *in vitro* fertilization *Biology of Reproduction* **51** 633–639

Funahashi H, Cantley TC and Day BN (1997) Synchronization of meiosis in porcine oocytes by exposure to dibutyryl cyclic adenosine monophosphate improves developmental competence following *in vitro* fertilization *Theriogenology* **47** 679–686

Geisert RD, Brookbank JW, Roberts RM and Bazer FW (1982) Establishment of pregnancy in the pig. II. Cellular remodelling of the porcine blastocyst during elongation on day 12 of pregnancy *Biology of Reproduction* **27** 941–955

Geisert RD, Zavy MT, Moffat RJ, Blair RM and Yellin T (1990) Embryonic steroids and the establishment of pregnancy in pigs *Journal of Reproduction and Fertility* **40** 293–305

Harvey MB, Leco KJ, Arcellana-Panlilio MY, Zhang X, Edwards DR and Schultz GA (1995) Roles of growth factors during peri-implantation development *Molecular Human Reproduction* **10** 712–718

Hay-Schmidt A, Viuff D, Greve T and Hyttel P (2001) Transcriptional activity in *in vivo* developed early cleavage stage bovine embryos *Theriogenology* **56** 167–176

Herrmann BG, Labiet S, Poustka A, King TR and Lerach H (1990) Cloning of the T gene required in mesoderm formation in the mouse *Nature* **343** 617–622

Heyman Y, Degrolard J, Adenot P, Chesne P, Flechon B, Renard JP and Flechon JE (1995) Cellular evaluation of bovine nuclear transfer embryos developed *in vitro*. *Reproduction, Nutrition and Development* **35** 713–723

Horwitz A, Duggan K, Buck RC, Beckerle MC and Burridge K (1986) Interaction between plasma membrane fibronectin receptor with talin, a transmembrane linkage *Nature* **320** 531–533

Hyttel P, Laurincik J, Rosenkranz C, Rath D, Niemann H, Ochs RL and Schellander K (2000) Nucleolar proteins and ultrastructure in pre-implantation porcine embryos developed *in vivo*. *Biology of Reproduction* **63** 1858–1866

Jacobs T (1992) Control of the cell cycle *Developmental Biology* **153** 1–15

Jarrel VL, Day BN and Prather RS (1991) The transition from maternal to zygotic control of development occurs during the 4-cell stage in the domestic pig, *Sus scrofa*:

quantitative and qualitative aspects of protein synthesis *Biology of Reproduction* **44** 62–68

Kanka J, Fulka J, Jr and Petr J (1991) Nuclear transplantation in bovine embryos: fine structural and autoradiographic studies *Molecular Reproduction and Development* **29** 110–116

Kanka J, Hozak P, Heyman Y, Chesne P, Degrolard J, Renard JP and Flechon JE (1996) Transcriptional activity and nucleolar ultrastructure of embryonic rabbit nuclei after transplantation to enucleated oocytes *Molecular Reproduction and Development* **43** 135–144

Kanka J, Smith SD, Soloy E, Holm P and Callesen H (1999) Nucleolar ultrastructure in bovine nuclear transfer embryos *Molecular Reproduction and Development* **52** 253–263

King WA, Shepherd DL, Plante L, Lavoir MC, Looney CR and Barnes FL (1996) Nucleolar and mitochondrial morphology in bovine embryos reconstructed by nuclear transfer *Molecular Reproduction and Development* **44** 499–506

Knudson K, Horwitz AF and Buck C (1986) A monoclonal antibody identifies a glycoprotein complex involved in cell–substratum adhesion *Experimental Cell Research* **157** 218–226

Ko Y, Choi I, Green ML, Simmen FA and Simmen RC (1994) Transient expression of the cytochrome P450 aromatase gene in elongating porcine blastocysts is correlated with uterine insulin-like growth factor levels during peri-implantation development *Molecular Reproduction and Development* **37** 1–11

Koo D-B, Kang Y-K, Choi Y-H *et al.* (2000) *In vitro* development of reconstructed porcine oocytes after somatic cell nuclear transfer *Biology of Reproduction* **63** 986–992

Kopecny V and Niemann H (1993) Formation of nuclear microarchitecture in the preimplantation bovine embryo at the onset of transcription: implications for biotechnology *Theriogenology* **39** 109–119

Kruip TAM and den Dass JHG (1997) *In vitro* produced and cloned embryos: effects on pregnancy, parturition and offspring *Theriogenology* **47** 43–52

Laurincik J, Rath D and Niemann H (1994) Pronucleus formation and early cleavage following *in vitro* fertilization of porcine oocytes matured *in vivo* and *in vitro*. *Journal of Reproduction and Fertility* **102** 277–284

Laurincik J, Thomsen PD, Hay-Schmidt A, Avery B, Greve T, Ochs RL and Hyttel P (2000) Nucleolar proteins and nuclear ultrastructure in pre-implantation bovine embryos produced *in vitro*. *Biology of Reproduction* **62** 1024–1032

Laurincik J, Zathartchenko V, Stozkovic M, Brem G, Wolf E, Müller M, Ochs RL and Hyttel P Nucleolar protein allocation and ultrastructure in bovine embryos produced by nuclear transfer from granulosa cells (in press)

Lavoir MC, Kelk D, Rumph N, Barnes F, Betteridge KJ and King WA (1997) Transcription and translation in bovine nuclear transfer embryos *Biology of Reproduction* **57** 204–213

Lavranos TC, Rathjen PD and Semark RF (1995) Trophic effect of myeloid leukemia inhibitory factor (LIF) on mouse embryos *Journal of Reproduction and Fertility* **105** 331–338

Macháty Z, Day BN and Prather RS (1998) Development of early porcine embryos *in vitro* and *in vivo*. *Biology of Reproduction* **59** 451–455

Meijer HA, Van De Pavert SA, Stroband HW and Boerjan ML (2000) Expression of the organizer specific homeobox gene goosecoid (gsc) in porcine embryos *Molecular Reproduction and Development* **55** 1–7

Miyoshi K, Taguchi Y, Sendai Y, Hiroyoshi H and Sato E (2000) Establishment of a porcine cell line from *in vitro*-produced blastocysts and transfer of the cells into enucleated oocytes *Biology of Reproduction* **62** 1640–1646

Niemann H and Elsaesser F (1986) Evidence for estrogen-dependent blastocyst formation in the pig *Biology of Reproduction* **35** 10–16

Niemann H and Elsaesser F (1987) Accumulation of oestrone by pig and its potential physiological significance for blastocyst development *in vitro. Journal of Reproduction and Fertility* **80** 221–227

Niemann H and Wrenzycki C (2000) Alterations of expression of developmentally important genes in preimplantation bovine embryos by *in vitro* culture conditions: implications for subsequent development *Theriogenology* **53** 21–34

Onishi A, Iwamoto M, Akita T, Mikawa S, Takeda K, Awata T, Hanada H and Perry AC (2000) Pig cloning by microinjection of fetal fibroblast nuclei *Science* **289** 1188–1190

Ouhibi N, Fulka J, Jr, Kanka J and Moor RM (1996) Nuclear transplantation of ectodermal cells in pig oocytes: ultrastructure and autoradiography *Molecular Reproduction and Development* **44** 533–539

Peters RM and Wells KD (1993) Culture of pig embryos *Journal of Reproduction and Fertility Supplement* **48** 61–73

Plante L, Plante C, Shepherd DL and King WA (1994) Cleavage and ^{3}H-uridine incorporation in bovine embryos of high *in vitro* developmental potential *Molecular Reproduction and Development* **39** 375–383

Polejaeva IA, Chen S-H, Vaught TD *et al.* (2000) Cloned pigs produced by nuclear transfer from adult somatic cells *Nature* **407** 86–90

Pope WF and First NL (1985) Factors affecting the survival of pig embryos *Theriogenology* **23** 91–105

Prather RS and Day BN (1998) Practical considerations for the *in vitro* production of pig embryos *Theriogenology* **49** 23–32

Prather RS, Sims MM and First NL (1989) Nuclear transplantation in early pig embryos *Biology of Reproduction* **41** 414–418

Rath D, Johnson LA, Dobrinsky JR, Welch GR and Niemann H (1997) Production of piglets preselected for sex following *in vitro* fertilization with X and Y chromosome bearing spermatozoa sorted by flow cytometry *Theriogenology* **47** 795–800

Rath D, Long CR, Dobrinsky JR, Welch GR, Schreier LL and Johnson LA (1999) *In vitro* production of sexed embryos for gender preselection: high speed sorting of X-chromosome bearing sperm to produce piglets after embryo transfer *Journal of Animal Science* **77** 3346–3352

Rouslahti E and Pierschbacher MD (1987) New perspectives in cell adhesion: RGD and integrins *Science* **238** 491–497

Schoenbeck RA, Peters MS, Rickords LF, Stumpf TT and Prather RS (1992) Characterization of deoxyribonucleic acid synthesis and the transition from maternal to embryonic control in the 4-cell porcine embryo *Biology of Reproduction* **47** 1118–1125

Stewart CL (1994) Leukemia inhibitory factor and the regulation of preimplantation development of the mammalian embryo *Molecular Reproduction and Development* **39** 233–238

Stroband HWJ and Van der Lende T (1990) Embryonic and uterine development during early pregnancy *Journal of Reproduction and Fertility Supplement* **40** 261–277

Tamkun JW, DeSimmone DW, Fonda D, Patel RS, Buck C, Horwitz AF and Hynes RO (1986) Structure of integrin, a glycoprotein involved in the transmembrane linkage between fibronectin and actin *Cell* **46** 271–282

Thompson EM (1996) Chromatin structure and gene expression in the preimplantation mammalian embryo *Reproduction, Nutrition and Development* **36** 619–635

Tomanek M, Kopecny V and Kanka J (1989) Genome reactivation in developing early pig embryos: an ultrastructural and autoradiographic analysis *Anatomy and Embryology* **180** 309–316

Trout WE, McDonnell JJ, Kramer KK, Baumbach GA and Roberts RM (1991) The retinol-binding protein of the expanding pig blastocyst: molecular cloning and expression in trophectoderm and embryonic disc *Endocrinology* **5** 1533–1540

Vajta G, Holm P, Greve T and Callesen H (1997) Vitrification of porcine embryos using the open pulled straw (OPS) method *Acta Veterinaria Scandinavica* **38** 349–352

Vaughan TJ, James PS, Pascall JC and Brown KD (1992) Expression of the genes for TGF alpha, EGF and the EGF receptor during early pig development *Development* **116** 663–669

Viuff D, Avery B, Greve T, King WA and Hyttel P (1996) Transcriptional activity in *in vitro* produced bovine two- and four-cell embryos *Molecular Reproduction and Development* **43** 171–179

Viuff D, Hyttel P, Avery B, Vajta G, Greve T, Callesen H and Thomsen PD (1998) Ribosomal ribonucleic acid is transcribed at the 4-cell stage in *in vitro* produced bovine embryos *Biology of Reproduction* **59** 626–631

Wachtler F and Stahl A (1993) The nucleolus: a structural and functional interpretation *Micron* **24** 473–505

Wang WH, Abeydeera LR, Prather RS and Day BN (1998) Morphological comparison of ovulated and *in-vitro* matured porcine oocytes, with particular reference to polyspermy after *in vitro* fertilization *Molecular Reproduction and Development* **49** 308–316

Yelich JV, Pomp D and Geisert RD (1997a) Ontogeny of elongation and gene expression in the early developing porcine conceptus *Biology of Reproduction* **57** 1256–1265

Yelich JV, Pomp D and Geisert RD (1997b) Detection of

transcripts for retinoic acid receptors, retinol binding protein, and transforming growth factors during rapid trophoblastic elongation in the procine conceptus *Biology of Reproduction* **57** 286–294

Ying C, Hsu WL, Hong WF, Cheng WT and Yang Y (2000) Estrogen receptor is expressed in pig embryos during preimplantation development *Molecular Reproduction and Development* **55** 83–88

Reproduction Supplement 58, 191–207

Functional analysis of autocrine and paracrine signalling at the uterine–conceptus interface in pigs

L. A. Jaeger[1,2], G. A. Johnson[2,3]*, H. Ka[2,3], J. G. Garlow[2,3], R. C. Burghardt[1,2], T. E. Spencer[2,3] and F. W. Bazer[2,3]

[1]Department of Veterinary Anatomy & Public Health, College of Veterinary Medicine, [2]Center for Animal Biotechnology and Genomics, and [3]Department of Animal Science, Texas A&M University, College Station, TX 77843–4458, USA

The complexity of implantation necessitates intimate dialogue between conceptus and maternal cells, and precise coordination of maternal and conceptus signalling events. Maternal and conceptus-derived steroid hormones, growth factors and cytokines, as well as integrins and their ligands, have important and inter-related roles in mediating adhesion between apical aspects of conceptus trophectoderm and maternal uterine luminal epithelium that leads to formation of an epitheliochorial placenta. Integrin receptors appear to play fundamental roles in the implantation cascade and may interact with extracellular matrix molecules and other ligands to transduce cellular signals through autocrine and paracrine mechanisms. Functional *in vitro* analyses can be used to monitor individual contributions of specific integrin receptors and ligands to the signalling cascades of the maternal–conceptus interface. Integrative studies of implantation in pigs, using *in vivo* and *in vitro* approaches, are required to understand conceptus attachment and implantation in this species, and provide valuable opportunities to understand the fundamental mechanisms of implantation in all species.

Introduction

The period of conceptus attachment and implantation in pigs, as in other species, is a critical time for embryonic survival. In pigs, marked morphological and functional changes occur in the peri-implantation blastocyst, including a change in shape from a relatively small (< 10 mm in diameter) sphere to a filamentous form that may exceed 100 mm in length in < 1 day. Coincident with and after this transformation, pig conceptuses produce a variety of secretory products, including oestrogens, interferons, proteases, growth factors and cytokines. Endometrial structure and function also change markedly and include alterations in expression of integral membrane glycoproteins as well as numerous secretory products such as protease inhibitors, growth factors and cytokines (for reviews see Burghardt *et al.*, 1997; Geisert and Yelich, 1997). Both maternal and conceptus factors play important roles in

Email: ljaeger@cvm.tamu.edu
*Present address: Department of Animal and Veterinary Science, Agricultural Sciences Building, University of Idaho, Moscow, ID 83844–2330, USA

maternal recognition of pregnancy and mediation of adhesion between the apical aspects of the apposing conceptus trophectoderm and maternal uterine luminal epithelium that lead to formation of an epitheliochorial placenta. The complexity of implantation necessitates intimate dialogue between conceptus and maternal cells, and precise coordination of maternal and conceptus signalling events.

Although the exact nature of the adhesive mechanisms responsible for successful implantation in pigs is not known, much evidence has been obtained that implicates interactions between integrins and extracellular matrix molecules as critical players in mammalian reproduction, particularly implantation. Which integrin–ligand combinations are required for successful implantation and maintenance of pregnancy in pigs, and the precise cellular signals they evoke to control these events, are still largely unknown. Similarly, regulation of expression of integrins and their ligands is incompletely understood, although considerable evidence points toward integrated control by steroid hormones and growth factors.

This review will focus on recent advancements in our understanding of the molecules involved in functional signalling interactions at the pre- and peri-implantation uterine–conceptus interface in pigs. In addition to examining current knowledge in pigs, signalling interactions in other species, which may provide insight into the mechanisms involved in successful implantation in pigs, will also be considered. Particular emphasis will be placed on interactions among molecules implicated directly in mediating peri-implantation differentiation and adhesion, and on analyses of their mechanistic functions, as determined using *in vitro* experimental models. Proteases, their inhibitors and products of protease activity are important factors in implantation, but will not be discussed in detail. The discussion will first explore interactions among soluble factors, such as steroid hormones, cytokines and growth factors, and their possible roles in controlling peri-implantation growth and differentiation at the pig uterine–conceptus interface. Specific growth factors will be discussed in the context of receptor-mediating actions, those associated with binding proteins and those that may transduce signals through integrin receptors. Finally, integrins, extracellular matrix proteins and other potential integrin ligands at the uterine–conceptus interface are discussed in the context of functional signals transmitted through these molecules, and in model systems for evaluating their role in the implantation cascade.

Steroid hormones and their receptors

Implantation in pigs entails adhesion between conceptus trophectoderm and maternal endometrial luminal epithelium, leading to formation of an epitheliochorial placenta. Although the absence of invasion in this placentation strategy implies that luminal epithelium and glandular secretions are important in accomplishing successful implantation, modulation of the process by steroid hormones may be direct, via epithelial–stromal interactions or both, as described for other tissues (for review see Cooke *et al.*, 1998). In particular, expression of receptors for progesterone, a steroid hormone that is a prerequisite for maintenance of pregnancy, decreases markedly in the luminal and glandular endometrial epithelium after day 5 of the oestrous cycle or pregnancy. Progesterone receptors are undetectable in luminal epithelium on days 12–18 of pregnancy, yet remain in the underlying stroma and myometrium (for review see Okulicz *et al.*, 1998). Thus, stromal-derived factors, expressed under the influence of progesterone (progestomedins), may exert paracrine effects on the luminal and glandular epithelia to achieve differentiation necessary for implantation.

Between day 11 and day 12 of gestation, preimplantation pig conceptuses produce oestrogens, which are believed to comprise a critical component of the signalling mechanism for maternal recognition of pregnancy in pigs. A second peri-implantation phase of oestrogen production occurs between day 15 and day 30 of pregnancy (for review see Bazer *et al.*, 1998). Oestrogen receptor mRNA and protein are present in pig endometrium during early pregnancy (for review see Okulicz *et al.*, 1998) and mRNA content appears to correlate significantly with immunoreactive oestrogen receptor protein content (Persson *et al.*, 1997). As oestrogen receptor α is present in epithelia of the pregnant uterus from day 5 to day 15 of pregnancy (for review see Okulicz *et al.*, 1998), conceptus-derived oestrogens could exert effects on endometrial function by direct interactions with epithelial oestrogen receptors. Although stromal oestrogen receptors were not detectable between day 15 and day 18 of pregnancy, the presence of oestrogen receptors in stromal cells underlying the luminal epithelium on days 10–12 of pregnancy indicates that oestrogens may have paracrine effects on preimplantation endometrial epithelium through stromal-derived factors produced in response to oestrogens (oestromedins).

Recently, progesterone receptors and oestrogen receptors α and β were identified in pig conceptuses, raising the possibility of paracrine and autocrine steroid hormone-induced effects on the conceptus during the peri-implantation phase of pregnancy.

Progesterone receptor mRNA and protein were not detectable in early (day 6) pig blastocysts (Ying *et al.*, 2000a); however, expression of progesterone receptor was detected in filamentous conceptuses by RT–PCR (Dekaney *et al*, 1998; Kowalski *et al.*, 2000). Progesterone receptor protein was localized immunohistochemically in embryonic and extraembryonic cells of conceptuses from day 10 to day 14 of gestation (Dekaney *et al.*, 1998).

Oestrogen receptor α mRNA was detected by RT–PCR in pig blastocysts on day 6 of gestation; however, the corresponding protein was not detectable by immunohistochemistry (Ying *et al.*, 2000b). In peri-implantation conceptuses from day 12 to day 14 of gestation, oestrogen receptor α expression was also detected by RT–PCR (Dekaney *et al.*, 1998; Kowalski *et al.*, 2000). Studies using immunohistochemical techniques have detected oestrogen receptor α protein in pig conceptus trophectoderm on days 10–12 of gestation (Dekaney *et al.*, 1998) and oestrogen receptor α protein has also been identified in embryonic disk and extraembryonic cells between day 10 and day 14 (L. A. Jaeger and N. H. Ing, unpublished). Presence of oestrogen receptor β in day 12 conceptuses has been detected via RT–PCR and western blot analysis (Kowalski *et al.*, 2000). The functions of conceptus steroid hormone receptors remain to be determined.

Growth factors and cytokines

Numerous growth factors and cytokines have been described in pig uterus and conceptus and implicated in control of the events surrounding implantation and early pregnancy (for review see Geisert and Yelich, 1997). Here, we will address recent results on expression and effects of growth factors, cytokines and their receptors at the pig uterine–conceptus interface, with particular emphasis on those with potential autocrine and paracrine effects on adhesive interactions between endometrium and conceptuses during early pregnancy.

Interferons are antiviral cytokines which, in domestic species, are of interest as possible mediators of pregnancy recognition and establishment of pregnancy. Tau interferons (IFN-τ) are members of a unique subclass of the type I IFN family that are produced by the conceptus trophectoderm to signal pregnancy recognition in ruminants. In sheep, IFN-τ prevents luteolysis by suppressing transcription of oestrogen receptor α and oxytocin receptor genes in the endometrial luminal epithelium and superficial glandular epithelium to impede the pulsatile release of $PGF_{2\alpha}$ (for review see Bazer *et al.*, 1998).

Peri-implantation pig conceptuses produce type I and type II interferons between day 12 and day 18 of pregnancy (for review see Bazer *et al.*, 1998); however, their physiological role is not clear. The major species is a member of the type II IFN family (IFN-γ) and the other component with antiviral activity is a novel type I IFN, IFN-δ (Lefèvre *et al.*, 1998a), which is co-expressed with IFN-γ in the trophectoderm. Type I and II interferons in pigs do not appear to be anti-luteolytic during early pregnancy, because neither intrauterine infusion of conceptus secretory proteins collected on day 15 of pregnancy nor a mixture of recombinant IFN-γ and IFN-δ extends the pig inter-oestrous interval (Harney and Bazer, 1989; Lefèvre *et al.*, 1998b). Paracrine effects for IFN-δ on the uterus are suggested by localization of type I IFN receptors on endometrial epithelial cells, but not on trophoblast (see Lefèvre *et al.*, 1998a). Chwetzoff and D'Andréa (1997) reported increased mRNA for β_2-microglobulin and Finkel–Biskis–Reilly murine sarcoma virus-associated ubiquitously secreted protein (FAU) in pig uterine luminal epithelial cells treated with a combination of IFN-γ and IFN-δ. A gene encoding the porcine UbA_{52} ubiquitin also increased in response to IFN treatment (Chwetzoff and D'Andréa, 1997) and is reminiscent of IFN induction of ISG17/UCRP, a functional homologue of ubiquitin, in ovine and bovine uterus (Hansen *et al*, 1997; Johnson *et al.*, 1999a). The physiological significance of interferons during pregnancy in pigs, as well as the specific signalling pathways activated in pig endometrium, is unknown.

Heparin-binding growth factors

A growing number of growth factors and cytokines has been identified on the basis of their ability to bind to immobilized heparin. *In vivo*, heparin-binding growth factors bind to heparan sulphate chains, such as components of heparan sulphate proteoglycans. Hence, these growth factors can be stored or sequestered in basement membranes and extracellular matrix compartments (for review see Vlodavsky *et al.*, 1996). As the actions of this heterogeneous group of growth factors can be altered by their interaction with extracellular matrix and regulated by release from the matrix, they are possible candidates to influence the dynamic events of implantation.

Fibroblast growth factors (FGFs) comprise a large family of growth factors with effects on cell proliferation, migration, angiogenesis, embryonic development and cellular differentiation in a variety of tissues. One of the earliest identified members, FGF-2, also known as basic FGF, has been identified in embryonic and uterine tissues of numerous species (for review see Rider and Piva, 1998). Brigstock *et al.* (1989) reported the presence of heparin-binding growth factors in pig uterine luminal flushings. Subsequently, several heparin-binding growth factors were purified from pig uteri, one of which was FGF-2, and another which displayed immunological crossreactivity with antiserum to FGF-1 (Brigstock *et al.*, 1990). FGF-2 mRNA has been identified in endometrial epithelium, stroma and myometrium of gilts during the oestrous cycle and the first 30 days of pregnancy; however, no changes in expression were detected during the oestrous cycle or pregnancy (Katsahambas and Hearn, 1996). Gupta *et al.* (1997) reported increases in FGF-2 expression in luminal epithelium and stroma between day 10 and day 14 of pregnancy. Expression of immunoreactive FGF-1 in tissues from the same gilts was limited to stromal compartments of the uterus. Immunoreactive FGF-2, but not FGF-1, was detected in pig conceptus trophectoderm, endoderm and embryonic disk. Four distinct genes encode FGF receptors and alternative splicing of FGF receptors leads to unique ligand binding specificity of each isoform (Ornitz *et al.*, 1996). Expression of most of these receptors at the pig maternal–conceptus interface has not been reported. Recently, FGF receptor 2IIIb, which binds FGF-1 (Ornitz *et al.*, 1996), was localized in endometrial luminal epithelium of pigs (Ka *et al.*, 2000, see below), indicating that luminal epithelium may be a target for stromally-derived or sequestered FGF-1 during the peri-implantation period. The roles of FGF-1 and FGF-2 during early pregnancy in pigs have not been established.

FGF-7, also called keratinocyte growth factor (KGF), binds with high affinity to FGF receptor 2IIIb, a transmembrane tyrosine kinase encoded by the *bek* gene. Activity of FGFs, including FGF-7, is modulated further by interactions with heparan sulphate proteoglycans (see Ornitz *et al.*, 1996). FGF-7 is a paracrine mediator of epithelial cell proliferation and expression of FGF receptor 2IIIb is restricted to epithelial cells (Finch *et al.*, 1989; Rubin *et al.*, 1989). In primates, FGF-7 is expressed in uterine stromal cells in response to progesterone (for review see Rider and Piva, 1998). Recently, Ka *et al.* (2000) cloned partial cDNAs encoding FGF-7 and FGF receptor 2IIIb from pig endometrium and detected endometrial expression of FGF-7 between day 9 and day 85 of pregnancy using slot blot hybridization. Endometrial FGF-7 expression reached a maximum on day 12 of pregnancy, coinciding with the period of oestradiol production by the conceptus and maternal recognition of pregnancy. Most surprising was localization of the FGF-7 mRNA to endometrial luminal epithelium, not stromal cells, during the pre- and peri-implantation phases and, later, to endometrial gland epithelium. Western blot analysis confirmed the presence of FGF-7 in uterine luminal flushings collected on day 12 of pregnancy. FGF receptor 2IIIb was detected in endometrial epithelia and conceptus trophectoderm, but conceptus trophectoderm does not express FGF-7 (Ka *et al.*, 2000). This finding is indicative of unique roles for FGF-7 in uterine epithelial–epithelial and epithelial–trophectoderm autocrine and paracrine communications in pregnant pigs, which were investigated further by Ka *et al.* (2001).

Treatment of pig endometrial explants with oestradiol in the presence or absence of progesterone increased endometrial FGF-7 expression, whereas progesterone alone had no effect (Ka *et al.*, 2001). Thus, conceptus oestrogens produced between day 11 and day 12 of pregnancy may be responsible for the peri-implantation peak in endometrial FGF-7 expression and, in pigs, FGF-7 appears to be an oestromedin. Possible paracrine effects of maternally derived FGF-7 on conceptus trophectoderm were investigated using a trophoblast cell line derived from day 12 pig conceptuses. Northern and slot blot analysis of FGF-7-treated trophectoderm cells revealed that FGF-7 increased expression of urokinase plasminogen activator (uPA), a conceptus protease produced *in vivo*, coincident with peri-implantation production of oestrogens. In addition, proliferation of trophectoderm was stimulated by FGF-7, as indicated by increased incorporation of tritiated thymidine into cellular DNA (Ka *et al.*, 2001).

In addition to marked rearrangement and remodelling of trophectoderm of conceptuses during peri-implantation elongation, conceptus trophectoderm is also mitotically active during both the pre-elongation and elongation phases of development, as shown by proliferating cell nuclear antigen (PCNA) immunostaining (Wilson and Ford, 1997; Ka *et al.*, 2001). This mitotic activity may be an important determinant of ultimate placental size and function. Wilson and Ford (2000) reported that administration of oestradiol to Meishan gilts, beginning on day 12 or day 13 of pregnancy and continuing for 48 h, which encompasses the time of conceptus elongation and initial attachment to the endometrium, resulted in placentae that were heavier and larger than those of controls near term, albeit less efficient (as determined by fetal weight:placental mass ratios). Conceptus oestradiol production results in increased endometrial production of secretory proteins, including growth factors, such as insulin-like growth factor I (IGF-I) (for review see Simmen *et al.*, 1995), which increases mitotic activity of trophectoderm. The increased placental size in oestrogen-treated gilts may be attributable to oestrogen-induced endometrial growth factors, such as IGF-I, which increase the rate of mitosis of peri-implantation conceptus trophectoderm (Wilson and Ford,

2000). The work of Ka *et al.* (2000, 2001) indicates that another effector of the placental growth response may be FGF-7. There is compelling evidence for an intricate series of paracrine communication events in which oestrogens of conceptus origin, acting through epithelial and stromal endometrial oestrogen receptors, increase production of luminal epithelial growth factors, which modulate further differentiation and growth of conceptus trophectoderm to achieve successful implantation.

Connective tissue growth factor (CTGF) is another heparin-binding growth factor identified in pig uterine luminal flushings. This 38 kDa cysteine-rich protein stimulates mitosis, migration, adhesion and extracellular matrix production in fibroblasts, and is a possible mediator of autocrine and paracrine signals in other cell types, including epithelial cells (for review see Moussad and Brigstock, 2000). In fibroblasts, CTGF mRNA is induced by TGF-β, indicating that it functions as a downstream modulator of the actions of TGF-β in fibroblastic cells (for review see Moussad and Brigstock, 2000). The receptor or receptors used by CTGF, as well as the downstream modulators of its cellular signals, are not known. Although CTGF does not contain an RGD (arginine-glycine-aspartic acid) recognition site, it appears to possess integrin-binding capabilities, and binds to integrin αvβ3 to promote migration of endothelial cells *in vitro* (for review see Lau and Lam, 1999).

Pig uterine luminal flushings, collected from pigs between day 0 and day 18 of the oestrous cycle or pregnancy, contain low molecular mass (10 kDa; 16–20 kDa) forms of CTGF (Ball *et al.*, 1998; for review see Moussad and Brigstock, 2000); however, only a single CTGF transcript was identified in RNA collected from pig endometrium during that period (Harding *et al.*, 1997). It was suggested that proteolytic processing was responsible for the mitogenically active low molecular mass forms of CTGF. Western blot analysis revealed that CTGF concentrations in luminal flushings on day 12 of pregnancy were higher than on day 10 of pregnancy and day 12 of the oestrous cycle. Expression of CTGF mRNA has been shown in pig endometrial stromal, vascular and endothelial cells (for review see Moussad and Brigstock, 2000); however, its detailed spatial and temporal expression patterns have not been reported. CTGF is expressed in murine embryonic and extraembryonic cells, including trophectoderm (Surveyor *et al.*, 1998), and in uterine tissues. In humans, CTGF is present in epithelial, stromal and vascular compartments of the uterus (Uzumcu *et al.*, 2000). In non-epithelial cells, CTGF stimulates expression of fibronectin and integrin α5 (for review see Moussad and Brigstock, 2000), two molecules implicated in facilitating adhesion at the pig maternal–conceptus interface; however, it is not known whether similar effects would occur in trophectoderm or uterine epithelia. The potential role of CTGF in pig implantation warrants further investigation.

Insulin-like growth factors and their binding proteins

Endometrial IGF-I is expressed coincident with maternal recognition of pregnancy in pigs. The IGF-I receptor has been identified in pig conceptus and uterine tissues, indicating potential effects of IGF-I on growth and development of the uterus and peri-implantation conceptuses (for review see Geisert and Yelich, 1997). The IGF-II/mannose-6-phosphate receptor (the role of which in IGF signalling remains unclear) has also been immunolocalized to trophectoderm of preimplantation pig conceptuses (for review see Rider and Piva, 1998). Possible roles for IGF-I in pig blastocyst development and early pregnancy have been reviewed previously (see Simmen *et al.*, 1995; Geisert and Yelich, 1997).

More recently, ligand blot analysis revealed the presence of several IGF-binding proteins (IGFBPs), including IGFBP-3, in pig uterine luminal flushings. Abundance of the IGFBPs decreased markedly between day 11 and day 12 of gestation (Lee *et al.*, 1998), which was associated temporally with conceptus transition from spherical to filamentous morphology. However, on day 12 of pregnancy, the abundance of endometrial IGFBP-3 mRNA from uteri containing spherical conceptuses was not different from that of uteri containing filamentous conceptuses. This finding indicates possible proteolytic regulation of IGFBP-3 abundance in uterine luminal flushings. *In vitro* analysis of IGFBP-3 proteolysis, using uterine flushes harvested on day 12 of pregnancy, indicated the presence of enzymes, including a serine protease, responsible for degradation of IGFBP-3 in uteri containing filamentous conceptuses. Regulation of intrauterine IGF actions by IGFBPs and proteases was suggested (Lee *et al.*, 1998). Subsequently, Geisert *et al.* (2001) demonstrated similar proteolysis of IGFBPs in uterine flushings collected during the oestrous cycle as well as during pregnancy. They provided evidence that increased activity of the serine protease kallikrein on day 12 of the oestrous cycle and pregnancy can result in cleavage of IGFBP-2 and -3, and that activation of matrix metalloproteinases by kallikrein may also contribute to IGFBP proteolysis within the uterine lumen.

Badinga *et al.* (1999) used cultures of endometrial glandular epithelial cells, established from uteri of pigs on day 12 of pregnancy, to study the effects of IGFs and IGFBPs on growth of uterine epithelial cells. Ligand blot analysis of conditioned media from the glandular epithelial cells revealed the presence of four IGFBP bands. IGF-I and IGF-II stimulated glandular epithelial cell DNA synthesis, as did an IGF-II analogue (Leu27-IGF-II), which binds the IGF-II receptor with normal binding affinity and the IGF-I receptor with low affinity. IGFBP-2, which was not identified in conditioned medium of cultured glandular epithelial cells, increased IGF-II-dependent DNA synthesis and also stimulated DNA synthesis in the absence of exogenous IGF-II. Therefore, IGF-II receptors may be involved in IGF mitogenic signalling, and IGFBP-2 may modulate uterine epithelial cell growth by IGF-dependent and -independent pathways (Badinga *et al.*, 1999).

Although not yet examined at the pig maternal–conceptus interface, IGFBP-5 binds with high affinity to extracellular matrix proteins such as osteopontin (Nam *et al.*, 2000). Furthermore, IGFBP-1 binds integrin $\alpha5\beta1$ and can alter human cytotrophoblast migration and attachment to fibronectin (Irwin and Guidice, 1998). It is possible that IGFBPs modulate activity of IGFs during early pregnancy in pigs and also affect conceptus and uterine growth and differentiation through interactions with extracellular matrix proteins or integrin receptors.

Transforming growth factor βs

Transforming growth factor βs (TGF-βs) 1, 2 and 3 are members of a large growth factor family. These three related TGF-β isoforms are 25 kDa homodimeric molecules derived from precursor proteins. Each is released from cells in a latent form, resulting from continued non-covalent association with its isoform-specific homodimeric peptide, the TGF-β latency-associated peptide (LAP). The latent TGF-β–LAP complex is often disulphide-bonded to a latent TGF-β binding protein implicated in secretion of the complex and its targeting to and storage in extracellular matrix. Although the mechanisms of physiological activation are still not understood fully, proteases, in particular the plasminogen activator–plasmin system, probably participate in conversion of latent TGF-βs to active forms (for review see Rifkin *et al.*, 1999). Once active, TGF-β1, -2 and -3 transmit their signals through transmembrane, serine-threonine kinase type I and type II TGF-β receptors (for review see Massague, 1998).

TGF-βs localized to the maternal–conceptus interface in numerous species have been implicated in maternal–conceptus interactions throughout pregnancy (for review see Rider and Piva, 1998). They are of particular interest in early pregnancy because of their stimulatory effects on production of extracellular matrix molecules, expression of integrins and their potential to limit conceptus invasiveness by altering expression of conceptus- and uterine-derived proteases and protease inhibitors.

Gupta *et al.* (1996) localized TGF-β1, -2 and 3, as well as type I and II receptors, to embryonic and extraembryonic cells of pig conceptuses from day 10 (spherical morphology) to day 14 (filamentous morphology) of gestation. Yelich *et al.* (1997a) found that TGF-β3 expression increased in spherical preimplantation conceptuses as they increased in size from 2–5 mm to 6–7 mm in diameter, and expression remained high throughout the tubular and filamentous stages of development. TGF-β2 was not detected. Subsequently, expression of all three TGF-β isoforms was detected in pig conceptuses between day 10 and day 14 of gestation. Expression of all three isoforms was greater in trophectoderm of day 14 filamentous conceptuses than in spherical day 10 conceptuses (Gupta *et al.*, 1998a). On the maternal side of the interface, expression of TGF-β1, -2 and -3 transcripts increased progressively in uterine luminal epithelium and stroma between day 10 and day 14 of gestation (Gupta *et al.*, 1998a), as did expression of the TGF-β proteins and type I and type II receptors (Gupta *et al.*, 1998b).

Possible regulation of TGF-β expression in the pig uterus and conceptus by maternal and possibly conceptus-derived steroids is likely. Hormonal modulation of TGF-β expression appears to be cell type- and also isoform-specific. For example, oestradiol decreases expression of TGF-βs in numerous cell types, but increases TGF-β1 mRNA expression slightly and increases TGF-β3 mRNA expression two- to three-fold in human endometrial stromal cells in culture, whereas treatment with a synthetic progestin decreases expression (Arici *et al.*, 1996). In explant cultures derived from human proliferative phase explants, TGF-β1 mRNA expression increased in response to a combination of oestradiol and progesterone compared with ethanol controls, but only after 4 days of culture, which may imply an indirect mechanism of induction (Casslen *et al.*, 1998). Therefore, it is possible that each of the TGF-βs may function as a progestomedin or oestromedin at the pig maternal–conceptus interface. Analyses of TGF-β expression are complicated further by TGF-β autoinduction (for review see Massague, 1998), which could occur through paracrine as well as autocrine pathways during implantation.

As TGF-βs are produced and secreted in latent forms, the activation process represents a critical step in determining the availability and biological activity of these growth factors. Analysis of pig uterine luminal flushings with an *in vitro* bioassay revealed significant increases in the amounts of biologically active TGF-βs between day 11 and day 13 of pregnancy (Gupta *et al.*, 1998b). Thus, the growth factors increase in both absolute amounts and activity during the implantation phase to interact with TGF-β receptors on conceptus trophectoderm, as well as maternal endometrial stromal and epithelial cells. The mechanisms responsible for activation of latent TGF-βs at the maternal–conceptus interface are not known. However, pig conceptuses produce plasminogen activator, as well as other proteases (for review see Geisert and Yelich, 1997), during this period, which could effect activation at the apical aspect of the trophectoderm. Expression of oncofetal fibronectin and several of the integrin subunits identified at the pig maternal–conceptus interface (see below) may be upregulated by active TGF-βs during the peri-implantation period (Gupta *et al.*, 1998b).

Recent studies have determined novel roles for TGF-βs in cell adhesion. Specifically, the latent TGF-β complex and its released LAP contain RGD sequences that serve as ligands for integrin receptors such as αvβ1 and αvβ5. The RGD of LAP, possibly due to a conformational change, binds integrins with greater avidity after release from the latent TGF-β complex (Munger *et al.*, 1998). As LAP and its potential integrin receptors are present at the pig maternal–conceptus interface, LAP interactions with pig trophectoderm and uterine luminal epithelial cell integrins have been explored using an *in vitro* integrin activation assay (see below).

Integrins and extracellular matrix proteins

Integrin receptors expressed by uterine endometrial epithelial cells and conceptus trophectoderm appear to play a fundamental role in the implantation adhesion cascade in mammals by virtue of their ability to bind extracellular matrix and other ligands. Integrin receptor ligation can lead to adhesion, migration, invasion and the induction of cytoskeletal reorganization and transduction of cellular signals through numerous signalling intermediates. Bi-directional signalling can involve ligand binding through an integrin receptor leading to specific effects on cytoskeletal organization and activation of signalling pathways resulting in regulation of gene expression (for review see Giancotti and Rouslahti, 1999). In addition, integrin cytoplasmic domains transduce cell type-specific signals that can modulate ligand-binding affinity. These functions of activated integrin are thought to be central to trophectoderm–uterine luminal epithelial cell interactions in pigs.

Bowen *et al.* (1996) reported expression of five alpha and two beta integrin subunits at the pig maternal–conceptus interface (for review see Burghardt *et al.*, 1997). Among the most significant of their findings was increased endometrial expression of subunits $\alpha 4$, $\alpha 5$ and $\beta 1$ during maternal recognition of pregnancy, and upregulation of these subunits by progesterone, both *in vivo* and in an *in vitro* model of polarized uterine luminal epithelium (Bowen *et al.*, 1996, 1997). This temporal and spatial modulation of integrin expression in luminal epithelium coincident with the reciprocal downregulation of the anti-adhesive glycoprotein Muc-1 by progesterone may be a prerequisite for conceptus attachment. Integrin subunits $\alpha 4$, $\alpha 5$, αv, $\beta 1$ and $\beta 3$ were localized at sites of contact between luminal endometrial epithelium and conceptus trophectoderm, and the heterodimers that can be formed from these subunit combinations are known receptors for extracellular matrix proteins that have been identified at the pig maternal–conceptus interface (Bowen *et al.*, 1997). Integrin subunit $\beta 5$ is also expressed by pig peri-implantation endometrial epithelium and trophectoderm (R. C. Burghardt and M. Kim, unpublished), revealing the possibility of another integrin heterodimer that may function at the maternal–conceptus interface ($\alpha v \beta 1$, $\alpha 4 \beta 1$, $\alpha v \beta 5$ and $\alpha v \beta 3$).

Vitronectin and fibronectin are among the extracellular matrix molecules identified at the pig maternal–conceptus interface that are capable of serving as ligands for these receptors. These extracellular matrix proteins have been implicated in murine trophoblast outgrowth and attachment, processes that can be blocked with RGD-containing peptides *in vitro* (Armant *et al.*, 1986; Campbell *et al.*, 1995). Tuo and Bazer (1996) determined that pig luminal and glandular epithelial cells, as well as trophectoderm, express a glycosylation variant of fibronectin, oncofetal fibronectin, constitutively. It is noteworthy that the human conceptus produces oncofetal fibronectin, which has been referred to as 'trophoblast glue' because it is present on invading human trophoblast (Feinberg *et al.*, 1991). The ability of integrins expressed at the apical surface of both the maternal and fetal interface to induce fibronectin polymerization at the maternal–fetal interface may allow fibronectin to serve as a bridging ligand or 'trophoblast glue' in pigs. The ability of fibronectin to affect morphology and motility is also relevant in the context of implantation. Fibronectin is a prototype cell adhesion protein recognized by as many as ten different integrins (Johansson *et al.*, 1997). The number of fibronectin receptors is not viewed simply as evidence of redundancy, but rather as receptors that generate different signals depending on the specific integrin receptor involved. For example, only a few fibronectin receptors play a role in the polymerization of fibronectin, two of which are relevant to implantation. Both $\alpha 5 \beta 1$ and $\alpha v \beta 3$ are involved in the formation of a fibronectin network that can be triggered on binding of the RGD sequence of fibronectin (Fogerty *et al.*, 1990; Wennerberg *et al.*, 1996).

In addition to vitronectin and fibronectin present at the maternal–conceptus interface in pigs (Tuo and Bazer, 1996; Bowen *et al.*, 1997), osteopontin is also present in pig endometrium and uterine luminal flushes from cyclic and pregnant gilts, and is expressed by endometrial epithelia (Garlow *et al.*, 2000). Expression of osteopontin mRNA is first evident in endometrial luminal epithelium on day 12 of pregnancy and increased by day 15 of pregnancy. Expression of osteopontin in endometrial glands was not detected during early pregnancy, but was detected in uterine gland epithelium by day 35 of pregnancy. Osteopontin protein was localized on the surface of pig peri-implantation trophectoderm, whereas osteopontin mRNA was not detected, indicating that osteopontin on conceptus trophectoderm is of uterine origin. In other species, including sheep, osteopontin is a product of glandular, not luminal, endometrial epithelia (Nomura *et al.*, 1988; Fazleabas *et al.*, 1997; Johnson *et al.*, 1999b,c). In fact, glandular epithelial expression of osteopontin in sheep occurs early in pregnancy, and osteopontin on the uterine luminal surface appears to be a component of histotroph from the uterine glands (Johnson *et al.*, 2000). The novel pattern of osteopontin expression in pig endometrium may reflect the importance of the luminal epithelium in the epitheliochorial placentation strategy used by this species.

Functional analysis of the implantation cascade

It is essential to define the specific integrin responses to available matrix molecules at the maternal–fetal interface and the repertoire of signalling cascades that are activated by specific receptor–ligand activation events to understand the functional role of integrins and their ligands in implantation better. A simplified *in vitro* strategy used by Miyamoto *et al.* (1995) to define experimentally the hierarchies of cytoskeletal and signalling molecules involved in organizing the cytoskeleton and signal transduction has been adapted to investigate integrin–matrix interactions in endometrial epithelium and conceptus trophectoderm of domestic animals.

Evidence that specific extracellular matrix proteins serve as ligands for maternal and conceptus integrins can be generated *in vitro* by monitoring rapid induction of large cytoskeletal complexes and associated signalling intermediates which mimic those organized in focal contacts after integrin receptor–ligand occupancy and aggregation. Initiation of these complexes results from the deposition of 6 μm polystyrene beads coated with relevant extracellular matrix protein ligands (Fig. 1). Controls for these experiments can include beads coated with poly-L-lysine, matrix molecules with mutated integrin recognition sequences or molecules that block integrin–matrix interactions (for example, neutralizing anti-integrin antibodies, soluble RGD-containing peptides or disintegrins). This general strategy is used to test the functional competence of integrins present at the apical surface of pig uterine luminal epithelial cells and conceptus trophectoderm cells to respond to ligands that have been identified at the maternal–conceptus interface. The induction of transmembrane aggregation of talin was selected as a response indicator in this assay because of its central role in binding cytoplasmic domains of β_1 and β_3 integrins, cytoskeletal proteins and focal adhesion kinase (Critchley, 2000).

Beads coated with LAP, the RGD-containing portion of the latent TGF-β complex, incubated with cultured pig trophectoderm and uterine luminal epithelial cells, activated integrins on apical surfaces of both cell types by aggregation of the cytoskeletal protein talin at bead–apical membrane interfaces (Fig. 1). This finding indicates that both the latent TGF-βs and LAP released at the time of activation play direct roles in integrin-mediated adhesion and signalling between conceptus and maternal cells. Similar responses in ovine trophectoderm and uterine luminal epithelial cells indicate that this novel role for TGF-βs in implantation is

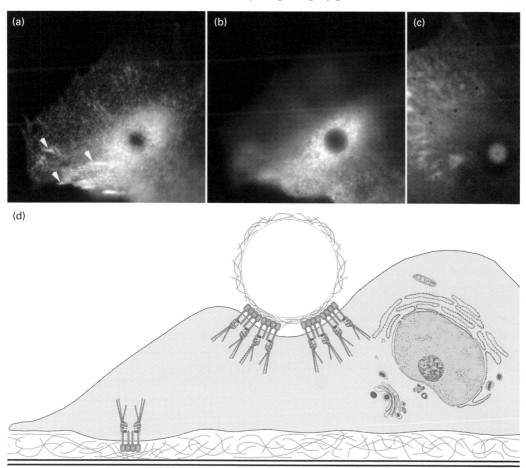

Fig. 1. Functional activation of integrin receptors on pig trophectoderm with latency-associated peptide (LAP) attached to a 6 μm polystyrene bead. Reorganization of the cytoskeleton resulting from integrin activation at the surface of the bead and assembly of cytoskeletal proteins and signalling molecules on the cytoplasmic side of the integrin subunits is shown using immunocytochemical localization of the cytoskeletal protein talin. Accumulation of this protein around the beads requires integrin attachment and aggregation. (a) An optical slice obtained at the focal plane where cell attachment to the substrate reveals a series of focal adhesions (arrows) formed as the result of integrin binding to the substrate. (b) An optical slice of the same cell recorded on a focal plane above the image recorded in (a), nearing the bead–apical membrane interface. Note that basal focal adhesions are not visible in this plane. Accumulation of talin around the bead demonstrates the formation of focal adhesions that were induced by LAP activation of integrins at the apical surface of the cell. (c) Poly-L-lysine-coated bead shows no evidence of focal aggregation of talin, indicating the absence of integrin involvement in the non-specific adhesive interaction of these beads with the cells. (d) Position of basal and apical focal adhesions and the basis for the assay used in these experiments. Cartoon images of aggregated integrins modified from Giancotti and Rouslahti (1999), with permission.

not unique to pigs (Jaeger *et al.*, 2000). The precise integrins with which LAP interacts in uterine and conceptus cells, as well as the downstream signals elicited by the interactions, are not known. However, TGF-βs may play numerous roles in modulating implantation through a complex interplay of autocrine and paracrine signalling involving binding proteins, extracellular matrix proteins and integrins, in addition to the type I and type II receptors.

Similar analyses using fibronectin- and osteopontin-coated beads also evoked integrin-activation responses in pig and ovine trophectoderm and uterine luminal epithelial cells (Johnson *et al.*, 2001; L. A. Jaeger, R. C. Burghardt, G. A. Johnson and F. W. Bazer, unpublished).

These studies are the first to reveal functional integrin activation and cytoskeletal reorganization in uterine luminal epithelium and trophectoderm cells in response to binding of the three matrix proteins identified in regions of initial contact between conceptus trophectoderm and uterine luminal epithelium. The receptor–ligand interactions potentially available during attachment in pigs are shown (Table 1). Clearly, dissection of the individual contributions of each receptor and each extracellular matrix protein will benefit from exploitation of *in vitro* models using biochemical approaches and modern imaging tools that facilitate non-invasive assessment of integrin-mediated signal transduction.

It is possible that each integrin heterodimer present at the apical surfaces of these cells (αvβ1, α4β1, α5β1, αvβ3 and αvβ5) functions as a receptor for the matrix proteins identified to date. However, this is not viewed as redundancy because different signalling cascades can be activated by different receptors. For example, α5β1 and αvβ3 are involved in fibronectin polymerization but the affinity of αvβ3 for fibronectin is much lower and contributes little to cell adhesion to fibronectin (Johansson *et al.*, 1997). Furthermore, these integrins trigger distinct intracellular signalling pathways (Schwartz and Denninghoff, 1994). Some integrins present on pig conceptus and endometrial epithelium may influence the actions of one another. In endothelial cells, for example, interactions between fibronectin and integrin α5β1 potentiate αvβ3-mediated migration on vitronectin (Kim *et al.*, 2000). This type of response may have a greater influence on the trophectoderm side of the maternal–fetal interface because of the dynamic events that bring trophectoderm in contact with the luminal epithelium. Finally, particular integrin–matrix protein interactions may occur in a precise, temporal sequence during the progressive attachment of the conceptus to the uterine luminal epithelium.

Several possible models of integrin–matrix protein interactions are apparent on the basis of expression of particular integrins and extracellular matrix proteins that may serve as ligands at attachment sites (Fig. 2). Firstly, these interactions may facilitate attachment by binding of conceptus integrins to matrix proteins expressed on the luminal epithelium, and vice versa. Secondly, molecules such as osteopontin, a component of histotroph with more than one potential integrin binding site, or fibronectin, which can exist in a polymerized state, may serve as 'bridging ligands' between the two apposing epithelia. Thirdly, localized autocrine actions of ligands expressed at the cell surface with apically expressed integrins may be important. This may be of particular importance as the elongating trophoblast undergoes marked morphological change in preparation for attachment. On approximately day 12 of gestation, the morphology of the conceptus undergoes a marked change from a small sphere to a long filamentous form, accompanied by alterations in trophectodermal cytoskeletal architecture (for review see Geisert and Yelich, 1997). In addition, gene expression in trophectoderm changes during the transition from non-filamentous to filamentous conceptuses (Yelich *et al.*, 1997b; Wilson *et al.*, 2000). The mechanisms responsible for the marked changes that occur in preparation for attachment are not known. Given the marked rearrangement of the trophectoderm actin cytoskeleton and the intimate relationship between activated integrins and the cytoskeleton it is possible that some of the morphological alterations and associated changes in gene expression result from integrin activation. Molecules produced by pig trophoblast, such as oncofetal fibronectin and the TGF-β LAP are possible candidate ligands for effecting this type of autocrine activation of integrin.

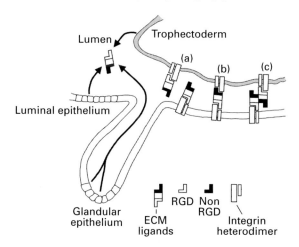

Fig. 2. Proposed model for extracellular matrix protein–integrin interactions at the maternal–conceptus interface. Extracellular matrix proteins (ECM ligands), produced by endometrial or conceptus epithelia, may interact with integrin heterodimers on apical aspects of trophectoderm and luminal epithelial cells via (a) arginine-glycine-aspartic acid (RGD) sequences and (b) non-RGD sequences. As ECM ligands such as osteopontin and fibronectin may contain more than one integrin binding site, they may function as 'bridging ligands' to facilitate conceptus attachment to the luminal epithelium in (b) monomeric or (c) polymeric forms. Modified from Johnson *et al.* (1999b), with permission.

Conclusion

Available results indicate that unravelling the complex signalling between maternal and conceptus cells requires integrative approaches using both *in vivo* and *in vitro* models. Pig trophectoderm cells, which are the source of conceptus-derived oestrogens, express numerous growth factors and growth factor receptors, and interact directly with maternal luminal uterine epithelium during implantation. Various *in vitro* models, including isolated trophectodermal cells and trophectodermal vesicles, have been used to study autocrine and paracrine activities of pig trophoblast and its contribution to successful establishment of pregnancy. In addition to primary culture models, feeder-dependent (Flechon *et al.*, 1995) and feeder-independent (Ramsoondar *et al.*, 1993; Ka *et al.*, 2001) pig trophectodermal cell lines have been developed from pre- and peri-implantation pig conceptuses. Similarly, primary cultures of uterine cells and tissues assist in evaluation of the complex signalling occurring at the maternal–conceptus interface. Co-culture models consisting of uterine stromal and epithelial cells, and culture of polarized epithelial cells supported by extracellular matrices, are useful for studying maternal autocrine and paracrine signalling during early pregnancy. Recently, immortalized cell lines representing luminal epithelium, glandular

Table 1. Possible ligand–integrin interactions at the pig uterine–conceptus interface

Ligands identified at the maternal–conceptus interface	Apically expressed integrin heterodimers
Oncofetal fibronectin/fibronectin	αvβ1, α5β1, α4β1
Osteopontin	αvβ1, α4β1, αvβ5, αvβ3
Vitronectin	αvβ1, αvβ5, αvβ3
TGF-β latency-associated peptide	αvβ1, αvβ5, αvβ3

TGF-β: transforming growth factor β.

epithelium, stroma and myometrium of pig uterus were developed using a retroviral vector containing the E6 and E7 human papillomavirus oncogenes (Wang *et al.*, 2000). These cells maintain many characteristics of their *in vivo* counterparts, including oestrogen and progesterone receptors, and thus provide useful models for studying cell-type specific uterine signalling.

Pigs, which have true epitheliochorial placentation, show some unique paracrine signalling, such as production of FGF-7 and osteopontin by luminal epithelium, which may provide insight into which molecules and mechanisms are critical for establishment of pregnancy in other species. As a result of the importance of 'histotroph' for pig conceptus development and maintenance of pregnancy, the pig is an attractive model for study of autocrine and paracrine signalling mediated by growth factors, cytokines and binding proteins. The non-invasive nature of placentation in this species offers unique opportunities to study mechanisms of adhesion that are not complicated by erosion of maternal endometrium. Other domestic species, such as sheep and goats, with syndesmochorial placentation, and horses, with chorionic girdle formation followed by diffuse epitheliochorial placentation, also offer distinctive features to aid in understanding the conceptus–maternal communication leading to successful implantation and placentation. Comparative studies of implantation in domestic livestock species with non-invasive implantation and in primates and rodents with invasive implantation provide valuable opportunities to understand fundamental mechanisms of implantation in all species.

Steroid hormones, growth factors and cytokines, as well as integrins and their ligands, are intertwined intricately in mediating pig implantation. Integrins, with their potential to transmit signals to maternal and conceptus cells, as well as bridge apposing epithelia, are probably major participants in mediation of peri-implantation differentiation of conceptus and maternal cells, and accomplishment of stable conceptus attachment to the endometrial epithelium. Maternal and conceptus steroids are critical components in the dialogue between maternal and conceptus cells and probably exert their effects directly and through growth factor mediators to affect epithelial cell functions. Current evidence supports roles for growth factors and their associated proteins to regulate expression of integrins and their ligands, and, importantly, to participate directly in integrin-mediated signalling.

Research was supported by USDA-NRICGP grants 98-35203-6223 and 95-37203-2185 to R. C. Burghardt and F. W. Bazer, USDA-NRICGP grant 2000-02290 to F. W. Bazer and L. A. Jaeger, and by NIH 1-F32-HD08501-01A1 to G. A. Johnson. Use of microscopy and imaging facilities in the College of Veterinary Medicine Image Analysis Laboratory, which are supported, in part, by NIH Grant P30 ES09106, is acknowledged.

References

Arici A, MacDonald PC and Casey ML (1996) Modulation of the levels of transforming growth factor β messenger ribonucleic acids in human endometrial stromal cell *Biology of Reproduction* **54** 463–469

Armant DR, Kaplan HA, Morer H and Lennarz WI (1986) The effects of hexapeptides on attachment and outgrowth of mouse blastocysts cultured *in vitro*: evidence for the involvement of the cell recognition tripeptide Arg-Gly-Asp *Proceedings National Academy of Sciences USA* **83** 6751–6755

Badinga L, Song S, Simmen RC, Clarke JB, Clemmons DR and Simmen FA (1999) Complex mediation of uterine endometrial epithelial cell growth by insulin-like growth factor-II (IGF-II) and IGF-binding protein-2 *Journal of Molecular Endocrinology* **23** 277–285

Ball DK, Surveyor GA, Diehl JR, Steffen CL, Uzumcu M, Mirando MA and Brigstock DR (1998) Characterization of 16- to 20-kilodalton (kDa) connective tissue growth factors (CTGFs) and demonstration of proteolytic activity for 38-kDa CTGF in pig uterine luminal flushings *Biology of Reproduction* **59** 828–835

Bazer FW, Ott TL and Spencer TE (1998) Endocrinology of the transition from recurring estrous cycles to establishment of pregnancy in subprimate mammals. In *Endocrinology of Pregnancy* pp 1–34 Ed. FW Bazer. Humana Press, New Jersey

Bowen JA, Bazer FW and Burghardt RC (1996) Spatial and temporal analyses of integrin and Muc-1 expression in porcine uterine luminal epithelium and trophectoderm *in vivo. Biology of Reproduction* **55** 1098–1106

Bowen JA, Bazer FW and Burghardt RC (1997) Spatial and temporal analyses of integrin and Muc-1 expression in porcine uterine luminal epithelium and trophectoderm *in vitro. Biology of Reproduction* **56** 409–415

Brigstock DR, Heap RB and Brown KD (1989) Polypeptide growth factors in uterine tissues and secretions *Journal of Reproduction and Fertility* **85** 747–758

Brigstock DR, Heap RB, Barker PJ and Brown KD (1990) Purification and characterization of heparin-binding growth factors from porcine uterus *Biochemical Journal* **266** 273–282

Burghardt RC, Bowen JA, Newton GR and Bazer FW (1997) Extracellular matrix and the implantation cascade in pigs *Journal of Reproduction and Fertility Supplement* **52** 151–164

Campbell S, Swann HR, Seif MW, Kimber SJ and Aplin JD (1995) Cell adhesion molecules on the oocyte and preimplantation human embryo *Human Reproduction* **10** 1571–1578

Casslen B, Sandberg T, Gustavsson B, Willen R and Nilbert M (1998) Transforming growth factor β1 in the human endometrium. Cyclic variation, increased expression by estradiol and progesterone, and regulation of plasminogen activators and plasminogen activator inhibitor 1 *Biology of Reproduction* **58** 1343–1350

Chwetzoff S and D'Andréa S (1997) Ubiquitin is physiologically induced by interferons in luminal epithelium of porcine uterine endometrium in early pregnancy – global RT–PCR cDNA in place of RNA for differential display screening *FEBS Letters* **405** 148–152

Cooke PS, Buchanan DL, Kurita T, Lubahn DB and Cunha GR (1998) Stromal–epithelial cell communication in the female reproductive tract. In *Endocrinology of Pregnancy* pp 491–506 Ed. FW Bazer. Humana Press, New Jersey

Critchley DR (2000) Focal adhesions – the cytoskeletal connection *Current Opinions in Cell Biology* **12** 133–139

Dekaney CM, Ing NH, Bustamante L, Madrigal MM and Jaeger LA (1998) Estrogen and progesterone peri-implantation porcine conceptuses *Biology of Reproduction* **58** (Supplement 1) 92 (Abstract)

Fazleabas AT, Bell SC, Fleming S, Sun J and Lessey BA (1997) Distribution of integrins and the extracellular matrix proteins in the baboon endometrium during the menstrual cycle and early pregnancy *Biology of Reproduction* **56** 348–356

Feinberg RF, Kliman HJ and Lockwood CJ (1991) Is oncofetal fibronectin a trophoblast glue for human implantation? *American Journal of Pathology* **138** 537–543

Finch PW, Rubin JS, Miki T, Ron D and Aaronson SA (1989) Human KGF is FGF-related with properties of a paracrine effector of epithelial cell growth *Science* **245** 752–755

Flechon JE, Laurie S and Notarianni E (1995) Isolation and characterization of a feeder-dependent, porcine trophectoderm cell line obtained from a 9-day blastocyst *Placenta* **16** 643–658

Fogerty FJ, Akiyama SK, Yamada KM and Mosher DF (1990) Inhibition of binding of fibronectin to matrix sites by anti-integrin (alpha5β1) antibodies *Journal of Cell Biology* **111** 699–708

Garlow JE, Ka H, Johnson GA, Jaeger LA, Burghardt RC and Bazer FW (2000) Role of osteopontin during early pregnancy in pigs *Biology of Reproduction* **62** (Supplement 1) 282 (Abstract)

Geisert RD and Yelich JV (1997) Regulation of conceptus development and attachment in pigs *Journal of Reproduction and Fertility Supplement* **52** 133–149

Geisert RD, Chamberlain CS, Vonnahme KA, Malayer JR and Spicer LJ (2001) Possible role of kallikrein in proteolysis of insulin-like growth factor binding proteins during the oestrus cycle and early pregnancy in pigs *Reproduction* **121** 719–728

Giancotti FG and Rouslahti E (1999) Integrin signalling *Science* **285** 1028–1032

Gupta A, Bazer FW and Jaeger LA (1996) Differential expression of TGFβs (TGFβ1, TGFβ2, TGFβ3) and their receptors (Type I and Type II) in peri-implantation porcine conceptuses *Biology of Reproduction* **55** 796–802

Gupta A, Bazer FW and Jaeger LA (1997) Immunolocalization of acidic and basic fibroblast growth factors in porcine uterine and conceptus tissues *Biology of Reproduction* **56** 15 227–155 36

Gupta A, Ing NH, Bazer FW, Bustamante LS and Jaeger LA (1998a) Beta transforming growth factors (TGFβs) at the porcine conceptus–maternal interface. Part I: expression of TGFβ1, TGFβ2, and TGFβ3 messenger ribonucleic acids *Biology of Reproduction* **59** 905–910

Gupta A, Dekaney CM, Bazer FW, Madrigal MM and Jaeger LA (1998b) Beta transforming growth factors (TGFβs) at the porcine conceptus–maternal interface. Part II: uterine TGFβ bioactivity and expression of immunoreactive TGFβs (TGFβ1, TGFβ2, and TGFβ3) and their receptors (Type I and Type II) *Biology of Reproduction* **59** 911–917

Hansen TR, Austin KJ and Johnson GA (1997) Transient ubiquitin cross-reactive protein gene expression in bovine endometrium *Endocrinology* **138** 5079–5082

Harding PA, Surveyor GA and Brigstock DR (1997) Characterization of pig connective tissue growth factor (CTGF) cDNA, mRNA and protein from uterine tissue *DNA Sequence – The Journal of Sequencing and Mapping* **8** 385–390

Harney JP and Bazer FW (1989) Effect of porcine conceptus secretory proteins on interestrous interval and uterine secretion of prostaglandins *Biology of Reproduction* **41** 277–284

Irwin JC and Guidice LC (1998) Insulin-like growth factor binding protein-1 binds to placental cytotrophoblast α5β1 integrin and inhibits cytotrophoblast invasion into decidualized endometrial stromal cultures *Growth Hormone and IGF Research* **8** 21–31

Jaeger LA, Burghardt RC, Johnson GA and Bazer FW (2000) Activation of conceptus and maternal integrins by transforming growth factor beta latency associated peptide *Biology of Reproduction* **62** (Supplement 1) 281 (Abstract)

Johansson S, Svineng G, Wennerberg K, Armulik A and Lohikangas L (1997) Fibronectin–integrin interactions *Frontiers in Bioscience* **2** 126–146

Johnson GA, Spencer TE, Hansen TR, Austin KJ, Burghardt RC and Bazer FW (1999a) Expression of the interferon-tau inducible ubiquitin cross-reactive protein in the ovine uterus *Biology of Reproduction* **61** 312–318

Johnson GA, Burghardt RC, Spencer TE, Newton GR, Ott TL and Bazer FW (1999b) Ovine osteopontin: II. Osteopontin and α$_v$β$_3$ integrin expression in the uterus and conceptus during the peri-implantation period *Biology of Reproduction* **61** 892–899

Johnson GA, Spencer TE, Burghardt RC and Bazer FW (1999c) Ovine osteopontin: I. Cloning and expression of mRNA in the uterus during the peri-implantation period *Biology of Reproduction* **61** 884–891

Johnson GA, Spencer TE, Burghardt RC, Taylor KM, Gray CA and Bazer FW (2000) Progesterone modulation of osteopontin gene expression in the ovine uterus *Biology of Reproduction* **62** 1315-1321

Johnson GA, Bazer FW, Jaeger LA, Ka H, Garlow JE, Pfarrer C, Spencer TE and Burghardt RC (2001) Muc-1, integrin and osteopontin expression during the implantation cascade in sheep *Biology of Reproduction* **65** 820–828

Ka H, Spencer TE, Johnson GA and Bazer FW (2000) Keratinocyte growth factor: expression by endometrial epithelia of the porcine uterus *Biology of Reproduction* **62** 1771–1778

Ka H, Jaeger LA, Johnson GA, Spencer TE and Bazer FW (2001) Keratinocyte growth factor is up-regulated by estrogen in porcine uterine endometrium and functions in trophectoderm cell proliferation and differentiation *Endocrinology* **142** 2303–2310

Katsahambas S and Hearn MTW (1996) Localization of basic fibroblast growth factor mRNA (FGF-2 mRNA) in the uterus of mated and unmated gilts *Journal of Histochemistry and Cytochemistry* **44** 1289–1302

Kim S, Harris M and Varner JA (2000) Regulation of integrin αvβ3-mediated endothelial cell migration and angiogenesis by integrin α5β1 and protein kinase A *Journal of Biological Chemistry* **275** 33 920–33 928

Kowalski AA, Graddy LG, Choi I, Katzenellenbogen BS, Simmen FA and Simmen RCM (2000) Expression of estrogen receptor (ER)-α and -β and progesterone receptor (PR) by porcine embryos suggests potential autocrine functions in development *Biology of Reproduction* **62** (Supplement 1) 106 (Abstract)

Lau LF and Lam SC-T (1999) The CCN family of angiogenic regulators: the integrin connection *Experimental Cell Research* **248** 44–57

Lee CY, Green ML, Simmen RC and Simmen FA (1998) Proteolysis of insulin-like growth factor-binding proteins (IGFBPs) within the pig uterine lumen associated with peri-implantation conceptus development *Journal of Reproduction and Fertility* **112** 369–377

Lefèvre F, Guillomot M, D'Andréa S, Battegay S and La Bonnardière C (1998a) Interferon-delta: the first member of a novel type I interferon family *Biochimie* **80** 779–788

Lefèvre F, Martinatbotte F, Locatelli A, Deniu P, Terqui M and La Bonnardière C (1998b) Intrauterine infusion of high doses of pig trophoblast interferons has no antiluteolytic effect in cyclic gilts *Biology of Reproduction* **58** 1026–1031

Massague J (1998) TGF-β signal transduction *Annual Reviews in Biochemistry* **67** 753–791

Miyamoto S, Teramoto H, Coso OA, Gutkind JS, Burbelo PD, Akiyama SK and Yamada KM (1995) Integrin function: molecular hierarchies of cytoskeletal and signaling molecules *Journal of Cell Biology* **131** 791–805

Moussad EE and Brigstock DR (2000) Connective tissue growth factor: what's in a name? *Molecular Genetics and Metabolism* **71** 276–292

Munger JS, Harpel JG, Giancotti FG and Rifkin DB (1998) Interactions between growth factors and integrins: latent forms of transforming growth factor-β are ligands for integrin αvβ1 *Molecular Biology of the Cell* **9** 2627–2638

Nam TJ, Busby WH, Jr, Rees C and Clemmons DR (2000) Thrombospondin and osteopontin bind to insulin-like growth factor (IGF)-binding protein-5 leading to an alteration in IGF-I-stimulated cell growth *Endocrinology* **141** 1100–1106

Nomura S, Wills AJ, Edwards JK, Heath JK and Hogan BLM (1988) Developmental expression of 2ar (osteopontin) and SPARC (osteonectin) RNA as revealed by *in situ* hybridization *Journal of Cell Biology* **106** 441–450

Okulicz WC, Hild-Petito S and Chilton B (1998) Expression of steroid hormone receptors in the pregnant uterus. In

Endocrinology of Pregnancy pp 177–197 Ed. FW Bazer. Humana Press, New Jersey

Ornitz DM, Xu J, Colvin JS, McEwen DG, MacArthur CA, Coulier F, Gao G and Goldfarb M (1996) Receptor specificity of the fibroblast growth factor family *Journal of Biological Chemistry* **271** 15 292–15 297

Persson E, Sahlin L, Masironi B, Dantzer V, Eriksson H and Rodriguez-Martinez H (1997) Insulin-like growth factor-I in the porcine endometrium and placenta – localization and concentration in relation to steroid influence during early pregnancy *Animal Reproduction Science* **46** 261–281

Ramsoondar J, Christopherson RJ, Guilbert LJ and Wegmann TG (1993) A porcine trophoblast cell line that secretes growth factors which stimulate porcine macrophages *Biology of Reproduction* **49** 681–694

Rider V and Piva M (1998) Role of growth factors of uterine and fetal–placental origin during pregnancy. In *Endocrinology of Pregnancy* pp 83–124 Ed. FW Bazer. Humana Press, New Jersey

Rifkin DB, Mazzieri R, Munger JS, Moguera I and Sung J (1999) Proteolytic control of growth factor availability *APMIS* **107** 80–85

Rubin JS, Osada H, Finch PW, Taylor WG, Rudikoff S and Aaronson SA (1989) Purification and characterization of a newly identified growth factor specific for epithelial cells *Proceedings National Academy of Sciences USA* **86** 8022–8026

Schwartz MA and Denninghoff K (1994) Alpha v integrins mediate the rise in intracellular calcium in endothelial cells on fibronectin even though they play a minor role in adhesion *Journal of Biological Chemistry* **269** 11 133–11 137

Simmen RCM, Green ML and Simmen FA (1995) IGF system in periimplantation uterus and embryonic development. In *Molecular and Cellular Aspects of Periimplantation Processes* pp 185–204 Ed. SK Dey. Springer-Verlag, New York

Surveyor GA, Wilson AK and Brigstock DR (1998) Localization of connective tissue growth factor during the period of embryo implantation in the mouse *Biology of Reproduction* **59** 1207–1213

Tuo WB and Bazer FW (1996) Expression of oncofetal fibronectin in porcine conceptuses and uterus throughout gestation *Reproduction, Fertility and Development* **8** 1207–1213

Uzumcu M, Homsi MF, Ball DK, Coskun S, Jaroudi K, Hollanders JM and Brigstock DR (2000) Localization of connective tissue growth factor in human uterine tissues *Molecular Human Reproduction* **6** 1093–1098

Vlodavsky I, Miao H-Q, Medalion B, Danagher P and Ron D (1996) Involvement of heparan sulfate and related molecules in sequestration and growth promoting activity of fibroblast growth factor *Cancer and Metastasis Reviews* **15** 177–186

Wang G, Johnson GA, Spencer TE and Bazer FW (2000) Isolation, immortalization, and initial characterization of uterine cell lines: an *in vitro* model system for the porcine uterus *In Vitro Cellular and Developmental Biology* **36** 650–656

Wennerberg K, Lohikangas L, Gullberg D, Pfaff M, Johansson S and Fässler R (1996) β1 integrin-dependent and -independent polymerization of fibronectin *Journal of Cell Biology* **132** 227–238

Wilson ME and Ford SP (1997) Differences in trophectoderm mitotic rate and P450 17-alpha-hydroxylase expression between late preimplantation Meishan and Yorkshire conceptuses *Biology of Reproduction* **56** 380–385

Wilson ME and Ford SP (2000) Effect of estradiol-17 beta administration during the time of conceptus elongation on placental size at term in Meishan pigs *Journal of Animal Science* **78** 1047–1052

Wilson ME, Sonstegard TS, Smith TPL, Fahrenkrug SC and Ford SP (2000) Differential gene expression in the preimplantation pig embryo *Genesis* **26** 9–14

Yelich JV, Pomp D and Geisert RD (1997a) Detection of transcripts for retinoic acid receptors, retinol-binding protein, and transforming growth factors during rapid trophoblastic elongation in the porcine conceptus *Biology of Reproduction* **57** 286–294

Yelich JV, Pomp D and Geisert RD (1997b) Ontogeny of elongation and gene expression in the early developing porcine conceptus *Biology of Reproduction* **57** 1256–1265

Ying CW, Yang YC, Hong WF, Cheng WTK and Hsu WL (2000a) Progesterone receptor gene expression in preimplantation pig embryos *European Journal of Endocrinology* **143** 697–703

Ying CW, Hsu WL, Hong WF, Cheng WTK and Yang YC (2000b) Estrogen receptor is expressed in pig embryos during preimplantation development *Molecular Reproduction and Development* **55** 83–88

Reproduction Supplement **58**, 209–222

Histological and immunohistochemical events during placentation in pigs

V. Dantzer and H. Winther

Department of Anatomy and Physiology, The Royal Veterinary and Agricultural University, Groennegaardsvej 7, DK-1870 Frederiksberg C, Denmark

The early morphological events in pig placental development are summarized and related to the known data on differences in placental vascular efficiency between Meishan and US breeds. The activation and localization of a number of factors, the ligands and their receptors, such as insulin-like growth factor (IGF), transforming growth factor β (TGFβ), platelet-derived growth factor (PDGF) and vascular endothelial growth factor (VEGF), as well as retinoids and calcium, is described. The comparison between these factors gives a strong impression of their complex interactions and hormonal relationships during placentation and vascular development in pigs. This review also emphasizes that retinoids are of great importance for placental function and that the transport of vitamin A appears to take place in the areolar gland complex only, whereas based on histochemistry and electron energy dispersive analysis, the calcium transport may be confined to the interareolar route across the interhaemal barrier.

Introduction

The placenta develops as a temporary organ to provide a highly regulated transfer of nutrients and waste products from mother to fetus and vice versa, including facilitation of the exchange of oxygen and carbon dioxide. Placenta is composed of a very close apposition between the uterine mucous membrane and the genetically different fetal allogenetic membrane, the allantochorion, which, in some species, may invade the endometrium in a highly regulated manner as seen during placentation in cows, horses, mustellids, mice and humans (Wooding and Flint, 1994).

However, pig placenta is non-invasive and, in addition, it is classified morphologically as diffuse, folded, epitheliochorial and indeciduate, with subunits composed by the interareolar part for haemothrophic exchange and the areolar gland complexes for transfer of large molecules called histiotroph (Wooding and Flint, 1994; Dantzer, 1999). Neovascularization of this 'new developing organ' very early in gestation is essential for cell growth and as an efficient transport route for gaseous and nutrient exchange between mother and embryo.

Morphological events during initial placentation

The morphological events preceding and during initial placentation in pigs have been described in detail (Dantzer, 1985; Keys and King, 1990; Stroband and Van der Lende, 1990).

Email: Vibeke.Dantzer@iaf.kvl.dk

In brief, at day 13 after coitus, conceptus elongation has almost ceased; conceptus migration within the uterine horns has taken place and the elongated conceptus (1.0–1.5 m) is now apposed closely to the elaborated circular folds of the endometrium. Anchoring of the conceptus to the uterine luminal surface occurs through newly developed epithelial proliferations in the endometrium that are initiated at the mesometrial side. These events are followed closely by adherence, close apposition and formation of interdigitating microvilli between maternal epithelium and developing trophoblast at days 15–16 after coitus.

At the same time, from day 15 after coitus, the vasculature of the subepithelial capillary network at the mesometrial side becomes distended, denser in its network and positioned very close to the base of the uterine epithelium (Keys and King, 1990; Dantzer *et al.*, 1991; Dantzer and Leiser, 1994; Leiser and Dantzer, 1994). With continued development, the maternal subepithelial capillary network appears to create the basis for the architecture of complex microscopic folding leading to the formation of maternal–fetal complementary ridges and furrows (Dantzer and Leiser, 1994). At day 32 after coitus, the vasculature develops a counter- to crosscurrent maternal–fetal interrelationship that maintains this basic architecture, although it is elaborated continually throughout gestation (Leiser and Dantzer, 1988).

Neovascularization in the fetal membranes is delayed by about 2 days compared with that of the maternal endometrium. Both are initiated close to the embryonic disc, progressing from the mesometrial side to the anti-mesometrial side as the blastocyst expands along the length of the uterine horn and continues along the elongated blastocyst towards its two tips (Dantzer *et al.*, 1991).

The uterine epithelium undergoes further changes in the composition of cell organelles and secretory activity as the materno–fetal contact becomes more and more close and indented. The endometrium undergoes mutual microscopic folding and under this process there must be an intimate interaction between the uterine epithelial cells, the stroma of the lamina propria, the vascular endothelial cells and developmental processes in the complementary allantochorion.

Signalling substances in the pig placental interhaemal barrier

Studies of Chinese Meishan pigs, which farrow 3–5 more viable piglets than do US or European breeds, have indicated that Meishan pigs remain relatively small compared with commercial breeds. Embryonic survival after day 30 after coitus is higher in Meishan pigs. Although Meishan fetuses in the later stages of gestation have smaller placentae compared with US breeds, placental efficiency is increased by a markedly increased growth of placental blood vessels at the fetal–maternal interface. Further experiments have indicated that uterine type modulates conceptus size and that the genotype of the conceptus controls placental vascular efficiency (Ford, 1997; Biensen *et al.*, 1999). In gilts evaluated for the different genotypes of oestrogen receptor, the B allele was associated with larger litter size and significantly longer placentae compared with AA genotype gilts. Hearts of AA×BA fetuses were significantly heavier compared with BB×AB and BB×BB fetuses, and the fetuses of AA×AA genotype were the lightest. Differences in heart weight would suggest that there is a relationship with placental vascularity; however, further investigations are required (Van Rens and Van der Lende, 2000; Van Rens *et al.*, 2000).

Insulin-like growth factor

Insulin-like growth factors (IGFs) are important mitogenic peptides that stimulate cell division and differentiation during fetal and placental growth (DeChiara *et al.*, 1990; Liu *et al.*,

1993). In a recent paper on expression of IGF and IGF binding proteins (IGFBPs) in guinea-pig placenta, Han *et al.* (1999) emphasized the importance of comparative studies between species, as there are significant differences in the spatial distributions of IGF-II and IGFBPs between the placentae of various species such as rhesus monkeys, sheep and rats. In a summary of the pig IGF system, Simmen *et al.* (1998) indicated that there is a relationship between nutrition and systemic/local IGF and that IGF is involved in the regulation of placental cellular responses to protein energy restriction to retain sufficient placental efficiency during gestation.

During the initial stages of placentation up to day 30 of gestation, IGF-I is immunolocalized in the uterine luminal and glandular epithelium, and in the endothelium and vascular smooth muscle cells, and there is weak activity in the trophoblast and fetal mesenchymal cells of the placenta (Persson and Rodriguez-Martinez, 1997; Persson *et al.*, 1997). In pregnant endometrium, expression of the oestrogen receptor gene is correlated with IGF-I gene expression, which is indicative of a common regulator, probably conceptus-derived oestrogens. Expression of IGF-I gene in the endometrium is consistent with variations in IGF-I immunoreactivity in the uterine glands and their secretory activity. The consistent strong immunostaining in the vascular smooth muscle cells indicates that IGF-I may be active in endometrial vascular development and function together with a number of other factors.

IGF-II gene expression in the interhaemal placental barrier was studied from day 8 to day 40 after coitus. IGF-II appears in the pig conceptus during early pregnancy, as it is activated in the extra-embryonic blood vessels between day 16 and day 24 after coitus, and at day 30 after coitus in the trophoblast, whereas IGF-II transcripts were not detected in pig endometrium. IGFBP-2 gene expression was present in both trophoblast and uterine epithelium at day 30 after coitus, and was very strong in the latter, whereas IGFBP-2 was not expressed in blood vessels (Fig. 1) (Persson, 1996). These results indicate an activation of IGF-II in the epitheliochorial placenta, in which IGF-II is first expressed in the trophoblast, thereby indicating that IGF-II interacts in the developmental pathways of pig placentation.

On the basis of *in vitro* experiments it was shown that an IGF-II analogue with selected affinity for IGF-II (type II) receptor increased thymidine uptake in pig uterine glandular cells two-fold compared with untreated cells. In addition, it was shown that a combination of IGF-I and IGF-II or IGF-II alone stimulated thymidine incorporation to a greater extent than did IGF-I alone. Therefore, it was suggested that IGFBP modulation of uterine gland cell growth may involve both IGF-dependent and -independent pathways in a complex interplay of IGF system components in regulation of uterine endometrial growth in pigs (Badinga *et al.*, 1999).

Transforming growth factor b (TGFb)

Gupta *et al.* (1998a,b) demonstrated that, in the peri-implantation period (day 10 to day 14 after coitus), uterine expression of TGFβ-1, -2 and -3 genes, as well as immunocytochemical localization of TGFβ receptors, is pregnancy-specific and that bioactive TGFβs are present at the conceptus–maternal interface. TGFβs may be involved in autocrine–paracrine interactions between these two genetically different tissues in a period during which marked uterine remodelling and conceptus differentiation take place by affecting cellular communication, proliferation, differentiation, extracellular matrix protein and integrin modification, tissue repair, angiogenesis and immunosuppression (Lawrence, 1996). However, the presence of TGFβs and, thus, suggested functional interaction with other factors during placentation, still needs to be investigated. Changes in glycan composition during gestation in pigs might be an important base for further studies (Jones *et al.*, 1995).

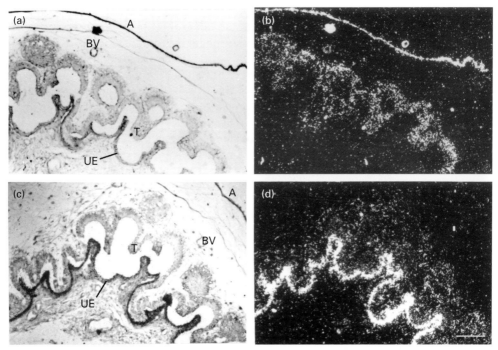

Fig. 1. The insulin-like growth factor binding protein 2 (IGFBP-2) gene was expressed in both the maternal and embryonic parts of the placenta and compared with the expression of the IGF-II gene. (a,c) Bright-field and (b,d) dark-field images of *in situ* hybridization of IGF-II and IGFBP-2 gene expression in the endometrium and placenta. (a,b) IGF-II transcripts are visible in the allantoic endoderm (A), trophoblast (T) and blood vessels (BV), but not in the uterine epithelium (UE). (c,d) IGFBP-2 transcripts are abundant in the surface epithelium of the endometrium (UE) and can also be detected in the trophoblast (T), but not in allantoic epithelium (A) or blood vessels (BV). Scale bar represents 100 µm. Reproduced from Persson (1996), with permission.

Retinoids in pig placentation

Retinoids, including vitamin A (retinol) and its active metabolite, retinoic acid, are unstable hydrophobic compounds that are indispensable for cellular differentiation and growth in general (Blomhoff, 1994), and for placental and embryonic development in particular (Soprano *et al.*, 1986; Baavik *et al.*, 1996). Transport mechanisms and metabolism are regulated tightly by the retinoid-binding proteins consisting of the 21 kDa plasma retinol-binding protein (RBP), the cellular RBPs (CRBP I and II) and cellular retinoic acid binding protein (CRABP I and II) of approximately 16 kDa. The RBPs are involved in cellular transport of retinol, whereas CRBP I participates in cellular transport of retinol and its metabolism into retinoic acid. In addition, the CRABPs are involved in the retinoic acid signalling pathways, regulation of the availability of retinoic acid to the nuclear receptors and modulation of retinoic acid metabolism (Chambon, 1996; Gustafson *et al.*, 1996; Li and Norris, 1996; Napoli, 1996). The relative amounts of RBP transcripts and the immunohistochemical location of RBP have been studied in pig placenta and uterus (Harney *et al.*, 1990, 1994a,b; Trout *et al.*, 1992; Schweigert *et al.*, 1999). However, Johansson *et al.* (2001) investigated the localization of RBP, CRBP-I and CRABP-I within the interareolar region and the areolar gland complex by immunohistochemistry and revealed the transepithelial route across the pig interhaemal barrier throughout gestation (Fig. 2). The results reveal that staining intensity of the RBPs in the pig placenta far exceeds the reactivity observed

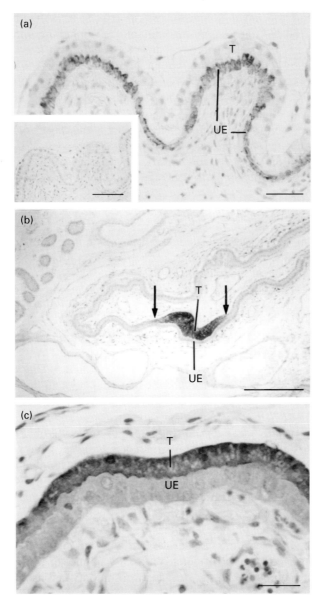

Fig. 2. Localization of retinol-binding protein (RBP) and cellular retinoid-binding protein (CRBP) in pig uterus and placenta during the first third of gestation. (a) In the interareolar region on day 20 after coitus, immunoreactivity of RBP is restricted to the uterine epithelium (UE) and uterine glands (not shown), whereas the trophoblast (T) is non-reactive. The control is shown in the inset. (b) At day 25 after coitus, the immunoreactivity for CRBP shows very strong reactivity in the trophoblast of the areola (T) and none in the areolar uterine epithelium (UE). The areola is marked by arrows. The low reactivity in the interareolar region and uterine gland (upper left side) is just visible at this low magnification with both regions included. (c) Detail from the interareolar region at day 25 after coitus showing the cellular retinoid acid binding protein (CRABP), which is located exclusively to the trophoblast (T), whereas the uterine epithelium (UE) is non-reactive. Scale bars represent (a) 100 μm, ((a) inset and (b)) 250 μm and (c) 50 μm. From Johansson *et al.* (2001), with permission.

in mouse and human placentae (Johansson et al., 1997, 1999; Sapin, 1998). The RBP immunoactivity was located to the uterine and glandular epithelium but not to the maternal epithelium lining the areolar cavity, whereas at the fetal side only the trophoblast of the areolae showed immunostaining. The CRBP immunostaining was co-localized with RBP in maternal endometrium, but appears as fine granularities within the cytoplasm. At the fetal side, strong staining was located in the trophoblast of areolae and there was less and finer granular staining in the trophoblast of the interareolar region. In contrast, CRABP immunostaining was located exclusively to the trophoblast of the interareolar regions of the placentae. These results were consistent with previous investigations in human and mouse placentae (Johansson et al., 1997, 1999), but revealed that the areolar gland complex is the transport route for vitamin A to the conceptus, and that RBPs are needed in the development and growth of pig placenta.

Vascular endothelial growth factors (VEGFs)

Recent reviews on angiogenesis in placentation and during implantation summarized different factors of importance for vascular growth, and inhibition during early placental growth and embryonic development (Reynolds and Redmer, 2001; Sherer and Abulafia, 2001). One of the most important growth factors involved with angiogenesis is vascular endothelial growth factor (VEGF). VEGF is a potent mitogen, morphogen and chemoattractant for endothelial cells, and is stimulated by hypoxia, cytokines and various hormones (Neufeld et al., 1994). In vitro experiments with endometrial carcinoma cell lines indicate that oestradiol and progesterone increase the expression of VEGF mRNA (Charnock-Jones et al., 1993). In pigs, embryonic production of oestrogens modulates the secretion of uterine proteins (Simmen and Simmen, 1990), secures the maternal recognition of pregnancy (Geisert et al., 1990; Bazer et al., 1998) and affects myometrial contractility (Pope et al., 1982; Scheerboom et al., 1987). The increase in angiogenesis observed at the mesometrial side of the uterus, where the first contact is established close to the embryonic disk (Keys and King, 1988; Dantzer and Leiser, 1994), may be stimulated by a paracrine effect of oestrogen secretion by the blastocyst, which may stimulate VEGF release (Charnock-Jones et al., 1993).

Neovascularization of pig placenta has been investigated recently with some surprising results (Winther et al., 1999). Immunohistochemical studies of VEGF and two of its receptors, Flt 1 (VEGFR-1) and KDR (VEGFR-2), revealed a high correlation in spatiotemporal distribution between the ligand and its receptors. Immunoreactivity of VEGF and VEGF receptors increased markedly in the capillary endothelium from day 13 after coitus through the first half of early pregnancy and remained almost constant until term compared with non-pregnant endometrial capillaries. In late stages of gestation there was a slight decrease in VEGF and KDR, whereas Flt-1 remained high. Vascular smooth muscle cells also showed a positive immunoreactivity for VEGF and its receptors. In addition, VEGF and its receptors were related to several non-endothelial cells such as uterine luminal and glandular epithelium, and trophoblast. The luminal epithelium shows a decrease in activity in the first half of early placentation (days 13–21), whereas in the trophoblast a decrease in immunostaining was observed in the second half of early gestation (days 21–31). Thereafter, the immunostaining increased and remained high to term with a slight decrease for KDR in late gestation (days 71–105 after coitus; Fig. 3a,b). Uterine glands also showed a marked increase in KDR staining from the late luteal phase of the oestrous cycle to days 13–21 after coitus and remained high in the late stage of gestation. These observations are in accordance with studies of human placenta concerning VEGF activity in uterine smooth muscle cells (Brown et al., 1997) and trophoblast (Clark et al., 1996). Furthermore, KDR is needed during the initial increase in angiogenesis, vasculogenesis and blood island formation (Shalaby et al.,

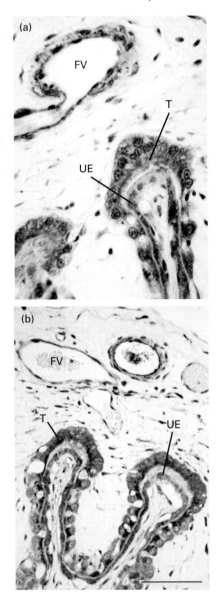

Fig. 3. Immunohistochemistry of vascular endothelial growth factor (VEGF) from the last third of gestation in pigs. (a) VEGF shows a strong reactivity in uterine epithelium (UE), trophoblast (T) and in endothelium and smooth muscle cells of fetal vessels (FV). (b) Localization of KDR (VEGF receptor 2) in the same cells as the ligand, namely uterine epithelium, trophoblast and in endothelial cells and smooth muscle cells of fetal vasculature. Scale bar represents 50 µm. From Winther *et al.* (1999), with permission.

1995), whereas Flt-1 plays a role in mediation of calcium-dependent nitric oxide release and regulation of human trophoblast activity (Ahmed *et al.*, 1997). These results imply that, during placentation in pigs, the VEGF ligand–receptor system may not only participate in the regulation of angiogenesis but also influences cellular differentiation and transport capabilities in the maternal–fetal interface, including the uterine glandular epithelium.

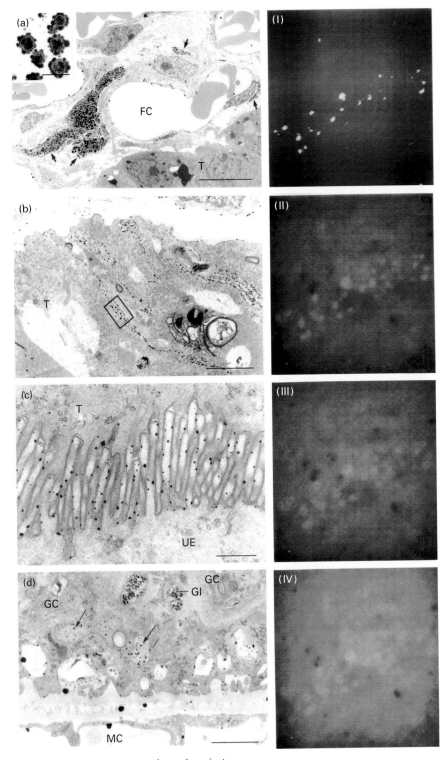

Fig. 4 (a)–(d) and (I)–(V). For legend see facing page.

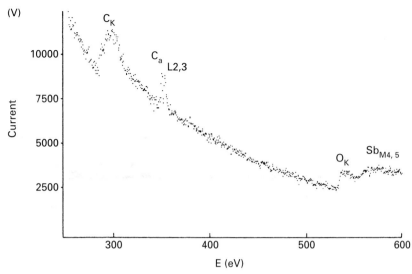

Fig. 4. Localization of calcium, seen as electron-dense antimonate precipitates, in the interhaemal barrier and mesenchyme of pig placenta from day 48 of gestation. Electron spectroscopic imaging (ESI) of the marked area in (b) is shown in the right-hand column (I, II, III, IV) and electron energy loss spectroscopy (EELS) is shown in (V). (a) Basal part of the trophoblast (T) and underlaying mesenchyme with fetal capillaries (FC) and prominent antimonate precipitates in the spherite-like inclusions (arrows). Notice also the precipitates at the luminal side of the fetal endothelium. Inset: a higher magnification view of the precipitate in the mesenchyme showing the concentric substructure. (b) Low magnification, of a 40 nm unstained Gauss image model, ESI at 250 eV, used for ESI (see panels I–IV) and EELS analysis (see panel V) in the marked area, showing the base of the trophoblast and the antimonate precipitates related closely to the lateral plasma membranes and in cytoplasmic vesicles. (c) Detail of the interdigitated microvilli between the uterine epithelium (UE) and the trophoblast, with antimonate precipitates related to the interdigitating microvilli. (d) The basal part of the uterine epithelium close to a maternal capillary (MC). Antimonate precipitates are visible in relation to the folded basal plasma membrane, in vesicles (arrows) as well as in a few stacks of the Golgi complex (GC). Glycogen: Gl. Scale bars represent (a) 10 µm, (inset to (a) and (c)) 500 nm, (b) 2 µm and (d) 1 µm. (I) Calcium distribution, pixel-wise, calculated from the other three images, II–IV, and here freed from background and reinforced to be clearly visible. (II) Electron spectroscopic image at 355 eV, containing a calcium-absorptive edge, the primary picture. (III) First background image for calcium at 355 eV. (IV) Second background image for calcium at 325 eV. (V) EELS analysis of the marked area in (b), showing the element distribution and demonstrating the content of calcium (Ca) and antimonate (Sb). Background for calcium at 320 eV and calcium edge, background for Sb+0 at 500 eV and Sb-O edge at 600 eV.

Platelet-derived growth factor (PDGF)

PDGF is a mitogen that exerts pleiotrophic effects on growth and motility of mesenchymal-derived cells. The PDGF-A ligand and receptors were immunolocalized in vascular smooth muscle cells. The PDGF receptors are expressed strongly in the endothelial and perivascular areas of the subepithelial layer, whereas PDGF is present in epithelial cell layers of the placenta (Persson and Rodriguez-Martinez, 1997). These findings indicate that PDGF interacts in an autocrine as well as a paracrine manner in the modulation of angiogenesis within the pig placenta.

Calcium

Calcium is important during fertilization (Lane and Bavister 1998) and during embryonic and fetal development, as intracellular calcium concentrations regulate many important cellular

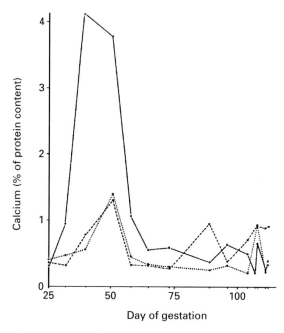

Fig. 5. Diagram showing the content of calcium in fetal pig membranes: allantochorion (——), amniochorion (----) and in the blind, non-vascularized paraplacental ends (........). It can be seen that calcium, measured as percentage of the protein content, accumulates mainly in the allantochorion, peaking between day 36 and day 55 of gestation.

functions such as cell division, membrane fusion, exocytosis, cell–cell communication and metabolism, as well as playing a role in many second messenger systems (Campbell, 1983). However, during gestation the increases in ossification and growth of the skeletal system will increase the demand for transfer of calcium from the dam to the fetus. During the 114 days of gestation in pigs, primary ossification centres appear at about day 34 after coitus, with a second period of ossification at day 100 (Patten, 1948; Hodges, 1953). There is a marked increase in fetal growth rate from day 60 of gestation to term (Marrable, 1971). After day 80 of gestation there is a three-fold increase in the deposition of fetal calcium: in ten fetuses evaluated on days 80 and 100 after coitus, 1.2 g and 4.0 g of calcium, respectively, were deposited daily (Moustgaard, 1971). In classical studies (Brambel, 1933; Wislocky and Dempsey, 1946) and studies with electron microscopy (Dantzer et al., 1989), large masses of lime infiltrations have been described in the mesenchyme between the chorionic and allantoic epithelium, which are seen as a temporal storage related to the interareolar regions.

Calcium deposits in placenta from 17 pregnant sows collected between day 25 and day 112 after coitus were investigated by measurement of calcium content and by using different methods for light and electron microscopy. Minor infiltrations, observed as spherite-like bodies, were localized in the mesenchyme just beneath the base of the interareolar trophoblast and related closely to vessels (Fig. 4a), particularly from day 33 to day 60 after coitus. However, calcium could not be measured by X-ray energy dispersive microanalysis after conventional processing for electronmicroscopy at pH 7.4, but could be measured in fresh cryofixed and ultrathin cryosectioned tissues (performed by Dr M. H. Nielsen and Dr L. Bastholm, University of

Copenhagen, Denmark) (data not shown). These results indicate that at this pH calcium may be bound loosely.

A histochemical method for calcium localization described by Borgers *et al.* (1983) was modified using 1% (w/v) potassium pyroantimonate in 7% (w/v) sucrose, 0.1 mol potassium phosphate buffer l^{-1} (> pH 8.5) in all preparatory steps from perfusion fixation in glutaraldehyde to embedding for electron microscopy to investigate the presence of calcium in the spherite-like inclusions in the mesenchyme and to locate and follow calcium intracellularly in the interhaemal barrier. For a negative control, the tissue was pretreated with EGTA, a calcium binder, before being processed by the calcium-binding potassium pyrantimonate solution. The presence of calcium in the antimonate precipitates was confirmed subsequently by electron spectroscopic imaging (ESI) (Fig. 4b; I–IV) taken at the specific element (calcium) edge and for estimation of the net calcium distribution by electron energy loss spectroscopy (EELS) (Fig. 4b; V) (analysis provided by Dr W. Probst, Zeiss, Oberkochen, Germany).

The antimonate precipitates indicate the presence of Ca^{2+}, Na^+ and Mg^{2+}, but in this study the precipitate was predominantly calcium as shown by the three different types of analysis. The precipitates, here described from the maternal to the fetal side, were scattered at the maternal endothelial plasma membrane and in the maternal uterine epithelium along the basal plasma membrane. Intracellularly, the precipitates were observed in large vesicles located basally and in the large membranous lysosomes typical of the maternal epithelium in pigs (Dantzer, 1984) and as fine precipitates in some of the inner stacks of the Golgi complexes (Fig. 4d). At the interdigitating microvilli between maternal and fetal epithelium, precipitates are mainly observed at the maternal side and at the inner side of vesicles opening to the narrow intercellular space between these two compartments (Fig. 4c). At the fetal side, calcium precipitates are visible apically in the trophoblast, in endocytic tubules and in large apical vesicles, as well as at the lateral plasma membranes and to some extent at the basal cell border (Fig. 4b,c). In both epithelia of the materno–fetal interface, fine precipitates were also detected in mitochondria. Precipitates are also clearly visible in the large spherite-like inclusions in the mesenchyme and at the luminal side of the fetal endothelium (Fig. 4a). The confirmation of calcium in these precipitates was done by electron spectroscopy imaging ESI (Fig. 4b; I–IV) and by electron energy loss spectroscopy EELS (Fig. 4b; V), using antimonate precipitates at the folded lateral plasma membranes of the trophoblast for demonstration (Fig. 4b). The localization of calcium to the basolateral plasma membranes of the trophoblast indicates that these membranes are linked to membrane bound Ca^{2+}-ATPase activity, which is one of the largest of the calcium transporters assisting in calcium extrusion (Carafoli *et al.*, 1990; Bronner, 1991).

The content of calcium was determined in fetal membranes collected between day 25 and day 112 after coitus. The fetal membranes were separated from the maternal endometrium and dissected into allantochorion, amniochorion and the blind nonvascularized ends of the conceptus (calcium analysis was done by Dr S. Boisen, Danish Agricultural Reseach Centre, Foulum, Denmark). The results (Fig. 5) indicate a rapid increase in calcium content from day 25 to day 36 after coitus and a rapid decrease from day 50 to day 65 after coitus in the allantochorionic membrane, with only a slight increase in the two other compartments of the fetal membranes. These findings, together with the observation that there were no apparent calcium antimonate precipitations in the areolar gland subunit, give a clear indication of transplacental transport of calcium across the interareolar compartment of pig placenta. This finding is in contrast to the supposed route for transepithelial placental transport in other species with an epitheliochorial placenta, such as sheep, cows and horses (Wooding *et al.*, 1996; Morgan *et al.*, 1997; Nikitenko *et al.*, 1998; Wooding *et al.*, 2000), determined by

9 kDa calcium binding protein, an apparent valid marker for epithelial-mediated active transcellular transporter protein (Kumar, 1995). These studies found that placental calcium transport in cow, sheep and mare placenta takes place over the areolar gland subunit only. Although the morphological methods differ, it appears that another pathway, the interareolar region, is used in pigs, which is also in accordance with the temporary storage of loosely bound calcium at the fetal side in the mesenchyme close to the fetal vessels of the interareolar regions described above.

Furthermore, these results also give a clear indication of the allantochorion as a reservoir for loosely bound calcium, preceding the rapid increase in growth and ossification of the skeleton. In a comparative study of carbonic anhydrase in six different types of placenta (Ridderstråle *et al.*, 1997), the highest activity in maternal capillaries, uterine epithelium and trophoblast was observed in pigs, in contrast to low activities in cows and horses. Therefore, it is possible that the high carbonic anhydrase activity in pig placenta is needed in placental transport and metabolism of calcium, as suggested for human placenta by Aliakbar *et al.* (1990).

Conclusion

This description of the activation and localization of a variety of important ligands and their receptors, including IGFs, TGFβ, VEGF and PDGF, during pig placentation gives a strong impression of the complex interactions between these factors and hormones during pig placentation and vascular development. However, it should also be emphasized that more studies combining analysis of genotypes, molecular biology, gene activation and a variety of histological techniques are required to achieve a better understanding of regulatory mechanisms during pig placentation. In addition, it is recognized that retinoids are of great importance for placental functions and that the transport of vitamin A from the maternal to the fetal side appears to take place in the areolar gland complex only, whereas calcium transport in pigs may be confined to the interareolar route across the interhaemal barrier.

The authors would like to thank W. Probst, M. H. Nielsen, L. Bastholm and S. Boisen for all their help, and H. Holm for excellent technical assistance.

References

Ahmed A, Dink C, Kniss D and Wilkes M (1997) Role of VEGF receptor-1 (Flt-1) in mediating calcium-dependent nitric oxide release and limiting DNA synthesis in human trophoblast cells *Laboratory Investigation* **76** 779–791

Aliakbar S, Brown PR and Nicolaides KH (1990) Localization of CA I and CA II isoenzymes in normal term human placenta by immunofluorescence techniques *Placenta* **11** 35–39

Baavik C-O, Ward SJ and Chamron P (1996) Developmental abnormalities in cultured mouse embryos deprived of retinoic acid by inhibition of yolk-sac retinol binding protein synthesis *Proceedings National Academy of Sciences USA* **93** 3110–3114

Badinga L, Song S, Simmen RC, Clarke JB, Clemmons DR and Simmen FA (1999) Complex mediation of uterine endometrial epithelial cell growth by insulin-like growth factor-II (IGF-II) and IGF-binding protein *Journal of Molecular Endocrinology* **23** 277–285

Bazer FW, Ott TL and Spencer TE (1998) Maternal recognition of pregnancy: comparative aspects review *Trophoblast Research* **12** 375–386

Biensen NJ, Wilson ME and Ford SP (1999) The impact of uterine environment and fetal genotype on conceptus size and placental vascularity during late gestation in pigs *Journal of Animal Science* **77** 954–959

Blomhoff R (1994) *Vitamin A in Health and Disease* Marcel Dekker, New York

Borgers M, Thone FJ, Xhonneux BJ and de Clerck FF (1983) Localization of calcium in red blood cells *Journal of Histochemistry and Cytochemistry* **31** 1109–1116

Brambel CE (1933) Allantochorionic differentiation of the pig studied morphologically and histochemically *American Journal of Anatomy* **52** 397–459

Bronner F (1991) Calcium transport across epithelia *International Review of Cytology* **131** 169–212

Brown LF, Detmar M, Tognazzi K, Abu-Jawdeh G and Iruela-Arispe ML (1997) Uterine smooth muscle cells express functional receptors (Flt-1 and KDR) for vascular permeability factor/vascular endothelial growth factor *Laboratory Investigation* **76** 245–255

Campbell AK (1983) *Intracellular Calcium: its Universal Role as a Regulator* pp 206–361. John Wiley and Sons, Chichester and New York

Carafoli E, James P and Strehler EE (1990) Structure–

function relationship in the calcium pump of plasma membrane. In *Molecular and Cellular Regulation of Calcium and Phosphate Metabolism* pp 181–193 Eds M Peterlik and F Bronner. Wiley-Liss, New York

Chambon P (1996) A decade of molecular biology of retinoic acid receptors *FASEB Journal* **10** 940–954

Charnock-Jones DS, Sharkey AM, Rajput-Williams J, Burch D, Schofield JR, Fountain SA, Boock CA and Smith SK (1993) Identification and localization of alternatively spliced mRNAs for vascular endothelial growth factor in human uterus and estrogen regulation in endometrial carcinoma cell lines *Biology of Reproduction* **48** 1120–1128

Clark DE, Smith SK, Sharkey AM and Charnock-Jones DS (1996) Localization of VEGF and expression of its receptors Flt and KDR in human placenta throughout pregnancy *Human Reproduction* **11** 1090–1098

Dantzer V (1984) An extensive lysosomal system in the maternal epithelium of the porcine placenta *Placenta* **5** 117–130

Dantzer V (1985) Electron microscopy of the initial stages of placentation in the pig *Anatomy and Embryology* **172** 281–293

Dantzer V (1999) Epithelichorial placentation. In *Encyclopedia of Reproduction* pp 18–28 Eds E Knobil and JD Neill. Academic press, New York

Dantzer V and Leiser R (1994) Initial vascularisation in the pig placenta: demonstration of nonglandular areas by histology and corrosion casts *Anatomical Record* **238** 177–190

Dantzer V, Nielsen MH and Boisen S (1989) Calcium in the pig placenta *Placenta* **10** 526–527

Dantzer V, Svendsen A-M and Leiser R (1991) Correlation between morphological events during initial stages of placentation in the pig. In *Placenta: Basic Research for Clinical Application* pp 188–199 Ed. H Soma. Karger, Basel

DeChiara TM, Efstradiadis A and Robertson EJ (1990) A growth-deficiency phenotype in heterozygous mice carrying an insulin-like growth factor II gene disrupted by targeting *Nature* **345** 78–80

Ford SP (1997) Embryonic and fetal development in different genotypes in pigs *Journal of Reproduction and Fertility Supplement* **52** 165–176

Geisert RD, Zavy MT, Moffatt RJ, Blair RM and Yellin T (1990) Embryonic steroids and the establishment of pregnancy in pigs *Journal of Reproduction and Fertility Supplement* **40** 293–305

Gupta A, Ing NH, Bazer FW, Bustamante LS and Jaeger LA (1998a) Beta transforming growth factor (TGFβ) at the porcine conceptus–maternal interface. Part I: expression of TGFβ1, TGFβ2, TGFβ3 messenger ribonucleic acids *Biology of Reproduction* **59** 905–910

Gupta A, Dekaney M, Bazer FW, Madrigal MM and Jaeger LA (1998b) Beta transforming growth factor (TGFβ) at the porcine conceptus–maternal interface. Part II: uterine TGFβ bioactivity and expression of immunoreactive TGFβs (TGFβ1, TGFβ2, TGFβ3) and their receptors (type I and type II) *Biology of Reproduction* **59** 911–917

Gustafson AL, Donovan M, Annerwall S, Dencker L and Eriksson U (1996) Nuclear import of cellular retinoic acid-binding protein type I in mouse embryonic cells *Mechanisms and Development* **58** 27–38

Han VKM, Carter AM, Chandarana S, Transwell B and Thompson K (1999) Ontogeny of expression of insulin-like growth factor (IGF) and IGF binding protein mRNAs in the guinea-pig placenta and uterus *Placenta* **20** 361–377

Harney JP, Mirando MA, Smith LC and Bazer FW (1990) Retinol-binding protein: a major secretory product of the pig conceptus *Biology of Reproduction* **42** 523–532

Harney JP, Smith LC, Simmen RCM, Fliss AE and Bazer FW (1994a) Retinol binding protein: immunolocalization of protein and abundance of messenger ribonucleic acid in conceptus and maternal tissues during pregnancy in pigs *Biology of Reproduction* **50** 1126–1135

Harney JP, Ali M, Vedeckis WV and Bazer FW (1994b) Porcine conceptus and endometrial retinoid-binding proteins *Reproduction, Fertility and Development* **7** 211–219

Hodges PC (1953) Ossification in the fetal pig *Anatomical Record* **116** 315–325

Johansson S, Gustafson AL, Donovan M, Romert A, Eriksson U and Dencker L (1997) Retinoid binding proteins in the mouse yolk sac and chorioallantoic placentas *Anatomy and Embryology* **195** 483–490

Johansson S, Gustafson AL, Donovan M, Eriksson U and Dencker L (1999) Retinoid binding protein expression patterns in the human placenta *Placenta* **20** 459–465

Johansson S, Dencker L and Dantzer V (2001) Immunohistochemical localisation of retinoid binding proteins at the materno–fetal interface of the porcine placenta *Biology of Reproduction* **64** 60–68

Jones CP, Dantzer V and Stoddart RW (1995) Changes in glycan distribution within the porcine interhaemal barrier during gestation *Cell and Tissue Research* **279** 551–564

Keys JL and King GJ (1988) Morphological evidence for increased vascular permeability at the time of embryonic attachment in the pig *Biology of Reproduction* **39** 473–487

Keys JL and King GJ (1990) Microscopic examination of porcine conceptus–maternal interface between 10 and 19 days of pregnancy *American Journal of Anatomy* **188** 221–238

Kumar R (1995) Calcium transport in epithelial cells of the intestine and kidney *Journal of Cell Biochemistry* **57** 392–398

Lane M and Bavister BD (1998) Calcium homeostasis in early hamster preimplantation embryos *Biology of Reproduction* **59** 1000–1007

Lawrence DA (1996) Transforming growth factor-beta: a general review *European Cytokine Network, The official journal of the European Cytokine Society, Montrouge* **7** 363–374

Leiser R and Dantzer V (1988) Structural and functional aspects of porcine placental microvasculature *Anatomy and Embryology* **177** 409–419

Leiser R and Dantzer V (1994) Initial vascularization in the pig placenta. II. Demonstration of gland and areola-gland subunits by histology and corrosion casts *Anatomical Record* **238** 326–334

Li E and Norris AW (1996) Structure/function of cytoplasmic vitamin A-binding proteins *Annual Review of Nutrition* **16** 205–234

Liu JP, Barker J, Perkins AS, Robertson EJ and Efstradiadis A (1993) Mice carrying null mutations of the genes encoding insulin-like growth factor I (IGF-I) and type IGF receptor (IGFIr) *Cell* **75** 59–72

Marrable AW (1971) *The Embryonic Pig: a Chronological Account* Pitman Medical, London

Morgan G, Wooding FBP, Care AD and Jones GV (1997) Genetic regulation of placental function: a quantitative *in situ* hybridisation study of calcium binding protein and calcium ATPase rRNAs in the sheep placenta *Placenta* **18** 211–220

Moustgaard J (1971) Nutritive influence upon reproduction *Journal of Reproductive Medicine* **7** 275–278

Napoli JL (1996) Retinoic acid biosynthesis and metabolism *FASEB Journal* **10** 993–1001

Neufeld G, Tessler S, Gitay-Goren H, Cohen T and Levi BZ (1994) Vascular endothelial growth factor and its receptors *Progress in Growth Factor Research* **5** 89–97

Nikitenko I, Morgan G, Kolesnikov SI and Wooding FBP (1998) Immunocytochemical and *in situ* hybridization studies of the distribution of calbindin D9K in the bovine placenta throughout pregnancy *Journal of Histochemistry and Cytochemistry* **46** 679–688

Patten BM (1948) *Embryology of the Pig* Blankistan Co., New York

Persson E (1996) *Studies of the Endometrium and Placenta During Early Pregnancy in the Pig: Morphology, Growth Factors and Steroid Receptors* PhD Thesis, University of Uppsala

Persson E and Rodriguez-Martinez H (1997) Immunocytochemical localization of growth factors and intermediate filaments during the establishment of the porcine placenta *Microscopic Research and Techniques* **38** 165–175

Persson E, Sahlin B, Masironi B, Dantzer V, Eriksson H and Rodriguez-Martinez H (1997) Insulin-like growth factor-I in the porcine endometrium and placenta. Localization and concentration in relation to steroid influence *Animal Reproduction Science* **46** 261–281

Pope WF, Maurir RR and Stormshak F (1982) Intrauterine migration of the porcine embryo: influence of estradiol-17β and histamine *Biology of Reproduction* **27** 575–579

Reynolds LP and Redmer DA (2001) Angiogenesis in the placenta *Biology of Reproduction* **4** 1033–1040

Ridderstråle Y, Persson E, Dantzer V and Leiser R (1997) Carbonic anhydrase activity in different placenta types: a comparative study of pig, horse, cow, mink, rat and human *Microscopic Research and Techniques* **38** 115–124

Sapin V (1998) Retinoids and mouse placentation *Trophoblast Research* **12** 57–76

Scheerboom JEM, Van Adrichem PWM and Taverne MAM (1987) Uterine motility of the sow during the oestrus cycle and early pregnancy *Veterinary Research Communication* **11** 253–269

Schweigert FJ, Bonitz K, Siegling C and Buchholz I (1999)

Distribution of vitamin A, retinol binding protein, cellular retinoic acid-binding protein I and retinoid X receptor beta in the porcine uterus during early gestation *Biology of Reproduction* **61** 906–911

Shalaby F, Rossant J, Yamaguch TP, Gertsenstein M, Wu XF, Breitman ML and Schuh AC (1995) Failure of blood island formation and vasculogenesis in Klk-1 deficient mice *Nature* **176** 62–66

Sherer DM and Abulafia O (2001) Angiogenesis during implantation, and placental and early embryonic development *Placenta* **22** 1–13

Simmen FA, Badinga L, Green ML, Kwak I, Song S and Simmen RC (1998) The porcine insulin-like growth factor system: at the interface of nutrition, growth and reproduction *Journal of Nutrition* **128** (Supplement 2) 315S–320S

Simmen RCM and Simmen FA (1990) Regulation of uterine and conceptus secretory activity in the pig *Journal of Reproduction and Fertility Supplement* **40** 279–292

Soprano DR, Soprano KJ and Goodman DS (1986) Retinol-binding protein and transthyretin mRNA levels in the visceral yolk sac and liver during fetal development in the rat *Proceedings National Academy of Sciences USA* **83** 7330–7334

Stroband HWJ and Van der Lende T (1990) Embryonic and uterine development during early pregnancy in pigs *Journal of Reproduction and Fertility Supplement* **40** 261–277

Trout WE, Hall JA, Stallings-Mann ML, Galvin JM, Anthony RV and Roberts MR (1992) Steroid regulation of the synthesis and secretion of retinol-binding proteins by the uterus of the pig *Endocrinology* **130** 2557–2564

Van Rens BT and Van der Lende T (2000) Fetal and placental traits at day 35 of pregnancy in relation to the estrogen receptor genotype in pigs *Theriogenology* **54** 843–858

Van Rens BT, Hazeleger W and Van der Lende T (2000) Periovulatory hormone profiles and litter size in gilts with different estrogen receptor (RSR) genotypes *Theriogenology* **53** 1375–1387

Winther H, Ahmed A and Dantzer V (1999) Immunohistochemical localization of vascular endothelial growth factor (VEGF) and its two specific receptors, Flt-1 and KDR, in the porcine placenta and non-pregnant uterus *Placenta* **20** 35–43

Wislocky GB and Dempsey EW (1946) Histochemical reactions of the placenta of the pig *American Journal of Anatomy* **78** 181–225

Wooding FBP and Flint APF (1994) Placentation. In *Marshall's Physiology of Reproduction* Chapter 4 Ed. GE Lamming. Chapman and Hall, London

Wooding FBP, Morgan G, Jones GV and Care AD (1996) Calcium transport and the localisation of calbindin-D9K in the ruminant placenta during the second half of pregnancy *Cell and Tissue Research* **285** 477–489

Wooding FBP, Morgan G, Fowden AL and Allen WR (2000) Separate sites and mechanisms for placental transport of calcium, iron and glucose in the equine placenta *Placenta* **21** 635–645

Reproduction Supplement **58**, 223–232

Comparative aspects of placental efficiency

M. E. Wilson[1] and S. P. Ford[2]*

[1]Division of Animal and Veterinary Science, West Virginia University, Morgantown, WV 26506-6108, USA; and [2]Department of Animal Science, Iowa State University, Ames, IA 50011-3150, USA

Litter size is often proposed as the trait that could have the greatest impact in improving reproductive efficiency of pigs. Efforts to select directly for increased litter size have generally been unsuccessful and highly variable. As a result, several attempts have been made to identify critical physiological components that control litter size, with the underlying assumption that augmenting these components would improve this important trait. One attempt at improving physiological components has involved the selection of animals for increased uterine capacity, as measured by the number of fetuses or piglets that a female can carry successfully to term. Recent evidence indicates that one critical component of the uterine capacity in pigs is placental efficiency, or the body weight of a piglet divided by the mass of its placenta. It is easy to determine the average placental efficiency in a litter, but variation among conceptuses within a litter for this trait can be substantial, leading to the conclusion that placental efficiency is an individual conceptus trait. It is suggested that the limited success of selection for an increased uterine capacity results, at least in part, from a misguided view that 'uterine capacity' is strictly a maternal trait. Uterine capacity is better defined as the mass of placental tissue that a pregnant female can support to term, and involves phenotypic variation in both the dam and her offspring. This definition of uterine capacity allows maximization of both uterine size and placental efficiency in future attempts to increase litter size in pigs.

Introduction

A critical element limiting reproductive efficiency in pigs is the large number of potential conceptuses that are lost during gestation (Dziuk, 1987; Lawrence, 1993; Pope, 1994; Rohrer *et al.*, 1999). A number of studies over the last 85 years have highlighted the impact of conceptus loss, particularly from day 12 to day 18 of gestation, on litter size (Hammond, 1914; Corner, 1923; Perry, 1954; Hanly, 1961; Perry and Rowlands, 1962; Scofield, 1972; Dziuk, 1987; Pope, 1994). In general, there is agreement that between 30 and 40% of the embryos formed are lost during this peri-elongation–attachment period (reviewed by Pope, 1994). Recent evidence indicates that embryo losses after day 18 of gestation are significant

Journal paper published with the approval of the Director of Agricultural and Forestry Experiment Station, West Virginia University as scientific paper no. 2781

*Current address: Department of Animal Science, University of Wyoming, Laramie, WY 82071-3684, USA
Email: mwilso25@wvu.edu

and that variation in placental function may contribute to these losses (Wilson *et al.*, 1998, 1999a, 2000). Late embryonic and early fetal losses are particularly critical in commercial crossbred sows in which the ovulation rate is very high (approximately 26 oocytes; Wilson *et al.*, 2000). Therefore, although 30–40% of the embryos are lost between day 12 and day 18 of gestation, the number of conceptuses present at day 25 of gestation is much greater than the number of embryos that survive to term (Foxcroft, 1997; Wilson *et al.*, 2000). In this review, recent work to elucidate the role of the conceptus in determining individual placental size and function, the role of modulation of the uterine environment in altering placental size and function, and the mechanism by which variation in placental size may influence the number of conceptuses that survive beyond days 20–25 of gestation, is described.

Ford (1997) presented the results of nearly a decade of research comparing the prolific Meishan pig to its distant relatives, the commercial occidental breeds. The overwhelming conclusion was that the Meishan pig embryo shows a reduced growth rate during early gestation compared with that of the other breed (Youngs *et al.*, 1993, 1994; Rivera *et al.*, 1996; Ford, 1997; Wilson and Ford, 1997) and concomitantly shows a markedly smaller and more vascular placenta in late gestation (Ford, 1997; Biensen *et al.*, 1998; Wilson *et al.*, 1998). Litter size was greater in Meishan gilts as compared with Yorkshire pigs (one of the occidental breeds used for comparison) despite similar uterine size and ovulation rate (Bazer *et al.*, 1988; Christenson, 1993; Galvin *et al.*, 1993; Lee *et al.*, 1995; Ford, 1997; Biensen *et al.*, 1998; Wilson *et al.*, 1998). Biensen *et al.* (1998) suggested that, in addition to the known impacts of ovulation rate or uterine size, variation in conceptus–uterine interaction must also limit conceptus survival and litter size. When both Yorkshire and Meishan embryos were co-transferred into a common uterine environment (either Meishan or Yorkshire gilts), fetal and piglet body weights at or near term were similar for the littermate Meishan and Yorkshire fetuses and piglets, despite the fact that Meishan conceptuses developed on smaller placentae (approximately 70% of the mass of the placentae of their Yorkshire littermates regardless of an overall breed-of-dam effect; Wilson *et al.*, 1998, 1999b). This critical observation indicates that the difference observed in placental size between straight bred Meishan and Yorkshire conceptuses is not simply a result of an overall smaller conceptus, but of an apparent dissociation of placental and fetal growth (Biensen *et al.*, 1998, 1999; Wilson *et al.*, 1998). As a result of this apparent dissociation, the ratio of fetal or piglet body weight to placental mass (placental efficiency) was used as a measure of placental function (Ford, 1997; Wilson *et al.*, 1999a). At farrowing Meishan conceptuses had placental efficiencies of 8.7 ± 0.4 and 6.3 ± 0.5 when gestated in Meishan and Yorkshire recipient female pigs, respectively. In contrast, Yorkshire conceptuses had placental efficiencies of 4.1 ± 0.9 and 3.4 ± 0.8 when gestated in Meishan and Yorkshire female pigs, respectively (Ford, 1997).

Pattern of placental growth and function

In general, placental growth, as measured by mass, increases exponentially between day 20 and day 60 of gestation (Pomeroy, 1960; Knight *et al.*, 1977). The growth of the placenta then plateaus from day 60 to day 110 of gestation, and this is followed by a secondary increase immediately before term (Pomeroy, 1960; Knight *et al.*, 1977; Biensen *et al.*, 1998; Wilson *et al.*, 1998). This pattern of growth emphasizes what has been observed in occidental breeds. This placental growth pattern was observed in Yorkshire pigs, but Meishan pigs have a smaller placenta throughout gestation and do not show a preterm increase in placental mass (Ford, 1997; Biensen *et al.*, 1998; Wilson *et al.*, 1998). Several workers have reported that placental mass does not change after day 70 of gestation; however, these authors all ceased measurement of placental mass on or before day 105 of gestation, the time of the initiation of the secondary increase (Knight *et al.*, 1977; Vallet *et al.*, 1996; Klemcke and Christenson, 1997). Data presented by Knight *et al.* (1977) indicate an evident increase (approximately 25%) in placental mass between day 90 and day 100 of gestation. This increase is obscured by a relatively uncharacteristic peak in placental mass in animals killed on day 70 of gestation (Pomeroy, 1960; Biensen *et al.*, 1998). In the study by Knight *et al.* (1997), a second set of animals was unilaterally hysterectomized–ovariectomized to establish a limiting uterine environment or capacity (Knight *et al.*, 1977). In these unilaterally hysterectomized–ovariectomized animals, a peak in placental mass was not observed at day 70 of gestation. However, there was a similar (approximately 25%) increase in placental mass between day 90 and day 100 of gestation; this difference was greater than the difference in placental mass between the intact and unilaterally hysterectomized–ovariectomized animals on day 80 of gestation (Knight *et al.*, 1977).

The surface area of the chorioallantoic membrane increases rapidly from day 35 to day 70 (Knight *et al.*, 1977). On day 35, the surface area is approximately 250 cm^2, whereas at day 70 it is approximately 1000 cm^2 (Knight *et al.*, 1977; Biensen *et al.*, 1998). By days 60–70 of gestation, there is an interlocking network of fetal and maternal microvilli, increasing the massive exchange surface of the placenta (Friess *et al.*, 1980; Björkman and Dantzer, 1987; Biensen *et al.*, 1998). From day 70 to day 100 of gestation, there is little change in the surface area of the placenta (Knight *et al.*, 1977). However, at some time after day 100 there is a marked increase in the surface area of the placenta, reaching approximately 1500 cm^2 (Biensen *et al.*, 1998), or doubling in size by day 110 of gestation (Wigmore and Strickland, 1985). The surface area for exchange is increased greatly by microscopic folding compared with that described by simply spreading out the intact chorioallantoic membrane (Björkman and Dantzer, 1987; Dantzer and Leiser, 1994; Biensen *et al.*, 1998).

The area for contact between the chorionic ectoderm and the luminal epithelium by the folding of the chorionic membrane into the permanent folds of the endometrium is increased markedly by the development of microscopic interdigitations, referred to as primary rugae, along the feto–maternal interface at about day 35 to day 40 of gestation (Friess *et al.*, 1980; Björkman and Dantzer, 1987; Leiser and Dantzer, 1988; Dantzer and Leiser, 1994). During the final third of gestation, the functional surface area for nutrient and waste exchange is increased further by the development of an additional tier of interdigitation along the primary rugae, referred to as secondary rugae (Friess *et al.*, 1980; Björkman and Dantzer, 1987). These microvilli are between 0.8 and 1.0 µm in length, and 0.08 µm in diameter, and occur at approximately 85 per µm^2 (Björkman, 1965).

An important component in the function of the placenta during gestation is the development of a sufficient absorptive area, not only in the physical size of the placenta, but also in the number and density of blood vessels for nutrient exchange (Friess *et al.*, 1980; Leiser and Dantzer, 1988; Reynolds and Redmer, 1995; Biensen *et al.*, 1998). By day 70 of gestation, the placental vasculature accounts for approximately 3.7% of the total volume of the chorioallantoic membrane (Biensen *et al.*, 1998). The density of blood vessels remains relatively constant during late gestation and occupies 3% of chorioallantoic membrane volume by day 90, and 2.5% of chorioallantoic membrane volume by day 110 of gestation (Biensen *et al.*, 1998). Furthermore, Wilson *et al.* (1998) reported that in farrowed placentae, the vascular volume was approximately 4% of placental volume. Pigs are described as having all six potential tissue layers present between the maternal and fetal blood supplies (that is, epitheliochorial as classified by Grosser, 1933). However, the maternal and fetal capillaries for exchange can migrate towards each other, reducing the thickness of the respective epithelial layers such that the distance between endothelial cell membranes is approximately 2 µm (Friess *et al.*, 1980, 1982).

The primary role of the placenta is to provide for fetal nutrition, gas exchange and waste removal throughout gestation (Dantzer, 1982; Munro, 1986). There are four main pathways whereby solutes can pass from maternal blood to fetal blood (Sibley et al., 1997). The first pathway is simple flow-limited diffusion. Molecules such as oxygen and carbon dioxide readily cross cell membranes and, therefore, their transfer from maternal to fetal circulation is limited only by the rate of delivery to the site of transfer (Björkman, 1973; Leiser and Dantzer, 1988; Sibley and Boyd, 1992). The second pathway is protein-mediated transport. The diverse transporter proteins involved can be active transporters or passive transporters, symporters or antiporters, or ion channels (Sibley et al., 1997). Finally, there are two types of transport of which the activity in the placenta is poorly understood: paracellular and endocytosis–exocytosis (Dantzer, 1982; Friess et al., 1982; Sibley et al., 1997). Paracellular transfer involves transfer through the extracellular fluid surrounding the cells of the placenta. Endocytosis–exocytosis involves engulfing solutes into an endocytotic vesicle, vesicular transport through the cell and exocytotic expulsion at the opposite pole. Endocytosis–exocytosis has been observed in pigs in structures referred to as transfer tubules (Sperhake, 1971 (in Friess et al., 1980); Friess et al., 1980, 1982; Dantzer, 1982). Simple flow-limited diffusion is regulated not only by the rate of maternal and fetal blood flows, but also by the arrangement of the endometrial and placental vasculature with respect to each other (Carter, 1989; Carter and Myatt, 1995). These arrangements are generally described by how closely they reflect particular fluid mechanical models, and include concurrent, crosscurrent and countercurrent exchange (Carter, 1989). Of these, concurrent exchange is least efficient (50% theoretical maximal transfer), countercurrent exchange is most efficient (100% theoretical maximal transfer) and efficiency of crosscurrent exchange is between these two values (Carter, 1989). In pigs, placental transfer of freely diffusible nutrients appears to rely on a vascular anatomy that is either concurrent or possibly crosscurrent (Friess et al., 1982; Leiser and Dantzer, 1988). Transporter protein-mediated transfer relies on the density and relative activity of the transporters, and is generally not limited by the rate of blood flow. In pigs, protein-mediated transfer appears to be concentrated in the troughs of the chorionic folds (adjacent to the ridges of endometrial folds; Friess et al., 1980, 1982; Poston, 1997; Sibley et al., 1997). Transported solutes include, but are not limited to, glucose, amino acids and ions, such as sodium, potassium, calcium and protons (Davies, 1960; Battaglia, 1986; Faber and Thornburg, 1986; Lester, 1986; Sibley et al., 1997). In addition to transfer across the interface between the uterine luminal epithelium and chorionic epithelium, large macromolecules (for example, uteroferrin) produced in the endometrial glands are absorbed intact by the placental areolae (Perry, 1981; Friess et al., 1982; Roberts et al., 1986; Leiser and Dantzer, 1994).

By using the gross measurement of placental efficiency as an indicator of overall placental function (for example, diffusion, active transport, umbilical and uterine blood flow, surface area and areolae number), total function has been emphasized over component function. However, the component that may be most important, and into which further investigation has been initiated (see below), is the density of blood vessels in the chorioallantoic membrane (and associated endometrium). Placental efficiency is very low (0.06–0.15) from day 30 to day 40 of gestation (Spies et al., 1959; Knight et al., 1977; Wilson et al., 2000; Fig. 1), but begins to increase very rapidly by day 50 (that is, approximately threefold; 0.6) and continues to increase, although at a reduced rate, until term (Knight et al., 1974, 1977; Dalton and Knight, 1983; Wilson et al., 2000; Fig. 1). This pattern of increased placental efficiency is critical to the exponential growth of the fetal component of the conceptus with regard to limited growth of the placenta after day 70 of gestation. It would appear that there is a second inflection point in the placental efficiency curve as the animal nears term (Fig. 1). It is suggested that the increase in placental efficiency is attenuated by the secondary increase in placental mass from

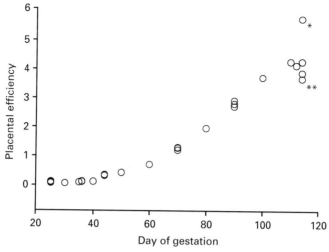

Fig. 1. Pattern of placental efficiency (fetal weight : placental mass) throughout gestation in pigs. Data summarized from several sources (Spies *et al.*, 1959; Knight *et al.*, 1974, 1977; Dalton and Knight, 1983; Ford, 1997; Wilson *et al.*, 1998, 1999a, 2000). *Individuals born to female pigs selected for greater than average placental efficiency. **Individuals born to female pigs selected for lower than average placental efficiency.

day 100 to day 110 of gestation to term. These data support the contention that the pig may be reaching a maximization of placental function coinciding with the end of gestation, which would probably be critical to the rapidity with which fetuses become nutritionally distressed in cases of delayed parturition.

Variation in placental size and function

The hallmark of placental efficiency is the marked variation that is present within a litter. This variation was characterized in an experiment using straight bred Yorkshire litters in which the umbilical cords of individual piglets were tagged at birth to allow piglets to be matched with their placentae. In eight litters, placental efficiency was 4.2 ± 0.2, which is very similar to that observed by Ford (1997) and Wilson *et al.* (1999a). However, the placental efficiency of individual conceptuses in all eight litters ranged from 2.7 to 7.4 (Wilson *et al.*, 1999a), and in one litter from 3.8 to 7.4. In this initial study, and in several subsequent studies, variation in placental efficiency was not associated with variation in the body weight of the fetus (prenatally) or piglet (natally), but was negatively associated with variation in the mass of the placenta (Biensen *et al.*, 1999; Wilson *et al.*, 1999a, 2000). This finding was observed not only near term when fetal growth is at a maximum and probably close to the limit for placental function, but was also evident as early as day 25 of gestation (Wilson *et al.*, 2000). Indeed, during the critical period between day 25 and day 45 of gestation when uterine capacity becomes limiting (that is, crowding reduces conceptus survival; Dziuk, 1968; Dhindsa and Dziuk, 1968; Fenton *et al.*, 1972; Pope *et al.*, 1972; Knight *et al.*, 1977; Huang *et al.*, 1987; Wilson *et al.*, 2000), there is a negative association between placental mass and placental efficiency (Wilson *et al.*, 2000). Furthermore, as uterine capacity becomes limiting, the number of viable conceptuses in a litter is no longer associated with ovulation rate and begins to be associated with the average placental efficiency for that litter (Wilson *et al.*, 2000). As expected, as placental mass reached a plateau at about day 60 of gestation, and the fetus continued to grow, placental efficiency was > 1 between day 60 and 70 of gestation (Fig. 1). Factors that result in variation in placental size have been investigated. Direct effects, generally via application of steroids during gestation, were examined by Spies *et al.* (1959), Knight *et al.* (1974), McGovern *et al.* (1981) and Wilson and Ford (2000). Indirect effects were observed by causing uterine crowding using superovulation, superinduction or unilateral hysterectomy–ovariectomy (Dhindsa and Dziuk, 1968; Dziuk, 1968; Fenton *et al.*, 1972; Pope *et al.*, 1972; Knight *et al.*, 1977; Huang *et al.*, 1987). Unfortunately, as variation in placental function *per se* was not the objective of these studies, only average placental efficiencies could be derived for treatment groups and the degree of variation within each litter was not evident. Treatment of sows with oestrogen, progestogen or a combination of both on different days of gestation can stimulate placental growth (Spies *et al.*, 1959; Knight *et al.*, 1974; McGovern *et al.*, 1981; Wilson and Ford, 2000) and crowding can limit placental growth (Knight *et al.*, 1974, 1977). However, neither steroid treatment nor uterine crowding appears to have much effect on placental efficiency during gestation (Spies *et al.*, 1959; Knight *et al.*, 1974, 1977; Dalton and Knight, 1983). It is suggested that placental efficiency is a unique trait of each individual conceptus and that treatments altering placental mass also alter fetal weight as a result of a fairly static functionality of an individual placenta. However, in contrast, in an experiment in which Meishan female pigs were treated with oestradiol on day 12 and day 13, or on day 13 and day 14 of gestation, a 40% increase in placental mass was observed at day 112 of gestation (Wilson and Ford, 2000). In these animals, placental efficiency was reduced compared with that of untreated controls. Whether the ability to alter placental efficiency markedly in Meishan female pigs is a result of a breed difference or is related to the lack of a secondary increase in placental mass after day 100 of gestation has not been established.

As pigs have a diffuse epitheliochorial type of placentation, its function is thought of as blood flow-limited, meaning that nutrient and gas fluxes across the maternal placental interface are limited by the rates of uterine and umbilical blood flows. Placentae of Meishan pigs do not increase in size from mid- to late gestation, but in contrast to placentae of Yorkshire pigs, undergo a marked increase in the proliferation of blood vessels in the chorioallantoic membrane that is in close contact with the associated endometrial vasculature (Biensen *et al.*, 1998; Wilson *et al.*, 1998). The marked increase in the density of placental blood vessels may increase the rate of nutrient and waste product exchange per unit area of placental–endometrial interface (Biensen *et al.*, 1998). Divergence in the strategy used to acquire the nutrients required by the developing fetus is most notable after day 70 of gestation when the fetus has grown to a size at which it begins to exert significant metabolic demands on the placenta (Biensen *et al.*, 1998; Wilson *et al.*, 1998). Between day 70 and day 110 of gestation, vascular density of the Meishan placenta increases twofold, whereas Yorkshire placental surface area increases by approximately 50%; however, significant littermate variation was observed in both breeds (Biensen *et al.*, 1998).

The potential role of placental-derived angiogenic factors in modulating placental efficiency has been investigated by Vonnahme *et al.* (2001). Vascular endothelial growth factor (VEGF) is a potent angiogenic and vascular permeability factor that is produced by the epithelium of both the placenta and endometrium during gestation in pigs (Winther *et al.*, 1999; Vonnahme *et al.*, 2001; Vonnahme and Ford, 2001). Expression of VEGF mRNA is relatively low during early gestation (that is, days 25–45). At some time after day 45 of gestation (mid-way through the initial period of rapid placental growth), expression of VEGF mRNA continues to increase until term (Vonnahme *et al.*, 2001). The potential significance of placental production of VEGF is evident by a positive correlation throughout gestation between the relative amount of mRNA being produced by a placenta and the density of blood vessels in the placenta (Vonnahme *et al.*, 2001). Furthermore, there was a positive association between the relative amount of VEGF mRNA present in a placenta and the efficiency of that placenta (Vonnahme *et al.*, 2001).

Impact of placental efficiency on uterine capacity

Several authors over the past 30 years have indicated that if the number of conceptuses surviving beyond day 18 of gestation is increased, the 'capacity' of the uterus will begin to have a negative impact on litter size at approximately day 30 of gestation (Fenton *et al.*, 1972; Pope *et al.*, 1972; Huang *et al.*, 1987; Wilson *et al.*, 2000). Development of the early conceptus was characterized in a commercial line of pigs that had a very high ovulation rate (> 26 oocytes), in which 40% of potential conceptuses were lost by day 25 (Wilson *et al.*, 2000). Between day 25 and day 35 of gestation there was an additional loss of approximately four conceptuses on average, supporting the role of the uterus in limiting litter size, even in a case in which no experimental manipulation was needed to increase the number of potential conceptuses. Conventionally, this limitation has been viewed simply as the absolute number of conceptuses that can be supported to a defined point of gestation, most notably parturition (Fenton *et al.*, 1972; Pope *et al.*, 1972; Chistenson *et al.*, 1987; Huang *et al.*, 1987). This view of uterine capacity has been instrumental in the advancement of our understanding of components important for limiting litter size (Christenson *et al.*, 1987; Vallet *et al.*, 1996; Rohrer *et al.*, 1999; Pearson *et al.*, 2000). However, in light of recent data, a revision of the terminology used is important (Wilson *et al.*, 1999a; Vallet *et al.*, 2001). In particular, uterine capacity should be defined more correctly as the total amount of placental mass a pregnant female pig can support to term. Therefore, it will include both an endometrial surface area for contact component and a component related to the average efficiency of the placentae in that litter (Wilson *et al.*, 1999a; Wilson and Ford, 2000). The uterine component of uterine capacity may not be adequately described strictly by a measure of surface area, but variation may occur in endometrial function per unit area. If so, a greater understanding of how to measure endometrial or uterine function and how it varies may allow for an even better understanding of how 'uterine capacity' is regulated and how it limits litter size.

Heritability of placental efficiency

Reproductive characteristics traditionally show a very low heritability. Indeed, it has been suggested by some authors that the critical nature of reproduction has resulted in the presence of a large number of genes that show few alleles and, therefore, have a low potential for selection. This modified view of uterine capacity was used to select male and female pigs of normal birth weight from within a herd that showed either greater than average or lower than average placental efficiency (Wilson *et al.*, 1999a). When gilts selected for high placental efficiency that had been mated to boars selected for high placental efficiency farrowed, the placental masses of their piglets were 40% lower than those farrowed by low placental efficiency gilts mated to low placental efficiency boars (Fig. 1). The resultant realized heritability was 0.37 (Wilson *et al.*, 1999a). More importantly, sows with high placental efficiency farrowed more than three live pigs per litter than did sows with low placental efficiency (12.8 ± 0.7 versus 9.5 ± 0.6, respectively). Furthermore, similar decreases in placental mass and increases in litter size were observed for sows with high placental efficiency than in sows with low placental efficiency when mated to the same boars and allowed to farrow a second time (Wilson *et al.*, 1999a). Vonnahme and Ford (2001) established that placentae of conceptuses resulting from mating boars and gilts selected for high placental efficiency have a greater placental expression of VEGF mRNA in addition to a greater placental efficiency, than conceptuses resulting from mating boars and gilts selected for low placental efficiency, with unselected controls being intermediate. Vallet *et al.* (2001) used gilts that were unilaterally hysterectomized–ovariectomized from lines selected for ovulation rate, uterine capacity or unselected controls and failed to find an increase in placental efficiency in those selected for uterine capacity (simply measured as number of conceputses) compared with controls. Vallet *et al.* (2001) observed an increase in placental efficiency in the line selected for ovulation rate. More importantly, in the 422 litters that were collected across all three lines, the heritability of placental efficiency was noteworthy for a reproductive trait (0.29 ± 0.08; Vallet *et al.*, 2001), particularly when compared with reported heritabilities for uterine capacity and litter size (0.09, Young *et al.*, 1996; and 0.16, Hertzer *et al.*, 1940, respectively).

Conclusion

A greater understanding of the physiological basis of traits such as litter size will probably result in more successful attempts to improve the character of interest through either alterations in management or genetic selection. The realization that gestation is an active and integrative process is key to furthering this understanding. Inherent variation as well as the apparent lack of plasticity in the relative efficiency of placental function in pigs is a critical component of uterine capacity. Such variation may explain why selection simply for the number of conceptuses present in a crowded uterus without regard to variation in placental efficiency has not been successful. In addition, an important concept of placental efficiency in pigs is the consistent lack of association with fetal or piglet weight and consistent negative association with placental mass. These associations indicate that either large or small fetuses or piglets can develop on small or large placentae, but that in general large placentae are relatively less efficient than smaller placentae. As we continue to develop and refine understanding of the reproductive biology of the pig, variation in the developmental regulation and final function of the placenta should provide an insight into conceptus loss after day 30 of gestation, as well as the size, number and potentially the uniformity of piglets at birth.

References

Battaglia FC (1986) Placental transport and utilization of amino acids and carbohydrates *Federation Proceedings* **45** 2508–2512

Bazer FW, Thatcher WW, Martinat-Botte F and Terqui M (1988) Sexual maturation and morphological development of the reproductive tract in Large White and prolific Chinese Meishan pigs *Journal of Reproduction and Fertility* **83** 723–728

Biensen NJ, Wilson ME and Ford SP (1998) Meishan and Yorkshire fetal and placental development in either a Meishan or Yorkshire uterus to days 70, 90 and 110 of gestation *Journal of Animal Science* **76** 2169–2176

Biensen NJ, Haussmann MF, Lay DC, Jr, Christian LL and Ford SP (1999) The relationship between placental and piglet birth weights and growth traits *Animal Science* **68** 709–715

Björkman N (1965) On the fine structure of the porcine placental barrier *Acta Anatomica* **62** 334–342

Björkman N (1973) Fine structure of the fetal–maternal area of exchange in the epitheliochorial and endotheliochorial types of placentation *Acta Anatomica* **86** 1–22

Björkman N and Dantzer V (1987) Placentation. In *Textbook of Veterinary Histology* 3rd Edn pp 340–360 Eds H-D Dellmann and EM Brown. Lea and Febiger, Philadelphia

Carter AM (1989) Factors affecting gas transfer across the placenta and the oxygen supply to the fetus *Journal of Developmental Physiology* **12** 305–322

Carter AM and Myatt L (1995) Control of placental blood flow: workshop report *Reproduction, Fertility and Development* **7** 1401–1406

Christenson RK (1993) Ovulation rate and embryonic survival in Chinese Meishan and white crossbred pigs *Journal of Animal Science* **71** 3060–3066

Christenson RK, Leymaster KA and Young LD (1987) Justification of unilateral hysterectomy–ovariectomy as a model to evaluate uterine capacity in swine *Journal of Animal Science* **65** 738–744

Corner GW (1923) The problem of embryonic pathology in mammals, with observations upon intrauterine mortality in the pig *American Journal of Anatomy* **31** 523–545

Dalton DL and Knight JW (1983) Effects of exogenous progesterone and estrone on conceptus development in swine *Journal of Animal Science* **56** 1354–1361

Dantzer V (1982) Transfer tubules in the porcine placenta *Bibliotheca Anatomica* **22** 144–149

Dantzer V and Leiser R (1994) Initial vascularization in the pig placenta. I. Demonstration of nonglandular areas by histology and corrosion casts *Anatomical Record* **238** 177–190

Davies J (1960) *Survey of Research in Gestation and the Developmental Sciences* pp 19–52. Williams and Wilkins, Baltimore

Dhindsa DS and Dziuk PJ (1968) Influence of varying the proportion of uterus occupied by embryos on maintenance of pregnancy in the pig *Journal of Animal Science* **27** 668–672

Dziuk PJ (1968) Effect of number of embryos and uterine space on embryo survival in the pig *Journal of Animal Science* **27** 673–676

Dziuk PJ (1987) Embryonic loss in the pig: an enigma. In *Manipulating Pig Production* pp 28–39 Eds JL Barnett, ES Batterham and GM Cronin. Australasian Pig Science Assoc, Werribee

Faber JJ and Thornburg KL (1986) Fetal nutrition: supply, combustion, interconversion and deposition *Federation Proceedings* **45** 2502–2507

Fenton FR, Schwartz FL, Bazer FW, Robison OW and Ulberg LC (1972) Stage of gestation when uterine capacity limits embryo survival in gilts *Journal of Animal Science* **35** 383–388

Ford SP (1997) Embryonic and fetal development in different genotypes in pigs *Journal of Reproduction and Fertility Supplement* **52** 165–176

Foxcroft GR (1997) Mechanisms mediating nutritional effects on embryonic survival in pigs *Journal of Reproduction and Fertility Supplement* **52** 47–61

Friess AE, Sinowatz F, Skolek-Winnisch R and Träutner W (1980) The placenta of the pig. I. Fine structural changes of the placental barrier during pregnancy *Anatomy and Embryology* **158** 179–191

Friess AE, Sinowatz F, Slolek-Winnisch R and Träutner W (1982) Structure of the epitheliochorial porcine placenta *Biblotheca Anatomica* **22** 140–143

Galvin JM, Wilmut I, Day BN, Ritchie M, Thomson M and Haley CS (1993) Reproductive performance in relation to uterine and embryonic traits during early gestation in Meishan, Large White and crossbred sows *Journal of Reproduction and Fertility* **98** 377–384

Grosser O (1933) Human and comparative placentation: including the early stages of human development *Lancet* **111** 999–1001

Hammond J (1914) On some factors controlling fertility in domestic animals *Journal of Agricultural Science* **6** 263–277

Hanly S (1961) Prenatal mortality in farm animals *Journal of Reproduction and Fertility* **2** 182–194

Hertzer HO, Lambert WV and Zeller HH (1940) Influence of inbreeding and other factors on litter size in Chester White swine *Circular-United States Department of Agriculture* **570** 1–10

Huang YT, Johnson RK and Eckardt GR (1987) Effect of unilateral hysterectomy and ovariectomy on puberty. Uterine size and embryo development in swine *Journal of Animal Science* **65** 1298–1305

Klemcke HG and Christenson RK (1997) Porcine fetal and maternal adrenocorticotropic hormone and corticosteroid concentrations during gestation and their relation to fetal size *Biology of Reproduction* **57** 99–106

Knight JW, Bazer FW and Wallace HD (1974) Effect of progesterone induced increase in uterine secretory activity on development of the porcine conceptus *Journal of Animal Science* **39** 743–746

Knight JW, Bazer FW, Thatcher WW, Franke DE and Wallace HD (1977) Conceptus development in intact and unilaterally hysterectomized–ovariectomized gilts: interrelations among hormonal status, placental development, fetal fluids and fetal growth *Journal of Animal Science* **44** 620–637

Lawrence J (1993) By the year 2000: more pigs from fewer sows *National Hog Farmer* **12 January** 22–24

Lee GJ, Ritchie M, Thomson M, MacDonald AA, Blasco A, Santacreu MA, Argente MJ and Haley CS (1995) Uterine capacity and prenatal survival in Meishan and Large White pigs *Animal Science* **60** 471–479

Leiser R and Dantzer V (1988) Structural and functional aspects of porcine placental microvasculature *Anatomy and Embryology* **177** 409–419

Leiser R and Dantzer V (1994) Initial vascularisation in the pig placenta. II. Demonstration of gland and areola-gland subunits by histology and corrosion casts *Anatomical Record* **238** 236–334

Lester GE (1986) Cholecalciferol and placental calcium transport *Federation Proceedings* **45** 2524–2526

McGovern PT, Morcom CB, de Sa WF and Dukelow WR (1981) Chorionic surface area in conceptuses from sows treated with progesterone and oestrogen during early pregnancy *Journal of Reproduction and Fertility* **61** 439–442

Munro HN (1986) Role of the placenta in ensuring fetal nutrition *Federation Proceedings* **45** 2500–2501

Pearson PL, Smith TP, Sonstegard TS, Klemcke HG, Christenson RK and Vallet JL (2000) Porcine erythropoietin receptor: molecular cloning and expression in embryonic and fetal liver *Domestic Animal Endocrinology* **19** 25–38

Perry JS (1954) Fecundity and embryonic mortality in pigs *Journal of Embryology and Experimental Morphology* **2** 308–322

Perry JS (1981) The mammalian fetal membranes *Journal of Reproduction and Fertility* **62** 321–335

Perry JS and Rowlands IW (1962) Early pregnancy in the pig *Journal of Reproduction and Fertility* **4** 175–188

Pomeroy RW (1960) Infertility and neonatal mortality in the sow. III. Neonatal mortality and foetal development *Journal of Agricultural Science* **54** 31–56

Pope WF (1994) Embryonic mortality in swine. In *Embryonic Mortality in Domestic Species* pp 53–77 Eds MT Zavy and RD Geisert. CRC Press, Boca Raton

Pope CE, Christenson RK, Zimmerman-Pope VA and Day BN (1972) Effect of number of embryos on embryonic survival in recipient gilts *Journal of Animal Science* **35** 805–811

Poston L (1997) The control of blood flow to the placenta *Experimental Physiology* **82** 377–387

Reynolds LP and Redmer DA (1995) Utero–placental vascular development and placental function *Journal of Animal Science* **73** 1839–1851

Rivera RM, Youngs CR and Ford SP (1996) A comparison of the number of inner cell mass and trophectoderm cells of preimplantation Meishan and Yorkshire pig embryos at similar developmental stages *Journal of Reproduction and Fertility* **106** 111–116

Roberts RM, Raub TJ and Bazer FW (1986) Role of uteroferrin in transplacental iron transport in the pig *Federation Proceedings* **45** 2513–2518

Rohrer GA, Ford JJ, Wise TH, Vallet JL and Christenson RK (1999) Identification of quantitative trait loci affecting female reproductive traits in a multigeneration Meishan-white composite swine population *Journal of Animal Science* **77** 1385–1391

Scofield AM (1972) Embryonic mortality. In *Pig Production* pp 367–383 Ed. DJA Cole. Butterworths, London

Sibley CP and Boyd RDH (1992) Mechanisms of transfer across the human placenta. In *Fetal and Neonatal Physiology* pp 62–74 Eds RA Polin and WW Fox. WB Saunders, Philadelphia

Sibley C, Glazier J and D'Souza S (1997) Placental transporter activity and expression in relation to fetal growth *Experimental Physiology* **82** 389–402

Sperhake B (1971) Zur Durchlässigkeit der Placenta des Schweines - Eine Literaturstudie *Inaug Diss Hannover*

Spies HG, Zimmerman DR, Self HL and Casida LE (1959) The effect of exogenous progesterone on formation and maintenance of the corpora lutea and on early embryo survival in pregnant swine *Journal of Animal Science* **18** 163–172

Vallet JL, Christenson RK and McGuire WJ (1996) Association between uteroferrin, retinol-binding protein, and transferrin within the uterine and conceptus compartments during pregnancy in swine *Biology of Reproduction* **55** 1172–1178

Vallet JL, Leymaster KA, Cassady JP and Christenson RK (2001) Are hematocrit and placental selection tools for uterine capacity in swine? *Journal of Animal Science Supplement* **79** 64 (Abstract)

Vonnahme KA and Ford SP (2001) Selection for increased placental efficiency (PE) results in increased placental expression of vascular endothelial growth factor (VEGF) in the pig *Journal of Animal Science Supplement* **79** 64 (Abstract)

Vonnahme KA, Wilson ME and Ford SP (2001) Role of vascular endothelial growth factor in modulating placental/endometrial vascularity in the pig *Biology of Reproduction* **64** 1821–1825

Wigmore PKC and Strickland NC (1985) Placental growth in the pig *Anatomy and Embryology* **173** 263–268

Wilson ME and Ford SP (1997) Differences in trophectoderm mitotic rate and P450 17α-hydroxylase expression between late preimplantation Meishan and Yorkshire conceptuses *Biology of Reproduction* **56** 380–385

Wilson ME and Ford SP (2000) Effect of estradiol-17β administration during the time of conceptus elongation on placental size at term in the Meishan pig *Journal of Animal Science* **78** 1047–1052

Wilson ME, Biensen NJ, Youngs CR and Ford SP (1998) Development of Meishan and Yorkshire littermate conceptuses in either a Meishan or Yorkshire uterine environment to day 90 of gestation and to term *Biology of Reproduction* **58** 905–910

Wilson ME, Biensen NJ and Ford SP (1999a) Novel insight into the control of litter size in the pig, using placental efficiency as a selection tool *Journal of Animal Science* **77** 1654–1658

Wilson ME, Vonnahme KA and Ford SP (1999b) Use of asynchronous embryo transfer to investigate the role of uterine-embryo timing on placental size *Journal of Animal Science Supplement* **77** 222 (Abstract)

Wilson ME, Vonnahme KA, Foxcroft GR, Gourley G, Wolff T, Quirk-Thomas M and Ford SP (2000) Characteristics of the reproductive biology of multiparous sows from a commercially relevant population *Journal of Animal Science Supplement* **78** 213 (Abstract)

Winther H, Ahmed A and Dantzer V (1999) Immunohistochemical localization of vascular endothelial growth factor (VEGF) and its two specific receptors, Flt-1 and KDR, in the porcine placenta and non-pregnant uterus *Placenta* **20** 35–43

Young LD, Leymaster KA and Christenson RK (1996) Opportunities for indirect selection for uterine capacity of swine *Journal of Animal Science Supplement* **74** 119 (Abstract)

Youngs CR, Ford SP, McGinnis LK and Anderson LH (1993) Investigation into the control of litter size in swine. I. Comparative studies on *in vitro* development of Meishan and Yorkshire preimplantation embryos *Journal of Animal Science* **71** 1561–1565

Youngs CR, Christenson LK and Ford SP (1994) Investigations into the control of litter size in swine. III. A reciprocal embryo transfer study of early conceptus development *Journal of Animal Science* **72** 725–731

Reproduction Supplement **58**, 233–246

Causes and consequences of fetal growth retardation in pigs

C. J. Ashworth[1], A. M. Finch[2], K. R. Page[3], M. O. Nwagwu[1]
and H. J. McArdle[2]

[1]*Animal Biology Division, SAC, Craibstone Estate, Bucksburn, Aberdeen AB21 9YA, UK;*
[2]*Division of Integrative and Developmental Biology, Rowett Research Institute, Bucksburn,
Aberdeen AB21 9SB, UK; and* [3]*Department of Biomedical Sciences, University of Aberdeen,
Aberdeen AB24 3FX, UK*

In pigs, as in other species, fetal growth retardation is associated with reduced birth weight and increased risk of fetal and neonatal death. As there are few opportunities after birth to remedy the detrimental effects of low birth weight, it is important to understand both the intrinsic and extrinsic factors associated with inadequate fetal growth and to determine when growth retarded fetuses deviate from the growth trajectory of their normal sized littermates. Inadequately grown pig fetuses can be identified statistically as early as day 30 of the 114 days of gestation, indicating that limited uterine space is not a primary determinant of fetal growth. Comparisons of the smallest fetus within a litter with a normal sized sibling reveal that inadequately grown fetuses have altered endocrine status and lower circulating concentrations of many essential amino acids. In addition, the placenta supplying the smallest fetus is disproportionately small and has a reduced capacity to transport amino acids. Understanding the timing and the causes of fetal growth retardation in pigs may help us to devise appropriate strategies to reduce the incidence and hence the detrimental postnatal consequences of runting.

Nature, timing and prevalence of fetal growth retardation

Piglet birth weights are the major determinant of subsequent survival and total weaning weights of the litter (Winters *et al.*, 1947). However, many litters contain at least one piglet that is significantly lighter than its littermates. In most cases, the piglet with low birth weight is an example of fetal growth retardation in the absence of obvious causes such as fetal anomaly or maternal illness. Low birth weight may be due to an intrinsic failure of fetal growth or arise as a consequence of inadequate placental function.

Several definitions have been used to identify inadequately grown fetuses within a litter. These include fetuses or neonates weighing less than two standard deviations below the mean body weight for gestational age, those weighing less than the tenth percentile (Bauer *et al.*, 1998), the smallest of each litter, those weighing less than two-thirds of the mean weight of the uterine horn, fetuses in the middle of the horn and those shown to be outliers in an otherwise

---

Email: c.ashworth@ab.sac.ac.uk

normally distributed population (Royston *et al.*, 1982; van der Lende *et al.*, 1990). Various terms including intrauterine growth retardation (IUGR), small for gestational age (SGA) and runt have been used to refer to piglets with low birth weights.

Clinical studies distinguish infants with low birth weight as either SGA or IUGR. SGA babies, usually defined as those weighing less than the tenth percentile at birth, are considered to have achieved their genetic potential for intrauterine growth and exhibit normal allometry. In contrast, IUGR infants do not achieve their normal intrauterine growth potential and exhibit asymmetrical growth characterized by normal brain growth at the expense of the growth of internal organs such as the liver and kidney. Similarly, in pigs, fetal growth restriction is characterized by asymmetrical organ growth, as demonstrated by differences in allometric coefficients for fetal liver, heart and lungs (Da Silva *et al.*, 2000). Widdowson (1971) suggested that such differences in relative organ size might arise as a consequence of hyperplasia rather than hypertrophy.

It is of interest that the within-litter distribution in piglet birth weight appears to be established by the end of the first month of pregnancy (Perry and Rowell, 1969; van der Lende *et al.*, 1990; Wise *et al.*, 1997). Furthermore, statistical assessment of the time at which growth-retarded fetuses first deviate from the growth trajectory of their normally grown siblings indicates that runting is apparent by day 44 of pregnancy (Cooper *et al.*, 1978). By plotting the cumulative probability of fetal weights within a litter, it is possible to distinguish small fetuses forming part of a normally distributed population from those lying outside an otherwise normally distributed population (Finch *et al.*, 1999; Fig. 1). Using this approach, we have confirmed that inadequately grown pig fetuses can be identified as early as day 30 of pregnancy and that the prevalence of inadequately grown fetuses does not increase between day 30 and parturition. This finding indicates that inadequate uterine space is not a major factor contributing to poor growth of pig fetuses. Instead, fetal growth may be related to the ability of the placenta to deliver nutrients. Indeed, placental mass on day 29 of pregnancy is an accurate determinant of fetal weight in late gestation (Knight *et al.*, 1977).

Possible causal factors of fetal growth retardation

Genotype

Meishan pigs give birth to a mean of four more live piglets per litter than do contemporary gilts or sows from indigenous breeds. This increase is achieved through a higher prenatal survival, which in late pregnancy is accommodated through limited fetal growth and reduced within-litter variability in fetal size (Lee and Haley, 1995).

Reciprocal embryo transfer between indigenous Landrace × Large White gilts and Chinese Meishan gilts demonstrated clearly that maternal genotype has a major influence on fetal size (Ashworth *et al.*, 1990). Day 30 fetuses carried by Meishan mothers were significantly lighter than fetuses carried by Landrace × Large White recipients, regardless of the genotype of the donor gilt. In this experiment, maternal genotype accounted for > 70% of the variation in fetal weight on day 30 of pregnancy. This is similar to the situation observed at term. Crossbreeding trials have shown that the 20–25% difference between the birth weight of Meishan and Large White piglets is almost entirely due to the maternal genotype and is explained only partially by differences in litter size *per se* (Lee and Haley, 1995). This finding indicates that the Meishan maternal environment may limit fetal growth.

Although placentae supplying Meishan fetuses are more vascular (Ashworth *et al.*, 1998a; Biensen *et al.*, 1999a), have a greater surface area (Ashworth *et al.*, 1998a) and secrete more protein *in vitro* (C. J. Ashworth and L. Beattie, unpublished) than do placentae from

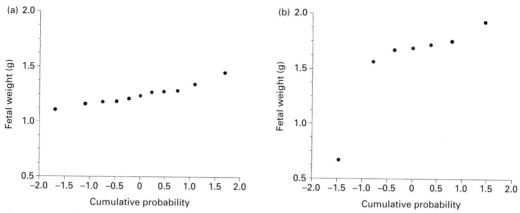

Fig. 1. Cumulative probability plots showing the within-litter range in pig fetal weights on day 30 of pregnancy. (a) Small for gestational age (SGA) fetuses are lighter than their littermates, but form part of a normally distributed population. (b) Intrauterine growth retarded (IUGR) fetuses lie outside an otherwise normally distributed population.

indigenous breeds, Meishan placentae are disproportionately lighter. Ford (1997) reported that the fetal weight:placental mass ratio was 8.7 ± 0.4 for Meishan conceptuses and 3.4 ± 0.8 for conceptuses from the control breed. The reason for this difference is unclear, but may be related to differences in the mitogenic potential of fetal fluids from different breeds. Allantoic fluid collected from Meishan gilts on day 100 of pregnancy was associated with a reduction in the proliferation of placental cells *in vitro* (Ashworth *et al.*, 1998b), whereas allantoic fluids from Large White × Landrace gilts did not alter proliferation of placental cells. The nature of the anti-proliferative agent in allantoic fluids from Meishan pigs remains to be determined, but it does not appear to involve cytokine tumour necrosis factor α (TNF-α) (C. J. Ashworth and M. Ewen, unpublished), which has been implicated in the regulation of placental growth in other species.

Both fetal insulin and thyroid hormones stimulate fetal growth by increasing the mitotic drive and nutrient availability for tissue accretion. Although Meishan fetuses are approximately one-third smaller than Large White × Landrace fetuses, Meishan fetal plasma concentrations of insulin, thyroxin and tri-iodothyronine are higher (Nwagwu *et al.*, 2000). The reason for this surprising finding is unclear. It does not appear to be related to differences in fetal body composition between breeds (M. Nwagwu, L. G. Yang and C. J. Ashworth, unpublished), but may reflect genotype differences in the relationship between fetal endocrinology and growth.

Maternal nutrition

There have been few comprehensive large-scale studies performed to address the effects of specific nutrients on fetal growth and subsequent litter size. Furthermore, the critical stages of pregnancy at which fetal development is most susceptible to changes in maternal nutrition and the postnatal consequences of inappropriate nutrition during fetal life are poorly understood. Although it is generally accepted that increased feed intake by sows during gestation increases piglet birth weight, this has not been adopted commercially because the increased feed costs outweigh the perceived financial benefits of a modest increase in birth weight. One study in which large numbers (*n* = 187) of pregnant sows were fed diets of different energy content for four successive parities (Young *et al.*, 1990) revealed a small increase in piglet birth weight in sows receiving higher dietary energy.

Some of the most interesting data describing the effects of nutritional status on fetal and postnatal development have been generated by feeding gilts or sows on diets deficient in protein. Schoknecht *et al.* (1993) found that the progeny of sows receiving a restricted protein diet (0.5% (w/w) protein) compared with those receiving a control (13% (w/w) protein) diet in pregnancy had reduced birth weight and growth rates until slaughter. Applying the protein restriction between day 1 and day 44, or between day 81 and term only, reduced birth weight, but not subsequent daily live weight gain. Other studies have shown that protein deficiency during early or mid-gestation decreases placental and fetal growth (Schoknecht *et al.*, 1994) and changes fetal plasma, amniotic and allantoic fluid amino acid concentrations (Wu *et al.*, 1998).

Of the various specific nutrients that may affect fetal and placental development, the effects of supplementary folic acid are worthy of note. The addition of folic acid (2 p.p.m.) to the diet of gilts for three oestrous cycles before mating and throughout pregnancy increased fetal crown–rump length, weight and both protein and RNA content (Harper *et al.*, 1996), thereby indicating that this nutrient may enhance fetal growth.

Litter size and uterine capacity

Superficially, it would be expected that as litter size increases, the demand for uterine space and maternal nutrients would also increase, leading to an inverse relationship between litter size and individual piglet birth weight. Whether this relationship holds over a spontaneously occurring range of litter sizes is equivocal. In a study involving 50 litters, Bauer *et al.* (1998) found a strong inverse correlation between the mean litter weight and litter size. Interestingly, Pere *et al.* (1997) observed that fetal weight on day 112 of pregnancy was related inversely to litter size on day 35 of pregnancy. This finding may be a reflection of the extent of placental development during early pregnancy, which, in turn, affects subsequent fetal growth.

Uterine capacity has been defined as the maximum number of fetuses that can be carried successfully to term when the number of potentially viable conceptuses is not limiting (Christenson *et al.*, 1987). Treatments imposed to exceed this uterine capacity, including unilateral ovariectomy–hysterectomy or transfer of supraphysiological numbers of embryos, tend to be associated with increased prenatal mortality (Wu *et al.*, 1989), rather than reduced fetal size.

Of particular interest in polytocous species is the naturally occurring variation in fetal size among siblings occupying the same uterus. Comparisons of normally and inadequately grown fetuses and their placentae within the same uterus allow intrinsic factors associated with differential fetal growth to be studied free from the confounding effects of maternal genotype, nutrition and husbandry. The remainder of this review will address the causes and consequences of within-litter variation in fetal size. Some local factors associated with inadequate fetal growth in pigs are highlighted (Fig. 2).

Location in the uterus

Within the normal range of litter sizes, the distribution and spacing of fetuses are not uniform throughout the length of the uterus. After a study of > 400 pregnant pigs, Dziuk (1985) reported that on day 25 the space available to each fetus decreased from the ovarian to the cervical end of the uterine horn. By day 40, the least space was available in the mid-portion of each horn, with similar space at each end. It may be expected that these differences in uterine space would be reflected in fetal size. However, the data relating position within the uterus and fetal size are equivocal.

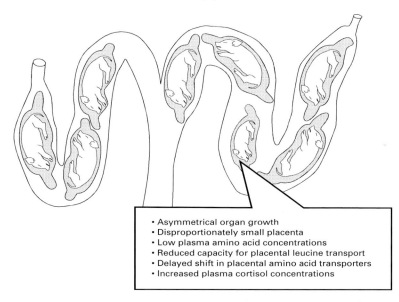

- Asymmetrical organ growth
- Disproportionately small placenta
- Low plasma amino acid concentrations
- Reduced capacity for placental leucine transport
- Delayed shift in placental amino acid transporters
- Increased plasma cortisol concentrations

Fig. 2. Schematic diagram showing differently sized pig fetuses in the uterus. The box highlights physiological and biochemical factors associated with the smallest fetus in the uterus.

In a study using 348 gilts, Wise *et al.* (1997) found no relationship between fetal weight and uterine position on day 30; however, on days 70 and 104 of pregnancy, the heavier fetuses were found at the ovarian ends and light fetuses at the cervical ends of the uterine horns. In contrast, Perry and Rowell (1969) found that fetuses at either end of the uterine horn tended to be larger compared with those in the mid-portion. It is often assumed that the mid-portion of the uterine horn may represent a disadvantaged site, because of increased competition for space or reduced arterial supply. However, Perry and Rowell (1969) found no relationship between fetal size and uterine vascular architecture. Most descriptions of the relationship between uterine position and fetal size are confounded by the litter size or by the number of fetuses in each uterine horn. The formula used to calculate relative uterine position described by Ashworth (1991), which expresses the position of each fetus within the uterine lumen on a uniform scale from 0 (ovarian) to 1 (cervical), overcomes this problem. When this formula is applied, there is no evidence that a particular position in the uterine horn is associated with advantages for fetal growth (A. M. Finch, P. F. N. Da Silva and C. J. Ashworth, unpublished; Fig. 3).

Fetal sex

From at least day 70 of pregnancy, male pig fetuses and their associated placentae are heavier than female fetuses and placentae (Wise and Christenson, 1992). These authors also presented data indicating that in late pregnancy (day 104) the sex of neighbouring fetuses within the uterus affected fetal size. Specifically, they reported that a fetus with both neighbours of the opposite sex was lighter than a fetus surrounded by neighbours of the same sex and proposed that fetuses with neighbours of the opposite sex may make up most of the piglets with low birth weight. As expected, plasma concentrations of the anabolic steroid testosterone were higher in male fetuses, but, in contrast to the situation in mice (vom Saal

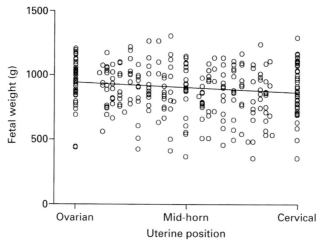

Fig. 3. Relationship between pig fetal weight and uterine location on day 100 of pregnancy. The position of each fetus within the uterine lumen was expressed on a uniform scale (uterine position) from 0 (ovarian) to 1 (cervical) ((fetal number − 1)/(total number in horn − 1)). The graph shows data from 305 fetuses obtained from 24 litters. $R^2 = 0.019$. (A. M. Finch, P. F. N. Da Silva and C. J. Ashworth, unpublished).

et al., 1990), female pig fetuses with two male neighbours did not have altered testosterone concentrations. Our preliminary data (C. J. Ashworth and H. J. McArdle, unpublished) also indicate that the sex of neighbouring fetuses can affect relative organ size, with positive relationships observed between relative liver mass and number of male neighbours in day 100 female fetuses.

Placental nutrient transport

The efficiency with which the placenta transports nutrients and oxygen to the fetus is determined by its surface area of contact with the uterine wall (chorionic villus surface area) and by blood flow at the maternal–fetal interface, and depends on transplacental transport kinetics and transporters. Pigs have a non-invasive diffuse epitheliochorial placenta in which the maternal blood supply is well separated from the absorptive surface of the chorion. The rate of oxygen transport is limited by placental blood flow. In contrast, the abundance and activity of specific transport proteins regulate placental transport of glucose, amino acids, ions and molecules. Placental glucose transport occurs by facilitated diffusion involving several glucose transporter (GLUT) protein isoforms. Many amino acids taken up by the placenta are transported against a feto–maternal concentration gradient by energy-dependent mechanisms. In pigs, as in other species, these include several sodium-dependent and sodium-independent amino acid transporter systems that have different levels of activity. Classically, amino acid transporters have been classified alphabetically according to their preferred substrates, with sodium-independent transporters having lower case letters and sodium-dependent transporters uppercase letters (Fig. 4).

Placentae supplying the smallest fetus in the uterus are disproportionately lighter than those supplying larger fetuses in the same litter (Ashworth and McArdle, 1999) (Table 1). This

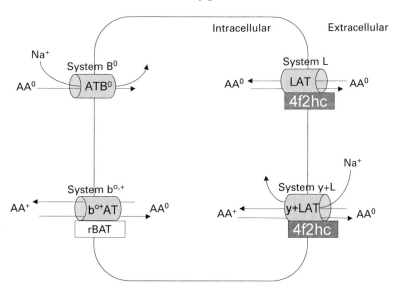

Fig. 4. Schematic diagram of amino acid transport systems. System L exchanges neutral amino acids, whereas sodium-dependent system y+L and sodium-independent system $b^{0,+}$ exchange cationic amino acids and neutral amino acids. These members of the glycoprotein-associated amino acid transporter family are heterodimeric in nature, with heavy chains (4f2hc/rBAT) and light chains (LAT, y+LAT, b^{0+}AT). Sodium-dependent system B^0 transports neutral amino acids. AA^+: cationic amino acids; AA^0, neutral amino acids.

observation, combined with the positive relationship between placental blood flow and fetal weight (Wootton *et al.*, 1977), implies that there is a generalized reduction in the ability of placentae supplying small fetuses to deliver nutrients.

There is increasing evidence in a variety of species, including rats, guinea-pigs, sheep and humans, of an association between placental amino acid transport and fetal growth (for review see Sibley *et al.*, 1997). Direct evidence that placental amino acid transport is defective came from *in vivo* studies in sheep in which ^{13}C-labelled leucine was infused during late (days 117–128) pregnancy (Ross *et al.*, 1996). Maternal leucine flux into the placenta supplying the growth-retarded fetus was reduced markedly. This finding, coupled with lower concentrations of several essential amino acids in fetal plasma obtained from growth-retarded pig fetuses (Ashworth and McArdle, 1999), indicates that the capacity of pig placentae to transport amino acids to the fetus may be associated with fetal growth.

Using membrane vesicles produced from pig chorioallantoic membrane, Ashworth and McArdle (1999) demonstrated that placentae supplying inadequately grown fetuses have a reduced capacity to transport the essential amino acid leucine. Leucine uptake is inhibited by 2-amino-2-norbornane-carboxylic acid, indicating that transport occurs via the system L amino acid transporter system. The reliance on sodium-dependent amino acid transport systems changes during gestation. These gestational changes in the nature of leucine uptake differ between placentae supplying normally and inadequately grown pig fetuses (Finch *et al.*, 2000; Fig. 5). On days 45 and 65 of pregnancy leucine uptake occurs predominantly by sodium-independent channels. By day 100 of pregnancy, placental leucine uptake to normally grown fetuses involves both sodium-dependent and sodium-independent transport.

Table 1. Weight of the smallest and normal sized pig fetuses and mass of their placentae on days 45, 65 and 100 of pregnancy

Day	n	Normal sized fetus			Smallest fetus		
		Fetal weight (g)	Placental mass (g)	Placental mass:fetal weight	Fetal weight (g)	Placental mass (g)	Placental mass:fetal weight
45	11	19.3 ± 0.6	77.3 ± 6.9	3.9 ± 0.3	16.3 ± 0.7***	35.6 ± 3.8***	2.2 ± 0.2***
65	10	199.5 ± 9.1	145.0 ± 23.2	0.7 ± 0.1	146.6 ± 12.3***	69.1 ± 13.1**	0.4 ± 0.1**
100	22	951.2 ± 27.4	213.6 ± 8.6	0.23 ± 0.01	572.9 ± 33.2***	110.0 ± 11.5***	0.20 ± 0.02

n = number of litters.
Values marked with an asterisk are significantly different compared with values from corresponding normal sized fetus;
**$P < 0.01$, ***$P < 0.001$ (paired t test between smallest and normal sized fetus on each day of pregnancy studied).

This shift in transport systems was not observed in placentae supplying the smallest fetuses, which continue to rely predominantly on sodium-independent transport.

At present, there are no data on the expression of the different transporters in pig placenta and it is not known how the ontogeny of expression is related to fetal development. Recent reports have demonstrated the heterodimeric nature of amino acid transporters, in which the transporter consists of a common heavy chain (4f2hc/rBAT) bound to different light chains, each conferring different transport characteristics (Deves and Boyd, 2000) (Fig. 4). It is possible that the differences in placental leucine uptake between the placentae supplying small and normal fetuses could result from differences in relative abundance of specific light chains. In the rat placenta, gestational changes in expression of system y+L amino acid transporters, involved in transport of lysine and arginine, correlate with changes in the abundance of 4f2hc expression. As 4f2hc is required for the cell surface expression and function of transporter light chains, the decrease in total transport observed in the placentae supplying small fetuses may result from delayed placental development leading to decreased 4f2 expression.

Endocrine and paracrine factors affecting fetal growth

Fetal hormones promote growth and development *in utero* by altering both metabolism and gene expression in fetal tissues. Their effects on growth may be mediated in part by other growth factors such as the insulin-like growth factors (IGFs) and cytokines such as TNF-α and colony stimulating factor 1 (CSF-1). Fetal hormones such as cortisol, thyroxin and insulin help to ensure that fetal growth is commensurate with nutrient supply and that prepartum maturation occurs in preparation for extrauterine life.

The IGFs have metabolic, mitogenic and differentiative activities, all of which play a role in promoting growth before and after birth. In most species, IGF-I concentrations are low during fetal life, and IGF-II plays a more prominent role in fetal growth. Our data show no effect of fetal size on day 100 plasma IGF-II concentrations; however, small fetuses have lower concentrations of both plasma IGF-I on day 100 (Nwagwu et al., 2000) and hepatic IGF binding protein 2 (IGFBP-2) on day 90 (Kampman et al., 1993) compared with normally grown fetuses in the same uterus.

We have observed inverse relationships between fetal weight and both plasma and allantoic fluid cortisol concentrations on day 100 and between fetal weight and plasma

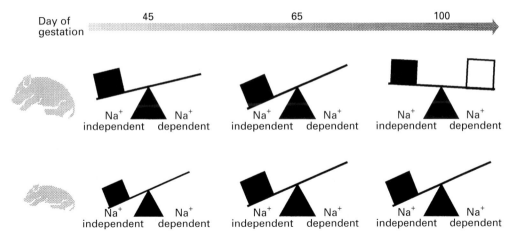

Fig. 5. Schematic diagram showing differences in leucine transport characteristics of placentae supplying normally (upper line) and inadequately (lower line) grown pig fetuses at key stages of gestation.

cortisol concentrations on day 65 (M. Nwagwu, K. Page and C. J. Ashworth, unpublished). It is not clear whether these inverse relationships reflect size-related alterations in fetal adrenal cortisol production or in placental 11β-hydroxysteroid dehydrogenase (11β-HSD) activity, which normally protects the fetus from high circulating concentrations of maternal cortisol. However, Klemcke and Christenson (1996) found no convincing evidence for an association between pig fetal size and placental 11β-HSD activity on days 50, 75 and 100 of pregnancy. A role for fetal pituitary hormones in fetal growth also appears unlikely, as decapitated pig fetuses grow and develop normally (Strkyer and Dziuk, 1975). Given that the fetal adrenal is the primary source of fetal plasma cortisol on days 50 and 100 (Klemcke, 1995), size-related differences in fetal cortisol concentrations are probably a function of differences in adrenal production or release *per se.*

The cause or effect nature of the relationship between cortisol concentrations and fetal size remains to be determined. In sheep fetuses, cortisol suppresses both IGF-I and IGF-II gene expression (for review see Fowden *et al.*, 1998), indicating that high cortisol concentrations may themselves reduce the drive for fetal growth. Early activation of the fetal hypothalamic–pituitary–adrenal (HPA) axis is likely to promote a premature cortisol-induced switch from cell proliferation to differentiation, leading to inappropriate growth for the developmental stage of the conceptus.

There is a positive correlation between fetal plasma cholesterol concentrations and fetal weight on day 104 of pregnancy (Wise *et al.*, 1997). The physiological significance of this observation is not clear, but may be related to the observation that brains from runt fetuses contain less cholesterol and, therefore, are less myelinated than the brains of normally grown littermates (Dickerson *et al.*, 1971).

Temporal changes in placental expression of CSF-1 in the pig mirror the pattern of placental growth and development in this species (Tuo *et al.*, 1995). Therefore, CSF has been proposed as an important regulator of placental development. Immunohistochemistry did not reveal a relationship between fetal size and localization of CSF-1 at the maternal–fetal interface; however, staining was more intense in endometrial and placental tissues supplying small fetuses compared with tissues surrounding normal sized fetuses (Ashworth *et al.*, 1998a). The reasons for this intriguing observation are unclear, but it does highlight local size-dependent differences in the abundance of CSF-1.

Consequences of fetal growth retardation

Low birthweight piglets are more likely to die from starvation (Hartsock et al., 1977) and thermoregulatory stress (Herpin and Le Dividich, 1995) than are their heavier littermates. The incidence of preweaning mortality is similar in light piglets which form part of a normally distributed population (SGA) and in those which are statistical outliers (IUGR) (van der Lende and de Jager, 1991). Low birthweight piglets that do survive grow more slowly, have reduced feed conversion efficiencies (Powell and Aberle, 1980) and reach a lower mature body weight (Widdowson, 1971) with a higher body fat to muscle ratio (Powell and Aberle, 1980) than do normally grown piglets. In addition, low birthweight piglets show compromised muscle (Bauer et al., 2000a), cardiac and renal (Bauer et al., 2000b) physiology. Cross-fostering runt piglets to a less competitive environment does little to improve these problems, indicating that there may be limited scope after birth to improve the consequences of prenatal growth restriction.

The ratio between piglet birth weight and the mass of its placenta does not affect subsequent weaning weight, growth rate or backfat depth (Biensen et al., 1999b), indicating that fetal weight per se is the major determinant of subsequent performance.

Neonatal growth and vigour

Although runt piglets experience a period of compensatory growth during the first 2 weeks of life, they never achieve the same mature body weight as their littermates (Widdowson, 1971). In addition, internal organs, including the liver, remain disproportionately small throughout the first 3 years. Feeding runt piglets with milk replacer to either mimic the intake a runt piglet would receive if left on the sow or to mimic an unrestricted intake from days 3 to 14 did not affect growth rate (Ritacco et al., 1997). These data indicate that growth-retarded piglets have a reduced absorptive capacity or altered postabsorptive metabolism. A reduced absorptive capacity appears unlikely, as the runt piglets consuming more milk replacer had an increased liver mass (Ritacco et al., 1997) and because IUGR is associated with the precocious occurrence of maltase and sucrase activities in the mucosa of the small intestine (Xu et al., 1994).

Low birthweight pigs take longer to suckle (Tuchscherer et al., 2000), indicating a possible compromise of behavioural development affecting subsequent neonatal vigour. This finding may explain why low birthweight piglets have lower circulating concentrations of IgG than do their heavier littermates (Antipatis et al., 2001).

As a consequence of the brain sparing associated with intrauterine growth retardation, a higher proportion of the weight of the runt piglet is represented by brain tissue. However, the brains of runt piglets are more poorly developed than those of normally grown siblings, with less myelination and dendritic development (Dickerson et al., 1971).

Muscle biology

Low birth weight in pigs is associated with a reduced total number of muscle fibres (Handel and Stickland, 1987a). Although the number of muscle fibres and the ratio between primary and secondary fibres are sensitive to nutrition during pregnancy (Dwyer et al., 1994), muscle fibre hyperplasia is complete by day 90 of gestation (Wigmore and Stickland, 1983). Therefore, the alterations in fibre number observed at birth are permanent. Except in very extreme cases of runting, reduced total number of muscle fibres is generated through a reduction in the ratio between secondary and primary fibres (Handel and Stickland, 1987a). More detailed investigation of the muscle fibre types affected by runting revealed that postnatal differentiation of muscle fibres was related more to physiological maturity (weight) than to chronological age (Handel and Stickland, 1987b). At equivalent live weights, the area of the semitendinosus muscle occupied by slow-twitch, oxidative metabolism fibres was greater in low birthweight piglets compared with normal sized littermates. The net effect of these observations is that animals developing from low birthweight piglets contain more slow muscle fibres than do littermates that were heavier at birth. In keeping with the greater prevalence of slow fibres, muscle blood flow and contractile function are more developed and calf muscles appear more tolerant to fatigue in newborn growth-retarded pigs (Bauer *et al.*, 2000a).

Thyroid hormones play a major role in muscle development and function. In particular, nuclear thyroid hormone receptors (TR) are important in fetal myogenesis and the ratio of TRα1:TRα2 receptor isoforms is believed to determine muscle type. In pigs, intrauterine growth retardation is associated with reduction in the number of skeletal muscle TRs (Dauncey and Geers, 1990) and a 50% downregulation of TRα1 expression in pig cardiac muscle (Dauncey *et al.*, 2001). Low cardiac muscle TRα1, combined with a reduction in plasma thyroid hormone concentrations, would reduce cardiac α-myosin transcription, which, in turn, would be expected to lead to a lower intrinsic contractile ability and operational heart rate. However, Bauer *et al.* (2000b) reported that heart rate, cardiac output, arterial blood gases and pH were similar in normal weight and IUGR piglets, although arterial blood pressure and glucose content were significantly lower.

Accompanying the changes in muscle fibre number and type associated with low piglet birth weights are increases in body fat. At equivalent live weight (96–109 kg), pigs that were light at birth had more adipocytes in the perirenal tissue and subcutaneous depot compared with their heavier birthweight siblings (Powell and Aberle, 1981).

Neonatal adrenal function

Plasma cortisol concentrations are related inversely to piglet weight on the day of birth (Wise *et al.*, 1991) and on days 3 and 7 after birth (Klemcke *et al.*, 1993). Inverse relationships between piglet weight and both adrenal weight and responsiveness of adrenal cells to ACTH *in vitro* are also evident on days 3 and 7 (Klemcke *et al.*, 1993). Differences in the sensitivity of the HPA axis are thought to originate during prenatal life and to be mediated by alterations in glucocorticoid receptor gene expression in the fetal hippocampus, which is involved in the feedback control of the HPA axis. Recent studies in rats have indicated that prenatal alterations in the sensitivity of the HPA axis may affect the subsequent stress responses of the individual (Welberg *et al.*, 2000).

In neonates, cortisol serves an essential physiological role, including glucose homeostasis and adaptation to enteric nutrition. Although increased neonatal cortisol concentrations may be associated with short-term advantage, in humans and rodent species increased neonatal glucocorticoid concentrations have been linked with hypertension and impaired glucose tolerance in adult life. Indeed, high neonatal glucocorticoid concentrations are thought to be central in explaining epidemiological relationships between low birth weight and later cardiovascular problems. However, such relationships have not yet been studied in domestic species.

Conclusion

In pigs, approximately one-third of litters contain at least one piglet that is substantially lighter than its littermates. The variability in fetal size within a litter appears to be established during the first month of pregnancy. Furthermore, the prevalence of inadequately grown pig fetuses is as great on day 30 of pregnancy as at term. Therefore, limited uterine space does not appear to be a primary determinant of inadequate fetal growth. Instead, the efficacy of placental attachment, coupled with the subsequent ability of that placenta to supply the developing fetus with nutrients, appears to be critical to ensure appropriate fetal growth.

Inadequate growth during intrauterine life has a detrimental effect on a diverse range of physiological functions in the offspring, many of which persist throughout life. There are limited opportunities to remedy the postnatal consequences of intrauterine growth retardation. Therefore, attempts to alleviate inadequate fetal growth in pigs should focus on opportunities to promote within-litter uniformity throughout pregnancy.

Unpublished results from the authors' laboratories were produced with funding from the Scottish Executive, Rural Affairs Department.

References

Antipatis C, Rooke JA, Ewen M and Ashworth CJ (2001) Both moderate vitamin A deficiency during pregnancy and birthweight affect piglet immunity *Proceedings of the Nutrition Society* **60** 72 (Abstract)

Ashworth CJ (1991) Effect of pre-mating nutritional status and post-mating progesterone supplementation on embryo survival and conceptus growth in gilts *Animal Reproduction Science* **26** 311–321

Ashworth CJ and McArdle HJ (1999) Both placental amino acid uptake and fetal plasma amino acid concentrations differ between small and normally-grown porcine fetuses *Early Human Development* **54** 90–91

Ashworth CJ, Haley CS, Aitken RP and Wilmut I (1990) Embryo survival and conceptus growth after reciprocal embryo transfer between Chinese Meishan and Landrace × Large White gilts *Journal of Reproduction and Fertility* **90** 595–603

Ashworth CJ, Cagney C, Hoggard N and Lea RG (1998a) Effect of breed and fetal size on porcine placental histology and immunolocalisation of leptin and CSF-1 *Journal of Reproduction and Fertility Abstract Series* **22** 56 (Abstract)

Ashworth CJ, Beattie L, Duthie SJ and McArdle HJ (1998b) Breed differences in mitogenic potential of porcine allantoic fluid *Biology of Reproduction* **58** (Supplement 1) 217

Bauer R, Walter B, Hoppe A, Gaser E, Lampe V, Kauf E and Zweiner U (1998) Body weight distribution and organ size in newborn swine (*Sus scrofa domestica*) – a study describing an animal model for asymmetrical intrauterine growth retardation *Experimental Toxicology and Pathology* **50** 59–65

Bauer R, Wank V, Walter B, Blickhan R and Zweiner U (2000a) Reduced muscle vascular resistance in intrauterine growth restricted newborn piglets *Experimental Toxicology and Pathology* **52** 271–276

Bauer R, Walter B, Ihring W, Kluge H, Lampe V and Zweiner (2000b) Altered renal function in growth-restricted newborn piglets *Pediatric Nephrology* **14** 735–739

Biensen NJ, Wilson ME and Ford SP (1999a) The impacts of uterine environment and fetal genotype on conceptus size and placental vascularity during late gestation in pigs *Journal of Animal Science* **77** 954–959

Biensen NJ, Haussmann MF, Lay DC, Christian LL and Ford SP (1999b) The relationship between placental and piglet birth weights and growth traits *Animal Science* **68** 709–715

Christenson RK, Leymaster KA and Young LD (1987) Justification of unilateral hysterectomy–ovariectomy as a model to evaluate uterine capacity in swine *Journal of Animal Science* **65** 738–744

Cooper JE, John M, McFadyen IR and Wootton R (1978) Early appearance of 'runting' in piglets *Veterinary Record* **102** 529–530

Dauncey MJ and Geers R (1990) Nuclear 3,5,3'-triodothyronine receptors in skeletal muscle of normal and small-for-gestational age newborn piglets *Biology of the Neonate* **58** 291–295

Dauncey MJ, White P, Burton KA and Katsumata M (2001) Nutrition–hormone receptor–gene interactions: implications for development and disease *Proceedings of the Nutrition Society* **60** 63–72

Da Silva PFN, Finch AM, Antipatis C and Ashworth CJ (2000) Changes in the relationship between porcine fetal size and organ development during pregnancy *Proceedings of the British Society of Animal Science* 123 (Abstract 24)

Deves R and Boyd CA (2000) Surface antigen CD98(4F2): not a single membrane protein, but a family of proteins with multiple functions *Journal of Membrane Biology* **173** 165–177

Dickerson JWT, Merat A and Widdowson EM (1971) Intra-uterine growth retardation in the pig. III. The chemical structure of the brain *Biology of the Neonate* **19** 354–362

Dwyer CM, Stickland NC and Fletcher JM (1994) The influence of maternal nutrition on muscle fiber number development in the porcine fetus and on subsequent post natal growth *Journal of Animal Science* **72** 911–917

Dziuk P (1985) Effect of migration, distribution and spacing of pig embryos on pregnancy and fetal survival *Journal of Reproduction and Fertility Supplement* **33** 57–63

Finch AM, Zuur G and Ashworth CJ (1999) Differential growth of porcine fetuses: timing of IUGR *Early Human Development* **55** 185–186

Finch AM, Ashworth CJ, Page KR and McArdle HJ (2000)

Gestational changes in leucine transport across porcine placentas supplying littermates of different sizes *Journal of Physiology* 528P 26P

Ford SP (1997) Embryonic and fetal development in different genotypes in pigs *Journal of Reproduction and Fertility Supplement* **52** 165–176

Fowden AL, Li J and Forhead AJ (1998) Glucocorticoids and the preparation for life after birth: are there long-term consequences of the life insurance? *Proceedings of the Nutrition Society* **57** 113–122

Handel SE and Stickland NC (1987a) Muscle cellularity and birthweight *Animal Production* **44** 311–317

Handel SE and Stickland NC (1987b) The growth and differentiation of porcine skeletal muscle fibre types and the influence of birthweight *Journal of Anatomy* **152** 107–119

Harper AF, Lindemann MD and Konegay ET (1996) Fetal survival and conceptus development after 42 days of gestation in gilts and sows in response to folic acid supplementation *Canadian Journal of Animal Science* **76** 157–160

Hartsock TG, Graves HB and Baumgardt BR (1977) Agonistic behaviour and the nursing order in suckling piglets *Journal of Animal Science* **44** 320–330

Herpin P and Le Dividich J (1995) Thermoregulation and the environment. In *The Neonatal Pig, Development and Survival* pp 57–95 Ed. MA Varley. CAB International, Oxford

Kampman KA, Ramsay TG and White ME (1993) Developmental changes in hepatic IGF-2 and IGFBP-2 mRNA levels in intrauterine growth-retarded and control swine *Comparative Biochemistry and Physiology B* **104** 415–421

Klemcke HG (1995) Placental metabolism of cortisol at mid- and late gestation in swine *Biology of Reproduction* **53** 1293–1301

Klemcke HG and Christenson RK (1996) Porcine placental 11β-hydroxysteroid dehydrogenase activity *Biology of Reproduction* **55** 217–223

Klemcke HG, Lunstra DD, Brown-Borg HM, Borg KE and Christenson RK (1993) Association between low birth weight and increased adrenocortical function in neonatal pigs *Journal of Animal Science* **71** 1010–1018

Knight JW, Bazer FW, Thatcher WW, Franke DE and Wallace HD (1977) Conceptus development in intact and unilaterally hysterectomised–ovariectomised gilts: interrelationships among hormonal status, placental development, fetal fluids and fetal growth *Journal of Animal Science* **44** 620–637

Lee GJ and Haley CS (1995) Comparative farrowing to weaning performance in Meishan and Large White pigs and their crosses *Animal Science* **60** 269–280

Nwagwu MO, Owens PC, Page KR and Ashworth CJ (2000) Effect of breed and fetal size on day 100 porcine fetal hormone concentrations *Journal of Reproduction and Fertility Abstract Series* **25** 18 (Abstract)

Pere M-C, Dourmad J-Y and Etienne M (1997) Effect of number of pig embryos in the uterus on their survival and development and on maternal metabolism *Journal of Animal Science* **75** 1337–1342

Perry JS and Rowell JG (1969) Variations in fetal weight and vascular supply along the uterine horn of the pig *Journal of Reproduction and Fertility* **19** 527–534

Powell SE and Aberle D (1980) Effects of birth weight on growth and carcass composition of swine *Journal of Animal Science* **50** 860–868

Powell SE and Aberle D (1981) Skeletal muscle and adipose tissue cellularity in runt and normal birth weight swine *Journal of Animal Science* **52** 748–756

Ritacco G, Radecki SV and Schoknecht PA (1997) Compensatory growth in runt pigs is not mediated by insulin-like growth factor I *Journal of Animal Science* **75** 1237–1243

Ross JC, Fennessey PV, Wilkening RB, Battaglia FC and Meschia G (1996) Placental transport and fetal utilization of leucine in a model of fetal growth retardation *American Journal of Physiology* **270** (*Endocrinology and Metabolism* **33**) E491–E503

Royston J, Flecknell PA and Wooton R (1982) New evidence that the intra-uterine growth-retarded piglet is a member of a discrete subpopulation *Biology of the Neonate* **42** 100–104

Schoknecht PA, Pond WG, Mersmann HJ and Maurer RR (1993) Protein restriction during pregnancy affects post-natal growth in swine progeny *Journal of Nutrition* **123** 1818–1825

Schoknecht PA, Newton GR, Weise DE and Pond WG (1994) Protein restriction in early pregnancy alters fetal and placental growth and allantoic fluid proteins in swine *Theriogenology* **42** 217–226

Sibley CJ, Glazier J and D'Souza S (1997) Placental transporter activity and expression in relation to fetal growth *Experimental Physiology* **82** 389–402

Stryker JL and Dziuk PJ (1975) Effects of fetal decapitation on fetal development, parturition and lactation in pigs *Journal of Animal Science* **40** 282–287

Tuchscherer, Puppe B, Tuchscherer A and Tiemann U (2000) Early identification of neonates at risk: traits of newborn piglets with respect to survival *Theriogenology* **54** 371–388

Tuo W, Harney JP and Bazer FW (1995) Colony-stimulating factor-1 in conceptus and uterine tissues in pigs *Biology of Reproduction* **53** 133–142

van der Lende T and de Jager D (1991) Death risk and preweaning growth rate of piglets in relation to the within-litter weight distribution at birth *Livestock Production Science* **28** 73–84

van der Lende T, Hazeleger W and de Jager D (1990) Weight distribution within litters at the early foetal stage and at birth in relation to embryonic mortality in the pig *Livestock Production Science* **26** 53–65

vom Saal FS, Quandagno DM, Even MD, Keisler LW, Keisler DH and Khan S (1990) Paradoxical effects of maternal stress on fetal steroids and postnatal reproductive traits in female mice from different intrauterine positions *Biology of Reproduction* **43** 751–761

Welberg LA, Seckl JR and Holmes MC (2000) Inhibition of 11beta-hydroxysteroid dehydrogenase, the feto–placental barrier to maternal glucocorticoids, permanently programs amygdala GR mRNA expression and anxiety-like behaviour in the offspring *European Journal of Neuroscience* **12** 1047–1054

Widdowson EM (1971) Intra-uterine growth retardation in the pig. I. Organ size and cellular development at birth and after growth to maturity *Biology of the Neonate* **19** 329–340

Wigmore PM and Stickland NC (1983) Muscle development in large and small pig fetuses *Journal of Anatomy* **137** 235–245

Winters LM, Cummings JN and Stewart HA (1947) A study of factors affecting survival from birth to weaning and total weaning weight of the litter of swine *Journal of Animal Science* **6** 288–296

Wise T and Christenson RK (1992) Relationship of fetal position within the uterus to fetal weight, placental weight, testosterone, estrogens and thymosin β4 concentrations at 70 and 104 days of gestation in swine *Journal of Animal Science* **70** 2787–2793

Wise T, Stone RT and Vernon MW (1991) Relationships of serum estriol, cortisol and albumin concentrations with pig weight at 110 days of gestation and at birth *Biology of the Neonate* **59** 114–119

Wise T, Roberts AJ and Christenson RK (1997) Relationships of light and heavy fetuses to uterine position, placental weight, gestational age and fetal cholesterol concentrations *Journal of Animal Science* **75** 2197–2204

Wootton R, McFadyen IR and Cooper JE (1977) Measurement of placental blood flow in the pig and its relation to placental and fetal weight *Biology of the Neonate* **31** 333–339

Wu MC, Chen ZY, Jarrell VL and Dziuk PJ (1989) Effect of initial length of uterus per embryo on fetal survival and development in the pig *Journal of Animal Science* **67** 1767–1772

Wu G, Pond WG, Ott T and Bazer FW (1998) Maternal dietary protein deficiency decreases amino acid concentration in fetal plasma and allantoic fluid of pigs *Journal of Nutrition* **128** 894–902

Xu RJ, Mellor DJ, Birtles MJ, Reynolds GW and Simpson HV (1994) Impact of intrauterine growth retardation on the gastrointestinal tract and the pancreas in newborn pigs *Journal of Pediatric Gastroenterology and Nutrition* **18** 231–240

Young LG, King GJ, Walton JS, McMillan I, Klevorick M and Shaw L (1990) Gestation energy and reproduction in sows over four parities *Canadian Journal of Animal Science* **70** 493–506

Reproduction Supplement **58**, 247–261

Prenatal development as a predisposing factor for perinatal losses in pigs

T. van der Lende[1], E. F. Knol[2] and J. I. Leenhouwers[1]

[1]*Animal Breeding and Genetics Group, Wageningen Institute of Animal Sciences (WIAS), Wageningen University, PO Box 338, 6700 AH Wageningen, The Netherlands; and* [2]*Institute for Pig Genetics, PO Box 43, 6640 AA Beuningen, The Netherlands*

The pig industry is confronted with substantial losses due to piglet mortality. With 3–8% stillbirths and generally > 10% preweaning mortality, approximately one fifth of all fetuses formed fully at the end of gestation die before weaning. Most of these losses occur in the perinatal period. Overall prenatal development (birth weight) and specific prenatal developmental and maturational processes in late gestation are predisposing factors for perinatal losses. Birth weight and variation in birth weight remain important risk factors for perinatal mortality. Genetic selection against piglet mortality will not necessarily increase birth weight but will affect body composition and proportional organ development. Many maturational processes that occur in late gestation in preparation for extrauterine life, for example specific biochemical changes in the gastrointestinal tract, are influenced by glucocorticosteroids and are, therefore, dependent on maturation of the pituitary–adrenal system. The carbohydrate metabolism of perinatal piglets is related closely to viability in the perinatal period. The prenatal deposition of carbohydrate reserves (glycogen) and prenatal effects on perinatal glucogenic capacity, glucose homeostasis, carbohydrate metabolism and thermostability are reviewed.

Introduction

The pig industry is confronted with substantial losses due to piglet mortality. Approximately one fifth of all fetuses formed fully at the end of gestation die before weaning. Most of these economically important losses occur during the perinatal period, which is the period from the onset of parturition to 2–3 days after completion of parturition. The ability of a piglet to withstand the stresses associated with birth and its competence to adapt to the postnatal environment are crucial to survive this period. Stillbirths and piglets with a low viability at birth reflect both suboptimal prenatal development and pathology associated with parturition. In this review, predisposing factors for perinatal losses that are related to impaired prenatal development and, more generally, to intra- and inter-litter variation in prenatal development, will be discussed. As many of the physiological and biochemical changes in preparation for birth occur during the period of rapid fetal growth in the second half of gestation, emphasis will be on this period. Genetic abnormalities in prenatal development leading to congenital anomalies at birth are relatively unimportant as a cause of perinatal piglet mortality and, therefore, will not be discussed in this review.

Email: tette.vanderlende@alg.vf.wag-ur.nl

Perinatal losses

Stillbirth

On average, 3–8% of all near-term fully grown fetuses are stillborn. Many sow factors influence the number of stillbirths per litter or the probability of stillbirth, including parity, condition of the sow, duration of gestation, total number of piglets in the litter and average birth weight of the litter. Post-mortem examinations indicate that approximately 10% of stillborn piglets died shortly before parturition (late prepartum deaths), approximately 75% died during parturition (intra-partum deaths) and approximately 15% died immediately after expulsion (immediate postpartum deaths) (Glastonbury, 1977; English and Morrison, 1984; J. I. Leenhouwers, unpublished). Piglets in the immediate postpartum category can be identified by the presence of air in their lungs and, strictly speaking, are not stillborn, but in practice are generally recorded as stillbirths.

Very little is known about the causes of prepartum deaths. In a study including 336 purebred litters, prepartum stillborn piglets were heavier on average than non-fresh stillborn, intra-partum stillborn and postpartum stillborn piglets (J. I. Leenhouwers, unpublished). Furthermore, prepartum stillborn piglets were heavier than live-born piglets that died within a day of birth, but were not different in weight from live-born piglets that survived the first day after birth. Although more data are needed to substantiate this observation, this study indicates that late prepartum death is not associated with retarded development but rather with precocious maturation. It is generally accepted that intra-partum and immediate postpartum deaths are predominantly a result of fetal asphyxiation (Sprecher *et al.*, 1974; Stanton and Carroll, 1974). Piglets that were exposed to 95% N_2:5% CO_2 immediately after birth survived < 5 min (Miller and Miller, 1965). Therefore, it can be concluded that, on average, intra-partum stillborn piglets experienced only a relatively short period of anoxia or a somewhat longer period of severe hypoxia. During normal delivery, fetal homeostasis is maintained, even in piglets delivered late in the farrowing order, providing that the umbilical circulation and placental exchange area are not compromised (Randall, 1982). Although cervicotubally directed myometrial contractions occur during farrowing to avoid untimely interruption of the fetal–placental–maternal connections (Taverne *et al.*, 1979), these contractions are obviously not fully effective, as most stillborn piglets occur in the second half of farrowing, often with broken umbilical cords (Randall, 1972a,b). The length of the umbilical cord correlates with the length and birth weight of the piglet, but not with piglet position in the uterus (Randall, 1989a). Zaleski and Hacker (1993) determined variables related to the progress of parturition and the probability of stillbirth, and found that the effect of a broken umbilical cord was additional to the effect of position in the birth order. These authors concluded that the effect of a later position in the birth order on the probability of stillbirth could not be explained only by the increased danger of breaking the cord as distance travelled through the uterus increased.

Early preweaning mortality

Owing to large herd to herd variation in environmental conditions, farrowing systems and management (for example, supervision during the perinatal period), the percentage of live-born piglets that die before weaning may show considerable variation, ranging from 5% to 30%. In most western countries, where labour is expensive and, therefore, the level of supervision at farrowing is generally low, preweaning mortality rates are often > 10%. Approximately 50% or more of all preweaning mortality occurs within 3–4 days after birth, during the period in which the piglet has to recover from the stress of birth and has to adapt to its new environment. In addition, it is generally accepted that a substantial part of the preweaning mortality after the first 3 days of life also results from problems of adaptation and development.

Undersized piglets and piglets with a low viability at birth have a higher probability of dying as a result of trauma, chilling or starvation than do their larger or more viable littermates (English and Smith, 1975; van der Lende and De Jager, 1991). Among the piglets with a low viability at birth are the piglets that suffered anoxia or severe hypoxia during parturition (Sprecher *et al.*, 1974). Although these piglets survive parturition, they may be lethargic or disoriented (Stanton and Carroll, 1974; Svendsen, 1992). They have a reduced ability to adapt to extrauterine life (Herpin *et al.*, 1996) and to compete with their littermates for colostrum at a critical period of life. The degree of anoxia in live-born piglets can be measured by blood lactate concentration (Dawes *et al.*, 1963). English and Smith (1975) found that live-born piglets dying before week 3 of age had a significantly higher average lactate concentration directly after birth than did those surviving at least 3 weeks (383.3 versus 303.0 µg lactate ml^{-1} blood, respectively; $P < 0.01$). According to more recent work by Herpin *et al.* (1999), the lower viability of piglets suffering from asphyxia during delivery is not due to impaired thermoregulatory ability after birth, but may be a consequence of reduced vigour and colostrum intake, and short term alterations in carbohydrate metabolism. As far as reduced vigour is concerned, many pathophysiological consequences of parturient hypoxia have been described, including circulatory, metabolic and neurological disturbances. Effects of parturient hypoxia on the central nervous system may include brain damage. Evidence for cellular injury in the hypoxic brain of perinatal piglets is provided, for example, from the expression of the heat shock protein gene *hsp*72 (Murphy *et al.*, 1996), and DNA fragmentation in different regions of the brain such as the cerebellum, cortex, hippocampus and striatum (David and Grongnet, 2000). The hypoxia-induced metabolic acidosis can cause defects in the brain microvascular endothelial cells, leading to breakdown of the blood–brain barrier (Hsu *et al.*, 1996).

The viability of piglets that suffer anoxia or hypoxia during parturition may also be affected by the secretion of β-endorphin into the fetoplacental circulation in response to the stress of delivery. Chiang and Rodway (1997) found a significant positive correlation between umbilical cord plasma pCO_2 and β-endorphin concentration. The correlation between umbilical cord plasma pH and β-endorphin concentration was significantly negative. β-endorphin is known to induce cardiorespiratory depression (Moss and Scarpelli, 1981). Therefore, the neonatal cardiorespiratory control may be affected in asphyxiated piglets, especially if the β-endorphin concentrations remain high or even increase for some time after birth.

Prenatal development in relation to perinatal mortality

Prenatal growth and birth weight

A large variation between and within litters in overall prenatal development is evident from the substantial variation in birth weight. Birth weight is an important risk factor for perinatal mortality in all breeds studied (for example see Leenhouwers *et al.*, 1999; Roehe and Kalm, 2000; Tuchscherer *et al.*, 2000). Therefore, it is evident that prenatal development is a predisposing factor for perinatal mortality. Birth weight is influenced by sow genotype rather than piglet genotype (Lee and Haley, 1995; Roehe, 1999). An important maternal trait in this respect is uterine capacity. At a given litter size, the fetuses in sows with larger uterine capacities will have an advantage in terms of placental development (mass, vascularity and surface area) compared with fetuses in sows with more limiting uterine capacities. Next to birth weight *per se*, within-litter variation in birth weight is also an important risk factor for piglet mortality (English and Smith, 1975). Within-litter variation in birth weight is largely a result of variation in placental mass (Waldorf *et al.*, 1975; Wise *et al.*, 1997; B. T. T. M. Van Rens, unpublished).

Various studies have shown that pig fetuses with a low weight at onset of farrowing have an increased likelihood of intra-partum death compared with heavier littermates (Björklund *et al.*, 1987; J. I. Leenhouwers, unpublished). On the basis of low body weight of many piglets that died intra-partum and the higher incidence of specific irregularities in the liver, kidneys and thyroid in such piglets, Björklund *et al.* (1987) suggested that at least some intra-partum deaths are related to disturbance in the fetal growth pattern. According to these authors, this contention supports the earlier suggestion of Svendsen (1982) that fetal asphyxiation during farrowing may be "...superimposed upon a prior disease or abnormality of the affected individuals, rendering them incapable of making a successful transition to extrauterine life...".

Birth weight as a risk factor for preweaning mortality is often related to the inability of low birthweight piglets to compete with littermates for colostrum, especially in litters with a large within-litter variation in birth weight (for review see Fraser *et al.*, 1995). In addition, there is evidence that there are developmental differences between low birthweight piglets and their heavier littermates that influence the likelihood of survival after birth. For example, Thornbury *et al.* (1993) found spontaneous necrotizing enterocolitis-like pathological lesions in low birthweight piglets (529–1510 g) of Large White × Landrace crossbred litters, but did not find such lesions in their littermates with average birth weights (1815–2140 g). The lesions were observed mainly in the distal ileum, with mucosal and submucosal necrosis, indicative of ischaemic injury. From a difference in the extent and severity of pathology between the gut and other organs, it was concluded that the processes finally leading to neonatal necrotizing enterocolitis-like lesions in low birthweight piglets had already started *in utero*. A second example comes from the work of Wise *et al.* (1997). These workers found lower cholesterol concentrations in day 104 lightweight fetuses in a white composite breed than in mean weight or heavyweight fetuses. From these studies it was concluded that the high mortality in lightweight piglets might be due not only to inadequate physical maturation and substandard nutrition, but also to inadequate development of the central nervous system. The possibility that inadequate development of the central nervous system might have a role was concluded from the fact that neonatal piglets from pig lines with genetically low cholesterol contents appear to be lethargic at birth and show reduced exploratory behaviour (Schoknecht *et al.*, 1994; Pond and Mersmann, 1995). The exploratory behaviour of low cholesterol piglets can be improved by feeding them additional cholesterol. Although these examples indicate that the developmental differences between low birthweight piglets and their littermates are negative in terms of survival, this is not always the case. The intestinal transmission of immunoglobulins in newborn piglets is of utmost importance for resistance against pathogens during the suckling period and even after weaning. In contrast to what might be expected, Svendsen *et al.* (1990) found that the ability of the small intestine of newborn piglets to transmit macromolecules into lymph and blood is negatively related to birth weight and, to a lesser extent, maturity. Small and immature piglets will generally ingest smaller quantities of colostrum as a result of competition with larger littermates, but probably also due to lower sucking vigour when they do successfully obtain a teat. Their greater ability to transmit macromolecules will compensate at least partially for the negative effect of lower ingestion of colostrum on acquired immunity.

Knowing the importance of birth weight as a risk factor for perinatal and preweaning mortality, strategies to increase birth weight by increasing food intake of sows during gestation or by genetic selection have been investigated and suggested, respectively. Attempts to increase birth weight of piglets by increasing food intake of sows in late gestation have had limited success (Hillyer and Phillips, 1980; Pond *et al.*, 1981; Sterling and Cline, 1986; Miller *et al.*, 2000). As far as the possibilities for genetic selection for birth weight are concerned, geneticists disagree about the correlated effect on piglet survival. Roehe (1999) and Roehe and Kalm (2000) suggested that direct selection for increased individual birth weight could increase piglet vitality. In contrast, Knol (2001) evaluated different selection strategies for improved piglet survival and concluded that selection for increased individual birth weight will not significantly increase piglet survival. Direct selection for piglet survival is possible but will affect body composition rather than birth weight. Effects on birth weight, although small, will probably be negative rather than positive (Knol, 2001). This seems contradictory to the accepted positive relationship between birth weight and piglet survival. However, within genetic lines and within litters this positive relationship may hold true, but between genetic lines, negative relationships between birth weight and piglet survival have been documented (Mersmann *et al.*, 1984; Kerr and Cameron, 1995).

Specific developmental and maturational processes

Much information is available about specific aspects of prenatal development, such as the development of specific organs (liver: Bielańska-Osuchowska, 1996; small intestine: Sangild *et al.*, 1995; Buddington and Malo, 1996; Sangild *et al.*, 2000; stomach: Sangild *et al.*, 1991), specific endocrine systems (adrenal/corticosteroid status: Kattesh *et al.*, 1997; thyroid/thyroid hormone status: Berthon *et al.*, 1993) and specific body tissues (fat deposits: Martin *et al.*, 1998). However, it is seldom clear how much variation there is within a population in any specific development and whether this variation merely reflects variation in fetal growth or also body weight-independent variation. As a consequence, little is known about the relative importance of weight-dependent and weight-independent variations in specific prenatal developmental patterns or processes as predisposing factors for perinatal mortality. A good example in this respect is our current knowledge about the prenatal development of the gastrointestinal tract. Maturational changes in the gastrointestinal tracts of fetal pigs during the weeks before birth have been studied intensively (for review see Sangild *et al.*, 2000). Changes that are important for the shift from parenteral nutrition before birth to enteral nutrition after birth include the production and activation of various enzymes involved in digestion (for example, prochymosin and pepsinogen A (Sangild, 1995), and intestinal brush-border disaccharidases and peptidases (Sangild *et al.*, 1995)). Despite the information now available, little is known about the early postnatal consequences of the observed between-piglet variation in enzyme activities for the survival and growth of piglets.

The pituitary–adrenal system. The maturation of the pituitary–adrenal axis in late gestation is essential for preparation of the fetus for the transition from intrauterine to extrauterine life. Experiments with corticotrophin-releasing hormone-deficient mice indicate strongly that the major role of glucocorticosteroids is during fetal rather than postnatal life (Muglia *et al.*, 1995). The glucocorticosteroids, cortisol and corticosterone, are important endocrine factors involved in the maturation of thyroid, lung, gastrointestinal tract, liver, kidney, brain and haemopoietic and lymphatic systems (for review see Liggins, 1994). The role of cortisol in the development and maturation of the gastrointestinal tract of fetal pigs has been reviewed by Sangild *et al.* (2000). The late prepartum increase in circulating fetal cortisol concentrations affects not only the growth and structure of the gastrointestinal tract, but also the concentrations of disaccharidase enzymes, peptidase enzymes and gastrointestinal hormones. Furthermore, it has a positive effect on the absorption of nutrients from colostrum. From studies in various species it is evident that glucocorticosteroids accelerate the morphological,

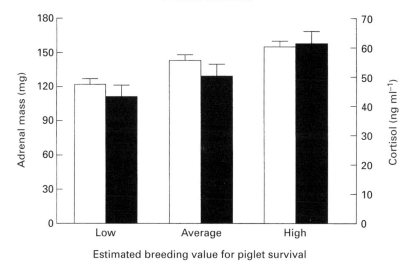

Fig. 1. Adrenal masses (□) and plasma cortisol concentrations (■) of late gestational pig fetuses with different breeding values for piglet survival. Both adrenal mass and cortisol concentration showed a significant positive linear relationship (P < 0.05) with the estimated breeding value for piglet survival (J. I. Leenhouwers, unpublished).

physiological and biochemical maturation of fetal lungs (for reviews see Gross, 1990; Hume *et al.*, 1996). Studies in pigs confirm the important role of cortisol in maturation of the lungs of fetal pigs (Ledwozyw, 1989). From research with rats it is clear that the combined effects of alveolar fluid dilation and glucocorticosteroids might co-ordinate the increased production of lung surfactant as birth approaches (Torday *et al.*, 1998).

Our current knowledge about the development and maturation of the pig hypothalamus–pituitary–adrenal axis is limited. The absolute and proportional masses of the adrenal glands in day 112–113 hypophysectomized fetuses were on average significantly lower (69.5 mg and 5.9 mg (100 g body weight)$^{-1}$, respectively) than in intact controls (154.5 mg and 15.0 mg (100 g body weight)$^{-1}$; Randall, 1989b). There were significant correlations between basal values of corticotrophin (ACTH) and cortisol in fetal plasma between day 70 and day 100 ($r = 0.47$) and between days 95–100 and delivery at days 111–114 ($r = 0.81$). The slope of the regression line was significantly higher for the latter period (Silver and Fowden, 1989). The results of Randall (1989b) and Silver and Fowden (1989) indicate pituitary control of fetal adrenal growth and activity, and an increased response of the adrenal to a given concentration of ACTH in late gestation.

There is large variation among pig fetuses in the responsiveness of adrenals to ACTH after day 103 of gestation (Randall *et al.*, 1990), and also in plasma cortisol concentrations on all days during the last weeks of gestation (Randall, 1983; Kattesh *et al.*, 1997). It is unclear to what extent this variation in responsiveness results in variation in fetal maturation and in piglet viability and adaptability after birth. Recently, significant positive relationships have been identified between the genetic merit (estimated breeding value) of piglets for survival and their adrenal masses, as well as plasma cortisol concentrations, at day 111 ± 1 of gestation (J. I. Leenhouwers, unpublished) (Fig. 1).

The pituitary–thyroid system. Thyroid hormones have an important role in maintaining and regulating thermogenesis (Dauncey, 1990). Immediately after expulsion, newborn piglets are confronted with a temperature that is 15–20°C lower than the intrauterine temperature. The consequential rapid cooling of the still wet, poorly insulated piglet is often associated with a temporary decrease in body temperature and induces vigorous thermogenic responses. The pituitary–thyroid system of piglets is well matured at birth (Ślebodziński, 1988). An important role for thyroid hormones in the control of thermogenesis in this period has been suggested by Berthon *et al.* (1993). In their experiments, newborn piglets with induced hypothyroidism during late fetal life had a significantly larger decrease in rectal temperature and a significantly reduced maximal heat production than did control piglets. An early postnatal surge of thyroxine, total 3,5,3′-triiodothyronine and free triiodothyronine occurred in both the hypothyroid and control piglets. During the prenatal period, in the constant thermoneutral environment of the uterus, low concentrations of thyroid hormones are necessary to maintain basal fetal metabolism. During late gestation, the thyroid must grow and develop the potential for the increased demand of thyroid hormones to sustain the increase in metabolic rate for thermostability after birth. According to Liggins (1994), the conflict between low prenatal and high postnatal demand is resolved in the following two ways. Firstly, the thyroid maintains a relatively high rate of secretion of thyroxine, but deiodination of thyroxine is predominantly to the biologically inactive reverse form of triiodothyronine rather than to triiodothyronine. Secondly, the placenta maintains a high rate of metabolic clearance of triiodothyronine.

Comparison of prenatal organ development in piglets with known differences in genetic merit for piglet survival

Experimentally, it is very difficult to relate variation in prenatal organ development to perinatal survival or preweaning survival. Therefore, fetal development was investigated in relation to the genetic merit of piglets to survive from the onset of parturition to weaning. Within a large breeding population in which stillbirth, preweaning mortality and individual birth weight have been registered accurately for many years in approximately 40 000 litters, the breeding values for piglet survival of all animals in the population were calculated (Knol, 2001). Knol (2001) showed that the actual difference in piglet survival between litters with a low versus a high estimated breeding value for piglet survival is almost equal to the expected difference as calculated from the breeding values. Regression coefficients of realised survival on predicted survival were close to the expected value of 1.0. A study of organ development on day 111 ± 1 of gestation using litters of known breeding values for piglet survival (J. I. Leenhouwers, unpublished) revealed positive relationships of this genetic merit with proportional masses (g kg^{-1} body weight) of liver ($P = 0.02$), small intestine ($P = 0.02$) and stomach ($P = 0.07$). The proportional length of the small intestine (cm kg^{-1} body weight) was also related positively to the genetic merit for piglet survival ($P = 0.08$). The proportional masses of heart, lung, spleen and kidney were not related to genetic merit for piglet survival. Both the liver glycogen concentration (mg g^{-1} wet weight) and the total amount of glycogen in the liver increased with increasing genetic merit for piglet survival ($P = 0.07$ and $P = 0.05$, respectively), as did the fat content of the carcasses of the fetuses ($P = 0.05$). No relationships with genetic merit for piglet survival were found for protein, ash and moisture content of the carcasses. Overall, these results indicate that piglets with a high genetic merit for survival are more mature at birth and better prepared for adaptation to extrauterine life than are piglets with a low genetic merit.

Prenatal effects on glycogen reserves, glucose homeostasis and carbohydrate metabolism in the perinatal period

As the carbohydrate metabolism of perinatal piglets is related closely to piglet viability in the perinatal period (for example see Stanton and Mueller, 1973), prenatal deposition of carbohydrate reserves (glycogen) and prenatal effects on perinatal glucogenic capacity, glucose homeostasis, carbohydrate metabolism and thermostability have received much attention.

Prenatal glycogen deposition

Glycogen is the main storage polysaccharide of animal cells. This polysaccharide of D-glucose in α(1,4) linkage is highly branched. The branches occur every 8–12 glucose residues and the branch linkages are α(1,6). The glycogen reserves of piglets at the onset of parturition, for example in heart, liver and muscle, have various important roles in carbohydrate metabolism in the perinatal period. Glycogen accounts for 60–70% of the total readily available energy reserves (Mellor and Cockburn, 1986). Heart glycogen is important for resistance against anoxia during farrowing (Dawes et al., 1959; Mott, 1961; Shelley, 1961). Liver glycogen is crucial for maintaining glucose homeostasis during parturition and the immediate postpartum period, and in situations of late or low colostrum ingestion. Owing to a lack of glucose 6-phosphatase in muscles and heart, muscle and heart glycogen reserves do not have a role in glucose homeostasis. Muscle glycogen reserves primarily have a function in postnatal thermogenesis, especially in the early neonatal period before colostrum consumption and in later periods of inadequate energy intake. The absence of functional brown adipose tissue in piglets as a readily available source for early neonatal thermogenesis (Trayhurn et al., 1989) and the initial inability of neonatal piglets to use fat for this purpose indicate further the importance of glycogen reserves for postnatal thermostability.

By the end of gestation, approximately 88% of all glycogen in fetal piglets can be found in the carcass (mainly skeletal muscle), approximately 11% in the liver and the remaining 1% in heart (0.4%), lung (0.5%) and kidneys (0.1%) (Okai et al., 1978). Deposition of liver glycogen starts as early as day 60 of gestation. The rate of increase of the total amount of liver glycogen (Fig. 2) is initially low but increases rapidly after day 80 of gestation and even more so after day 100 of gestation (Randall and L'Ecuyer, 1976; Okai et al., 1978; Fowden et al., 1995). Ultrastructural and stereological investigation of hepatocytes of developing fetuses have also indicated that the late prepartum period is the period of glycogen accumulation in the liver (Bielańska-Osuchowska, 1996). Deposition of glycogen in skeletal muscle may begin earlier (Randall and L'Ecuyer, 1976), and the pattern of deposition in the carcass is similar to that in the liver (Randall and L'Ecuyer, 1976; Okai et al., 1978). In several species investigated (guinea-pig, rabbit, sheep and rhesus monkey), the cardiac glycogen content (mg g^{-1} wet weight) reaches its highest values before the last third of gestation and decreases thereafter (Shelley, 1961). However, in pigs, the cardiac glycogen content (Fig. 2) appears to remain fairly constant throughout the second half of gestation (Randall and L'Ecuyer, 1976; Okai et al., 1978). As the mass of the heart increases during this period, the total amount of cardiac glycogen increases from only a few to > 200 mg (Okai et al., 1978). In the lungs, glycogen concentrations are highest at about day 80 of gestation (Fig. 2) and decrease to very low concentrations at birth (Randall and L'Ecuyer, 1976; Okai et al., 1978). Glycogen in fetal lung tissue is concentrated in the fetal alveolar epithelium and the decrease in lung glycogen concentrations towards birth is associated with the loss of this epithelium (Shelley, 1961).

Control of prenatal glycogen synthesis

The enzymes involved in the synthesis of glycogen from glucose are hexokinase, phosphoglucomutase, UDP glucose pyrophosphorylase, glycogen synthetase and branching enzyme. Branching enzyme is involved in the formation of mature glycogen from the

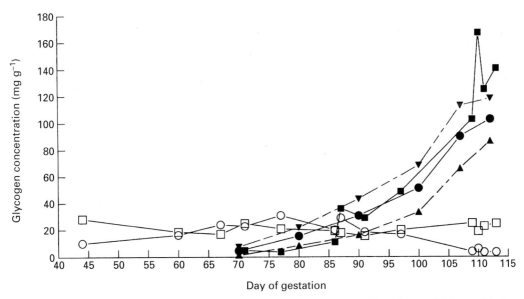

Fig. 2. Changes in liver, lung and heart glycogen concentrations in prenatal pig fetuses (□: heart, Okai *et al.*, 1978; ○: lung, Okai *et al.*, 1978; ■: liver, Okai *et al.*, 1978; ●: liver, Randall and L'Ecuyer, 1976; ▲ and ▼: maximum and minimum liver glycogen concentrations, respectively Randall and L'Ecuyer, 1976).

glycogen α(1,4) polymer. The rate-limiting enzyme in glycogen synthesis is glycogen synthetase. There are two forms of glycogen synthetase: the 'a' form (active form) and the 'b' form (inactive form) (Hers *et al.*, 1969). The interconversion of these two forms is achieved by phosphorylation (inactivation) and dephosphorylation (activation) and can be influenced by glucocorticosteroids (De Wulf *et al.*, 1968).

Our current knowledge about the control of glycogen deposition in fetal pigs is incomplete. The large increase in liver glycogen deposition during the last weeks of gestation coincides with the prepartum increase in circulating fetal glucocorticosteroid concentrations. Evidence that cortisol is involved in glycogen deposition comes from experiments in which cortisol was infused into intact (Fowden *et al.*, 1985, 1995) or hypophysectomized (Randall, 1987, 1988) pig fetuses. Fowden *et al.* (1985) showed that hepatic glycogen deposition could be stimulated by cortisol well before the normal increase in prepartum deposition. Furthermore, it has been shown that 6 days of s.c. cortisol infusion into fetal pigs, starting at days 82–84 or 92–94 of gestation, significantly increases the already ongoing hepatic glycogen deposition (Fowden *et al.*, 1995). Although the experiment of Randall (1988) with chronically catheterized hypophysectomized fetal pigs confirmed that cortisol is an important stimulant for liver glycogen deposition, other hormones may be necessary for maximal response, especially in muscle glycogen deposition. For example, insulin may be involved. Chronic hyperinsulinaemia in euglycaemic pig fetuses increases both liver and muscle glycogen concentrations (Garssen *et al.*, 1983).

Knowledge about the regulation of glycogen synthesis in other species confirms the role of glucocorticosteroids in liver glycogen synthesis (Liggins, 1994) and also indicates other hormones that may be involved. Hepatic glycogen deposition in sheep is stimulated by endogenous placental lactogen (Schoknecht *et al.*, 1996) and is mediated through binding to specific placental lactogen receptors (Freemark and Handwerger, 1986). A role for placental lactogens in pigs is not likely, as at present there is no evidence for the production of lactogenic factors by pig placenta. Studies in other species have also indicated the involvement of growth factors in prenatal glycogen deposition. In a study with insulin-like growth factor II (IGF-II)-deficient mice, Lopez _et al._ (1999) showed that IGF-II is involved in the regulation of glycogen synthesis. These authors suggested that IGF-II might operate through stimulation of glycogen synthetase activity. The role of IGF-II on glycogen deposition in fetal pigs has, to our knowledge, not been investigated, but indirect evidence indicates that its role may be either small or facilitating. The IGF-II concentration in fetal pigs is relatively low ($\pm$ 125 ng ml^{-1}) and increases after birth (Peng _et al._, 1996). Hypophysectomy of fetal pigs did not appear to affect serum and tissue IGF-II concentrations (Latimer _et al._, 1993), but decreased the amount of glycogen in liver (from 7.2 $\pm$ 0.6 to 2.0 $\pm$ 0.5% wet weight) and skeletal muscle (from 6.1 $\pm$ 0.3 to 3.0 $\pm$ 0.5% wet weight) at days 103–108 of gestation (Randall, 1988). Infusion of cortisol in these hypophysectomized fetuses between day 100 and day 104 of gestation increased the liver and skeletal muscle glycogen concentrations (+112% and +44%, respectively). However, these concentrations were still below the concentrations in intact fetuses (Randall, 1988). These results indicate at most a limited role for IGF-II in glycogen synthesis in pig fetuses, but the possibility that the presence of IGF-II may be necessary for the effect of cortisol cannot be ruled out.

Manipulating prenatal glycogen deposition

Glycogen reserves of piglets at birth can be influenced by restricting the feed intake of sows during late gestation (Elliot and Lodge, 1977; Ojamaa _et al._, 1980) or by feeding sows additional energy during late gestation (Seerley _et al._, 1974; Coffey _et al._, 1982; Seerley, 1989). Elliot and Lodge (1977) and Ojamaa _et al._ (1980) restricted the feed intake of sows and gilts from day 100 and day 87 of gestation, respectively, and observed negative effects on liver glycogen concentrations (–19.3% and –7.9%, respectively) relative to controls. Muscle glycogen concentration was hardly affected in the study of Elliot and Lodge (1977) but was slightly decreased (–6% relative to controls) in the study of Ojamaa _et al._ (1980). Both studies were performed with relatively low numbers of experimental animals and no information on piglet survival was reported in either study. Seerley _et al._ (1974) fed sows additional cornstarch or corn oil from day 109 of gestation and found higher glycogen concentrations (mg g^{-1} wet tissue) in liver (on average +12%) and longissimus muscle (on average +16%) in both groups compared with the control group. All increases were significant except that of the liver glycogen content in the group fed additional corn oil. Nevertheless, this increase was comparable to that in the group fed with cornstarch. In the study of Seerley (1989), piglets of sows fed additional fat from day 80 (5% added solid fat pellets) or day 100 (10% added solid fat pellets) of gestation were compared with those of sows fed the same diet without additional fat. In both experimental groups, the liver glycogen concentration increased significantly by 16% and the total amount of liver glycogen increased by 41%. These results are in agreement with the results of Coffey _et al._ (1982), who found 11–23% higher piglet liver glycogen concentrations in sows fed additional animal fat compared with sows fed additional cornstarch. In the studies of Seerley _et al._ (1974) and Seerley (1989), the increased glycogen reserves in the experimental groups had only a small positive effect on piglet survival. In the corn oil group of the study by Seerley _et al._ (1974), a significantly higher percentage of piglets weighing < 1.0 kg at birth survived to day 21 compared with the control group. In an experiment by Boyd _et al._ (1978a,b) in which gilts were fed additional tallow or cornstarch from day 100 of gestation, no significant effects on fetal liver glycogen were found relative to the control group (Boyd _et al._, 1978a), but survival until day 14 after parturition among piglets weighing < 1.0 kg at birth was also increased significantly (mortality rates: tallow group:

46.3%; cornstarch group: 57.1%; control group: 72.5%; Boyd *et al.*, 1978b). Effects of sow nutrition in late gestation on the survival of piglets weighing < 1.0 kg have also been found by Okai *et al.* (1977), but these authors did not report data on piglet liver glycogen content.

Prenatal effects on glucose concentrations in the perinatal period

Blood glucose concentrations in fetal pigs remain relatively constant until the end of gestation and increase rapidly during or after expulsion of the piglet (Randall, 1982). This increase is almost certainly a result of increased secretion of catecholamines (adrenaline and noradrenaline). Injections of adrenaline or noradrenaline in newborn piglets increased plasma glucose concentrations in a dose-dependent manner, although adrenaline had a larger effect than noradrenaline (Stanton and Mueller, 1973). The timing of the rapid increase in blood glucose concentration is related to the course of expulsion. In normal deliveries, the increase occurs as late as several minutes after expulsion. In deliveries associated with asphyxiation, a rapid increase is observed during expulsion. Herpin *et al.* (1996) showed a curvilinear relationship between the glucose concentration of the piglet immediately after expulsion and the extent of asphyxia during delivery. The earlier increase in glucose concentrations in asphyxiated piglets may prevent or at least reduce the pathophysiological effects of hypoxia on the brain (McGowan *et al.*, 1995).

In addition to the progress of farrowing, perinatal blood glucose concentrations in piglets are also affected by the glucose tolerance of the sow during late gestation. Variation in glucose tolerance of apparently normal sows was recognized as early as the late nineteenth century (see Bunding *et al.*, 1956). As in many other mammalian species, the glucose tolerance in sows is affected adversely by gestation and results in a diabetogenic state of the dam (George *et al.*, 1978; Bouillon-Hausman *et al.*, 1986; Schaefer *et al.*, 1988; Schaefer *et al.*, 1991; Kemp *et al.*, 1996; Père *et al.*, 2000). The available data show that the diabetogenic state of sows increases with the stage of gestation (George *et al.*, 1978; Père *et al.*, 2000) and indicate that, for a given day of gestation, the glucose tolerance varies largely among individual sows (George *et al.*, 1978; Kemp *et al.*, 1996). Fetuses developing in diabetogenic sows with mild hyperglycaemia are both hyperglycaemic and hyperinsulinaemic. As soon as the piglet is expelled and maternal glucose is no longer maintaining high glucose concentrations in the blood of the piglet, the high piglet insulin concentrations are maintained by its hyperplasic pancreatic islets of Langerhans. Although the piglets are born hyperglycaemic, they soon become hypoglycaemic for some time (Phillips *et al.*, 1980). This transient hypoglycaemia leads to reduced vigour, suboptimal colostrum intake and chilling, thereby increasing the risk of mortality. Under normal practical conditions in a well-managed pig unit, Kemp *et al.* (1996) found a significant increase in piglet mortality rate until day 7 after farrowing with an increase in the preparturient diabetogenic state of the dam. As piglets from diabetogenic sows have larger glycogen reserves (Ezekwe *et al.*, 1984), they may have a better ability to withstand long-term adverse conditions after they have survived the short-term hypoglycaemia. In agreement with this, Kasser *et al.* (1982) found that newborn piglets of alloxan-induced diabetogenic sows had a better ability to survive long-term (> 36 h) fasting at 32°C than did piglets from control (non-alloxan-treated) sows kept at the same temperature. Thus, the overall effect of the degree of glucose tolerance of the sow during late gestation on the perinatal survival rate will probably depend on the nutritional state of the piglets and on the ambient temperature.

To our knowledge, it is still unknown whether fetal hyperglycaemia in late gestation of pigs may affect specific fetal maturational processes and, thus, influence early neonatal viability. Work in other species indicates negative effects of fetal hyperglycaemia during the later stages

T. van der Lende et al.

of gestation on lung maturation. For example, in sheep, chronic hyperglycaemia with secondary hyperinsulinaemia inhibits the maturational response of fetal lungs to cortisol (Warburton, 1983). In streptozotocin-diabetic rats, the ensuing fetal hyperglycaemia, in the absence of hyperinsulinaemia, was also associated with delayed lung maturation. The lungs showed a decrease in surfactant phospholipid synthesis, decreased surfactant apoprotein and a decrease in the activity and mRNA of Na^+, K^+-ATPase (Warshaw, 1990). On the basis of the knowledge currently available (for example see Bourbon and Farrell, 1985), it can be concluded that hyperglycaemia has direct effects on lung maturation (for example see Warshaw, 1990), as well as indirect effects through secondary hyperinsulinaemia (for example see Engle *et al.*, 1983; Biasini *et al.*, 1994).

References

Berthon D, Herpin P, Duchamp C, Dauncey MJ and Le Dividich J (1993) Modification of thermogenic capacity in neonatal pigs by changes in thyroid status during late gestation *Journal of Developmental Physiology* **19** 253–261

Biasini A, Casadei G and Cerasoli G (1994) Il figlio di madre diabetica *Minerva Endocrinologica* **19** 91–94

Bielańska-Osuchowska Z (1996) Ultrastructural and stereological studies of hepatocytes in prenatal development of swine *Folia Morphologica (Warsz.)* **55** 1–19

Björklund N-E, Svendsen J and Svendsen LS (1987) Histomorphological studies of the perinatal pig: comparison of five mortality groups with unaffected pigs *Acta Veterinaria Scandinavica* **28** 105–116

Bouillon-Hausman D, Kasser TR, Seerley RW and Martin RJ (1986) Studies of gestational diabetes using the pig as a model. In *Swine in Biomedical Research Volume 1* pp 561–572 Ed. ME Tumbleson. Plenum Press, New York

Bourbon JR and Farrell PM (1985) Fetal lung development in the diabetic pregnancy *Pediatric Research* **19** 253–267

Boyd RD, Moser BD, Peo ER and Cunningham PJ (1978a) Effect of energy source prior to parturition and during lactation on tissue lipid, liver glycogen and plasma levels of some metabolites in the newborn pig *Journal of Animal Science* **47** 874–882

Boyd RD, Moser BD, Peo ER and Cunningham PJ (1978b) Effect of energy source prior to parturition and during lactation on piglet survival and growth and on milk lipids *Journal of Animal Science* **47** 883–892

Buddington RK and Malo C (1996) Intestinal brush-border membrane enzyme activities and transport functions during prenatal development of pigs *Journal of Pediatric Gastroenterology and Nutrition* **23** 51–64

Bunding IM, Davenport ME and Schooley MA (1956) The glucose tolerance test in swine and its implications *Journal of Animal Science* **15** 234–241

Chiang FE and Rodway RG (1997) Determinations of umbilical cord β-endorphin concentration and blood gas parameters in newborn piglets *Research in Veterinary Science* **63** 107–111

Coffey MT, Seerley RW, Martin RJ and Mabry JW (1982) Effect of level, source and duration of feeding of supplemental energy in sow diets on metabolic and hormonal traits related to energy utilization in the baby pig *Journal of Animal Science* **55** 329–336

Dauncey MJ (1990) Thyroid hormones and thermogenesis *Proceedings of the Nutrition Society* **49** 203–215

David J-C and Grongnet J-F (2000) Effect of hypoxia on DNA fragmentation in different brain regions of the newborn piglet *Molecular Reproduction and Development* **57** 153–158

Dawes GS, Mott JC and Shelley HJ (1959) The importance of cardiac glycogen for the maintenance of life in foetal lambs and new-born animals during anoxia *Journal of Physiology* **146** 516–538

Dawes GS, Jacobson HN, Mott JC, Shelley HJ and Stafford A (1963) The treatment of asphyxiated, mature, foetal lambs and rhesus monkeys with intravenous glucose and sodium carbonate *Journal of Physiology, London* **169** 167–184

De Wulf H, Stalmans W and Hers HG (1968) The influence of inorganic phosphate, adenosine triphosphate and glucose 6-phosphate on the activity of liver glycogen synthetase *European Journal of Biochemistry* **6** 545–551

Elliot JI and Lodge GA (1977) Body composition and glycogen reserves in the neonatal pig during the first 96 hours postpartum *Canadian Journal of Animal Science* **57** 141–150

Engle MJ, Langan SM and Sanders RL (1983) The effects of insulin and hyperglycaemia on surfactant phospholipid sunthesis in organotypic cultures of type II pneumocytes *Biochimica et Biophysica Acta* **753** 6–13

English PR and Morrison V (1984) Causes and prevention of piglet mortality *Pig News and Information* **5** 369–376

English PR and Smith WJ (1975) Some causes of death in neonatal piglets *The Veterinary Annual* **15** 95–104

Ezekwe MO, Ezekwe EI, Sen DK and Ogolla F (1984) Effects of maternal streptozotocin-diabetes on fetal growth, energy reserves and body composition of newborn pigs *Journal of Animal Science* **59** 974–980

Fowden AL, Comline RS and Silver M (1985) The effects of cortisol on the concentration of glycogen in different tissues in the chronically catheterized fetal pig *Quarterly Journal of Experimental Physiology* **70** 23–35

Fowden AL, Apatu RSK and Silver M (1995) The glucogenic capacity of the fetal pig: developmental regulation by cortisol *Experimental Physiology* **80** 457–467

Fraser D, Phillips PA, Thompson BK, Pajor EA, Weary DM and Braithwaite LA (1995) Behavioural aspects of piglet survival and growth. In *The Neonatal Pig: Development and Survival* pp 287–312 Ed. MA Varley. CAB International, Wallingford

Freemark M and Handwerger S (1986) The glycogenic effects of placental lactogen and growth hormone in ovine fetal liver are mediated through binding to specific fetal ovine placental lactogen receptors *Endocrinology* **118** 613–618

Garssen GJ, Spencer GSG, Colenbrander B, Macdonald AA and Hill DJ (1983) Lack of effect of chronic hyper-insulinaemia on growth and body composition in the fetal pig *Biology of the Neonate* **44** 234–242

George PB, England DC, Siers DG and Stanton HC (1978) Diabetogenic effects of pregnancy in sows on plasma glucose and insulin release *Journal of Animal Science* **46** 1694–1700

Glastonbury JRW (1977) Preweaning mortality in the pig. Pathological findings in piglets dying before and during parturition *Australian Veterinary Journal* **53** 282–286

Gross I (1990) Regulation of fetal lung maturation *American Journal of Physiology* **259** L337–L344

Herpin P, Le Dividich J, Hulin JC, Fillaut M, De Marco F and Bertin R (1996) Effects of the level of asphyxia during delivery on viability at birth and early postnatal vitality of newborn pigs *Journal of Animal Science* **74** 2067–2075

Herpin P, Wosiak F, Le Dividich J and Bertin R (1999) Effects of acute asphyxia at birth on subsequent heat production capacity in newborn pigs *Research in Veterinary Science* **66** 45–49

Hers HG, De Wulf H, Stalmans W and Van den Berghe G (1969) The control of glycogen synthesis in the liver *Advances in Enzyme Regulation* **8** 171–190

Hillyer GM and Phillips P (1980) The effect of increasing feed level to sows and gilts in late pregnancy on subsequent litter size, litter weight and maternal body-weight change *Animal Production* **30** 469 (Abstract)

Hsu P, Haffner J, Albuquerque MLC and Leffler CW (1996) pH$_i$ in piglet cerebral microvascular endothelial cells: recovery from an acid load *Proceedings of the Society for Experimental Biology and Medicine* **212** 256–262

Hume R, Conner C and Gilmour M (1996) Lung maturation *Proceedings of the Nutrition Society* **55** 529–542

Kasser TR, Gahagan JH and Martin RJ (1982) Fetal hormones and neonatal survival in response to altered maternal serum glucose and free fatty acid concentrations in pigs *Journal of Animal Science* **55** 1351–1359

Kattesh HG, Baumbach GA, Gillespie BB, Schneider JF and Murai JT (1997) Distribution between protein-bound and free forms of plasma cortisol in the gilt and fetal pig near term *Biology of the Neonate* **72** 192–200

Kemp B, Soede NM, Vesseur PC, Helmond FA, Spoorenberg JH and Frankena K (1996) Glucose tolerance of pregnant sows is related to postnatal pig mortality *Journal of Animal Science* **74** 879–885

Kerr JC and Cameron ND (1995) Reproductive perform-ance of pigs selected for components of efficient lean growth *Animal Science* **60** 281–290

Knol EF (2001) *Genetic Aspects of Piglet Survival* PhD thesis, Wageningen University

Latimer AM, Hausman GJ, McCusker RH and Buonomo FC (1993) The effects of thyroxine on serum and tissue concentrations of insulin-like growth factors (IGF-I and –II) and IGF-binding proteins in the fetal pig *Endo-crinology* **133** 1312–1319

Ledwozyw A (1989) Changes in the content of lung surfactant phospholipid and fatty acid in pigs during ontogenesis and in a nearly post-natal period *Medycyna Weterynaryjna* **45** 369–374

Lee GJ and Haley CS (1995) Comparative farrowing to weaning performance in Meishan and Large White pigs and their crosses *Animal Science* **60** 269–280

Leenhouwers JI, van der Lende T and Knol EF (1999) Analysis of stillbirth in different lines of pig *Livestock Production Science* **57** 243–253

Liggins GC (1994) The role of cortisol in preparing the fetus for birth *Reproduction, Fertility and Development* **6** 141–150

Lopez MF, Dikkes P, Zurakowski D, Villa-Komaroff L and Majzoub JA (1999) Regulation of hepatic glycogen in the insulin-like growth factor II-deficient mouse *Endo-crinology* **140** 1442–1448

McGowan JE, Marro PJ, Mishra OP and Delivoria-Papadopoulos M (1995) Brain cell membrane function during hypoxia in hyperglycemic newborn piglets *Pediatric Research* **37** 133–139

Martin RJ, Hausman GJ and Hausman DB (1998) Regulation of adipose cell development *in utero*. *Proceedings of the Society for Experimental Biology and Medicine* **219** 200–210

Mellor DJ and Cockburn F (1986) A comparison of energy metabolism in the newborn infant, piglet and lamb *Quarterly Journal of Experimental Physiology* **71** 361–379

Mersmann HJ, Pond WG, Stone RT, Yen JT and Lindvall RN (1984) Factors affecting growth and survival of neonatal genetically obese and lean swine: cross fostering experi-ments *Growth* **84** 209–220

Miller HM, Foxcroft GR and Aherne FX (2000) Increasing food intake in late gestation improved sow condition throughout lactation but did not affect piglet viability or growth rate *Animal Science* **71** 141–148

Miller JA and Miller FS (1965) Studies on prevention of brain damage in asphyxia *Developmental Medicine and Child Neurology* **7** 607–619

Moss IR and Scarpelli EM (1981) β-Endorphin: central depression of respiration and circulation *Journal of Applied Physiology* **50** 1011–1016

Mott JC (1961) The ability of young mammals to withstand total oxygen lack *British Medical Bulletin* **17** 144–148

Muglia L, Jacobson L, Dikkes P and Majzoub JA (1995) Corticotropin-releasing hormone deficiency reveals major fetal but not adult glucocorticoid need *Nature* **373** 427–432

Murphy SJ, Song D, Welsh FA, Wilson DF and Pastuzko A (1996) The effect of hypoxia and catecholamines on regional expression of heat-shock protein-72 mRNA in neonatal piglet brain *Brain Research* **727** 145–152

Ojamaa KM, Elliot JI and Hartsock TG (1980) Effects of gestation feeding level on glycogen reserves and blood parameters in the newborn pig *Journal of Animal Science* **51** 620–628

Okai DB, Aherne FX and Hardin RT (1977) Effects of sow nutrition in late gestation on the body composition and survival of the neonatal pig *Canadian Journal of Animal Science* **57** 439–448

Okai DB, Wyllie D, Aherne FX and Ewan RC (1978) Glycogen reserves in the fetal and newborn pig *Journal of Animal Science* **46** 391–401

Peng M, Pelletier G, Palin M-F, Véronneau S, LeBel D and Abribat T (1996) Ontogeny of IGFs and IGFBPs mRNA levels and tissue concentrations in liver, kidney and skeletal muscle of pig *Growth, Development and Aging* **60** 171–187

Père MC, Etienne M and Dourmad JY (2000) Adaptations of glucose metabolism in multiparous sows: effects of pregnancy and feeding level *Journal of Animal Science* **78** 2933–2941

Phillips RW, Panepinto LM, Will DH and Case GL (1980) The effects of alloxan diabetes on Yucatan miniature swine and their progeny *Metabolism* **29** 40–45

Pond WG and Mersmann HJ (1995) Genetically diverse pig models in nutrition research related to lipoprotein and cholesterol metabolism. In *International Symposia of Swine in Biomedical Research* pp 843–864 Eds M Tumbelson and L Schook. Plenum Press, New York

Pond WG, Yen JT, Maurer RR and Christenson RK (1981) Effect of doubling daily energy intake during the last two weeks of pregnancy on pig birth weight, survival and weaning weight *Journal of Animal Science* **52** 535–541

Randall GCB (1972a) Observations on parturition in the sow. I. Factors associated with the delivery of the piglets and their subsequent behaviour *Veterinary Record* **90** 178–182

Randall GCB (1972b) Observations on parturition in the sow. II. Factors influencing stillbirth and perinatal mortality *Veterinary Record* **90** 183–186

Randall GCB (1982) Changes in fetal and maternal blood at the end of pregnancy and during parturition in the pig *Research in Veterinary Science* **32** 278–282

Randall GCB (1983) Changes in the concentrations of corticosteroids in the blood of fetal pigs and their dams during late gestation and labor *Biology of Reproduction* **29** 1077–1084

Randall GCB (1987) Effect of hypophysectomy on tissue glycogen concentrations in the fetal pig *Biology of the Neonate* **52** 174–180

Randall GCB (1988) Tissue glycogen concentrations in hypophysectomized pig fetuses following infusion with cortisol *Journal of Developmental Physiology* **10** 77–83

Randall GCB (1989a) Form and development of the umbilical cord in pigs and their association with delivery of viable pigs *American Journal of Veterinary Research* **50** 1512–1515

Randall GCB (1989b) Effect of hypophysectomy on body and organ weights and subsequent development in the fetal pig *Canadian Journal of Animal Science* **69** 655–661

Randall GCB and L'Ecuyer C (1976) Tissue glycogen and blood glucose and fructose levels in the pig fetus during the second half of gestation *Biology of the Neonate* **28** 74–82

Randall GCB, Kendall JZ, Tsang BK and Taverne MAM

(1990) Endocrine changes following infusion of fetal pigs with corticotropin in litters of reduced numbers *Animal Reproduction Science* **23** 109–122

Roehe R (1999) Genetic determination of individual birth weight and its association with sow productivity traits using Bayesian analyses *Journal of Animal Science* **77** 330–343

Roehe R and Kalm E (2000) Estimation of genetic and environmental risk factors associated with pre-weaning mortality in piglets using generalized linear mixed models *Animal Science* **70** 227–240

Sangild PT (1995) Stimulation of gastric proteases in the neonatal pig by a rise in adrenocortical secretion at parturition *Reproduction, Fertility and Development* **7** 1293–1298

Sangild PT, Foltmann B and Cranwell PD (1991) Development of gastric proteases in fetal pigs and pigs from birth to thirty-six days of age. The effect of adrenocorticotropin (ACTH) *Journal of Developmental Physiology* **16** 229–238

Sangild PT, Sjöström H, Norén O, Fowden AL and Silver M (1995) The prenatal development and glucocorticoid control of brush-border hydrolases in the pig small intestine *Pediatric Research* **37** 207–212

Sangild PT, Fowden AL and Trahair JF (2000) How does the foetal gastrointestinal tract develop in preparation for enteral nutrition after birth? *Livestock Production Science* **66** 141–150

Schaefer AL, Jones SDM, Newman JA, Sather AP and Tong AKW (1988) Reproductive performance, fetal growth, carcass composition and glucose tolerance in pregnant gilts given a dietary protein supplement *Canadian Journal of Animal Science* **68** 677–687

Schaefer AL, Tong AKW, Sather AP, Beltranena E, Pharazyn A and Aherne FX (1991) Preparturient diabetogenesis in primiparous gilts *Canadian Journal of Animal Science* **71** 69–77

Schoknecht PA, Ebner S, Pond WG et al. (1994) Dietary cholesterol supplementation improves growth and behavioural response of pigs selected for genetically high and low serum cholesterol *Journal of Nutrition* **124** 305–314

Schoknecht PA, McGuire MA, Cohick WS, Currie WB and Bell AW (1996) Effect of chronic infusion of placental lactogen on ovine fetal growth in late gestation *Domestic Animal Endocrinology* **13** 519–528

Seerley RW (1989) Survival and postweaning performance of pigs from sows fed fat during late gestation and lactation *Journal of Animal Science* **67** 1889–1894

Seerley RW, Pace TA, Foley CW and Scarth RD (1974) Effect of energy intake prior to parturition on milk lipids and survival rate, thermostability and carcass composition of piglets *Journal of Animal Science* **38** 64–70

Shelley HJ (1961) Glycogen reserves and their changes at birth and in anoxia *British Medical Bulletin* **17** 137–143

Silver M and Fowden AL (1989) Pituitary adrenocortical activity in the fetal pig in the last third of gestation *Quarterly Journal of Experimental Physiology* **74** 197–206

Ślebodziński AB (1988) Hyperiodothyroninaemia of

neonates, its significance for thermogenesis *Acta Physiologica Poland* **39** 364–379

Sprecher DJ, Leman AD, Dziuk PD, Cropper M and DeDecker M (1974) Causes and control of swine stillbirths *Journal of the American Veterinary Medical Association* **165** 698–701

Stanton HC and Carroll JK (1974) Potential mechanisms responsible for prenatal and perinatal mortality or low viability of swine *Journal of Animal Science* **38** 1037–1044

Stanton HC and Mueller RL (1973) Metabolic responses to cold and catecholamines as a function of age in swine (*Sus domesticus*). *Comparative and Biochemical Physiology* **45A** 215–225

Sterling LG and Cline TR (1986) The effect of energy level in late gestation and lactation on the sow and litter: growth and reproductive performance *Journal of Animal Science* **63** (Supplement 1) 115 (Abstract)

Svendsen J (1992) Perinatal mortality in pigs *Animal Reproduction Science* **28** 59–67

Svendsen LS (1982) Organ weights of the newborn pig. Characterization and comparison of the organ weights of pigs dying within 48 hours of birth with those of unaffected, growing pigs: stillborn intra partum pigs, weak pigs, splayleg pigs, splayleg and weak (splayweak) pigs, and traumatized pigs *Acta Veterinaria Scandinavica Supplementum* **78** 1–205

Svendsen LS, Weström BR, Svendsen J, Olsson A-Ch and Karlsson BW (1990) Intestinal macromolecular transmission in underprivileged and unaffected newborn pigs: implication for survival of underprivileged pigs *Research in Veterinary Science* **48** 184–189

Taverne MAM, Naaktgeboren C and Van der Weyden GC (1979) Myometrial activity and expulsion of fetuses *Animal Reproduction Science* **2** 117–131

Thornbury JC, Sibbons PD, Van Velzen D, Trickey R and Spitz L (1993) Histological investigations into the relationship between low birth weight and spontaneous bowel damage in the neonatal piglet *Pediatric Pathology* **13** 59–69

Torday JS, Sun H and Qin J (1998) Prostaglandin E$_2$ integrates the effects of fluid distension and glucocorticoid on lung maturation *American Journal of Physiology* **274** L106–L111

Trayhurn P, Temple NJ and Van Aerde J (1989) Evidence from immunoblotting studies on uncoupling protein that brown adipose tissue is not present in the domestic pig *Canadian Journal of Physiology and Pharmacology* **67** 1480–1485

Tuchscherer M, Puppe B, Tuchschere A and Tiemann U (2000) Early identification of neonates at risk: traits of newborn piglets with respect to survival *Theriogenology* **54** 371–388

van der Lende T and De Jager D (1991) Death risk and preweaning growth rate of piglets in relation to the within-litter weight distribution at birth *Livestock Production Science* **28** 73–84

Waldorf DP, Foote WC, Self HL, Chapman AB and Casida LE (1975) Factors affecting fetal pig weight late in gestation *Journal of Animal Science* **16** 976–985

Warburton D (1983) Chronic hyperglycemia with secondary hyperinsulinemia inhibits the maturational response of fetal lamb lungs to cortisol *Journal of Clinical Investigation* **72** 433–440

Warshaw JB (1990) Nutritional correlates of fetal growth *Developmental Pharmacology and Therapeutics* **15** 153–158

Wise T, Roberts AJ and Christenson RK (1997) Relationship of light and heavy fetuses to uterine position, placental weight, gestational age, and fetal cholesterol concentrations *Journal of Animal Science* **75** 2197–2207

Zaleski HM and Hacker RR (1993) Variables related to the progress of parturition and probability of stillbirth in swine *Canadian Veterinary Journal* **34** 109–113

Reproduction Supplement **58**, 263–276

Endocrine regulation of periparturient behaviour in pigs

C. L. Gilbert

MAFF Welfare and Behaviour Laboratory, Department of Neurobiology, The Babraham Institute, Babraham, Cambridge CB2 4AT, UK

Pigs begin behavioural preparations for birth about 1–2 days before parturition. Prepartum sows wander to select a suitable site and then construct a maternal nest. The signal that initiates this behavioural cascade probably results from fetal maturation but is unknown. However, endogenous $PGF_{2\alpha}$ appears to be involved early on in an endocrine pathway that projects to the brain and can generate most of the prepartum behavioural components. This period of intense activity is followed by a quiescent phase of lying in the nest for some hours before fetal ejection occurs. Feedback from a completed nest or abdominal discomfort may both contribute to the end of nest building. In the postpartum phase, sows have to deal with the apparently conflicting drives of remaining passive to reduce accidental or deliberate damage to piglets, while at the same time responding actively to their needs. In commercial environments, animals frequently fail in this task. Although environmental influences on piglet survival have received much experimental attention, the genetic, social and endocrine drives that control sow behaviour after parturition remain poorly understood and their clarification is a major challenge for the future.

Introduction

Behavioural changes associated with birth consist of much more than the process of fetal expulsion alone. For the purposes of this review the onset of periparturient behaviour is defined as the first observable prepartum behavioural change and the end as the establishment of stable neonatal–maternal relationships with the onset of regular nursing.

Variations in maternal behaviour result from the product of genetic background, individual previous experience and immediate environmental feedback impinging upon innate drives. Although modern domestic sows are many generations removed from their wild boar ancestors, innate periparturient behaviours appear to be similar (Špinka *et al.*, 2000). As the sequence of behaviours seen during birth are not observed at other times and their timing is crucial for reproductive success, it seems likely that signals from mature fetuses or placentae are likely to trigger these behavioural changes. Such signals could be relayed from the uterus to the brain by afferent nerve stimulation via ascending spinal pathways or through the bloodstream and across the blood–brain barrier via areas of 'leakiness' such as the

Email: colin.gilbert@bbsrc.ac.uk

circumventricular organs (McKinley *et al.*, 1998) or by specific carrier systems. The initiation of the physiological and endocrine events that lead to parturition in sheep has been traced to fetal pituitary adrenocorticotrophic hormone (ACTH) secretion (for review see Challis and Lye, 1994). However, there is no clear evidence that a similar system operates in pigs (Randall *et al.*, 1990). This is an example of an argument (Naaktgeboren, 1979) that multiparous animals (for example, pigs, rabbits, carnivores and rodents) and usually uniparous animals (for example ungulates) should be considered in two broadly separate categories in most aspects of their periparturient physiology.

With the advent of intensive husbandry systems, the environment in which commercial pigs give birth is frequently very different from that of their wild ancestors. Concern over the extent to which intensification prevents or alters normal behaviour patterns, potentially causing maternal stress, has been the subject of much recent research. However, this review will concentrate on describing parturient behaviours unhindered by potentially impoverished environments, and what is known of their endocrine regulation, in an attempt to place these applied studies in context.

The prepartum period

Normal behaviour

Preparatory behaviours for birth in domestic sows with space to roam through different environments and terrain in large semi-natural enclosures have been described in a series of reports (for example, Jensen, 1986; Jensen *et al.*, 1987, 1991, 1993). The first observable changes in behaviour occur about 48 h before giving birth, when animals become restless before a period of concentrated walking, interpreted as nest-site seeking and selection behaviour. During this time, either as an indirect consequence of increased locomotion or as a result of deliberate action, animals tend to leave the herd home range. They may walk several kilometres and build one or more 'mock nests' before final nest-site selection and construction. The nest is built by first digging a hollow in the ground using the snout and raking movements with the front hooves. A mixture of vegetation is gathered from nearby and arranged within the hollow using the snout and hooves to form a nest with a deep bed. This sequence of behaviours may continue for more than a day, declining 3–7 h before birth of the first piglet. In preparation for this phase, sows characteristically push their bodies into the nest using a lowered, turned head and forelegs before lying recumbent on their sides. Nest building does not normally occur after this time (Petersen *et al.*, 1990), although some repairs and improvements after parturition have been observed (Jensen *et al.*, 1987). Nest quality is an important determinant of the timing of the end of nest building, as sows with access to fewer types of material continued to build, in some cases into the postpartum period (Damm *et al.*, 2000).

Motivation to change behaviour in the prepartum period may initially be the result of 'internal factors' such as endocrine change, with 'external factors' such as environmental feedback becoming increasingly important as nest-building progresses (Jensen *et al.*, 1993).

Endocrine regulation

Although a great deal is now known about how pig plasma concentrations of substances relevant to parturition vary over time, we are still a long way from understanding how these variations translate, if at all, into the molecular and neuronal events that drive behavioural change. However, plasma concentrations of many reproductive hormones are in a rapid state of change in the prepartum period, when behavioural change occurs (see Fig. 1) and some

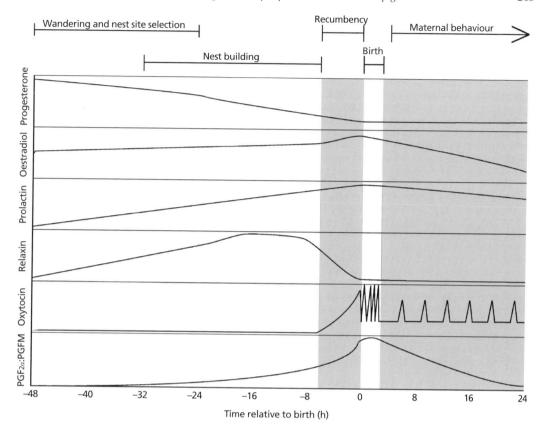

Fig. 1. Trends in plasma concentrations of key hormones about the time of parturition in pigs and their relationship to behavioural change. No scaling of absolute values is given. Sources of data include: Ellendorff *et al.* (1979); Taverne *et al.* (1982); Watts *et al.* (1988); King and Wathes (1989); Whitely *et al.* (1990); Meunier-Salaün *et al.* (1991); Castrén *et al.* (1993a,b); Gilbert *et al.* (1994); and Gilbert (1999).

experiments have been performed in which alteration in plasma hormone content has led to behavioural change. Of these, the main known causal relationship between the endocrine system and nest building is the strong evidence that endogenous $PGF_{2\alpha}$ initiates and mediates these behaviours (see Fig. 2).

$PGF_{2\alpha}$ and nest building behaviour. Peripheral injection of luteolytic doses of $PGF_{2\alpha}$ to late pregnant sows rapidly induced behaviours very similar to nest building, whereas a synthetic analogue of $PGF_{2\alpha}$, cloprostenol, had a minimal behavioural effect (Widowski *et al.*, 1990). Remarkably, $PGF_{2\alpha}$ has also been shown to induce nest building behaviours in postpartum (Blackshaw, 1983), pseudopregnant (Boulton *et al.*, 1997a) and cyclic (Blackshaw, 1983; Burne *et al.*, 2000a) sows. Behavioural elements that have been recorded include increased locomotion and isolation in outdoor enclosures, comparable to prepartum wandering (Gilbert *et al.*, 2000a), snout rooting and front leg pawing at the ground, and carrying and arranging straw (Burne *et al.*, 2000a,b). These induced behaviours appear to be dependent on environment (outdoors, strawed pen or farrowing crate), but are separate from the nest building associated with temperature regulation (Burne *et al.*, 2001). This is an important distinction as thermoregulatory motivators can also generate nest building, particularly in

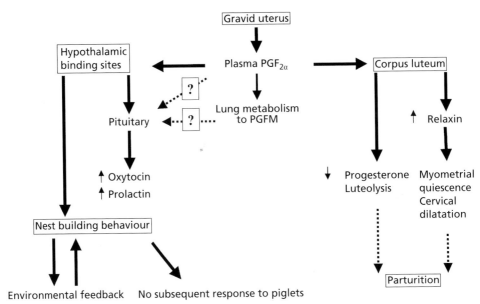

Fig. 2. Schematic representation of proposed regulation of parturient behaviour in pigs by endogenous PGF$_{2\alpha}$. Although PGF$_{2\alpha}$ is able to bring about all of the changes shown, it remains unclear whether it is the primary endogenous regulator in all cases. PGFM: 13,14 dihydro-15-keto-PGF$_{2\alpha}$.

rodent species (Bhatia *et al.*, 1995). Recently, Burne *et al.* (2000c) suggested that the development of PGF$_{2\alpha}$-induced nest building is dependent upon age and appears at about the time of puberty.

PGF$_{2\alpha}$ can be synthesized by the uterine endometrium (Uzumcu *et al.*, 1998) and may be released by the placenta in preparturient animals (Silver *et al.*, 1979), although the stimulation of release is not understood. Studies in other species support the idea that feto–placental synthesis of prostaglandins occurs in late pregnancy (Mitchell *et al.*, 1995). Plasma secretion of PGF$_{2\alpha}$ in the prepartum period has been measured (Watts *et al.*, 1988; Whitely *et al.*, 1990) through assay of the major metabolite 13,14,dihydro-15-keto-PGF$_{2\alpha}$ (PGFM). Metabolism of PGF$_{2\alpha}$ to PGFM in the lungs of pigs is only 80% efficient, whereas in a non-nest-building species, sheep, this figure approaches 100% (Davis *et al.*, 1979). Therefore, it is likely that some peripherally secreted PGF$_{2\alpha}$ could access the brains of pigs. However, no study so far has convincingly demonstrated an increase in circulating concentrations of PGF$_{2\alpha}$ or PGFM coincident with the nest-building phase. Insufficient sampling frequencies plus the use of a metabolite assay may have contributed to this deficiency. In addition, prostaglandin synthesis in the brain may be occurring that is not measurable by peripheral sampling. However, there is clearly a sharp increase in PGFM immediately before parturition, after nest building has finished and during the behaviourally quiescent, recumbent phase (Fig. 1). This presents the hypothesis with a problem. Behaviours that are readily inducible with exogenous PGF$_{2\alpha}$ are not observed at the time when endogenous PGFM concentrations are at their peak. This paradox is a good example of the danger inherent in trying to understand endocrine control of behaviour from the standpoint of plasma concentrations alone, without related data on receptor kinetics and signalling events. Unfortunately, information of this latter type is very scarce for pigs (especially in the central nervous system). However, if the PGF$_{2\alpha}$-induced nest-building hypothesis is correct, the continuing increase in plasma prostaglandin concentrations during the recumbent phase requires either alterations in the sensitivity of central behavioural receptor systems to $PGF_{2\alpha}$ or other systems acting to override the stimulatory effect of $PGF_{2\alpha}$ on nest-building. Increasing prepartum peripheral oxytocin concentrations (Gilbert, 1999) correlates with the end of nest building in pigs (Castrén *et al.*, 1993a), together with the associated increase in intensity of uterine concentrations and abdominal discomfort (Naaktgeboren, 1979; Taverne *et al.*, 1979). Whether recumbency and behavioural quiescence are a simple function of a response to abdominal discomfort or specific effects produced directly by an altered endocrine state is unclear, but the former option seems plausible. However, central neuronal activation has been observed after prepartum increases in peripheral oxytocin concentrations (Antonijevic *et al.*, 1995) and central oxytocin is an important mediator of postpartum behaviour in rodents (see below).

Receptors to $PGF_{2\alpha}$ are synthesized in pig hypothalamic nuclei (Burne, 2000). Cells in similar areas are activated by peripheral $PGF_{2\alpha}$ treatment (Walton *et al.*, 2001). This is a possible site of action for the initiation of prepartum behavioural change. Although it is uncertain which cell type possesses $PGF_{2\alpha}$ receptors, glial cells express $PGF_{2\alpha}$ mRNA in rats (Kitanaka *et al.*, 1996) and brain microvessels possess these receptors in pigs (Chemtob *et al.*, 1996). In rats, local $PGF_{2\alpha}$ infusion altered the firing rate of neurones in the supraoptic nucleus (Setiadji *et al.*, 1998). However, no information is available on $PGF_{2\alpha}$ modulation of neuronal activity in pigs and the downstream central mechanisms that result in behavioural changes are unknown.

In addition to altering behaviour, $PGF_{2\alpha}$ also generates rapid increases in plasma concentrations of prolactin and oxytocin (Boulton *et al.*, 1997b). Plasma concentrations of progesterone increase acutely, followed by a longer-term decrease associated with luteolysis (Boulton *et al.*, 1997b). It is possible that these induced increases may account for some of the reported correlative data between these hormones and nest building behaviours. For example, the preparturient increase in plasma prolactin concentrations may be responsible for the initiation of nest building, as these events occur at similar times (Castrén *et al.*, 1993a). However, these data do not imply causality and Boulton *et al.* (1998) showed that profound reduction of peripheral prolactin concentrations with bromocriptine failed to prevent $PGF_{2\alpha}$-induced nest-building behaviours. It is possible that central mechanisms that generate nest building also produce downstream prolactin secretion. Similarly, the duration of straw gathering behaviour has been positively correlated with plasma progesterone concentrations (Castrén *et al.*, 1993a), but neither the sex steroid ratio (Boulton *et al.*, 1997b) nor oestradiol supplementation (Burne *et al.*, 1999) affected $PGF_{2\alpha}$-induced nest-building behaviour. However, endocrine control of nest building appears to be species-specific, as both prolactin and variations in the ratio of circulating oestrogen:progesterone affect digging, straw-carrying and hair-pulling (to line a nest) behaviours in late pregnant rabbits (Gonzalez-Mariscal *et al.*, 1996).

Relaxin. The timing of the endogenous prepartum relaxin surge is not fully understood. Some experiments have shown that corpora lutea of pregnancy produce a relaxin surge 112–114 days after mating even in the absence of a gravid uterus (for example see Felder *et al.*, 1988). This raises the intriguing idea of an 'internal clock' in the ovary or central nervous system that measures the duration of gestation independently of uterine signals and initiates endocrine events leading to parturition. Although $PGF_{2\alpha}$ stimulates relaxin secretion (Sherwood *et al.*, 1979; King and Wathes, 1989) and prepartum plasma concentrations of relaxin appear to be closely related in time to nest-building behaviour (Fig. 1), relationships between the prepartum relaxin surge and behaviour have not been tested systematically. In rodents, relaxin can affect neuronal activity in the hypothalamus through binding to receptors in areas of blood–brain barrier weakness (Heine *et al.*, 1997; McKinley *et al.*, 1998). Summerlee *et al.* (1998) proposed that in rats a central relaxin system controlling the timing of birth exists discretely from the peripheral system regulating uterine motility and cervical softening, but the only report of centrally applied relaxin affecting behaviour relates to drinking (Summerlee and Robertson, 1995).

In addition to central effects, relaxin has important functions in the late pregnant uterus, preventing inappropriate early myometrial contractions and inducing cervical softening (Bagnall *et al.*, 1993). The co-ordination of cervical softening, prevention of inappropriate early uterine contraction and prepartum behaviour by a single system is an attractive hypothesis, as the events clearly need to be co-ordinated in time. It is possible that relaxin may act to counteract the uterotonic influences of $PGF_{2\alpha}$ during nest building, with the end of the relaxin surge allowing myometrial activity to increase, which would in turn adjust behaviour away from nest building towards recumbency and expulsive effort.

Fetal delivery

Notwithstanding effects on nest-building behaviour, prostaglandins also appear to be required for parturition to occur (Nara and First, 1981). This effect is probably due to a peripheral action of $PGF_{2\alpha}$ on the corpora lutea of pregnancy to remove luteal support to the pregnancy, as has been shown clearly in $PGF_{2\alpha}$ receptor knockout mice (Sugimoto *et al.*, 1997). Indeed, $PGF_{2\alpha}$ analogues are frequently used commercially to induce parturition and various combinations of $PGF_{2\alpha}$ and oxytocin have been tested experimentally (for review see Gilbert, 1999).

Piglets are nearly always born with sows lying in lateral recumbency and fetal expulsion through the birth canal is accompanied by visible and powerful contractions of the external abdominal musculature (Randall, 1972). The rate at which piglets are expelled is variable. Mean duration of second stage labour has been reported as 2.5 h with a range of 0.5–10.5 h, and mean piglet interval as 16.0 min with a range (per litter) of 4.2–48.4 min with animals in a variety of commercial environments (Randall, 1972). Data sets from semi-natural environments are much smaller, but report somewhat slower (Petersen *et al.*, 1990) or similar (Jensen, 1986) birth rates. Although nest building is discontinued during parturition, some postural changes occur. Typically, sows stand, inspect piglets and lie down again (Petersen *et al.*, 1990). This behaviour has been studied more systematically in more intensive conditions (Edwards and Furniss, 1988) and appears to be observed more frequently after birth of the first piglet compared with later littermates. Similarly, Jarvis *et al.* (1999) showed that maternal responsiveness to piglets was high at the onset of farrowing, decreased over the following 4 h and was restored by the following day.

Endocrine regulation

The physiology underlying the initiation of powerful uterine contractions at birth has been described elsewhere (for example see Ellendorff *et al.*, 1979; Taverne *et al.*, 1982; Silver *et al.*, 1983). The powerful and visible contractions of the external abdominal muscles that accompany delivery have been described as the 'fetal ejection reflex' in rats, which requires intact pelvic nerves and may be initiated by cervical dilatation (Higuchi *et al.*, 1987). Once the cervix is open, fetal expulsion is achieved by a combination of uterine smooth muscle and abdominal striated muscle contractions. Much of the increase in uterine smooth muscle activity may be attributable to an increase in circulating oxytocin secretion, which begins to increase above baseline values at about 7 h before birth (Gilbert, 1999). However, oxytocin gene knockout mice were able to give birth normally (Nishimori *et al.*, 1996), indicating that other uterotonic agents (Challis and Lye, 1994) are able to compensate for a lack of oxytocin, and implying considerable flexibility and redundancy in the system (Russell and Leng, 1998).

Oxytocin secretion during parturition is under inhibitory regulation by central endogenous opioids (Leng and Russell, 1989), which are responsible for inhibiting parturition in stressful circumstances (Lawrence *et al.*, 1992). However, as parturition is likely to be inherently both stressful and painful, opioid systems may also be involved normally in regulating oxytocin secretion to time parturition (Gilbert *et al.*, 2000b), help space births (Jarvis *et al.*, 2000) and, through separate spinal systems, attenuate pain perception (Jarvis *et al.*, 1997).

Cervical dilatation and maternal behaviour. In sheep, recognition of individual lambs and selective bonding occur rapidly after birth and are triggered by mechanical cues from the fetus passing down the birth canal modulating hypothalamic relays, involving centrally released oxytocin with progesterone and oestrogen priming (Kendrick and Keverne, 1991). In pigs, individual recognition of piglets by sows is not observed reliably at day 1 after parturition, but develops by day 7 after parturition (Horrell and Hodgson, 1992; Maletínská *et al.*, 2000). Although vagino–cervical dilatation at birth increases peripheral oxytocin secretion in pigs (Gilbert *et al.*, 1997), there is no evidence that this process contributes to maternal behaviour.

Oxytocin secretion and nursing behaviour. During parturition, oxytocin secretion is increased above pre-term values with pulsatile release superimposed (Castrén *et al.*, 1993b): additional pulses associated with fetal ejection are measurable as increases in intra-mammary pressure (Gilbert *et al.*, 1994). This may aid the release of colostrum, which can be expressed continually during birth. Newborn piglets are highly precocious and often vocal. Having cleared the fetal membranes from around their heads, piglets normally rise rapidly (within 2 min of birth) and begin to nuzzle their dam, seeking a nipple (Randall, 1972). The discrete milk ejection reflexes characterized by maternal behavioural (Algers *et al.*, 1990; Jensen *et al.*, 1991), endocrine (Ellendorff *et al.*, 1982) and neuronal (Jiang and Wakerley, 1995) changes that develop as lactation progresses are not behaviourally apparent immediately after parturition (Herskin *et al.*, 1999). This apparently minimal maternal constraint to suckling may help neonates, as teats may initially be hard to find or regain once lost, due to sibling competition, so a continuous letdown maximizes the chance of an early meal (for review see Fraser *et al.*, 1995).

The postpartum period

Normal maternal behaviour

Normal pig maternal behaviour is rather different in the 24 h after birth compared with later periods during lactation (Jensen *et al.*, 1991) and is characterized by high nest occupancy (Stangel and Jensen, 1991). In the immediate postpartum period, removal of placental membranes and licking of individual piglets by sows does not normally occur. Furthermore, in contrast to species such as the rat (Bridges, 1990), carrying of offspring in the mouth and retrieval to the nest is not observed. Duration of maternal lateral lying in the first day after parturition is high (Meunier-Salaün *et al.*, 1991; Cronin and Smith, 1992). Newborn piglets may be weak (Fraser, 1990) and are often located at or near the udder on the day after birth

(Cronin and Smith, 1992), such that relatively minor postural changes by the mother (such as rolling over) can endanger piglets (Weary *et al.*, 1996), with a greater likelihood of accidental damage or death to piglets than later on in lactation (Marchant *et al.*, 2001). Newborn piglets are relatively small ($\leq 0.5\%$ of maternal weight) but highly precocious and will fight for access to teats. They normally establish a stable teat order and dominance hierarchy within a few days, thereby minimizing further antagonistic interactions (Fraser *et al.*, 1995).

Throughout this period of maternal behaviour there is a conflict between the sow investing in her own wellbeing and that of her piglets. The inability of some sows to adapt sufficiently to perform adequately the tasks associated with maternal care is shown by the existence of 'death-prone litters' (Fraser, 1990; Fraser *et al.*, 1995), in which too many deaths occur for the overall frequency of mortality to conform to a Poisson distribution (Fraser, 1990). Large litter size, maternal disease or low milk yield may account for some death-prone litters, but many are the result of poor maternal care. In sows with an equivalent metabolic status and similar husbandry systems (such as housing and temperature regulation), there is still large variation in maternal behaviour (van der Steen *et al.*, 1988; Fraser, 1990), which must be caused by either genetic predisposition or the consequences of an individual's previous experience. An example of selective breeding producing effects on maternal behaviour has recently been published (McPhee *et al.*, 2001). The effects of earlier maternal experience (Jarvis *et al.*, 2001) and other physical and social experiences also appear to influence the subsequent maternal behaviour of pigs (for example, Varley and Stedman, 1993; Beattie *et al.*, 1995). For example, sows that are dominant during pregnancy are more active immediately before farrowing and allow their piglets to suckle more freely than do lower ranking sows. In contrast, low ranking sows are more restless in the early phase after farrowing and can show stereotyped and redirected behaviour patterns (Csemmely and Nicosia, 1991).

Underprivileged piglets may eventually die as a result of overlying, hypothermia or intercurrent disease. However, excessive maternal activity for whatever reason is likely to contribute to accidental damage to offspring. Indeed, Jarvis *et al.* (1999) suggested that optimum maternal behaviour in the first day after parturition is characterized by passivity, unresponsiveness to piglets and lateral lying, allowing both a reduced risk of crushing and maximum access to teats. However, it is also clear that later in lactation, as maternal–piglet relationships develop, responsiveness to piglet distress calls plays an important part in reducing crush injuries (Wechsler and Hegglin, 1997).

Aggressive infanticide

In addition to accidental injury, deliberate maternal aggression of sows towards offspring has been described in large surveys of commercial piggeries with incidences of 8% (Knap and Merks, 1987) and 7–12% (van der Steen *et al.*, 1988) of sows giving birth, a significant heritability and prevalence in primparous sows (gilts). The behaviour is characterized by sows killing some or all of their offspring by biting them to death. Most piglets are killed within day 1 after parturition. Although animals that are predisposed to aggressive infanticide do not show obvious warning signs before farrowing, recent evidence suggests that variations in posture in the day before birth might be useful as behavioural predictors (Appleyard *et al.*, 2000), and animals that show maternal aggression appear to be less aggressive to pen-mate sows during pregnancy (McLean *et al.*, 1998).

Whether this phenotype is part of a continuum of poor maternal behaviour related to a failure in maternal passivity (Jarvis *et al.*, 1999) or an entirely separate event is unknown. Carcasses may be consumed but are often discarded, so hunger is unlikely to be the cause.

Whether this aggressive behaviour is limited to a sow's own offspring, or would be directed to any piglets or other foreign objects, has not been tested. This would be useful information as it might show whether the sow's aggression is a response to a general increase in reactivity or fearfulness or is a specific rejection of her own piglets.

Endocrine regulation

Most studies on maternal behaviour support regulation by neuro–endocrine systems that originate in and are co-ordinated by hypothalamic nuclei, particularly the medial pre-optic area, paraventricular nucleus, supraoptic nucleus and associated projections. These brain areas are responsive to the changes in ovarian and uterine hormone secretion that occur in late pregnancy. Much of this evidence is derived from studies in laboratory rodents (for example see Bridges *et al.*, 1999) but some studies have also been performed in pigs.

Sex steroids. In rats, increased circulating concentrations of oestrogens with progesterone promote maternal behaviour in virgin rats exposed to newborn pups (for review see Bridges, 1990), whereas in mice, marginal progesterone concentrations during pregnancy increased maternal rejection of pups (Wang *et al.*, 1995). Although similar studies have not been performed in pigs, sedative treatment of sows for maternal aggression was associated with high prepartum oestrogen:progesterone ratios and high postpartum plasma oestradiol concentrations (McLean *et al.*, 1998). Both oestrogen receptor α and β are found in the brain in rodents, with high concentrations of both subtypes again located in the hypothalamus (Laflamme *et al.*, 1998). Progesterone receptors are found in rat hypothalamus, preoptic area, hippocampus and frontal cortex, with hypothalamic expression of the B-isoform being sensitive to reproductive status (GuerraAraiza *et al.*, 2000). Both genomic and non-genomic effects of progesterone on central neurotransmitters relevant to reproductive behaviour have been reported (Schumacher *et al.*, 1999). Many neurones that contain either oestrogen or progesterone receptors are neuroendocrine in type, as they have been shown to project to the median eminence (Goldsmith *et al.*, 1997).

Oxytocin. Central oxytocin appears to be important in mediating maternal behaviour, although this has not been proven in pigs. For example, administration of oxytocin into the cerebrospinal fluid of mice reduced aggressive infanticide (McCarthy, 1990) and similar treatment with an oxytocin antagonist inhibited postpartum maternal behaviour in rats (van Leengoed *et al.*, 1987). However, oxytocin gene knockout mice did not show any gross deficits in maternal care apart from an inability to nurse, which is probably due to peripheral effects (Nishimori *et al.*, 1996). Oxytocin injection into the medial pre-optic area or paraventricular nucleus reduced maternal rejection of lambs in sheep (Kendrick *et al.*, 1992). In our laboratory, we have evidence that gilts displaying aggressive behaviour to offspring also had lowered peripheral oxytocin concentrations at birth (C. L. Gilbert, T. H. J. Burne, J. A. Goode and P. J. E. Murfitt, unpublished; Fig. 3). This could be a clue to causality but it could also simply be that aggressive sows receive less tactile stimulation of the nipples (Algers *et al.*, 1990). Furthermore, endogenous opioid systems may mediate passivity in parturient sows (Jarvis *et al.*, 1999) but generally also reduce oxytocin secretion.

PGF$_{2\alpha}$. Despite its effects on prepartum behaviour, peripheral PGF$_{2\alpha}$ could not be shown to influence responses of female pigs to newborn piglets (Gilbert *et al.*, 2001). Although only a single study of this kind has been performed, this permits the hypothesis that pre- and postpartum mechanisms regulating behaviour may be separate.

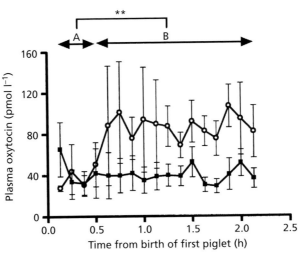

Fig. 3. Plasma oxytocin concentrations in pigs during parturition. Animals were classified as aggressive (■, $n = 4$) if they attacked or bit any of their piglets during the period shown. Non-aggressive controls (○, $n = 4$) gave birth under the same conditions. Data are derived from a large experiment (C. L. Gilbert, T. H. J. Burne, J. A. Goode and P. J. E. Murfitt, unpublished) in which maternal aggression occurred sporadically. All animals had previously received 10 mg $PGF_{2\alpha}$ to induce parturition. Mean values in period A were subtracted post-hoc from those in period B for each animal separately and compared using a one-way ANOVA. **Indicates significant difference ($P < 0.01$) ($F = 14.5$, df = 7).

Prolactin. Studies in rodents have established a clear role for prolactin receptors in maternal behaviour (Lucas *et al.*, 1998). Central receptors (particularly the long form) are located predominantly in the choroid plexus and are also distributed widely in hypothalamic nuclei (Pi and Grattan, 1998).

Conclusion

The active maternal prepartum phase followed by a relatively passive postpartum response to active (but not individually recognized) offspring are features of pig behaviour that, when combined, differ from other domestic or laboratory species and represent a distinctive model for the study of maternal behaviour. Endocrine regulation of prepartum behaviour is becoming more clearly understood, although central relays turning peripheral cues into co-ordinated behavioural output are unknown. Postpartum maternal behaviour has been well described, but what we know of its endocrine control amounts to no more than a few disconnected snippets. Similarities in some aspects of behaviour with other multiparous species allow comparisons of the mechanisms of regulation to be made when information is unavailable in pigs, but these must be treated with caution. An inability to resolve the apparently opposite behavioural requirements of postpartum sows to be generally passive yet responsive to piglet distress may be partly responsible for sows that go on to show inadequate maternal behaviour.

This review has not touched on the large body of work that has examined environmental influences on sow behaviour and endocrinology at birth from the perspective of animal welfare. A thorough understanding of basic mechanisms, once established, will help to place these studies in context and improve the well-being of parturient pigs and their offspring.

The author is grateful to J. Bicknell and T. H. J. Burne for constructive comments on the manuscript. Experiments performed in this laboratory were funded by the UK Ministry for Agriculture, Fisheries and Food (commissions AWO117 and AWO118).

References

Algers B, Rojanasthian S and Uvnäs-Moberg K (1990) The relationship between teat stimulation, oxytocin release and grunting rate in the sow during nursing *Applied Animal Behaviour Science* **26** 267–276

Antonijevic IA, Leng G, Luckman SM, Douglas AJ, Bicknell RJ and Russell JA (1995) Induction of uterine activity with oxytocin in late pregnant rats replicates the expression of c-*fos* in neuroendocrine and brain stem neurons as seen during parturition *Endocrinology* **136** 154–163

Appleyard SJ, Hall AD and Lawrence AB (2000) Pre-farrowing behaviour distinguishes piglet-savaging gilts from non-savaging gilts. *Proceedings of the 34th International Congress of the ISAE* pp 62 Eds A Ramos, LCP Machado Filho and MJ Hotzel

Bagnall CA, Zhang Q, Downey B and Ainsworth L (1993) Sources and biological actions of relaxin in pigs *Journal of Reproduction and Fertility Supplement* **48** 127–138

Beattie VE, Walker N and Sneddon IA (1995) Effect of rearing environment and change of environment on the behavior of gilts *Applied Animal Behaviour Science* **46** 57–65

Bhatia AJ, Schneider JE and Wade GN (1995) Thermoregulatory and maternal nestbuilding in Syrian hamsters: interaction of ovarian steroids and energy demand *Physiology and Behavior* **58** 141–146

Blackshaw JK (1983) Prostaglandin $F_{2\alpha}$ induced nest building behavior in the non-pregnant sow, and some welfare considerations *International Journal for the Study of Animal Problems* **4** 299–304

Boulton MI, Wickens A, Brown D, Goode JA and Gilbert CL (1997a) Prostaglandin F2alpha-induced nest-building in pseudopregnant pigs. I. Effects of environment on behaviour and cortisol secretion *Physiology and Behavior* **62** 1071–1078

Boulton MI, Wickens A, Brown D, Goode JA and Gilbert CL (1997b) Prostaglandin F2alpha-induced nest-building in pseudopregnant pigs. II. Space restriction stress does not influence secretion of oxytocin, prolactin, oestradiol or progesterone *Physiology and Behavior* **62** 1079–1085

Boulton MI, Wickens A, Goode JA and Gilbert CL (1998) Prolactin and induced nest-building behaviour in pseudopregnant gilts treated with bromocriptine *Journal of Neuroendocrinology* **10** 601–609

Bridges RS (1990) Endocrine regulation of parental behaviour in rodents. In *Mammalian Parenting Biochemical, Neurobiological, and Behavioural Determinants* pp 93–117 Eds NA Krasnegor and RS Bridges. Oxford University Press, Oxford

Bridges RS, Mann PE and Coppeta JS (1999) Hypothalamic involvement in the regulation of maternal behaviour in the rat: inhibitory roles for the ventromedial hypothalamus and the dorsal/anterior hypothalamic areas *Journal of Neuroendocrinology* **11** 259–266

Burne THJ, Murfitt PJE, Goode JA, Boulton MI and Gilbert CL (1999) Effects of oestrogen supplementation and ace restriction on $PGF_{2\alpha}$-induced nest-building in pseudopregnant gilts *Animal Production Science* **55** 255–267

Burne THJ (2000) Expression of PGF-2-alpha receptor mRNA in the female pig brain *European Journal of Neuroscience* **12** 407

Burne THJ, Murfitt PJE and Gilbert CL (2000a) Behavioural responses to intramuscular injections of prostaglandin $F_{2\alpha}$ in female pigs *Pharmacology, Biochemistry and Behavior* **66** 789–796

Burne THJ, Murfitt PJE and Gilbert CL (2000b) Deprivation of straw bedding alters $PGF_{2\alpha}$-induced nesting behaviour in female pigs *Applied Animal Behaviour Science* **69** 215–225

Burne THJ, Murfitt PJE and Gilbert CL (2000c) Effects of ovariohysterectomy and age on $PGF_{2\alpha}$ induced nest building in female pigs *VIth International Conference on Hormones, Brain and Behaviour (Madrid, Spain) Trabajos del Instituto Cajal Tomo* **77** 350–352

Burne THJ, Murfitt PJE and Gilbert CL (2001) The effect of temperature on prostaglandin $F_{2\alpha}$-induced nesting behaviour in pigs (*Sus scrofa*). *Applied Animal Behaviour Science* **71** 293–304

Castrén H, Algers B, de Passillé A-M, Rushen J and Uvnäs-Moberg K (1993a) Parturient variation in progesterone, prolactin, oxytocin and somatostatin in relation to nest building in sows *Applied Animal Behaviour Science* **38** 91–102

Castrén H, Algers B, de Passillé A-M, Rushen J and Uvnäs-Moberg K (1993b) Early milk ejection, prolonged parturition and periparturient oxytocin release in the pig *Animal Production* **57** 465–471

Challis JRG and Lye SJ (1994) Parturition. In *The Physiology of Reproduction* pp 985 Eds E Knobil and JD Neill. Raven Press Ltd, New York

Chemtob S, Li D-Y, Abran D, Peri KG and Varma DR (1996) Regulation of cerebrovascular prostaglandin E_2 (PGE_2) and $PGE_{2\alpha}$ receptors and their functions during development *Seminars in Perinatology* **20** 164–172

Cronin GM and Smith JA (1992) Suckling behaviour of sows in farrowing crates and straw-bedded pens *Applied Animal Behaviour Science* **33** 175–189

Csemmely D and Nicosia E (1991) Maternal behavior in sows of different social rank *Journal of Endocrinology* **9** 83–93

Damm BI, Vestergaard KS, Schrøder-Petersen and Ladewig J (2000) The effects of branches on prepartum nest building in gilts with access to straw *Applied Animal Behaviour Science* **69** 113–124

Davis AJ, Fleet IR, Harrison FA and Maule Walker FM (1979) Pulmonary metabolism of prostaglandin $F_{2\alpha}$ in the conscious non-pregnant ewe and sow *Journal of Physiology* **301** 86P

Edwards SA and Furniss SJ (1988) The effects of straw in crated farrowing systems on peripartal behaviour of sows and piglets *British Veterinary Journal* **144** 139–147

Ellendorff F, Taverne M, Elsaesser F, Forsling ML, Parvizzi N, Naaktgeboron C and Smidt D (1979) Endocrinology of parturition in the pig *Animal Reproduction Science* **2** 323–334

Ellendorff F, Forsling ML and Poulain DA (1982) The milk ejection reflex in the pig *Journal of Physiology* **333** 577–594

Felder FJ, Klindt J, Bolt DJ and Anderson LL (1988) Relaxin and progesterone secretion as affected by luteinizing hormone and prolactin after hysterectomy in the pig *Endocrinology* **122** 1751–1760

Fraser D (1990) Behavioural perspectives on piglet survival *Journal of Reproduction and Fertility Supplement* **40** 355–370

Fraser D, Phillips PA, Thompson BK, Pajor EA, Weary DM and Braithwaite LA (1995) Behavioural aspects of piglet survival and growth. In *The Neonatal Pig Development and Survival* pp 287–312 Ed. MA Varley. CAB International, Wallingford

Gilbert CL (1999) Oxytocin secretion and management of parturition in the pig *Reproduction of Domestic Animals* **34** 193–200

Gilbert CL, Goode JA and McGrath TJ (1994) Pulsatile secretion of oxytocin during parturition in the pig: temporal relationship with fetal expulsion *Journal of Physiology* **475** 129–137

Gilbert CL, Boulton MI, Forsling ML, Goode JA and McGrath TJ (1997) Restricting maternal space during parturition in the pig: effects on oxytocin, vasopressin, and cortisol secretion following vagino–cervical stimulation and administration of naloxone *Animal Reproduction Science* **46** 245–259

Gilbert CL, Murfitt PJE, Boulton MI, Pain J and Burne THJ (2000a) Effects of prostaglandin $F_{2\alpha}$ treatment on the behavior of pseudopregnant pigs in an extensive environment *Hormones and Behavior* **37** 229–239

Gilbert CL, Boulton MI, Goode JA and McGrath TJ (2000b) The timing of parturition in the pig is altered by intravenous naloxone *Theriogenology* **53** 905–923

Gilbert CL, Murfitt PJE and Burne THJ (2001) Effects of prostaglandin $F_{2\alpha}$ treatment of pseudopregnant pigs on nest building behavior and subsequent interactions with newborn piglets *Hormones and Behavior* **39** 206–215

Goldsmith PC, Boggan JE and Thind KK (1997) Estrogen and progesterone receptor expression in neuroendocrine and related neurons of the pubertal female monkey hypothalamus *Neuroendocrinology* **65** 325–334

Gonzalez-Mariscal G, Melo AI, Jiménez P, Beyer C and Rosenblatt JS (1996) Estradiol, progesterone, and prolactin regulate maternal nest-building in rabbits *Journal of Neurochemistry* **8** 901–907

GuerraAraiza C, Cerbon MA, Morimoto S and CamachoArroyo I (2000) Progesterone receptor isoforms expression pattern in the rat brain during the estrous cycle *Life Sciences* **66** 1743–1752

Heine PA, Di S, Ross LR, Anderson LL and Jacobson CD (1997) Relaxin-induced expression of *Fos* in the forebrain of the late pregnant rat *Reproductive Neuroendocrinology* **66** 38–46

Herskin MS, Jensen KH and Thodberg K (1999) Influence of environmental stimuli on nursing and suckling behaviour in domestic sows and piglets *Animal Science* **68** 27–34

Higuchi T, Uchide K, Honda K and Negoro H (1987) Pelvic neurectomy abolishes the fetus-expulsion reflex and induces dystocia in the rat *Experimental Neurology* **96** 443–455

Horrell I and Hodgson J (1992) The bases of sow–piglet identification. 1. The identification by sows of their own piglets and the presence of intruders *Applied Animal Behaviour Science* **33** 319–327

Jarvis S, McLean KA, Chirnside J, Deans LA, Calvert SK, Molony V and Lawrence AB (1997) Opioid-mediated changes in nociceptive threshold during pregnancy and parturition in the sow *Pain* **72** 153–159

Jarvis S, McLean KA, Calvert SK, Deans LA, Chirnside J and Lawrence AB (1999) The responsiveness of sows to their piglets in relation to the length of parturition and the involvement of endogenous opioids *Applied Animal Behaviour Science* **63** 195–207

Jarvis S, Lawrence AB, McLean KA, Chirnside J, Deans LA, Calvert SK, Gilbert CL, Goode JA and Forsling ML (2000) The effect of opioid antagonism and environmental restriction on plasma oxytocin and vasopressin concentrations in parturient gilts *Journal of Endocrinology* **166** 39–44

Jarvis S, Van der Vegt BJ, Lawrence AB, McLean KA, Deans LA, Chirnside J and Calvert SK (2001) The effect of parity and environmental restriction on behavioural and physiological responses of pre-parturient pigs *Applied Animal Behaviour Science* **71** 203–216

Jensen P (1986) Observations on the maternal behaviour of free-ranging domestic pigs *Applied Animal Behaviour Science* **16** 131–142

Jensen P, Florén K and Hobroh B (1987) Peri-parturient changes in behaviour in free-ranging domestic pigs *Applied Animal Behaviour Science* **17** 69–76

Jensen P, Stangel G and Algers B (1991) Nursing and suckling behaviour of semi-naturally kept pigs during the first 10 days postpartum *Applied Animal Behaviour Science* **31** 195–209

Jensen P, Vestergaard K and Algers B (1993) Nestbuilding in free-ranging domestic sows *Applied Animal Behaviour Science* **38** 245–255

Jiang QB and Wakerley JB (1995) Analysis of bursting responses of oxytocin neurons in the rat in late pregnancy, lactation and after weaning *Journal of Physiology* **486** 237–248

Kendrick KM and Keverne EB (1991) Importance of progesterone and estrogen priming for the induction of maternal behavior by vaginocervical stimulation in sheep: effects of maternal experience *Physiology and Behavior* **49** 745–750

Kendrick KM, Keverne EB, Hinton MR and Goode JA (1992) Oxytocin, amino acid and monoamine release in the region of the medial preoptic area and bed nucleus of the stria terminalis of the sheep during parturition and suckling *Brain Research* **569** 199–209

King GJ and Wathes DC (1989) Relaxin, progesterone and estrogen profiles in sow plasma during natural and induced parturitions *Animal Reproduction Science* **20** 213–220

Kitanaka J, Hashimoto H, Gotoh M *et al.* (1996) Expression pattern of messenger RNAs for prostanoid receptors in glial cell cultures *Brain Research* **707** 282–287

Knap PW and Merks JWM (1987) A note on the genetics of aggressiveness of primiparous sows towards their piglets *Livestock Production Science* **17** 161–167

Laflamme N, Nappi RE, Drolet G, Labrie C and Rivest S (1998) Expression and neuropeptidergic characterization of estrogen receptors (ER alpha and ER beta) throughout the rat brain: anatomical evidence of distinct roles of each subtype *Journal of Neurobiology* **36** 357–378

Lawrence AB, Petherick JC, McLean K, Gilbert CL, Chapman C and Russell J (1992) Naloxone prevents interruption of parturition and increases plasma oxytocin following environmental disturbance in parturient sows *Physiology and Behavior* **52** 917–923

Leng G and Russell JA (1989) Opioids, oxytocin and parturition. In *Brain Opioid Systems in Reproduction* pp 231–256 Eds RG Dyer and RJ Bicknell. Oxford University Press, Oxford

Lucas BK, Ormandy CJ, Binart N, Bridges RS and Kelly PA (1998) Null mutation of the prolactin receptor gene produces a defect in maternal behavior *Endocrinology* **139** 4102–4107

McCarthy MM (1990) Oxytocin inhibits infanticide in female house mice (*Mus domesticus*). *Hormones and Behavior* **24** 365–375

McKinley MJ, Allen AM, Burns P, Colvill LM and Oldfield BJ (1998) Interaction of circulating hormones with the brain: the roles of the subfornical organ and the organum vasculosum of the Lamina terminalis *Clinical and Experimental Pharmacology and Physiology* **28** S61–S67

McLean KA, Lawrence AB, Petherick JC, Deans L, Chirnside J, Vaughan A, Nielsen BL and Webb R (1998) Investigation of the relationship between farrowing environment, sex steroid concentrations and maternal aggression in gilts *Animal Reproduction Science* **50** 95–109

McPhee CP, Kerr JC and Cameron ND (2001) Peri-partum posture and behaviour of gilts and the location of their piglets in lines selected for components of efficient lean growth *Applied Animal Behaviour Science* **71** 1–12

Maletinská J, Špinka M, Vichová J, Stehulová I, Panamá J and Šimunek J (2000) Sow–piglets recognition in early postpartum period. *Proceedings of the 34th International Congress of the ISAE* pp 161 Eds A Ramos, LCP Machado Filho and MJ Hotzel

Marchant JN, Broom DM and Corning S (2001) The influence of sow behaviour on piglet mortality due to crushing in an open farrowing system *Animal Science* **72** 19–28

Meunier-Salaün MC, Gort F, Prunier A and Schouten WPG (1991) Behavioural patterns and progesterone, cortisol and prolactin levels around parturition in European (Large-White) and Chinese (Meishan) sows *Applied Animal Behaviour Science* **31** 43–59

Mitchell MD, Romero RJ, Edwin SS and Trantman MS (1995) Prostaglandins and parturition *Reproduction, Fertility and Development* **7** 623–632

Naaktgeboren C (1979) Behavioural aspects of parturition *Animal Reproduction Science* **2** 155–166

Nara BS and First NL (1981) Effect of indomethacin and prostaglandin $F_{2\alpha}$ on parturition in swine *Journal of Animal Science* **52** 1360–1369

Nishimori K, Young LJ, Guo Q, Wang Z, Insel TR and Matzuk MM (1996) Oxytocin is required for nursing but is not essential for parturition or reproductive behaviour *Proceedings National Academy of Sciences USA* **93** 11 699–11 704

Petersen V, Recén B and Vestergaard K (1990) Behaviour of sows and piglets during farrowing under free-range conditions *Applied Animal Behaviour Science* **26** 169–179

Pi XJ and Grattan DR (1998) Distribution of prolactin receptor immunoreactivity in the brain of estrogen-treated, ovariectomized rats *Journal of Comparative Neurology* **394** 462–474

Randall GCB (1972) Observations on parturition in the sow. II. Factors influencing stillbirth and perinatal mortality *Veterinary Record* **90** 183–186

Randall GCB, Kendall JZ, Tsang BK and Taverne MAM (1990) Endocrine changes following infusion of fetal pigs with corticotropin in litters of reduced numbers *Animal Reproduction Science* **23** 109–122

Russell JA and Leng G (1998) Sex, parturition and motherhood without oxytocin? *Journal of Endocrinology* **157** 343–359

Schumacher M, Coirini H, Robert F, Cuennoun R and ElEtr M (1999) Genomic and membrane actions of progesterone: implications for reproductive physiology and behavior *Behavioral Brain Research* **105** 37–52

Setiadji VS, Shibuya I, Kabashima N, Ibrahim N, Harayama N, Ueta Y and Yamashita H (1998) Actions of prostaglandin E_2 on rat supraoptic neurones *Journal of Neuroendocrinology* **10** 927–936

Sherwood OD, Nara BS, Crnekovic VE and First NL (1979) Relaxin concentrations in pig plasma after the administration of indomethacin and prostaglandin $F_{2\alpha}$ during late pregnancy *Endocrinology* **104** 1716–1721

Silver M, Barnes RJ, Comline RS, Fowden AL, Clover L and Mitchell MD (1979) Prostaglandins in the foetal pig and prepartum endocrine changes in mother and foetus *Animal Reproduction Science* **2** 305–322

Silver M, Comline RS and Fowden AL (1983) Fetal and maternal endocrine changes during the induction of parturition with the PGF analogue, cloprostenol, in chronically catheterized sows and fetuses *Journal of Developmental Physiology* **5** 307–321

Špinka M, Illmann G, de Jonge F, Andersson M, Schuurman T and Jensen P (2000) Dimensions of maternal behaviour characteristics in domestic and wild × domestic crossbred sows *Applied Animal Behaviour Science* **70** 99–114

Stangel G and Jensen P (1991) Behaviour of semi-naturally kept sows and piglets (except suckling) during 10 days postpartum *Applied Animal Behaviour Science* **31** 211–217

Sugimoto Y, Yamasaki A, Segi E *et al.* (1997) Failure of parturition in mice lacking the prostaglandin F receptor *Science* **277** 681–683

Summerlee AJS and Robertson GF (1995) Central administration of porcine relaxin stimulates drinking behaviour in rats: an effect mediated by central angiotensin II *Endocrinology Journal* **3** 337–381

Summerlee AJS, Ramsey DG and Poterski RS (1998) Neutralization of relaxin within the brain affects the timing of birth in rats *Endocrinology* **139** 479–484

Taverne MAM, Naaktgeboron C, Elsaesser F, Forsling ML, van der Weyden GC, Ellendorff F and Smidt D (1979) Myometrial electrical activity and plasma concentrations of progesterone, oestrogens and oxytocin during late pregnancy and parturition in the miniature pig *Biology of Reproduction* **21** 1125–1134

Taverne M, Bevers M, Bradshaw JMC, Dieleman SJ, Willemse AH and Porter DG (1982) Plasma concentrations of prolactin, progesterone, relaxin and oestradiol 17β in sows treated with progesterone, bromocriptine or indomethacin during late pregnancy *Journal of Reproduction and Fertility* **65** 85–96

Uzumcu M, Braileanu GT, Carnation KG, Ludwig TE and Mirando MA (1998) Oxytocin stimulated phospho-inositide hydrolysis and prostaglandin $F_{2\alpha}$ secretion by luminal epithelial glandular epithelial and stromal cells from pig endometrium. I. Response of cyclic pigs on day 16 post-oestrus *Biology of Reproduction* **59** 1259–1265

van der Steen HAM, Schaeffer LR, de Jong H and de Groot PN (1988) Aggressive behavior of sows at parturition *Journal of Animal Science* **66** 271–279

van Leengoed E, Kerker E and Swanson HH (1987) Inhibition of post-partum maternal behaviour in the rat by injecting an oxytocin antagonist into the cerebral ventricles *Journal of Endocrinology* **112** 275–282

Varley MA and Stedman RC (1993) The influence of the early life environment on personality development and reproduction in multiparous sows *Proceedings of the British Society for Animal Production* **56** 422 (Abstract 14)

Walton SL, Burne THJ and Gilbert CL (2001) $PGF_{2\alpha}$-induced nesting behaviour increases hypothalamic c-fos and c-jun mRNA expression *Proceedings of the British Neuroscience Association* **16** 116 (Abstract)

Wang M-W, Crombie DL, Hayes JS and Heap RB (1995) Aberrant maternal behaviour in mice treated with a progesterone receptor antagonist during pregnancy *Journal of Endocrinology* **143** 371–377

Watts AD, Flint APF, Foxcroft GR and Porter DG (1988) Plasma steroid, relaxin and dihydro-keto-prostaglandin F2alpha changes in the minipig in relation to myometrial electrical and mechanical activity in the pre-partum period *Journal of Reproduction and Fertility* **83** 553–564

Weary DM, Pajor EA, Fraser D and Honkanen A-M (1996) Sow body movements that crush piglets: a comparison between two types of farrowing accommodation *Applied Animal Behaviour Science* **49** 149–158

Wechsler B and Hegglin D (1997) Individual differences in the behaviour of sows at the nest-site and the crushing of piglets *Applied Animal Behaviour Science* **51** 39–49

Whitely JL, Hartmann PE, Willcox DL, Bryant-Greenwood GD and Greenwood FC (1990) Initiation of parturition and lactation in the sow: effects of delaying parturition with medroxyprogesterone acetate *Journal of Endocrinology* **124** 475–484

Widowski TM, Curtis SE, Dziuk PJ, Wagner WC and Sherwood OD (1990) Behavioral and endocrine responses of sows to prostaglandin $F_{2\alpha}$ and cloprostenol *Biology of Reproduction* **43** 290–297

Reproduction Supplement **58**, 277–292

Applying functional genomics research to the study of pig reproduction

D. Pomp, A. R. Caetano, G. R. Bertani, C. D. Gladney
and R. K. Johnson

Department of Animal Science, University of Nebraska, Lincoln, NE 68583–0908, USA

Functional genomics is an experimental approach that incorporates genome-wide or system-wide experimentation, expanding the scope of biological investigation from studying single genes to studying potentially all genes at once in a systematic manner. This technology is highly appealing because of its high throughput and relatively low cost. Furthermore, analysis of gene expression using microarrays is likely to be more biologically relevant than the conventional paradigm of reductionism, because it has the potential to uncover new biological connections between genes and biochemical pathways. However, functional genomics is still in its infancy, especially with regard to the study of pig reproduction. Currently, efforts are centred on developing the necessary resources to enable high throughput evaluation and comparison of gene expression. However, it is clear that in the near future functional genomics will be applied on a large scale to study the biology and physiology of reproduction in pigs, and to understand better the complex nature of genetic control over polygenic characteristics, such as ovulation rate and litter size. We can look forward to generating a significant amount of new data on differences in gene expression between genotypes, treatments, or at various temporal and spatial coordinates within a variety of reproductively relevant systems. Along with this capability will be the challenge of collating, analysing and interpreting datasets that are orders of magnitude more extensive and complex than those currently used. Furthermore, integration of functional genomics with traditional genetic approaches and with detailed analysis of the proteome and relevant whole animal phenotypes will be required to make full use of this powerful new experimental paradigm as a beneficial research tool.

General background

Improvement of reproductive traits in pigs remains of great importance and interest to the pork industry. The sow is the unit of production, and increases in litter size and preweaning viability have been highlighted as major factors for reducing the costs of producing pork (Tess *et al.*, 1983a,b). Although geneticists have made much progress in the improvement of production efficiency and carcass quality traits in pigs with the use of traditional quantitative genetic methods (Clutter and Brascamp, 1998), reproductive traits have been more difficult to

Email: dpomp@unl.edu

enhance due to low heritability (10–15%). For this reason, several studies have focused on genomic technologies to study pig reproduction, primarily in the form of quantitative trait loci (QTL) and candidate gene identification for traits such as ovulation rate, litter size and age at puberty (see, Rothschild, 2000; Table 5 in Cassady *et al.*, 2001). Although there have been some successes, large variation in results and lack of power to localize the underlying genes have limited the use of DNA marker-assisted selection for improvement of reproduction. In addition, these efforts have yielded very little basic information regarding the biology of reproduction. Detected QTL represent only broad regions containing potentially hundreds or even thousands of genes, and even evidence for candidate gene associations (for example, oestrogen receptor; Rothschild *et al.*, 1996) may be caused by other genes (known or unknown) in linkage disequilibrium with the candidate locus.

Thus, new methods and models for identification of genes are required to understand better the genetics underlying reproduction in pigs. Furthermore, an approach that better integrates genetic and physiological investigation is well overdue, and promises to provide synergistic discoveries leading to alternative ways to improve these traits through genetic selection, therapeutics and management practices. Functional genomics, along with its 'sister technology' proteomics, is currently the most appropriate technology to achieve this aim.

What is functional genomics?

The term 'functional genomics' is widely used, but is often poorly understood given a lack of common definition. In its broadest sense, functional genomics encompasses all methods that enable a better understanding of the function of a gene, and includes a wide variety of techniques including DNA sequencing, evaluation of gene expression, and even mutational and transgenic analysis. However, a more useful definition of functional genomics incorporates the genome-wide or system-wide experimentation, expanding the scope of biological investigation from studying single genes or proteins to studying all genes or proteins at once in a systematic manner. This definition will be used in this review.

In some organisms (including humans and mice), functional genomics is built upon the framework of knowing the near-complete sequence of the genome, and is used to narrow the gap between sequence and function. In livestock species, including pigs, data are limited to fairly extensive collections of partially sequenced regions of expressed genes. Although this may limit the scale (and progress) of functional genomic studies, it does not change the nature or overall goals of investigation.

Large-scale functional genomic studies that attempt to understand pig reproduction are fairly new and ongoing. Thus, this review must be based primarily on progress reports, abstracts and updates rather than on a large body of published data. The aims of this review are to define the strategies of functional genomics applied to understanding the genetic and physiological control of pig reproduction, to describe the primary existing resources and research efforts, and to speculate on the future utility and benefit of this approach in increasing our understanding of the genetics and physiology of reproduction in pigs. Although it is recognized that analysis of the proteome is critical and mandatory for understanding the connection between genotype and phenotype, the focus will be on analysis of gene expression at the mRNA level, or the transcriptome.

Functional genomics – transcriptome analysis

The development of a new approach to investigate the expression of thousands of genes, in parallel, in complex biological samples has produced a paradigm shift in biology (Lander,

1999). It is now possible to look at patterns of expression of the entire genome of an organism (for example, yeast) during normal cell processes, or in response to environmental changes (Schena *et al.*, 1995, 1996; Brown and Botstein, 1999). This technology has also been used to gain new insights into human gene expression in cancerous compared with normal cells (DeRisi *et al.*, 1996), or the response of fibroblasts to serum starvation (Iyer *et al.*, 1999). Thus, this exploratory paradigm can be used in the absence of complete genome information without losing its intrinsic power, because of the high throughput and relative low cost of the technology.

Expression microarrays can be thought of as reverse northern blots, in which thousands of DNA 'probes' are individually spotted (printed) on to a solid support (glass slide) in defined patterns or grids. The probes are usually derived from partially sequenced cDNA clones or from sets of oligonucleotides representing expressed genes. Subsequently, fluorescent targets are produced from mRNA isolated from two distinct biological samples (for example, cancerous cells and normal cells, or tissue samples from two genetic lines). Each mRNA population is labelled with a different fluorescent dye (usually Cy3 and Cy5), mixed in equimolar proportions and hybridized to the microarray. After stringent washes, detection of the remaining fluorescent material at each spot is made with a microarray laser scanner, which can accurately estimate the intensity of each fluorescent dye at each spot. Thus, it is possible to determine the expression of each mRNA in both samples at the same time. The data are usually represented as the ratio of the expression detected between the two mRNA samples used. These experiments produce large sets of data, which require specialized computer software to manage and analyse them (Ermolaeva *et al.*, 1998; Bassett *et al.*, 1999). Indeed, bioinformatics may be the most important, complex and challenging aspect of using microarrays to dissect complex traits, such as reproduction at the transcription level.

Reports of changes in gene expression associated with reproductive phenotypes in pigs have been mostly gene specific. The evaluation of differences in expression profiles of thousands of genes in parallel offers powerful new opportunities for gene discovery. Although the advent of differential display PCR has enabled preliminary investigations of changes in gene expression in whole tissue, the methods are laborious and not facilitative of large-scale analysis of various time points, tissue sources and treatments. Thus, the ability to analyse the expression of thousands of genes simultaneously makes microarray technology a valuable tool for studying biological events in domestic species. The advantage of the technology is its high throughput and relatively low cost. Furthermore, microarray analysis is likely to be more biologically relevant than the conventional paradigm of reductionism because it has the potential to uncover new biological connections between genes and biochemical pathways. This ability may be especially important for biological events that are specific to pigs and that have not been studied in model species.

Although several studies are underway to develop microarrays containing thousands of pig genes, no research data have been published to date. However, functional genomic analysis of gene expression using microarrays has been applied to the study of reproduction in other species, providing an example of what might be forthcoming for scientists working with pigs. These studies range from identification of sex-regulated transcriptional changes in *Caenorhabditis elegans* (Jiang *et al.*, 2001), the evaluation of gene expression profiles during folliculogenesis (Liu *et al.*, 2001) and mid-gestation embryo and placenta (Tanaka *et al.*, 2000) in mice, to identification of differentially expressed genes in human myometrium during pregnancy and labour (Aguan *et al.*, 2000).

The ability to examine the transcriptome on a system-wide or genome-wide basis enables not only a thorough comparison between treatments, developmental stages or genotypes, but also the opportunity to identify and link pathways that play critical roles in regulating important reproductive phenotypes. This bridge between genetics and physiology will be critical for implementing a fully integrated research programme combining quantitative genetics, genomics, proteomics, metabolomics and phenomics. It is likely that such an approach will be required to dissect fully the complex and polygenic nature of reproductive traits in pigs, and lead to discoveries that will have a strong impact on improvement of reproduction in the pork industry.

Functional genomics in pigs – early studies

For many years, researchers have focused on analysis of expression of individual genes involved in pig reproductive processes. For example, Li *et al.* (1997) evaluated the expression of follistatin and inhibin/activin alpha, beta (A) and beta (B) subunit genes in pig ovarian follicles during the follicular phase of the oestrous cycle, whereas Yelich *et al.* (1997a,b) focused on gene expression during the period of rapid trophoblastic elongation in the pig conceptus. Although much has been learned from these (and many other) single gene investigations, the use of functional genomic approaches promises to carry transcriptome analysis further by providing access to many genes in parallel. Although current and future efforts are focused on microarrays, functional genomic analysis of transcription differences has been taking place in the absence of genomic sequence or even large, defined sets of expressed sequence tags (ESTs). Differential display PCR (Liang and Pardee, 1992) has been used successfully to isolate genes that have important roles in the reproductive biology of pigs.

Li *et al.* (1996) used differential display PCR to isolate transcripts that are differentially expressed in the anterior pituitary gland of Meishan and White Composite sexually mature boars. Several transcripts showing differential amplification were isolated including the gene for the β-subunit of thyroid stimulating hormone (TSH-β). Several attempts have been made to isolate genes that are expressed by the uterus and the conceptus during early pregnancy using differential display PCR. Green *et al.* (1996) used differential display PCR to isolate putative transcripts differentially expressed in the peri-implantation (days 11–12) endometrium of unilaterally pregnant pigs, including the pig gene homologous to human spermidine/spermine N1-acetyltransferase (SSAT). Chang *et al.* (2000) conducted differential display PCR experiments to isolate transcripts from the epithelium of oviducts from gilts carrying embryos at various stages of early development. Wilson *et al.* (2000) used RNA arbitrarily primed-PCR (RAP–PCR) to search for genes differentially expressed by trophectodermal cells during elongation of the pig conceptus. The pig heterogeneous nuclear ribonucleoprotein (hnRNP) A2/B1 was found to be differentially expressed by trophectodermal cells during the elongation process.

Differential display PCR has also been used to isolate genes that are differentially expressed by cell cultures derived from pig gonadal tissue. Clouscard-Martinato *et al.* (1998) used differential display PCR to isolate transcripts differentially expressed by pig primary granulosa cells in culture in the presence or absence of FSH. A total of 16 differentially amplified differential display PCR fragments were isolated and sequenced, of which 12 were regulated by FSH. Tosser-Klopp *et al.* (1997) isolated 238 clones by differential hybridization from a pig granulosa cell cDNA library, using probes prepared from RNA extracted from either untreated or FSH-treated cells. In a follow-up study (Tosser-Klopp *et al.*, 2001), several of these clones were functionally evaluated in granulosa cells (with or without FSH treatment) and in fresh isolated ovarian follicles using comparative RT–PCR analysis.

In addition, differential display PCR has been used in attempts to dissect the genetic response to long-term selection for components of litter size in pigs, using both anterior pituitary gland (Bertani *et al.*, 2000a,b) and ovarian follicle tissue (Gladney *et al.*, 2000a,b). This work is described in more detail below.

EST development

The raw material for large-scale functional genomics research in pigs is DNA sequence. Although whole genome sequencing in pigs is unlikely to occur in the near future (at least in the public domain), several large-scale studies to develop extensive catalogues of expressed sequence tags from a variety of relevant pig tissues are in progress.

Scientists at the Roman L. Hruska US Meat Animal Research Center (MARC) are sequencing (5' single pass reads) from two normalized cDNA libraries constructed from pooled tissues (library 1: embryos from day 10 to day 30; and library 2: testes, ovary, pituitary, hypothalamus, placenta and endometrium). Over 43 000 EST sequences have been submitted to Genbank (B. A. Freking, personal communication). Sequencing within these libraries is continuing, and a third pooled-tissue library is currently being processed for creation of a new normalized cDNA library.

The Animal Science Department at the University of Missouri (principal investigators: R. S. Prather and B. N. Day), through primary funding from Monsanto Company, is focusing EST discovery efforts on female reproductive tissues (oocyte, preimplantation stage embryo, oviduct and uterus). To date, this project has generated 29 658 EST sequences (ascswine. rnet.missouri.edu).

The Pig Reproduction EST Project is a publicly funded (USDA-NRICGP) consortium comprising Iowa State University (Coordinating Institution; pigest.genome.iastate.edu), the University of Iowa, the University of Missouri, the University of Nebraska and the National Center for Genomic Resources (NCGR; Albuquerque, NM). The consortium has produced a total of 17 libraries from the following tissues: whole embryo (day 14, day 20 and day 45 of gestation); term placenta; anterior pituitary (day 0, day 5 and day 12 of oestrus); hypothalamus (day 0, day 5 and day 12 of oestrus); ovary (day 0, day 5 and day 12 of oestrus); and uterus (day 12 and day 14 of gestation). By January 2001 (Tuggle *et al.*, 2001), a total of 10 124 EST sequences (out of an overall goal of 20 000) had been produced and most have been submitted to Genbank. As assessed by cluster analysis of 9911 sequences, these data represent 6655 different genes for a novelty rate of 67.2%. In addition, selected ESTs (*n* = 700) will be localized physically using radiation hybrid mapping to improve the density of genes in the pig genetic maps and to facilitate more powerful comparative mapping. Approximately 10% of this mapping has been completed. Such comparative maps will be critical for capitalizing on the large-scale studies undertaken to sequence the complete human and mouse genomes.

Our group is focusing on ESTs from a normalized library developed from ovarian follicles (2–10 mm in diameter) at various stages of folliculogenesis (Caetano *et al.*, 2001). A total of 5231 processed sequences were assembled into 3479 clusters (33.5% of the sequences were redundant). BLAST searches of the Genbank nucleotide database (non-redundant; does not include EST database) were performed with sequences from each cluster. A total of 1037 sequences did not match any of the sequences in the nucleotide database (42% novelty rate). All sequences have been released into Genbank.

At the University of Illinois, libraries have been made from whole fetuses at various stages of early gestation, and from skeletal muscle from fetuses at the mid- and late stages of gestation (J. Beever, personal communication). Over 5000 clones have been sequenced from these libraries.

In addition, several smaller studies have contributed numerous ESTs to Genbank from reproductively relevant tissues, including granulosa cells (Tosser-Klopp *et al.*, 1997, 2001;

Clouscard-Martinato *et al.*, 1998), ovarian follicles (Gladney *et al.*, 2000a,b) and anterior pituitary (Bertani *et al.*, 2000a,b). All of these ESTs have resulted from projects focusing directly on functional analysis using differential display PCR or differential hybridization.

A pig gene index has been generated through collaboration between MARC and The Institute for Genomic Research (TIGR; Rockville, MD) and this index clusters all public EST sequences. As of August 2001, 13 017 tentative consensus clusters comprising 53 082 ESTs have been identified and there are an additional 30 014 single ESTs (Release 3.0; tigr.org/tdb/ssgi). Thus, it is likely that publicly available ESTs represent over 50% of the genes in the expressed pig genome.

The Nebraska functional genomics effort – a case study

Unique University of Nebraska (UN-L) genetic model

The UN-L selection lines represent a unique biological resource that will be valuable for identifying genes that control variation in ovulation rate, litter size and embryo survival in pigs, and for discovering pathways and mechanisms regulating reproduction. The high index (I) line has advantages of 7.4 ova, three fully formed pigs and 1.4 live pigs per litter compared with the randomly selected contemporary control (C) line (Johnson *et al.*, 1999). This research model differs considerably from others such as the Meishan paradigm, because the pigs are highly viable in a commercial setting. Understanding the genetics and biology of reproduction in these pigs can thus lead to immediate technology transfer to the industry, and the I line is now an important component of commercial pig production.

The observed difference in ovulation rate in the UN-L selection lines is primarily the result of changes in the dynamics of follicular development (Yen, 1999), which in turn have been shown by independent studies to be controlled by the expression of several genes. Our work to understand the genetic and physiological control of reproduction in these lines began with a genome-wide QTL screen (Cassady *et al.*, 2001) and analysis of selected candidate genes (Linville *et al.*, 2001). We next focused on gene expression analysis using differential display PCR methods (Bertani *et al.*, 2000a,b; Gladney *et al.*, 2000a,b). Recently, we have created and partially characterized a normalized ovarian follicle cDNA library (Caetano *et al.*, 2001), and production of follicle-specific expression microarrays is nearly completed, allowing for comprehensive investigation of the transcriptional factors that have changed as correlated responses to selection for components of litter size. We have thus created the resources necessary to monitor simultaneously the expression of thousands of genes normally expressed in ovarian follicles, and to use these resources to determine the expression profile of developing ovarian follicles in the UN-L selection lines.

QTL and candidate gene analysis

A three-generation resource population was developed by crossing low indexing animals from the randomly selected C line with high indexing animals from the high I selection line (Cassady *et al.*, 2001). Phenotypic data were collected in F_2 females for ovulation rate, age at puberty, litter size and number of nipples. Litter size data included number of fully formed, live, stillborn and mummified pigs. The genotypes of grandparent, F_1 and F_2 ($n = 423$) animals were determined for 151 microsatellite markers distributed across all 19 chromosomes. Average spacing between markers was approximately 19 cm. LOD scores were calculated by least squares, including fixed effects of sire–dam combination and replicate. Genome-wide significance thresholds of 5% and 10% were calculated using an empirical permutation approach. There was evidence at the 5% significance level that QTL affects ovulation rate on SSC9, age at puberty on SSC7 and SSC8, number of stillborn pigs on SSC5 and SSC13, and number of fully formed pigs on SSC11. At the 10% significance level there was evidence of additional QTL affecting age at puberty on SSC7, SSC8, and SSC12, and number born live on SSC11.

In addition, a candidate gene approach was used to determine whether specific loci explain responses in ovulation rate and number of fully formed, live, stillborn and mummified pigs at birth observed in two lines selected for ovulation rate and litter size compared with a randomly selected C line (Linville *et al.*, 2001). The IOL line was selected for an index of ovulation rate and embryonic survival for eight generations, followed by eight generations of two-stage selection for ovulation rate and litter size. The C line was selected at random for 16 generations. The COL line, derived from the C line at generation eight, underwent eight generations of two-stage selection. IOL and C lines differed in mean estimated breeding value by 6.1 ova and 4.7 fully formed pigs, whereas COL and C lines differed by 2.2 ova and 2.9 fully formed pigs (Ruiz-Flores and Johnson, 2001). The genotype of pigs was determined for the retinal-binding protein 4 (*RBP4*), epidermal growth factor (*EGF*), oestrogen receptor (*ESR*), prolactin receptor (*PRLR*), follicle stimulating hormone β (*FSHβ*) and prostaglandin-endo-peroxide synthase 2 (*PTGS2*) loci. On the basis of a chi-squared analysis for homogeneity of genotypic frequencies, distributions for *PRLR*, *FSHβ* and *PTGS2* were significantly different among lines. Differences in gene frequencies between IOL versus C and COL versus C were: 0.33 ± 0.25 and 0.16 ± 0.26 for *PRLR*, 0.35 ± 0.20 and 0.15 ± 0.24 for *FSHβ*, and 0.16 ± 0.16 and 0.08 ± 0.18 for *PTGS2*. Although these differences are consistent with a model of selection acting on these loci, estimates of additive and dominance effects at these loci did not differ from zero and several of them had signs that were inconsistent with the changes in allele frequencies. We were not able to find significant associations between the polymorphic markers and phenotypes studied; however, it cannot be ruled out that other genetic variation within these candidate genes has an effect on the traits studied.

The QTL studies in the UN-L selection lines, taken together with the other primary pig reproduction QTL experiments (Rohrer *et al.*, 1999; Wilkie *et al.*, 1999), demonstrate relatively inconsistent results and poorly resolved localizations of putative genes. The small number of detected reproduction QTL and the low detection resolution attained may be a consequence of the highly polygenic control of these traits, by loci with small effects that interact with each other and with the environment. Given current resources and power of investigation, it is extremely unlikely that the underlying polygenes controlling the inheritance of reproductive phenotypes will be identified.

Functional genomics, differential display PCR studies

Reproductive tissues (anterior pituitary gland and ovarian follicles) were collected from I and C sows from the UN-L selection lines on day 2 and day 4 after $PGF_{2\alpha}$ administration between day 12 and day 14 of the oestrous cycle (that is, follicular phase). Differential display PCR was conducted in both ovarian follicles and in anterior pituitaries, using 200 primer combinations (10 anchor oligo-dT 3′ primers and 20 arbitrary 5′ 10-mers), to compare gene expression between the selection lines.

Anterior pituitary. Differential display PCR yielded 372 putative differentially expressed bands; 151 of these were cloned and sequenced yielding anterior pituitary ESTs that were deposited into Genbank (Bertani *et al.*, 2000a,b). Confirmation of differential expression by northern blotting was undertaken for several of the most promising results, confirming that FSHβ, ferritin (heavy chain) and G-beta-like protein are expressed differently in the two lines (Fig. 1).

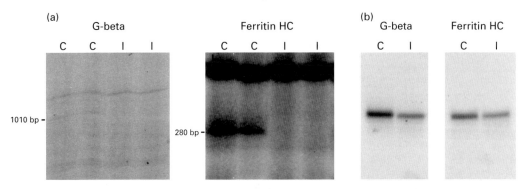

Fig. 1. (a) Differentially expressed genes in anterior pituitaries from the Nebraska high index and control selection lines of pigs. cDNA samples were amplified using PCR with 200 combinations of differential display PCR primers. (b) Differentially expressed bands were isolated, sequenced and used as probes in northern blots for confirmation of differences. Two confirmed differentially expressed genes are shown: G-beta-like protein and ferritin heavy chain (HC). C: control line; I: index line.

Ovarian follicles. Twelve pools of mRNA from follicles of different size classes dissected on day 2 or day 4 (Gladney *et al.*, 2000a,b) were used in the differential display PCR, resulting in 282 putative differentially expressed bands. Of these, 107 were cloned and sequenced, yielding 84 unique follicle ESTs that were deposited in Genbank. Northern blot hybridization confirmed expression results for calpain I light subunit, cytochrome C oxidase subunit III, cytochrome P450 aromatase and cytochrome P450 side chain cleavage. In addition to differences among selection lines, changes in gene expression were found between days of the follicular period, and between sizes of follicle (Fig. 2).

Further confirmation. Unfortunately, differential display PCR is labour intensive and is prone to a high rate of false positives. Given that each putative change in gene expression must be confirmed individually, we have printed all of the clones representing putative differentially expressed genes (*n* = approximately 250) from the above two experiments on to glass slides as microarrays. These microarrays are being used to confirm simultaneously each potential change in gene expression. In this manner, it is likely that many additional genes will be confirmed to have differential expression between the high I and C selection lines.

These two differential display PCR studies demonstrate changes in pituitary and follicular gene expression as the result of long-term selection for reproduction. Integration of QTL and expression studies will help to determine whether these changes represent actual genetic variation within predisposition genes (QTL), or whether they are the result of regulation of physiological genes that represent correlated responses to selection manifested downstream from the causative genetic variation. On the basis of comparison of the map locations of these differentially expressed genes and the QTL identified for reproductive traits in the same populations, it appears that the latter explanation is more likely.

In these studies, although interesting results were obtained that could result in potentially new mechanisms to investigate as contributors to genetic control of reproduction, it is difficult to examine simultaneously correlated genes and multiple members of pathways. Given that a plethora of EST data are now available in the pig, microarray analysis will be a much more powerful method for analysis of gene expression and large-scale functional genomics experimentation.

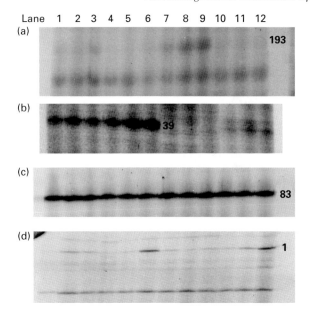

Lane	Line	Day	Size (mm)
1	I	2	4.0–4.25
2	I	2	4.5–4.75
3	I	2	5.0–5.25
4	I	4	4.0–4.5
5	I	4	5.0–5.5
6	I	4	6–7
7	C	2	4.0–4.25
8	C	2	4.5–4.75
9	C	2	5.0–5.25
10	C	4	4.0–4.5
11	C	4	5.0–5.5
12	C	4	6–7

Fig. 2. Differential display gel images of ovarian follicle mRNA showing (a) differences between days of folliculogenesis (day 2 versus day 4; band 193), (b) differences between lines (high index versus control; band 39), (c) bands demonstrating equal expression (band 83) and (d) differences between different follicle sizes (band 1). C: control line; I: index line.

Functional genomics, microarrays – cross-species hybridization

Before the development of pig ESTs and microarrays, the only opportunity to use microarray technology was to attempt cross-species hybridization with arrays developed for humans or mice. Incyte UniGEM human gene chips were used to examine changes in follicular gene expression between the UN-L selection lines (C. D. Gladney and D. Pomp, unpublished). For microarray analysis, two mRNA pools, containing follicles (day 2; 4.50–4.75 mm) from two I or two C line sows were evaluated on the Incyte UniGEM V1.0 human chip (approximately 7000 gene probes). An additional evaluation on the Incyte UniGEM V2.0 human chip (approximately 9100 gene probes) was performed using follicles (day 2; 4.50–5.00 mm) from four sows selected from the I line and five sows selected from the C line sows. UniGEM V1.0 results indicated significant differences between I and C lines (statistical significance defined as two-fold or greater relative expression when comparing I and C lines, following adjustment for expression of control probes) for 33 genes. UniGEM V2.0 results indicated 21 significant differences between C and I lines. Results were inconsistent between the two array hybridizations. However, expression differences for two genes, *follistatin* and *nuclear receptor subfamily 4, group A, member 1*, were confirmed using northern blot hybridization. This study represents the first application of microarray techniques to livestock populations and to study the underlying effects of long-term selection on gene expression. However, the current development of significant EST resources in pigs will enable pig-specific microarray experimentation, thus eliminating the need for future cross-species hybridization studies.

Functional genomics, microarrays – pig follicle microarray

Although the ultimate tool for transcriptome analysis will be a genome-wide microarray encompassing all pig genes, smaller, more directed projects could now be initiated with existing techniques and resources. Given our focus on understanding the changes that have occurred in the ovarian follicle as the result of selection for litter size, we have established resources to investigate this in a high throughput and powerful manner. Our experimental paradigm is presented as a flow-chart (Fig. 3).

cDNA library construction. Gilts from high and low UN-L ovulation rate selection lines (Lamberson *et al.*, 1991) were injected with $PGF_{2\alpha}$ on day 13 (day 0 of treatment) of the oestrous cycle. Ovaries were harvested by ovariectomy on days 0–6 after treatment, and follicles were dissected. mRNA isolated from ovarian follicles (2.0–10.0 mm in diameter) was used to construct a cDNA library (5×10^6 c.f.u.) with an average insert size of 1.2 kb. This cDNA library was subsequently normalized to decrease the relative number of redundant messages derived from highly transcribed genes (Soares *et al.*, 1994; Bonaldo *et al.*, 1996).

Plasmid DNA was isolated from clones derived from the normalized ovarian follicle cDNA library for sequencing. Raw sequences obtained with Li-Cor 4200 (Lincoln, NE) sequencers were processed with an automated sequence-processing software pipeline. A total of 5231 processed sequences were assembled into 3479 clusters (33.5% of the sequences were redundant). BLAST searches of the nucleotide database (all non-redundant GenBank + EMBL + DDBJ + PDB sequences, but no EST, STS, GSS, or HTGS sequences) were performed with sequences from each cluster (for reference, see www.ncbi.nlm.nih.gov/BLAST). A total of 1037 sequences did not match any of the sequences in the nucleotide database (42% novelty rate).

Microarray construction. Clones representing the 3479 unique EST clusters, the 107 follicle ESTs isolated in the differential display PCR study and several other genes known to be expressed in follicles but not represented in the clone list were arrayed on glass slides in duplicate. A total of 120 duplicated arrays have been produced to support an experimental design to compare gene expression between the I and C selection lines (Fig. 4).

Expression studies. The UN-L selection lines have different numbers of follicles of different size classes during the follicular phase. Labelled mRNA will be hybridized to the follicle microarrays from whole ovaries and dissected follicles from gilts (generation 18; high I and C selection lines). Studies with whole ovaries will provide a complete, overall picture of follicular gene expression, by including follicles of all sizes and health status. Studies within pools of healthy follicles of similar size are designed to search for expression differences within and between standardized conditions, to provide insights into the mechanisms underlying differences in ovulation rate in the I and C selection lines.

The merging of genetics and reproductive biology

The chromosomal regions that have been found to harbour reproduction QTL do not appear to coincide with many of the most prominent candidate genes, selected based on physiological evidence. Consider QTL to represent 'redisposition genes' or those within which heritable genetic variations (DNA polymorphisms) explain phenotypic variation in traits. Alternatively, consider genes the protein products of which are key regulators of reproduction to represent 'physiological genes'. Merging of existing databases and genetic maps indicates a

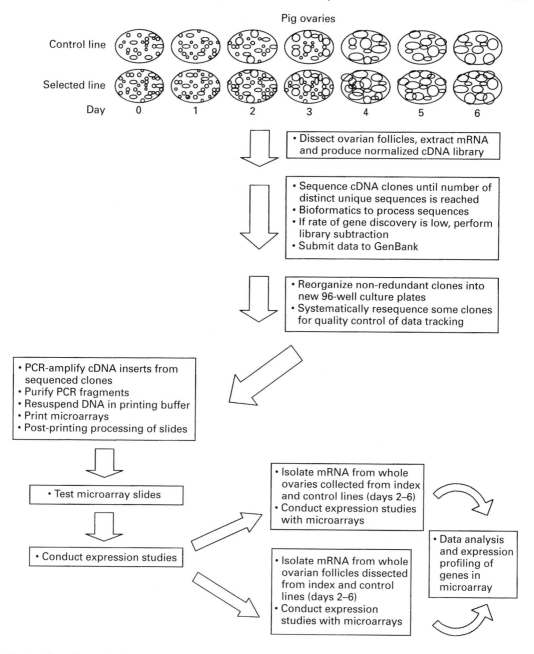

Fig. 3. Flow chart of Nebraska Functional Genomics Project. Initially, a normalized library was created and characterized by sequencing genes. Microarrays were printed on glass slides and expression analysis was used in an attempt to determine the transcriptional changes caused by selection for enhanced reproduction.

potential 'polygenic paradox', whereby predisposition and physiological genes appear to represent two distinct subsets of genes. In other words, evidence for an important role of a protein in regulation of a phenotype does not necessarily implicate the underlying gene as a QTL. This may represent our relatively poor knowledge of existing genes (that is, many

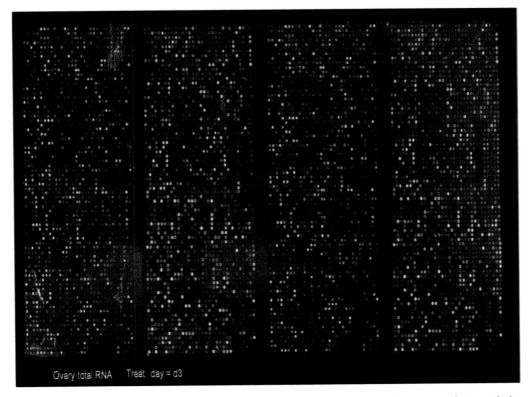

Fig. 4. Representative image of hybridization of control (Cy3) and index (Cy5) line mRNA from a whole ovary to the ovarian follicle microarray. The array is organized into four quadrants. The two left quadrants contain 4608 spots with clones representing 3479 unique gene clusters, several hundred random duplicates, the 107 follicle-expressed sequence tags (ESTs) isolated in the differential display PCR study, several other candidate genes known to be expressed in follicles and a panel of control yeast transcripts. The two right quadrants contain the same clones, providing replication of results within each array. For this hybridization, green and red indicate over-expression in the control and index lines, respectively, whereas yellow indicates relatively equal expression.

candidate genes have yet to be discovered) and of how genes function and interact. However, it can also be hypothesized that QTL primarily represent regulatory elements or initiation factors in a cascade of events, culminating in expression of physiological genes. Fuller understanding of this 'polygenic paradox' will require broad evaluation at the DNA, mRNA, protein and detailed phenotypic levels. The merging and integrating of quantitative genetics, functional genomics, proteomics, metabolomics and phenomics will establish linkages between predisposition and physiology, enhancing our understanding of how economically important traits in domestic animals are controlled and regulated, and facilitating improvement via genetics, intervention and management.

In particular, functional genomics will be a very powerful tool for studying the quantitative polygenic control of reproduction, as well as for understanding the underlying biology and physiology. Gene expression profiles between selection lines (or for example between divergent breeds) will allow for the dissection of selection response (or genetic variation) into two major categories: (i) loci that have been selected for (by definition, the QTL); and (ii) genes the expression of which (quantity or quality of mRNA) has changed as the result of direct or

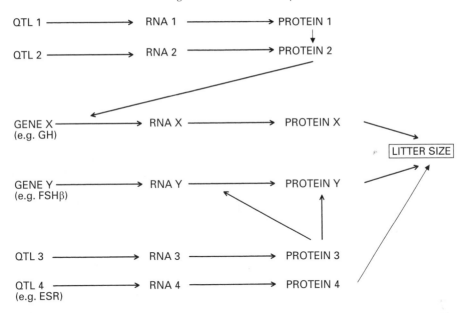

Fig. 5. Schematic diagram representing a simplified hypothesis of the genetic architecture of a complex polygenic trait, such as litter size or ovulation rate in pigs. Quantitative trait loci (QTL) represent predisposition genes, or those within which heritable genetic variations (DNA polymorphisms) explain phenotypic variation in traits. Alternatively, genes that produce proteins that are key regulators of reproduction, but within which may be no important genetic variation, represent 'physiological genes'. In this hypothesis, some QTL may directly influence a reproductive phenotype (for example, oestrogen receptor (ESR)), but more often (for example QTL 1, 2, 3) will exert effects by interacting with and regulating expression of 'physiological genes' (for example, FSHβ, growth hormone (GH)) or other QTL.

indirect interaction with QTL (Fig. 5). It is within this second category that we are most likely to identify the key components underlying the biology of reproduction.

These results support the traditional hypothesis that quantitative traits are controlled by a large number of genes, each with a small or moderate effect. In other words, there are many QTL that operate in tandem and with potentially complex interactions to control reproduction genetically. Although the heritable genetic variation must, by definition, reside within QTL, it is likely that these genes are regulatory and initiate critical changes in the transcription or translation of other genes, within which heritable sequence variation does not occur (Fig. 5). For example, FSH is clearly a critical rate-limiting protein in the determination of ovulation rate in pigs, and has been implicated definitively as an important correlated response to selection for increased ovulation rate and litter size. However, there is no evidence that the FSHβ locus is a QTL for reproduction. Thus, reproductive QTL must stimulate changes in FSHβ mRNA profiles through direct interaction, or through a cascade of regulatory events, which may also be manifested at the mRNA or protein levels. Further support for this contention is provided by recent work searching for QTL for FSH concentrations in Meishan–White composite boars (G. Rohrer, personal communication). Although several chromosomal regions were found to harbour genes with effects on FSH concentrations, the FSHβ locus itself was not implicated as a QTL.

Conclusion

One important issue in relation to the use of functional genomics as a tool to study reproduction is that, by nature, the use of microarrays for discovery is more 'question-driven' than 'hypothesis-driven'. At least initially, large-scale and high throughput determination of differentially expressed genes will potentially uncover vast databases of putative genes involved in reproductive processes. Many of these may not have been considered to have important roles in reproduction. In addition, new pathways and links between pathways may be uncovered. Indeed, it is this potential for new discovery that makes functional genomics such an appealing paradigm.

However, it is still critical that the design of functional genomics experiments is based on relevant scientific hypotheses, which will be required for determining which samples to study, and the temporal and spatial coordinates to be used. Furthermore, perhaps the most important outcome of functional genomics is that it will be 'hypothesis-generating', revealing significant new opportunities for experimentation as the plethora of collected expression data becomes organized and better understood.

Finally, this discussion would be remiss if it were not emphasized that evaluation of the transcriptome is but one important component of understanding how the genome influences reproduction. Amounts of mRNA are themselves phenotypes, under the potentially strong influence of environmental factors and interactions with other genetic components. Importantly, they may not be directly correlated with concentrations or activity of their respective translated proteins, or with the economically relevant end-point phenotypes such as litter size or age at puberty. Although functional genomics may uncover a large amount of information, significant efforts will be required to confirm and corroborate the influences of changes in gene expression within the broader, complex genetic and physiological models that are currently used.

References

Aguan K, Carvajal JA, Thompson LP and Weiner CP (2000) Application of a functional genomics approach to identify differentially expressed genes in human myometrium during pregnancy and labour *Human Reproduction* **6** 1141–1145

Bassett DE, Jr, Eisen MB and Boguski MS (1999) Gene expression informatics – it's all in your mine *Nature Genetics* **21** (Supplement 1) 51–55

Bertani GR, Gladney C, Johnson RK and Pomp D (2000a) Differentially expressed genes in anterior pituitary of pigs selected for reproduction *Plant and Animal Genome VIII, San Diego* 201 (Abstract)

Bertani GR, Gladney C, Johnson RK and Pomp D (2000b) Pig anterior pituitary EST's isolated by differential display in gene expression study of two lines selected for fertility *27th International Conference on Animal Genetics, Minneapolis, July* 73 (Abstract)

Bonaldo MF, Lennon G and Soares MB (1996) Normalization and subtraction; two approaches to facilitate gene discovery *Genome Research* **6** 791–806

Brown PO and Botstein D (1999) Exploring the new world of the genome with DNA microarrays *Nature Genetics* **21** (Supplement 1) 33–37

Caetano AR, Johnson RK and Pomp D (2001) Characterization of a normalized cDNA library of pig ovarian

follicles *Plant and Animal Genome IX, San Diego* 77 (Abstract)

Cassady JP, Johnson RK, Pomp D, Rohrer GA, Van Vleck LD, Spiegel EK and Gilson KM (2001) Identification of quantitative trait loci affecting reproduction in pigs *Journal of Animal Science* **79** 623–633

Chang HS, Cheng WT, Wu KH and Choo KB (2000) Identification of genes expressed in the epithelium of porcine oviduct containing early embryos at various stages of development *Molecular Reproduction and Development* **56** 331–335

Clouscard-Martinato C, Mulsant P, Robic A, Bonnet A, Gasser F and Hatey F (1998) Characterization of FSH-regulated genes isolated by mRNA differential display from pig ovarian granulosa cells *Animal Genetics* **29** 98–106

Clutter AC and Brascamp EW (1998) Genetics of performance traits. In *The Genetics of the Pig* pp 427–462 Eds MF Rothschild and A Ruvinsky. CAB International, Wallingford

DeRisi J, Penland L, Brown PO, Bittner ML, Meltzer PS, Ray M, Chen Y, Su YA and Trent JM (1996) Use of a cDNA microarray to analyse gene expression patterns in human cancer *Nature Genetics* **14** 457–460

Ermolaeva O, Rastogi M, Pruitt KD *et al.* (1998) Data

management and analysis for gene expression arrays *Nature Genetics* **20** 19–23

Gladney C, Bertani GR, Johnson RK and Pomp D (2000a) Evaluation of gene expression in ovarian follicles of pigs selected for reproduction using microarray and differential display PCR technologies *Plant and Animal Genome VIII, San Diego* **201** (Abstract)

Gladney C, Bertani GR, Johnson RK and Pomp D (2000b) Differential display PCR and microarray evaluation of ovarian follicle gene expression in pigs selected for reproduction *27th International Conference on Animal Genetics, Minneapolis, July* **73** (Abstract)

Green ML, Blaeser LL, Simmen FA and Simmen RC (1996) Molecular cloning of spermidine/spermine N1-acetyltransferase from the periimplation porcine uterus by messenger ribonucleic acid differential display; temporal and conceptus-modulated gene expression *Endocrinology* **137** 5447–5455

Iyer VR, Eisen MB, Ross DT *et al.* (1999) The transcriptional program in the response of human fibroblasts to serum *Science* **283** 83–87

Jiang M, Ryu J, Kiraly M, Duke K, Reinke V and Kim SK (2001) Genome-wide analysis of development and sex-regulated gene expression profiles in *Caenorhabditis elegans*. *Proceedings National Academy of Sciences USA* **98** 218–223

Johnson RK, Nielsen MK and Casey DS (1999) Responses in ovulation rate; embryonal survival, and litter traits in swine to 14 generations of selection to increase litter size *Journal of Animal Science* **77** 541–557

Lamberson WR, Johnson RK, Zimmerman DR and Long TE (1991) Direct responses to selection for increased litter size, decreased age at puberty or random selection following selection for ovulation rate in swine *Journal of Animal Science* **69** 3129–3143

Lander ES (1999) Array of hope *Nature Genetics* **21** (Supplement) 3–4

Li MD, Matteri RL, Macdonald GJ, Wise TH and Ford JJ (1996) Overexpression of beta-subunit of thyroid-stimulating hormone in Meishan swine identified by differential display *Journal of Animal Science* **74** 2104–2111

Li MD, DePaola LV and Ford JJ (1997) Expression of follistatin and inhibin/activin subunit genes in porcine follicles *Biology of Reproduction* **57** 112–118

Liang P and Pardee AB (1992) Differential display of eukaryotic messenger RNA by means of the polymerase chain reaction *Science* **257** 967–971

Linville RC, Pomp D, Johnson RK and Rothschild MF (2001) Candidate gene analysis for loci affecting litter size and ovulation rate in swine *Journal of Animal Science* **79** 60–67

Liu H, He Z and Rosenwaks Z (2001) Application of complementary DNA microarray (DNA chip) technology in the study of gene expression profiles during folliculogenesis *Fertility and Sterility* **75** 947–955

Rohrer GA, Ford JJ, Wise TH, Vallet JL and Christenson RK (1999) Identification of quantitative trait loci affecting female reproductive traits in a multigeneration Meishan–White composite swine population *Journal of Animal Science* **77** 1385–1391

Rothschild MF (2000) Advances in pig molecular genetics, gene mapping and genomics. *X Reunion Nacional de Mejora Genetica Animal, Caldes de Montbui, June 8–9* (http://www.etsia.upv.es/acteon/docs/final.pdf)

Rothschild MF, Jacobson C, Vaske D *et al.* (1996) The estrogen receptor locus is associated with a major gene influencing litter size in pigs *Proceedings National Academy of Sciences USA* **93** 201–205

Ruíz-Flores A and Johnson RK (2001) Direct and correlated responses to two-stage selection for ovulation rate and number of fully formed pigs at birth in swine *Journal of Animal Science* **79** 2286–2297

Schena M, Shalon D, Davis RW and Brown PO (1995) Quantitative monitoring of gene expression patterns with a complementary DNA microarray *Science* **270** 467–470

Schena M, Shalon D, Heller R, Chai A, Brown PO and Davis RW (1996) Parallel human genome analysis; microarray-based expression monitoring of 1000 genes *Proceedings National Academy of Sciences USA* **93** 10 614–10 619

Soares MB, Bonaldo MF, Jelene P, Su L, Lawton L and Efstratiadis A (1994) Construction and characterization of a normalized cDNA library *Proceedings National Academy of Sciences USA* **91** 9228–9232

Tanaka TS, Jaradat SA, Lim MK *et al.* (2000) Genome-wide expression profiling of mid-gestation placenta and embryo using a 15 000 mouse development cDNA microarray *Proceedings National Academy of Sciences USA* **97** 9127–9132

Tess MW, Bennett GL and Dickerson GE (1983a) Simulation of genetic changes in life cycle efficiency of pork production I. A bioeconomic model *Journal of Animal Science* **56** 336–353

Tess MW, Bennett GL and Dickerson GE (1983b) Simulation of genetic changes in life cycle efficiency of pork production II. Effects of components on efficiency *Journal of Animal Science* **56** 354–368

Tosser-Klopp G, Benne F, Bonnet A, Mulsant P, Gasser F and Hatey F (1997) A first catalog of genes involved in pig ovarian follicular differentiation *Mammalian Genome* **8** 250–254

Tosser-Klopp G, Bonnet A, Yerle M and Hatey F (2001) Functional study and regional mapping of 44 hormono-regulated genes isolated from a porcine granulosa cell library *Genetics Selection Evolution* **33** 69–87

Tuggle CK, Green JA, Fitzsimmons C *et al.* (2001) Production of 17 cDNA libraries and successful EST sequencing of 10 124 clones from porcine female reproductive tissues *Journal of Animal Science* **79** 338 (Abstract)

Wilkie PJ, Paszek AA, Beattie CW, Alexander LJ, Wheeler MB and Schook LB (1999) A genomic scan of porcine reproductive traits reveals possible quantitative trait loci (QTLs) for number of corpora lutea *Mammalian Genome* **10** 573–578

Wilson ME, Sonstegard TS, Smith TP, Fahrenkrug SC and Ford SP (2000) Differential gene expression during elongation in the preimplantation pig embryo *Genesis* **26** 9–14

Yelich JV, Pomp D and Geisert RD (1997a) Detection of

D. Pomp et al.

transcripts for retinoic acid receptors, retinol-binding protein, and transforming growth factors during rapid trophoblastic elongation in the porcine conceptus *Biology of Reproduction* **57** 286–294

Yelich JV, Pomp D and Geisert RD (1997b) Ontogeny of elongation and gene expression in the early developing porcine conceptus *Biology of Reproduction* **57** 1256–1265

Yen HW (1999) *Follicular Development, Maturation and Atresia during the Estrous Cycle in Gilts Expressing High and Low Ovulation Rates* PhD Thesis, University of Nebraska-Lincoln

Reproduction Supplement **58**, 293–300

Cloning pigs: advances and applications

I. A. Polejaeva

PPL Therapeutics Inc., 1700 Kraft Drive, Suite 2400, Blacksburg, VA 24060, USA

Although mouse embryonic stem cells have been used widely for over a decade as an important tool for introducing precise genetic modification into the genome, demonstrating the great value of this technology in a range of biomedical applications, similar technology does not exist for domestic animals. However, the development of somatic cell nuclear transfer has bypassed the need for embryonic stem cells from livestock. The production of offspring from differentiated cell nuclei provides information and opportunities in a number of areas including cellular differentiation, early development and ageing. However, the primary significance of cloning is probably in the opportunities that this technology brings to genetic manipulation. Potential applications of gene targeting in livestock species are described with particular emphasis on the generation of pigs that can be used for xenotransplantation, and the production of improved models for human physiology and disease. The development of techniques for somatic cell nuclear transfer in pigs and the challenges associated with this technology are also reviewed.

Why clone pigs?

The continuously expanding gap between availability of organs and the number of patients awaiting an organ transplant is the major driving force behind most efforts to clone pigs. Between 1990 and 1999 the number of patients in the US waiting for organ transplants more than tripled from 21 914 in 1990 to 72 110 in 1999 (Transplant Patient Data Source, 2000). The organ donation programme initiated by the US Department of Health and Human Services was not able to reduce this gap. Annual cadaveric and living donor transplants over the same period increased at a far slower rate, from 15 009 in 1990 to 21 715 in 1999 (Fig. 1). This critical shortage of human organs for allotransplantation has forced researchers to look for alternative sources, one of which is xenotransplantation. Pig organs are the most compatible in terms of size and biology, and are ethically less controversial than alternative species (primates). However, pig organs must be genetically modified to overcome the natural destruction of pig organs by the human immune system. Gene targeting is likely to play a major role in preventing hyperacute rejection in organ xenotransplantation. Hyperacute rejection is the initial and most marked response to vascularized pig organs and is triggered by pre-formed antibodies binding to the endothelium lining of blood vessels in the pig organ. The bound human antibodies rapidly activate the complement cascade, as well as activating the endothelium and inducing a response causing it to become pro-coagulatory. The result of this process is total destruction of the graft within minutes to hours of transplantation.

Email: ipolejaeva@ppl-therapeutics.com

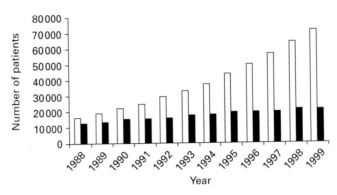

Fig. 1. Expanding gap between the number of patients waiting for organ transplantation (□) and the number of available donor transplants (■). Transplant Patient Data Source (2000).

Evidence has emerged that hyperacute rejection is due primarily to a carbohydrate epitope, galactose, linked via an α $(1{\rightarrow}3)$ linkage to a second molecule of galactose (α-1,3 gal), to which about 1% of human immunoglobulins crossreact (Sandrin *et al.*, 1993). The high concentration of circulating antibodies to this epitope is thought to form a first line of defence against pathogens that express α-1,3 gal. The most direct method of preventing the adverse immunological response involves the production of α-1,3 galactosyl transferase gene knockout donor animals. Removal of this enzyme activity would lead to the total lack of expression of the α-1,3 gal epitope on the cell surface, which should reduce hyperacute rejection markedly. It should also prevent acute vascular rejection, which is anti-α-1,3 gal antibody-mediated, and which occurs approximately 5 days after transplantation. It has been reported that a homozygous knockout of α-1,3 galactosyl transferase is not lethal in mice (Thall *et al.*, 1995; Tearle *et al.*, 1996). Knockout mice have normal organ development and although tissues of α-1,3 galactosyl transferase knockout mice show a reduction in activation of human complement, they still retain binding capacity for human xenogenic antibodies (Tanemura *et al.*, 2000). Gene targeting in murine embryonic stem cells has been used widely for over a decade as a powerful tool for introducing modifications of the germ line (Moreadith and Radford, 1997). However, embryonic stem cells that contribute to the germ line are not available for any other species. Nuclear transfer using targeted somatic cells offers a method for producing precise genetic modification in a range of livestock species. Unfortunately, recombination frequencies in somatic immortal cells are on average much lower than in embryonic stem cells (Arbones *et al.*, 1994). Furthermore, homologous recombination events are even less frequent in primary cells than in immortalized cell lines (Finn *et al.*, 1989). Another problem is that primary cultures have a limited lifespan and many of the clonal populations reach proliferative senescence. Nevertheless, two reports indicate that gene targeting insertion (McCreath *et al.*, 2000) and deletions (Denning *et al.*, 2001) can occur in primary sheep fibroblasts and that animals can be generated from targeted primary cells using nuclear transfer. Production of α-1,3 galactosyl transferase knockout pigs has not yet been accomplished, but the recent achievement of cloning pigs (Betthauser *et al.*, 2000; Onishi *et al.*, 2000; Polejaeva *et al.*, 2000) gives rise to increased expectation that it will be possible to produce knockout pigs.

In addition to their roles in xenotransplantation, pigs are often better models for human physiology and disease than rodents because of similarities in anatomy, physiology and size

(Petters, 1994). For example, pigs have a multipyramidal kidney with an undivided cortex; this occurs in only two other species, humans and dwarf water buffalo (Terris, 1986). Similarities in coronary anatomy make the pig an ideal model for ischaemic heart disease and atherosclerosis (Armstrong and Heistad, 1990). Pigs could also be a model for human eye diseases such as retinitis pigmentosa, because of the similarity in eye size and retinal anatomy (Adams, 1988). However, due to the previous low efficiency of transgenic livestock production and a lack of availability of homologous recombination techniques, these applications have been very limited. Somatic cell cloning could also be used as an alternative to microinjection for generating heteroplasmic animal models of mitochondrial DNA diseases. Genetic modifications in pigs also have a number of agricultural applications. A few examples of potential future benefits include: enhancement of resistance to disease and parasites, increased feed efficiency and modification of growth characteristics.

Techniques for nuclear transfer

The technique of nuclear transfer was proposed originally more than 60 years ago by Spemann (1938) as a method to study cellular differentiation. However, it was limited almost entirely to amphibians until McGrath and Solter (1983) demonstrated the possibilities of mammalian cloning. Robl and First (1985) were the first to describe nuclear transfer in pig embryos using a method for pronuclear exchange between zygotes as well as transfer of nuclei between two-cell stage embryos. Prather *et al.* (1988) demonstrated that metaphase II-arrested oocytes could be enucleated, activated and used as recipients for transferred nuclei. The nuclei of two- to eight-cell stage embryos were used as nuclear donors and after nuclear transfer they directed development to mid-gestation.

Techniques for nuclear transplantation involve a number of key factors, each of which potentially has a significant effect on cloning efficiency. These include: (i) removal of metaphase chromosomes from a metaphase II-arrested oocyte (enucleation); (ii) transfer of donor cell nuclei, in which a donor cell is either placed next to an 'enucleated' oocyte and fused using a precise electrical pulse, or the donor cell can be injected directly into the cytoplasm of the enucleated oocyte; (iii) activation of the reconstructed oocytes; (iv) embryo culture; and (v) transfer of the cloned embryos into a synchronized recipient.

Some of these factors have been addressed successfully and others require further investigation. Enucleation of recipient metaphase II oocytes using DNA-specific dyes to verify enucleation and transfer of donor cells are both highly efficient processes (near 100% efficiency).

Oocyte activation has been the most difficult technical component of the nuclear transfer procedure to refine. In all species, when metaphase II oocytes are used as recipients, the method of activation is crucial for subsequent development. Under normal conditions the fertilizing spermatozoon induces oocyte activation by generating a transient increase in the intracellular free Ca^{2+} concentration ($[Ca^{2+}]_i$). Activation of oocytes can be induced artificially by a variety of physical and chemical agents (for reviews see Whittingham, 1980; Prather *et al.*, 1999). Activation can be achieved either by a calcium-dependent mechanism or by a pathway downstream of the calcium signal through inhibition of protein synthesis or kinase inhibition. An increase in $[Ca^{2+}]_i$ can be generated by the entry of external Ca^{2+} through the oocyte plasma membrane, by exposing the oocytes to electric field pulses resulting in the formation of plasma membrane pores (Zimmermann and Vienken, 1982). This method of oocyte activation resulted in the production of viable offspring after transfer of a nucleus from a four-cell stage embryo (Prather *et al.*, 1989). Another method to increase $[Ca^{2+}]_i$ is by stimulating the release of Ca^{2+} from the smooth endoplasmic reticulum stores through Ca^{2+}

release channels using inisitol 1,4,5-triphosphate (IP_3) agonists. Ca^{2+}, Mg^{2+} ionophore is able to increase $[Ca^{2+}]_i$. Presicce and Yang (1994) reported that a combination of an increase in $[Ca^{2+}]_i$ and inhibition of protein synthesis or protein kinase resulted in higher rates of pronuclear formation.

Methods of embryo culture, which are not as advanced in pigs as in cows, may also play a crucial role in cloning. The results presented by Machaty *et al.* (1998) indicate that cultured embryos are developmentally competent (formed conceptuses), even though *in vitro* culture is not able to provide an environment comparable to *in vivo* conditions (lower cell number). A detailed study conducted by Wang *et al.* (1999) showed that abnormal embryonic division begins with the first cell cycle under *in vitro* culture conditions. Morphological abnormalities include fragmentation and binucleation. These morphological abnormalities were not observed in *in vivo*-derived embryos. Day 6 pig blastocysts produced *in vitro* have more than four times fewer cells than do *in vivo*-derived embryos (37.3 ± 11.7 versus 164.5 ± 51.9 nuclei per blastocyst, respectively). Wang *et al.* (1999) also observed an abnormal distribution of actin filaments in the *in vitro*-cultured embryos, which is a possible explanation for abnormal embryo cleavage. A combination of low efficiency of activation with suboptimal culture conditions can be detrimental to the success rates of nuclear transfer procedures.

The relative stage of the cell cycle of the donor and recipient cell is also crucial to the success of nuclear transfer and the production of live offspring. In mammalian species, enucleated metaphase II oocytes are the preferred recipient, owing to the lack of development obtained using enucleated zygotes (Robl *et al.*, 1987; Prather *et al.*, 1989). The use of a diploid donor cell allows the cycles of the donor and recipient to be co-ordinated, while the use of metaphase II oocytes as recipients maximizes the number of mitotic events that the donor chromatin undergoes before initiation of zygotic transcription. The importance of co-ordination of the cell cycle between the recipient cytoplasm and the incoming nuclear component has been discussed in great detail elsewhere (Collas *et al.*, 1992; Campbell *et al.*, 1993; Cheong *et al.*, 1993).

Somatic cell nuclear transfer

Successful somatic cell nuclear transfer using an embryo-derived differentiated cell population was first demonstrated in sheep by Campbell *et al.* (1996). The technique was repeated and extended subsequently using cell populations derived from fetal and adult donors in sheep (Wilmut *et al.*, 1997). The technique has been developed successfully for cattle (Cibelli *et al.*, 1998), goats (Baguisi *et al.*, 1999), mice (Wakayama *et al.*, 1998) and pigs (Polejaeva *et al.*, 2000). The somatic cell nuclear transfer system has an advantage compared with embryonic stem cell technology for producing transgenic animals, because the entire animal is derived from a single transgenic donor nucleus, thereby eliminating the need for generation of an intermediate chimaera before the effect of genetic modification can be assessed (Polejaeva and Campbell, 2000).

At the time of writing, three groups have reported the birth of cloned pigs (Table 1). In the first published report of cloned pigs, Polejaeva *et al.* (2000) used *in vivo*-matured oocytes and a double nuclear transfer procedure. Granulosa cell nuclei were transferred into enucleated recipient oocytes by electrofusion. Oocytes were activated at the time of fusion and an additional electrical activation pulse was applied 30–60 min later to induce a second wave of calcium. The fused embryos were placed into culture. The following day, a second round of nuclear transfer was performed by removing karyoplasts from 1-day-old nuclear transfer embryos, and transferring them into *in vivo*-derived zygotes from which the two pronuclei had been removed. Couplets were fused using an electrical pulse and transferred into

Table 1. Live births resulting from somatic cell nuclear transfer in pigs

Cell type	Cell donor	Donor cell culture conditions	Oocyte maturation	Oocyte activation	Embryo stage at the time of transfer	Live births/ number transferred (%)*	Reference
Granulosa	Adult	Confluent 0–2 days	*In vivo*	Electrical	One-cell	5/72 (6.9)	Polejaeva *et al.* (2000)
Fibroblast	Fetal	Confluent 16 days	*In vivo*	Electrical	Two- to eight-cell	1/36 (2.8)	Onishi *et al.* (2000)
Fibroblast	Fetal	Confluent 0–4 days	*In vitro*	Ionomycin and DMAP	One-cell	2/143 (1.4)	Betthauser *et al.* (2000)
Genital ridge	Fetal	Confluent 0–4 days	*In vitro*	Ionomycin and DMAP	Four-cell stage or later	2/164 (1.2)	Betthauser *et al.* (2000)

*This figure does not include the trials that have resulted in no offspring.

synchronized recipient gilts within 2 h after fusion. Five cloned piglets were produced. This system, which uses fertilized oocytes as cytoplast recipients, bypasses the inefficiencies of artificial activation procedures and may promote more successful development. However, it is very labour intensive and time-consuming. With the recent success in cloning pigs using a standard (single round) nuclear transfer (Betthauser *et al.*, 2000; Onishi *et al.*, 2000), coupled with the further optimization of activation and embryo culture conditions, the double nuclear transfer approach may be replaced by single nuclear transfer techniques.

Onishi *et al.* (2000) produced one cloned piglet by microinjection of somatic cell nuclei into enucleated oocytes, similar to a technique used previously to produce cloned mice (Wakayama *et al.*, 1998). Onishi *et al.* used *in vivo*-matured oocytes as recipients, as did Polejaeva *et al.* (2000), and fetal fibroblast cells were used as nuclear donors. Oocytes were activated by an electrical pulse applied 3–4 h after nuclear microinjection. After immersion in a short-term culture, 110 cloned embryos (two- to eight-cell stage) were transferred to four recipients, resulting in one pregnancy, which yielded one live offspring. It has been suggested that mitochondrial DNA heteroplasmy, resulting from the fusion of donor and recipient cells, could result in high rates of death and abnormal development in fused nuclear transfer embryos. Factors contained within the cytoplasm of a donor cell such as protein and mRNA transcripts could theoretically interfere with reprogramming and development of cloned embryos. This would favour the technique of nuclear transfer by microinjection, which removes much of the donor cell cytoplasm selectively. However, Steinborn *et al.* (2000) demonstrated that mitochondrial DNA heteroplasmy in cloned animals does not necessarily impede normal development.

Betthauser *et al.* (2000) applied techniques similar to those used in bovine cloning. *In vitro*-matured oocytes were used for nuclear transfer and electrofusion was applied to deliver the cell nucleus into an enucleated oocyte. The activation procedure involved increasing calcium concentrations using calcium ionophore (ionomycin) and inhibition of the activity of maturation-promoting factors using the kinase inhibitor, 6-dimethylaminopurine (DMAP). Two types of cell were used in this study: cells from the genital ridge and a population of cells derived from 47- to 51-day-old pig fetuses. Cloned embryos were cultured for up to 3 days and transferred into recipients, resulting in four cloned male pigs.

Many factors contribute to the development of reconstructed embryos. These factors include the quality of the recipient oocyte, method and timing of activation, and culture methodology. Similarly, induction and maintenance of pregnancy are dependent upon a range of factors, influenced by the quality of the transferred embryos, in combination with the age and hormonal status of the recipient. At the present time it is difficult to determine to what extent each factor or combination of factors has contributed to making pig cloning successful.

We have observed, as have a number of other scientists, significant pre- and post-natal mortality in both ovine and bovine nuclear transfer programmes. Placental (hydroallantois, reduced number of placentomes) and fetal (kidney defects, liver and brain pathology, metabolic and cardiovascular problems) developmental abnormalities associated with somatic cell nuclear transfer have been reported by several research groups (Cibelli *et al.*, 1998; Kato *et al.*, 1998; Wells *et al.*, 1999; Hill *et al.*, 2000). However, problems with developmental abnormalities and death at birth or soon after birth have not been observed in the cloned pigs (Polejaeva *et al.*, 2000; Betthauser *et al.*, 2001). In addition, no fetal losses have been observed after day 40 of gestation. Two factors that may contribute to the low rate of fetal loss are the very different type of placentation in pigs and the limited duration of embryo culture *in vitro*.

Conclusion

The use of nuclear transplantation for livestock species promises to provide enormous benefits. The impact of nuclear transfer on the fields of biotechnology, biomedicine and agriculture looks increasingly promising as new technology and scientific research continue to refine the process of nuclear transfer. However, the efficiency of this procedure is still low in relation to pregnancy and development-to-term rates. Significantly more research is needed to determine how cloning by somatic cell nuclear transfer is achieved. The mechanism of somatic cell nuclear reprogramming, the effect of karyoplast source and its differentiation on reprogramming, the effect of mismatches between nuclear and mitochondrial genes on development, as well as potential species-specific differences, are still unknown. For applied research, somatic cell nuclear transfer offers a new method for transgenesis and allows the production of disease models in species that are physiologically more similar to humans, thereby allowing the progression of disease and the benefits of any potential new therapies to be assessed more effectively. The successful development of nuclear transfer in pigs provides opportunities for multiple applications of gene targeting technology, allowing very precise genetic modifications, including gene knockouts, to be made.

The author would like to acknowledge the staff at PPL Therapeutic Inc. who have contributed to the nuclear transfer experiments: S-H. Chen, T. Vaught, R. Page, P. Jobst, S. Walker, B. Gragg and S. Ball. In addition, the support and helpful advice of D. Ayares, R. Greene and J. Robl in preparation of this manuscript are greatly appreciated.

References

Adams RJ (1988) Ophthalmic system. In *Experimental Surgery and Physiology: Induced Animal Models of Human Disease* pp 125–153 Eds MM Swindle and RJ Adams. Williams and Wilkins, Baltimore

Arbones ML, Austin HA, Capon DJ and Greenburg G (1994) Gene targeting in normal somatic cells: inactivation of the interferon-gamma receptor in myoblasts *Nature Genetics* **6** 90–97

Armstrong ML and Heistad DD (1990) Animal models of atherosclerosis *Atherosclerosis* **85** 15–23

Baguisi A, Behboodi E, Melican D et al. (1999) Production

of goats by somatic cell nuclear transfer *Nature Biotechnology* **17** 456–461

Betthauser J, Forsberg E, Augenstein M et al. (2000) Production of cloned pigs from *in vitro* systems *Nature Biotechnology* **18** 1055–1059

Betthauser J, Forsberg E, Jurgella G et al. (2001) Cloning pigs using *in vitro* systems *Theriogenology* **55** 255 (Abstract)

Campbell KH, Ritchie WA and Wilmut I (1993) Nuclear–cytoplasmic interactions during the first cell cycle of nuclear transfer reconstructed bovine embryos:

implications for deoxyribonucleic acid replication and development *Biology of Reproduction* **49** 933–942

Campbell KH, McWhir J, Ritchie WA and Wilmut I (1996) Sheep cloned by nuclear transfer from a cultured cell line *Nature* **380** 64–66

Cheong NT, Takahashi Y and Kanagawa H (1993) Birth of mice after transplantation of early cell-cycle-stage embryonic nuclei into enucleated oocytes *Biology of Reproduction* **48** 958–963

Cibelli JB, Stice SL, Golueke PJ, Kane JJ, Jerry J, Blackwell C, Ponce de Leon A and Robl JM (1998) Cloned transgenic calves produced from non-quiescent fetal fibroblasts *Science* **280** 1256–1258

Collas P, Pinto-Correia C, Ponce de Leon A and Robl JM (1992) Effect of donor cell cycle stage on chromatin and spindle morphology in nuclear transplant rabbit embryos *Biology of Reproduction* **46** 501–511

Denning C, Burl S, Ainslie A *et al.* (2001) Deletion of the α(1,3) galactosyl transferase (GGTA1) gene and the prion protein (PrP) gene in sheep *Nature Biotechnology* **19** 559–562

Finn GK, Kurz BW, Cheng RZ and Shmookler Reis RJ (1989) Homologous plasmid recombination is elevated in immortally transformed cells *Molecular Cell Biology* **9** 4009–4017

Hill JR, Winger QA, Long CR, Looney CR, Thompson JA and Westhusin ME (2000) Development rates of male bovine nuclear transfer embryos derived from adult and fetal cells *Biology of Reproduction* **62** 1135–1140

Kato Y, Tani T, Sotomaru Y, Kurokawa K, Kato J, Doguchi H, Yasue H and Tsunoda Y (1998) Eight calves cloned from somatic cells of a single adult *Science* **282** 2095–2098

McCreath KH, Howcroft J, Campbell KH, Colman A, Schnieke AE and Kind AJ (2000) Production of gene-targeted sheep by nuclear transfer from somatic cells *Nature* **405** 1066–1069

McGrath J and Solter D (1983) Nuclear transplantation in the mouse embryo by microsurgery and cell fusion *Science* **220** 1300–1302

Machaty Z, Day BN and Prather RS (1998) Development of early porcine embryos *in vitro* and *in vivo. Biology of Reproduction* **59** 451–455

Moreadith RW and Radford NB (1997) Gene targeting in embryonic stem cells: the new physiology and metabolism *Journal of Molecular Medicine* **75** 208–216

Onishi A, Iwamoto M, Akita T, Mikawa S, Takeda K, Awata T, Hanada H and Perry ACF (2000) Pig cloning by microinjection of fetal fibroblast nuclei *Science* **289** 1188–1190

Petters RM (1994) Transgenic livestock as genetic models of human disease *Reproduction, Fertility and Development* **6** 643–645

Polejaeva IA and Campbell KHS (2000) New advances in somatic cell nuclear transfer: application in transgenesis *Theriogenology* **53** 117–126

Polejaeva IA, Chen S, Vaught TD *et al.* (2000) Cloned pigs produced by nuclear transfer from adult somatic cells *Nature* **407** 86–90

Prather RS, Sims MM and First NL (1988) Nuclear

transplantation in early porcine embryos *Theriogenology* **29** 290 Abstract

Prather RS, Sims MM and First NL (1989) Nuclear transplantation in early pig embryos *Biology of Reproduction* **41** 414–418

Prather RS, Tao T and Machaty Z (1999) Development of the techniques for nuclear transfer in pigs *Theriogenology* **51** 487–498

Presicce GA and Yang X (1994) Nuclear dynamics of parthenogenesis of bovine oocytes matured *in vitro* for 20 and 40 hours and activated with combined ethanol and cycloheximide treatment *Molecular Reproduction and Development* **37** 61–68

Robl JM and First NL (1985) Manipulation of gametes and embryos *Journal of Reproduction and Fertility Supplement* **33** 101–114

Robl JM, Prather R, Barnes F, Eyestone W, Northey D, Gilligan B and First NL (1987) Nuclear transplantation in bovine embryos *Journal of Animal Science* **64** 642–647

Sandrin MS, Vaughan HA, Dabkowski PL and McKenzie IF (1993) Anti-pig IgM antibodies in human serum react predominantly with Gal(alpha 1-3)Gal epitopes *Proceedings National Academy of Sciences USA* **90** 11 391–11 394

Spemann H (1938) *Embryonic Development and Induction* pp 210–211. Yale University Press, New Haven

Steinborn R, Schinogl P, Zakhartchenko V, Achmann R, Schernthaner W, Stojkovic M, Wolf E, Muller M and Brem G (2000) Mitochondrial DNA heteroplasmy in cloned cattle produced by fetal and adult cell cloning *Nature Genetics* **25** 255–257

Tanemura M, Maruyama S and Galili U (2000) Differential expression of alpha-Gal epitopes (gal alpha1-3Gal beta1-4GlcNAc-R) on pig and mouse organs *Transplantation* **69** 187–190

Tearle RG, Tange MJ, Zannettino ZL *et al.* (1996) The alpha-1,3-galactosyltransferase knockout mouse: implications for xenotransplantation *Transplantation* **61** 13–19

Terris JM (1986) Swine as a model in renal physiology and nephrology: an overview. In *Swine in Biomedical Research* pp 1673–1689 Ed. ME Tumbleson. Plenum Press, New York

Thall AD, Malý P and Lowe JB (1995) Oocyte Gal alpha 1,3Gal epitopes implicated in sperm adhesion to the zona pellucida glycoprotein ZP3 are not required for fertilization in the mouse *Journal of Biochemistry* **270** 21 437–21 440

Transplant Patient Data Source (2000) February 16. Richmond, VA: *United Network for Organ Sharing:* http://www.patients.unos.org/data.html

Wakayama T, Perry ACF, Zucotti M, Johnson KR and Yanagimachi R (1998) Full-term development of mice from enucleated oocytes injected with cumulus cell nuclei *Nature* **394** 369–374

Wang W, Abeydeera LR, Han Y, Prather R and Day B (1999) Morphologic evaluation and actin filament distribution in porcine embryos produced *in vitro* and *in vivo. Biology of Reproduction* **60** 1020–1028

Wells DN, Misica PM and Tervit HR (1999) Production of cloned calves following nuclear transfer with cultured adult mural granulosa cells *Biology of Reproduction* **60** 996–1005

Whittingham DG (1980) Parthenogenesis in mammals. In *Oxford Reviews of Reproductive Biology* pp 205–231 Ed. CA Finn. Clarendon Press, Oxford

Wilmut I, Schnieke AE, McWhir J, Kind AJ and Campbell KHS (1997) Viable offspring derived from fetal and adult mammalian cells *Nature* **385** 810–813

Zimmermann U and Vienken J (1982) Electric field-induced cell-to-cell fusion: topical review *Journal of Membrane Biology* **67** 158–174

Reproduction Supplement **58**, 301–311

Deep intrauterine insemination and embryo transfer in pigs

E. A. Martinez[1], J. M. Vazquez[1], J. Roca[1], X. Lucas[1], M. A. Gil[1] and J. L. Vazquez[2]

[1]*Department of Animal Pathology, University of Murcia, 30071 Murcia, Spain; and* [2]*Department of Surgery, University Miguel Hernandez, Elche, Spain*

A new method for non-surgical deep intrauterine catheterization of pigs, without sedation of the sow, is described. Insemination results obtained with this method using fresh spermatozoa demonstrate that, in comparison to conventional artificial insemination (AI) (3×10^9 spermatozoa in 80–100 ml), a 20–60-fold reduction in the number of spermatozoa inseminated and at least a 8–10-fold reduction in the dose volume can be used without affecting fertility if spermatozoa are deposited deep (middle or upper) into one of the uterine horns. Results from deep intrauterine insemination with frozen–thawed spermatozoa and flow-sorted spermatozoa are also presented and the effect of deep intrauterine insemination on sperm transport is discussed. In addition, a brief description of the advances made in non-surgical embryo transfer technology is reported.

Introduction

Artificial insemination (AI) is gaining importance in the pig industry. Over the past 15 years, there has been an increase in the development of on-farm AI services in many countries, and the percentage of sows artificially inseminated can be more than 80% (Weitze, 2000). The demand for higher quality pork together with the optimal fertility results that can be achieved by using improvements to the AI technique have contributed to the growth in the use of AI. As a consequence of this increase, a more efficient use of semen samples of high quality and high genetic value would be of great importance for the pig industry because a larger number of females could then be inseminated with semen from boars that are genetically superior.

Numerous investigations have been carried out on the development of several semen extenders for short- or long-term storage of spermatozoa. Different tests for evaluating the quality and functionality of semen, and predicting boar fertility *in vivo* have been proposed. Other investigations have focused on the effect of timing of insemination relative to ovulation, the role of seminal plasma in sperm transport and the addition of different compounds to the insemination doses to enhance reproductive performance. Nevertheless, few investigations have been performed regarding three important aspects of the AI technique: site of deposition of the insemination dose, number of spermatozoa per dose and dose volume. A large volume of liquid (50–200 ml) and a large number of spermatozoa (5–10 $\times 10^9$ per insemination dose) deposited intracervically during AI were recommended 40 years ago to achieve maximum

---

Email: emilio@um.es

fertility in pigs (Polge, 1956; Stratman and Self, 1960; Baker *et al.*, 1968). Few modifications of these recommendations have been introduced since these studies. Thus, current AI procedures in pigs use two inseminations during oestrus with a concentration of 2.5–4.0 × 10^9 spermatozoa in a large volume of liquid (80–100 ml) deposited intracervically at each insemination, which limits the number of doses that can be prepared from one semen sample to approximately 20.

However, it is now known that the number of spermatozoa per insemination can be reduced if the sperm dose is deposited into the uterine horn. Successful non-surgical deep intrauterine inseminations using very small numbers of spermatozoa have been reported in cattle (Seidel *et al.*, 1997) and horses (Morris *et al.*, 2000). In pigs, a 100-fold reduction of the standard AI dose (3 × 10^9 spermatozoa in 80 ml) can be made when spermatozoa are surgically deposited close to the uterotubal junction (Krueger *et al.*, 1999; Krueger and Rath, 2000).

This article describes a new procedure for non-surgical deep intrauterine insemination in pigs and subsequently focuses on the effectiveness of this procedure in sows using a small number of fresh, frozen or flow-sorted spermatozoa. Implications about transport of spermatozoa into the genital tract will also be discussed. Finally, a brief description of the advancements achieved in non-surgical embryo transfer in pigs is presented.

Procedure for non-surgical deep uterine catheterization

Non-surgical transcervical catheterization of the uterus has been successfully performed in cows, horses and dogs (Devine and Lindsay, 1984; Bracher *et al.*, 1992; Watts and Wright, 1995). However, there are no reports of transcervical catheterization of the uterus in sows. The main obstacle to this procedure is the complex anatomy of the cervix and uterus of the pig. The cervical folds and the length and coiled nature of the uterine horns have discouraged attempts at non-surgical transcervical introduction of a catheter into the uterine horn for AI.

Vazquez *et al.* (1999) reported a procedure to gain access to the uterine horn through the cervix by using a flexible fibreoptic endoscope (length 1.35 m, outer diameter 3.3 mm) and the difficulties of this technique when applied in oestrous sows. In their study, deep uterine catheterizations were performed in weaned sows in their own crates at 30–40 h after hCG treatment, without sedation. With this technique, it was possible to pass the cervical canal and to reach the depth of one uterine horn in 96.7% of sows and the procedure was completed within 3–7 min in about 90% of sows. The behaviour of the sows during the procedure was similar to the reaction of the sows during standard AI, indicating that this procedure is a relatively stress-free method that is well tolerated by sows, as is also the case for cows (Devine and Lindsay, 1984). After uterine catheterization, no symptoms of uterine infection were observed during the days after the hysteroscopy, and sows returned to oestrus after a normal period of time. Endoscopic images obtained during insertion of the fibrescope are shown (Fig. 1a–c). Upon entering the uterine body, the endometrial folds were apparent and occluded visualization of the bifurcation between the uterine horns. However, the fibrescope progressed without difficulty along one uterine horn until its total length was inserted. The tip of the fibrescope reached approximately the middle or the beginning of the anterior third of the uterine horn, which adapted to the fibrescope and formed a spiral shape, as determined by laparoscopy (Fig. 1d).

Although endoscopic deep intrauterine insemination is a successful technique for inseminating sows with a small number of spermatozoa, the fibrescope is expensive and fragile, and unsuitable for use under field conditions. As it is not necessary to have an optic system to pass through the cervix or to gain entry into the uterine horn, a new flexible catheter (1.8 m in length, 4.0 mm in outer diameter) was made on the basis of the propulsion force and

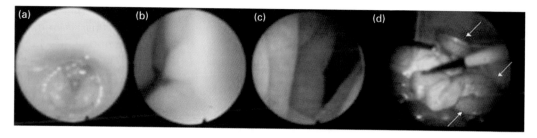

Fig. 1. Endoscopic (a,b,c) and laparoscopic (d) photographs of the sow genital tract during oestrus. The insertion of the endoscope was performed in sows housed in gestation crates. Sows were not sedated. (a) Artificial insemination spirette (blue) inserted into the cervix. (b) Cervical canal with cervical folds. (c) Lumen of a uterine horn. (d) Image illustrating the silhouette (arrows) of the endoscope in one uterine horn.

flexibility of the fibrescope used in the previous studies (Martinez *et al.*, 2001). With this new device, similar results in the passage of the catheter through the cervix into one uterine horn to those obtained with the fibrescope have been achieved, but the time required to complete the procedure was reduced (3–4 min). The tip of the flexible catheter was located in the anterior third of one uterine horn, as determined by laparotomy of sows of 2–3 parities.

Deep intrauterine insemination with a small number of spermatozoa in sows

Several experiments to determine the effectiveness of deep intrauterine insemination using a small number of spermatozoa have been, or are in the process of being, performed, including the use of fresh, frozen or flow-sorted spermatozoa.

Deep intrauterine insemination using fresh semen

Successful surgical intrauterine insemination with small numbers of spermatozoa has been reported for hormonally stimulated prepubertal gilts (Krueger *et al.*, 1999) and for sows (Krueger and Rath, 2000). These investigations demonstrated that the number of spermatozoa used for surgical intrauterine insemination (next to the uterotubal junction) can be reduced to 1×10^7 spermatozoa per uterine horn, without compromising fertility. Preliminary results (Martinez *et al.*, 2000) indicate that when spermatozoa are deposited non-surgically using the fibrescope deep into one of the uterine horns of hormonally treated post-weaning sows, normal farrowing rates and litter sizes are obtained by inseminating a concentration of 5×10^7 spermatozoa per sow (Fig. 2). Further experiments have been conducted in our laboratory to determine the minimum number of spermatozoa required to maintain optimal fertility using the flexible catheter for non-surgical deep intrauterine insemination in weaned sows undergoing induced oestrus (Martinez *et al.*, 2001). Farrowing rates and litter sizes after deep intrauterine insemination with 1.5×10^8 or 5.0×10^7 spermatozoa at 36 h after hCG treatment did not differ from those obtained after standard AI with 3×10^9 spermatozoa; however, a significant decrease in the farrowing rates was observed in sows inseminated with 2.5×10^7 or 1.0×10^7 spermatozoa (Fig. 3). An additional study is being conducted to evaluate the pregnancy rates, farrowing rates and litter sizes when deep intrauterine insemination is performed in sows undergoing natural oestrus after weaning. The possibility of carrying out deep intrauterine inseminations in natural oestrous sows after weaning would allow the application of this new technique under the same conditions as the conventional procedures of AI used in commercial pig units.

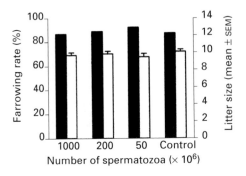

Fig. 2. Farrowing (■) rates and litter size (□) in oestrous-induced weaned sows that were inseminated once into one uterine horn with a concentration of 1000 ($n = 15$), 200 ($n = 18$) or 50 ($n = 13$) $\times 10^6$ spermatozoa in 10 ml of Beltsville thawing solution diluent using an endoscope. Control sows ($n = 48$) were inseminated twice by the standard artificial insemination method.

Deep intrauterine insemination with frozen semen

The first pregnancies using frozen semen in pigs were obtained 30 years ago by surgical insemination into the oviducts (Polge *et al.*, 1970) or by intracervical insemination of thawed spermatozoa (Crabo and Einarsson, 1971; Graham *et al.*, 1971). The fertility achieved with frozen semen from 1970 to 1999 was about 20–30% and two to three piglets fewer than that obtained using fresh semen or semen stored for a short time. Recently, increased fertility rates have been reported using spermatozoa frozen in a new flat plastic package of 5 ml (Eriksson and Rodriguez-Martinez, 2000) or in 0.5 ml straws (Bussiere *et al.*, 2000). Nevertheless, fertility and prolificacy are still lower than that expected with fresh semen and standard AI. It is established that boar spermatozoa are more susceptible to cold shock than spermatozoa of other species and that a high proportion of spermatozoa die during the freezing procedure.

After thawing, a large proportion of motile spermatozoa has decreased or suppressed fertilizing ability because the freezing–thawing causes destabilization of the sperm membrane (Watson, 1996). This process resembles capacitation, although it is not identical (Watson and Green, 2000). Consequently, a greater number of thawed spermatozoa ($5–6 \times 10^9$) extended in 80–100 ml of diluent are usually inseminated intracervically close to the time of ovulation to increase the fertility results.

Results of numerous studies on freezing procedures, diluents, cryoprotectants and other aspects of frozen boar semen have been published (for a review, see Johnson *et al.*, 2000a). However, the effect of frozen–thawed semen deposition in different parts of the uterine horn on fertility has not been reported. A preliminary field trial was performed to determine the effectiveness of deep intrauterine insemination with frozen–thawed semen (J. Roca, G. Carvajal, C. Cuello, I. Parrilla, X. Lucas, J. M. Vazquez and E. A. Martinez, unpublished). Sows ($n = 49$) were hormonally treated after weaning and subjected to one deep intrauterine insemination at 40 h after hCG treatment with 1×10^9 thawed spermatozoa extended in BTS diluent (Beltsville thawing solution; Pursel and Johnson, 1975) in a total volume of 7.5 ml,

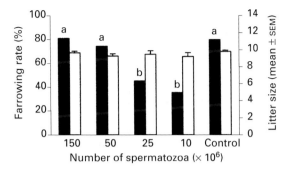

Fig. 3. Farrowing (■) rates and litter size (□) in oestrous-induced weaned sows inseminated once with a flexible catheter deep into one uterine horn with 150 ($n = 84$), 50 ($n = 82$), 25 ($n = 31$) or 10 ($n = 34$) × 10^6 spermatozoa in 10 ml of Beltsville thawing solution diluent. Control sows ($n = 99$) were inseminated twice by the standard artificial insemination method. [ab]Significantly different at $P < 0.01$.

using the flexible catheter for deep intrauterine insemination. Surprisingly, farrowing rates and litter sizes were approximately 80.0% and 9.5%, respectively, and did not differ from those obtained with traditional AI (sows ($n = 52$) inseminated twice with 3 × 10^9 fresh spermatozoa by the standard AI method, two inseminations per oestrus). Unfortunately, standard intracervical inseminations with a concentration of 5–6 × 10^9 frozen spermatozoa extended in 80–100 ml of medium were not performed in this experiment. Therefore, it was not possible to evaluate whether the results achieved after deep intrauterine insemination using frozen semen are attributable to the insemination method or other factors, such as the quality of thawed spermatozoa used. As the quality of spermatozoa inseminated was considered as normal for frozen–thawed semen (40–50% motility and 35–45% of normal apical ridge) it is possible that when thawed semen is deposited in the depth of a uterine horn, an improvement in fertility can be achieved by using a small number of thawed spermatozoa and a small dose volume.

Deep intrauterine insemination using flow-sorted semen

Currently, the only means of farrowing pre-sexed offspring in pigs is by using flow cytometric sorting of spermatozoa bearing X and Y chromosomes (for a review, see Johnson *et al.*, 2000b). The effectiveness of this method has been demonstrated using surgical intratubal inseminations (Johnson, 1991) and *in vitro* fertilization (Rath *et al.*, 1997; Abeydeera *et al.*, 1998). The flow-sorting method produces populations of weak spermatozoa and changes in spermatozoa similar to those that occur during capacitation. The current technique of high speed and high pressure sorting (Johnson and Welch, 1999) also produces a small number of sexed spermatozoa, which is limited to a concentration of 5–6 × 10^6 X or Y spermatozoa per h. Therefore, the practical application of the current technology for gender preselection in pigs depends partially on efficient techniques for non-surgical inseminations with a very small number of spermatozoa. Farrowing rates of 26.7 and 50.0%, and litter sizes of 7.8 and 9.5 were obtained in our laboratory when weaned oestrous sows were deeply inseminated once with 2–5 × 10^7 ($n = 15$) or 6–15 × 10^7 ($n = 12$) flow-sorted spermatozoa, respectively, using non-surgical deep intrauterine methods (J. M. Vazquez, I. Parrilla,

N. Garcia, C. Cuello, X. Lucas, J. Roca and E. A. Martinez, unpublished). Although the litter size could be considered as excellent after insemination with flow-sorted spermatozoa, the farrowing rate using a concentration of $2-5 \times 10^7$ flow-sorted spermatozoa is still too low to have economic advantages using both techniques together. Further investigations are being conducted on this matter to improve the fertility of sows undergoing deep intrauterine insemination with sex-sorted spermatozoa.

Possible mechanisms implicated in the effectiveness of deep intrauterine insemination

Our results from deep intrauterine insemination with fresh semen indicate that if spermatozoa are non-surgically deposited deep into one uterine horn, normal farrowing rates and litter sizes can be obtained when a dose of 5×10^7 spermatozoa per sow is used.

The mechanisms by which the number of spermatozoa per insemination can be reduced during insemination in the depth of the uterine horn are not clear. Billions of spermatozoa in a large volume of liquid are deposited intracervically during natural mating or artificial insemination. However, only about 1000 spermatozoa reach the sperm reservoir (Mburu et al., 1996) that is located in the caudal 1–2 cm of the isthmus (Hunter, 1981, 1984), where the cells maintain their fertilizing ability and are released just before ovulation (Hunter, 1984). Most of the spermatozoa are eliminated rapidly from the uterus by back flow of semen at insemination or during 2 h after insemination (Steverink et al., 1998) and by local phagocytosis (Rozeboom et al., 1998), which occurs 2 h after insemination (Pursel et al., 1978). Some spermatozoa are found in the oviducts within 15 min after insemination (First et al., 1968) and sufficient spermatozoa to ensure subsequent fertilization are present in the isthmus reservoir within 1–2 h of mating (Hunter, 1981, 1984).

During natural mating, different stimuli from the boar, such as tactile, ejaculate volume and seminal plasma components can facilitate transport of spermatozoa in the female genital tract by increasing oxytocin and $PGF_{2\alpha}$ concentrations, which should stimulate myometrial contractions (for a review, see Soede, 1993). AI has a positive affect on uterine motility, probably as a result of a cervical stimulus. Hunter (1982) suggested that although uterine contractions should assist transport and redistribution of semen between the two uterine horns, an initial distribution of semen into the uterus might be achieved during natural mating due to the force of ejaculation and the volume of fluid involved. Thus, the large volume of semen deposited during natural mating ensures that the uterotubal junction is bathed in a sperm suspension by the completion of mating (Hunter, 1982). Therefore, spermatozoa from this suspension could enter the oviducts and establish the sperm reservoir soon after mating. A similar situation could occur when animals are artificially inseminated with a dose of 80–100 ml. In fact, when 100 ml is used, fluid can be collected from uterine cannulae inserted near the uterotubal junction as early as 1.5 min after the onset of insemination (Baker and Degen, 1972). The requirement for a large volume when semen is deposited intracervically is supported by the observation that neither spermatozoa in the oviducts nor accessory spermatozoa were found 12 h after insemination in gilts inseminated intracervically with only 20 ml of semen containing 10×10^9 spermatozoa (Baker et al., 1968). Stratman and Self (1960) also found a positive effect of the insemination volume (50 versus 10 or 20 ml) on embryo survival and percentage of conception regardless of the number of spermatozoa used ($2.5–10.0 \times 10^9$). The requirement for a large volume of semen for intracervical deposition also supports the finding that high fertilization rates (92%) and numbers of accessory spermatozoa (approximately 100) have been found in sows inseminated intracervically with only 5×10^8 spermatozoa in a total volume of 100 ml (Waberski et al., 1996). In contrast, it has been demonstrated that the dose volume is not important when the inseminations are carried out close to the uterotubal junction. Optimal fertility has been obtained after surgical inseminations next to the uterotubal junction with an insemination volume of only 0.5 ml containing 1×10^7 spermatozoa (Krueger and Rath, 2000) or after non-surgical deep intrauterine inseminations with 5×10^7 spermatozoa in a dose volume of only 10 ml (Martinez *et al.*, 2000, 2001). Thus, the deposition of a small number of spermatozoa in a small volume of liquid close to the uterotubal junction may be similar to an aliquot of the ejaculate or of a standard AI dose arriving at the uterotubal junction during natural mating or AI, as has been suggested in horses (Morris *et al.*, 2000). This finding is not surprising, as it was hypothesized by Hunter (1982) that for the future development of AI, a technique that permits deposition of a few milliliters of semen at the top of each uterine horn against the uterotubal junction should be beneficial.

Our results with endoscopic inseminations of fresh semen (Martinez *et al.*, 2000) indicate that it is not necessary to deposit spermatozoa at the uterotubal junction to obtain adequate farrowing rates and litter sizes by inseminating a small number of spermatozoa in a small volume of medium. Semen was deposited once near the middle of one uterine horn. These conditions were sufficient to enable formation of a sperm reservoir in the caudal isthmus of at least one oviduct, because no significant differences were observed in farrowing rates from those obtained after standard AI. When deep intrauterine insemination is performed closer to the uterotubal junction by using the flexible catheter (length 1.80 m), the number of spermatozoa cannot be lower than 5×10^7 without a reduction in fertility (Martinez *et al.*, 2001).

Other alternatives must be considered. Comparable fertility results to those obtained using deep intrauterine insemination might be obtained after insemination of a reduced number of spermatozoa in a small dose volume into the uterine body, as has been shown in horses (Woods *et al.*, 2000). In a study by Johnson *et al.* (2000c), two pregnancies in five sows and five pregnancies in six sows resulted after insemination once or twice, respectively, into the uterine body with $1–3 \times 10^8$ fresh spermatozoa in a total volume of 25 ml. Moreover, litter sizes obtained after one insemination into the depth of one uterine horn with fresh or frozen semen were not significantly different from the standard inseminated control groups (Martinez *et al.*, 2000, 2001; J. Roca, G. Carvajal, C. Cuello, I. Parrilla, X. Lucas, J. M. Vazquez and E. A. Martinez, unpublished). Although it was not evaluated in these studies, it is possible that the hormonal treatment of sows inseminated in the depth of one uterine horn probably increased the number of ovulations in each ovary and, as a result, a greater number of oocytes may be fertilized in the oviduct ipsilateral to the uterine horn inseminated. This might explain the large number of piglets born under our experimental conditions if fertilization had occurred in only one oviduct. However, embryos at four- to eight-cell stages could be collected from the tip of both uterine horns 2 days after deep uterine insemination with a concentration of 1.5×10^8 fresh spermatozoa in five of six sows (E. A. Martinez, J. M. Vazquez, X. Lucas, X. Roca, J. L. Vazquez and B. N. Day, unpublished). No significant difference was observed in the yield of embryos in each the uterine horns. This finding demonstrated that when spermatozoa are deposited close to the uterotubal junction in only one uterine horn, spermatozoa reach the contralateral oviduct and fertilize the oocytes. Whether spermatozoa reach the contralateral oviduct by a transperitoneal or intrauterine pathway is being investigated. Therefore, in addition to dose volume and site of deposition of the spermatozoa, other factors could be implicated in the differences in requirements between intracervical and deep intrauterine insemination procedures. There are two basic differences between the procedures. Firstly, during intracervical insemination the spermatozoa contact the cervical canal and its secretions, which does not occur during deep intrauterine insemination. As the traditional deposition of semen in pigs has generally been considered 'intrauterine', little attention has been given to the sperm–cervical mucus interaction in this species. Secondly, deep intrauterine insemination produces a large distension of the cervix and uterine horn, which might induce a greater release of hormones implicated in uterine contractility and sperm transport compared with the traditional insemination method. Investigations are currently in progress to clarify some of these issues.

Non-surgical embryo transfer

Practical application of embryo transfer in pigs is limited because of the necessity to use surgical procedures for the collection and transfer of the embryos. Although Polge and Day (1968) demonstrated that pregnancy could be established in pigs by non-surgical embryo transfer, this procedure was considered impossible for many years. The complex anatomy of the cervix and uterus in pigs were the principal obstacles to the insertion of a catheter during metoestrus. In the 1990s, new procedures were developed to transfer embryos non-surgically (for a review, see Hazeleger and Kemp, 1999), although most of them have not been successful. Only one research group has performed non-surgical embryo transfer directly into the uterine body without sedation of the recipient sows (Hazeleger and Kemp, 1994, 1999). Hazeleger and Kemp (1994) showed that deposition of embryos in 0.1 ml of medium into the uterine body is possible in non-sedated sows using a specially designed flexible instrument. Use of this device resulted in a relatively high pregnancy rate of 59% and an average of eleven normal fetuses at day 37 after embryo transfer when 28–30 expanded blastocysts per embryo transfer were used. The farrowing rate was lower when the same embryo transfer procedure was used under field conditions (41% farrowing rate and 7.4 piglets born) (Ducro-Steverink *et al.*, 2001). Although the results achieved by this research group are similar to those obtained surgically, in which a pregnancy rate of 60–80% and an embryonic survival rate of 50–70% at 30 days have been reported (Polge, 1982; Wallenhorst and Holtz, 1999), further improvements are required to increase fertility results after non-surgical embryo transfer.

Results from surgical embryo transfer indicate that the uterine body is an inadequate site for embryo transfer in pigs. The pregnancy rate of the recipients is low when expanded blastocysts are deposited surgically in the uterine body (12%), compared with blastocysts deposited in the middle (88%) or the caudal quarter of the uterine horn (81%) (Wallenhorst and Holtz, 1999). Although these results are poor and not in agreement with those found after non-surgical embryo transfers into the uterine body (Hazeleger and Kemp, 1994; Galvin *et al.*, 1994; Li *et al.*, 1996; Hazeleger *et al.*, 1999), the possibility that the uterine body is not an optimum site to deposit embryos should be considered. However, with the current procedures for non-surgical embryo transfer, the embryos cannot be deposited into a uterine horn and, therefore, it has not been possible to determine whether embryo transfer results could be increased by depositing the embryos in the middle or even further up the uterine horn. In addition, another limitation of the current non-surgical embryo transfer systems is that only sows can be used as recipients because the cervix of gilts is too restrictive to allow penetration.

On the basis of the flexible catheter used for deep intrauterine insemination, a new device for non-surgical embryo transfer in the depth of one uterine horn of gilts and sows at days 4–6 of the oestrous cycle (day 0 = onset of oestrus) is being developed. The embryo transfer catheter (1.20 m in length, 4 mm outer diameter and 0.7 mm of working canal) can be inserted quickly and appropriately through the cervix into the uterus in about 90% of gilts (determined by laparotomy) and 95% of sows (determined by the flow of the catheter through the cervix and uterus, and by the shape of the catheter after removal, whether it was straight or bent). The overall correct prediction of the location of the catheter in the uterus was 96.1% (25 correct predictions of 26 insertions performed) in gilts and 97.1% (34 correct predictions of 35 insertions performed) in sows, and no perforations of the cervix or uterine wall were observed. This procedure offers new possibilities to transfer embryos non-surgically in pigs and other experiments are being conducted to determine the overall effectiveness of this procedure. It is possible that a simple, effective and practical procedure for non-surgical embryo transfer in pigs will be available in the next few years and important advances in the commercial applications of this technique can be achieved.

Conclusion

A new technique for non-surgical deep intrauterine insemination in pigs is being developed. With this technique, it is possible to pass the cervical canal and to reach the depth of one uterine horn in about 95% of sows, and the time required is similar to that required to perform traditional AI. In comparison with standard AI (3×10^9 spermatozoa in 80–100 ml of liquid), a 20–60-fold reduction in the number of spermatozoa inseminated and at least an 8–10-fold reduction in the dose volume can be achieved without a decrease in fertility. Deep intrauterine insemination might have a high impact on the fresh semen AI industry by decreasing the number of boars that are used. Selection of the boars could be more rigorous and only boars that have high genetic value would be included in the AI centres. A decrease in space, food, management and replacement of boars and a decrease in the time required for semen collection, sperm evaluation and sperm dose preparation would be secondary benefits using this insemination procedure. Preliminary results indicate that the non-surgical deep intrauterine technique may also be a practical method for obtaining satisfactory fertility in sows inseminated with a low number of cryopreserved spermatozoa. The number of frozen spermatozoa per ejaculate could be increased at least five to six times (about 60 doses per ejaculate). In addition, deep intrauterine insemination could provide a technique for practical application of biotechnologies, such as flow-sorted spermatozoa or non-surgical embryo transfer and could be used for new investigations on sperm transport in the female reproductive tract. However, this technology is in the preliminary stages and many investigations will be necessary to elucidate numerous questions that cannot be answered now.

The authors are grateful to B. N. Day for reading the manuscript critically. Financial support from EUREKA (EU 1713), FEDER (1FD97-370), CDTI B288/98, MEC of Spain (No. PR2000-179), Miller Fund of the University of Missouri (C-4-22481), and Monsanto Company (G-2929) projects in many of the studies reported is also most gratefully acknowledged.

References

Abeydeera LR, Johnson LA, Welch GR, Wang WH, Boquest AC, Cantley TC, Riecke A and Day BN (1998) Birth of piglets preselected for gender following *in vitro* fertilization of *in vitro* matured pig oocytes by X and Y chromosome bearing spermatozoa sorted by high speed flow cytometry *Theriogenology* **50** 981–988

Baker RD and Degen AA (1972) Transport of live and dead boar spermatozoa within the reproductive tract of gilts *Journal of Reproduction and Fertility* **28** 369–377

Baker RD, Dziuk PJ and Norton HW (1968) Effect of volume of semen, number of sperm and drugs on transport of sperm in artificially inseminated gilts *Journal of Animal Science* **27** 88–93

Bracher V, Mathias S and Allen WR (1992) Videoendoscopic evaluation of the mare's uterus: II. Findings in subfertile mares *Equine Veterinary Journal* **24** 279–284

Bussiere JF, Bertaud G and Guillouet P (2000) Conservation de la semence congelée de verrat. Resultats *in vitro* et après insemination *32emes Journees de la Recherche Porcine en France* **32** 429–432

Crabo BG and Einarsson S (1971) Fertility of deep frozen boar spermatozoa *Acta Veterinaria Scandinavica* **12** 125–127

Devine DA and Lindsay FEF (1984) Hysteroscopy in the cow using a flexible fibrescope *Veterinary Record* **115** 627–628

Ducro-Steverink DWB, Smits JM, Hazeleger W and Merks JWM (2001) Reproduction results after non-surgical embryo transfer in pigs *Theriogenology* **55** 361 (Abstract)

Eriksson BM and Rodriguez-Martinez H (2000) Export of frozen boar semen in a new flat package. In *Boar Semen Preservation IV* 244 (Abstract) Eds LA Johnson and HD Guthrie. Allen Press Inc., Lawrence, KS

First NL, Short RE, Peters JB and Stratman FW (1968) Transport and loss of boar spermatozoa in the reproductive tract of the sow *Journal of Animal Science* **27** 1037–1040

Galvin JM, Killian DB and Stewart ANV (1994) A procedure for successful nonsurgical embryo transfer in swine *Theriogenology* **41** 1279–1289

Graham JK, Rajamannan AHJ, Schmehl MKL, Maki-Laurila M and Bower RE (1971) Fertility studies with frozen boar spermatozoa *Artificial Insemination Digest* **19** 16–18

Hazeleger W and Kemp B (1994) Farrowing rate and litter size after transcervical embryo transfer in sows *Reproduction in Domestic Animals* **29** 481–487

Hazeleger W and Kemp B (1999) State of the art in pig embryo transfer *Theriogenology* **51** 81–90

Hazeleger W, Bouwman EG, Noordhuizen JPTM and Kemp B (1999) Effect of superovulation induction on embryonic development on day 5 and subsequent development and survival after nonsurgical embryo transfer in pigs *Theriogenology* **53** 1063–1070

Hunter RHF (1981) Sperm transport and reservoirs in the pig oviduct in relation to the time of ovulation *Journal of Reproduction and Fertility* **63** 109–117

Hunter RHF (1982) Interrelationships between spermatozoa, the female reproductive tract and the egg investments. In *Control of Pig Reproduction* pp 585–601 Eds DJA Cole and GR Foxcroft. Butterworth, London

Hunter RHF (1984) Pre-ovulatory arrest and peri-ovulatory redistribution of competent spermatozoa in the isthmus of the pig oviduct *Journal of Reproduction and Fertility* **72** 203–211

Johnson LA (1991) Sex preselection in swine: altered sex ratios in offspring following surgical insemination of flow sorted X- and Y-bearing sperm *Reproduction in Domestic Animals* **26** 309–314

Johnson LA and Welch GR (1999) Sex preselection: high-speed flow cytometric sorting of X and Y sperm for maximum efficiency *Theriogenology* **52** 1323–1341

Johnson LA, Weitze KF, Fiser P and Maxwell WMC (2000a) Storage of boar semen *Animal Reproduction Science* **62** 143–172

Johnson LA, Dobrinsky JR, Guthrie HD and Welch GR (2000b) Sex preselection in swine: flow cytometric sorting of X- and Y-chromosome bearing sperm to produce offspring. In *Boar Semen Preservation IV* pp 107–114 Eds LA Johnson and HD Guthrie. Allen Press Inc., Lawrence, KS

Johnson LA, Guthrie HD, Dobrinsky JR and Welch GR (2000c) Low dose artificial insemination of swine with sperm sorted for sex using an intrauterine technique in sows *Proceedings of 14th International Congress on Animal Reproduction* Vol II 244 (Abstract). Stockholm, Sweden

Krueger C and Rath D (2000) Intrauterine insemination in sows with reduced sperm number *Reproduction, Fertility and Development* **12** 113–117

Krueger C, Rath D and Johnson LA (1999) Low dose insemination in synchronized gilts *Theriogenology* **52** 1363–1373

Li J, Riecke A, Day BN and Prather RS (1996) Porcine non-surgical embryo transfer *Journal of Animal Sciences* **74** 2263–2268

Martinez EA, Vazquez JM, Vazquez JL, Lucas X, Gil MA, Parrilla I and Roca J (2000) Successful low-dose insemination by a fiberoptic endoscope technique *Theriogenology* **53** 201 (Abstract)

Martinez EA, Vazquez JM, Roca J, Lucas X, Gil MA and Vazquez JL (2001) Deep intrauterine insemination in sows with a low number of spermatozoa: a new simple procedure *Theriogenology* **55** 248 (Abstract)

Mburu JN, Einarsson S, Lundeheim N and Rodriguez-Martinez H (1996) Distribution, number and membrane integrity of spermatozoa in the pig oviduct in relation to spontaneous ovulation *Animal Reproduction Science* **45** 109–121

Morris LHA, Hunter RHF and Allen WR (2000) Hysteroscopic insemination of small numbers of spermatozoa at the uterotubal junction of preovulatory mares *Journal of Reproduction and Fertility* **118** 95–100

Polge C (1956) Artificial insemination in pigs *Veterinary Record* **68** 62–76

Polge C (1982) Embryo transplantation and preservation. In *Control of Pig Reproduction* pp 277–291 Eds DJA Cole and GR Foxcroft. Butterworth, London

Polge C and Day BN (1968) Pregnancy following non-surgical egg transfer in pigs *Veterinary Record* **82** 712

Polge C, Salamon S and Wilmut I (1970) Fertilizing capacity of frozen boar semen following surgical insemination *Veterinary Record* **87** 424–428

Pursel VG and Johnson LA (1975) Freezing of boar spermatozoa: fertilizing capacity with concentrated semen and a new thawing procedure *Journal of Animal Science* **40** 99–102

Pursel VG, Schulman LL and Johnson LA (1978) Distribution and morphology of fresh and frozen–thawed sperm in the reproductive tract of gilts after artificial insemination *Biology of Reproduction* **19** 69–76

Rath D, Johnson LA, Dobrinsky JR and Welch GR (1997) Production of piglets preselected for sex following *in vitro* fertilization with X and Y chromosome-bearing spermatozoa sorted by flow cytometry *Theriogenology* **47** 795–800

Rozeboom KJ, Troedsson MHT and Crabo BG (1998) Characterization of uterine leukocyte infiltration in gilts after artificial insemination *Journal of Reproduction and Fertility* **114** 195–199

Seidel GE, Allen CH, Johnson LA, Holland MD, Brink Z, Welch GR, Graham JK and Cattell MB (1997) Uterine horn insemination of heifers with very low numbers of non-frozen and sexed spermatozoa *Theriogenology* **48** 1255–1264

Soede NM (1993) Boar stimuli around insemination affect

reproductive processes in pigs: a review *Animal Reproduction Science* **32** 107–125

Steverink DWB, Soede NM, Bouwman EG and Kemp B (1998) Semen backflow after insemination and its effect on fertilization results in sows *Animal Reproduction Science* **54** 109–119

Stratman FW and Self HL (1960) Effect of semen volume and number of sperm on fertility and embryo survival in artificially inseminated gilts *Journal of Animal Science* **19** 1081–1088

Vazquez JL, Martinez EA, Vazquez JM, Lucas X, Gil MA, Parrilla I and Roca J (1999) Development of a non-surgical deep intrauterine insemination technique *IV International Conference on Boar Semen Preservation* p 35 Beltsville, MD

Waberski D, Soares JAG, Bandeira de Arruda E and Weitze KF (1996) Effect of a transcervical infusion of seminal plasma prior to insemination on the fertilizing competence of low numbers of boar spermatozoa at controlled AI–ovulation intervals *Animal Reproduction Science* **44** 165–173

Wallenhorst S and Holtz W (1999) Transfer of pig embryos to different uterine sites *Journal of Animal Sciences* **77** 2327–2329

Watson PF (1996) Cooling of spermatozoa and fertilizing capacity *Reproduction in Domestic Animals* **31** 135–140

Watson PF and Green CE (2000) Cooling and capacitation of boar spermatozoa: what do they have in common? In *Boar Semen Preservation IV* pp 52–60 Eds LA Johnson and HD Guthrie, Allen Press Inc., Lawrence, KS

Watts JR and Wright PJ (1995) Investigating uterine disease in the bitch: uterine cannulation for cytology, microbiology and hysteroscopy *Journal of Small Animal Practice* **36** 201–206

Weitze KF (2000) Update on the worldwide application of swine AI. In *Boar Semen Preservation IV* pp 141–145 Eds LA Johnson and HD Guthrie. Allen Press Inc., Lawrence, KS

Woods J, Rigby S, Brinsko S, Stephens R, Varner D and Blanchard T (2000) Effect of intrauterine treatment with prostaglandin E_2 prior to insemination of mares in the uterine horn or body *Theriogenology* **53** 1827–1836

Reproduction Supplement **58**, 313–324

Transgenic alteration of sow milk to improve piglet growth and health

M. B. Wheeler[1], G. T. Bleck[1] and S. M. Donovan[2]

Departments of [1]Animal Sciences and [2]Food Science and Human Nutrition, University of Illinois, Urbana, IL 61801, USA

There are many potential applications of transgenic methodologies for developing new and improved strains of livestock. One practical application of transgenic technology in pig production is to improve milk production or composition. The first week after parturition is the period of greatest loss for pig producers, with highest morbidity and mortality attributed to malnutrition and scours. Despite the benefits to be gained by improving lactation performance, little progress has been made in this area through genetic selection or nutrition. Transgenic technology provides an important tool for addressing the problem of low milk production and its detrimental impact on pig production. Transgenic pigs over-expressing the milk protein bovine α-lactalbumin were developed. α-Lactalbumin was selected for its role in lactose synthesis and regulation of milk volume. Sows hemizygous for the transgene produced as much as 0.9 g bovine α-lactalbumin l^{-1} pig milk. The outcomes assessed were milk composition, milk yield and piglet growth. First parity α-lactalbumin gilts had higher milk lactose content in early lactation and 20–50% greater milk yield on days 3–9 of lactation than did non-transgenic gilts. Weight gain of piglets suckling α-lactalbumin gilts was greater (days 7–21 after parturition) than that of control piglets. Thus, transgenic over-expression of milk proteins may provide a means for improving the lactation performance of pigs.

Introduction

The insertion of DNA into livestock and its stable integration into the germline have been major technical advances in agriculture. Production of transgenic livestock provides a method for introducing 'new' genes rapidly into cattle, pigs, sheep and goats without crossbreeding (Pursel and Rexroad, 1993). It is an extreme methodology but, in essence, its result is not really different from crossbreeding or genetic selection. Two basic strategies are used when producing transgenic animals. These are the so-called 'gain of function' or 'loss of function' transgenics. The basic idea behind the 'gain of function' paradigm is that by adding a cloned fragment of DNA to the genome of an animal, several aims can be achieved. One aim is to obtain new expression of a gene product that did not exist previously in that cell or tissue type. An example of this is the expression of human growth hormone (hGH) in mouse liver (Palmiter *et al.*, 1982).

Email: mbwheele@uiuc.edu

The 'loss of function' paradigm has many similar applications to the 'gain of function' strategy, especially when considering over-expression, insertional mutations and antisense situations. The major difference is the ability to disrupt genes in a targeted fashion. This strategy relies on the ability of embryonic cells to undergo homologous recombination. The generation of transgenic animals is dependent on the ability of the cell to form stable recombinants between the exogenous DNA and the endogenous chromosomal DNA in the genome of the host. Most of these events are non-homologous recombinations, in which the DNA inserts are introduced randomly into the genome. However, some cells possess the enzymatic machinery required for recombination between the introduced DNA sequence and the homologous or identical sequence in the genome of the host. This is called homologous recombination, which is often referred to as 'gene targeting'. Gene targeting permits the transfer of genetic alterations created *in vitro* into precise sites in the embryonic or cell genome (Wheeler and Choi, 1997). If the host's cells are totipotent or pluripotent embryonic cells (embryonic stem cells, embryonic germ cells or primordial germ cells) or re-programmable somatic cells, then these homologous recombination events can be transferred to the germ line of the offspring. The use of this strategy has great potential for making specific genetic changes for use in medicine and agriculture, and for furthering our understanding of the genetic control of developmental processes.

Recent advances in transgenic technology in pigs

Microinjection of cloned DNA into the pronucleus of a fertilized ovum has been the most widely used and successful method for producing transgenic mice and livestock (Hammer *et al.*, 1985). Microinjection has produced most of the transgenic pigs obtained to date. Two recent developments will have profound impacts on the use of transgenic technology in livestock: (i) the ability to isolate and maintain embryonic and somatic cells directly from embryos, fetuses and adults *in vitro*; and (ii) the ability to use these embryonic and somatic cells as nuclei donors in nuclear transfer or 'cloning' strategies. These strategies have several distinct advantages for use in the production of transgenic livestock that cannot be attained using pronuclear injection of DNA.

The use of nuclear transfer (cloning) techniques may have the potential to increase the number of offspring from a single female into the thousands and, possibly, tens of thousands (Bondioli *et al.*, 1990). Since the cloned sheep 'Dolly' was born (Wilmut *et al.*, 1997), nuclear transfer technology has become another methodology available for the production of transgenic animals.

The nuclear transfer procedure (for review see Wheeler and Walters, 2001) uses either *in vitro* or *in vivo* oocytes as the cytoplasm donor (cytoplast). The genetic material of the cytoplast is removed (enucleation) leaving only the cytoplasm. After enucleation of the oocyte, a donor nucleus (karyoplast) is injected into the perivitelline space or into the cytoplasm of the enucleated oocyte (cytoplast). The enucleated oocyte and the donor nucleus are fused by electrofusion. Electrofusion of the cytoplast and karyoplast is highly species-dependent in terms of the duration, fusion medium, fusion medium equilibration and amplitude of the pulse required. After fusion of the donor nucleus and the enucleated oocyte, the oocyte is activated by either chemical or electrical stimulation. Successful activation initiates development to the blastocyst stage, followed by transfer into a pseudopregnant recipient.

These new methods for production of genetically identical individuals from embryonic (Campbell *et al.*, 1996; Wilmut *et al.*, 1997) and somatic (Wilmut *et al.*, 1997; Polejaeva *et al.*, 2000) cells, via nuclear transfer, should allow the rapid development of genetically identical animals with a targeted gene insertion. These developments will enhance our ability to produce transgenic animals with genes inserted into specific sites in the genome.

Recently, the birth of the world's first two sets of cloned piglets produced using fetal fibroblasts and adult somatic cells was announced (Onishi *et al.*, 2000; Polejaeva *et al.*, 2000). This achievement will allow nuclear transfer technology to be used to produce transgenic pigs.

Mammary-specific gene expression in transgenic animals

The expression of transgenes in mammary tissue has been studied in numerous laboratories (Simons *et al.*, 1987; Clark *et al.*, 1989; Vilotte *et al.*, 1989; Bleck and Bremel, 1994; Bleck *et al.*, 1996, 1998). The 5′ flanking regions of many milk protein genes, which have a regulatory function, have been used to drive expression of foreign proteins in mammary epithelial cells of transgenic animals (Simons *et al.*, 1987; Vilotte *et al.*, 1989). Of all the bovine milk protein genes, the expression of bovine α-lactalbumin is regulated most tightly and is lactation-specific (Goodman and Schanbacher, 1991; Mao *et al.*, 1991). The unique expression pattern of the bovine α-lactalbumin gene makes its promoter and regulatory elements a useful mammary expression system in transgenic animals. In contrast to the caseins and β-lactoglobulin, the production of α-lactalbumin mRNA and protein shows a marked increase at parturition, remains high during lactation and decreases sharply during cessation of lactation and involution.

Regulatory regions of milk proteins have been linked to genes that have been expressed as transgenes in a variety of animals (pigs, sheep and goats; Clark *et al.*, 1989; Ebert *et al.*, 1991; Wall *et al.*, 1991). Levels and patterns of expression have been very similar to those observed in numerous transgenic mouse experiments. These regulatory regions have shown little or no species specificity and have even been regulated properly in species that do not express those proteins (Simons *et al.*, 1987; Wall *et al.*, 1991).

Transgenic mice have been produced using the α-lactalbumin 5′ region to drive the expression of bovine, caprine or guinea-pig α-lactalbumin transgenes in the mammary gland (Vilotte *et al.*, 1989; Mashio *et al.*, 1991; Soulier *et al.*, 1992; Bleck and Bremel, 1994). Production of exogenous α-lactalbumin in the milk of these mice ranged from undetectable concentrations to up to 3.7 mg ml^{-1} in a line of mice producing caprine α-lactalbumin. However, although a number of α-lactalbumin-expressing transgenic animals have been produced, our studies are the only experiments in which lactose and milk production have been examined in transgenic pigs over-expressing α-lactalbumin (Bleck *et al.*, 1998).

Applications for modification of milk

Practical applications of transgenics in livestock production include improved milk production and composition, increased growth rate, improved feed usage, improved carcass composition, increased disease resistance, enhanced reproductive performance, increased prolificacy, and altered cell and tissue characteristics for biomedical research (Wheeler and Choi, 1997) and manufacturing. The production of transgenic pigs with growth hormone serves as an excellent example of the value of this technology (Vise *et al.*, 1988). Transgenic alteration of milk composition has the potential to enhance the production of certain proteins or growth factors that are deficient in milk (Bremel *et al.*, 1989). The improvement of the nutrient or therapeutic value of milk may have a profound impact on survival and growth of both newborn humans and animals.

Advances in recombinant DNA technology have provided the opportunity to either change the composition of milk or produce entirely novel proteins in milk. These changes may add value to, as well as increase the potential uses of, milk.

The improvement of livestock growth or survival through the modification of milk composition requires production of transgenic animals that: (i) produce a greater quantity of milk; (ii) produce milk of higher nutrient content; or (iii) produce milk that contains a beneficial 'nutriceutical' protein. The major nutrients in milk are protein, fat and lactose. Increasing any of these components can have an impact on the growth and health of the developing offspring. In many species such as cattle, sheep and goats, the nutrients available to the young may not be limiting. However, milk production in sows limits piglet growth and, therefore, pig production (Hartmann *et al.*, 1984). In fact, studies indicate that milk yield and total milk solids composition from the sow account for 44% of the variation in weight gain of piglets (Lewis *et al.*, 1978). Methods that increase the growth of piglets during suckling result in an increase in weaning weights, a decrease in the number of days required to reach market weight and, thus, a decrease in the amount of feed needed for the animals to reach market weight.

The high percentage in growth rate attributed to milk indicates the potential usefulness of this technology for developing piglets. An approach to increase milk production in pigs may be accomplished by alteration of milk components such as lactose, a major constituent of milk in mammary gland cells. The over-expression of lactose in the milk of pigs will increase the carbohydrate intake of the developing young, resulting in improvement of piglet growth.

Cattle, sheep and goats used for meat production might also benefit from increased milk yield or composition. In tropical climates, *Bos indicus* cattle breeds do not produce copious quantities of milk. Improvement in milk yield by as little as 2–4 litres per day may have a profound effect on weaning weights in cattle such as the Nelore breed in Brazil. Similar comparisons can be made with improving weaning weights in meat type breeds such as Texel sheep and Boer goats. This application of transgenic technology could lead to improved growth and survival of offspring.

A second mechanism by which the alteration of milk composition may affect animal growth is the addition of beneficial hormones, growth factors or bioactive factors to milk through the use of transgenic animals. It has been suggested that bioactive substances in milk possess important functions in the neonate with regard to regulation of growth, development and maturation of the gut, immune system and endocrine organs (Grosvenor *et al.*, 1993). Transgenic alteration of milk composition has the potential to enhance the production of certain proteins and growth factors that are deficient in milk (Wall *et al.*, 1991). The over-expression of a number of these proteins in milk through the use of transgenic animals may improve growth, development, health and survival of the developing offspring. Some factors that have important biological functions in neonates are obtained through milk; these factors include insulin-like growth factor I (IGF-I), epidermal growth factor (EGF), transforming growth factor α (TGF-α) and lactoferrin (Grosvenor *et al.*, 1993). Alexander and Carey (1999) have suggested that oral administration of IGF-I might also improve nutrient absorptive function.

Other properties of milk that should be considered for modification are those that affect human and animal health. Pre-formed specific antibodies can be produced in transgenic animals (Storb, 1987). It should be possible to produce antibodies in the mammary gland that are capable of preventing mastitis in cattle, sheep and goats, and MMA (mastitis-metritis-agalactia) in pigs, or antibodies that aid in the prevention of domestic animal or human diseases (Pursel and Rexroad, 1993). Another example is to increase the content of proteins that have physiological roles within the mammary gland itself, such as lysozyme (Maga *et al.*, 1995) or other anti-microbial peptides.

It is important to consider the use of transgenics to increase specific components that are already present in milk for manufacturing purposes. An example might be to increase one of the casein components in milk. This could increase the value of milk in manufacturing processes such as production of cheese or yoghurt. The physical properties of a protein could also be altered, for example glycosylation of β-casein could be increased (Choi *et al.*, 1996). This would result in increased β-casein solubility. Increasing the β-casein concentration of milk would reduce the time required for rennet coagulation and whey expulsion, thereby producing firmer curds that are important in cheese making. The deletion of phosphate groups from β-casein would result in softer cheeses. Changes in other physical properties could result in dairy foods with improved characteristics, such as better-tasting low fat cheese (Bleck *et al.*, 1995). Increasing the β-casein content would result in increased thermal stability of milk that could improve manufacturing properties, as well as the storage properties of fluid milk and milk products. Eventually, it may be possible to increase the concentration of milk components while maintaining a constant volume. This could lead to greater product yield – more protein, fat or carbohydrate from a litre of milk. This would also aid in manufacturing processes, as well as potentially decreasing the transportation costs of the more concentrated products in fluid milk. The end result would be a more saleable product for the dairy producer.

An important application of transgenic technology is the production of therapeutic proteins for human clinical use in so-called 'bio-reactors'. Through genetic engineering it has become possible to produce any protein from any animal, plant or bacterial species in the milk of mammals (Bremel *et al.*, 1989; Rudolph, 1999). For example, it is possible to express milk proteins and other proteins of pharmaceutical value in the milk of mice, rabbits, pigs, goats and sheep (Simons *et al.*, 1987; Buehler *et al.*, 1990; Ebert *et al.*, 1991; Wall *et al.*, 1991; Wright *et al.*, 1991; Velander *et al.*, 1992). Advantages of the mammary synthesis of proteins include the ability of the mammary secretory cells to modify the protein properly so it is biologically active and to then secrete the protein-containing fluid (milk) in large quantities. The ability to produce large quantities of bioactive proteins and peptides transgenically has resulted in the development of a new segment of the pharmaceutical industry, which has become known as 'bio-pharming' (Rudolph, 1999).

Genes coding for proteins with pharmaceutical value such as human blood clotting factor IX, which is genetically deficient in haemophiliacs, may be incorporated into transgenic sheep, goats and cows. This protein can be harvested from the milk, purified and provided therapeutically to serum albumin for artificial blood substitute. Hepatitis antigens could also be made available for vaccine production.

The overall result of the transgenic modification of milk will be the creation of more uses of milk and milk products in both agriculture and medicine. This truly is a 'value-added' opportunity for animal agriculture by increasing the concentrations of existing proteins or producing entirely new proteins in milk.

Improvement of lactation performance of sows

Large increases in average milk production of dairy cattle have been achieved over several decades because of intense selection for a trait that is easy to measure objectively, milk yield. However, despite the importance of milk production for fast growth of the offspring of pigs, negligible increases in milk production have been made in pigs. High milk production is particularly important given the emphasis on increasing litter size. Although research has provided more insight into the process of milk secretion, understanding of the physiological factors that control the amount of milk a mammal produces is limited. Previous work has suggested that the volume of milk produced is directly dependent on the amount of lactose synthesized. Lactose is synthesized in the Golgi apparatus of mammary secretory cells by the lactose synthase complex (Brew and Grobler, 1992). This complex is composed of the mammary specific protein α-lactalbumin and the enzyme β1,4 galactosyltransferase. Secretory vesicles are budded off from the Golgi complex, transported to the apical membrane of the epithelial cell and secreted into the lumen. As lactose cannot diffuse out of the vesicles, it acts to draw water by osmosis into the vesicle. Lactose synthase is critical in the control of milk secretion: it is necessary for the production of lactose and the movement of water into the mammary secretory vesicles and into the lumen of the gland (Hayssen and Blackburn, 1985). There is evidence to suggest that milk volume is related directly to expression of the α-lactalbumin gene (Goodman and Schanbacher, 1991). α-Lactalbumin is a normal constituent of milk and its expression correlates with the induction of copious milk secretion at the onset of lactation (Goodman and Schanbacher, 1991).

High milk production is vital for growth of offspring. Low milk production is manifested not only by slow growth before weaning but also by slow growth later in life, as animal performance also suffers through the growing and finishing stages. Current pig production management schemes attempt to maximize the number of piglets born per litter and piglet survival (Hartmann *et al.*, 1984). In addition, pork producers have reduced the duration of lactation to maximize the number of piglets born per sow per year. Currently, 10–14 days of lactation is becoming common in the pig industry. Thus, increased milk production in early lactation must be obtained to get maximum growth from larger litter sizes and shorter lactation periods. Early weaning, gains in decreasing neonatal mortality and increased litter sizes from selected high genetic merit sows make milk production one of the most important limiting factors in piglet growth. In fact, studies indicate that milk production and milk composition of the sow account for 44% of the growth weight of the piglets (Lewis *et al.*, 1978).

The effect of increased sow milk production on US pork production is marked. Using current milk production values (Auldist *et al.*, 1998), we estimate that increasing milk production by 10% would result in an additional $2.46 per litter, which would be worth $28.4 million per year in the USA due to increased weight gains before weaning, using a typical hog price of $50 per cwt. Modern sows can produce approximately 1 kg of milk per piglet for litter sizes of ≤ 14 pigs (Auldist *et al.*, 1998). This calculation does not consider decreased feed and labour costs associated with rearing pigs with heavier weaning weights.

Results from studies of α-lactalbumin transgenic pigs have several applications in animal agriculture. Firstly, lines of breeding stock to improve milk production and piglet growth can be established as a result of increased milk production and piglet growth. Secondly, as overproduction of α-lactalbumin increases milk yield, assays for α-lactalbumin can be used as a selection method for increased milk production in sows.

Production and characterization of transgenic pigs expressing bovine α-lactalbumin

Production of transgenic pigs expressing bovine α-lactalbumin

Two lines of transgenic pigs have been produced containing the bovine α-lactalbumin gene. DNA was isolated from ear biopsies for each of the piglets. PCR was performed using two separate primer sets specific for the bovine α-lactalbumin 5′ flanking region. This transgene is inherited in a normal Mendelian fashion in F_1 crosses (Bleck *et al.*, 1996, 1998). The two lines have also been mated to produce homozygous individuals. Tissue collected from nine transgenic animals was subjected to northern blot analysis. Results showed that expression of the transgene was specific to the mammary gland and not to other tissues (brain,

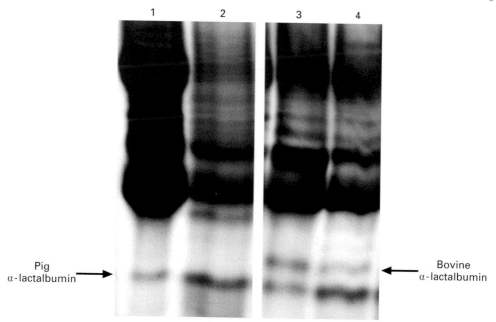

Fig. 1. Transgenic bovine α-lactalbumin is more abundant at the start of lactation than on day 5. Milk from a transgenic pig and her control full sister was separated by non-reducing urea PAGE. Lane 1: control pig milk on day 0 of lactation. Lane 2: control pig milk on day 5 of lactation. Lane 3: transgenic pig milk on day 0 of lactation. Lane 4: transgenic pig milk on day 5 of lactation.

heart, muscle, kidney, liver, skin, spleen, lung, stomach, intestine and ovary; M. B. Wheeler, M. Monaco and S. M. Donovan, unpublished).

Characterization of transgenic pigs expressing bovine α-lactalbumin

Expression of bovine α-lactalbumin in milk. Milk samples were collected from one line of transgenic pigs. In the analysis, five hemizygous transgenic gilts were matched by breed, age and farrowing season with eight control gilts of the same breed, age and farrowing season. Gilts were mated, allowed to farrow and litter size was set at ten piglets. Milk samples were collected from each animal on day 0 (after the completion of farrowing) and days 5, 10, 15 and 20 of lactation. Milk was analysed for the presence of bovine α-lactalbumin using an ELISA specific for bovine α-lactalbumin (Mao *et al.*, 1991). Transgenic sows produced bovine α-lactalbumin in their milk at concentrations ranging from 0.3 to 0.9 mg ml^{-1}. The concentration of bovine α-lactalbumin in pig milk was highest on days 0 and 5 of lactation and decreased as lactation progressed. Sows hemizygous for the transgene produced an average of 0.68 g bovine α-lactalbumin l^{-1} pig milk on day 0 of lactation (Fig. 1). The production of the bovine protein caused an approximate 50% increase in the total α-lactalbumin concentration of pig milk throughout a lactation (although the increase was dependent on the stage of lactation). The production of bovine α-lactalbumin in a single animal from day 0 to day 5 is shown (Fig. 1). The ratio of bovine to pig α-lactalbumin also appears to change during this interval. Milk from five first lactation transgenic sows was analysed to compare the relative concentrations of pig and bovine α-lactalbumin. The ratio of bovine α-lactalbumin:pig α-lactalbumin was 4.3:1.0 on day 0 of lactation, but by day 20 of

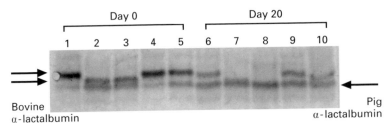

Fig. 2. Western blot of a non-reducing urea PAGE of transgenic pig milk. Milk samples were collected from five first parity transgenic sows. Lanes 1–5: milk samples from day 0 of lactation. Lanes 6–10: milk samples from day 20 of lactation.

lactation the ratio was 0.43:1.0 (Bleck *et al.*, 1998), indicating that the bovine transgene and the endogenous pig gene are under slightly different control mechanisms. These ratios were calculated by densitometry of the western blot shown (Fig. 2). A non-reducing urea PAGE system was used to separate bovine from pig α-lactalbumin (Kim and Jiménez-Flores, 1993) and bovine α-lactalbumin was found to migrate slightly slower than the pig protein (Bleck *et al.*, 1998).

Milk protein and total solids of control and transgenic pigs. No consistent significant differences were observed in the concentration of total milk protein and total solids between control and transgenic animals. Total milk protein percentage in both transgenic and control sows decreased as lactation advanced, reaching a relatively constant percentage at day 10 of lactation. This pattern is similar to that observed for the concentration of bovine α-lactalbumin, indicating that expression of the transgene is regulated in a manner analogous to that of most pig milk proteins. There was a trend for the transgenic animals to have a lower percentage of protein; however, the difference was not significant in this small sample of animals. The total solids data showed much more variation than did the protein data. Transgenic sows had a significantly higher total solids percentage than did control sows on days 10 and 20 of lactation ($P < 0.01$). However, this difference was not consistent throughout lactation (Bleck *et al.*, 1998). Recently, these results have been confirmed with pairs of full sibling (20 control and 20 transgenic) gilts (Noble *et al.*, 2000a,b; in press).

Lactose concentration of control and transgenic pig milk. The higher concentration of total α-lactalbumin present on day 0 of lactation was correlated with higher lactose percentage on day 0 in transgenic sows (3.8%) compared with controls (2.6%) ($P < 0.01$) (Fig. 3). There was also a trend for higher lactose percentage in transgenic sows on days 5 and 10 of lactation, but no significant differences were observed. Mean lactose percentage over the entire lactation period (days 0, 5, 10, 15 and 20) was also calculated. Mean lactose percentage of transgenic sows averaged 5.43%, whereas for control sows the average was 4.89%; this difference is not significant. The significant difference in mean lactose percentage on day 0 of lactation was also observed in the second lactation of these pigs. The lactose analysis for the second lactation was performed on four transgenic animals and five control animals. The lactose percentage on day 0 was 3.7% for transgenic sows and 2.6% for control sows ($P < 0.01$). These data suggest that α-lactalbumin is a limiting factor early in lactation of pigs. Furthermore, it is possible that higher concentrations of α-lactalbumin early in lactation may boost lactation, causing maximal milk output at an earlier time (Noble *et al.*, 2000b).

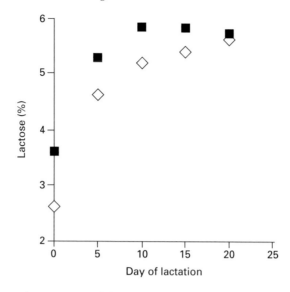

Fig. 3. Mean milk lactose percentage from first parity transgenic α-lactalbumin sows (■; $n = 5$) compared with control sows (◇; $n = 8$) over a 20 day lactation (first parity). Lactose percentage was significantly different between transgenic and control sows on day 0 of lactation ($P < 0.01$). A trend towards higher lactose percentage in the transgenic sows was also observed on days 5 and 10 of lactation; however, the difference was not significant.

Milk production in transgenic pigs

The bovine gene construct used in these experiments (see above) induced the production of α-lactalbumin at approximately 50% of normal endogenous pig α-lactalbumin expression. The bovine α-lactalbumin produced by sows appeared to be the same size as endogenous bovine α-lactalbumin. Interestingly, the concentration of bovine α-lactalbumin was highest on day 0 of lactation and decreased as lactation progressed. That pattern was similar to the trend shown for total milk protein concentration. In contrast to bovine α-lactalbumin, pig α-lactalbumin concentration was lowest on day 0 of lactation and became higher later in lactation. These data suggest that in these transgenic pigs the bovine α-lactalbumin gene was regulated differently from pig α-lactalbumin and was behaving more like other pig milk proteins.

These findings show that α-lactalbumin concentration in pig milk can be increased by the use of transgenic pigs, indicating that lactose production in early lactation can be improved. Furthermore, because of the osmoregulatory role of lactose, it is possible that higher concentrations of α-lactalbumin early in lactation may boost milk yield. We are currently examining early lactation performance in greater detail using a larger number of animals.

Recently, the milk production by and the growth of piglets suckling first parity gilts that express this bovine α-lactalbumin transgene in addition to their endogenous pig α-lactalbumin gene were examined (Noble *et al.*, 2000a). Weigh-suckle-weigh analysis was used to assess milk production from transgenic ($n = 16$) and control ($n = 20$) gilts on days 3, 6, 9 and 12 of lactation. Overall, milk production in transgenic gilts was greater than in controls

(P < 0.01). Milk yields for transgenic gilts were 5.18 ± 0.14, 7.33 ± 0.19 and 7.40 ± 0.22 kg day^{-1} on days 3, 6 and 9, respectively. Milk yields for the controls were 4.33 ± 0.13, 5.86 ± 0.17 and 6.68 ± 0.19 kg day^{-1} on the corresponding days of lactation. By day 12 of lactation, milk yields from transgenic gilts were similar to those of their full-sibling controls (7.21 ± 0.22 kg day^{-1} for transgenic gilts and 6.94 ± 0.2 kg day^{-1} for control gilts). Daily weights of piglets reared on transgenic and control gilts were used to assess piglet growth throughout lactation. The weight gain of piglets suckling transgenic gilts was significantly greater (P < 0.05) than the weight gain of control reared piglets throughout the 21 days of lactation. These results indicate that milk production is increased in early lactation by the expression of the bovine α-lactalbumin transgene in first parity gilts and that this increased milk production results in enhanced piglet growth rates.

Conclusion

These results demonstrate that the bovine α-lactalbumin gene can be expressed in the pig mammary gland and that the protein can be secreted subsequently into milk. Animals containing the transgene showed no obvious abnormal phenotype. The transgenic animals grew at the same rate as controls, reached puberty at the same time, farrowed normally, lactated normally, and their litters grew at rates consistent with or faster than controls. This is different from transgenic pigs that expressed the mouse whey acidic protein gene. In these sows, high production of the transgene resulted in poor lactational performance and agalactia in some animals (Shamay et al., 1991; Wall et al., 1991).

Producers have continued to reduce the duration of lactation in an attempt to maximize the number of piglets born per sow per year. This production system creates a need for sows that produce more milk in early lactation to obtain maximal piglet growth during the short lactation period. This is difficult to do in sows, as maximum milk production does not normally occur until days 21–28 of lactation (Hartmann et al., 1984). In addition, the number of piglets born per litter has increased in recent years, thereby also adding to the demand for higher milk production. This study indicates that lactose production in early lactation may be increased through the over-expression of α-lactalbumin in the mammary gland. Higher lactose concentrations in early lactation would provide the developing piglet with greater energy intake leading to faster growth. Furthermore, owing to the role of lactose as the major constituent in milk, increased lactose concentrations may be associated with greater milk production at the start of lactation.

The authors would also like to thank their colleagues who have contributed to the work described here: M. S. Noble, M. Monaco-Siegel, J. B. Cook, W. L. Hurley, D. Bidner and S. Hughes. This material is based on work supported partially by the Illinois Council for Food and Agricultural Research (C-FAR) Project No. 971-136-3, and the Cooperative State Research, Education and Extension Service, USDA National Research Initiative under Project No. NRI-960-3240.

References

Alexander AN and Carey HV (1999) Oral IGF-I enhances nutrient and electrolyte absorption in neonatal piglet intestine American Journal of Physiology 277 G619–G625

Auldist DE, Morrish L, Eason P and King RH (1998) The influence of litter size on milk production of sows Animal Science 60 501–507

Bleck GT and Bremel RD (1994) Variation in expression of a bovine α-lactalbumin transgene in milk of transgenic mice Journal of Dairy Science 77 1897–1904

Bleck GT, Jiminez-Flores R and Wheeler MB (1995) Pro-

duction of transgenic animals with altered milk as a tool to modify milk composition, increase animal growth and improve reproductive performance. In Animal Production and Biotechnology pp 1–19 Eds GF Greppi and G Enne. Elsevier, Amsterdam

Bleck GT, White BR, Hunt ED, Rund LA, Barnes J, Bidner D, Bremel RD and Wheeler MB (1996) Production of transgenic swine containing the bovine α-lactalbumin gene Theriogenology 45 1:347 (Abstract)

Bleck GT, White BR, Miller DJ and Wheeler MB (1998)

Production of bovine α-lactalbumin in the milk of transgenic pigs *Journal of Animal Science* **76** 3072–3078

Bondioli KR, Westhusin ME and Looney CR (1990) Production of identical bovine offspring by nuclear transfer *Theriogenology* **33** 165–174

Bremel RD, Yom H-C and Bleck GT (1989) Alteration of milk composition using molecular genetics *Journal of Dairy Science* **72** 2826–2833

Brew K and Grobler JA (1992) α-Lactalbumin. In *Advanced Dairy Chemistry, Proteins* pp 191–229 Ed. PF Fox. Elsevier Science Publications Ltd, New York

Buehler TA, Bruyere T, Went DF, Stranzinger G and Buerki K (1990) Rabbit β-casein promoter directs secretion of human interleukin-2 into the milk of transgenic rabbits *Bio/Technology* **8** 140–143

Campbell KHS, McWhir J, Ritchie WA and Wilmut I (1996) Sheep cloned by nuclear transfer from a cultured cell line *Nature* **380** 64–66

Choi BK, Bleck GT, Wheeler MB and Jiminez-Flores R (1996) Genetic modification of bovine β-casein and its expression in the milk of transgenic mice *Journal of Agricultural and Food Chemistry* **44** 953–960

Clark AJ, Bessos H and Bishop JO (1989) Expression of human anti-hemophilic factor IX in the milk of transgenic sheep *Bio/Technology* **7** 487–492

Ebert KM, Selgrath JP, Ditullio P *et al.* (1991) Transgenic production of a variant of human tissue-type plasminogen activator in goat milk: generation of transgenic goats and analysis of expression *Bio/Technology* **9** 835–840

Goodman RE and Schanbacher FL (1991) Bovine lactoferrin mRNA: sequence, analysis and expression in the mammary gland *Biochemical and Biophysical Research Communications* **180** 75–84

Grosvenor CE, Picciano MF and Baumrucker CR (1993) Hormones and growth factors in milk *Endocrine Reviews* **14** 710–728

Hammer RE, Pursel VG, Rexroad CE, Jr, Wall RJ, Bolt DJ, Ebert KM, Palmiter RD and Brinster RL (1985) Production of transgenic rabbits, sheep and pigs by microinjection *Nature* **315** 680–683

Hartmann PE, McCauley I, Gooneratne AD and Whitely JL (1984) Inadequacies of sow lactation: survival of the fittest. In *Lactation Strategies* Eds M Peaker, RG Vernon and CH Knight. *Symposia, Zoological Society of London* **51** 301–326

Hayssen V and Blackburn DG (1985) α-Lactalbumin and the origins of lactation *Evolution* **39** 1147–1149

Kim H and Jiménez-Flores R (1993) Two-dimensional analysis of skim milk proteins using preparative isoelectric focusing followed by polyacrylamide gel electrophoresis *Journal of Food Biochemistry* **16** 307–321

Lewis AJ, Speer VC and Haught DG (1978) Relationship between yield and composition of sows milk and weight gains of nursing pigs *Journal of Animal Science* **47** 634–638

Maga EA, Anderson GB and Murray JD (1995) The effect of mammary gland expression of human lysozyme on the properties of milk from transgenic mice *Journal of Dairy Science* **78** 2645–2652

Mao FC, Bremel RD and Dentine MR (1991) Serum concentrations of the milk proteins α-lactalbumin and α-lactoglobulin in pregnancy and lactation: correlations with milk and fat yields in dairy cattle *Journal of Dairy Science* **74** 2952–2958

Mashio A, Brickell PM, Kioussis D, Mellor AL, Katz D and Craig RK (1991) Transgenic mice carrying the guinea-pig α-lactalbumin gene transcribe milk protein genes in their sebaceous glands during lactation *Biochemical Journal* **275** 459–467

Noble MS, Wheeler MB, Cook JS and Hurley WL (2000a) Milk production and piglet growth in first parity gilts transgenic for bovine α-lactalbumin *Theriogenology* **53** 519 (Abstract)

Noble MS, Bleck GT, Cook JS, Wheeler MB and Hurley WL (2000b) Milk composition in early lactation is affected by expression of a bovine α-lactalbumin transgene in sows *Journal of Animal Science* **78** (Supplement 1) 708 (Abstract)

Noble MS, Cook JS, Bleck GT, Wheeler MB and Hurley WL Lactational performance of first parity transgenic gilts expressing bovine α-lactalbumin in their milk: milk production, milk composition, milk component intake and piglet growth rate (in press)

Onishi A, Iwamoto M, Akita T, Mikawa S, Takeda K, Awata T, Hanada H and Perry ACF (2000) Pig cloning by microinjection of fetal fibroblast nuclei *Science* **289** 1188–1190

Palmiter RD, Brinster RL, Hammer RE, Trumbauer ME, Rosenfeld MG, Birnberg NC and Evans RM (1982) Dramatic growth of mice that develop from eggs microinjected with metallothionein-growth hormone fusion genes *Nature* **300** 611–615

Polejaeva IA, Chen SH, Vaught TD *et al.* (2000) Cloned pigs produced by nuclear transfer from adult somatic cells *Nature* **407** 505–509

Pursel VG and Rexroad CE (1993) Status of research with transgenic farm animals *Journal of Animal Science* **71** (Supplement 3) 10–19

Rudolph NS (1999) Biopharmaceutical production in transgenic livestock *Trends in Biotechnology* **17** 367–374

Shamay A, Solinas S, Pursel VG, McKnight RA, Alexander L, Beattie C, Hennighausen L and Wall RJ (1991) Production of the mouse whey acidic protein in transgenic pigs during lactation *Journal of Animal Science* **69** 4552–4562

Simons JP, McClenaghan M and Clark AJ (1987) Alteration of the quality of milk by expression of sheep β-lactoglobulin in transgenic mice *Nature* **328** 530–532

Soulier S, Vilotte JL, Stinnakre MG and Mercier J-C (1992) Expression analysis of ruminant α-lactalbumin in transgenic mice: developmental regulation and general location of important *cis*-regulatory elements *FEBS Letters* **297** 13–18

Storb U (1987) Transgenic mice with immunoglobin genes *Annual Review of Immunology* **195** 151–174

Velander WH, Johnson JL, Page RL, Russell CG, Subramanian A, Wilkins TD, Gwazdauskas FC, Pittius C and Drohan WN (1992) High-level of expression of a heterologous protein in the milk of transgenic swine using the cDNA encoding human protein C *Proceedings National Academy of Sciences USA* **89** 12 003–12 007

Vilotte JL, Soulier S, Stinnakre MG, Massoud M and Mercier JC (1989). Efficient tissue-specific expression of bovine α-lactalbumin in transgenic mice *European Journal of Biochemistry* **186** 43–48

Vise PD, Michalska AE, Ashuman R, Lloyd B, Stone AB, Quinn P, Wells JRE and Seamark RR (1998) Introduction of a porcine growth hormone fusion gene into transgenic pigs promotes growth *Journal of Cell Science* **90** 295–300

Wall RJ, Pursel VG, Shamay A, McKnight RA, Pittius CW and Hennighausen L (1991) High-level synthesis of a heterologous milk protein in the mammary glands of transgenic swine *Proceedings National Academy of Sciences USA* **88** 1696–1700

Wheeler MB and Choi SJ (1997) Embryonic stem cells and transgenics: recent advances *Arquivos da Faculdade de Veterinaria, Universidade Federal Rio Grande do Sul (UFRGS), Brazil* **25** 64–83

Wheeler MB and Walters EM (2001) Transgenic technology applications in swine *Theriogenology* **56** 1345–1370

Wilmut I, Schneieke AE, McWhir JM, Kind AJ and Campbell KHS (1997) Viable offspring from fetal and adult mammalian cells *Nature* **385** 810–813

Wright G, Carver A, Cottom D, Reeves D, Scott A, Simons P, Wilmut I, Garner I and Colman A (1991) High level of expression of active alpha-1-antitrypsin in the milk of transgenic sheep *Bio/Technology* **9** 830–834

Reproduction Supplement **58**, 325–333

Cryopreservation of pig embryos: adaptation of vitrification technology for embryo transfer

J. R. Dobrinsky

Germplasm and Gamete Physiology Laboratory, Agricultural Research Service, US Department of Agriculture, Beltsville, MD 20705, USA

Great advancements in cryopreservation of pig embryos have been made since the last International Conference on Pig Reproduction (ICPR). In 1997, there were standard methods to cryopreserve germplasm and embryos of most livestock species, except for the pig, and development of this technology for use in the international pig industry was slow and in the early stages. Since 1997, there have been advancements in cryopreservation of pig embryos, with reports of production of live offspring after transfer of frozen–thawed and vitrified–warmed pig embryos. This review summarizes the progress in cryopreservation of pig embryos since 1997. Cellular and molecular biology have been used to understand the hypothermic sensitivity of pig embryos. Development of delipation technology has provided the first evidence that intracellular lipids are linked to hypothermic sensitivity. Cytoskeletal stabilization and vitrification have led to the production of live offspring from vitrified–warmed and transferred embryos. Recently, technology has been developed for cryopreservation of pig morulae. Development of open pulled straws has provided more rapid rates of cooling during vitrification and has been effective for cryopreservation of pig embryos. Although improvements and refinements of the technologies will continue, it is now time for the pig industry to consider cryopreservation of pig embryos as a tool for pig production and for propagation of select herd genetics, while maintaining germplasm resources for the future.

Introduction

Conservation of genetic resources is essential for making desirable genes and germplasm available to meet the needs of the future. Banking of germplasm from animals with desirable genetic, production or disease resistance traits will facilitate acquisition and characterization of potentially useful germplasm, ensure genetic variation through preservation of selected stocks and facilitate the use of useful germplasm in research and industry in the future. Implementation of methodologies for long-term preservation and transfer of pig embryos would provide a foundation for effective use of the world's most valuable genetic resources, while modernizing production and enhancing genetic improvement programmes (Dobrinsky, 1997).

Disease transmission and other health concerns limit the transport of live animals and, hence, subsequent propagation globally. The use of embryos in addition to spermatozoa

Email: bigjohn@anri.barc.usda.gov

represents a major increase in the global efficiency of transmitting improved genetic potential. The ability to preserve maternal genetic material enables improvement of genetic potential in a form other than the live animal. The development of reliable techniques for preservation of pig embryos could not have been more timely for the pig industry, considering the most recent outbreaks of foot and mouth disease (FMD) in Europe and other parts of the world in February 2001 (Brownlie, 2001; N. C. Steele, personal communication). After starting in England, the infection had spread throughout the UK within a few weeks and cases were reported in the Netherlands, France and the Republic of Ireland. The most proven methodology for eradication of FMD is 'stamping out', which involves extermination of all animals, with no exceptions, from the ring perimeter inwards toward the site of infection, which denies the virus a host to support replication. Restriction of movement is integral to this strategy, as no movement of hosts or passive vectors (humans, equipment and product) beyond the ring radius is permitted. Pursuit of a stamping out policy implies that the long-term value of commodities for export is more valuable than the short-term losses incurred by mass slaughter. Attempts to control and eradicate the epidemic resulted in the slaughter of over 4 million head of livestock in the UK alone, while FMD outbreaks in other parts of the world (for example, Taiwan in the mid-1990s) and attempts to control and eradicate the disease have caused the unintentional loss of germplasm resources worldwide (Brownlie, 2001; N. C. Steele, personal communication). If embryos had been cryopreserved and held in long-term storage, permanent germplasm losses could have been averted, as present lines could be regenerated through embryo transfer once the threat of the disease outbreak has subsided. Herd repopulation by genetic rescue from cryopreservation and embryo transfer of stored genetic lines, as well as import of genetically superior embryos for transfer, would enhance genetic repopulation.

The development of a repeatable method for the long-term preservation of pig embryos, coupled with embryo transfer, would provide numerous applications for production, research and medicine, including indefinite embryo storage, line regeneration, line proliferation, increased selection pressure in select herds, rescue of premium genetics from diseased herds, international export and import of potential breeding stock, and insurance for select genetic lines that are critical for the advancement of animal production and biotechnology. Furthermore, the global transport of genetically superior embryos to developing countries will enhance indigenous pig populations greatly to meet the needs of a growing world population. The conservation and preservation of pig genetics would enhance the improvement and usage of animal production techniques such as sperm sexing, artificial insemination, *in vitro* fertilization and development of non-surgical transfer of pig embryos. Collectively, these technologies would have a major impact on pig production worldwide (Dobrinsky *et al.,* 2000).

Early research on cryopreservation of pig embryos has been reviewed in great detail (Dobrinsky, 1997). Since then, new technology has been developed to cryopreserve early hatched blastocyst stage pig embryos, which has resulted in the world's first live piglets born after cryopreservation by vitrification. This technology was an interim solution suitable only for local movement of embryos within the country of origin; international rules on embryo transport outside the country of origin mean that only aseptic embryos with an intact zona pellucida can be exported. In this review, the most recent developments in pig embryo cryopreservation technology are summarized. The methodology for cryopreservation of morula stage pig embryos is described, including adaptation of delipation for cryo-preservation of embryos in the absence of much of their intracellular lipids. Furthermore, the USDA swine embryo cryopreservation technology (USECT), a non-invasive methodology designed to cryopreserve zona pellucida intact, non-micromanipulated, pre-blastocyst stage pig embryos, is described. Data on development of live offspring after transfer of delipated–cryopreserved embryos and USECT embryos are also presented.

Cryopreservation of pig embryos

Cytoskeletal stabilization

Dobrinsky (1997) reported ongoing pregnancies after transfer of cytoskeletal-stabilized, vitrified hatched blastocysts. Dobrinsky (1996, 1997) and Dobrinsky *et al.* (2000) reported cellular disruption, specifically to the embryonic cytoskeleton, during and after cryopreservation, for developing methodologies to circumvent such disruptions that would lead to the production of live offspring after cryopreservation and subsequent embryo transfer. Microfilament damage during vitrification of pig embryos and the use of cytochalasins before and during cryopreservation were assessed to help prevent damage and to stabilize the plasma membrane. Our hypothesis was based on the observation that cryoprotectants and cryopreservation disrupted the embryonic cytoskeleton, specifically filamentous actin. If the actin microfilaments were dismantled reversibly (or depolymerized) before cryopreservation, they might reform (or repolymerize) normally after rehydration. When embryos were treated and vitrified under the influence of a depolymerizing agent (cytochalasin b), after rehydration the filamentous actin repolymerized normally in the absence of cytochalasin b and embryos resumed development *in vitro* (Dobrinsky *et al.*, 2000). Morulae and early blastocysts did not survive cryopreservation with or without cytochalasin b (Table 1). Expanded and hatched blastocysts showed low rates of survival after vitrification (22–29%). However, vitrification under the influence of cytochalasin b improved the survival of expanded and early hatched blastocysts significantly. Although cytochalasin b-treated expanded blastocysts had improved viability after vitrification (60%), their development was still lower than that of early hatched blastocysts (90%). Cytochalasin b did not improve development of expanded hatched blastocysts after vitrification (41%).

Trans-oviductal uterine catheterization was used for transfer of cytoskeletal-stabilized and vitrified embryos to seven surrogate females (29–33 embryos per female; Table 2). Two surrogate females were examined on day 25 of presumptive gestation; one recipient had four normal fetuses. Of the other five surrogate females, two farrowed five live and normal offspring each. These piglets were normal in appearance and had birth weights within the normal range for these hybrids. The surrogate mothers weaned eight of the ten offspring, which grew normally as assessed by growth rates and phenotypes, and no anatomical abnormalities were observed by macroscopic examination after weaning at day 28 after birth. Of these mature offspring, two boars and two gilts were retained for breeding and have successfully proven their fecundity, as the boars each inseminated three gilts, and the two gilt offspring were mated. The females farrowed normal litters.

In a second cryopreservation–embryo transfer trial (Table 3), all embryos were cultured for 3–5 h after warming and recovery. Only morphologically excellent to good recavitating embryos were transferred by trans-oviductal uterine catheterization with surgical embryo transfer. Of seven recipient surrogate females, four farrowed a total of 29 live offspring, with litter sizes of 10, 10, 6 and 3. Select offspring from these litters have been raised to maturity to study their fecundity. At least three generations of normal pigs have been produced from this founder line of offspring produced from cryopreserved embryos. Stabilized vitrification is a viable method for the long-term preservation of pig embryos. This work enabled the repeatable production of live offspring after transfer of cytoskeletal-stabilized and vitrified–warmed embryos into surrogate females.

Table 1. Development of morphologically different stages of pig embryos after cryopreservation by vitrification under the influence of microfilament stabilizer cytochalasin b

Stage of development	Vitrification control			Vitrification + cytochalasin b		
	n	Development	% Development	n	Development	% Development
Morula or blastocyst	17	0	0[a]	17	1	6[a]
Expanded blastocyst	27	6	22[ab]	25	15	60[bx]
Hatched blastocyst < 400 μm in diameter	36	10	28[b]	48	43	90[cx]
Hatched blastocyst > 400 μm in diameter	14	4	29[ab]	22	9	41[b]

[a-c]Values with different superscripts within columns are significantly different ($P < 0.05$; ANOVA-GLM).
[x]Value with superscript is significantly different from control value within the row ($P < 0.01$; chi-squared analysis).
Data are from Dobrinsky et al. (2000).

Table 2. Development of cytoskeletal-stabilized and vitrified hatched blastocyst stage pig embryos after embryo transfer

Recipient	Number of embryos transferred	Embryo quality*	Embryo development
H	33	16	5 offspring
I	33	17	None
J	32	19	5 offspring
K	29	17	None
L	30	12	None
Total	157	81 (52%)	10 offspring ($n = 5.0$ average litter size)

*Number of excellent to good quality embryos at the time of transfer, 3–5 h after rehydration.
Data are from Dobrinsky et al. (2000).

Vitrification research

Kuwayama et al. (1997) reported that, of a range of pig embryos from the morulae to the hatched blastocyst stage, blastocysts achieved the highest survival rates in vitro with the vitrification treatments described. Much of the earlier reviewed literature (Dobrinsky, 1997) supports the contention that peri-hatching blastocysts are able to survive some forms of cryopreservation. Vajta et al. (1997) introduced 'open pulled straw' (OPS) vitrification. This methodology, which is based on a decreased diameter of straws that subsequently increases surface area to volume ratio, is designed to increase the rate of cooling of solutions during vitrification. Vajta et al. (1997) showed high rates of embryo development from morulae and blastocysts to hatched blastocyst stages (70–90%) in vitro. Unfortunately, at the time of these experiments, the authors did not transfer embryos to study the developmental competence of OPS-vitrified embryos. Holm et al. (1999) also reported high rates of survival in vitro after OPS vitrification of 346 pig blastocysts. After warming, the embryos were cultured for 24 or 48 h or transferred surgically to synchronized recipients. In vitro, 88% and 71% of warmed blastocysts were reported to re-expand or hatch in culture, respectively. After embryo transfer, no recipients farrowed.

Table 3. Development of cytoskeletal-stabilized and vitrified hatched blastocyst stage pig embryos after embryo transfer

Recipient	Number of embryos transferred	Embryo quality*	Embryo development
M	32	26	10 offspring
N	33	27	None
O	31	20	None
P	31	19	10 offspring
Q	32	20	6 offspring
R	33	16	None
S	32	15	3 offspring
Total	224	143 (64%)	29 offspring ($n = 7.25$ average litter size)

*Number of excellent to good quality embryos at the time of transfer, at 3–5 h after rehydration; remainder of embryos transferred were marginally developing, showing some cellular disruption but maintaining recavitation.
Data are from Dobrinsky *et al.* (2000).

Berthelot *et al.* (2000) reported the first live offspring after OPS vitrification of pig embryos. Morulae and unhatched blastocysts from Large White hyperprolific (LWh) and Meishan gilts were used to test the OPS vitrification method with two media. The viability of vitrified–warmed embryos was estimated by the percentage of embryos that developed to the hatched blastocyst stage *in vitro* or by birth after transfer. In the first experiment, two cryoprotectant dilution media were compared for cryopreservation of Meishan and LWh blastocysts: the culture medium was a standard Hepes-buffered TCM199 + 20% new born calf serum (NBCS) medium and PBS was a PBS + 20% NBCS medium. After a two-step equilibration in ethylene glycol, dimethyl sulphoxide and sucrose, 2–5 blastocysts were loaded into OPS and plunged into liquid nitrogen. The embryos were warmed and a four-step dilution with decreasing concentrations of sucrose was applied. In PBS, LWh blastocysts (27%) had a lower viability *in vitro* than did Meishan blastocysts (67%; $P = 0.001$). No significant difference was observed between genotypes (41% for LWh and 43% for Meishan blastocysts) in TCM and both viability rates were lower than that of the control group. In the second experiment, morula stage LWh and Meishan embryos were vitrified and warmed using PBS. The viability rate was low and was not significantly different between LWh (11%) and Meishan (14%) embryos. In the third experiment, 200 Meishan and 200 LWh blastocysts were vitrified–warmed as described in the first experiment (PBS). Twenty embryos were transferred to each of 20 Meishan recipients. The farrowing rate was 55% and recipients farrowed four and five piglets (median) for Meishan and LWh blastocysts, respectively. In this experimental design, the OPS vitrification method was appropriate for cryopreservation of unhatched pig blastocysts.

Embryo delipation

The emphasis in our laboratory has been on cryopreservation of morula or early blastocyst stage pig embryos. Pig embryos suffer from severe sensitivity to hypothermia, which limits their ability to withstand conventional cryopreservation. Research has focused on the high lipid content of pig embryos and its role on hypothermic sensitivity and cryosurvival. Our previous data indicate, as do most reports in the literature, that morula stage pig embryos have little or no survival after cryopreservation (Dobrinsky, 1997). Nagashima *et al.* (1995)

provided the first real evidence that intracellular lipid was associated with cooling or cryosensitivity of pig embryos. These workers isolated lipid from the embryo by centrifugation, used micromanipulation to remove (or suck) lipid from the embryo (delipation) and cooled or cryopreserved two- to eight-cell pig embryos. More than half of the delipated embryos survived cryopreservation, whether they had been frozen immediately after delipation or after further culture (to determine mitotic competence) before freezing, whereas none of the control embryos survived. Normal piglets were obtained from at least one recipient after unfrozen delipated and frozen delipated embryos were transferred. It is clear that pig embryos gain some form of tolerance to chilling when their lipid content is reduced. This was the first direct evidence that early cleavage stage embryos can survive cryopreservation after delipation and that the loss of cytoplasmic lipid is compensated for later in development. These observations by Nagashima *et al.* (1995) are a landmark in understanding the sensitivity of pig embryos to cooling and cryopreservation.

Dobrinsky *et al.* (1999) aimed to determine whether morulae and early blastocysts could survive delipation and cryopreservation. Embryos were delipated and frozen by conventional freezing using procedures described by Nagashima *et al.* (1995); delipated–vitrified embryos were cryopreserved with cytoskeletal stabilization throughout micromanipulation and vitrification. Control and delipated non-cryopreserved embryos developed at high rates *in vitro*. After cryopreservation, 89% of delipated–frozen embryos and 83% of delipated–vitrified embryos underwent advanced embryonic development in culture for 48 h, including cavitation and blastocyst expansion. After cryopreservation and subsequent embryo transfer, three of seven recipients that received delipated–frozen embryos delivered a total of 14 live piglets, and three of four recipients that received delipated–vitrified embryos delivered a total of 13 live piglets. These studies confirm that morulae and early blastocyst stage pig embryos can withstand cryopreservation by conventional freezing or vitrification after removal of their cytoplasmic lipid and remain developmentally competent after transfer.

Although these results indicate that intracellular lipid is involved directly in hypothermic sensitivity of morulae and early blastocyst stage embryos, delipation disrupts the zona pellucida of the embryos. It is a requirement that embryos to be transported internationally must have an intact zona pellucida (Stringfellow and Seidel, 1998). Dobrinsky *et al.* (2001) aimed to develop non-invasive methodology for cryopreservation of non-micromanipulated, zona pellucida intact morula and early blastocyst stage pig embryos to enable long-term preservation and future global transfer of uterine stage pig embryos.

Non-invasive embryo vitrification

In a preliminary study, we cryopreserved centrifuged, intact morulae and early blastocyst stage embryos (Dobrinsky *et al.*, 2001). Embryos were either centrifuged to isolate lipid or not centrifuged (intact whole embryos), and cryopreserved by conventional freezing or vitrification. Embryos were recovered from cryopreservation and cultured for 48 h. Non-centrifuged frozen and non-centrifuged vitrified morulae and early blastocyst stage embryos did not develop *in vitro*. Centrifuged frozen–thawed and centrifuged vitrified–warmed embryos showed 60–70% survival *in vitro* after cryopreservation, and most developed a morphologically acceptable blastocoel after 48 h of culture. However, embryos that developed to early blastocysts did not continue to develop or hatch *in vitro*, which is typical for control embryos cultured for 48 h. Blastocysts that developed did not expand and the zona pellucida did not undergo any thinning, which was typical for culture control embryos. Vital staining by propidium iodide exclusion indicated that most embryos with a blastocoel were alive and intact, but their development appeared to be arrested, as they did not undergo any further cell

Table 4. Effect of centrifugation before cryopreservation and development *in vitro* (72 h) of control and cryopreserved morula and early blastocyst stage pig embryos after zona pellucida removal

Type of cryopreservation	Centrifugation	Number of embryos cultured	Number of embryos that developed (%)	Number of cells in blastocysts
Frozen	+	25	24 (96)[a]	100.3 ± 16.2[a]
Frozen	–	22	4 (18)[b]	64.3 ± 17.2[b]
Vitrified	+	25	21 (84)[a]	115.4 ± 14.0[a]
Vitrified	–	26	2 (8)[b]	60.0 ± 4.0[b]
None	+	20	20 (100)[a]	216.6 ± 13.4[c]

[a–c]Values within columns with different superscripts are significantly different ($P < 0.05$).
Data are from Dobrinsky *et al.* (1999).

division or morphological progression of development in culture. It was then investigated whether centrifuged cryopreserved morulae and early blastocyst stage embryos can continue to develop normally *in vivo*. Centrifuged–vitrified embryos were warmed and transferred to recipient females, but pregnancies were not established. Furthermore, embryos could not be recovered from three recipients at slaughter 72 h after embryo transfer. No embryos were found when uterine flushings from the recipients were examined. Lipid isolated but undelipated, zona pellucida intact embryos cease to develop *in vitro* and did not develop *in vivo*. It is possible that embryo lysis might result from a local cytotoxic effect of the isolated lipid remaining inside the intact zona pellucida. In centrifuged, cryopreserved morulae and early blastocyst stage embryos either the embryo itself or the zona pellucida is altered in a way that prevents further development. However, the surviving embryos did develop a morphologically acceptable blastocoel before they became dormant.

Embryos were cryopreserved by conventional freezing or vitrification, with or without centrifugation (Dobrinsky *et al.*, 2001), and after indefinite storage in liquid nitrogen the embryos were warmed and processed through dilution and rehydration. After rehydration, the zona pellucida was removed and zona-free embryos were placed into culture medium to monitor development after thawing. Centrifuged, non-cryopreserved, zona pellucida-removed embryos served as a culture control group. As expected, non-centrifuged, cryopreserved morulae and early blastocyst stage embryos with their zona pellucida removed did not develop *in vitro* (Table 4). However, centrifuged, cryopreserved morulae and early blastocyst stage embryos with zona pellucida removed developed at high rates into blastocysts after 72 h in culture and, morphologically, resembled expanding hatched blastocysts. Furthermore, the type of cryopreservation had no effect on embryo survival in embryos with zonae pellucidae removed. Interestingly, centrifuged, non-cryopreserved, control embryos with zonae pellucidae removed, recovered from the same embryo donors and distributed randomly to treatment or control groups, also developed well in culture and underwent a two-fold increase in number of cells after 72 h of culture compared with centrifuged, cryopreserved embryos with zonae pellucidae removed. Recovery from the entire cryopreservation procedure did slow down the rate of cryopreserved embryo development *in vitro*, as indicated by reduced cell numbers; however, the type of cryopreservation had no effect on mitotic activity in culture after zona pellucida removal.

Centrifuged, cryopreserved morulae and early blastocyst stage embryos were transferred to asynchronous surrogate females to determine whether this reduction in number of cells would affect developmental competence (Dobrinsky *et al.*, 2001). As type of cryopreservation had no effect on *in vitro* embryo development to blastocysts and number of blastocyst cells, vitrification was selected as the method of cryopreservation as it is a simple and rapid

Table 5. Development of centrifuged, cytoskeletal-stabilized and vitrified morulae and early blastocyst stage pig embryos after zona pellucida removal and embryo transfer

Recipient	Status	Live offspring	Total offspring
		Litter size	
A	Not pregnant	–	–
B	Pregnant	8	8
C	Pregnant	7	7
D	Pregnant	4	5
E	Not pregnant	–	–
F	Pregnant	9	10
G	Pregnant	7	7
H	Pregnant	7	8
I	Pregnant	4	5
J	Pregnant	8	8
K	Pregnant	7	7
Total		61 live offspring ($n = 7$ per litter)	

Trial 1: recipients A–D; trial 2: recipients E–K.
Data are from Dobrinsky et al. (2001).

procedure for cryopreservation of large numbers of embryos destined for transfer in a short period of time. Large numbers of embryo donors underwent oestrous synchronization and superovulation, and embryos were recovered in bulk and cryopreserved using the new USDA swine embryo cryopreservation technology. All centrifuged and vitrified embryos were cryopreserved in bulk and stored in liquid nitrogen for 3–6 months. Naturally cyclic gilts at day 4 after oestrus (oestrus = day 0), with at least two previous normal oestrous cycles, served as asynchronous (–24 to –36 h) recipients. In the first trial, centrifuged and vitrified embryos were warmed, rehydrated and their zona pellucida was removed and transferred (Table 5); three of four gilts farrowed eight, seven and four live healthy offspring. In the second trial, six of seven gilts farrowed a total of 42 offspring. Total recipient farrowing rate was 82% (9/11) with 61 live piglets born, averaging seven pigs per litter.

Select male and female offspring from these litters were retained on our farm and raised to sexual maturity (Dobrinsky et al., 2001). Their growth rates to day 165 of age were not different from the farm average. Three centrifuged and vitrified female offspring entered puberty normally and maintained normal oestrous cycles before mating. The gilts underwent normal pregnancies and each had a litter of piglets that grew normally and established normal fecundity. Two boars that developed from centrifuged and vitrified embryos entered puberty normally. One boar was trained for semen collection and was placed in our boar facility. Semen was collected from this boar, processed and extended for use in artificial insemination of three hybrid gilts in oestrus. These gilts became pregnant and had litters of piglets that grew normally and established normal fecundity. The other boar was placed on the farm and was used in natural mating of three hybrid gilts in oestrus. These gilts also became pregnant and had litters of piglets that grew normally and established normal fecundity.

Conclusion

In the conclusion of my last paper at ICPR, I began with the remarks '... Methods for preservation of pig embryos are in early stages of development, as are other technologies in pigs, such as non-surgical embryo transfer (Li *et al.*, 1996), that could make embryo cryopreservation practical and usable by the producer. Technologies available for embryo transfer in cattle, such as non-surgical embryo recovery and *in vitro* embryo production, are not readily available to the pig industry or are in early stages of development, making it impractical for the producer to use these biotechnical advances in swine. (Dobrinsky, 1997). In 2001, this is no longer the case. In our laboratory and others, vitrification technologies have been used to overcome the cooling sensitivity of pig embryos and methodologies have been developed that can produce high rates of live offspring after cryopreservation and embryo transfer. Although delipated morulae and early blastocysts can survive cryopreservation and maintain developmental competence to live offspring, the USDA swine embryo cryo-preservation technology provides a non-invasive methodology to cryopreserve pig embryos at all stages of preimplantation, from zygotes to hatched blastocysts, and can produce live, healthy piglets that grow normally and are of excellent fecundity when mature. The *in vivo* development of cryopreserved embryos after transfer could be improved, as in most reports < 30% of transferred embryos actually develop to live offspring. Furthermore, a better understanding of the physiology, endocrinology and synchrony of embryo recipient (surrogate) females at the time of embryo transfer is required.

Implementation of methodologies for long-term embryo preservation and transfer in pigs would provide a foundation for effective use of the world's most valuable genetic resources on a global basis while modernizing production and enhancing genetic improvement programmes. It is now time for breeders and producers to adopt cryopreservation and transfer of pig embryos into pig production for propagating select genetic traits and maintaining germplasm resources for the future. Collectively, these technologies will have a major impact on pig production worldwide.

References

Berthelot F, Martinat-Botte F, Locatelli A, Perreau C and Terqui M (2000) Piglets born after vitrification of embryos using the open pulled straw method *Cryobiology* **41** 116–124

Brownlie J (2001) Strategic decisions to evaluate before implementing a vaccine programme in the face of a foot-and-mouth disease (FMD) outbreak *British Cattle Veterinary Association Bulletin* **22 March** 1–5

Dobrinsky JR (1996) Cellular approach to cryopreservation of embryos *Theriogenology* **45** 17–26

Dobrinsky JR (1997) Cryopreservation of pig embryos *Journal of Reproduction and Fertility* **52** 301–312

Dobrinsky JR, Nagashima H, Pursel VG, Long CR and Johnson LA (1999) Cryopreservation of swine embryos with re-duced lipid content *Theriogenology* **51** 164 (Abstract)

Dobrinsky JR, Pursel VG, Long CR and Johnson LA (2000) Birth of piglets after transfer of embryos cryopreserved by cytoskeletal stabilization and vitrification *Biology of Reproduction* **62** 564–570

Dobrinsky JR, Nagashima H, Pursel VG, Schreier LL and Johnson LA (2001) Cryopreservation of morula and early

blastocyst stage swine embryos: birth of litters after embryo transfers *Theriogenology* **55** 303 (Abstract)

Holm P, Vajta G, Machaty Z, Schmidt M, Prather RS, Greve T and Callesen H (1999) Open pulled straw (OPS) vitrification of porcine blastocysts: simple procedure yielding excellent *in vitro* survival but so far no piglets following transfer *Cryo-Letters* **20** 307–310

Kuwayama M, Holm P, Jacobsen H, Greve T and Callesen H (1997) Successful cryopreservation of porcine embryos by vitrification *Veterinary Record* **141** 365

Nagashima H, Kashiwazaki N, Ashman RJ, Grupen CG and Nottle MB (1995) Cryopreservation of porcine embryos *Nature* **374** 416

Stringfellow DA and Seidel SM (1998) Ethical and sanitary recovery, handling, preservation, movement and transfer of embryos. In *Manual of the International Embryo Transfer Society* pp 79–84. International Embryo Transfer Society, Savoy, Illinois

Vajta G, Holm P, Greve T and Callesen H (1997) Vitrification of porcine embryos using the open pulled straw (OPS) method *Veterinaria Scandinavica* **38** 349–352

Author Index

Abeydeera, L. R.	159	Laurincik, J.	175
Ashworth, C.	233	Leenhouwers, J. I.	247
		Liu, J.	31
Barb, C. R.	1	Lucas, X.	301
Bazer, F. W.	191	Lucy, M. C.	31
Bertani, G. R.	277		
Bleck, G. T.	313	McArdle, H. J.	233
Boyd, C. K.	31	Maddox-Hyttel, P.	175
Bracken, C. J.	31	Mandon-Pepin, B.	65
Burghardt, R. C.	191	Martinez, E. A.	301
Burkin, H. R.	147	Matthijs, A.	113
		Miller, D. J.	147
Caetano, A. R.	277	Moor, B.	91
Coté, F.	47	Murphy, B. D.	47
Cotinot, C.	65		
		Niemann, H.	175
Dai, Y.	91	Nwagwu, M. O.	233
Dantzer, V.	209		
Dinnyés, A.	175	Page, K. R.	233
Dobrinsky, J.	325	Pailhoux, E.	65
Donovan, S. M.	313	Polejaeva, I. A.	293
Downey, B. R.	47	Pomp, D.	277
		Prather, R. S.	105
Ekwall, H.	129		
		Rampacek, G. B.	1
		Rath, D.	175
Finch, A. M.	233	Roca, J.	301
Ford, S. P.	223	Rodriguez-Martinez, H.	129
Funahashi, H.	129	Rosenkranz, C.	175
		Ruiz-Cortés, T.	47
Garlow, J. G.	191		
Garrett, W. M.	17	Sirois, J.	47
Gévry, N.	47	Spencer, T. E.	191
Gil, M. A.	301	Suzuki, K.	129
Gilbert, C. L.	263		
Gladney, C. D.	277	Telfer, E. E.	81
Guthrie, H. D.	17	Tienthai, P.	129
Jaeger, L. A.	191	van der Lende, T.	247
Johannisson, A.	129	Vazquez, J. L.	301
Johnson, G. A.	191	Vazquez, J. M.	301
Johnson, R. K.	277		
		Wheeler, M. B.	313
Ka, H.	191	Wilmut, I.	175
Knol, E. F.	247	Wilson, M. E.	223
Kraeling, R. R.	1	Winther, H.	209
		Woelders, H.	113

Subject Index

Apoptosis
during folliculogenesis — 17

Behaviour
periparturient, endocrine regulation of — 263

Cloning — 293
Corpus luteum
development of — 47
Cryopreservation
of embryos — 325

Development
prenatal, and perinatal mortality — 247

Embryo
development, and *in vitro* fertilization — 159
gene expression in — 175
transfer — 301, 325
vitrification — 325

Fertilization — 105
adhesion molecules in — 147
in vitro, and embryo
development — 159
Fetus
retardation of growth of — 233
Follicular development
in ovary — 31
preantral, *in vitro* — 81
Folliculogenesis
apoptosis during — 17
Functional genomics
and reproduction — 277

Gamete adhesion molecules — 147
Gene expression
in embryos — 175
Gonadal differentiation — 65
Growth
fetal — 233
improvement of, by transgenic
alteration of milk — 313

Hypothalamic–pituitary axis
nutritional regulators of — 1

Intrauterine insemination
deep, and embryo transfer — 301

Milk
transgenic alteration of — 313

Nutrition
and regulation of hypothalamic–
pituitary axis — 1

Oocyte
activation — 105
maturation *in vivo* and *in vitro* — 91
Ovary
follicular development in — 31
Oviduct
in sperm capacitation and oocyte
development — 129

Parthenogenesis — 105
Periparturient behaviour
endocrine regulation of — 263
Phagocytosis
of spermatozoa — 113
Pituitary hormones
nutritional control of — 1
Placenta
efficiency of — 223
growth factors and calcium during
development of — 209
Preantral follicle
development of, *in vitro* — 81
Prenatal development
and perinatal mortality — 247

Signalling
at uterine–conceptus interface — 191
Spermatozoa
capacitation of, in oviduct — 129
phagocytosis of, *in vitro* and *in vivo* — 113

Transgenic alteration
of milk — 313

Uterine–conceptus interface
autocrine and paracrine signalling at — 191